# GLOBAL ECONOMY AND DIGITAL SOCIETY

EDITED BY

Erik Bohlin
*Department of Innovation,*
*Chalmers Institute of Technology, Götenburg, Sweden*

Stanford L. Levin
*Department of Economics,*
*Southern Illinois University Edwardsville, USA*

Nakil Sung
*Department of Economics,*
*University of Seoul, Korea*

Chang-Ho Yoon
*Department of Economics,*
*Korea University, Korea*

2004

ELSEVIER

Amsterdam – Boston – Heidelberg – London – New York – Oxford
Paris – San Diego – San Francisco – Singapore – Sydney – Tokyo

**ELSEVIER B.V.**  ,ELSEVIER Inc.  ELSEVIER Ltd  ELSEVIER Ltd
**Sara Burgerhartstraat 25**  525 B Street, Suite 1900  The Boulevard, Langford Lane  84 Theobalds Road
**P.O. Box 211, 1000 AE Amsterdam**  San Diego, CA 92101-4495  Kidlington, Oxford OX5 1GB  London WC1X 8RR
**The Netherlands**  USA  UK  UK

1st edition 2004

Library of Congress Cataloging in Publication Data
A catalog record is available from the Library of Congress.

British Library Cataloguing in Publication Data
A catalogue record is available from the British Library.

ISBN:   0-444-51335-3

♾ The paper used in this publication meets the requirements of ANSI/NISO Z39.48-1992 (Permanence of Paper).
Printed in The Netherlands.

## PREFACE AND ACKNOWLEDGEMENTS

The International Telecommunications Society (ITS) convened its 14th Biennial Conference in Seoul, South Korea, August 18-22, 2002. Organized by KATP (Korea Association for Telecommunications Policies), KT and SK Telecom, the conference had the theme "Challenges and Opportunities in the Digital Century: The Role of Information and Telecommunications." In a time of economic downturn and uncertainty about future prospects, the conference provided the opportunity to systematically assess and discuss the state of global information and telecommunication markets and to re-affirm the importance of digital society for the global economy.

This theme attracted approximately 120 high-quality research paper presentations, and nearly 300 attendees from 27 countries. Bringing to the fore papers covering a variety of topics related to the digital society, the conference built on the ITS long research tradition in telecom policy. This book includes 20 conference papers in the area of global economy and digital society. As the implications of digitalization become more and more pervasive, the editors have aimed to provide a balanced overview of current and emerging issues of high relevance for policymakers, researchers and private companies.

The selection for the book was made independently by the book editors, but this volume would not have been possible without the conference to start with. Therefore, we would like to acknowledge the following people and organizations for their role in supporting and organizing the conference. The editors would like to thank the main sponsors of the conference, KATP (Korea Association for Telecommunications Policies), KT and SK Telecom. Our thanks also go to the conference organizers, in particular staff from the hosting organizations, the Conference Co-Chairs Jae-Cheol Kim, Kyung Joon Lee and Shin-Bae Kim, the Conference Coordinators Cheolkyu Hong and Daesu Park and the Conference Program Coordinators Nakil Sung and Jae-Hyeon Ahn. We would also like to acknowledge all the organizing committee members, especially the other sub-theme coordinators Joong-Ho Ahn, Suk-Gwon Chang, Daewon Choi, Kap-Young Jeong, In-Soo Kang, Bong Ho Lee, Jae Kyu Lee, Jürgen Müller, Tatsuya Omura, P.M. Rao, Ed Steinmueller and Marcio Wohlers. In addition, our special thanks go to Dr. Hansuk Kim of KT and Dr. Shin Cho of SK Telecom, without whose timely intervention and critical support there would have been no ITS conference in Seoul. Likewise, the decision of the ITS to endorse the event was a necessary prerequisite for the conference to take place, and the editors would like to thank the ITS Executive Committee, ITS Board of Directors, ITS Treasurer Leland Schmidt and ITS Chair Loretta Anania.

For the completion of this volume, we would like to thank VINNOVA for providing a grant to facilitate editorial work. The editorial assistance of Ms. Eva Burford and Mr. Mikael Olsson is gratefully acknowledged. Finally, our sincere thanks and acknowledgement go to the authors of the chapters for this book. We appreciate the creativity, commitment and command with which they prepared and revised drafts and met deadlines, and welcome the international cooperative efforts that many of the individual papers in the book represent.

Erik Bohlin
Chalmers University of Technology

Stanford L. Levin
Southern Illinois University Edwardsville

Nakil Sung
University of Seoul

Chang-Ho Yoon
Korea University

# List of Contents

## Part V: Policy Aspects of the Digital Society

## Author Information

## Index

**List of Tables**

## List of Figures

# INTRODUCTION

Global Economy and Digital Society
E. Bohlin, S. Levin, N. Sung and C-H. Yoon (Editors)

# CHAPTER 1

# Global Economy and Digital Society: An Introduction

Erik Bohlin
*School of Technology Management and Economics,*
*Chalmers University of Technology, Göteborg*

Stanford L. Levin
*Department of Economics and Finance,*
*Southern Illinois University Edwardsville, Edwardsville*

Nakil Sung
*Faculty of Economics, University of Seoul, Seoul*

Chang-Ho Yoon
*Department of Economics, Korea University, Seoul*

## 1 INTRODUCTION

The effects of Information and Communication Technologies (ICTs) on globalization, innovation, growth and productivity are immense. It is an accepted view that ICTs contribute to the globalization of production and capital markets by reducing the cost of information and communication. These technologies have certainly made it easier for multinationals and other companies to spread production facilities all over the world, to co-ordinate international marketing campaigns, and to ease collaboration in projects taking place on different continents. While the anti-globalization movement may claim otherwise, individuals and consumers also have a lot to gain from the internationalization of trade and commerce. Using the Internet, consumers can today find products on sale in other countries or not available in their own countries, and compare their standard of living to that of others. It is also, as a result of the Internet, much easier for consumers to become better informed. As a result of this increased access to information, markets work more efficiently. Furthermore, globalization has speeded up the diffusion of innovation, bringing new knowledge, products and services to developing countries in months rather than years or decades.

On the other hand, following the boundless optimism of the late 1990s, it is becoming clear that several factors limit the actual effect of ICTs. There is evidence that ICTs do play a role in spurring economic growth, but this growth is spread rather unevenly. Only certain industries have been able to make substantial gains from ICTs, and the effect varies dramatically from country to country. Recent studies also show that these technologies may actually be more effective in complementing physical presence than in extending reach. Concerning the contribution of ICTs to more efficient markets, it seems that we are still far from a perfect, frictionless market, even for the trade that takes place over the Internet. The same goes for other types of trade and for the liberalization of markets: policy reform and liberalization take time, and, unlike technological progress, these political changes can be reversed. In spite of these qualifying factors, the linkage between a digital society and globalization cannot be denied, and the objections outlined here make it all the more important to establish how theoretical gains can be turned into reality.

From a research perspective, there is now a wealth of evidence of changes and events related to the digital society and globalization that can be used to study these linkages. The IT and telecommunication industries have gone through spectacular booms and busts, with high expectations having been replaced by a widespread shakeout and pessimism about market prospects. At the same time, the services related to these industries have matured, and a number of years have passed since they were first applied to companies' business processes. Even the so-called productivity paradox is now outdated, since organizations have been able to adapt themselves enough for the output of ICTs to be visible and quantifiable; as a result, it is now possible to measure the effect of ICT tools more accurately. The meaning of the concept of convergence, while still used in different circumstances, is also becoming more clear, and the erasing of boundaries between the telecommunication and IT industries has proceeded far. Furthermore, telecommunications markets in North America, Europe, Asia and other parts of the world have been liberalized, leading to the breaking up of monopolies, incumbents being challenged, and a new industry structure emerging. Unlike ten years ago, these sweeping changes are not phenomena that are predicted to occur but realities that provide a rich source of empirical evidence.

Considering the dependence of society on digital technologies, research based on this evidence is urgent. ICTs have moved beyond an initial stage of experimentation to a situation in which society is dependent on the Internet and other digital services. These services supply people with vital information in everyday situations as well as in times of crisis, allow business transactions to be completed, and provide cheap and convenient communication between people. When digital applications cease to function, so does society. At the moment, society's dependence on these technologies is not matched by a sufficiently high level of reliability and security. With this background, it should be a priority task to investigate how markets, regulation and technologies can function together to improve the reliability and use of ICTs and the functioning of international markets, helping to reap the gains from the digital society.

Taking into account the wide-ranging impact of ICTs, it is hardly surprising that the research field encompassing ICTs and globalization has attracted many writers and publications. The field is comparatively new and rapidly growing, with a number of subfields that differ with regard to their emphasis on market, policy and civil society issues. Major problems in ICT and globalization research include the relationship between markets and states, industrial policy, innovation and diffusion, information society, cohesion and sustainability, and privacy and security. A prominent perspective in the field has been that based on neo-classic economics, which has resulted in important contributions in the areas of liberalization, privatization and (de)regulation. In addition, the post-industrial school has had significant influence on the thinking about information society developments among political decision-makers and administrators.

The contributions to ICT and globalization presented in this book belong to the subfield of telecom policy research. As the book will show, research efforts in this field often take their starting point in an analysis of data or evidence based on economic models but have the ultimate goal of providing concrete policy recommendations. The mechanisms linking telecom investment and use to growth and other economic measures - involving not only market forces but also policy interventions - are the main focus. In other words, telecom policy research addresses practical issues in the telecommunications sector, studying the interplay between markets and the political domain. This line of inquiry is, moreover, developed in a multidisciplinary fashion, building upon neo-classical economics as well as other perspectives. As a whole, this book provides a broad cross-section of telecom policy research, including research with an e-policy perspective, while the individual studies provide deep insights into various aspects of ICTs and the global economy.

In this introductory chapter, the subfield of telecom policy research is discussed in greater detail. The field's content and international profile are outlined, and a case is made for the continued relevance of telecom policy research, provided the research agenda is broadened to include the full range of factors influencing telecommunications. Finally, an overview of the book, with a description of how the chapters fit together and a brief summary, is provided.

## 2 TELECOM POLICY RESEARCH: OVERVIEW AND THE ROLE OF THE ITS[1]

The International Telecommunications Society (ITS) has long been a driving force in international telecom policy research. For almost three decades, the ITS has gathered representatives from the telecom industry, research and political communities in an international forum. By bringing together 300-400 of the leaders in telecom research at regular conferences, the ITS has contributed to setting the agenda for telecom policy research and to creating a consensus around the most urgent problem areas. In the course of these activities, the ITS has created a discourse and approach to problem solving for issues in the "information sector." Many of the network's members have published research in the leading telecommunications journals for years and share a techno-economic perspective in analyzing developments in the sector. As a result, the ITS has created a research tradition in the growing field of telecommunications and information society policy research. By publishing the strongest contributions from the ITS 2002 14th Biennial Conference in Seoul, this book is a continuation of that tradition and aims to provide a broad picture of important questions for the digital society.

### 2.1 International Overview

A majority of stakeholders in the ITS are from the three leading regions in telecom policy research: USA, Europe and Asia (in this case, in particular, Japan and Korea). Since the USA has been leading the transformation of telecom policy, its telecom policy research has stayed ahead of that in other regions. To begin, research received an important stimulus from the

---

[1] For a more in-depth discussion of telecom policy research history and agendas, see Bohlin, E. (2003), "Telecommunications Policy Research in Information Society Discourse", *World Telecommunications Markets, Vol III of the International Handbook* on Telecommunication Economics, edited by Gary Madden, Edward Elgar Publication, 2003.

antitrust lawsuit against AT&T, which began in 1969. During the trial, AT&T built up economic competence within Bell Laboratories and at several universities, and new professorships were established from a variety of sources during the 1980s and 1990s. Similarly, key research was encouraged by the state regulatory authorities and the federal authority (the Federal Communications Commission (FCC)) as well as other interested parties in the divestiture debate. There is also a more independent tradition of research that focuses chiefly on modeling and theory development. Many universities have a School of Communications or similar program where telecom policy research is supported, as it is as well in economics programs. Generally speaking, American telecom policy research is strongly influenced by the economic outlook, and traditional approaches are predominant.

Japan's telecom policy research has been even more been influenced by stakeholders than America's. This is largely due to the protracted and partly unresolved conflict between the dominant telecom operator NTT and the telecom ministry. The latter has organized loosely connected advisory councils including prominent researchers (together with practitioners), and the ministry finances external research in addition to its own research institutes. Nonetheless, NTT finances a major portion of telecom policy research, external as well as internal, besides having external councils. It is unusual for an academic to be a member of both NTT's and the ministry's councils. Several other interested parties, too, have external advisory bodies to which noted academics belong, not only to stimulate debate but also to legitimize positions. The research's orientation, on the whole, closely follows the methods, concepts and perspectives which have been developed in the USA. There is no specifically Japanese perspective or approach in telecom policy; the USA has served as an explicit forerunner and object of comparison in practice and research alike.

In Korea, the situation surrounding telecom policy research was similar to that in Japan in the 1980s. As a matter of fact, Korea often followed Japanese telecom policies at that time. In particular, both Korea and Japan took advantage of a former public monopoly to boost their domestic telecom equipment industry. On the other hand, telecom policies in Korea have gradually diverged from those in Japan and become more influenced by the US and the EU from the 1990s. This was clearly affected by the fact that an increasing number of telecom experts in Korea studied at US universities. As a result, the Korean government sometimes pursued a more radical approach to telecom policies than either Japan or EU countries. For example, the Korean incumbent carrier (KT) is completely privatized, while many European dominant carriers are still partly owned by their governments. Also, the Korean government left high-speed Internet access to competition between local carriers, i.e., a market mechanism, which contributed to its world-record diffusion rate. However, as in Japan, there is no specifically Korean perspective or approach to telecom policy.

In Europe the picture is more heterogeneous as regards research perspectives and stakeholders. The European Commission has lent limited support to telecom policy research within the research Framework Programmes. Here the research is generally oriented toward broader issues, with the information society as a shared concept. Further, the European Commission has to a limited degree engaged academics as external consultants for expert investigations, but has mainly relied on specialized consultancy firms. It has also organized semi-independent external councils loosely connected with the European Commission, on which both academics and practitioners collaborate, and that have published a number of works intended to present a broad approach to information-society policy.

In national terms, the scope of telecom policy research varies. For example, a major national 10-year effort was made in Great Britain within the so-called PICT program, where several competence centers and professorships were built up in a very successful way. In Germany and France, large research institutes exist that are financed partly with public funds. Smaller centers attached to universities can be found in many countries. In Sweden, research traditions are more multidisciplinary.

Generally, the focus on telecom policy research is more heterogeneous in Europe than in both the USA and Japan. There is a wider range of perspectives and methods and a stronger emphasis on qualitative approaches. Apart from the ITS, the European Communications Policy Research Conference (Euro-CPR) has served as an important forum for European telecom policy research in recent years, and a European network, the European Network for Communication and Information Perspectives (ENCIP), has been a driving force of late.

## 2.2 Telecom Policy Research: Towards a Definition

But what, then, is the field of telecom policy research? As defined here, such research deals with the ends and means of telecom policy on theoretical and empirical grounds. The objects of study comprise actors, institutions, technologies and markets which telecom policy influences and is influenced by. Market issues are thus to be placed in a political context, but more than political issues are included in this research. It is of interest to study the interplay between markets and politics. For example, a market study of how mobile telephone operators develop over time may contain questions about telecom policy. It is, therefore, natural to distinguish telecom policy research from technology research or from research solely on economic issues, while keeping in mind that telecom policy's objects of study are obviously concerned with both economic and technological aspects.

From a longer and more dynamic perspective, it is important for telecom policy research to address the radical changes in preconditions and consequences that have occurred during the last two decades, a rate of change that will scarcely decrease. In this respect, a broadening towards e-policy is particularly urgent, as will be discussed further below.

In general, the dominant issues within telecom policy research have closely followed practical needs. The practical needs have also influenced the research perspectives. Dominant perspectives within practically-oriented telecom policy research have consisted primarily of economic theory in different shades and applications. This is natural, given that most telecom policy instruments are of an economic character (price regulation, cost issues, etc.). Relatively little telecom policy research with practical applications has emerged from political science, sociology or engineering sciences, although interdisciplinary efforts are increasing. Moreover, the research perspectives have been influenced by the stakeholder structure and institutional environment on both a national and a regional basis. Therefore, telecom policy research has at times been highly politicized.

Research in Korea is an example of the high priority attached to telecom policy research and its close link to practical policy decisions. The Korean government has been actively involved in organizing research efforts and establishing several governmental institutes to promote the in-depth analysis of IT policy issues, as have private companies. These national institutes have played an important advisory role in building modern telecom infrastructure and establishing workable competition among service providers. A number of prominent researchers and practitioners have been able to participate in policy fora and academic seminars on topics including analysis of information technology adoption, critical assessment and further advancement of ICTs, comparative evaluations of telecommunications and broadcasting convergence in the global economy, and broader normative issues such as regulatory reform and fair competition. These telecom policy research endeavors have contributed to the clarification of policy issues and have enhanced the transparency of the implementation process.

Telecom policy has been an active field of research and orientation in academia internationally (as have tele-economics and tele-technology) and has been so for many years. The field's leading journal, *Telecommunications Policy*, was founded just over 20 years ago. Area-specific conferences have drawn participants since the mid-1970s. The number of conference participants as well as the number and frequency of conferences have increased during the 1980s and 1990s. The most important periodic research conferences are the Telecommunications Policy Research Conference (TPRC), International Telecommunications Society conferences (ITS), the European Communications Policy Research Conference (Euro-CPR), the International Communications Forecasting Conference (ICFC), and the Pacific Telecommunications Council Research Conference (PTC). The number of journals has also grown; in addition to *Telecommunications Policy*, some of the most important publications are *Information Economics and Policy, Communications and Strategies, Info, Media and Communications Review, Infomedia, Journal of Information*, and *Law and Technology*.

## 3  CONTINUED RELEVANCE OF TELECOM POLICY RESEARCH AND THE NEED FOR A BROAD PERSPECTIVE

For researchers and policymakers, it is important to establish if telecom policy research will continue to be relevant, and, if so, in what form. On the one hand, some commentators believe that the convergence of telecommunications, IT and broadcasting, and calls for general rather than sector-specific regulation, point to a smaller role for telecom policy. Instead, they argue, regulation should be broad and address the vision of an "information" or "digital" society. On the other hand, several factors indicate that the role of telecom policy and related research will not disappear because of the convergence phenomenon.

There is considerable inertia in the change of regulations and legislation all over the world. For instance, in the European context, the democratic decision processes have their own rhythm and logic. A phase-out of telecom policy, in this environment, will take time – at least ten years more. In the United States, it took a long time to get the Telecommunications Act of 1996 into effect, despite numerous revision attempts in the 1980s and 1990s, and a further revision does not seem likely. In Japan, the telecommunications legislation from 1985 still forms the backbone of legislation, and it is not expected to change in any material way in the next few years. In Korea, bureaucratic inertia still remains strong, partly because the regulatory body is also responsible for structural adjustment and promotion of ICT.

It is not even certain that a prospective phase-out of telecom policy is desirable. Increasingly, telecom policy has become intertwined with several of the political contexts and agendas, ranging from trade policy to education. Telecom policy interacts with, and supports, ambitions within so-called IT policy and e-policy. These political fields are areas of increasing political ambition, extent, and strategic significance. Telecom policy is becoming ever more a means of strengthening and supplementing comprehensive political objectives. Telecom policy also has connections with media policy, an area that touches upon constitutional issues.

While telecom policy as a practical phenomenon is here to stay for the foreseeable future, future research in this field will have to address broader and more comprehensive questions. Today, policies for telecommunications do not fully take into account the complexity of the evolving system for the provision of telecommunication services. This system is characterized by complex interactions among a number of variables, including technology, regulation, demand and adoption, financial markets, innovation, and the complementarities between systems and technologies. Clearly, the system will not become less complicated as we move into an environment characterized by increasing technological diversity.

Thus, to produce results that can be applied to the complex and changing environment in the sector, telecom policy research should address the entire system of actors and processes supplying telecommunication services. Among the processes to be addressed are those of competition, substitution and complementarities among technologies. As interdependencies between technologies in the form of substitution and complementarities are no longer confined to narrow application areas but occur across generations, systems and industries, an understanding of the interdependencies among technologies is essential. It has become clear that technology cannot be viewed in isolation: technology affects regulation, economics and consumers, but regulation and economic forces also shape technology. In addition, the processes driving demand and the role of regulation, standardization and financial markets must be understood. With an overview of the technologies, actors, processes and users that make up the telecommunications system, policymakers will be able to prevent tensions, promote standardization, and maintain the balance between co-ordination and competition that is needed for innovation.

To capture all these interconnected factors, a number of areas need to be addressed by telecom policy research (see Figure 1): past lessons, industrial dynamics, demand analysis, international comparisons and critical infrastructures and institutions.

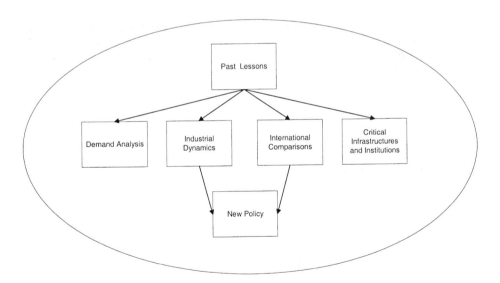

Figure 1. Dimensions to be Addressed in a Broader Telecom Policy Research Agenda

As the figure shows, an understanding of the dynamics of an industry requires insight into the rapid development that has led up to the current state, in other words, an historical analysis. In particular, the past interaction between demand and technologies, and the effect of regulatory interventions such as the 3G auctions are of interest. For policymakers to be able to influence a techno-economic system, they must understand the dynamic industrial processes driving the system and the possible evolutionary paths that the system may follow. The dynamic industrial processes and institutional factors such as regulation, standardization, legal frameworks, and financial markets should be addressed by telecom policy research. Furthermore, end user demand has and will continue to act as a selection mechanism for technology and applications. Identification of trends in the development of demand, and how these affect the different players that together deliver products and services to end users, is the key task. Another urgent research issue concerns critical infrastructures required for secure and dependable communications, data transfers and payments. Society's widespread dependence on ICTs should make critical infrastructures a priority area for research.

Finally, in addition to the specific issues on the telecom policy research agenda, two general research tools deserve mention: international benchmarking and forecasting. Benchmarking across regions or countries with regard to different aspects of performance, including innovation, telecommunications services uptake, and growth, is a useful tool for telecom policy research. These international comparisons must be built on a definition of what characterizes strong performance, which in itself is a complex issue. Apart from understanding the dynamics of the supply of telecommunications services, policy research must be extrapolated to include the telecommunications landscape in 10-15 years. To avoid unnecessarily vague results, any forecasting undertaken should be built on a clear structure and be firmly tied to an analysis of the industry.

In conclusion, telecom policy research should strive to answer the question: How should a new, dynamic policy capable of dealing successfully with a diverse, complex and changing structure of small as well as larger companies and competing technologies be formulated? To provide the basis for such a framework for regulatory, industrial and competition policies, the analysis concerning each of the above dimensions must be synthesized into a coherent set of concrete recommendations. Clearly, individual research projects will not be able to cover the full set of issues relevant for telecom policy; however, a recognition of the wide range of actors and processes influencing telecommunications will make it easier to work toward a more comprehensive understanding of the sector and contribute to an informed process of policy formulation.

## 4   AN OVERVIEW OF THE BOOK

### 4.1  Parts of the Book

This book is divided into five parts, each addressing a different aspect of the global economy and the digital society and the relationship between the two.

- Part 1: Global Economy and Digital Markets: Boom and Bust?
- Part 2: Global Economy and Digital Technology
- Part 3: Digital Goods: Theoretical Investigation
- Part 4: ICT Market Evolution and the Digital Society
- Part 5: Policy Aspects of the Digital Society

Part 1 contains several perspectives on the boom and bust of the ICT industries in the late 1990s and early 2000s. Part 2 is empirically focused, examining data on the relationship between ICTs and economic growth in different regions. More theoretically-oriented studies of markets for digital goods are presented in Part 3, followed by Part 4's analysis of market evolution for some of the main sub-sectors of the ICT industry. Finally, Part 5 analyzes policy aspects of the digital society.

While the separate chapters are summarized in the following section, the organization of chapters within parts of the book is described here. In Part 1, two studies describing and analyzing the telecoms boom and bust as a phenomenon (and its implications) are followed by a chapter concerning new perspectives on the role of e-commerce in business transactions. The chapters in Part 2 all deal with the relationship between ICT and various economic performance variables, with a focus on, respectively, the OECD, Japan and Korea. In Part 3 the chapters address, in turn, three different phenomena relevant for the digital society: price dispersion on the Internet, disclosure of source code, and information society indices. Part 4 commences with a study concerning flexible architectures for Internet QoS model design, followed by two chapters focusing on broadband market evolution, and closing with a chapter examining drivers of demand growth for mobile telecommunications services. Part 5 begins with four chapters offering traditional analyses of interconnection and other policy aspects in telecommunications; newer policy aspects, convergence and resilience, close the book in the final three chapters of Part 5.

## 4.2  Part 1: Global Economy and Digital Markets: Boom and Bust?

Why did investors believe that the telecoms industry would provide significantly above-average returns? In Chapter 2, Fransman explores possible answers to this key question through an examination of three hypotheses: the Biased Incentive Hypothesis, the Information Processing/Bounded Rationality Hypothesis, and the Guru Hypothesis of Information Selection. Although elements of all three hypotheses are found leading up to the telecoms boom, these hypotheses, taken individually or collectively, fail to provide a sufficient explanation for the boom. In order to explain the telecoms boom more must be known about how investors constructed the interpretive frameworks that shaped their understanding of how the telecoms industry worked. The discussion is linked to Keynesian and Austrian theories of the business cycle, and suggestions are made for further research, drawing on the ideas associated with Thomas Kuhn's concept of paradigms.

Noam argues in Chapter 3 that the telecom industry is entering a chronic pattern of volatility and instability, with boom-bust patterns becoming a common occurrence rather than an aberration. With a discussion of six main explanations for economic cyclicality and their relation to the telecom industry as a starting point, the chapter analyzes possible responses to the emerging cyclicality of three types of participants in the market: telecom companies, investors, and governments. For the industry, many of the strategies in a downturn have common elements that make them successful: expansion and consolidation of surviving firms within the industry, and collaboration, to the extent possible, with one's competitors. For government, Noam argues, the most realistic response may be to implement a dynamic policy that permits the industry to stabilize the market by creating oligopolies and to deal with the inevitable negative fall out by regulations that protect consumers and others.

Electronic commerce development was shaped by a number of assumptions about how it adds value to economic exchange. These assumptions focused attention on the ability of e-commerce to transcend distance and reach into markets without physical presence, replace costlier in-person transactions with electronic ones, and demonstrate network effects that reward rapid growth. In Chapter 4, Steinfield presents an alternative perspective in which electronic commerce complements a firm's physical location, works in concert with other modes of interaction, and emphasizes services to pre-existing exchange partners. A review of both business-to-consumer and business-to-business electronic commerce research is provided in support of this alternative perspective. In essence, the point of the chapter is to encourage a more realistic approach to e-commerce that is sensitive to the potential complementary benefits it offers to existing offline business activities.

### 4.3  Part 2: Global Economy and Digital Technology

Although the role of information and communications technology (ICT) in the productivity boom of the 1990s is disputed, a number of studies suggest that new economy gains are contained completely within ICT production or use. Chapter 5, written by Madden and Coble-Neal, examines the role that new technology activity plays in economic growth for a sample of 12 OECD member countries from 1976 to 2000. An empirical model that relates TFP to domestic and foreign technology spillovers and human capital is estimated. The study reveals a substantial increase in TFP growth over the late-1990s for 9 of 12 OECD member countries, coinciding with the new economy thesis, but with four countries exhibiting a superior ability to convert innovation into higher growth. This suggests that the new economy is not confined to specific industrial sectors nor just to the US. Also, the chapter suggests that increasing education levels and sustained capital deepening enhanced the ability to innovate in the best performing countries.

Chapter 6 presents a quantitative analysis of the impact of information technology adoption on the manufacturing and non-manufacturing sectors in Japan. More specifically, the authors, Hiromatsu, Ohira, Kobayashi, Tsubone and Kurita, analyze the labor productivity of each sector by relying on the growth accounting method as well as financial data, and then measure efficiency change in the sectors by using data envelopment analysis (DEA). The four sectors are manufacturing related to consumption, manufacturing related to raw materials, manufacturing related to machinery and non-manufacturing. The time span encompassed by the study is 1986-1998. The results show that the contribution of information equipment in the 1990s declined compared to that of the second half of the 1980s and that significant slack is seen in the Information Equipment Ratio and in employees with a college degree or above in the 1990s. The implication is that the non-production sector of the Japanese economy is unable to make effective use of information equipment.

In Chapter 7, Kim and Oh present findings on the impacts of telecommunications development in one country on both other industries in the country and all industries in other countries. In particular, the chapter examines the industrial linkages among 30 industries in 10 countries in the Asia-Pacific region. The analysis is carried out with the 1990 input-output data and by relying on a multi-regional variable input-output (MRVIO) model. In general, most studies on the impact of information technology (IT) on productivity or economic growth are based on the growth accounting of a national economy or micro-economic analysis of a specific industry. The use of the MRVIO model allows the authors to consider inter-industry (and even inter-country) spillover of development in the IT sector. In this sense, the chapter is clearly complementary to existing studies. One of the interesting findings is that technological improvement in the Korean telecommunications industry causes the Korean economy to improve the trade account with all nine countries. Also, the chapter puts emphasis on the role of non-IT industries in the Korean economy for international competitiveness.

### 4.4 Part 3: Digital Goods: Theoretical Investigation

As e-commerce has many of the characteristics associated with a perfect or "frictionless" market, one would expect limited price dispersion in a cyber market. However, there is broad empirical evidence that e-markets are characterized by significant price dispersion, as Grilli states in Chapter 8. Past contributions on price dispersion have advanced three main reasons for its occurrence: the immature nature of the market, service-premium strategies employed by firms, and the presence of uninformed consumers in the market. This chapter presents an empirical investigation that aims at testing the service-premium hypothesis. Results indicate that the superior quality of some services (in particular, customer support and reliability of delivery times) allows retailers to raise prices, while other features (web site quality and ease of ordering) have a negligible impact on price dispersion.

Chapter 9 examines the effect on the market of the enforced disclosure by an antitrust agency of private technological information and the role played by compatibility and the technological gap among competing goods in determining market structure. To this end, Sohn and Yang apply a two-period, two-firm model, in which a firm exists as a monopoly in the first period and another firm with a technologically advanced good enters in the second period. On the basis of this modeling and a review of case studies, the authors conclude that, in situations where a monopolistic incumbent wields its private technological information as an entry barrier, disclosure of source code to competitors contributes to improving social welfare by addressing the inefficient allocation of resources caused by path dependence. An open source software policy can also be justified for eliminating an entry barrier when technology improves gradually.

In Chapter 10, Grigorovici, Schement and Taylor have as an objective making a contribution to a conceptual model of information indicators. A variety of statistics are currently used to measure Internet access and the level of ICT deployment, but the underlying theory is tenuous at best, with data that are often not comparable and indicators that are chosen subjectively. This chapter includes a survey of the history of Information Society Indicators (ISIs) and of where, how and in what forms information indicators are currently being applied. The authors argue that most existing indicators are not based on a comprehensive, deductive theory and that the "unweighted" measures are used too frequently in inter-sector and inter-country comparisons. As an alternative, the steps involved in constructing an "e-readiness" index based on a Structural Equation Modeling approach are presented, and its potential application to social development issues is discussed.

### 4.5 Part 4: ICT Market Evolution and the Digital Society

As uncertainty in the network industry increases, network service providers need a flexible architecture in order to maintain a competitive advantage, Kim and Weiss argue in Chapter 11. Since complete replacement of existing networks is not practical, modularity in network design may be an efficient approach. The goal of the chapter is to construct a theoretical framework to support the decisions of network service providers in network design: to modularize or not, and if so, by how much. To achieve this goal, a theory is developed to show the extent of modularity in network design by combining two important concepts: modularity from management and complementarity from economics. For empirical testing, a simple QoS service model network is designed and simulated, with preliminary results showing that modularity in network design has value, but that its effect is limited by complementarity.

The number of high-speed Internet subscribers in Korea, which has been growing rapidly every year since high-speed services were launched in 1998, reached more than 10 million by the end of 2002. Until now, service providers have concentrated on marketing activities to attract new customers, to some extent neglecting service quality and customer satisfaction for existing customers. In Chapter 12, Kim, Park and Yeon analyze the relationships between service quality, customer satisfaction, and customer retention. The authors find that six key quality elements are major determinants of customer retention. Implications for management are, for instance, that service providers should establish quality indices to foster continuous quality management and that service providers may need a short-term performance improvement plan as well as a long-term network development plan.

As the Internet grows, an increasing number of households are demanding higher-speed access, primarily through digital subscriber line (DSL) or cable modem service. The analysis of Rappoport, Taylor and Kridel in Chapter 13 focuses on the demand for these two forms of high-speed access, making use of willingness-to-pay (WTP) data from a survey conducted in 2002. Findings include (1) the inverse importance of age as a determinant of willingness-to-pay; (2) the emergence of what would appear to be a material difference between the demand for cable modem access and DSL access; (3) cable modem access, but not DSL access, appearing to be largely independent of income and education. One would think that the two forms of access (assuming that both were available) would be fairly strong substitutes, but the correlation between the willingnesses-to-pay suggests otherwise.

In Chapter 14, Banerjee and Ros report the results from an econometric analysis of global mobile telephony demand growth as a function of various market and regulatory variables and unobservable country and region-specific factors. Using panel data from 1996-2000, the authors investigate the drivers of mobile services demand growth in selected developed and developing countries. In particular, the effect on demand growth of the quality of the existing fixed network, the presence of a separate regulator, and the offering of innovative pricing arrangements, such as calling party pays and prepaid services, are explored. The study finds that although those effects are, for the most part, as expected, there is mixed evidence on the role of the regulator and of the price structure innovations. In addition, the study points to technological, rather than economic, substitution as the more powerful underlying source of movement in mobile telephony markets.

### 4.6  Part 5: Policy Aspects of the Digital Society

The liberalization of telecommunications markets has been accompanied by a growing tendency towards regionalization and internationalization of regulatory regimes. Chapter 15 examines the Europeanization of telecommunications regulation, focusing on the European Community (EC), by far the most advanced regionalization movement at present. In particular, the chapter concentrates on the regulatory and institutional arrangements following the 1999 Communications Review. The author, Michalis, puts forward two main arguments. First, despite the transfer of regulatory authority to the European arena, the role of national regulation remains significant. Second, the greater flexibility of the new EC communications regulatory framework is likely to result in renewed diversity at the national level. Although the resulting degree of harmonization may be low, the new framework will give national governments more freedom to pursue their own policy objectives.

In Chapter 16, Jamison examines how incumbents and entrants respond to prices for network interconnection in telecommunications, including prices for unbundled network elements. Most studies of the effects of these prices find that lower prices encourage entry and encourage entrants to use more unbundled network elements. Missing from this literature are studies of how incumbents respond to the interconnection prices they charge. US telecommunications laws place an obligation on incumbents to provide interconnection at any technically feasible point, implying that interconnection prices should not affect incumbents' provision of interconnection services. Using data from 1998, the author finds evidence that low unbundled network element prices result in lower entry, perhaps indicating that US incumbents limit entry. No evidence is found that incumbents hinder entrants from gaining market share for customers who receive more calls than they make (such as Internet Service Providers) or from gaining market share using resold services.

Chapter 17 explores interconnection and unbundling policies that will be required for packet networks. Kolesar and Levin analyze these policies both for the case when packet networks interconnect with each other and for the case where packet networks interconnect with circuit-switched networks. Required regulations are identified both for end-state packet networks and for the transition period; the authors conclude that the only point of interconnection that theoretically could require regulatory intervention is interconnection at the last router to the terminating customer's device and that the interconnection model proposed for a packet-to-packet network interconnection will also prevail for interconnection between packet and circuit-switched networks. Furthermore, the negative consequences of alternative regulatory approaches that depart from the preferred regulations, including rules requiring incumbents to share their facilities outside what is necessary to ensure access to essential facilities, are examined.

As part of a broader investigation of how interconnection policy regimes influence strategic alliance activity in the telecom industry, Lee and Madhavan present a preliminary analysis of the relationship between telecom traffic networks and strategic alliance networks in Chapter 18. In order to quantitatively analyze the interconnection network at the global level, the authors use international traffic flows as a proxy for interconnection. While the alliance networks point to several interesting features of the alliance landscape, including increasing complexity, decreasing centralization, and increasing regionalization, the traffic flow network appears to be relatively stable, although there is some evidence of increasing regionalization in traffic volume as well. A preliminary analysis to compare lagged cross-year correlation between alliance activity and traffic flow was attempted but failed to throw light on whether traffic drove alliances or vice versa.

As a result of convergence in the telecommunications industry, the conventional one-service-via-one-network concept is changing to multiple services via multiple networks. However, understanding of this convergence phenomenon is vague, thereby resulting in confusion and uncertainty about the market environment. To address the issues related to the convergence phenomenon, Chapter 19 introduces a Service-Network matrix. Using this matrix, the authors, Han, Ahn and Skudlark, explain the convergence phenomenon from both a service and a network viewpoint. The framework is intended to help managers identify new service opportunities, especially during the idea-generation stage of the new service development process. Furthermore, a scenario-planning approach for initial screening of new service concepts is suggested. Finally, the convergence framework and scenario-planning approach are applied to an actual Internet access via WLAN service development case.

In Chapter 20, Noam addresses how communications networks coped with the aftermath of the attacks on the World Trade Center and the Pentagon, and the lessons for the future about the nature of emergency communications. The chapter documents how domestic and international fixed-line and mobile networks, business communication systems, and the internet responded to the huge increase in traffic volume that followed the attacks. While the limitations of cellular networks and major internet content servers in serving millions of users simultaneously were demonstrated, decentralized forms of communication such as email, instant messaging, and bulletin boards performed well. Noam concludes that we should revise the basic philosophy of emergency communication from that of the traditional military-style, top-down approach of public safety agencies to a more decentralized system building on lessons from the spontaneous efforts of using internet technology following September 11.

Finally, in Chapter 21, Alleman and Liebenau explore the rules, regulations, and company actions that impede network resilience. The chapter begins with a definition of network resilience and a discussion of factors that affect it. These fall into three interacting categories: standards, regulations, and government practices and policies. This analysis allows the authors to identify barriers to network resilience related to local exchange carriers (LECs) and electromagnetic spectrum issues, with a focus on rules and regulation that resulted from the Telecommunications Act of 1996. The chapter proposes four main action areas, involving pro-active roles for industry and government actors, for enhancing network resilience: ensuring inter-modal competition, stimulating demand for resilience by raising standards, subsidies to build out critical infrastructure, and devising new governmental roles and priorities. Addressing these concerns, while perhaps expensive, will stimulate new business development in the telecommunications industry and is, therefore, potentially economically justifiable.

In conclusion, the papers collected in this volume address a number of issues that will affect the development of the digital society in the coming decades: growth patterns and underlying drivers, market evolution and company strategies, the effect of ICTs on productivity, and urgent policy requirements. They present a clear picture of the specific ways in which the global economy is linked to the digital society and suggest various measures for increasing the benefits of ICTs and improving the functioning of digital markets. But while the issues are addressed separately here, the effect on growth will be determined by the techno-economic system of communications as a whole. Crucially, the social fabric and institutional arrangements are critically influenced by the growth of ICTs. Future research, therefore, could profitably incorporate continued efforts to define and understand the complex relationships between industries, technologies, regulation, firms, and user adoption.

In addition to presenting work at the cutting edge of telecom policy research, the editors hope that this book will contribute to fostering international research collaboration. Different regions have much to learn from each other in the areas of globalization, economic development and digital society, and thus there is a strong case for promoting cooperative inter-regional research on these issues. In the long run, such international collaboration will lead to a more thorough understanding of a global economy and digital society and will help to multiply the benefits for all.

# PART I


# GLOBAL ECONOMY AND DIGITAL
# MARKETS: BOOM AND BUST?

Global Economy and Digital Society
E. Bohlin, S. Levin, N. Sung and C-H. Yoon (Editors)

# CHAPTER 2

# The Telecoms Boom and Bust, 1996-2002: Puzzles, Paradoxes, and Processing*

Martin Fransman

*Institute for Japanese-European Technology Studies, The University of Edinburgh, Edinburgh*

**Abstract**. Why did investors believe that the Telecoms Industry would provide significantly above-average returns? In this chapter possible answers to this key question are explored through the examination of three hypotheses: the Biased Incentive Hypothesis, the Information Processing/Bounded Rationality Hypothesis, and the Guru Hypothesis of Information Selection. It is shown that although elements of all three hypotheses are to be found in the processes that led to the Telecoms Boom, these hypotheses, taken individually or collectively, fail to provide a sufficient explanation for the boom. It is concluded that in order to explain the Telecoms Boom we need to know more about how investors constructed the interpretive frameworks that shaped their understanding of how the Telecoms Industry worked and what would happen to it in the future. The discussion is then linked to Keynesian and Austrian theories of the business cycle. In the penultimate section suggestions are made for further research, drawing on some of the ideas associated with Thomas Kuhn's concept of paradigms.

## 1   INTRODUCTION

"Soros explains something that most observers of the recent stock market bubble know intuitively, but that market fundamentalists deny: 'Financial markets, left to their own devices, are liable to go to extremes and eventually break down'. Robert Shiller, in his book Irrational Exuberance, has documented this tendency of markets to excess volatility" (Stiglitz, 2002, p.26).

Why are financial markets "liable to go to extremes"? This chapter examines this question within the context of the Telecoms Boom and Bust, 1996-2002. In the first part of the chapter the main beliefs that drove the Telecoms Boom are reconstructed. These beliefs formed a Consensual Vision regarding the Telecoms Industry and its dynamics. There were, however, fundamental flaws in this vision that are analysed in this chapter. These flaws contributed to the ensuing Telecoms Bust. The main question posed in this chapter, however, is why did so many key players come to accept this Consensual Vision despite its shortcomings, many of

---

* This chapter draws on the author's recently published book, *Telecoms in the Internet Age: From Boom to Bust to...?*, Oxford University Press, 2002. The author would like to acknowledge, without implicating, useful comments from Arno Penzias and Steve Klepper.

which could have been anticipated? This question is examined through an analysis of three hypotheses which all deal with how decision-makers handle information in the attempt to derive knowledge about how their world works, what will happen to it, and what the implications are for what they should be doing. The three hypotheses are the Biased Incentive Hypothesis, the Information Processing/Bounded Rationality Hypothesis, and the Guru Hypothesis of Information Selection. It is concluded that the paradox of the 'Information Society' and the 'Knowledge Economy' is that they do not provide the information and knowledge that is necessary to eliminate the extremes. We have little option, it seems, but to live with booms and busts as best we can.

## 2   PUZZLES

According to Business Week, in the second half of the 1990s Jack Benjamin Grubman "may have been the most influential person in the telecom industry".[1] Between 1998 and 2000 Grubman helped his firm, Salomon Smith Barney, to raise $53 billion for telecoms companies, more than any other firm on Wall Street. However, after the onset of the Telecoms Bust from March 2000, Grubman's influence quickly crumbled. At least ten of the major telecoms companies he strongly supported – including the most prominent such as WorldCom and Global Crossing – have filed for bankruptcy.

What did Grubman, in retrospect, make of the Telecoms Boom and Bust? According to Grubman, "Everyone was culpable: the debt markets, the equity markets, the issuers, the companies. Anyone who tries to point a finger at a single group is not being fair".[2] But Grubman's conclusion poses a puzzle. To say that everyone was culpable is to imply that they could have, and should have, known and done better. If events were beyond their control they could not be culpable. But if they could have, and should have, known and done better, why did they not?

### 2.1   The Consensual Vision of the Telecoms Industry

To take this further, it is worth attempting to reconstruct the key beliefs that underpinned the Telecoms Boom from around 1996 to March 2002. These beliefs were widely shared amongst the debt markets, equity markets, issuers and companies that Grubman refers to, and even by regulators. Accordingly, I refer to these beliefs as comprising a Consensual Vision. In my book I suggest that there were four key beliefs that underpinned the Consensual Vision, expressing the conventional wisdom about what would happen in the Telecoms Industry. These beliefs are shown in Table 1.

---

[1] *Business Week*, May 13, 2002, p.42.

[2] *Financial Times*, 7 September 2001.

Table 1. The Beliefs Underpinning the Consensual Vision Regarding the Telecoms Industry

| Belief 1 | The Internet will drive an explosive demand for bandwidth |
|----------|----------------------------------------------------------|
| Belief 2 | New telecoms operators will out-compete the incumbents in providing this bandwidth |
| Belief 3 | Financial markets will support the fittest new operators |
| Belief 4 | Technical change will further reinforce the processes referred to in the first three beliefs |

Source: Fransman (2002).

These beliefs together provided the building-blocks for the interpretive framework[3] that shaped thinking about what would happen to the Telecoms Industry and its companies and, by inference, how decision-makers should play their cards. Most visibly, this interpretive framework drove share prices. More specifically, the interpretive framework was responsible for the rapid rise in the price of the shares of the main telecoms companies (operators as well as equipment suppliers) and for the rise in the share price of the major new entrant telecoms operators (such as WorldCom, Qwest, Level 3, Global Crossing and Colt) relative to the incumbent operators (like AT&T, BT, etc.).[4]

The rise in the share price of the telecoms operators (and also the telecoms equipment companies who supplied them) continued until about March 2000. At this time the generalised bull stock market ended and the decline began. Simultaneously, doubts emerged regarding the validity of the beliefs underlying the Consensual Vision that had reigned. These doubts may be summarised in the form of three questions regarding the Consensual Vision. These questions are presented in Table 2.[5]

Table 2. Questions Regarding the Consensual Vision

| Question 1 | At what rate will the demand for bandwidth increase? |
|------------|------------------------------------------------------|
| Question 2 | What will happen to the supply of bandwidth and how will demand and supply interact? |
| Question 3 | How many competitors will there be in the market for telecoms services? |

Source: Fransman (2002).

## 2.2 The Rocks on which the Consensual Vision Foundered[6]

In retrospect, it is clear that the implicit assumptions on which Belief 1 (that the Internet will drive an explosive demand for bandwidth) were based were overly optimistic. Although, as a result of the rapid global diffusion of the Internet, there was an "explosive demand for bandwidth" – as the new operators and their supporting financial analysts put it in their public pronouncements – it was not explicitly acknowledged that this rate of increase in demand could not continue indefinitely. Telecoms operators – just as their counterparts producing PCs and mobile phones – would soon be forced to live with this fact.

---

[3] For recent writing on interpretive frameworks in economics see Loasby (2003, 2001) and Witt (2000).

[4] See Fransman (2002) for an elaboration on the rationale behind the four beliefs and for empirical evidence on the share price movements of the incumbents and their main new operator competitors in the US and UK.

[5] For a more detailed examination of these three questions see Fransman (2002).

[6] The arguments in this section are elaborated upon in Fransman (2002).

Even more surprising was the under-emphasis in the Consensual Vision of the supply side (Question 2). As the 19th century economist Alfred Marshall noted, price is determined by both blades of the scissors, a fact recognised by any first-year economics student. Curiously, however, in their eagerness to address the new demand opportunities opened up by the Internet, the proponents of the Consensual Vision neglected the supply side.

But crucial changes were taking place on the supply side. In 2000 it was announced, for example, that Lucent Technologies' Bell Labs had pushed 1.6 trillion bits, or terabits, of information through a single optical fibre by using the dense wavelength division multiplexing technique (DWDM).[7] This is enough for 25 million conversations or 200,000 video signals simultaneously and one cable may contain a dozen such fibres. The effects of such technical change were dramatic. In September 2001 it was estimated that "only 1 or 2 percent of the fibre optic cable buried under Europe and North America has even been turned on or 'lit'… A similar overcapacity exists in undersea links, where each new Atlantic cable adds as much bandwidth as all the previous infrastructure put together".[8]

However, it was not only technical change per se that was rocking the foundations of the Consensual Vision. The evolving structure and organisation of the entire Telecoms Industry constituted a fundamental challenge to this Vision. The problem was that very few of the participants in this industry understood how the Telecoms Industry worked and how it was changing.[9]

As had happened in the Computer Industry, processes of vertical specialisation were radically transforming the Telecoms Industry. Until the 1980s, the engine of change in the Telecoms Industry lay in the central research laboratories of the incumbent telecoms operators – famous institutions such as AT&T's Bell Labs, BT's Martlesham Laboratories, France Telecom's CNET laboratories, and NTT's Electrical Communications Laboratories. The research and advanced development that took place in these laboratories created the new generations of technology and equipment that drove the Telecoms Industry. The equipment itself, however, was manufactured by a group of specialist telecoms equipment suppliers such as Lucent (then an integrated part of AT&T) and Nortel in North America, Siemens, Alcatel, Ericsson and Nokia in Europe, and NEC, Fujitsu and Hitachi in Japan. Closed markets and long-term obligational relationships bound the incumbent telecoms operators closely to their equipment suppliers.

By the 1990s, however, this pattern of industrial organisation had changed dramatically. The forces of vertical specialisation that had, at first unnoticed, begun to transform the Telecoms Industry decades earlier were given legal vent from the mid-1980s when government liberalisation introduced the first elements of competition in telecoms services markets in Japan, the UK and US. In the US, MCI and Sprint emerged to challenge AT&T; in the UK, Mercury took on BT; and in Japan, DDI, Japan Telecom and Teleway Japan fought with NTT.

The entry path of these 'original new entrant operators' was smoothed by the decades of learning and knowledge accumulation undertaken by the specialist equipment suppliers who in most cases had cut their teeth through manufacturing equipment for their national incumbent telecoms operator. Rapidly the knowledge of these specialist suppliers had deepened with

---

[7] DWDM is an optical technology that uses different coloured light waves as communications channels in a single optical fibre, thereby increasing significantly the carrying capacity of that fibre.

[8] *Financial Times*, 4 September 2001.

[9] A detailed analysis of the evolution of the Telecoms Industry is contained in Chapters 1 and 2 of Fransman (2002).

the result that by the late-1990s they were collectively some four times as R&D-intensive as the incumbent operators who hitherto had powered the engine of technical change in the Telecoms Industry. By the end of the 1990s, however, the incumbent operators had handed over a large part of their R&D requirements, in addition to their equipment requirements, to the specialist suppliers. With falling R&D intensities, the incumbent operators became less research and development intensive than the average in industries normally not considered to be 'high-tech' industries such as automobiles, personal care products, and media and photography, and about as R&D-intensive as the beverages industry.[10] In this way, the R&D engine of the Telecoms Industry moved decisively from the central research laboratories of the incumbent operators to the specialist equipment suppliers. But this would have crucial consequences for the evolving structure and dynamics of the entire industry.

One of the most important consequences was that technological entry barriers into the network operator layer of the Telecoms Industry were dramatically lowered. The reason, simply, was that telecoms equipment suppliers such as Nortel and Lucent were willing to supply state-of-the-art equipment to any company that wanted to enter the telecoms operator market, provided they were able to pay. And financial markets, enthused by the Consensual Vision, were willing to provide the funds that enabled the new entrant operators to pay. Furthermore, labour markets, oiled by the granting of generous stock options to newly recruited top managers, provided the new operators with the knowledgeable staff they needed, often head-hunted from the incumbent operators. Between 1996 and 1999 in the US alone 144 new telecoms companies went public, raising more than $25 billion.

These events seemed to represent a vibrant market response to the major new business opportunities opened up by the Internet. They seemed to provide empirical support for the assumptions made in the Consensual Vision (summarised in Table 1). Even regulators were delighted, arguing that the market forces which their deregulation measures had unleashed were creating the competitive pressures and incentives that, in marked contrast to the earlier telecoms monopoly era, would stimulate innovation and improve services.

Unfortunately, however, things did not turn out so happily. The problems arose largely from Question 3 in Table 2 (How many competitors will there be in the market for telecoms services?). The substantial number of new entrant operators – together with the great increase in investment in new network capacity embodying much improved technology – undermined prices and profitability. This was particularly the case in long-distance and international voice and data services.[11] Only local services and mobile services provided relief from this trend. (In the US the Telecommunications Act of 1996 had attempted, unsuccessfully, to dislodge the market dominance of the local phone companies such as Verizon and SBC. Particularly in Europe, mobile services remained profitable into 2002 but in the US strong competition between the mobile operators soon put an end to above-average rates of profitability.)

The collapse in prices meant that both the revenue and the earnings of incumbents and new operators alike were significantly below what investors had expected. The problem in this high fixed-cost industry was that large sums of money had to be spent on rolling out networks well in advance of the compensating revenues that would eventually pay for these invest-ments. During the Telecoms Boom the exuberant expectations of investors (shaped by the

---

[10] This remarkable fact is documented in Table 8.2 (p.281) and is analysed in Chapters 2 and 8 of Fransman (2002).

[11] This was the general picture although some sub-areas were profitable, such as private lines (data networks for businesses) and frame relay services (switched data access). However, Internet transmission provided little profit. (I am grateful to Arno Penzias for pointing this out to me.)

Consensual Vision) plugged the gap between investment costs and the anticipated revenue streams that would cover them. The collapse in prices, however, meant that these future revenue streams were unlikely to be forthcoming. Financial markets that were exuberant quickly became disenchanted.

The collision between Consensual Vision-shaped expectations and the reality of falling prices and profitability put enormous pressure on telecoms operators. It was this pressure that explains the transgressions of WorldCom – accused of fraudulently reporting an excess of up to $9 billion in earnings – and the somewhat lesser misdemeanours by companies such as Qwest and Global Crossing. Caught in the web of false expectations that they themselves had created, these companies did everything they could to avoid disappointing the markets that fed them and kept them alive. In short, the bonanza foreseen by the Consensual Vision proved illusory. The rest is history.

## 3   PARADOXES

"Investors took everything at face value, which was understandable. There wasn't a lot of information, and it was of varying quality" (Michael E. Kenneally, co-Chairman and Chief Investment Officer, Bank of America Capital Management Inc. quoted in Business Week, 2002, p.37).

This statement is remarkable, implying as it does the existence of a significant paradox. In the so-called Information Society, when supposedly a greater proportion of the workforce are 'knowledge workers' than ever before, there is not enough information and the information that does exist is of 'varied quality'! Jack Grubman, the telecoms guru, alone was paid about $20 million annually (Business Week, 2002, p.42) while the compensation of his colleague, Henry Blodget, the "Superstar Internet Analyst", increased from $3 million in 1999 to $12 million in 2001 (Business Week, 2002, p.39). And there were many, though less well-compensated, Grubmans and Blodgets. Why then, collectively, did they produce so little information and of such varied quality?

## 4   THE REMAINING BIG QUESTION: WHY WAS THE CONSENSUAL VISION BELIEVED IN THE FIRST PLACE?

The biggest puzzle is why the Consensual Vision became the conventional wisdom in the first place. If the argument in this chapter is correct, it was the Consensual Vision that drove the Telecoms Boom. But why were the beliefs that underlay the Consensual Vision (shown in Table 1) so readily accepted? This question is puzzling because, as shown in the last subsection, there were many reasons – some of which were summarised in the three questions raised in Table 2 – to be sceptical of the Consensual Vision. And some of these reasons could have, and should have, been anticipated before the Telecoms Boom turned into the Telecoms Bust. Neither was the history of the Telecoms Industry between 1996 and 2002 so very different from that of other industries, such as the railway and electricity industries in earlier periods. In short, why is it that the 'Information Society' and 'Knowledge Economy' of the late 1990s failed to provide the information and knowledge that might have led to the avoidance of the excesses of the Telecoms Boom and Bust?

## 5    THREE HYPOTHESES

In attempting to answer this intriguing question, three hypotheses will be examined. They are the Biased Incentive Hypothesis, the Information Processing/Bounded Rationality Hypothesis, and what will be called the Guru Hypothesis of Information Selection.

### 5.1    The Biased Incentive Hypothesis

One answer that has been given to this question is that the incentive system governing the provision of information and the creation of knowledge about how industries, markets and companies were working and performing was responsible for the production of biased 'information and knowledge'. One version of this biased incentive hypothesis is provided in the following quotation from Business Week (2002, p.36): "Wall Street has always struggled with conflicts of interest. Indeed, an investment bank is a business built on them. The same institution serves two masters: the companies for which it sells stock, issues bonds, or executes mergers; and the investors whom it advises. While companies want high prices for their newly issued stocks and low interest rates on their bonds, investors want low prices and high rates. In between, the bank gets fees from both and trades stocks and bonds on its own behalf as well, potentially putting its own interests at odds with those of all its customers. But in recent years, those inherent conflicts have grown worse…"

More generally, the argument is that the analysts working for an investment bank might bias the recommendations they make in order to suit the interests of the corporate clients of the bank. It is this biased incentive hypothesis that supposedly explains the remarkable fact discovered by New York Attorney General Eliot Spitzer in an investigation into the stock market boom and bust. In Business Week's (2002, p.37) words, "In some of the e-mail turned up by Spitzer, analysts disparage stocks as 'crap' and 'junk' that they were pushing at the time".

Another variant of the biased incentive hypothesis applies the argument to the incentive regime governing the behaviour of managers. According to Robert J. Shiller, author of Irrational Exuberance, "It's finally dawning on people that this incentive system we've given managers based on the value of stock options has encouraged management to puff up their companies a lot" (Business Week, 2002, p.39).

*Strengths*

The main strength of the Biased Incentive Hypothesis is that it goes a long way towards explaining the behaviour of some of the individuals governed by these incentive regimes and the 'information and knowledge' they created. The power of the hypothesis lies in the causal link that it postulates between incentive, behaviour, and the 'information and knowledge' that is created.

*Weaknesses*

However, the Biased Incentive Hypothesis also has several weaknesses. To begin with, the causal link that it postulates does not always operate. For example, in his book Dot.con, John Cassidy discusses the bears whose views contradicted those of the dot.com bulls who were sometimes in the same financial organisation. In some cases, as Cassidy shows, the bears remained bears even when the tide of consensual opinion was flowing decisively in favour of the bulls (although in other cases the bears eventually succumbed and conformed). There were, however, instances where recalcitrant bears, refusing to conform to the incentive regime, were "shunted aside" by their financial institution determined to impose the desired answer.[12] As these examples show, the causal link – incentive-behaviour-'information and knowledge' – is not a deterministic one.

The second problem with the Biased Incentive Hypothesis is that it fails to take account of all the other players in the economic system who were subject to different incentive regimes that, arguably, encouraged them to tell the 'truth' (or at least – to the extent that it is impossible to create 'true' information and knowledge that is uninfluenced by the incentive regime – to create 'information' with different biases). Examples include independent financial analysts, independent consultants, large institutional investors, academics and regulators.

Of these, possibly the most problematical are the large institutional investors such as the mutual funds that controlled many billions of dollars. Are we to believe that they were unaware of the biases in the information provided by analysts tied to investment banks? Even if they were unaware, these analysts would frequently have come up with contradictory advice amongst themselves, raising the question of the resources that the institutional investors put into attempts to get an independent view of what was happening. If it was all a matter of incentives, surely the institutional investors had an equally strong incentive to attempt to 'get at the truth'? The subsequent losses that they and their clients took seem to provide grounds for this suggestion. However, if there were different incentive regimes in the economic system, and if 'information and knowledge' is caused by the incentive regime, then there must have been different, perhaps contradictory, sets of 'information and knowledge'. This raises the question of how selection was made between these sets.

A third problem with the Biased Information Hypothesis is that it fails to distinguish between short-run and long-run incentives, confining attention to the former. Implicit in the hypothesis, therefore, is the tacit assumption of short-sightedness on the part of those supposedly driven by the incentive regime. While the creation of 'information and knowledge' that conforms with the incentive regime may benefit the individual analyst in the short term, their incorrectness may produce problems for the individual in the longer term. It is not at all clear that Jack Grubman, for example, would have given the same advice if he could rewind the 'video of time'. Although it is possible that even now - punished after public investigation with a $15 million fine and banned from employment in financial institutions, and suffering from the resulting social stigma - Grubman might feel that his short-term gains outweigh the longer-term ill-effects, it is by no means obvious that the same calculation would be made by all the other analysts involved.

In the event, however, there seems to have been little discussion and debate around different analyses, views and opinions – based on different sets of information and knowledge – regarding how the Telecoms Industry works and what would happen to the profitability of its companies. Rather, as argued earlier in this chapter, it seems that a Consensual Vision emerged, took root and held sway, shaping beliefs about the Telecoms Industry until early 2000 when boom turned to bust. If this account of events is correct, it is the rise to dominance

---

[12] According to Cassidy (2002, p.120), "One by one, most of the bears either changed their views or found themselves shunted aside".

of the Consensual Vision that needs to be explained.[13] The biased incentive hypothesis, it would appear, is insufficient by itself to provide the explanation.

### Conclusion

It may be concluded, therefore, that although incentives certainly were an important part of the story, they are not sufficient to explain the Telecoms Boom and Bust.

## 5.2    The Information Processing/Bounded Rationality Hypothesis

Another view of how individuals and organisations work is contained in the Information Processing/Bounded Rationality Hypothesis, originally put forward by Nobel Prize-winning economist Herbert Simon. Until his death in February 2001, Herbert Simon held the view of "human beings ... as information processors". Furthermore, he believed that "human beings are serial information processors: we can attend to at most one thing at a time" and that this was a "fundamental axiom underlying the principle of scarcity of attention" (Simon, 2002). Simon argued that "bounded rationality" was one of the major consequences of the scarcity of attention. In his view human beings are competent calculators who are attempting to make informed decisions and choices through the processing of information but who are inevitably constrained by the scarcity of attention. To what extent, if at all, can the consensual belief that super-normal profits could be made in the Telecoms Industry be attributed to bounded rationality?

### Strengths

The principal strength of the Information Processing/Bounded Rationality Hypothesis lies in its axiomatic deduction of the principle of scarcity of attention. While this principle is deduced from the assumption of human beings as serial information processors, we all, through our own experiences (painful and otherwise) are made aware of the fact of scarcity of attention. Indeed, it seems difficult to imagine the truth of an alternative, contradicting, hypothesis. Accordingly, it seems necessary to incorporate the principle of scarcity of attention in any explanation of the Telecoms Boom and Bust. However, the question is to what extent was scarce attention the cause of the belief in super-normal profits in the Telecoms Industry.

### Weaknesses

How would the Simonian decision-maker, essentially an information processor working under the constraints of scarce attention, say in 1998, have decided whether or not to invest in the Telecoms Industry?[14] The emphasis on 'information' in the Information Processing/Bounded Rationality Hypothesis suggests that our decision-maker would have searched for information relating to the Telecoms Industry. Given his or her scarce attention, it would not have been

---

[13] If, however, this account is incorrect then we need to, first, clarify why it is incorrect, secondly, replace it with a more accurate account of events driving the Telecoms Boom and Bust, and, third, explain why the boom emerged to begin with and why it turned into a bust. In short, we need an alternative explanation of why markets in this case "went to extremes", to use Stiglitz's phrase used at the outset of this chapter.

[14] Following Grubman above, these were the decision-makers in the debt markets, the equity markets, the issuers, and the telecoms companies.

possible to collect and process all the relevant information in existence. However, being by assumption a competent calculator, he or she would be expected to collect and process as much relevant information as possible (within the scarce attention constraint[15]) and, on the basis of this information, make the investment decision.

While this seems to be the procedure that Simon had in mind when he referred to human beings as essentially information processors, further investigation into the problems confronting our hypothetical decision-maker reveal a number of issues that need to be addressed. These issues begin to emerge once we ask how our decision-maker is to decide what constitutes 'relevant information'. Simon's writings provide an answer to this question although, as we shall see, the logical implications of his arguments contradict one of his basic assumptions, namely that human beings are essentially information processors.

It is clear from Simon's writings that in tackling the question of what, from the decision-maker's point of view, constitutes 'relevant information' it is necessary to make three conceptual distinctions.[16] The first is what may be termed the objective set of relevant information, that is the total amount of information in existence relating to the Telecoms Industry. Because, by axiomatic definition, the decision-maker's attention is scarce, the decision-maker will be unable to access all the information in the objective set of information. It will only be possible to access a subset of this information. But this raises the question of what determines the subset that the decision-maker ends up acquiring.

It is here that Simon's second conceptual distinction comes in. This is the notion of attention as a selection mechanism. Not only is attention scarce, it also serves as a mechanism for focusing on, and therefore selecting, a subset of the objective set of relevant information.[17] But this is not the end of the Simonian story. The reason is that there may be many alternative ways of dealing with the subset of information selected by the decision-maker's attention. According to Simon, the decision-maker goes through a second selection procedure when he or she chooses a problem-solving strategy[18]. The problem-solving strategy, accordingly, is the third conceptual distinction.

Returning to our poor hypothetical decision-maker - grappling with the decision about whether to invest in the Telecoms Industry and, if so, how much to invest and in which companies – an important conclusion is implied by Simon's tripartite conceptual distinction. This conclusion is that what drives the ultimate decision is not the objective set of information on the Telecoms Industry 'out there', but rather the attention and the problem-solving strategy

---

[15] In addition to scarce attention, there is also an organisational constraint. This organisational constraint is determined by the individual's responsibilities and the priority attached to these responsibilities. In the case, say, of a typical fund manager a relatively small proportion of working time would have been available to decide how much of a portfolio should be invested in the Telecoms Industry and which company shares should be purchased.

[16] For a more detailed discussion, with relevant quotations from Simon, see Fransman (1994), pp725-734.

[17] "Perception is sometimes referred to as a 'filter'. This term is as misleading as 'approximation', and for the same reason: it implies that what comes through into the nervous system is really quite a bit like what is 'out there'. In fact, the filtering is not merely a passive selection of some part of a presented whole, but an active process involving attention to a very small part of the whole and exclusion, from the outset, of almost all that is not within the scope of attention." (Simon 1959, 272-3)

[18] "there are hosts of inferences that might be drawn from the information stored in the brain that are not in fact drawn. The consequences implied by information in the memory become known only through active information-processing, and hence through active selection of particular problem-solving paths from the myriad that might have been followed." (Simon 1959, 273) This quotation illustrates Simon's concern with what he called procedural rationality.

of the decision-maker. However, instead of solving the problem under discussion – namely the extent to which bounded rationality explains the belief that super-normal profits were to be made in the Telecoms Industry – this conclusion merely pushes the problem one stage back: what determines the decision-maker's 'attention' and 'problem-solving strategy' that drive the final decision. Attention and the problem-solving strategy cannot be the ultimate cause because they themselves are not given but are determined by other factors. It seems that the purported explanation of how decision-makers used information about the Telecoms Industry in order to make their investment decisions has run into a dead-end.

In order to try and find a way out let us return to Simon's notion of 'attention'. As the present discussion has implied, there are two aspects to Simon's concept of attention. The first, on which he primarily concentrates, is the scarcity of attention, deriving from the axiomatic assumption that human beings can only attend to one thing at a time. The derived notion of bounded rationality draws primarily on the scarce aspect of attention. The second aspect is that of attention as selection mechanism. It is this aspect that raises further important issues. Specifically, since it is possible for the decision-maker to pay attention to numerous parts of the objective information set we have to ask why it is that his or her attention focuses on the specific parts that it does. More concretely, for example, why does our decision-maker focus attention on the financial reports of Jack Grubman, rather than trying to understand the relevance of the boom and bust in the Nineteenth Century railways industry?

To answer this question, it is necessary to link 'attention' to the concept of an 'interpretive framework'. An interpretive framework may be thought of as the set of constructs, connections, conduits and constraints that together will influence the focus of the decision-maker's attention in selecting a subset of the objective set of information and in interpreting that information. This process, however, is not determined but is open-ended, allowing for flexibility, creativity and novelty. In the process of selecting and interpreting the subset of information, existing constructs, connections, conduits and constraints may be modified or abandoned and new ones formed. Furthermore, although these constructs, connections, conduits and constraints exist at the level of the individual human mind, they are influenced by social (including institutional) processes. For example, the interpretive framework of an individual fund manager working in a financial organisation may be influenced by institutionalised practices such as routinely reading the reports of financial analysts from the major investment banks. In the same way, the interpretive framework will also influence the decision-maker's choice of problem-solving strategy, emphasised by Simon as the second selection mechanism (the first being attention) that determines the knowledge that the individual derives from the subset of information that is selected.

But what determines the individual's interpretive framework at a particular point in time? The general answer is the evolution of the individual's earlier interpretive frameworks as they have been modified and changed through the processes of application plus feedback and learning.

The point to emphasise, however, is that it is misleading to see "human beings... as [essentially] information processors" as Simon does. That they process information goes without saying. The key question is what information they select from amongst that potentially available within the constraint of their scarce attention, and how they interpret this information. The answer to this question, as we have seen, does not depend on information processing per se. Rather than understanding human beings as information processors it is more meaningful to conceive of them as the creators and adopters of interpretive frameworks.

## Conclusion

Relating this discussion to the key question examined in the present chapter, namely why investors believed that the Telecoms Industry would provide significantly above-average returns, the answer has more to do with the interpretive frameworks of the key decision-makers than with the scarcity of their attention. This leads directly on to a consideration of one of the 'stylised facts' of the Telecoms Boom and Bust, namely the apparent influence wielded by 'Gurus' such as Jack Grubman over the decisions made by key decision-makers. This issue is discussed in the following section.

### 5.3    The Guru Hypothesis of Information Selection

At first sight the Guru Hypothesis seems to help in dealing with some of the weaknesses of both the Biased Incentive Hypothesis and the Information Processing/Bounded Rationality Hypothesis. The Guru Hypothesis suggests that what decision-makers do is not process as much information as their scarce attention will allow, but rather they select other human beings who they believe will provide them with appropriate answers. Indeed, there is a significant amount of evidence suggesting that such human beings – the Gurus – carried disproportionate weight in influencing the decisions of many of the key players whose decisions shaped the evolutionary path of the Telecoms Industry over the period under consideration. Jack Grubman, already referred to, was probably the most prominent of these people in the US Telecoms Industry and his counterparts in the so-called dot.com field included individuals such as Mary Meeker, Henry Blodget, and Abby Cohen.[19]

### Strengths

One strength of the Guru Hypothesis is that it deals with some of the shortcomings of the Information Processing/Bounded Rationality Hypothesis. Instead of attempting the tortuous, costly and perhaps impossible process of collecting and processing all relevant information (within the attention constraint), the decision-maker turns to one or more Gurus. A solution is similarly offered to one of the implications of the Biased Incentive Hypothesis, namely to the problem that is caused by the existence of more than one incentive regime and, correspondingly, more than one set of 'information and knowledge'. By choosing Gurus, the decision-maker sidesteps the problem of multiple sets of 'information and knowledge'. Likewise, the Guru 'solves' the problem of uncertainty by purporting, implicitly or explicitly, to know what will happen.

### Empirical Evidence: Investing Billions of Dollars in Telecoms in the Latter 1990s

Mr X is a famous investor in the US. According to Forbes he is amongst the richest in the US. Crucial for present purposes, he is also one of the largest investors in the Telecoms Industry in the US, having made a number of major investments in new entrant telecoms operating companies. He was personally interviewed in the US by the present author in May 2002.

Significantly, Mr X made his fortune outside the Telecoms Industry. What made him interested in the Telecoms Industry and what made him decide to commit a significant

---

[19] See, for example, Cassidy (2002).

proportion of his own and his company's fortune to investment in this industry? What are the implications for the three hypotheses under investigation in this chapter?

Having accumulated investible funds in his core businesses, Mr X was always searching for other areas for profitable investment. He first came into contact with the profitable opportunities being opened up by telecoms deregulation in the US when one of his companies did contracting work for the original new entrants, MCI and Sprint, who competed with the incumbent, AT&T. As a result of this experience, Mr X made significant investments in a start-up telecoms operating company. However, the business of this company was not essentially Internet-driven.

In 1995 he went through what might be described as a defining moment in the construction of the cognitive framework that would shape his thinking about the changing Telecoms Industry, the impact of the Internet, and the profitable opportunities that it provided. The occasion was a private meeting of investors at which Bill Gates was the invited speaker.

At the time, Gates himself was going through a defining moment when his own cognitive framework regarding the future of computing was undergoing a fundamental transformation. This was a time when computers were becoming linked in larger networks. Hitherto, Gates had believed that Microsoft itself could both create and dominate these networks. This he made clear in a memorandum dated October 6, 1994 titled "Sea Change" which spelled out plans for networked computing by Microsoft.[20] However, by May 1995 Gates – influence by Microsoft's technical guru, Nathan Myrhvold, a Cambridge University trained physicist, and younger staff in the company who were more in touch with the growing uses of the Internet on American campuses than Gates was – had changed his cognitive framework significantly. On May 26, 1995 Gates issued a memorandum, "The Internet Tidal Wave", which confirmed his conversion to the view that the Internet had become the dog, with Microsoft, after all, only its tail.[21]

Prior to this private meeting of investors, Mr X and his colleagues in his company had thought about the Internet. "We talked about the Internet substantially prior to that [meeting] but I don't know that we had a good understanding of it. We had a reasonable understanding but did not have, I don't think, what you'd call really a good understanding." The problem was not that they lacked the necessary technical background. "Y [the top manager running the company's telecoms interests] is very able technically." However, Mr X himself lacked technical knowledge. "I'm not [technically able]. I tend to look at things from an economic standpoint and a business standpoint."

How did Mr X react to Bill Gates' comments at the meeting? "From my perspective, if Bill really thought the Internet was important and he needed to understand it, I thought it was important we needed to understand it. And I thought that because I have a lot of faith and confidence in Bill knowing and understanding a lot more about those things than I do. And with the interest that Bill had in it, I just came back and told [Y] that I thought it was something we now needed to do something about." Very shortly thereafter Mr X made one of the largest acquisitions in the US of a leading Internet-related telecoms company.

---

[20] This information is provided in a particularly illuminating special report on Microsoft in *Business Week*, July 15, 1996, pp.38-44.

[21] ibid.

*Discussion*

As this important example makes clear, Mr X, a sophisticated investor with excellent technical information and advice at his fingertips – rather than making sure that he and his team themselves selected, collected and processed what they thought was all the relevant information regarding the Internet and the Telecoms Industry – instead selected another human being whom he trusted to come up with the right answers. The procedure provided important benefits. By selecting a Guru who, by assumption, had already obtained the relevant information and had processed it to arrive at the right answers, Mr X was bypassing the complex and costly process that would have been involved had he and his team attempted to do the same thing. The result was a significant economising on the costs of information selection and processing.

*The Cautionary Tale of Warren Buffett, The Sage of Omaha*

However, another investor, perhaps the most famous independent investor in the US, also turned his attention to the Telecoms Industry. He was Warren Buffett, the legendary 'Sage of Omaha' and one of the richest Americans. However, he came to a fundamentally different conclusion regarding the returns to investing in the Telecoms Industry; he avoided not only the Telecoms Industry but also the so-called tech sector generally.

Why was this? According to one of his close associates, personally interviewed by the present author,[22] "Warren looked at [the Telecoms Industry] as a technology business and he's never really gotten into things that are involved in technology. His most recent purchase was Fruit of the Loom, which is underwear, and that's not what you'd call technology". But why did Buffett not want to invest in the telecoms and tech sectors, even when most others were doing so? "I'll try to repeat what he said. He said, 'I want to stay within my circle of competence. I really don't understand the technology business, therefore it's out of my circle of competence'." As these quotations clearly imply, different people make different choices even when they are in the same situation. While some may decide to follow the advice of trusted Gurus, others may shun the same advice. Diversity of beliefs and expectations is the rule, even in times of consensual visions.[23]

*Weaknesses of the Guru Hypothesis*

If this account of the process involving Mr X's investment decisions (or at least some of them) in the Telecoms Industry is correct, and if it is generalisable beyond Mr X, then a further question becomes central. How is the decision made regarding which Guru to select? Once again, the answer does not appear to depend on collecting all the relevant information (within the constraints of the attention span) on all the possible Gurus that could be chosen, and selecting the most appropriate. Once again, a bypassing mechanism is used. This involves

---

[22] In May 2002.

[23] On 8 July 2002, when the telecoms bust was at its depths and some of the industry's main heroes had been slain – including Global Crossing and WorldCom – Warren Buffett announced that his main investment vehicle, Berkshire Hathaway, would join two other companies in a $500 million investment in Level 3 Communications, one of the main US alternative operators. According to the *Financial Times* (July 8, 2002), this marked "a dramatic departure from Mr Buffett's previous caution towards technology stocks". As part of the deal, Berkshire Hathaway agreed to buy $100 million worth of 10-year convertible bonds.

using "faith and confidence" (in Mr X's words) to make the selection. Faith and confidence provide the short-circuiting mechanism that allows for the economising of the costs of information selection and processing.

But if this is the case, then the question shifts to how this "faith and confidence" is established. By our assumption, faith and confidence are not the result of complex and costly processes of information selection and processing. Rather, there is a 'leap of faith', a socio-psychological process, that allows the decision-maker to feel confident in his or her choice of Guru without having attempted to collect all the relevant information that might support this selection.

A further problem with the Guru Hypothesis as an explanation of the Telecoms Boom and Bust is that the hypothesis deals essentially with the mechanisms encouraging individuals to select Gurus based on the degree of faith and confidence they have in them. Less clear is why in the Telecoms Boom from 1996 to 1999 so many of the Gurus concurred with the Consensual Vision. The consensus suggests that there is also an inter-Guru process simultaneously occurring. In explaining this inter-Guru process the Biased Incentive Hypothesis may provide some illumination through an analysis of the similarity of the incentive regimes governing different Gurus. However, an explanation is still needed of why significant investors did not have faith and confidence in some potential Gurus who were operating under different incentive regimes and who refused to buy into the Consensual Vision. Where, for example, were the Guru academics who refused to go along with the Consensual Vision and its shortcomings and biases?

Further problems arise, not so much regarding the Guru hypothesis as an explanation of the Telecoms Boom and Bust, but rather as a result of the practical difficulties that may emerge from the use of a Guru. We have seen that Gurus obviate the need to process information while they provide a way (though not a rational way) of coping with uncertainty. But Gurus do not provide their followers with a way of deciding whether the 'information and knowledge' they are offering is biased or not. Indeed, precisely because their role eliminates or reduces the need of their followers to process their own information in order to arrive at their own conclusions, Gurus may be offered a screen behind which they can hide their biases. This may be referred to as Guru Hazard. There seem to be strong grounds for concluding that Guru Hazard played an important role in both the Telecoms and the Dot.Com Booms and Busts.

Finally, a necessary implication of the Guru Hypothesis is that Gurus may be wrong. Unfortunately, however, their followers may have no way of knowing they are wrong until it is too late. For example, there is scant comfort for telecoms investors to read in Business Week (2002, p.42) that "Grubman argues that he truly believed in the stocks he recommended, even if he was wrong".

*Conclusion*

The Guru Hypothesis, as shown in this section, has some important shortcomings. Nevertheless, in view of the important role that several gurus seem to have played in the Telecoms Boom, it is concluded that it is necessary to include an analysis of the role of such gurus in an explanation of the Telecoms Boom and Bust.

## 6    INTERPRETIVE FRAMEWORKS

Our discussion of the three hypotheses suggests that there may be no completely reliable way for decision-makers, within the bounds of their scarce attention, to handle information in order to derive knowledge (justified true beliefs) about how their world works, what will happen in it, and what the implications are for what should be done. While there is an abundance of 'information' available (although we have also seen that some of it may be biased), there remains a black hole with regard to the knowledge that this information implies.[24] The selection of Gurus, it was suggested, provides one way of attempting to fill this hole. However, the unavoidable existence of Guru Hazard suggests that this way may not turn out to be particularly satisfactory.

So how do decision-makers cope with the black hole in their knowledge? The answer, it seems, is through the construction of interpretive frameworks.[25] These frameworks, based on the decision-maker's beliefs (justified by information or not), shape the way the decision-maker understands the world and acts within it. In short, the interpretive framework fills the black hole by substituting for the information-derived knowledge (justified true belief) that, for the reasons analysed, cannot be created.

The advantage of the interpretive framework is that it allows the decision-maker to act in the world with a degree of confidence, rather than to remain inert in the face of the black hole. The disadvantage, however, is that the beliefs from which the framework is constructed are not necessarily justified by existing unbiased information and therefore are not necessarily true.[26] In short, interpretive frameworks, while serving their purpose, may be wrong. The Consensual Vision that ruled the Telecoms Industry during the crucial years of 1996 to 2000 seems to be a significant case in point.

## 7    THE LINK TO ECONOMIC THEORIES OF THE BUSINESS CYCLE

The link between the present discussion and economic theories of the business cycle is closer than might at first sight appear. Take the Keynesian and Austrian theories as examples. To simplify, the main driver in the Keynesian theory is the volatility of investment demand. Investment, in Keynes' memorable phrase, is subject to the 'animal spirits' of investors. A sufficient increase in investment, caused by optimistic spirits, may increase household incomes and expenditure that will have further effects leading to an economic upturn. . However, later a downturn may occur as optimism turns to pessimism.

According to Hayek's version of the Austrian theory, if short term interest rates fall below their 'natural' equilibrium level (which equates the savings of households with the investment of firms) credit and investment will increase too rapidly relative to savings. This will lead to a mismatch between future output (driven by the increase in investment) and future spending

---

[24] The philosopher Dretske (1982), for example, argues that "information is that commodity capable of yielding knowledge" (p.44). Knowledge, in turn, "is identified with information-produced (or sustained) belief" (p.86). However, the three hypotheses discussed in this paper, and the Telecoms Boom and Bust more generally, deal with circumstances where the causal link between information and knowledge has been ruptured. Hence, the black hole.

[25] Elsewhere I have referred to these interpretive frameworks as visions.

[26] Of course, knowledge, in order to be 'knowledge', does not necessarily have to be justified by existing information. Karl Popper's black swans provide an example.

(which will be reduced by the fall in short term savings). Accordingly, there will be over-investment (leading to excess capacity) as well as unsustainable investment in inappropriate areas.

Both these theories depend on investors' expectations of opportunities for future profit. These expectations are shaped by investors' interpretive frameworks. As *The Economist* (2002, p.4) put it in its own Austrian-like explanation of the recent boom and bust: "Firms overborrowed and overinvested on unrealistic expectations about future profits and the belief that the business cycle was dead. Consumers ran up huge debts and saved too little, believing that an ever rising stockmarket would boost their wealth. The boom became self-reinforcing as rising profit expectations pushed up share prices, which increased investment and consumer spending. Higher investment and a strong dollar helped to hold down inflation and hence interest rates, fuelling faster growth and higher share prices. That virtuous circle has now turned vicious. (emphasis added)"

The question is why were these "unrealistic expectations", which play a key role in the causal explanation, formed in the first place? The answer must necessarily depend on an understanding of how the interpretive frameworks of the investors were constructed.

## 8   FUTURE RESEARCH

Many questions remain if we are to provide a robust explanation of the 1996-2002 Telecoms Boom and Bust, an explanation which includes not only the processes analysed and debated in economic theories of the business cycle but also an understanding of how 'unrealistic expectations' are formed which ultimately drive the processes referred to. As this chapter has made clear in the specific case of the Telecoms Boom and Bust, the formation of a 'consensual vision' played a key role in driving the boom that, for the reasons analysed earlier, inevitably collapsed into a bust. But how was this consensual vision constructed?

In answering this crucial question future research may benefit from some of the ideas developed by Thomas S. Kuhn in The Structure of Scientific Revolutions. Although it would be unwise to drive the analogy too far, there are some important parallels between Kuhn's concept of a scientific paradigm and what has been referred to in this chapter as an interpretive vision. Both refer to "the entire constellation of beliefs, values, techniques, and so on shared by the members of a given community", which is one way in which Kuhn defines a paradigm (p.175). Furthermore, as is evident in the last part of this definition, both are constructs of a 'given community', in the one case a scientific community, in the other an investment community. Kuhn's definition of 'community structure' is also relevant. According to Kuhn, "a scientific community consists...of the practitioners of a scientific special-ity...they have undergone similar educations and professional initiations; in the process they have absorbed the same technical literature and drawn many of the same lessons from it....Communities of this sort are the units that this book has presented as the producers and validators of scientific knowledge. Paradigms are something shared by the members of such groups." (p.177-8)

In order to better understand the consensual vision that emerged in the latter 1990s in the Telecoms Industry it would be helpful to know more about the communities of investors that provided the bulk of the funds that drove the boom (and led, indirectly, to the subsequent bust). Who were they? What did they read and who did they speak to in constructing their visions/expectations of the future of the telecoms industry? Which were the gurus they followed, and why these particular individuals? How did they form a consensus regarding what would happen in the telecoms industry? What institutional procedures did they follow in going about their work? Answers to these and similar questions would help to fill a gap in our understanding of the causes of the 1996-2002 Telecoms Boom and Bust and, by providing an insight into the processes involved in the construction of 'unrealistic expectations', improve our explanation of the causes of business cycles more generally.

## 9   CONCLUSION

To return to Stiglitz, why are financial markets "liable to go to extremes"? The present study of the Telecoms Boom of 1996-2002 and of the explanatory power of the three hypotheses suggests one reason (which, obviously, is not the only reason). Financial markets at times go to extremes as a result of the problems that decision-makers sometimes confront in attempting to handle information in order to derive knowledge about how their world works, what will happen in it, and what the implications are for what should be done. Some of the problems that decision-makers confront, and some of the solutions that they attempt to use, have been analysed in this chapter.

All the three hypotheses imply – as the detailed discussion showed – that there is no completely satisfactory way of deriving this knowledge. However, in the absence of such knowledge the conditions are created for the possible emergence of exuberance and disillusionment. And it is this exuberance and disillusionment that can help to drive cycles of boom and bust. Accordingly, it may be concluded that the paradox of the 'Information Society' and the 'Knowledge Economy' is that they do not provide the information and knowledge that it necessary to eliminate the extremes. We have little option, it seems, but to live with booms and busts as best we can.

## 10   REFERENCES

*Business Week* (2002), Special Report – "How Corrupt is Wall Street?" 13 May.

Cassidy, J. (2002), *Dot.con*, Allen Lane, London.

Dretske, F.I. (1982), *Knowledge and the Flow of Information*, MIT Press, Cambridge, Mass.

*Economist* (2002), "The Unfinished Recession. A survey of the world economy", 28 September.

Fransman, M. (2002), *Telecoms in the Internet Age: From Boom to Bust to …?*, Oxford University Press, Oxford.

Fransman, M. (1994), "Information, Knowledge, Vision and Theories of the Firm," *Industrial and Corporate Change*, Vol.3, No. 3, pp.713-758.

Kuhn, T. S. (1996), *The Structure of Scientific Revolutions*, third edition, University of Chicago Press, Chicago.

Loasby, B. (2003), *"The Innovative Mind,"* paper presented at the DRUID Conference on Creating, Sharing and Transferring Knowledge, Copenhagen, June 12-14.

Loasby, B. (2001), "Cognition, Imagination and Institutions in Demand Creation," *Journal of Evolutionary Economics*, Vol. 11, No. 1, pp.7-22.

Simon, H.A. (2002), "Organizing and Coordinating Talk and Silence in Organizations," *Industrial and Corporate Change*, Vol. 11, No. 3, pp.616-617.

Simon, H.A. (1959), "Theories of Decision Making in Economics and Behavioral Science," *American Economic Review*, 49, pp.253-283.

Stiglitz, J.E. (2002), "A Fair Deal for the World," *The New York Review of Books*, May 23.

Witt, U. (2000), "Changing Cognitive Frames – Changing Organizational Forms: An Entrepreneurial Theory of Organizational Development," *Industrial and Corporate Change*, Vol. 9, No. 4, pp. 733-756.

CHAPTER 3

# The Emerging Cyclicality of the Telecom Industry

Eli M. Noam[1]
*Columbia University, New York*

**Abstract**. This chapter analyzes the long-term lessons of the recent upturn and downturn in the telecommunications industry. It concludes that cyclicality will be an inherent part of the telecom sector in the future. To deal with such instabilities, the most effective responses by companies and investors is to seek consolidation and co-operation. Hence, an oligopoly is likely to be the equilibrium market structure. This means that government, if seeking stabilization, will need to reassess its basic policy approach that has long been focused on the enabling of competition. And this, in turn, means that the structure of the future network industry will look a lot more like the old telecom industry and less like the new Internet.

## 1    THE NEW CYCLICALITY

The telecommunication industry is in deep crisis in the United States, Europe, and other regions. Quite likely, the present downturn is only temporary and the industry will recover, though not at the hyper level of the bubble years. That, however, is not the real problem for the industry. It is not a one-time recovery from a one-time boom and bust. The main problem is that the telecom industry is entering a chronic pattern of volatility and instability, with boom-bust patterns becoming a common occurrence rather than an aberration. Thus the telecommunications network environment is leaving linearity and entering volatility. A pattern of ups and downs may be emerging, a cycle.

Yet many participants and observers of the industry miss or deny the emergence of cyclicality, sometimes interpreting the term too literally and needlessly implying it to mean a regularity of ups and downs. Most observers believe that the present downturn is merely a one-time accident, that things will return to their past stability because we have learned from past mistakes, and that we will not repeat them. This view is one of denial. True, we do not have much experience with volatility in telecom to make long-term predictions. And true, we are learning from the recent past. But if we analyze the drivers of the recent volatility, we must conclude that they will be with us into the foreseeable future, and cyclicality with them, just as they are in some other industries unless, that is, we take steps that are at variance with telecom strategy and policy of two decades.

---

[1] Assistance by Alok Bhardwaj, Uriel Cohen, and Robert Russell is gratefully acknowledged, as are helpful comments by James Alleman, David Allen, Bob Atkinson, Kenneth Carter, Larry Darby and Jonathan Liebenau.

While business cycles are not new to many industries, in telecom they are a new phenomenon. In the past, the network industry progressed in only one direction: up. Telecom used to be less volatile than the economy as a whole. It grew steadily, with long planning horizons hardly ruffled by the business cycle. (The only time the industry declined in volume was in the Great Depression, when subscribers dropped temporarily by 16%). One company, AT&T, accounted for 80% of network activity and equipment manufacturing, and provided stability, planning, and an industry-wide umbrella. Its stocks with their steady dividends were treated like bonds by investors. The equipment industry, being also globally diversified, was almost as stable as the carriers. But today, in sharp contrast, the telecom sector may well have become more volatile than the economy, more like the construction business, less like water utilities.

## 2   WHY CYCLICALITY?

This question is important, because if we do not know why something happened we cannot predict, prevent, or encourage recurrence.[2]

There are many competing explanations for economic cyclicality, from sunspots to the alignment of the planets, and to the political election cycle. Over more than a century and a half, many distinguished economists have contributed their views[3]. I will discuss six main approaches and relate them to the telecom industry.

### 2.1   The Monetarist View

According to that theory, associated especially with Friedrich von Hayek (1933, 1950) and Milton Friedman (1982), cycles are caused by flawed monetary policy that causes instability. For example, if a central bank changes interest rates incorrectly, consumers and businesses get wrong signals and their expectations lead to reactions that set off instabilities. (Fischer 1997). Whether this theory is correct or not for the aggregate economy, it is probably not applicable to the telecom industry. Interest rates were moderated, and maybe contributed to the bubble; were low but they were much lower in the bust, and yet did not turn the industry around.

### 2.2   The Keynesian Perspective

Aggregate demand is affected by the mood swings of market participants that often become self-fulfilling. (Keynes 1936, Hicks 1950, Tobin 1975). The key trigger is psychological and on the demand side. Keynes called it the "animal spirits" of entrepreneurs. More recently Allan Greenspan described it as an "irrational exuberance" (Shiller, 2001).

---

[2] It is necessary to differentiate telecom from the internet sector. The latter, though interrelated, operates under its own dynamics. Most internet projects were uncertain and unproven due to their novelty, and one should expect exuberance and failures. In contrast, in telecommunications the basic business was well established and stable. The internet's inherent riskiness was clearer understood than that of the telecom sector.

[3] Some of them will be listed as part of the subsequent discussion. Others include, chronologically, Marx (1867), Malthus(1820,), Mitchell (1913), Kuznets (1926), Pigou (1927), Kondratief (1935), Schumpeter (1939), Kaldor (1940), Burns (1946), Abramovitz (1950), Hicks (1950), Lundberg (1955), Duesenberry (1958), Moore (1961), Tobin (1975), Nordhaus (1975), Kindelberger (1978), Blinder (1983). For a review of the earlier literature, see Zarnowitz (1985).

The demand orientation of the Keynesian approach leads Wall Street analysts to look closely at data for consumer spending as leading indicators. But for telecom and the Internet, one cannot really blame a drop in consumer demand on the downturn. True, the growth rate in the Internet subscribership is not as torrid as before – it was "only" 30-40% in 2001 – and Internet minutes per user and day have dropped a bit, as one would expect as more marginal subscribers are signed up. Internet connections increased in America by about 20 million in 2001. Broadband Internet subscribership is up and with it the aggregate bit flow for the Internet. Similarly, the usage of long-distance minutes, data communications, and wireless minutes keeps rising. With double-digit growth rates in actual consumption, it is hard to blame the downturn on insufficient demand.

## 2.3   Real Business Cycles Theory (RBC)

This theory is a supply side story, going back to Prescott (1983) and others. For RBC advocates, cycles are caused by random shocks and their impact on total factor productivity. The internet was a positive shock. September 11 was a negative shock. Random positive shocks lead to higher productivity, higher output, higher real wages, consumption, etc. For RBC advocates, causality does not run from consumption to output but the other way around. (Espinosa-Vega and Guo, 2001). The theory therefore rejects explanations based on consumer psychology such as "exuberant irrationality." RBC proponents believe that there is really nothing that governments can do about a cycle since it is based on random shocks.

How does this perspective fit telecommunications? Empirical studies show that single shocks do rarely trigger downturns. But a shock can topple an already weak structure. In telecommunications, several shocks occurred in the same period and added their impact cumulatively. Local competition failed; long distance competition, on the other hand, worked only too well, lowering prices and profits; Wall Street became irrationally depressed when stocks declined from their unrealistic heights; governments extracted future expected profits by auctioning access to a vital resource, spectrum; regulators, often beholden to incumbents' well-being, held back competitors; etc. But note that most of these events are not the kind of exogenous, technology-oriented shocks that affect productivity, as hypothesized by RBC advocates. They are endogenous financial and institutional variables of the sector itself. They are thus not truly random but systemic.

There is, however, one important factor that can be interpreted as a technologically-based shock, if we take a generous definition of the term. It is the re-emergence of economies of scale through network technologies such as fiber-optic transmission cables and of wireless distribution systems. On the supply side, the fixed costs of networks are rising and the marginal costs are dropping – strengthening the classic attributes of "natural" monopoly. Scale effects are compounded by "indivisibilities" or "lumpiness" in investment, which leads to short-term excess capacity (Darby, 2002). Hence, the advantages of being large are greater than before. As a result, for example, the market share of mobile wireless telecom providers (i.e., relative size) has been a predictor of profitability (Waverman, 2002). And the cost characteristics of wireless firms are inversely related to the absolute and relative size of wireless companies. (Katz et al, 2002).

Similar effects have long been identified for the telecom long distance market (see, for example, Denny, Fuss, and Waverman (1981), Nadiri and Schankerman (1981), Alleman (1983)), as well as for cable TV (Noam 1983,1985). They generally show cost elasticities with respect to size of 5-15 %. In addition, the technological expansion in capacity has not only increased but accelerated (Noll, 2002).

For a long time, these size advantages in telecom were submerged under the accumulated inefficiencies of the incumbents. But having had to shape up under the pressure of real or threatened competition, they reduced their inefficiencies sufficiently for their scale to overcome the efficiency of small entrants. This is not the classic RBC story, but it is inspired by it.

## 2.4 Lag and Accelerator Models

These models go back to Samuelson (1939). Small changes in desired capacity levels lead to large differences in capacity expansion, which drives investment. Where there is a delivery lag, unanticipated shifts in desired capacity can generate cycles of investment spending. The key here is the adjustment lag. These lags induce oscillation in the same way that a slowly reacting bathroom shower induces cycles of hot and cold water. The famous "cobweb" cycle is a model of such overshooting. Industry examples are cattle, airline services, and office space – and now telecommunications. Here, investments take a long time to get on line, and disinvestments may take even longer (it took more than a decade for the excess supply of 1980s Texas office space to dissipate.) The lumpiness of investments in telecommunications, coupled with an even slower regulatory and court system, makes the feedback loop very slow. On top of this is the "chicken and egg" problem of applications development depending on networked buildouts and vice versa. Since it is difficult to synchronize the two, developments often progress in spurts. The build-out of networks for broadband-internet capability is a recent example.

## 2.5 The "Austrian" Theory

This view is associated with Mises (1928), Hayek (1933, 1990), Haberler (1937), Böhm-Bawerk (1895), Wicksell (1936), and Schumpeter (1939). It is focused on overcapacity. Such overcapacity has been created for some reason—whether due to exuberance, excessive bank lending, monetary policy, or other factors. After an adjustment lag there is eventually a downturn. The pattern is one of boom, overcapacity, price war, bust, shakeout. A young industry tends to start off with small firms, and once their product fetches a high price it attracts entry, which expands output and lowers price. This goes on for a while. Industry growth rate slows below that of individual firms, and a shakeout occurs. For example, there used to be 275 tire manufacturers in the US in 1922. Today, less than a dozen survive, even though the tire production as a whole is vastly larger. This view is common-sensical, with numerous examples such as snowmobiles, pocket calculators, bowling alleys, PCs, or movie theaters.

The Austrian view seems to be a fitting description of the telecom industry, in which the various network companies over-optimistically projected long distance market shares that added up to over twice the actual market. Everybody built capacity to overwhelm competitors and gain size. Capital expenditures grew by an annual rate of 29% from 1996-2001. The incremental cost of bandwidth fell by about 54% annually. Overcapacity was assisted by the lumpiness and irreversabilities of telecom investments such as oceanic cables. It was further assisted by the tendency of Wall Street analysts to value a firm's progress by physical measures of its infrastructure, such as cell-sites and fiber-miles. As the result of these factors, some carriers had over 90% of their fiber "dark" and prices dropped dramatically.

The Austrian theory has its detractors. Paul Krugman, the Princeton economist and New York Times columnist, has called it a "hangover theory" and "about as worthy of serious study as the phlogiston theory of fire" (Krugman 1998), largely because it places the blame for a downturn on the boom itself, and does not explain why each company systematically over-estimates its market. Krugman's critique is focused on the macro-economy rather than specific industries, where he accepts the notion of over-expansion. For telecommunications, then, one would need to understand why so many companies were so wrong about their prospects, and why none engaged in a meaningful counter-cyclical strategy.

Paul Samuelson indirectly addressed this criticism by observing that economists have no theory to predict when a bubble in asset prices will burst. It is therefore not "irrationally exuberant" but rather economically logical for an individual to participate in a bubble. An individual's micro behavior may be efficient even if the system is macro-inefficient.

## 2.6   Externalities

The RBC theory discussed earlier assumes constant returns to scale. That is, if one increases the capital and labor inputs of the firms proportionately, their outputs would grow by the same proportion. But for network industries this ignores the network effects, also known as positive network externalities (Farmer and Guo, 1994) or the Metcalfe effect. An increase in usage leads to greater utility of the product and to increased demand. This increases productivity and real wages and enables further consumption. Growth of other network participants is factored in as part of the value of the product, and leads to still further growth. At some point, however, the expectations of further growth decline, for example as saturation occurs. This leads consumers to reassess the value of the service, and to adjust their consumption to the new value. This reduces demand or at least its growth, which creates negative network effects. And thus, the dynamics that had led the system to go up now take it down faster, too. Network externalities strengthen the oscillations of market demand rather than dampen it[4]. If the firms could coordinate their action they could jointly reduce these externality effects, but in a competitive environment they cannot easily or legally do so. This story fits well with the telecom and internet markets of the '90s and beyond.

## 2.7   Adding up the Theories of Cyclicality

Like the proverbial six blind observers of an elephant, each of these theories gets something right in its views of the drivers of cyclicality. Demand growth has slowed. Investment and regulatory lags prevented adjustment. Network externalities and lumpiness in investments amplified the swings. Economies of scale and network externalities created strong incentives for growth strategies, at the expense of profitability. Financial markets encouraged this strategy. Managers benefited from it in the short run. Yet while expansion made sense for each firm individually, it created a major oversupply in the aggregate.

In telecommunications, technological and economic obsolescence will gradually take capacity out of circulation. Satellites, for example, eventually leave their orbit or burn up. But disinvestment takes time. For Texas office space, it took over a decade in the 1980s to dissipate the excess supply. For railroads, it took many decades. Thus, the capacity overhang in telecom will remain for a long time if it is reduced merely by obsolescence. The key for a

---

[4] This idea originated with Kenneth Carter.

recovery is a substantial growth in demand, probably from mass-media uses of the internet such as video. When demand has caught up with supply, prices will rise, supply will expand, new entrants will emerge, and every firm will aim at increasing its market share. A new cycle emerges.

## 3    THE IMPLICATIONS OF CYCLICALITY

Given this emerging cyclicality in the telecom market, what should be the response? I will discuss three types of participants: telecom companies, investors, and governments. The conclusion will be that for the private sector participants the strongest strategy is to deal with cyclicality by seeking (or financing) an oligopolistic market structure. This, in turn, has implications for government policy.

### 3.1    Telecom Companies

There is, of course, no shortage of potential actions for telecom companies to take. They must start with an intense self-analysis. Firms, managers and owners need to disentangle their firm's performance from that of their industry, their customers and suppliers, and the regional, national, and global economies. This is not easy. But it is necessary in order to judge management's performance. Following such analysis, several strategic options exist.

- *Cut cost and contract.* A downturn puts pressures on the firm and makes cost-cutting more acceptable. Similarly, a downturn provides an opportunity to change the internal structure and shed marginal operations. It may also include the deferral of innovation due to its riskiness. This strategy works best if competitors, too, follow it and slow the rate of their own investment in innovation.

- *Expand in the downturn.* The opposite strategy from contraction may also make sense. The prices to acquire other firms through mergers or to expand by internal investment drop in a downturn, and it is a good time to get ready for the upturn, especially where lag times for investments are long. However, in many countries the dominant telecom incumbent cannot easily be contrarian, because it may account for 80% or more of the market. This strategy might work better for a small firm—assuming it can raise the capital in a downturn, which is a fundamental dilemma. One conclusion is that a strategy of expansion of capacity by internal growth makes less sense than the acquisition of a competitor's capacity. Such a merger does not add to overall industry capacity (which would lower prices and profitability) but instead eliminates a competitor, which may result in higher returns.

- *Design the firm for downward (and upward) flexibility.* Firms need to operate with built-in adjustments for the cycle. They need to implement scalable technology and flexible labor costs, for example, through profit sharing, commissions, and outsourcing. However, the labor component is becoming smaller as capital-labor ratios increase in the economy, and is therefore becoming less of a factor than it was in more labor intensive days. Similarly, firms need to engage in financial hedging. And in their capital structure, firms need to substitute corporate debt for convertible debt or preferred equity because this enables them to reduce a debt load in a downturn. In contrast, the capital structure of large telecom firms has become weighed by debt: it was 325% of market capitalization of France Telecom in 2001/2; 163% of Deutsche Telekom; 60% of BT; 66% of Telefonica.

- *Diversify in product markets and geography.* Diversification reduces risk in some ways, but may also get a firm to move outside its core area of competence, which raises risk again. Expansion into other countries creates exposure to political vagaries. Vertical expansion into related elements of the value-chain may create synergies (economies of scope) but may tie one part of the firm to others within the same corporate family, even if their inputs are costlier and less desirable. It can also lead to competition with one's own customers. And, any expansion into multiple product lines inevitably creates and requires changes in the firm's corporate culture, which may entail significant and mostly hidden costs.

- *Avoid a heavy debt load.* In the downturn, cash is king. It reduces payment obligations and enables acquisitions. In the recent past, even established telecom firms have loaded up on debt in dramatic ways, and the result is that they are hurting in the downturn. Some of the reasons for such debt load was that the resource requirements of global and product expansion are huge, for example for the move to next generation wireless. Add to that the expense of firms engaging in empire building and the shortening of product cycles of technology, and the debt begins to balloon. Deutsche Telekom paid over $40 billion for the second-tier mobile carrier Voicestream; France Télécom paid $30 billion for Orange; and Vodafone paid $180 billion for Mannesmann. After the 1996 Telecom Act a huge investment boom took place in the industry, in the order of $1.3 trillion. Between 1999-2001 alone, US telecom firms borrowed over $320 billion from banks. Credit was not difficult to obtain, and banks often accepted a subordinated creditor status without much collateral. But the revenues per investment dollar dropped. In 1996, according to Lehman Brothers, it was $5.08. But in 2001 it had fallen to $2.84 (Darby, 2002). Merril Lynch estimates that return on equity for the telecom industry declined from 13.8 % in 1996 to 5.9 % in 2001. In consequence, investments are expected to decline by an annual average rate of –14%. Verizon alone invested 33.7 billion over the period 1999-2002 with limited impact (Stern, 2002). Qwest's debt load in 2002 was $25 billion. Around the world, the same story can be told. Deutsche Telekom's debt is $64 billion, France Télécom's $68 billion, and Telefonica's $20 billion. As a percentage of revenues, France Télécom's debt is 141%, Deutsche Telekom's 140%, Telefonica's 92%, BT's 75%, and Telecom Italia's 67%. Even these mountains of debt are being understated by various accounting practices. The cumulative debt of the seven largest European telecom firms exceeded $210 billion in 2002, greater than GDP of Belgium. It required some firms, on a daily basis, to commit over $10 million for debt service. In theory, firms without leverage will do better in downturn. But economy-wide studies also show that some highly leveraged firms have been helped in downturn by banks which cancelled payments rather than foreclosed. (Field, 1985, in Mascarenhas and Aaker 1989). Similarly, governments may be helpful in the downturn when it affects several firms in an essential industry. Given such a safety net, big telecom firms had fewer reasons to be prudent. But they had an incentive to be too big and were not permitted to fail, and this, encouraged expansion.

- *Engage in price-cutting.* This strategy has drawbacks when price-cuts are matched by competitors. Hence, there are incentives to oligopolistic cooperation entailing the mutual reduction of capacity rather than engaging in price wars.

To conclude: many of the strategies in a downturn have common elements that make them successful: expansion and consolidation of surviving firms within the industry, and collaboration, to the extent possible, with one's competitors.

## 3.2  Investors

In the past, the underlying assumption for government policy in telecommunications policy had been that if one gets a competitive structure in place, investment will follow efficiently and plentifully (Darby, 2002). The present downturn negates this assumption in the short run (which is tolerable) and possibly in the long-run (which is much less tolerable).

For better or for worse, there have been increasingly close linkages between financial markets and the real economy, with the links forged through such instruments as securitization, derivatives, and leveraged investments. Financial markets are also becoming increasingly volatile, as risk taking becomes easier but risk assessment harder. These trends, taken together, mean that financial turbulence makes industries more vulnerable to financial shocks.

Wall Street has thus been part of the problem, though it has also paid dearly for it, in money as well as credibility. Risk and market power should have been factored in, as should have been the price deflation due to competition and over-capacity. Share prices seem to move in ways that seem unrelated to the underlying discounted value of cash flows. In fairness, it is hard to value companies in volatile industries, both conceptually and institutionally. "Consensus" earnings forecasts have been useless for investors in cyclical industries, especially for startup firms in high-growth, high-risk industries. Forecasts tend to be rosy and asymmetrical. According to a McKinsey study, for volatile industries the forecasts are generally upbeat, and "the forecasts don't acknowledge even the existence of a cycle" (de Heer and Koller, 2000). Why this positive bias? Maybe it is the pressure of the investment banking part of the firms to avoid unfavorable evaluations of companies which would lose them as clients. Maybe it is the opaque accounting practices, and proliferating derivative securities and stock options that make assessments difficult.

According to Joseph Stiglitz (2002), deregulations are always associated with periods of frenzied activity that tend to go wrong. And indeed, after the 1996 Telecommunications Act, financial markets gave the wrong signals to firms by raising stock values enormously. They evaluated unprofitable startup firms by proxies such as fiber miles and cellsites. This led telecom firms to over-invest in such physical elements, and to an over-investment in such firms. The bubble was further fed by the ability to borrow against the rising value of the stock; later, when stock values dropped, this necessitated sell-offs and led to further price declines. Traditional theory has it that investors look at total risk – market risk plus financial risk. If they are additive, then high market risk in this sector should have been offset by investor unwillingness to support highly leveraged capital structures. But, it seems just the opposite happened. Eventually, rapid changes in market expectations led to rapid reassessment of asset prices. This caused massive reductions in asset-holder's wealth, which lowered expectations further. As that happened, zooming share prices ceased to be a motivation for investments, and the new entrants rapidly fell out of favor since they could not offer any earnings or service their debt. Confidence was further shaken by questionable accounting practices.

Studies show that the inability of lenders like banks to discover the relevant characteristics of borrowers' projects, e.g., when information is asymmetrical, leads to poor projects driving out good projects. This is Akerlof's "lemon" principle (1970). In the new media and telecom sectors, lenders' and investors' ability to evaluate projects has declined, and with it the quality of loans. When this became obvious even to the investment bankers, they raised the threshold, cutting off in the process projects they could evaluate before.

Investors now favored incumbent telecom firms, which looked much better than before when they had been derided as "dinosaurs" by the financial community. In contrast, the financing of new entrants largely dried up. If anything, further stability was desired. The incumbents' traditional shareholders seek a utility-style stock with predictably steady dividends. When the industry becomes volatile, such investors leave. Market power, on the other hand, lowers risk, and raises prices and cash flows. One can see how market power benefits market valuations. In America, rural LECs, facing little prospect of competition, maintained their value much better than other telecom firms. In other countries, Telmex did better than most large incumbents, mostly because of its hold over the Mexican market. Its stock rose 28% in the first four months of 2002.

## 3.3   Government

The wisest thing for government would be to ride out the cycle, but a hands-off policy might not be easy to maintain. Cyclicality is undesirable to government. When it comes to Schumperterian dynamics of "creative destruction", governments dislike destruction even more than they fear creativity. Clearly, too much stability is also undesirable. See the example of Japan. What is the proper level of stability? Too little of it reduces innovation, but too much stability does the same. An optimum instability might exist, but it is difficult to agree on that level. Entire political philosophies hinge on the different views on the acceptable societal risk.

To the extent that volatility raises uncertainty it also raises the cost of producing telecom services, which is an essential and universal input. This also has some distributional implications such as fluctuations in employment. And through network effects, everybody is negatively affected. The losses from cyclicality can be substantial. Estimates of the economic losses from the oversupply in US of office space in the 1980s are $130 billion, in lost rents only, without counting the secondary effects of reduced tax receipts and negative multiplier impacts on the rest of the economy.

Imagine the impact of a telecom downturn on smaller countries where a telecom firm has a large presence and is affected by shocks originating from the outside. In Finland, Nokia accounts for 35% of exports and 14% of GNP. Similarly, the telecom sectors of less developed countries have become more volatile as they have opened up to the rest of the world and become engulfed in external instabilities over which they have no control.

All of this and more are reasons for government to fear cyclicality and to engage in counter-vailing policies, even though government policy may also be a contributing cause to cyclicality, for example through regulatory delay. If such involvement is likely, for better or for worse, what are the potential tools of government for dampening the cycles of the telecommunications industry? Some such tools are discussed in the following and they should be read as a list of potential actions rather than as recommendations.

- *Flexibility in taxes and other payments.* The US telecom industry is subject to telecom taxes beyond the regular business taxes. Those taxes could be automatically adjusted through the cycle if the tax rates were levied on earnings rather than on revenues.

Similarly, spectrum license auctions could be structured in a way that would collect payments over the life of the license, with annual collections based on earnings, and would thus become an automatic stabilizer.

- *Flexibility of retail price regulation.* Retail prices, if regulated, could be adjusted through the cycle, again by automatic adjustments such as the inclusion of a growth rate factor in the price-cap formula.

- *Flexibility of wholesale prices.* If one can pick a single variable that is potentially most effective in influencing telecom prices and the relation of incumbent and competitors, it is the wholesale price of interconnection.

That price, charged by carriers to each other, is regulated, and is usually set by some result-oriented economic methodology such as TELRIC or ECPR (Noam 2001). Such a price could be made variable and dependent on the state of the telecom market. If the entrants falter as a group, the interconnection prices could be lowered. If incumbents weaken as a group, on the other hand, one would raise interconnection prices. Some formula might be established in advance to deal with those situations. Or, the regulatory agency could vary the price to affect the sector in the same way that a central bank uses the discount rate.

Such variability of prices may seem to create uncertainty. But certainty does not mean a fixed stability. It can also mean a dynamic regulation that adjusts predictably over the cycle. In practical terms, it means that counter-cyclical government policies need to be as automatic as possible, and indexed to defined variables. Even then, such measures increase the complexity and extent of government involvement.

- *Industrial Policy.* Government could support the creation of demand in order to increase utilization of networks, or support new entry. Examples might be the creation or distribution of content such as distance education or health delivery, and the release of spectrum to new service providers.

- *Competition Policy.* Perhaps most important is the government's policy in permitting or preventing market power. The process of consolidation is far from over. Where competition exists, especially in long-distance and wireless, the number of carriers is likely to decline. The challenge is therefore to deal with an environment of potential oligopoly. On the one hand, oligopolies help generate greater profitability and lower volatility. The downside, of course, is that the users pay for this greater profitability in higher prices, potentially lower service quality, and slower innovation. Several of these problems might be dealt with onside of the market structure, by regulation such as price caps or minimum service level requirements, triggered by high levels of market concentration. Similarly, rules that keep the market open to potential entrants might establish a "contestability" that can be an effective dampener on oligopolistic behavior.

## 4   CONCLUSION

Overexpansion, by itself, is a hallmark of health, not weakness. At one time or another, there were hundreds of companies making automobiles, motorcycles, airplanes, tires, and microcomputers. One of the functions of slowdown is consolidation. That is, to reduce competition, to reduce the commodification that lowers profitability and future investments. This must be a telecom firm's overriding strategy (together with designing the firm for downward flexibility and avoiding excessive debt, to deal with the next cycle if they survive the present one). The present contraction will therefore inevitably raise industry concentration, slow innovation, reduce capacity expansion, and raise prices. (This strategy will, of course, be publicly denied by the survivors.) Regrettably but realistically, what will turn the telecom industry around will not be more competition but more of an oligopolistic market structure, coupled with increasing demand. (A positive technology shock might also do the job, but one cannot base the future of essential infrastructure industries on unexpected events.)

For public policy, this suggests several alternatives. The first alternative is to let nature take its course through the business cycle, relying on natural contractions and expansion cycles. This approach recognizes realistically the difficulty in identifying problems and creating timely and workable solutions to them. However, this policy is less likely to be chosen by politically sensitive regulators when the downturn persists, when essential service providers falter, and when service quality deteriorates.

The second option is for government to take an activist, almost macro-economic, approach to the sector and try to raise it from recession. This would involve significant and ongoing intervention. A related but less intrusive strategy would be to automatically adjust existing rules and requirements over the business cycle, as discussed in the section above.

The third option is to permit industry to stabilize the market by creating oligopolies, and to deal with the inevitable negative fall out by regulations that protect consumers and others. This would require a fairly radical departure from the regulatory philosophy of the past 20 years. For a generation now, liberalization, deregulation, and competition have been the keystones of telecom policy and strategy. Now, one business cycle later, and facing future volatility, we may have to get used to the idea of living with a regulated oligopoly in telecom rather than the hoped-for unregulated competition.

The volatility of the telecom sector thus points to a scenario of market power and regulation, not of competition and of the withering away of governmental intervention. Government policy, investor behavior, and telecom management will all have to become responsive to periodic volatility and vary across it. The cyclicality of the industry will thus lead to a cyclicality of behavior within and towards the industry. And the effect of such volatility on the telecom market structure will lead to a new model of regulatory policy.

## 5   REFERENCES

Abramovitz, Moses (1950), *Inventories and Business Cycles, with Special Reference to Manufacturers' Inventories*, NY: NBER.

Akerlof, George (1970), "The Market For Lemons: Quality Uncertainty and the Market Mechanism," *The Quarterly Journal of Economics*, Vol. 84, No. 3, pp. 488-500.

Blinder, Alan S and Joseph E Stiglitz (1983), "Money, Credit Constraints, and Economic Activity," *Amer. Econ. Rev.*, Vol. 73, No. 2, pp. 297-302.

Böhm-Bawerk, Eugen (1895), "The Positive Theory of Capital and Its Critics", *The Quarterly Journal of Economics*, Vol. 9, No. 2, pp. 113-131.

Burns, Arthur F. and Wesley C. Mitchell (1946), *Measuring Business Cycles.* NY: NBER.

Darby, Larry (2000), "Telecom Regulation and Capital Markets," presentation at Columbia Institute for Tele-Information, Conference on Telecommunications Volatility, April 2002.

De Heer, Marco and Timothy M Koller (2000), "Valuing Cyclical Companies," *McKinsey Quarterly*, Vol. 2, pp. 62-69.

Duesenberry, James S. (1958), *Business Cycles and Economic Growth*, NY: McGraw-Hill.

Espinosa-Vega, Marco A. and Jang-Ting Guo (2001), "On Business Cycles and Countercyclical Policies," *Fed. Res. Bank Atl. Econ. Rev.*, Fourth Quarter 2001, pp. 1-11.

Farmer, Roger E.A., and Jang-Ting Guo (1994), "Real Business Cycles and the Animal Spirits hypothesis," *Journal of Economic Theory*, Vol. 63, pp. 42-72.

Field, A. (1985), "Bad Economics Drives Out Good," *Forbes*, 18 November, pp.78-82.

Fischer, Stanley. (1977), "Long-Term Contracts, Rational Expectations, and the Optimal Money Supply Rule," *J. Polit. Econ.*, Vol. 85, No. 1, pp. 191-205.

Friedman, Milton (1982), *Monetary Trends in the United States and the United Kingdom: Their Relation to Income, Prices, and Interest Rates, 1867-1975*, Chicago: U. of Chicago Press for NBER.

Haberler, Gottfried ([1937] 1964), *Prosperity and Depression*, New edition, first published by the League of Nations, Cambridge, MA: Harvard U. Press.

von Hayek, Friedrich A. (1933), *Monetary Theory and the Trade Cycle*, NY: Harcourt, Brace & Co.

Hicks, John R. (1950), *A Contribution to the Theory of the Trade Cycle*, Oxford: Clarendon Press.

Kaldor, Nicholas (1940), "A Model of the Trade Cycle," *Econ. J.*, Vol. 50, No. 197, pp. 78-92.

Keynes, John M. (1936), *The General Theory of Employment, Interest, and Money*, London: Macmillan & Co.

Kindleberger, Charles P. (1978), *Manias, Panics, and Crashes: A History of Financial Crises*, NY: Basic Books.

Kondratieff, N.D. and W.F. Stolper (1935), "The Long Waves in Economic Life," *The Review of Economic Statistics*, Vol. 17, No. 6, pp. 105-115.

Krugman, Paul (1998), "The Hangover Theory," *Slate*, December 3, 1998.

Kuznets, Simon Smith (1926), *Cyclical Fluctuations; Retail and Whole-Sale Trade, United States, 1919-1925*, New York: Adelphi.

Lundberg, Erik, ed. (1955), *The Business Cycle in the Postwar World*, London: Macmillan Co.

Malthus, Thomas Robert (1820), *Principles of Political Economy Considered with a View to their Practical Application*, London: J. Murray.

Marx, Karl, and Friedrich Engels (1867), *Capital: A Critique of Political Economy*, Hamburg, O. Meissner; New-York, L. W. Schmidt.

Mascarenhas, Briance and David A. Aaker (1989), "Strategy Over the Business Cycle," *Strategic Management Journal*, Vol. 10, pp. 199-210.

von Mises, Ludwig (1928), *Geldwertstabilisierung and Konjunkturpolitik* [Monetary Stabilization and Cyclical Policy], Jena: Gustav Fischer.

Mitchell, Wesley C (1913), *Business Cycles*, Berkeley: U. of California Press.

Moore, Geoffrey H, *Business cycles indicators*, 2 vols., Princeton U. Press for NBER, 1961.

Noam, Eli ((1983-84)), "Is Cable Television a Natural Monopoly?" *Communications: International Journal of Communications Research*, Vol 9, No. 2-3, pp. 241-59.

Noam, Eli (1985), "Economies of Scale in Cable Television," *Video Media Competition: Regulation, Economics, and Technology*, E. Noam, ed., New York: Columbia University Press, pp. 93-120.

Noam, Eli (2001), *Interconnecting the Network of Networks*, MIT Press, Cambridge, MA.

Noll, A. Michael (2002), "Accelerating Technology: The Pace of Transmission Systems," *Prometheus*, Vol. 20, No. 1.

Nordhaus, William D. (1975), "The Political Business Cycle," *Rev. Econ. Stud.*, vol. 42, No. 2, pp. 169-90.

Pigou, A. C. (1927), *Industrial fluctuations*, London: Macmillan.

Prescott, Edward C. (1986), "Theory ahead of Business Cycle Measurement," *Federal Reserve Bank of Minneapolis, Quarterly Review*, Fall 1986, pp. 9-22.

Samuelson, Paul A. (1939), "Interactions Between the Multiplier Analysis and the Principle of Acceleration," *Rev. Econ. Statist.*, Vol. 21, No. 2, pp. 75-78.

Schumpeter, Joseph A. (1939), *Business cycles: A theoretical, historical, and statistical analysis of the capitalist process*, 2 vols., NY: McGraw-Hill.

Shiller, Robert J. (2000), *Irrational Exuberance*, Princeton, NJ : Princeton University Press.

Stern, Christopher (2002), "Testing the Telecom Giants' Economic Resilience," *Washington Post*, Saturday, April 27, 2002, p. E01.

Stiglitz, Joseph (2002), keynote presentation at Columbia Institute for Tele-Information, Conference on Telecommunications Volatility, April 2002.

Tobin, James (1975), "Keynesian Models of Recession and Depression," *Amer. Econ. Rev.*, Vol. 65, No. 2, pp. 195-202.

Wicksell, Knut ([1898] 1936), *Interest and Prices: A Study of the Causes Regulating the Value of Money*, London: Macmillan.

Zarnowitz, Victor (1985), "Recent Work on Business Cycles in Historical Perspective: A Review of the Theories and Evidence," *J. Econ. Lit.*, 23, pp. 523-580.

Global Economy and Digital Society
E. Bohlin, S. Levin, N. Sung and C-H. Yoon (Editors)

CHAPTER 4

# Rethinking the Role of E-commerce in B2B and B2C Transactions: Complementing Location, Personal Interactions and Pre-existing Relations

Charles Steinfield

*Department of Telecommunication, Michigan State University, East Lansing*

**Abstract.** Electronic commerce development was shaped by a number of assumptions about how it adds value to economic exchange. These assumptions focused attention on the ability of e-commerce to transcend distance and reach into markets without physical presence, replace costlier in-person transactions with electronic ones, and demonstrate network effects that reward rapid growth. In this chapter, an alternative perspective is presented in which electronic commerce complements a firm's physical location, works in concert with other modes of interaction, and emphasizes services to pre-existing exchange partners. A review of both business-to-consumer and business-to-business electronic commerce research is provided in support of this alternative perspective.

## 1  INTRODUCTION

As electronic commerce flourished in the late 1990s, a number of assumptions implicitly, - and, at times, explicitly - came to dominate perceptions of its role in economic exchange. Awed by the power of e-commerce as a transaction medium, researchers, policy makers and practitioners alike focused on the opportunities e-commerce offered to enable firms to access new markets, replace outmoded or inefficient supply chains and distribution channels, and achieve dramatic growth in the number of customers served (Cairncross, 1997; Choi, Stahl and Whinston, 1997; Wigand and Benjamin, 1995). These perceived opportunities stem from several basic assumptions that shaped much of the e-commerce activity leading up to the widespread failure of "dot.com" firms in 2000 and 2001. Three of the most influential beliefs shaping e-commerce practices and strategies at the time were:

- IP networks make distance irrelevant. Unlike circuit-switched networks, Internet protocols allow telecommunications traffic to be insensitive to distance (Cairncross, 1997). Hence, electronic mails, file transfers, web hosting, and other Internet services cost the same regardless of the distance between sender and receiver. Indeed, on the Web, unless a site explicitly highlights geographical information, the physical address of the destination site is unknown to most users. The implication for economic exchange is that buyers and sellers no longer have to be co-located, because the Internet has reduced the transaction costs associated with doing business with a distant partner to the point where distant sellers are competitive with local ones (Bakos, 1997;1998).

- Internet transactions are substitutable for transactions formerly occurring in person or via other forms of direct communication. Unlike former generations of network-based transactions, the Web supports rich graphics and multimedia, enabling even highly complex products to be sold. Moreover, innovations in web programming enable Web-based enterprises to complete transactions, including complex customization and personalization features (Rayport and Sviokla, 1995). Modern logistics and transport systems complete the picture by ensuring rapid fulfillment of online orders. Hence all the elements needed to effectively automate transactions are present, and enable online transactions to substitute for offline ones (Choi et al., 1997).

- E-commerce is highly susceptible to network efforts, meaning those with the largest number of users will achieve sustainable competitive advantage (Afuah and Tucci, 2001; Choi et al., 1997; Kaplan and Sawhney, 2000; Shapiro and Varian, 1999). According to this assumption, the more users an e-commerce site has, the more value it offers any individual user. This occurs in many ways for a variety of different business models. Network effects are thought to be crucial, for example, for sites that function as third-party market makers offering brokerage services. In order to improve the liquidity of the market such sites must be able to attract a critical mass of buyers and sellers. The more of each a market maker can attract, the better the probability any member has of finding a desired match. Another common type of network effect is evident in sites that offer recommendation systems, since the ability to develop such recommendations improves with more users and more data (Dieberger, Dourish, Hook, Resnick and Wexelblat, 2000). The belief in such network effects justified a continuing drive to increase the number of users, perhaps at the expense of a focus on using e-commerce to better support pre-existing business relationships.

These assumptions formed the basis of the dominant perspective in e-commerce, shaping its development and use in both business-to-business (B2B) and business-to-consumer (B2C) exchange. In this chapter, I argue that this dominant perspective has led to an underestimation and underutilization of e-commerce in local and regional settings, with a corresponding lack of emphasis on the ways that e-commerce works in concert with traditional forms of transactions, and with established trading partners. Based on a review of research findings, an alternative perspective is offered. In direct contrast to the above three assumptions, I argue that there is sufficient evidence now to conclude that 1) physical location still matters, both for B2C and B2B e-commerce, 2) for many firms with an existing physical retail presence, e-commerce may be better viewed as complementary to, rather than a substitute for in-person transactions, and 3) particularly in B2B situations, e-commerce may be best used to strengthen, not bypass pre-existing relationships, and hence a focus purely on market-share growth and the resulting network effects may be misguided.

The chapter is organized as follows. First, an analysis of e-commerce in retail environments is provided, based upon a review of recent research. In particular, the dynamics of click and mortar business models are discussed in order to highlight the critical importance of physical presence in a market, due to the opportunities it offers when combined with e-commerce for generating cross-channel synergies. The chapter then explores the business-to-business arena, noting the lack of success of so many B2B e-hubs. Here I argue that, unlike the flourishing click and mortar retailers, there is limited evidence to date of a prominent role of location in B2B e-commerce. However, by extrapolation from the growing attention being paid to the economics of regional and local business clusters, the inattention to location appears misguided. Moreover, substantial evidence suggests that B2B e-hubs ignore pre-existing business trading relationships at their peril. The arguments are summarized in the concluding section.

## 2    TOWARDS AN ALTERNATIVE PERSPECTIVE ON B2C E-COMMERCE

In the early years of Web-based commerce, much emphasis was placed on sources of competitive advantage that Internet firms had over traditional ones, primarily using a transaction cost logic (Bakos, 1997; Choi et al., 1997). Transaction cost economics emphasizes the nature of costs that firms incur in the process of conducting transactions with buyers or sellers (Williamson, 1975;1985). Such costs include information gathering and search costs, negotiation and settlement costs, and monitoring costs to ensure that trading partners adhere to the terms of any agreements made. Initially, transaction cost economics focused on business-to-business trading, and directed our attention to how such costs exert an influence on market structure. The classic question was whether high transaction costs caused firms to avoid the market altogether, and develop an in-house production ability in order to avoid being taken advantage of by opportunistic sellers (Williamson, 1975;1985).

Information systems researchers relied heavily on transaction cost theory to predict that a major effect of the Internet would be to lower critical transaction costs, such as search and monitoring costs (Bakos, 1997; Malone, Yates and Benjamin, 1987). Once search costs were reduced, buyers could then find sellers in distant geographic markets who had lower prices, provided better service, offered higher quality, or had products that better matched needs (Bakos, 1997; Cairncross, 1997; Choi et al., 1997; Malone et al., 1987; Wigand, 1997; Wigand and Benjamin, 1995; Wildman and Guerin-Calvert, 1991). Hence, even though first applied to inter-firm relationships, transaction cost economics also provided the conceptual underpinnings for explaining how distant Internet firms may be able to compete with local, physically present businesses (Choi et al., 1997). E-commerce researchers and practitioners thus arrived at the first dominant assumption noted above: that distant was irrelevant. Because of the ease of product information search on the Internet, the basic raison d'etre for many local retailers – the fact that they had a geographic monopoly and could therefore charge high enough prices to overcome their inefficiencies and limited selection – no longer applied (Cairncross, 1997).

In addition to the transaction cost advantages offered by e-commerce, researchers have spelled out numerous economic advantages that virtual firms enjoy over physical firms. During the dot.com boom, Web-based businesses were perceived to hold many operational, cost, scale and scope advantages over firms confined to physical channels, including: access to wider markets, lower inventory and building costs, flexibility in sourcing inputs, improved transaction automation and data mining capabilities, ability to bypass intermediaries, lower menu costs enabling more rapid response to market changes, ease of bundling complementary products, ease of offering 7X24 access, and no limitation on depth of information provided to potential customers (Afuah and Tucci, 2001; Anonymous, 2000; Bailey, 1998; Choi et al., 1997; Wigand, 1997; Wigand and Benjamin, 1995).

These analyses, however, mainly contrast traditional firms with Internet firms. They ignore the potential synergies that arise when firms have a combination of physical and e-commerce channels. A growing body of conceptual and empirical work has sharply criticized the early expectations that virtual firms will drive out physical ones and make distance irrelevant (Friedman and Furey, 1999; Otto and Chung, 2000; Rosen and Howard, 2000; Steinfield, Adelaar and Lai, 2002a; Steinfield, Bouwman and Adelaar, 2002b; Steinfield, DeWit, Adelaar, Bruin, Fielt, Smit, Hoofslout and Bouwman, 2001; Steinfield and Klein, 1999; Ward, 2001). In these works, the authors emphasize the theoretical advantages of hybrid, "click and mortar" approaches to e-commerce. Importantly, these works suggest that advantages arise not only from the ability that a multi-channel approach offers for reaching new customers and offering new services, but also because each channel can have spillover effects that result in increased purchases and reduced costs in the other channel (Ward, 2001).

The history of e-commerce provides strong empirical support for the notion that click and mortar approaches to e-commerce are more successful than non-integrated approaches. The dot.com firms followed the dominant paradigm by attempting to reach markets without physical presence, relying on web-based automation over any form of human intervention, and heavily emphasizing market share growth to capitalize on scale economies and network effects. Yet, by one estimate, only ten percent of the dot.com firms that began in 1995 still survived in 2001 (Laudon and Traver, 2001). Moreover, Laudon and Traver also note that click and mortar retailers began to rapidly replace dot.com retailers in lists of top e-commerce firms in the years following the dot.com bust.

The underlying sources of advantage of click and mortar firms have been extensively analyzed by Steinfield and colleagues (Steinfield et al., 2002a; Steinfield et al., 2002b; Steinfield et al., 2001). The basic framework used by Steinfield and colleagues is depicted in Figure 1.

## 2.1 Sources of Synergy Between Physical and Virtual Channels

Click and mortar firms have a number potential sources of synergy not necessarily available to pure Internet firms or traditional firms without an e-commerce channel. Among the sources spelled out in classic competitive advantage theory are common infrastructures, common operations, common marketing, and common customers (Porter, 1985) (see Figure 1). An example of the use of a common infrastructure is when a firm relies on the same logistics system (warehouses, trucks, etc.) for handling distribution of goods for e-commerce activities as well as for delivery to its own retail outlets. Another critical infrastructure that can be shared is the IT infrastructure. Recent empirical work suggests, in fact, that the more firms build their e-commerce capability in conjunction with an existing IT infrastructure the more likely they will see performance improvements (Zhu and Kraemer, 2002). An order processing system shared between e-commerce and physical channels is a good example of a common operation as a source of synergy. This can enable, for example, improved tracking of customers' movements between channels, in addition to potential cost savings. E-commerce and physical channels may also share common marketing and sales assets, such as a common product catalogue, a sales force that understands the products and customer needs and directs potential buyers to each channel, or advertisements and promotions that draw attention to both channels. Finally, an alternative perspective on the cannibalization issue is the fact that e-commerce and physical outlets in click and mortar firms often target the same potential buyers. This enables a click and mortar firm to be able to meet customers' needs for both convenience and immediacy, enhancing customer service and improving retention. Hence, to the extent that virtual and physical channels are able to share these various assets in a coordinated fashion, a variety of benefits can emerge.

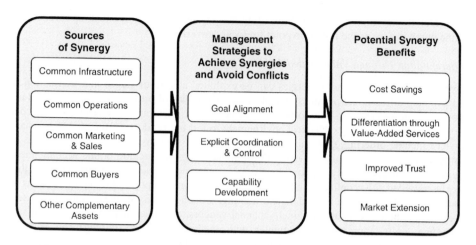

Figure 1. Sources, Management Requirements, and Benefits of Click and Mortar Synergies

Adapted from Steinfield, Adelaar and Lai, 2002.

Another way to view these various sources of synergy is that they represent the many forms of complementary assets that click and mortar firms possess that purely Internet firms may not. Established firms have existing supplier and distributor relationships, experience in the market, a customer base, and other complementary assets that can enable them to take better advantage of an innovation like e-commerce (Afuah and Tucci, 2001; Teece, 1986).

## 2.2  Click and Mortar Case Studies Reveal Importance of a Complementary Logic

The right-hand side of the framework in Figure 1 focuses on the potential benefits that click and mortar firms may achieve when synergies between the Web and existing physical assets are exploited. Based on a series of case studies conducted in both the Netherlands (Steinfield et al., 2002b) and the United States (Steinfield et al., 2002a), four broad areas of benefit have been identified. These include: 1) lower costs, 2) increased differentiation through value-added services, 3) improved trust, and 4) geographic and product market extension. In general, each area of benefit reveals the importance of leveraging each firm's existing physical presence, and treating e-commerce as a complementary rather than a substitute channel to customers.

*Lower Costs*

Cost savings may occur in a number of areas, including labor, inventory, marketing/promotion, and distribution. Labor savings result when costs are switched to consumers for such activities as looking up product information, filling out forms, and relying on online technical assistance for after-sales service. Inventory savings arise when firms find that they can avoid having to stock infrequently purchased goods at local outlets, while still offering the full range of choices to consumers via the Internet. Marketing and promotion efficiencies are garnered when each channel is used to inform consumers about services and products available in the other. Delivery savings may result from using the physical outlet as the pick-up location for online purchases, or as the initiation point for local deliveries.

### Differentiation Through Value-added Services

Physical and virtual channel synergies can be exploited at various stages in a transaction in order to help differentiate products and add value. Examples of pre-purchase services include various online information aids to help assess needs and select appropriate targets, or, conversely, opportunities in the physical environment to test out products. Examples of purchase services include ordering, customization, and reservation services, as well as easy access to complementary products and services. Post-purchase services include online account management, social community support, loyalty programs and various after-sales activities that may be provided either online or in the physical store. Typical opportunities are in the areas of installation, repair, service reminders and training. Although many of these value-added services are potentially available to single-channel vendors, combined deployment of such services (e.g. online purchase of computer with in-store repair or training) can enhance differentiation and lock-in effects (Shapiro and Varian, 1999).

### Improved Trust

Three reasons for improved trust, relative to pure Internet firms, derive from the physical presence of click and mortar firms, including reduced consumer risk, affiliation with and embeddedness in recognized local social and business networks, and the ability to leverage brand awareness. Lower perceived risk results from the fact that there is an accessible location to which goods can be returned or complaints can be registered (Tedeschi, 1999). Affiliation and embeddedness in a variety of social networks can facilitate the substitution of social and reputational governance for expensive contracts or legal fees (Granovetter, 1985). DiMaggio and Louch (DiMaggio and Louch, 1998) show that, particularly for risky transactions, consumers are likely to rely on social ties as a governance mechanism. Such ties are more likely to exist between geographically proximate buyers and sellers, suggesting that there may indeed be a preference for doing business with firms that are already physically present in the local market. Finally, marketing theorists have long recognized the power of branding as a means of building consumer confidence and trust in a product (Kotler, 1999). Established firms are able to leverage their familiar name to make it easier for consumers to find and trust their affiliated online services (Coates, 1998).

### Geographic and Product Market Extension

It is, of course, very true that many click and mortar firms can and do seek to extend their reach beyond traditional physical outlets, addressing new geographic markets with e-commerce. This fact does not negate our basic argument that physical location is important for e-commerce, for several reasons. First, as noted above, many of the other benefits derive from the fact that existing customers also use existing physical locations in concert with e-commerce. Second, Steinfield and colleagues found in several of their cases that those supposedly new customers in distant markets were actually former customers of the physical outlet who had moved away but wanted to continue doing business with the firm. It is also worth pointing out that some of the market extension comes not from reaching into new geographical locations, but from expanding into new product markets. Virtual channels can extend the product scope and product depth of physical channels by enabling firms to offer new products that they do not have to physically stock locally. Moreover, firms may add new revenue generating information services online that would not be feasible to offer in physical outlets. Finally, the Internet may help reach customers within an existing market who may not have visited the physical outlet, but are otherwise attracted to the virtual channel due to its special characteristics (Anderson, Day and Rangan, 1997).

## 2.3 Realizing Synergies and Avoiding Channel Conflict

The kinds of benefits discussed above are certainly not guaranteed to all firms. Indeed, firms with such multiple channels may fall prey to channel conflict. Channel conflicts can occur when the alternative means of reaching customers (e.g. a Web-based store) implicitly or explicitly competes with or bypasses the existing physical channels, and are nothing new to e-commerce (Balasubramanian, 1998; Stern and Ansary, 1992). One common problem is that one channel may simply cannibalize sales from the other. Perceived threats caused by competition and conflict across channels can have other harmful effects, including limited cooperation across the channels, confusion when customers attempt to engage in transactions using the two uncoordinated channels, and even sabotage of one channel by the other (Friedman and Furey, 1999; Useem, 1999; Ward, 2001). A critical finding from the Steinfield and colleagues' click and mortar cases, highlighted by the center column of Figure 1, is that management must act to diffuse conflicts and ensure the necessary alignment of goals, coordination and control, and development of capabilities to achieve synergy benefits.

In the successful click and mortar companies, firms went through a process of goal alignment across physical and virtual channels. They worked to ensure that all employees involved realized that the parent firm benefits from sales originating in either channel. Management and employees recognized the value of existing physical assets and did not seek to replace them with e-commerce, nor did they expect e-commerce to function as a stand-alone business. One problem faced by click and mortar firms is that the contributions made by the Internet channel may be intangible and hard to measure (Tedeschi, 2001a). Managers have to be open to such intangible benefits and not, for example, evaluate e-commerce divisions purely on the basis of their own sales and profitability. Moreover, there must be agreement on what types of customers (e.g. existing vs. new) are targeted by the new e-commerce channel.

Aligning goals is only a first step. The more successful cases go further and implement explicit coordination and control mechanisms that help to exploit the various synergy opportunities. These include mechanisms such as IT systems integration for ensuring interoperability so that customers may move freely between channels. In most cases, firms also demonstrated coordination by using each channel to promote the other. One of the most common strategies for enforcing cross-channel cooperation is to build in incentives, such as the allocation of e-commerce sales credit to specific outlets based on customers' addresses. Here again, the physical location of customers and of outlets matters greatly. Finally, the successful click and mortar firm manager recognized the differing cost structures and capabilities associated with each channel, and developed measures that encouraged customers to use the most appropriate channel for the services they were seeking.

In many situations, traditional firms may lack important competencies needed to achieve synergy benefits with e-commerce. For example, traditional firms may lack Web development skills, or logistics skills needed to serve distant markets. In these situations, alliances may be more useful than attempting to develop a virtual channel in-house.

## 2.4   B2C Summary

Based on this analysis, it is clear that many of the advantages of click and mortar firms stem directly from the fact that such firms can leverage their existing physical presence in a given community, complement online services with in-person customer interactions, and build on customer retention with an established customer base rather focusing primarily on costly customer acquisition. Hence, this review of B2C developments directly contradicts the three assumptions outlined at the outset of the chapter that characterized the dominant e-commerce paradigm.

## 3   TOWARDS AN ALTERNATIVE PERSPECTIVE ON B2B E-COMMERCE

Business-to-business electronic trade has a much longer history than B2C e-commerce, beginning with the emergence of automated order entry systems and EDI in the 1970s and continuing with proprietary interorganizational networks since then (Laudon and Traver, 2001; Steinfield, Kraut and Plummer, 1995). Throughout the 1980s, in fact, many well-known interorganizational systems, such as those implemented by American Hospital Supply, American Airlines (Sabre) and McKesson, demonstrated that electronic transactions could be important competitive weapons (Malone et al., 1987). Moreover, with the increasing globalization of trade and the rise of large multinational firms, such interorganizational networks clearly became global in scope, connecting producers with suppliers around the world (Bradley, 1993). These interorganizational networks were based upon proprietary standards, and typically were only open to those firms with an existing business relationship with the sponsoring firm (Steinfield et al., 1995). In addition to procurement functions, such proprietary linkages supported all forms of interaction between a closed set of trading partners, including inventory management, joint product design and development, scheduling, and interfirm conferencing. However many believed that the rise of standard and open electronic networks would permit the establishment of electronic marketplaces that would ultimately connect any buying firm to a much wider group of sellers, including new ones from other parts of the world (Malone et al., 1987). When Internet-based electronic commerce appeared, many believed that such an open network was here, and predicted the growth of vast electronic marketplaces that would add value by reducing search costs, increasing transaction efficiencies, and aggregating buyers and sellers to improve the likelihood that firms would be able to find a trading partner (Kaplan and Sawhney, 2000). Hence, just as with B2C e-commerce, the three dominant assumptions - distance irrelevance, substitution for costlier in-person interactions, and importance of network effects - were influential in shaping a significant amount of B2B e-commerce activity. Since these assumptions are mainly related to the establishment of Internet-based B2B marketplaces, we focus on them in this section rather than all forms of B2B electronic trade. Such a focus yields a contrasting view to the three assumptions about e-commerce with which this chapter began, and reveals why we will continue to see most B2B electronic trade occurring over private networks for some time to come.

### 3.1   The Rise and Fall of B2B Electronic Marketplaces

E-commerce researchers generally expect the value of B2B electronic transactions to vastly exceed business-to-consumer (B2C) retail trade due to the enormous volume of goods and services traded between firms (Garicano and Kaplan, 2001; Kaplan and Sawhney, 2000; Laudon and Traver, 2001; Subramami and Walden, 2000). Laudon (2001), reporting figures from a Jupiter Media Metrix report, estimated U.S. B2B trade at \$12 trillion in 2001, a surprising figure in that it exceeds the estimated GDP of the U.S. that year. As e-commerce began to take off in the late 1990s, the potential for even a small fraction of this trade to be conducted over the Internet attracted hundreds of new entrants seeking to established B2B marketplaces. As early as 2000, the U.S. Department of Commerce (2000) reported that more than 750 B2B e-markets were operating worldwide in a range of different industries. Laudon and Traver (2001) estimated that up until the dot.com bust, more than a thousand B2B network marketplaces had been created.

B2B electronic marketplaces have mainly focused on the opportunities for improved efficiencies in procurement processes (Kaplan and Sawhney, 2000; Laudon and Traver, 2001; Segev, Gebauer and Färber, 1999). The logic is similar to B2C e-commerce, with higher stakes. Transaction efficiencies arise from the ability of B2B electronic marketplaces to reduce the search and monitoring costs for participating firms (Bakos, 1997;1998; Garicano and Kaplan, 2001; Segev et al., 1999; Steinfield, Chan and Kraut, 2000). In the height of the dot.com euphoria, the B2B e-hub was one of the most prominent new business models in what was then called the "digital economy" (Timmer, 1998). However, despite the widespread optimistic projections by industry consultants, academic analysts and government policy makers (Katsaros, Shore, Leathern and Clark, 2000; U. S. Department of Commerce, 2000), most third party-provided B2B marketplaces have not met with much success, and many have failed entirely (Laudon and Traver, 2001; Tedeschi, 2001b).

The failure of third party B2B marketplaces does not mean that B2B e-commerce is unimportant. Just as with B2C e-commerce, B2B e-commerce continues to grow. It just is based upon different approaches that are not shaped so forcefully by the earlier dominant assumptions. In particular, it is important to distinguish between Internet-based network marketplaces and the private industrial networks mentioned at the start of our discussion about B2B electronic trade (Laudon and Traver, 2001). These differing approaches to B2B electronic trade are described in the sections below.

## 3.2   Classifying B2B Marketplaces

B2B Internet marketplaces have been classified according to two important dimensions of business purchasing: how businesses buy and what businesses buy (Kaplan and Sawhney, 2000). The "how" dimension distinguishes between spot purchasing to fill an immediate need, and systematic purchasing for planned, long term needs. The former is often done using ephemeral, market-based transactions, without long term contracts. The latter is often done after significant negotiation, and is used for purchasing in large volumes from trusted trading partners. The "what" dimension normally distinguishes between vertical (also called direct or manufacturing) inputs that relate to the core products of a firm and horizontal (often called indirect or MRO for maintenance, operating and repair) inputs, such as office supplies, that are acquired by all firms. Laudon and Traver (2001) distinguish between the following four types of Internet-based B2B marketplaces.

- E-distributors such as Grainger.com or Staples.com offer electronic catalogues representing thousands of suppliers in support of spot purchasing for horizontal inputs. Laudon and Traver (2001) call them the Amazon.coms for industry since they operate much like retailers. The main benefit for buyers is simply the reduced search cost, although additional services like credit and account management are offered to help further reduce transaction costs.

- E-procurement services such as Ariba.com also offer MRO supplies, but focus on systematic purchasing rather than spot purchasing. Such B2B intermediaries offer a range of procurement services, including the licensing of procurement software that supports a range of value-added services. They do not own the supplies, but offer the catalogues of thousands of suppliers from whom they also obtain fees and commissions. They theoretically bring value by aggregating both buyers and sellers, decreasing search costs for both parties, and therefore are subject to significant positive network externalities.

- Exchanges, such as E-steel.com are intermediaries that focus on bringing together buyers and sellers within a particular industry, and concentrate on the spot purchasing of manufacturing inputs. They charge commissions, but offer a range of purchasing services to buyers and sellers, supporting price negotiations, auctions, and other forms of bidding in addition to normal fixed-price selling. Buyers benefit from greater choice and lower prices, while sellers gain access to large numbers of buyers. Often these vertical markets are used to unload surplus materials, for example, via auctions. They are also subject to network externalities.

- Industry consortia are best represented by Covisint, the electronic procurement system developed by the leading automobile manufacturers. These exchanges are typically jointly owned by large buying firms seeking to rely on electronic networks to support long term relationships with their suppliers. Entrance is by invitation only, and the buying clout of the founders influences suppliers to make the investments needed to participate.

In contrast to these various forms of network marketplaces, as noted above, private industrial networks are closed user group affairs, mainly linking a small set of strategic partners together with private infrastructure (Laudon and Traver, 2001). These strategic partners may be organized by a focal firm such as a manufacturer, which, together with its suppliers and downstream channels is seeking greater efficiencies in serving their common market. Well known examples of such interorganizational networks organized by large focal firms include those set up by WalMart, Siemens, and Procter & Gamble, to name a few (Laudon and Traver, 2001). These private industrial networks often encompass a particular value chain enabling just-in-time inventory, efficient consumer response, and collaborative design and production. Increasingly, industry observers are focusing on value-webs, in which the respective value chains of all the strategic partners are incorporated into the network to seek out new ways to gain efficiencies and add value for end-customers. Clearly, these networks span distances, allowing firms to do business more efficiently with remote suppliers. However, an important caveat is that the empirical evidence suggests that such buyer seller relations are more likely to have preceded the formation of the network, rather than having resulted from it (Kraut, Steinfield, Chan, Butler and Hoag, 1998).

According to the logic of the three assumptions provided at the outset of this chapter, B2B electronic exchanges would bring together large numbers of businesses regardless of location, enabling firms to find the lowest cost provider without additional transaction costs. B2B hubs would support electronic procurement, enabling automated ordering and fulfillment, rather than relying on human intervention. Finally, B2B hubs would experience network externalities, so that the more firms that join any particular hub, the more value it would offer to its members. However, as noted at the start of the discussion of B2B e-commerce, in most cases, the B2B marketplace business model did not achieve these expected successes. In fact, the vast majority of B2B electronic trade occurs over private industrial networks. Laudon and Traver (2001), in fact, estimated that 93% of electronic B2B trade occurred on private networks, rather than Internet-based e-marketplaces. Moreover, among the network marketplace models described above, the fastest growth is in the area of industry consortia, not in the area of open B2B exchanges. The alternative perspective offered here, questioning the three dominant assumptions, helps to explain these trends.

### 3.3    The Role of Location, Personal Relations, and Small Networks

The high failure rate of third-party B2B e-hubs, coupled with the dominance of private networks and the growth of industry consortia reflects an important dynamic. Businesses have established relations with their suppliers, and the trust engendered by reliable performance and commitment over the long term may be more valuable to firms than any short term price advantages offered by the supposedly neutral marketplaces. Indeed an important trend in the B2B electronic trade arena is the rise of "collaborative e-commerce" where networks are used for far more than simple transaction support. Joint product design, more tightly integrated inventory databases, and other forms of coordination between producers and suppliers occur over private intranets. In a sense, these developments are merely the latest manifestation of what Malone and colleagues (1987) referred to as electronic hierarchies, where firms rely on networks to facilitate outsourcing, but only to a small number of firms with which they are tightly integrated. Substantial empirical evidence exists suggesting that these inter-organizational forms are more common and long-lasting than the market exchanges (Kraut et al., 1998; Steinfield et al., 1995).

Rarely is the role of location discussed in the literature on B2B electronic markets, and the relationship between geography and B2B e-commerce is not as straightforward as with B2C click and mortar e-commerce. There is some empirical evidence, however, suggesting that even over public Internet-based B2B exchanges, geography remains relevant. A recent study of public B2B e-markets in Korea examined two types of markets - those in which buyers and sellers found each other and completed transactions and those in which the marketplace functioned as an agent, completing the transaction on behalf of the buyer (Choi, 2003). The spatial patterns of transactions over a six month period in 2002 were examined, revealing that when buying firms made the purchases themselves, they were more likely to purchase from suppliers within their own region of Korea. However, agent-mediated purchases were more likely to be directed toward suppliers outside the region, and mainly to suppliers located in the Seoul metropolitan area. The former finding suggests that firms prefer to buy from known local trading partners, even when using a public e-marketplace. The latter finding at first suggests that e-marketplaces do provide access to distant suppliers. However, some locational impact exists even here, since nearly all public B2B e-marketplaces in Korea are based in the Seoul region and it may be that the agent that prefers known local trading partners.

Another argument for the potential relevance of geography may be derived from the growing body of work by economists and geographers studying the significant role that location plays in the formation and maintenance of business trading communities, primarily within the context of discussions about business clusters (Porter, 1990;1998;2000).

Porter (1998; 2000) defines a cluster as a "critical mass of companies in a particular field in a particular location..." He further notes that they can include "...a group of companies, suppliers of specialized inputs, components, machinery, and services, and firms in related industries." They can also include "firms in downstream industries, producers of complementary products, specialized infrastructure providers, and other institutions that provide specialized training, and technical support" as well as industry groups such as trade associations. This description parallels the structure of many of the electronic business trading communities established in the past several years, except that Porter's cluster members are physically co-located in a particular region.

Several of the primary economic benefits ascribed to business clusters are similar to the main benefits of participation in a B2B electronic market: improved access to specialized inputs, lower transaction costs, and access to complementary goods and services. Clusters are also thought to enhance the rate of innovation among member firms.

Rather than relying on electronic networks and automation to achieve these transactional and informational advantages, clusters capitalize on proximity. A concentration of skilled workers, for example, increases access to needed labor inputs. Proximity helps in many less formal ways, however. As has been shown repeatedly in analyses of such clusters as Silicon Valley, knowledge sharing can occur through spontaneous or chance encounters between professionals living in the same community, enhancing overall innovation capacity (Maskell, 2001; Rogers and Larsen, 1984; Saxenian and Hsu, 2001). Porter (1998) further refers to the advantages of common language, culture, and social institutions in reducing transaction costs, and notes that local institutions are likely to be more responsive to the specialized needs of a cluster (e.g. for creating public infrastructure). He even points to peer pressure and the presence of rivals as causes for the enhanced competitiveness of firms that are embedded in a local cluster.

The research on IT use in local business clusters is somewhat mixed regarding the potential of e-commerce. In the early years of e-commerce, there were some efforts to establish regionally-oriented malls to highlight area businesses and activities, such as the Electronic Mall Bodensee (Zimmermann, 1997). However, such regional malls were quite broad, and often were driven by local chambers of commerce, rather than focusing on a particular industry sector as in the above discussion of clusters. Many had a retail focus, as well, and were not built mainly for B2B trade support.

Additional hints regarding the importance of geography on B2B trade can be found in studies of Internet traffic. That electronic transactions might follow from physical proximity is suggested by Castell's (2001) fascinating account of the geography of the Internet, where he points out the spatial concentration associated not only with producers of Internet content and infrastructure, but among firms that use the Internet. The following quote illustrates this line of reasoning (Castells, 2001): "...these advanced service centers are territorially concentrated, built on interpersonal networks of decision-making processes, organized around a territorial web of suppliers and customers, and increasingly communicated by the Internet among themselves (page 228)." Indeed, one study of Internet traffic demonstrated that the majority of IP traffic flows within, rather across locations (Kolko, 2000). Business-to-business transactions are embedded in an enabling social and cultural context, yet in striving for transaction efficiencies, most efforts to create electronic networks to support transactions go to great lengths to ignore and even bypass this context.

Such analyses of Internet traffic are suggestive, but more specific analyses of IT use for commerce and coordination in local business clusters reveal the fundamental challenges of replacing highly developed social exchange processes with electronic transactions. In these more specific studies, the outcomes of inter-organizational systems suggest a lack of fit between B2B marketplace design and local business cluster needs. They offer insights into why private networks continue to dominate in B2B commerce.

A good deal of research on IT use in a geographically defined business cluster has been conducted in the industrial region of Northern Italy. Some years ago, Johnston and Lawrence's (1988) seminal work on value-adding partnerships focused extensively on the Prato area textile industry. Their analysis examined how the large textile mills formed had disaggregated into small, specialized firms that focused on one part of the overall value chain in textile production (e.g. washing, coloring, cutting,, etc.). They showed how networks of firms worked in concert to meet the market demands for the good of the network, and pointed out how an inter-organizational information system was being used to facilitate coordination (Johnston and Lawrence, 1988). However, a decade later, Kumar and colleagues revisited the merchants of Prato, and found that the information system had been all but abandoned (Kumar, van Dissel and Bielli, 1998). The system offered no real added value in terms of transaction cost reductions over the personal forms of coordination that had evolved over centuries of textile production in the region. Kumar et al (1998) suggest that trust and personal relationships – the social capital of the region – were effective substitutes for the inter-organizational system, rendering it unnecessary.

Other research on B2B electronic transactions further disputes the assumptions that e-commerce can be an adequate substitute for personal relations and that network effects are critical in B2B trade. A case study of media buyers and sellers in France illustrates the sometimes oppositional nature of information systems built from a transaction cost rationality and existing practices based upon personal relationships (Caby, Jaeger and Steinfield, 1998). The market for TV advertising had become more complex due to the liberalization of the market and the resulting increase in private channels. An electronic marketplace was created by the media industry, allowing media buyers to find available time slots and reserve them. Theoretically this would reduce selling costs and improve transaction efficiencies. It was built on France's Minitel system, and so required minimal investment by the buyers. However, it soon failed, largely because it prevented many of the relationship-based selling strategies that media representatives preferred. They could not offer the best times and prices to their preferred customers, for example. Moreover, customers behaved strategically, often reserving time slots only to prevent competitors from obtaining them. Before long, the media representatives were bypassing their own system, and returned to their prior methods of selling media time.

Finally, a large scale empirical study by Kraut and colleagues (Kraut et al., 1998) investigated personal and electronic forms of transaction coordination between 250 producers and their suppliers in four different industries. Their research extends the Kumar findings in important ways and further supports the application of the alternative assumptions for B2B trade. In contrast to the Prato case, Kraut and colleagues found that electronic networks were more likely to be used precisely when there were existing relationships between producers and suppliers, and greater use was associated with more tightly-coupled producer-supplier relations. Kraut et al. (1998) explain this by pointing out that to be able to conduct electronic transactions, investments are required by the participants. Suppliers are unlikely to make such investments unless they can expect a certain amount of business. Note how this contradicts a rationality based on network effects, and predisposes firms to see more value when the number of participants in a B2B system is smaller rather than larger. In addition, e-commerce was complementary to, rather than a substitute for personal relationships. This was evident in the finding of a positive association between the presence of personal links and the extent to which firms engaged in electronic transactions. Moreover, there was an interesting interaction between the two: the more firms attempted to substitute electronic transactions for personal forms of coordination, the more errors and quality problems they experienced with transactions. If they complemented electronic transactions with personal coordination, such problems were mitigated.

## 3.4  B2B Summary

The analysis of B2B electronic trade, focusing especially on the dramatic rise and fall of Internet-based, third party B2B marketplaces, provides further evidence for questioning the three assumptions outlined at the start of the chapter. Although there are clearly many examples of global B2B electronic trade, most occurs over private industrial networks rather than via open B2B exchanges (Laudon and Traver, 2001). Moreover, there is some evidence of a preference for locally based suppliers, even on public B2B exchanges (Choi, 2003). Further arguments for the relevance of geography are suggested by the continuing focus on the importance of regional business clusters (Porter, 2000). To the extent that there is a higher probability of pre-existing relations among geographically proximate firms, then there is a role for B2B networks, albeit perhaps smaller, more closed user group ones, in such local business clusters. Regarding the substitution of electronic transactions for personal linkages, the limited research on IT use in local business clusters suggests that traditional forms of coordination often supercede electronic coordination, although some studies do find that the two can be complementary (Kraut et al., 1998). Finally, the importance of network effects is somewhat contradicted by the experience of the dot.com B2B electronic marketplaces, where we are beginning to see a movement away from an emphasis on arms-length transactions, to one where the networks are used to support existing relationships in collaborative e-commerce ventures. In fact, one might view some of the trade facilitation features common in B2B marketplaces as compensation for the lack of familiarity and trust that might have been present in trade between established partners. Such compensatory features include the need for member qualification and reputation and ratings services. The rise of industry consortia, and the growth of collaborative e-commerce suggest that pre-existing relationships have an important place in B2B electronic trade and the emphasis exclusively on network effects may have unwittingly made electronic marketplaces less valuable to potential participants.

## 4    CONCLUSION

This review of B2C and B2B electronic commerce has attempted to illustrate the dangers of overly focusing on the distance insensitivity, transaction automation capability, and network externality characteristics as the overriding logic guiding business model development. In place, an alternative perspective emphasizing the coupling of e-commerce to physical presence in a market, offline modes of interaction, and existing customers and other exchange partners has been presented. For the sake of illustration, a somewhat one-sided argument has been provided, although it should be obvious that it is not an either/or situation. E-commerce certainly is a distance spanning technology. It clearly does enable automated transactions that are often at a much lower cost than offline transactions. In many cases, the arguments for network effects are definitely justified. The point of the chapter is to encourage a more realistic approach to e-commerce that is sensitive to the potential complementary benefits it offers to existing offline business activities. In so doing, some new lines of inquiry are suggested. How, for example, can firms best blend e-commerce with physical channels, and what does this imply for e-commerce system developers? How can firms create incentives for offline channels to promote e-commerce? How can the potential synergies be exploited? What should the role of e-commerce be in local business clusters? How can B2B e-commerce better support smaller value webs while at the same time remaining flexible enough to accommodate change? As e-commerce becomes more pervasive, addressing such questions related to how it can work with, rather than replace, existing business approaches will only become more important.

## 5 REFERENCES

Afuah, A. and C. Tucci (2001). *Internet Business Models and Strategies: Text and Cases.* New York, NY, McGraw-Hill Irwin.

Anderson, E., G. S. Day and V. K. Rangan (1997). "Strategic Channel Design." *Sloan Management Review,* Vol. 38, No. 4, pp. 59-69.

Anonymous (2000). "The 10 Driving Principles of the New Economy." *Business 2.0.*

Bailey, J. (1998). *Internet Price Discrimination: Self-regulation, Public Policy, and Global Electronic Commerce.* Telecommunications Policy Research Conference, Washington, D.C.

Bakos, J. Y. (1997). "Reducing Buyer Search Costs: Implications for Electronic Marketplaces." *Management Science,* Vol. 43, No.12, pp. 1676-1692.

Bakos, J. Y. (1998). "The Emerging Role of Electronic Marketplaces on the Internet." *Communications of the ACM,* Vol. 41, No. 8, pp. 35-42.

Balasubramanian, S. (1998). "Mail Versus Mall: A Strategic Analysis of Competition between Direct Marketers and Conventional Retailers." *Marketing Science,* Vol. 17, No 3, pp. 181-195.

Bradley, S. (1993). *The Role of IT Networking in Sustaining Competitive Advantage. Globalization, Technology, and Competition: The Fusion of Computers and Telecommunications in the 1990s.* S. Bradley, J. Hausman and R. Nolan. Boston, MA, Harvard University Press, pp. 113-142.

Caby, L., C. Jaeger and C. Steinfield (1998). "Explaining the Use of Inter-firm data Networks for Electronic Transactions: The Case of the Pharmaceutical and Advertising Industries in France." *Telecommunications and Socio-Economic Development.* S. MacDonald and G. Madden. Amsterdam, Elsevier, pp. 191-204.

Cairncross, F. (1997). *The Death of Distance.* Boston, MA, Harvard Business School Press.

Castells, M. (2001). *The Internet Galaxy.* Oxford, Oxford University Press.

Choi, J.-S. (2003). *Spatial Analysis of Transactions that Use e-Catalogs in Public Business-to-Business Electronic Marketplaces by Business Model.* International Geographical Union Special Symposium, Dynamics of Economic Spaces in E-Commerce, Incheon, Korea.

Choi, S., D. O. Stahl and A. Whinston (1997). *The Economics of Electronic Commerce: The Essential Economics of Doing Business in the Electronic Marketplace.* Indianapolis, IN, MacMillan.

Coates, V. (1998). *Buying and Selling on the Internet: Retail Electronic Commerce.* Washington, D.C., The Institute for Technology Assessment.

Dieberger, A., P. Dourish, K. Hook, P. Resnick and A. Wexelblat (2000). "Social Navigation: Techniques for Building more Usable Systems." *Interactions,* November-December, pp. 37-45.

DiMaggio, P. and H. Louch (1998). "Socially Embedded Consumer Transactions: For What Kinds of Purchases do People Most Often Use Networks?" *American Sociological Review*, Vol. 63, No. 5, pp. 619-637.

Friedman, L. G. and T. R. Furey (1999). *The Channel Advantage: Going to Market with Multiple Sales Channels to Reach More Customers, Sell More Products, Make More Profit.* Boston, Butterworth Heinemann.

Garicano, L. and S. N. Kaplan (2001). Beyond the Hype: Making B2B e-Commerce Profitable. *Capital Ideas,* 2.

Granovetter, M. (1985). "Economic Action and Social Structure: The Problem of Embeddedness." *American Journal of Sociology*, Vol. 91, No. 3, pp. 481-510.

Johnston, R. and P. Lawrence (1988). "Beyond Vertical Integration: The Rise of the Value-added Partnership." *Harvard Business Review*, pp. 94-101.

Kaplan, S. N. and M. Sawhney (2000). "E-hubs: The New B2B Marketplaces." *Harvard Business Review* 78, pp. 97-103.

Katsaros, H., M. Shore, R. Leathern and T. Clark (2000). *U.S. Business-to-Business Internet Trade Projections.* New York, Jupiter Research.

Kolko, J. (2000). *The Death of Cities? The Death of Distance? Evidence from the Geography of Commercial Internet Usage. Internet Upheaval: Raising Questions, Seeking Answers in Communications Policy.* I. Vogelsang and B. Compaine. Cambridge, MA, MIT Press, pp. 73-98.

Kotler, P. (1999). *Marketing Management,* 10th Edition. Upper Saddle River, NJ, Prentice Hall.

Kraut, R., C. Steinfield, A. Chan, B. Butler and A. Hoag (1998). "Coordination and Virtualization: The Role of Electronic Networks and Personal Relationships." *Journal of Computer Mediated Communication,* Vol. 3, No. 4.

Kumar, K., H. van Dissel and P. Bielli (1998). "The Merchant of Prato – Revisited: Toward a Third Rationality of Information Systems." *MIS Quarterly*, Vol. 22, No. 2, pp. 199-226.

Laudon, K. and C. Traver (2001). *E-commerce: Business, Technology, Society.* Boston, Addison-Wesley.

Malone, T., J. Yates and R. Benjamin (1987). "Electronic Markets and Electronic Hierarchies: Effects of Information Technology on Market Structure and Corporate Strategies." *Communications of the ACM*, Vol. 30, No. 6, pp. 484-497.

Maskell, P. (2001). "Towards a Knowledge-based Theory of the Geographical Cluster." *Industrial and Corporate Change*, Vol. 10, No. 4, pp. 921-944.

Otto, J. and Q. Chung (2000). "A Framework for Cyber-enhanced Retailing: Integrating e-Commerce Retailing with Brick and Mortar Retailing." *Electronic Markets*, Vol. 10, No. 4, pp. 185-191.

Porter, M. E. (1985). *Competitive Advantage: Creating and Sustaining Superior Performance.* New York, Free Press.

Porter, M. E. (1990). *The Competitive Advantage of Nations.* New York, Free Press.

Porter, M. E. (1998). "The Adam Smith Address: Location, Clusters, and the 'New' Microeconomics of Competition." *Business Economics*, Vol. 33, No. 1, pp. 7-13.

Porter, M. E. (2000). "Location, Competition, and Economic Development: Local Clusters in a Global Economy." *Economic Development Quarterly*, Vol. 14, No. 1, pp. 15-34.

Rayport, J. F. and J. J. Sviokla (1995). "Exploiting the Virtual Value Chain." *Harvard Business Review*, Vol. 73, No. 6, pp. 75-87.

Rogers, E. and J. Larsen (1984). *Silicon Valley Fever: Growth of High-technology Culture*. New York, Basic Books.

Rosen, K. T. and A. L. Howard (2000). "E-retail: Gold Rush or Fool's Gold?" *California Management Review*, Vol. 42, No. 3, pp. 72-100.

Saxenian, A. and J. Y. Hsu (2001). "The Silicon Valley-Hsinchu Connection: Technical Communities and Industrial Upgrading." *Industrial and Corporate Change*, Vol. 10, No 4, pp. 893-920.

Segev, A., J. Gebauer and F. Färber (1999). "Internet-based Electronic Markets." *Electronic Markets*, Vol. 9, No. 3, pp. 138-146.

Shapiro, C. and H. R. Varian (1999). *Information Rules: a Strategic Guide to the Network Economy*. Boston, Mass., Harvard Business School Press.

Steinfield, C., T. Adelaar and Y.-j. Lai (2002a). *Integrating Brick and Mortar Locations with e-Commerce: Understanding Synergy Opportunities*. Hawaii International Conference on Systems Sciences, Big Island, Hawaii, IEEE Computer Society.

Steinfield, C., H. Bouwman and T. Adelaar (2002b). "The Dynamics of Click and Mortar e-Commerce: Opportunities and Management Strategies." *International Journal of Electronic Commerce*, Vol. 7, No. 1, pp. 93-119.

Steinfield, C., A. Chan and R. Kraut (2000). "Computer-mediated Markets: An Introduction and Preliminary Test of Market-structure Impacts." *Journal of Computer Mediated Communication*, Vol. 5, No. 3.

Steinfield, C., D. DeWit, T. Adelaar, A. Bruin, E. Fielt, A. Smit, M. Hoofslout and H. Bouwman (2001). "Pillars of Virtual Commerce: Leveraging Physical and Virtual Presence in the New Economy." *Info*, Vol. 3, No. 3, pp. 203-213.

Steinfield, C. and S. Klein (1999). "Local vs. Global Issues in Electronic Commerce." *Electronic Markets*, Vol. 9, No. 1/2, pp. 45-50.

Steinfield, C., R. Kraut and A. Plummer (1995). "The Effect of Networks on Buyer-Seller Relations." *Journal of Computer Mediated Communication*, Vol. 1, No.3.

Stern, L. W. and A. I. Ansary (1992). *Marketing Channels*. Englewood Cliffs, NJ, Prentice Hall.

Subramami, M. and E. Walden (2000). *Economic Returns to Firms from Business-to-business Electronic Commerce Initiatives: An Empirical Investigation*. 21th International Conference on Information Systems, Brisbane, Australia.

Tedeschi, R. (1999). Dealing with Those Pesky Returns. *New York Times*. New York.

Tedeschi, R. (2001a). Bricks-and-Mortar Merchants Struggling to Assess Web Sidelines. *New York Times*. New York.

Tedeschi, R. (2001b). E-commerce Report: Companies in no Hurry to Buy over the Internet. *New York Times*. New York.

Teece, D. J. (1986). "Profiting from Technological Innovation: Implications for Integration, Collaboration, Licensing and Public Policy. " *Research Policy*, Vol. 15, pp. 285-306.

Timmer, P. (1998). "Business Models for Electronic Markets." *Electronic Markets*, Vol. 8, No. 2, pp. 3-8.

U. S. Department of Commerce (2000). *The Emerging Digital Economy*. Washington, D. C., U. S. Department of Commerce.

Useem, J. (1999). "Internet Defense Strategy: Cannibalize Yourself." *Fortune*, Vol. 140, p. 121.

Ward, M. R. (2001). "Will Online Shopping Compete More with Traditional Retailing or Catalog Shopping?" *Netnomics*, Vol. 3, No. 2, pp. 103-117.

Wigand, R. (1997). "Electronic Commerce: Definition, Theory, and Context." *The Information Society*, Vol. 13, pp. 1-16.

Wigand, R. and R. Benjamin (1995). "Electronic Commerce: Effects on Electronic Markets." *Journal of Computer Mediated Communication*, Vol. 1, No. 3.

Wildman, S. and M. Guerin-Calvert (1991). *Electronic Services Networks: Functions, Structures, and Public Policy. Electronic Services Networks: A Business and Public Policy Challenge*. M. Guerin-Calvert and S. Wildman. New York, Praeger, pp. 3-21.

Williamson, O. (1975). *Markets and Hierarchies: Analysis and Antitrust Implications*. New York, Free Press.

Williamson, O. (1985). *The Economic Institutions of Capitalism*. New York, Free Press.

Zhu, K. and K. Kraemer (2002). "Electronic Commerce Metrics: Assessing the Value of e-Commerce to Firm Performance with Data from the Manufacturing Sector." *Information Systems Research*, Vol. 13, No. 3, pp. 275-295.

Zimmermann, H.-D. (1997). "The Electronic Mall Bodensee (EMB): An Introduction to the EMB and its Architectural Concepts." *Electronic Markets*, Vol. 7, No. 1, pp. 1-7.

# PART II

# GLOBAL ECONOMY AND DIGITAL TECHNOLOGY

# CHAPTER 5

# OECD Growth Blocs and the Role of ICT[*]

Gary Madden and Grant Coble-Neal

*Communication Economics and Electronic Markets Research Centre, School of Economics and Finance, Curtin University of Technology, Perth*

**Abstract.** The role of information and communications technology (ICT) in the productivity boom of the 1990s has been the subject of vigorous recent debate. Gordon (2000) claims that production of ICT is the sole source of new-economy productivity growth. Nordhaus (2001) and Stiroh (2001) disagree and attribute most of the gains to ICT use. However, these studies suggest that new economy gains are contained completely within ICT production or its use. If these arguments are correct, then growth blocs within the OECD could emerge and contribute to divergence in wealth creation by 'new' and 'old' economies. This chapter examines the role that new technology activity plays in economic growth for a sample of 12 OECD member countries from 1976 to 2000. An empirical model that relates total factor productivity to domestic and foreign technology spillovers and human capital is estimated. The empirical results and policy implications are discussed.

## 1    INTRODUCTION

The role of information and communications technology (ICT) in the US productivity boom of the late-1990s is the subject of recent debate. Gordon (2000) claims that, once temporary cyclical effects are accounted for, ICT production is the sole source of 'new economy' productivity growth. Nordhaus (2001) disagrees. He finds new economy (machinery, electric equipment, telephone and telegraph, and software) productivity growth increased at 13.3% per annum from 1998 through 2000. After deducting this contribution, Nordhaus concludes the US productivity rebound is not confined to the new economy. Further, Oliner and Sichel (2000) observe that while US business investment in computing and peripheral equipment rose four-fold between 1995 and 1999, only two-thirds of the acceleration in labour productivity is contained within the ICT production sector. Moreover, ICT capital deepening contributed over 40% of the rise in US labour productivity in the late-1990s. By contrast, ICT production contributed 25% of the increase in productivity. Finally, Jorgenson and Stiroh (2000) find little evidence of spillovers from production of ICT with industries that use ICT

---

[*] We thank Christiano Antonelli, Karl-Heinz Neumann and seminar participants at the Investment, Productivity and the Digital Divide Session presentation at the 14th Biennial Conference of the International Telecommunications Society, Seoul, Korea, August 2002. Data collection by Michael Schipp is gratefully acknowledged. The usual disclaimer applies.

relatively intensively such as finance, insurance and real estate displaying high rates of substitution of ICT for other inputs, but low productivity growth.

Recent analysis by Baily (2002) reports the US ICT capital deepening observed by Jorgenson and Stiroh, and Oliner and Sichel, has resulted in increased total factor productivity (TFP) growth in the Finance and Wholesale and Retail Trade sectors. Within the Finance sector, TFP growth acceleration was initially confined to security and commodity brokers, but more recently has broadened to include the banking sector. Stiroh (2001) also finds that industries with above median ICT intensity experienced above average labour productivity growth. Taking up Gordon's claim that cyclical variation accounts for much of the TFP surge, Brynjolfsson and Hitt (2001) find that in the short-term, computers contribute to output growth, but not productivity growth. In the longer term, however, they calculate that output elasticity with respect to ICT stock is up to eight times the ICT factor share.

This debate highlights the fact that growth accounting procedures cannot adequately capture the productivity effects of ICT investment. Brynjolfsson and Hitt explain that the introduction of general-purpose technology (GPT) (such as ICT) requires new production processes to exploit efficiency gains.[1] It is therefore likely that growth accounting will not accurately reflect the gains derived from GPT until the associated processes are firmly established. Moreover, Brynjolfsson and Hitt argue that ICT investment is intended to generate value-chain improvements through new product development. These gains will not be captured in standard output measures. As Bresnahan and Greenstein (2002) observe, there is a substantial gap between technical advance and realised welfare enhancement. Knowledge of new invention travels more quickly among OECD countries, but co-invention is localised. Co-invention or new product development is part of a process of adapting GPT to specific uses. Firms, industries and countries realise different co-invention and so obscure the relationship between ICT investment and productivity measurement.

To date, research concerning the link between ICT investment and TFP growth has been dominated by US-oriented studies. Accordingly, there is a need to conduct analysis of ICT and productivity growth to see whether ICT has similar impacts on TFP in other countries. Unfortunately, the paucity of available data on ICT investment limits the scope of this study. As a first step towards this objective, this paper provides a cross-country study that tests whether new technology 'growth blocs' exist within the OECD, based on the ability to translate new knowledge into superior growth, and examines implications of membership on growth.

Identification of distinct technology-based growth blocs is the first step to identifying the country-specific factors that lead to endogenous economic growth and enhanced welfare. Essentially, the two innovation paths that lead to higher TFP are embodied and disembodied technical change. Embodied technical change refers to the increased level of technology embodied in new physical and human capital. For example, the latest generation of ICT capital will be more efficient than earlier generations of ICT. If fully utilised, the new capital will lead to enhanced TFP, which translates to a higher level of GDP. Similarly, workers with advanced skills are likely to produce a higher output. Combining new capital with higher skill levels yields a co-invention effect as the workers integrate new capital into production processes. Countries exhibiting the same effectiveness in acquiring and integrating new

---

[1] GPT is defined by Ames and Rosenberg (1984) as technology that fundamentally affects the business processes of many sectors.

capital will share identical output elasticities.[2] Hence, countries can be ranked in groups according to their output responses. Clearly, those with the most elastic output elasticities will be the countries that react fastest to technology change and therefore, have the greatest potential to extract the most from capital-embodied technical change. Disembodied technical change refers to the fundamental discoveries and breakthroughs that are typically produced via research and development. These advances are not yet integrated into physical and human capital. The economic effects of these discoveries may not be realised for a considerable period of time. However, eventually the new knowledge will begin to be incorporated into production via co-invention with the effect that steady-state output will be raised to a new level. Countries vary according to their ability to make use of these discoveries. Some, such as the US will be able to absorb these discoveries more quickly than others. The reason is that some countries have advanced and highly effective research and development sectors. In many cases, these advanced sectors will be able to extract use from discoveries, irrespective of where the breakthroughs originated. Therefore, there are likely to be technology spill-overs from one country to others. The determining factor will be the ability to absorb the information.

In both the embodied and disembodied technical change cases, once countries have been identified in terms of ability to translate knowledge into efficiency gains, country differences can be analysed to determine the factors that lead to maximal TFP growth. Therefore, this study develops a model that identifies countries in terms of growth blocs. The ability to innovate via capital embodied technical change is conducted in the form of a test for parameter homogeneity across countries. The disembodied case is assessed by developing 'pure' TFP indexes. These indexes are then included as arguments in a standard form vector-autoregressive (VAR) system. The VAR approach permits direct testing for technology spillovers between countries. The approach used here thus permits an assessment of the impacts of new technology and groups countries according to the degree and form that such activity plays in TFP growth for a sample of 12 OECD Member Countries from 1976 to 2000. The paper is organised as follows. Section 2 develops an econometric model of productivity growth designed to directly measure the impact of technical advance. Section 3 describes the data and presents descriptive statistics of TFP. Section 4 assesses the econometric results with a particular emphasis on the implications, and two growth blocs are identified. An ancillary analysis is conducted that focuses on the role of ICT for a Member Country from each group. Section 5 concludes.

## 2 ECONOMETRIC MODEL

An economy with non-constant TFP is in disequilibrium. The extent of disequilibrium is assessed by measuring departure from the steady state framework established by Solow (1957). Consider the two-input production function for country i at time t as

$$Q_{it} = F\left(A_{it}, K_{it}, L_{it}\right),$$ (1)

---

[2] Output elasticity measures the percentage change in production output given one percent increase in a given production input.

where Q, A, K and L are indices of output, technology, capital and labour, respectively. Conventional TFP measures typically assume perfectly competitive product and factor markets, constant returns, and fully employed factors that are flexible and homogenous in quality through time. Together these assumptions formulate an economic model of well-established equilibrium production processes that remain unchanged. A functional form that embodies these properties is the Cobb-Douglas

$$Q_{it} = A_{it} K_{it}^{\alpha_{it}} L_{it}^{\beta_{it}} ,$$ (2)

where $\alpha_{it}$ and $\beta_{it}$ are output elasticities defined as

$$\alpha_{it} = \frac{MP_{K,it}}{AP_{K,it}} \text{ and } \beta_{it} = \frac{MP_{L,it}}{AP_{L,it}} .$$ (3)

MPK, APK, MPL and APL are the marginal product (MP) and average product (AP) of capital and labour, respectively. Assuming linear homogeneity (3) is written

$$\alpha_{it} = \frac{P_{K,it} K_{it}}{P_{it} Q_{it}} \text{ and } \beta_{it} = \frac{P_{L,it} L_{it}}{P_{it} Q_{it}} .$$ (4)

Equation (4) shows that output elasticities are equal to the share of expenditure of capital and labour in total revenue. Shifts in the shares imply input substitution. Considering sources of deviation from this state incorporates production disequilibrium. In particular, Brynjolfsson and Hitt (2001) argue when new forms of capital are introduced, adjustment and learning take place as organizations combine new capital with complementary changes in work practices, human capital and firm organization. Accordingly, (1) is modified to allow the capital elasticity to vary by time t and human capital H,

$$Q_{it} = A_{it} K_{it}^{\alpha_{it} + \alpha_{1,i} t + \alpha_{2,i} H_{it}} L_{it}^{\beta_{it} + \beta_{1,i} H_{it}} .$$ (5)

*t* is correlated with unobserved organisational adjustment as production processes are integrated to adapt to new capital.

Equation (5) is rearranged to yield,

$$\ln Q'_{it} = \ln A_{it} + \alpha_{1,i} t \ln K_{it} + \alpha_{2,i} H_{it} \ln K_{it} + \beta_{1,i} H_{it} \ln L_{it}$$ (6)

where $\ln Q'_{it} = \ln Q_{it} - \alpha_{it} \ln K_{it} - \beta_{it} \ln L_{it}$ and $\ln Q'_{it}$ is the remaining output in excess of the long-run equilibrium component. Equation (6) allows for Nelson's (1964) argument that interaction between technology, education and the stock of capital are important in explaining economic growth. Such interaction creates endogenous growth and increasing returns. Further, Coe and Helpman (1995), Frantzen (1998), Madden and Savage (2000) and Edmond (2001) present empirical evidence of the spillover effects of research and development (R&D). These studies model the impact of foreign and domestic technology using R&D expenditure to proxy for discovery and knowledge. However, by its experimental nature the outcome of R&D

expenditure is uncertain. So TFP is modelled as a random walk with drift.[3] This specification establishes (6) as Watson's (1986) unobserved components model where $\ln A_{it}$ is the time-varying drift term. Accordingly, the technology argument in (6) is restated as

$$\ln A_{it} = \gamma_i + \ln A_{it-1} + e_{it},\tag{7}$$

where $A_{it-1}$ is the past period's level of technology and $e_{it}$ are random technology shocks. The constant term $\gamma_i$ in (7) is the country-specific long-run trend rate of growth in technology. The random positive technology shocks ($e_{it}$) temporarily raise the growth rate of technology above its long-run rate while negative shocks temporarily lower growth below the long-run rate. The random shocks do, however, have a permanent impact on the level of technology. Thus, the model states that there are permanent gains from the new economy technology. However, because the discoveries underlying the technology are random, the perceived above-trend growth in GDP is temporary.

Assessing the magnitude of the increased technology gains derived from new economy discoveries requires identification, via econometric estimation, of the unobserved growth components ($\gamma_i$ and $e_{it}$). However, since technology is a random walk, consistent estimation requires using the first-difference of (6),

$$\Delta \ln Q'_{it} = \gamma_i + \alpha_{1,i}\Delta t \ln K_{it} + \alpha_{2,i}\Delta H_{it} \ln K_{it} + \beta_{1,i}\Delta H_{it} \ln L_{it} + \varepsilon_{it}.\tag{8}$$

Equation (8) establishes disequilibrium output growth as a function of the integration speed of new capital, growth generated via interaction between production inputs, and growth in technology. Possible paths for cross-country technology spillover are factor embodied technical change and disembodied technology shocks. Variation in output elasticities through other country impact reflects differences in the composition of aggregate capital and labour. Growth blocs are identified by tests for parameter homogeneity across countries. Equality of cross-country parameters is assessed by the Greene (2000) likelihood ratio test

$$\lambda = \frac{\hat{L}_R}{\hat{L}_U},\tag{9}$$

where $\hat{L}_R$ and $\hat{L}_U$ are the value of the restrained and unrestrained likelihood functions. The large sample distribution of $-2\ln\lambda$ is $\chi^2(N)$ distributed, where N is the number of countries comprising the group.

Estimation of (8) permits construction of country-specific TFP measures, where TFP growth is defined as $\Delta \ln A_{it} = \gamma_i + \varepsilon_{it}$. Further, rearranging (8) provides,

$$\Delta \ln A_{it} = \Delta \ln Q'_{it} - \alpha_{1,i}\Delta t \ln K_{it} - \alpha_{2,i}\Delta H_{it} \ln K_{it} - \beta_i\Delta H_{it} \ln L_{it}.\tag{10}$$

The log-level of technology is then constructed as

$$\ln A_{it} = \gamma_i t + \ln A_{i0} + \sum_{p=1}^{T}\varepsilon_{it-p},\tag{11}$$

---

[3] This specification captures the effects of all innovations, not just those relating to R&D.

where $t = \{1, 2, 3, \ldots, T\}$ is a time index and $\ln A_{i0}$ is the initial level of technology. Since the initial technology is not observed, (11) is rearranged to

$$\ln \frac{A_{it}}{A_{i0}} = \gamma_i t + \sum_{p=1}^{T} \varepsilon_{it-p} \,. \tag{12}$$

Hence, the technology index is the cumulative level of technology relative to the base year. Initial estimates of the technology level ($\gamma_i$) provide a basis to measure country technology differences. The construction of TFP in (12) permits direct testing of the influence of cross-country spillovers. Country-specific shocks influencing another country's economic growth is captured through the vector auto-regressive specification

$$\ln\mathbf{TFP}_t = \tilde{\mathbf{A}}_0 + \sum_{p=1}^{T} \tilde{\mathbf{A}}_p \ln\mathbf{TFP}_{t-p} \,, \tag{13}$$

where p denotes lag length, $\tilde{\mathbf{A}}_0$ and $\tilde{\mathbf{A}}_p$ are matrices of estimated coefficients and TFP is a vector of country-specific TFP indexes. The Granger causality test is employed to detect cross-country spillover.


## 3   DATA AND VARIABLES

Data required to estimate (6) are collected for a sample of 12 OECD Member Countries from 1976 to 2000.[4] Source data is obtained primarily from the OECD (2002) STAN Database for Industrial Analysis. The main reason for using the STAN database is that it is based on the United Nations (1989) International Standard Industrial Classification of all Economic Activities, Revision 3 and so includes consistent measurement of the services sector. Supplementary time series are sourced from the OECD (2001a) National Accounts 2001 database, and United Nations Organization for Education, Science and Culture (UNESCO) Statistical Yearbook 2001.

A standard TFP growth index ($\Delta \ln Q'_{it}$) is constructed using annual time-series for Value Added at current prices (VALU), Gross Fixed Capital Formation (volume) (GFCFK), Labour Compensation of Employees (LABR), Total Employment (persons) (EMPN), and Operating Surplus and Mixed Income (OPS). Net Capital Stock series are constructed using the perpetual inventory method assuming a constant depreciation rate (3.04%). The rate chosen is a simple average of Hulten and Wykoff's (1981) Best Geometric Rates for commercial and industrial sectors.[5] Initial (1975) capital stock estimates are sourced from Nehru and Dhareshwar (1995). The growth rate of capital is then calculated as the percentage change in the Net Capital Stock. The growth rate of labour is percentage change in EMPN. For Japan and the US, Labour Share ($\beta_{it}$) is calculated according to the OECD Productivity Manual (2001b) as

---

[4] Countries included are Austria, Belgium, Canada, Denmark, Finland, France, Italy, Japan, Rep. of Korea, the Netherlands, the UK and the US.

[5] The depreciation rates correspond to the censored sample selection estimates and allows for capital retirement.

$$\beta_{it} = \frac{LABR + I_L + t_L T}{VALU} \qquad (14)$$

where IL is the Labour Component of Gross Mixed Income, tL is the Share of Labour in Net Taxes, and T is Net Taxes.[6] For the remaining countries (where VALU is not available), the labour share is

$$\beta_{it} = \frac{LABR + I_L + t_L T}{GDP_C}, \qquad (15)$$

where GDPc is Gross Domestic Product at current factor cost. Once Labour Share is obtained, the Capital Share is defined as

$$\alpha_{it} = 1 - \beta_{it}. \qquad (16)$$

The Human Capital index H is the ratio of Graduates to Total Labour Force. The Graduate series is comprised of data sourced from UNESCO Statistical Year Book 2001. Missing values for Canada (1999 and 2000) are sourced from Statistics Canada (2002), CANSIM, Cross-Classified Tables 00580701 and 00580702. Missing data for the United States, 1976-79, 1985, 1987, 1996-2000 is sourced from National Center for Education Statistics (2001), Digest of Education Statistics 2001. Missing values for the remaining countries (1976-1979) are interpolated. Total Labour Force is from the World Bank World Development Indicators 2001.

Table 1 reports sample averages for the constructed series, Labour and Capital Share, Output and conventional TFP Growth $(\Delta \ln Q'_{it})$. Observations not able to be calculated for Canada (1998, 1999 and 2000), France (2000), Japan (1999 and 2000) and the UK (2000) are sourced from Colecchia and Schreyer (2001). Table 1 reveals 11% variation in average Labour Share from a minimum of 66.31 for Italy to a maximum of 74.35 for Korea. Average Output Growth exhibits a difference of 5.3% across countries from a minimum of 2.07% (Denmark) to a maximum of 7.37% for Korea. TFP varies in a tighter 2.33% range from France (0.11%) to Austria (2.44%). Average Output and TFP Growth for the group is 3.19% and 1.17%, respectively. For the two fastest growing economies, Austria and Korea, TFP growth accounts for 61% and 30% of Output Growth, respectively. The average group share of TFP in Output Growth is 37%. Using the group average as a basis for comparison, it is apparent Austria, Belgium, Finland and Korea have the most unexplained growth. By contrast, France has the least with its average share 90% below the group average.[7]

---

[6] See the Appendix for calculations of $I_L$, $t_L$ and T.

[7] Given US TFP growth is known, TFP growth calculated from the OECD STAN database for the US is compared to US Bureau of Labor Statistics (BLS) multifactor productivity estimates. There is a discrepancy, which is explained by Scarpeta *et al* (2000) as being due to the BLS' exclusion of government enterprises.

Table 1. Sample Means 1976-2000

| Country | Labour share | Capital Share | Output Growth (%) | TFP Growth (%) |
|---|---|---|---|---|
| Austria | 69.60 | 30.40 | 4.00 | 2.44 |
| Belgium | 73.94 | 26.06 | 2.35 | 1.59 |
| Canada | 67.07 | 32.28 | 2.77 | 0.75 |
| Denmark | 67.51 | 32.49 | 2.07 | 0.71 |
| Finland | 68.40 | 31.52 | 2.93 | 1.89 |
| France | 66.59 | 33.41 | 2.70 | 0.11 |
| Italy | 66.31 | 33.39 | 2.30 | 0.56 |
| Japan | 74.72 | 25.28 | 3.32 | 1.27 |
| Rep. of Korea | 74.35 | 25.65 | 7.37 | 2.24 |
| The Netherlands | 68.31 | 31.69 | 2.59 | 0.71 |
| UK | 71.70 | 28.30 | 2.34 | 0.92 |
| US | 68.44 | 31.56 | 3.52 | 0.80 |
| Average | 69.75 | 30.17 | 3.19 | 1.17 |

## 4   ESTIMATION RESULTS

Seemingly unrelated regression (SUR) estimation results by country for (8) are presented in Table 2. A cursory examination of Table 2 reveals considerable variation among factors driving disequilibrium growth. Moreover, for most countries the magnitudes of the estimated coefficient differences are significant. Likelihood ratio tests for parameter homogeneity across countries identify 2 country groups, Austria-Finland and Japan-Korea. The null hypothesis that the coefficients within a group are identical yields a $\chi^2(6)$ statistic of 2.20. With a 10% critical value of 10.64, the country groupings are accepted. Other potential country groupings are selected on the basis of proximity, e.g., North America and Western Europe. Possible groupings are also suggested by similar coefficient estimates. However, likelihood ratio tests of these groupings are rejected by the data.

Table 2. Estimation Results

| Country | Parameter | Coefficient Estimate | t-Ratio |
|---|---|---|---|
| Austria | $\alpha_1$ | -0.00 | -0.55 |
| | $\alpha_2$ | -2.47 | -1.99[1] |
| | $\beta$ | 4.13 | 2.01[1] |
| | $\gamma$ | 0.07 | 0.73 |
| Belgium | $\alpha_1$ | -0.00 | -0.95 |
| | $\alpha_2$ | -0.00 | -2.75[1] |
| | $\beta$ | 0.00 | 2.83[1] |
| | $\gamma$ | 0.09 | 1.10 |
| Canada | $\alpha_1$ | 0.00 | 2.19[1] |
| | $\alpha_2$ | -0.88 | -0.84 |
| | $\beta$ | 1.50 | 0.84 |
| | $\gamma$ | -0.19 | -2.21[1] |
| Denmark | $\alpha_1$ | -0.00 | -0.07 |
| | $\alpha_2$ | -15.19 | -6.95[1] |
| | $\beta$ | 25.23 | 7.21[1] |
| | $\gamma$ | 0.00 | 0.08 |
| Finland | $\alpha_1$ | -0.00 | -0.55 |
| | $\alpha_2$ | -2.47 | -1.99[1] |
| | $\beta$ | 4.13 | 2.01[1] |
| | $\gamma$ | 0.07 | 0.71 |
| France | $\alpha_1$ | -0.03 | -3.28[1] |
| | $\alpha_2$ | -5.87 | -2.70[1] |
| | $\beta$ | 10.14 | 2.69[1] |
| | $\gamma$ | 1.01 | 3.39[1] |
| Italy | $\alpha_1$ | 0.00 | 1.45 |
| | $\alpha_2$ | -8.44 | -4.86[1] |
| | $\beta$ | 18.26 | 4.99[1] |
| | $\gamma$ | -0.27 | -1.47 |
| Japan | $\alpha_1$ | 0.00 | 0.55 |
| | $\alpha_2$ | -2.36 | -4.25[1] |
| | $\beta$ | 4.56 | 4.33[1] |
| | $\gamma$ | -0.07 | -0.57 |
| Rep. of Korea | $\alpha_1$ | 0.00 | 0.55 |
| | $\alpha_2$ | -2.36 | -4.25[1] |
| | $\beta$ | 4.56 | 4.33[1] |
| | $\gamma$ | -0.03 | -0.25 |

[1] Significant at the 5% level.

(cont.)

Table 2. Estimation Results (Continued)

| Country | Parameter | Coefficient Estimate | t-Ratio |
|---------|-----------|---------------------|---------|
| The Netherlands | $\alpha_1$ | 0.00 | 1.80 |
| | $\alpha_2$ | -6.94 | -3.82[1] |
| | $\beta$ | 10.94 | 3.90[1] |
| | $\gamma$ | -0.21 | -1.77 |
| UK | $\alpha_1$ | 0.00 | 0.82 |
| | $\alpha_2$ | 6.13 | 2.12[1] |
| | $\beta$ | -9.64 | -2.09[1] |
| | $\gamma$ | -0.12 | -0.82 |
| US | $\alpha_1$ | -0.03 | -7.31[1] |
| | $\alpha_2$ | -1.93 | -0.53 |
| | $\beta$ | 3.17 | 0.55 |
| | $\gamma$ | 1.10 | 7.64[1] |

[1] Significant at the 5% level.

Further inspection of Table 2 reveals France and the US have a significant $\alpha_1$ parameter. France's negative coefficient suggests slight diseconomies through time. There is no interaction between physical and human capital ($\alpha_2$) for Austria, Canada, Finland and the US. Belgium, Denmark, France, Italy, Japan, Rep. of Korea and the Netherlands record negative coefficient estimates. A negative $\alpha_2$ coefficient implies that the effect of capital stock on TFP decreases as the level of human capital increases and also indicates that the capital share decreases as human capital accumulates.[8] Finally, the interaction between labour demand and education ($\beta$) is consistently positive, except for the UK. $\beta>0$ suggests that the effectiveness of capital increases as the number of graduates to total labour force rises. However, there is substantial variation by country, e.g., the UK estimate suggests that a 1% increase in graduates leads to a 10% decrease in capital's contribution to TFP, while the same increases has no impact for Canada or the US, and a 25% increase for Denmark.[9]

Estimation of (8) by country permits a 'pure' TFP growth index to be constructed by (11).[10] This approach filters out systematic components of TFP growth, leaving only random effects. While these shocks are likely to be an aggregation of a multitude of economy-wide shocks, the new economy thesis suggests that positive technology shocks emanating from the ICT sector are captured, and possibly form a substantial part of aggregate shocks. Figure 1 presents the constructed TFP index comprised entirely of random shocks.[11] Inspection reveals large differences across countries. Figure 1A displays those countries that have a statistically insignificant drift term ($\gamma$) while Figure 1B illustrates the countries with a significant drift

---

[8] We thank an anonymous referee for making this point.

[9] Care should be exercised in interpreting country parameter estimates. For instance, the proportion of Graduates to Total Labour Force in the US is three times that of Denmark. Further, between 1976 and 2000 the proportion of Graduates to Total Labour Force has doubled for Denmark while remaining constant for the US. This suggests that Denmark is experiencing increasing returns to human capital enhancement while the US has exhausted scale economies from education.

[10] Only statistically significant parameters are used to filter the TFP series.

[11] Figure 1 is split into two charts for clear exposition.

terms (γ). Inspection of Figure 1 in terms of the divergence between countries shows substantial variation across countries. In Figure 1A, Korea, Finland and Austria produce
consistently faster TFP growth than Belgium, Denmark, Japan and the UK. Korea averages
2.9% annual TFP growth, while Finland and Austria average 2.4% and 1.6%, respectively. By
contrast, UK average TFP growth is a relatively flat 0.5%, while Japan exhibits a negative
trend. The cumulative indexes shown in Figure 1A give the impression of a trend, but this is
an illusion due to the cumulative summation of the random shocks over the years. Inspection
of the growth series reveals considerable volatility, highlighting the randomness of the impact
of R&D on economic growth. The cumulative series does, however, clearly reveal that
countries are consistent in their responses to the shocks. Indeed, Korea is shown as the best
able to take advantage of new knowledge. Figure 1B shows the impact of random shocks on
the trended TFP series, resulting in oscillation around the stochastic trend. Moreover, ranking
across countries in Figure 1B is less clear. France is the exception, with average TFP growth
of 6.5% per annum. The US appears to have the fastest improvement in TFP, growing an
average 22% since 1995. Canada is the next fastest with TFP growth of 7.9% since 1995.
Italy, however, exhibits a slightly negative trend. Perhaps most noticeable across the two
charts is that Canada, France and the US all experienced a surge in TFP since 1996, while
Korea appeared to plateau somewhat.

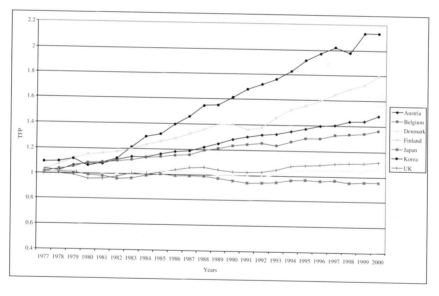

Figure 1A. TFP Series 1976-2000

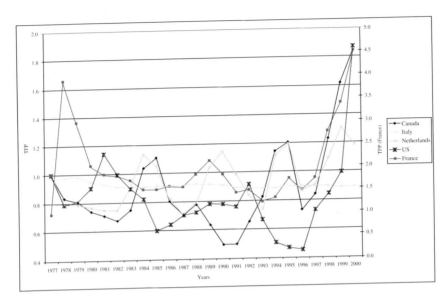

Figure 1B. TFP Series 1976-2000

Further analysis is conducted by calculating long-run averages pre- and post-1995. These sub-samples permit comparison of the new economy versus the 'old economy' that existed prior to 1995. All countries exhibit a positive increase in trend TFP over the post-1995 era. Canada and France exhibit the largest trend changes while for the US, the trend change is actually a reversal of trend from -4.1% for the pre-1995 era. Belgium, Japan and Italy exhibit the smallest increase in trend.

Table 3 presents those countries that recorded significant Granger causality test results. The results reveal mutual feedback in TFP between Austria-Belgium, Canada-Finland and Finland-UK. The remaining results show one-way causality. The impact on the US appears exclusively one-way, with Denmark, Finland, France and the UK revealed to have significant influence on the US. Japan has a one-way impact on the Rep. of Korea, The Netherlands and the UK. Both the Netherlands and the UK appear to have substantial influence on the other European countries. Statistically significant links between Japan-US and Korea-US cannot be found. Overall, it appears that all countries are open to external influences.

Table 3. Granger Causality Tests

| Country 1 | Country 2 | Country 1 → Country 2 | Country 2 → Country 1 |
|---|---|---|---|
| Austria | Belgium | 6.37 | 7.94 |
| | Canada | 3.55 | |
| | Finland | | 5.24 |
| | France | | 4.82 |
| | The Netherlands | 4.96 | |
| | UK | 4.37 | |
| Belgium | Canada | 3.12 | |
| | Finland | | 12.30 |
| | Rep. of Korea | | 6.80 |
| | The Netherlands | 4.73 | |
| | UK | 4.08 | |
| Canada | Denmark | 10.2 | |
| | Finland | 4.08 | 3.10 |
| | France | 6.75 | |
| | Italy | | 5.12 |
| | Japan | | 9.00 |
| Denmark | US | 11.8 | |
| Finland | Rep. of Korea | | 3.50 |
| | The Netherlands | 6.77 | |
| | UK | 3.99 | 4.44 |
| | US | 3.94 | |
| France | UK | | 5.23 |
| | US | 8.95 | |
| Italy | Japan | | 8.35 |
| | Rep. of Korea | 15.50 | |
| | The Netherlands | 4.08 | |
| | UK | 20.80 | |
| Japan | Rep. of Korea | 4.40 | |
| | The Netherlands | 4.11 | |
| | UK | 3.21 | |
| Rep. of Korea | The Netherlands | 4.25 | |
| | UK | 3.79 | |
| The Netherlands | UK | | 5.41 |
| UK | US | 3.94 | |

Note. Critical values for the F distribution: 5% level is 3.49 and 1% level is 5.85. Null hypothesis is that Country 1 TFP does not affect Country TFP and vice versa.

Comparing the results from Table 3 with the reported surge in trend TFP post-1995, it is apparent that the superior TFP growth experienced by the Rep. of Korea and Finland is internally driven. To sum, a group of 4 countries, Finland, France, Rep. of Korea and the US are substantially outperforming the remaining sample in terms of TFP growth. The relative sluggishness of Finland and Korea casts doubt over the existence of a growth bloc between the 4 high-performing countries. Overall, the results suggest the 4 best performing countries have an increasing ability to translate knowledge into accelerated economic growth.

## 4.1 Ancillary Analysis

To isolate the role of ICT in the growth process the definition of $\ln Q'_{it}$ in (6) is expanded to separate ICT capital (C) from aggregate capital to yield,

$$\ln Q'_{it} = \ln Q_{it} - \alpha_{K,it} \ln K_{it} - \alpha_{C,it} \ln C_{it} - \beta_{it} \ln L_{it} . \tag{17}$$

Similarly, (8) is expanded to measure the effects of ICT capital,

$$\Delta \ln Q'_{it} = \gamma_i + \alpha_{1K,i}\Delta \ln K_{it} t + \alpha_{1C,i}\Delta \ln C_{it} t + \alpha_{2K,i}\Delta \ln K_{it} H_{it} \tag{18}$$
$$+ \alpha_{2C,i}\Delta \ln C_{it} H_{it} + \beta_{1,i}\Delta \ln L_{it} H_{it} + \varepsilon_{it} .$$

ICT capital stock data for Finland and the US is sourced from the STAN database, industry sectors Machinery and Equipment, and Post and Telecommunications. Finland is of special interest since, as observed by Jalava and Pohjola (2002), it is one of the leading producers and consumers of ICT in Europe. ICT capital stock is removed from Total Net Capital using the Törnqvist index.[12] ICT Net capital stocks are calculated using the perpetual inventory method and a depreciation rate of 27.29%.[13] The ICT share of initial total stock level (1975) is assumed to be in proportion to the ratio of ICT gross fixed capital formation (GFCF) to Total GFCF.

Table 4 presents estimation results for (18). Estimation results for Finland indicate that there are no systematic components to disequilibrium growth. However, the stochastic trend is statistically significant and positive. By contrast, the results for the US indicate all factors; Capital, ICT Capital and Human Capital have significant effects on US TFP growth. In addition, the coefficient for the Labour-Human Capital effect (β) suggests a substantial skill-bias. The likelihood ratio test again rejects equality of parameters

---

[12] Total and ICT Net Capital Stock are first converted to growth rates. The ICT Capital growth rate weighted by its average value share is subtracted from the growth rate for Total Net Capital Stock. The Net Capital Stock less ICT is then reconstructed using the proportion of initial Total Net Capital Stock less ICT to Total Net Capital in 1975.

[13] Depreciation rate is based on Jorgenson and Sullivan (1981) and relates to the category Office , Computing, and Accounting Machinery.

Table 4. Ancillary Estimation Results

| Country | Parameter | Coefficient Estimate | t-Ratio |
|---------|-----------|----------------------|---------|
| Finland | $\alpha 1K$ | -0.02 | -1.90 |
|         | $\alpha 1C$ | 0.01 | 0.90 |
|         | $\alpha 2K$ | -2.22 | -0.21 |
|         | $\alpha 2C$ | 6.74 | 0.63 |
|         | $\beta$ | -4.74 | -0.58 |
|         | $\gamma$ | 0.49 | 2.33 |
| USA | $\alpha 1K$ | 0.05 | 2.42 |
|     | $\alpha 1C$ | -0.01 | -2.08 |
|     | $\alpha 2K$ | -17.03 | -2.01 |
|     | $\alpha 2C$ | -9.58 | -3.97 |
|     | $\beta$ | 39.79 | 2.67 |
|     | $\gamma$ | -1.21 | -2.31 |

The resulting TFP series for Finland is virtually unchanged while the residual TFP for the US, after removing systematic components of disequilibrium growth, is non-existent. Overall, the results for the US support the thesis that the benefits are derived from ICT use rather than production. Finally, the Granger causality tests between Finland and the US (presented in Table 5) suggest one-way technology spillovers from the US to Finland.

Table 5. Granger Causality Test

| Country 1 | Country 2 | Country 1 $\rightarrow$ Country 2 | Country 2 $\rightarrow$ Country 1 |
|-----------|-----------|-----------------------------------|-----------------------------------|
| Finland | USA | | 3.48 |

## 5   CONCLUSION

This study specifies a disequilibrium model to capture the systematic components of TFP growth. Filtering out both the equilibrium components of growth and the systematic effects explaining disequilibrium permits the creation of a TFP index comprised of pure technology shocks. Utilising OECD STAN data, the study reveals a substantial increase in TFP growth over the late-1990s, coinciding with the new economy thesis, for all of the OECD Member Countries. This suggests that the new economy is not confined to specific industrial sectors, nor just the US. Direct parameter homogeneity tests of the systematic components of disequilibrium growth shows Austria-Finland and Korea-Japan respond identically to changes in capital and labour quality. However, the remainder of the sample respond differently. Moreover, this paper reports that 4 countries (Finland, France, Rep. of Korea and the US) have a superior ability to convert innovation into higher economic growth. In seeking an explanation, Granger causality tests are conducted to determine the extent of technology spillover. The tests suggest no direct connection between the 4 best performing economies, although the UK may be an important conduit. It appears that increasing education levels and sustained capital deepening enhanced the ability to innovate in the best performing countries. These factors may be contributing to a co-invention effect as advanced labour skills are applied to integrate GPT.

To isolate ICT's role in growth the model is expanded to separate ICT from aggregate capital for Finland and the US. Ancillary estimation for Finland indicates no systematic components to disequilibrium growth. However, the stochastic trend is positive and significant. Results for the US show substantial increase in capital productivity with rising human capital. However, after removing systematic components, the US TFP series is practically eliminated. Finally, Granger causality tests suggest one-way technology spillover from the US to Finland.

## 6   APPENDIX: DATA DEFINITIONS

### 6.1   Constructed Variables

The definitions of the variables, Labour Component of Gross Mixed Income (IL) and the Share of Labour in Net Taxes (tL), defined in the OECD Productivity Manual 2001, page 108. IL is calculated as

$$I_L = \frac{LABR}{EMPE} SE \tag{A.1}$$

where LABR is Labour Compensation of Employees, EMPE is the number of Employees Persons and SE is Number of Self Employed (persons). LABR and EMPE are sourced from the OECD STAN database. SE is derived from the STAN database as the difference between Total Employed Persons (EMPN) and EMPE. tL is calculated as

$$t_L = \frac{LABR + I_L}{LABR + OPS} \tag{A.2}$$

where OPS is Net Operating Surplus. Net taxes (taxes less subsidies) is defined as

$$T = VALU\_P - VALU\_B \qquad (A.3)$$

where VALU_P is Value Added at producer's prices and VALU_B is Value Added at factor prices. Both VALU_P and VALU_B are sourced from the STAN database.

# 7  REFERENCES

Ames, E. and Rosenberg, N. (1984), "Technological Change in the Machine Tool Industry, 1840-1910," in Rosenberg, N. (ed.) (1984), *Perspectives on Technology*, Cambridge Press, Cambridge: MA.

Baily, M.N. (2002), "The New Economy: Post Mortem or Second Wind?," *Journal of Economic Perspectives*, Vol. 16, pp. 3-22.

Bresnahan, T. and Greenstein, S. (2002), "The Economic Contribution of Information Technology: Value Indicators in International Perspective," *mimeo*.

Brynjolfsson, E. and Hitt, L.M. (2001), "Computing Productivity: Firm-Level Evidence," *mimeo*.

Coe, D.T. and Helpman, E. (1995), "International R&D Spillovers," *European Economic Review*, Vol. 39, pp. 859-887.

Colecchia, A. and Schreyer, P. (2001), "ICT Investment and Economic Growth in the 1990s: Is the United States a Unique Case? A Comparative Study of Nine OECD Countries," *Directorate for Science, Technology and Industry*, DSTI/DOC(2001)7, OECD, Paris.

Edmond, C. (2001), "Some Panel Cointegration Models of International R&D Spillovers," *Journal of Macroeconomics*, Vol. 23, pp. 241-260.

Frantzen, D. (1998), "R&D, International Technical Diffusion and Total Factor Productivity," *Kyklos*, Vol. 51, pp. 489-508.

Gordon, R.J. (2000), "Does the 'New Economy' Measure up to the Great Inventions of the Past?," *Journal of Economic Perspectives*, Vol. 14, pp. 49-74.

Greene, W.H. (2000), *Econometric Analysis*, Prentice Hall, New Jersey.

Hulten, C.R. and Wykoff, F.C. (1981), "Economic Depreciation and the Taxation of Structures in United States Manufacturing Industries: An Empirical Analysis," in Usher, D. (ed.) (1981), *The Measurement of Capital*, University of Chicago Press, Chicago.

Jalava, J. and Pohjola, M. (2002), "Economic Growth in the New Economy: Evidence from Advanced Economies", *Information Economics and Policy*, Vol. 14, pp. 189-210.

Jorgenson, D.W. and Stiroh, K. (2000), "Raising the Speed Limit: US Economic Growth in the Information Age," *Brookings Papers on Economic Activity*, Vol. 1, pp. 125-135.

Jorgenson, D.W. and Sullivan, M.A. (1981), "Inflation and Corporate Capital Recovery", in Hulten C.R. (ed.), *Depreciation, Inflation, and the Taxation of Income from Capital*, pp. 311-313. Washington : Urban Institute Press.

Madden, G. and Savage, S. (2000), "R&D Spillovers, Information Technology and Telecommunications, and Productivity in Asia and the OECD," *Information Economics and Policy*, Vol. 12, pp. 367-392.

National Center for Education Statistics (2001), Digest of Education Statistics 2001, Office of Educational Research and Improvement, NCES 2002-130, US Department of Education, Washington DC.

Nehru, V. and Dhareshwar, A. (1995), "A New Database on Physical Capital Stock: Sources, Methodology and Results," *Rivista de Analisis Economico*, Vol. 8, pp. 37-59.

Nelson, R. (1964), "Aggregate Production Functions and Medium-Range Growth Projections," *American Economic Review*, Vol. 54, pp. 575-606.

Nordhaus, W.D. (2001), "Productivity Growth and the New Economy," NBER Working Paper, No.W8096, New York.

Oliner, S.D. and Sichel, D.E. (2000), "The Resurgence of Growth in the Late 1990s: Is Information Technology the Story?," *Journal of Economic Perspectives*, Vol. 14, pp. 3-22.

OECD (2001a), National Accounts, Volume II, OECD, Paris.

OECD (2001b), *OECD Productivity Manual: A Guide to the Measurement of Industry-Level and Aggregate Productivity Growth,* OECD, Paris.

OECD (2002), *STAN Database for Industrial Analysis*, OECD, Paris.

Scarpeta, S., Bassanini, A., Pilat, D. and Schreyer, P. (2000), "Economic Growth in the OECD Area: Recent Trends at the Aggregate and Sectoral Level," Economics Department Working Papers, No. 248, OECD, Paris.

Stiroh, K. (2001), "Information Technology and the US Productivity Revival: What Do the Industry Data Say?," Mimeo, Federal Reserve Bank of New York, December.

Solow, R.M. (1957), "Technical Change and the Aggregate Production Function," *Review of Economics and Statistics*, Vol. 39, pp. 214-231.

Statistics Canada (2002), CANSIM Cross-Classified Table 00580601, Statistics Canada, Ottawa.

Statistics Canada (2002), CANSIM Cross-Classified Table 00580602, Statistics Canada, Ottawa.

UNESCO (2001), *Statistical Yearbook 2001*, United Nations, New York.

United Nations (1989), *International Standard Industrial Classification of all Economic Activities*, Revision 3, United Nations publication (St/ESA/STAT/ SER.M/4 /Rev.3), Sales No. E.90XVII.11, United Nations, New York.

Watson, M.W. (1986), "Univariate Detrending Methods With Stochastic Trends", *Journal of Monetary Economics*, Vol. 18, pp. 49-75.

World Bank (2001), *World Development Indicators 2001*, World Bank, Washington DC.

# CHAPTER 6

# Information Technology, Efficiency, and Productivity Growth in the Japanese Manufacturing and Non-Manufacturing Sectors[*]

Takeshi Hiromatsu
*Graduate School and College of Arts and Science, The University of Tokyo, Tokyo*

Gohsei Ohira
*Faculty of Economics, Tokyo International University, Saitama*

Minoru Kobayashi
*Faculty of Economics, Wako University, Tokyo*

Naoki Tsubone
*Information Technology Research & Development Division,
Daiwa Institute of Research Ltd., Tokyo*

Manabu Kurita
*Information Technology Research & Development Division,
Daiwa Institute of Research Ltd., Tokyo*

**Abstract**. The purpose of this paper is to make a quantitative analysis of the impacts of informatization. The Information Equipment Ratio is defined as an index to show the progress of informatization, and its impacts on the amount of Value-added per Employee (Labor Productivity) is analyzed and examined for each sector using growth accounting and DEA (Data Envelopment Analysis). The results show that the contribution of Information Equipment in the 1990s declined compared to that of the second half of the 1980s, and that significant slack is seen in the Information Equipment Ratio and in Employees with a college degree or above in the 1990s. This fact suggests strongly that the non-production sector of Japanese business is unable to make effective use of Information Equipment.

[*] Acknowledgement. The authors would like to thank to Hajime Oniki, participants at International Telecommunication Society, Seoul, 18-21 August 2002, and an anonymous referee for very useful comments. Erik Bohlin, Sandy Levin, Nakil Sung and Chang-Ho Yoon, editors of this book, are gratefully acknowledged.

## 1  INTRODUCTION

Since 1980, many industrial sectors in U.S. have promoted the introduction of IT (Information Technology) with OA (Office Automation) as its core. However in the late 80s, the economist Robert Solow, among others, warned against the introduction of IT without serious assessment, with his Productivity Paradox theory, which claims that the introduction of information system does not lead to the higher productivity. This argument has caused many controversial issues thereafter.

Meanwhile, the U.S. economy since 1991 has enjoyed the extreme prosperity for over 10 years until 2001, as the result of the policy efforts focused on cultivating IT industry such as National Information Infrastructure Plan, and achieved the economic expansion without inflation. Consequently, New Economy theory advocated by Greenspan, Chairman of FRB (Federal Reserve Bank), attracted the public attention in the late 90s, which attributed the long-term economic growth with no inflation coming to the surface, to the productivity growth achieved by the aggressive introduction of IT. Besides, several researches and articles, such as the one by Brynjolfsson (1994), reported in the first half of 90s that Productivity Paradox was solved.

On the other hand, Japan entered into the bubble economy backed by the extremely low interest rate policies brought about by Plaza Accord since 1986. Firms raised a large sum of fund at a very low cost by equity finance and promoted the excessive capital investments. Investment on IT was no exception and IT capital stock in firms expanded rapidly. However, entering in 90s, the attitude of firms toward IT introduction changed radically with the collapse of bubble economy, and IT investment decreased greatly. This can be interpreted as a corporate behavior resulted from the management's doubt as to the ability of IT investment to improve the productivity, as pointed out by the Productivity Paradox theory (Hiromatsu et al. 1998).

The problem here is the fact that the impacts of introducing IT into the industry on business performance have not been identified. It is necessary to analyze particularly the effect of IT investment quickly reinforced in the latter half of 80s, the impact of the explosive diffusion of PC (Personal Computer) with the release of Windows 95 in 1995, and that of the spread of information networks such as the Internet and LAN (Local Area Network). Our research team have kept measuring since 1985 the economic effects of IT introduction on the industry, by using the various macro-economic statistics and other statistic materials for each industry. This paper presents, as a part of our research outcomes on the issue, the economic impacts of IT introduction since the latter half of 80s. A part of analyses presented here is carried out with 2 different data sources, in order to eliminate the data errors and to make possible the more objective examination.

In Japan so far, the researches and analyses on the impact of IT investment on the macro-economic level have been published by, among others, the research section of Development Bank of Japan, but no analysis has been done on the economic impact of IT investment on each sector. Therefore, the quantitative analysis of its economic impacts on each sector and the examination of their factors and causes will be a very useful decision making material for each industry to consider the future IT investment. Each of the following measurement results has been published as papers or presented at the academic conferences (Hiromatsu et al. 2002, 2001 and so on). In this paper, the results by those different measurement methods will be analyzed and examined comprehensively and the informatization in Japanese industry and its impact since the latter half of 80s will be examined with consideration to overall IT trend as its background.

## 2   ANALYSIS OF LABOR PRODUCTIVITY BY FINANCIAL INDICATORS

In this section, the realities of Labor Productivity are examined through the relevant data, before discussing the impact of IT on its improvement. Herein, Labor Productivity is defined as Value-added per Employee, and Value-added is defined as the sum of Operating Profit, Labor Cost / Service Cost, Welfare Cost, and Depreciation Cost.

Figure 1 shows the change in Labor Productivity between 1985 and 1998 for Manufacturing Related to Consumption, Materials, and Machinery, and Non-Manufacturing sectors, calculated from the data in the financial reports of TSE (Tokyo Stock Exchange) -listed (1 and 2 sections) firms and OTC (Over The Counter) firms[1].

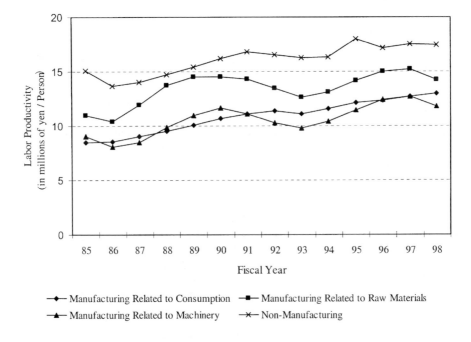

Figure 1. Change of Labor Productivity in Each Sector

---

[1] The firms whose stock can be traded in the Japanese stock markets and the OTC markets. They must satisfy certain criteria for their stock to be traded in these markets respectively. Therefore, those whose stock is traded in them can be considered as fairly large firms.

It shows the improvement of Labor Productivity itself in each sector[2]. Then the financial indicators are used to investigate the causes of such change in Labor Productivity. Labor Productivity is reduced into follows:

$$\text{Labor Productivity} = \frac{\text{Value-added}}{\text{Sales Amount}} \times \frac{\text{Sales Amount}}{\text{Fixed Capital}} \times \frac{\text{Fixed Capital}}{\text{No. of Employees}}$$
$$\equiv \text{Value-added Ratio} \times \text{Turnover Ratio of Tangible Fixed Capital} \times \text{Labor Equipment Ratio} \tag{1}$$

This shows that either further efficiency improvement, more Value-added to the products, or improvement of Labor Equipment Ratio is required to improve Labor Productivity.

Figure 2 shows the result of breaking down Labor Productivity into the changes in Capital Investment Efficiency and in Labor Equipment Ratio, where

Capital Investment Efficiency
$$\equiv \text{Value-added Ratio} \times \text{Turnover Ratio of Tangible Fixed Capital} \tag{2}$$

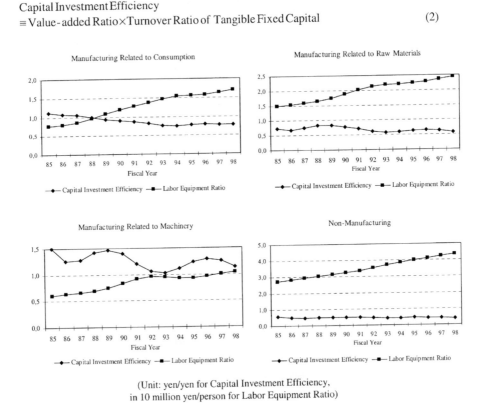

(Unit: yen/yen for Capital Investment Efficiency,
in 10 million yen/person for Labor Equipment Ratio)

Figure 2. Change of Capital Investment Efficiency and Labor Equipment Ratio

---

[2] The industries included in each sector are shown in Appendix A.

It shows that Labor Equipment Ratio is constantly increasing in all categories of sectors. This indicates that the main factor to improve Labor Productivity is the improvement of Labor Equipment Ratio. Then, on which part has this increase of Labor Equipment Ratio given the positive impact so as to bring about the growth of Productivity? Figure 3 shows the ratios of sales cost and administration expenditure to the sales amount during 1985 to 1998.

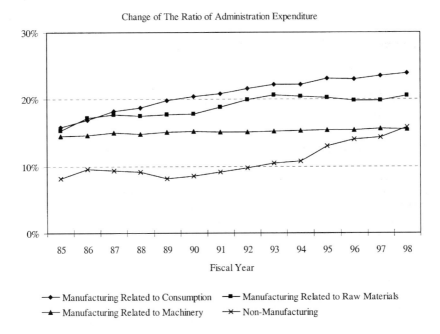

Figure 3. The Ratio of Cost of Sales and Administration Expenditure to the Sales Amount

In all sectors, the ratio of sales cost is declining, but that of administration expenditure is constantly increasing. Since the sales cost is the cost of the sections directly related to production and the administration expenditure is that of the sections not directly related to production, it can be assumed that the change in the ratio of the former indicates the efficiency improvement of production sections, while the change in the ratio of the latter indicates that of indirect sections. Therefore, Figure 3 shows that the improvement of Labor Equipment Ratio seen in Figure 2 has contributed mainly to the efficiency improvement of production sections, and that, as for the indirect sections, it has contributed not to the efficiency improvement but to its corpulence.

From the beginning of 1990s, a large amount of PC and other IT devices began to be deployed and their networks started spreading in the offices. However, there has been no proof of improved productivity in the indirect sections seen from the data. Certainly, the assessment based upon such financial indicators alone is not totally acceptable, because of the subtle influence of the relative relationship between wage and prices involved in the argument of Labor Productivity. But it is true that the indirect sections have expanded considerably as suggested by the large-scale introduction of IT equipment in the offices (IT investment in the indirect sections), the improved Labor Productivity, and the increase of administration expenditure in contrast to the decrease of sales cost. In the following section on, an attempt is made to give the rational explanations to this fact employing the information equipment and labor classified by educational level estimated for this particular purpose.

## 3   ANALYSIS OF ECONOMIC IMPACT OF INFORMATION EQUIPMENT BY GROWTH ACCOUNTING MODEL

In the previous section, the trend suggested by various financial indicators after the second half of 1980s is described. It is highly possible that the stock accumulated as the result of IT investment have given an impact on these indicators. Consequently, in this section, the influence of IT investment on the cash flow that takes place as a result of the corporate business activities is analyzed. The period is the fiscal years from 1985 to 1998, and the sectors analyzed are Manufacturing Related to Consumption, Materials and Machinery, and Non-Manufacturing.

The statistics used as the base for cash flow are Financial Statements Statistics of Corporations and Financial Reports. The former includes medium and small companies, while the latter is limited to the relatively large companies that are listed and/or public. By employing these statistics with somewhat distinct characters, residuals and specificities can be eliminated, and the more detailed study becomes possible by analyzing the difference in the results obtained through the different data sources.

### 3.1   Model

Formula (3) shows Growth Accounting Model employed herein. The growth rate of the amount of Value-added per Employee $q$ (hereafter referred as Labor Productivity) is measured, broken down into its determinant factors, which are the Annual Working Hour per Employee $h$, the amount of Information and Communication- related Capital Stock per Employee $k_i$ (hereafter referred as Information Equipment Ratio), the Capital Stock other than Information and Communication- related Capital Stock per Employee $k_o$ (hereafter referred as Capital Equipment Ratio), and External Factor (technological progress and so on).

$$G(q) = A + \alpha G(h) + \beta G(k_o) + \gamma G(k_i) \tag{3}$$

where

$G(X)$ : Annual Growth Rate of X

$$\alpha = (\partial q / \partial h) / (q / h) \tag{4}$$

$$\beta = (\partial q / \partial k_o) / (q / k_o) \tag{5}$$

$$\gamma = (\partial q / \partial k_i) / (q / k_i) \tag{6}$$

$q$ : Labor Productivity (the amount of Value-Added per Employee)

$h$ : Annual Working Hours per Employee

$k_o$ : Capital Equipment Ratio (the amount of Capital Stock other than Information and Communication- related Capital Stock per Employee)

$k_i$ : Information Equipment Ratio (the amount of Information and Communication- related Capital Stock per Employee)

$A$ : Constant indicating the impact of External Factor


Assuming primary homogeneity, the following equations hold:

$$\alpha + \beta + \gamma = 1 \tag{7}$$

$$\alpha = w h \tag{8}$$

where

$\alpha$ : Labor Share

$w$ : Wage Rate

$$\beta = r_o k_o \tag{9}$$

where

$\beta$ : Capital Share of Capital Stock other than Information and Communication- related Capital Stock

$r_o$ : Profit Rate of Capital Stock other than Information and Communication- related Capital Stock

$$\gamma = r_i k_i \tag{10}$$

where

$\gamma$ : Capital Share of Information and Communication- related Capital Stock

$r_i$ : Profit Rate of Information and Communication- related Capital Stock

However, since the calculation of $r_o$ and $r_i$ is very difficult, $\alpha$ is calculated by the equation (8) and $\gamma$ by (6) from the data series, and using these results and (7), $\beta$ is calculated.

### 3.2   Data

*Information Equipment Ratio*

Information Equipment Ratio is defined as Information and Communication- related Capital Stock (hereafter referred as Information Equipment) per Employee. In this paper, $k_i$ ,

Information Equipment Ratio for each sector, is obtained, based upon the Research on Survey on Information Processing Activities by Industry, using "Research Report on Comprehensive Indicators of Informatization" by Information Processing Society of Japan as reference.

The flow of calculation for $k_i$ in the year t, that is $k_i(t)$, is shown in Figure 4. First, the amount of hardware depreciation and software investment is aggregated for each sector. The amount of Average Hardware Investment per Employee for 6 years up to the year t, $i^h(t)$, is the sum of Depreciation, Rental/Leasing Cost and Other Hardware-related Costs per Employee in the research on "Survey on Information Processing Activities by Industry", all recalculated to fit the actual prices of 1990. Hardware Capital Stock per Employee in the year t, $k_i^h(t)$, of each sector is determined by multiplying this $i^h(t)$ by the number of employees of each sector shown in "Survey on Employment Trends", $L_n^2(t)$, and then by six, and then by dividing it by $L_n^2(t)$.[3]

The amount of Software Investment per Employee in the year t, $i^s(t)$, is the sum of Labor Cost for External Staff, Software Fee, Software Purchase Cost, Software Rental/Leasing Cost, Software Development Fee in the Software-related Cost items and Data Creation/Input Cost, and Other Information Services Cost in the same research report, all recalculated to fit the actual prices of 1990. Then, Software Capital Stock per Employee in the year t, $k_i^s(t)$, of each sector is determined by multiplying $i^s(t)$ by $L_n^2(t)$, totaling them for the past 5 years including the year t, and then dividing it by $L_n^2(t)$.

Lastly, the Information Equipment Ratio of the year t, $k_i(t)$, is defined as the mean value of the sum of this $k_i^h$ and $k_i^s$ in the year t and the year (t-1), because the number of employees in the year t is the average of number of employees at the end of the year t and the year (t-1) in "Financial Statements Statistics of Corporations" used in this paper. Therefore, the same technique is employed in calculating not only $k_i(t)$ but also $k_o(t)$ (Capital Equipment Ratio). However, it should be noted that the results of calculation is not considered as a two-year moving average in this context, but what should be called an "interim average", which indicates an average of relevant variables in the middle of the year analyzed and is an useful representation of one year term.

---

[3] Refer to Appendix B for more details.

Note: This method is used to prepare the data for each sector.

Figure 4. Calculation of the Information Equipment Ratio

*Labor Productivity*

It is necessary first to define Value-added in order to calculate Labor Productivity $q$. Value-added in this paper is the sum of Labor Cost, Operational Profit, and Depreciation. The base materials are Financial Statements Statistics of Corporations and Financial Reports.

The equation (11) shows how to calculate Labor Productivity for each sector from Financial Statements Statistics of Corporations.

$$q^c(t) = Q^c(t) / L_n^c(t) \tag{11}$$

where

$q^c(t)$ : Labor Productivity based upon Financial Statements Statistics of Corporations (Value-added per Employee)

$Q^c(t)$ : Actual amount of Value-added based upon Financial Statements Statistics of Corporations[4] (Sum of wage, executive compensation, welfare cost, operating profit, and depreciation, all recalculated to suit the actual prices of the year)

$L_n^c(t)$ : Sum of executives and employees on regular basis

The calculation based on Financial Reports is shown in (12).

$$q^f(t) = Q^f(t) / L_n^f(t) \tag{12}$$

where

$q^f(t)$ : Labor Productivity based upon Financial Reports (Value-added per Employee)

$Q^f(t)$ : Actual amount of Value-added based upon Financial Reports[5] (Sum of wage, executive compensation, welfare cost, operating profit, and depreciation, all recalculated to suit the actual prices of the year)

$L_n^f(t)$ : Sum of executives and employees on regular basis

*Capital Equipment Ratio*

Capital Equipment Ratio in the year t, $k_o(t)$, is the amount of Capital Stock other than Information Equipment per Employee for each sector, calculated first by subtracting the amount of Information Equipment used for hardware purchase from the amount of Capital Stock for each sector, and then by dividing it the number of employees of the sector. Its calculation based on Financial Statements Statistics of Corporations is shown by (13) below.

$$k_o^c(t) = \left\{ K^c(t) - k_i^d(t) L_n^c(t) \right\} / L_n^c(t) \tag{13}$$

where

$k_o^c(t)$ : Capital Equipment Ratio based upon Financial Statements Statistics of Corporations (Amount of Capital Stock other than Information Equipment per Employee)

---

[4] Actualized by GDP deflator with 1990 as reference.

[5] Actualized by GDP deflator with 1990 as reference.

$K^c(t)$ : Sum of Other Tangible Fixed Asset and Temporary Account in Financial Statements Statistics of Corporations, recalculated to fit to the actual prices with 1990 as its standard, using Net Fixed Asset Deflator (corporations other than financial firms) calculated by SNA (System of National Accounts)

$k_i^d(t)$: Amount of Information Equipment per Employee used for hardware purchase (Depreciation in Survey on Information Processing Activities by Industry, actualized with 1990 standard, multiplied by 6 and divided by Number of Employees in the same)

$L_n^c(t)$ : Already calculated by (11)

The same calculation based on Financial Reports is shown by (14) below.

$$k_o^f(t) = \left\{ K^f(t) - k_i^d(t)L_n^f(t) \right\} / L_n^f(t) \tag{14}$$

where

$k_o^f(t)$ : Capital Equipment Ratio based upon Financial Reports (Amount of Capital Stock other than Information Equipment per Employee)

$K^f(t)$ : Sum of Other Tangible Fixed Asset and Temporary Account in Financial Reports, recalculated to fit to the actual prices with 1990 as its standard, using Net Fixed Asset Deflator (corporations other than financial firms) calculated by SNA

$k_i^d(t)$ : Already calculated by (13)

$L_n^f(t)$ : Already calculated by (12)

*Labor Input*

Labor Input is the Aggregate Net Working Hours per Employee in the year t, $h(t)$, for each sector. First the Annual Aggregate Working Hours in the year t for each sector is calculated.

$$H^c(t) = C(t) \times l_m \times 12 \times w^c(t) \tag{15}$$

$$H^f(t) = C(t) \times l_m \times 12 \times w^f(t) \tag{16}$$

where:

$H^c(t)$ : Annual Aggregate Working Hours based on Financial Statements Statistics of Corporations for each industry[6]

$H^f(t)$ : Annual Aggregate Working Hours based on Financial Reports for each industry

$C(t)$ : Monthly Indicator of Aggregate Net Working Hours for each sector in the Monthly Labor Statistics

$l_m(t)$ : Monthly Aggregate Net Working Hours per Employee for each sector in 1990

---

[6] Refer to Appendix A.

$w^c(t)$ : Number of Executives and Employees on regular basis for each industry in Financial Statements Statistics of Corporations

$w^f(t)$ : Average Number of Employees for each industry in the period analyzed in Financial Reports

Then, expressing $H^c(t)$ and $H^f(t)$ aggregated at each sector level as $\tilde{H}^c(t)$ and $\tilde{H}^f(t)$ and by dividing them by $L_n^c(t)$ and $L_n^f(t)$ respectively, $h^c(t)$ and $h^f(t)$ are calculated.

$$h^c(t) = \tilde{H}^c(t) / L_n^c(t) \tag{17}$$

$$h^f(t) = \tilde{H}^f(t) / L_n^f(t) \tag{18}$$

where

$h^c(t)$ : Annual Aggregate Net Working Hours per Employee in each sector in Financial Statements Statistics of Corporations

$h^f(t)$ : Annual Aggregate Net Working Hours per Employee in each sector in Financial Reports

$\tilde{H}^c(t)$ : $H^c(t)$ (Already calculated by (15)) of each industry aggregated by each sector

$\tilde{H}^f(t)$ : $H^f(t)$ (Already calculated by (16)) of each industry aggregated by each sector

$L_n^c(t)$ : Already calculated by (11)

$L_n^f(t)$ : Already calculated by (12)

The following Table 1 shows the data from those two data sources to be used for the Growth Accounting analysis.

Table 1. The Data for The Growth Accounting Analysis

| Data Source | Labor Productivity | Labor Input | Capital Equipment Ratio | Information Equipment Ratio |
|---|---|---|---|---|
| Financial Statements Statistics of Corporations | $q^c(t)$ $\left( = Q^c(t)/L_x^c(t) \right)$ | $h^c(t)$ $\left( = H^c(t)/L_x^c(t) \right)$ | $k_a^c(t)$ $\left( = (K^c(t) - k_i^d(t)L_x^c(t))/L_x^c(t) \right)$ | $k_i(t)$ (See Figure 4) |
| Financial Reports | $q^f(t)$ $\left( = Q^f(t)/L_x^f(t) \right)$ | $h^f(t)$ $\left( = H^f(t)/L_x^f(t) \right)$ | $k_a^f(t)$ $\left( = (K^f(t) - k_i^d(t)L_x^f(t))/L_x^f(t) \right)$ | $k_i(t)$ (See Figure 4) |

As can be seen, the only common data is that of Information Equipment Ratio. Therefore, though it must be assumed that the Information Equipment Ratio does not vary by the sizes of firms, other Inputs and Output are considered strongly unique, so the comparison of the data from two different sources is highly meaningful.

## 3.3 Results

Table 2 and 3 show the results of analysis. Table 2 is based on Financial Statements Statistics of Corporations and Table 3 is based on Financial Reports.

Table 2. Contribution of Each Input Factor to Value-added Productivity

(Financial Statements of Corporations by Industry)

| Industrial Sector | Period | $G(q)$ (%) | $A$ (%) | $\alpha$ | $G(h)$ (%) | $\alpha G(h)$ (%) | $\beta$ | $G(k_a)$ (%) | $\beta G(k_a)$ (%) | $\gamma$ | $G(k_i)$ (%) | $\gamma G(k_i)$ (%) |
|---|---|---|---|---|---|---|---|---|---|---|---|---|
| Manufacturing | 85-90 | 0.2 | -2.2 | 0.64 | -0.9 | -0.6 | 0.33 | 7.5 | 2.5 | 0.03 | 16.3 | 0.4 |
| Related | 90-95 | 0.6 | -0.4 | 0.66 | -1.2 | -0.8 | 0.25 | 2.9 | 0.7 | 0.09 | 12.0 | 1.1 |
| to Consumption | 95-98 | 0.8 | -3.6 | 0.67 | 2.0 | 1.3 | 0.20 | 4.5 | 0.9 | 0.13 | 16.9 | 2.2 |
| Manufacturing | 85-90 | 4.6 | -0.5 | 0.54 | -0.2 | -0.1 | 0.07 | 3.5 | 0.3 | 0.39 | 12.8 | 5.0 |
| Related | 90-95 | 1.0 | -0.6 | 0.56 | -1.1 | -0.6 | 0.35 | 3.5 | 1.2 | 0.09 | 11.4 | 1.0 |
| to Materials | 95-98 | 1.6 | -2.0 | 0.57 | 2.4 | 1.4 | 0.32 | 1.6 | 0.5 | 0.11 | 15.7 | 1.7 |
| Manufacturing | 85-90 | 8.8 | 0.2 | 0.60 | -0.1 | -0.1 | -0.25 | 5.4 | -1.4 | 0.66 | 15.4 | 10.1 |
| Related | 90-95 | 3.7 | -1.2 | 0.62 | -1.5 | -0.9 | -0.30 | 1.6 | -0.5 | 0.68 | 9.3 | 6.3 |
| to Machinery | 95-98 | 6.4 | -1.5 | 0.61 | 3.0 | 1.9 | -0.26 | 5.1 | -1.3 | 0.65 | 11.3 | 7.3 |
| Non- | 85-90 | 4.5 | 2.7 | 0.64 | -0.6 | -0.4 | 0.29 | 4.4 | 1.3 | 0.07 | 12.9 | 0.9 |
| Manufacturing | 90-95 | -0.7 | 0.1 | 0.65 | -1.3 | -0.8 | 0.48 | 3.2 | 1.5 | -0.13 | 12.1 | -1.5 |
| | 95-98 | -0.6 | -1.7 | 0.68 | 1.7 | 1.1 | 0.37 | 1.5 | 0.5 | -0.05 | 12.0 | -0.6 |
| Industries | 85-90 | 4.8 | 0.5 | 0.62 | -0.5 | -0.3 | 0.07 | 4.5 | 0.3 | 0.32 | 13.6 | 4.3 |
| Covered | 90-95 | 0.3 | -0.1 | 0.63 | -1.3 | -0.8 | 0.35 | 2.9 | 1.0 | 0.02 | 11.3 | 0.2 |
| | 95-98 | 1.3 | -2.2 | 0.65 | 2.0 | 1.3 | 0.22 | 2.2 | 0.5 | 0.13 | 12.5 | 1.7 |

Table 3. Contribution of Each Input Factor to Value-added Productivity (Financial Report)

| Industrial Sector | Period | $G(q)$ (%) | $A$ (%) | $\alpha$ | $G(h)$ (%) | $\alpha G(h)$ (%) | $\beta$ | $G(k_a)$ (%) | $\beta G(k_a)$ (%) | $\gamma$ | $G(k_i)$ (%) | $\gamma G(k_i)$ (%) |
|---|---|---|---|---|---|---|---|---|---|---|---|---|
| Manufacturing | 85-90 | 2.5 | -1.2 | 0.62 | -0.9 | -0.5 | 0.23 | 7.8 | 1.8 | 0.15 | 16.3 | 2.4 |
| Related | 90-95 | 2.9 | -1.3 | 0.65 | -1.2 | -0.8 | -0.10 | 5.2 | -0.5 | 0.46 | 12.0 | 5.5 |
| to Consumption | 95-98 | 0.4 | -1.8 | 0.65 | 2.0 | 1.3 | 0.35 | 2.6 | 0.9 | 0.01 | 16.9 | 0.1 |
| Manufacturing | 85-90 | 6.1 | -0.2 | 0.53 | -0.3 | -0.2 | -0.06 | 3.2 | -0.2 | 0.52 | 12.8 | 6.7 |
| Related | 90-95 | 1.6 | -0.6 | 0.57 | -1.0 | -0.6 | 0.27 | 3.3 | 0.9 | 0.16 | 11.4 | 1.9 |
| to Materials | 95-98 | 2.6 | -2.0 | 0.56 | 2.1 | 1.2 | 0.27 | 2.7 | 0.7 | 0.17 | 15.7 | 2.7 |
| Manufacturing | 85-90 | 9.5 | -0.3 | 0.64 | -0.1 | -0.1 | -0.41 | 4.9 | -2.0 | 0.77 | 15.4 | 11.8 |
| Related | 90-95 | 4.1 | -1.5 | 0.68 | -1.6 | -1.1 | -0.47 | 1.4 | -0.7 | 0.79 | 9.3 | 7.3 |
| to Machinery | 95-98 | 4.3 | -2.8 | 0.67 | 3.3 | 2.2 | -0.14 | 3.1 | -0.4 | 0.48 | 11.3 | 5.4 |
| Non- | 85-90 | 1.4 | -1.9 | 0.49 | -0.4 | -0.2 | 0.28 | 2.1 | 0.6 | 0.23 | 12.9 | 2.9 |
| Manufacturing | 90-95 | 1.3 | -0.6 | 0.53 | -1.2 | -0.6 | 0.39 | 4.1 | 1.6 | 0.08 | 12.1 | 1.0 |
|  | 95-98 | -0.2 | -2.5 | 0.53 | 2.4 | 1.3 | 0.51 | 3.0 | 1.5 | -0.04 | 12.0 | -0.5 |
| Industries | 85-90 | 5.0 | -1.2 | 0.55 | -0.3 | -0.2 | -0.03 | 3.7 | -0.1 | 0.48 | 13.6 | 6.5 |
| Covered | 90-95 | 2.5 | -0.3 | 0.59 | -1.3 | -0.8 | 0.15 | 4.1 | 0.6 | 0.26 | 11.3 | 3.0 |
|  | 95-98 | 2.0 | -2.6 | 0.59 | 2.7 | 1.6 | 0.24 | 3.8 | 0.9 | 0.17 | 12.5 | 2.1 |

First, take notice of the contribution of Information Equipment Ratio ( $\gamma G(k_i)$ ) and compare those values in each sector and each period of analysis in Table 2 and 3. The following formula holds for all the periods and sectors, except for Manufacturing Related to Consumption and Manufacturing Related to Machinery in the period 1995-98:

( $\gamma G(k_i)$ in Table 2) < ( $\gamma G(k_i)$ in Table 3)

This seems to reflect the different characters of the databases. Financial Statements Statistics of Corporations include many small and medium size firms, while Financial Reports include only listed and public companies with very few small and medium companies. Therefore, it can be interpreted as the more effective use of Information Equipment by larger firms than small and medium companies.

Then, the observation of $\gamma G(k_i)$ in time series shows the following formula holds for all the sectors in Table 2 and 3, except for Manufacturing Related to Consumption:

(Values of 1985-90) > (Values of 1990-95)

This means that Information Equipment contributed to the improvement of Labor Productivity less in the first half of 1990 than in the second half of 1980. Information Equipment in 1990-95 was the results of the investment around the Bubble Economy, and even in 1991-92, when the collapse of the Bubble became clear to all, firms pursued the active IT investment[7]. However, from the macro-economic viewpoint, their business performance declined after that, in spite of such huge amount of IT investment. Therefore, the declining contribution of Information Equipment in the first half of 90s can be considered as the result of IT investment during and after the Bubble Economy when Informatization was held sacred and its investment was carried out without sufficient consideration for its effect. Thus, the existence of Productivity Paradox in Japan is inferred from this result.

On the other hand, the values of $\gamma G(k_i)$ in 1990-95 and 1995-98 do not show any significant improvement both in Table 2 and 3. Moreover, in Table 3 that is mainly comprised of large firms, $\gamma G(k_i)$ shows the decline except for the Manufacturing Related to Materials. The contribution of Information Equipment has not improved greatly in 1990s, though its effect is somewhat mixed depending on the type of sector and the scale of corporation. This becomes clear with the following formula of $\gamma G(k_i)$ in 1985-90 and 1995-98, which holds for all except for Manufacturing Related to Consumption in Table 2:

(Values of 1985-90) > (Values of 1995-98)

The decline of $\gamma$ contributes greatly to this trend. The following formula holds for $\gamma$ in Table 2 and 3, except for Manufacturing Related to Consumption in Table 2:

(Values of 1985-90) > (Values of 1995-98)

What this formula means in terms of Growth Accounting Model expressed by (3) is as follows:

$$\gamma = (\partial q / \partial k_i) / (q / k_i)$$

so $\partial k_i$ and $\partial q$ have a great impact on $\gamma$. The decline of $\gamma$ is caused by the fact that, in spite of the large value for $\partial k_i$, $\partial q$ is not increasing. In order to give an explanation for the movement of $\partial k_i$, the changes of Information Equipment Ratio of Employees with college degree or above, $\partial k_{iU}$, and of those without college degree, $\partial k_{iO}$, are expressed as follows:

$$\partial k_{iU} = \partial (K_{iU} / L_U) \tag{19}$$

$$\partial k_{iO} = \partial (K_{iO} / L_O) \tag{20}$$

where

$\partial k_{iU}$ : Change of Information Equipment Ratio of Employees with college degree or above

$\partial k_{iO}$ : Change of Information Equipment Ratio of Employees without college degree

$K_{iU}$ : Amount of Information Equipment of Employees with college degree or above

$K_{iO}$ : Amount of Information Equipment of Employees without college degree

$L_U$ : Number of Employees with college degree or above

$L_O$ : Number of Employees without college degree

---

[7] It was in 1993 when the sales of information service industry turned to decline for the first time in Japan.

According to Basic Survey on Wage Structure done by the Ministry of Labor and Welfare, the labor force of the production section is mainly composed of $L_o$. Therefore, approximately all the $L_U$ Employees can be considered to belong to the non-production section. During the analysis period (1985-1998), the ratio of $L_o$ to $L_U$ is 3-5 times in the sector as a whole. Therefore, in order that the following formula

$$\partial k_{iU} = \partial k_{iO} \tag{21}$$

holds, $K_{iO}$ is needed as 3-5 times as $K_{iU}$. In other words, IT investment is required more in the production section.

However, the actual history of IT utilization in Japan shows the gradual shift from its initial use for efficiency improvement in the production section, with Kanban method of Toyota and the use of factory robot as its typical examples, to the non-production section. Moreover, it has become more important in the non-production section to share the intangible assets such as business know-how and to create the new Value-added. This suggests the high possibility of the weight of IT investment being placed not in the production section but in the non-production section. In other words,

$$\partial k_{iU} > \partial k_{iO} \tag{22}$$

is expected. Therefore, the increase of contribution of $\partial k_{iU}$ in $\partial k_i$ and the decrease of that of $\partial k_{iO}$ are expected.

Thus, it has become highly possible that the decline of contribution of Information Equipment Ratio $\gamma G(k_i)$ is greatly attributed to that of $\gamma$, and that such decline is caused by the inability of the non-production section to make effective use of Information Equipment so that it may contribute to the increase of Value-added. In the following section, further analyses are carried out by the model with split labor input.

## 4    EFFICIENCY ANALYSIS BY DEA

One of the most important issues we have been strongly aware of throughout the survey is the possible decline of productivity of the white-color employees. In this paper, those with college degree and above are considered as the white-color employees. As pointed out in Section 3, a notable contribution of Information Equipment to the rise of Labor Productivity was seen in the latter half of 1980s, but 1990s showed its declining tendency, with a high possibility of the white-color employees being its cause.

In order to prove this hypothesis using the Growth Accounting, it is necessary to estimate the Information Equipment Ratio of the white-color and the blue-color employees respectively. However, this estimation is greatly difficult with the statistics available at present in Japan. Therefore, there is no other way than employing some other methods to make indirect comparison of those two kinds of employees. The method employed here is an attempt to prove the results of the analysis with Growth Accounting indirectly, by finding the years in which the annual output is relatively smaller than the relevant input factors, assuming the existence of input factors which do not contribute to the Output of the pertinent year, determining them and observing the change over the years.

The reason for the use of DEA as analysis method is the Slack calculated with DEA. Slack is an input factor with strong implication of "surplus". So it is used as a substitute to indicate the input factor not contributing to the output.

## 4.1 D-efficiency and Slack

In the analysis by DEA, the efficiency is measured as the output amount against the input amount. The measured value (D-efficiency) $\theta$ is

$$0 \leq \theta \leq 1$$

and judged to be most efficient when its value is 1. For instance, in Figure5 which shows the amount of inputs (Input 1 and Input 2) against 1 unit of output in a particular sector in the years A, B, and C , $\theta$ equals 1 in the years B and C, and on all the points on the line segment BC, $\theta$ equals 1. Meanwhile, $\theta$ in the year A is obtained as

$$\theta = OP / OA (< 1)$$

In other words, the efficiency in the year A is considered lower than in the years B and C, because of the larger input to obtain the same output. In order for the year A to be efficient (that is, $\theta = 1$ ), it is necessary to multiply Input 1 and Input 2 by $\theta$, and use them as the inputs at the point P. Similarly, if the input required for 1 unit of output is as described as the year A',

$$\theta = OP' / OA' (< 1)$$

holds. If Input 1 and Input 2 are multiplied by $\theta$, it moves to P' and the value of $\theta$ becomes 1. But, as seen in Figure 5, Input 2 is smaller in the year B than in P'.

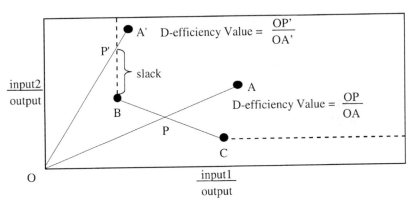

Figure 5. Image of D-efficiency and Slack

Therefore, in order for the year A' to be really efficient, it is necessary to reduce Input 2 by the amount of P'B. This reduced amount P'B is called Slack. Slack is not the kind of factor that can be reduced in the same ratio as other factors, and therefore considered to have a stronger implication as surplus compared to the amount of reduction indicated by D-efficiency $\theta$.

## 4.2   Data

In the analysis by DEA, following data are used:

$Q^c(t)$ : Already calculated by (11)

$L_v$ : Number of graduates of colleges and universities, both in the new and old systems, in $L_n^c(t)$

$L_o$ : Number of those finished primary schools, middle schools in the new systems, high schools in the old and new systems, vocational high school, and junior colleges, in $L_n^c(t)$

$K_o$ : Capital Stock Amount other than Information Equipment (Already calculated by (13) as $K^c(t) - k_i^d(t)L_n^c(t)$ )

$K_i$ : Amount of Information Equipment (Calculated by $k_i(t)L_n^c(t)$ )

## 4.3   Results

The result of analysis of D-efficiency is shown in Table 4.

Table 4. D-Efficiency Values $\theta$ of Each Sector

| Fiscal Year | Manufacturing Related to Consumption | Manufacturing Related to Materials | Manufacturing Related to Machinery | Non-Manufacturing |
|---|---|---|---|---|
| 1985 | 1 | 1 | 1 | 1 |
| 1986 | 0.956 | 0.946 | 0.911 | 0.967 |
| 1987 | 0.939 | 0.955 | 0.905 | 0.980 |
| 1988 | 0.962 | 0.995 | 1 | 1 |
| 1989 | 0.974 | 1 | 1 | 0.955 |
| 1990 | 0.987 | 1 | 1 | 1 |
| 1991 | 0.966 | 1 | 0.949 | 0.986 |
| 1992 | 0.974 | 0.948 | 0.851 | 0.980 |
| 1993 | 0.922 | 0.890 | 0.824 | 0.943 |
| 1994 | 0.986 | 0.941 | 0.868 | 0.943 |
| 1995 | 0.991 | 0.953 | 0.957 | 0.975 |
| 1996 | 1 | 1 | 0.979 | 1 |
| 1997 | 0.987 | 1 | 1 | 0.997 |
| 1998 | 1 | 0.951 | 0.979 | 0.986 |

In all the sectors, $\theta$ started to decline in 1986 when the depression caused by strong yen began in response to the Plaza Accord in 1985. However, during the Bubble period of 1988-

90, it increased in all the sectors, and became 1 in 1990 in all the sectors except for Manufacturing Related to Consumption, showing that all the input factors were made effective use of and lead to the creation/increase of Value-added. Then, due to the impact of collapse of the Bubble, the number of industries considered to be efficient rapidly decreased. However, during the Heisei Boom after 1994, $\theta$ rose again. Though its values vary depending on the sectors, its movement is considered to have agreed with the actual feeling on economy at the moment.

Table 5. Ratio of Sector-Average Slack to Input

| Industrial Sector | Period | $K_i$ (%) | $L_U$ (%) | $L_O$ (%) |
|---|---|---|---|---|
| Manufacturing Related to Consumption | 85-90 | 0.1 | 1.9 | 0 |
| | 90-95 | 2.0 | 4.0 | 0 |
| | 95-98 | 0.1 | 2.3 | 0 |
| Manufacturing Related to Materials | 85-90 | 0 | 0.8 | 0.7 |
| | 90-95 | 0 | 1.5 | 0 |
| | 95-98 | 4.7 | 1.6 | 0 |
| Manufacturing Related to Machinery | 85-90 | 0 | 0.5 | 0 |
| | 90-95 | 0 | 1.4 | 0.3 |
| | 95-98 | 2.8 | 1.5 | 0.5 |
| Non-Manufacturing | 85-90 | 0 | 1.5 | 0 |
| | 90-95 | 13.7 | 0.2 | 0 |
| | 95-98 | 15.0 | 2.0 | 0 |

Table 5 shows the change of ratio of Slack to $K_i$, $L_U$, and $L_O$. At a glance, it is clear that in many sectors Slack is seen in $L_U$, employees with college degree or above, indicating that there are many sectors with Slack in Labor Input in their non-production sections, since the number of such employees in the production section is very small.

In Manufacturing Related to Consumption, no Slack is seen throughout the period in $L_O$, but it does exist in $L_U$. Slack is also seen in $K_i$ throughout the period. The decreasing trend of Slack in both seen after 1990 is a sign of improved contribution of the non-production section and Information Equipment to Value-added.

In Manufacturing Related to Materials, Slack in Information Equipment first appeared in 1995-98. The increasing trend of Slack in $L_U$ and the zero Slack in $L_O$ after 1990, are interpreted as the high possibility of inability on the part of the non-production section, to which most of $L_U$ belongs, to make effective use of Information Equipment. These trends exist in Manufacturing Related to Machinery as well, and Slack in Information Equipment is seen first in 1995-98. But, since some slack is also seen in $L_O$, unlike other sectors, more detailed analysis is required to determine whether it exists in the production section or in the non-production section.

Meanwhile, Slack in Non-Manufacturing sector is distinctive. Slack in $K_i$ appeared greatly in 1990-95, proving the excessive investment during the Bubble period. This Slack increased further in 1995-98 period. On the other hand, in spite of the zero Slack in $L_O$ throughout the period, Slack is seen in $L_U$ throughout the period. Moreover, though it diminished in 1990-95, it increased greatly again in 1995-98. Non-Manufacturing sector, where the production of goods is minimal, has a relatively small portion of work that can be replaced or substituted by computers, compared to the manufacturing sectors. In other words, it is the sector where the creation of Value-added by the effective use of computers is strongly required. However, as Table 5 shows, the possibility is very small that this purpose has been accomplished, and this sector has much room for improvement in this sense.

In the latter half of 1990s, the increase of Labor Input of $L_U$ and the reduction of that of $L_O$ is a common trend in all the sectors. This means the relative increase of the kind of Labor Input, for which the important issue in the use of Information Equipment is not to produce the goods, but to effectively create Value-added. However, in reality, Slack in $K_i$ and Labor Input of $L_U$ exist in all the sectors in the latter half of 1990s, and in some sectors, even its increase from the past is seen.

It should be noted that these results are derived from the time-series data, applied to DEA, for the research period of 14 years, during which no frontier shift is assumed[8]. In order to mitigate the impact of such assumption, the whole research period was divided into 3 periods, namely 1985-90, 1990-95, and 1995-98, and the window analysis was carried out to them. The results are shown in Table 6, which shows the similar tendency as those in Table 5.

Table 6. Ratio of Sector-Average Slack to Input (Window Analysis)

| Industrial Sector | Period | $K_i$ (%) | $L_U$ (%) | $L_O$ (%) |
|---|---|---|---|---|
| Manufacturing Related to Consumption | 85-90 | 2.5 | 0.3 | 0 |
| | 90-95 | 2.2 | 0 | 0 |
| | 95-98 | 3.3 | 0.2 | 0 |
| Manufacturing Related to Materials | 85-90 | 0 | 0.8 | 0.7 |
| | 90-95 | 2.8 | 0.7 | 0 |
| | 95-98 | 4.7 | 1.0 | 0 |
| Manufacturing Related to Machinery | 85-90 | 0 | 0.5 | 0 |
| | 90-95 | 1.2 | 0.9 | 0.7 |
| | 95-98 | 2.8 | 0.2 | 0.5 |
| Non-Manufacturing | 85-90 | 0 | 1.5 | 0 |
| | 90-95 | 20.8 | 2.1 | 0.3 |
| | 95-98 | 10.8 | 2.0 | 0 |

In both Tables, large Slack is seen for $L_U$ and $K_i$, though their ratios slightly differ, and Slack is hardly seen for $L_O$. This proves the outcomes of this section, even with the impact of frontier shift taken into consideration.

These results suggest strongly that Information Equipment is not utilized effectively in the non-production section in Japan, which confirms the results of Growth Accounting analysis. Therefore, one of the crucial factors of decline of Labor Productivity in Japan is the inability on the part of white-color employees to generate the Value-added by making a good use of Information Equipment.

---

[8] Malmquist Productivity Index can be employed to examine the change of Frontier during the research period (M.J. Farrell 1957). Refer to Appendix C for the results. Note that it is difficult to identify which input factor caused the change of productivity by this method.

## 5   CONCLUSIONS

In this paper, the analysis was carried out with the focus on Labor Productivity of the production and non-production sections, with Labor Input classified by the educational levels. As noted in Section 2, the ratio of sales administrative cost has been increasing in spite of the decline of that of the sales cost in all the sectors. If they are considered as the indicators of Productivity for the non-production and the production sections respectively, its decline in the non-production section and its increase in the production section are expected. Though Information Equipment assumes an important role in the daily business operation in both sectors, it accounts for an especially large portion of the tools for creating Value-added in the non-production section. Therefore, the inability of the non-production section to make an effective use of Information Equipment is supposed, which are supported by the results of analysis in Sections 3 and 4.

One of the most typical examples of the "creation of Value-added" in the non-production section is grasping the customers' needs. The information obtained through the use of Information Equipment is made the best use of, in order to grasp the customers' needs, and it becomes the task of the production section to produce efficiently the goods and/or service to satisfy such needs, based on the information obtained.

If such relationship between the two sections is taken into consideration, the limit in the creation of Value-added by only one of these two sections becomes clear. A significant growth in the creation of Value-added can be expected only when the two sections work harmoniously like the two wheels of a cart. The recent trend of introduction of SCM (Supply Chain Management) is truly descriptive of such case.

What is important to be considered here is the fact that the actual creators of Value-added are the men and organizations that make the effective use of information and information systems (Brynjolfson and Hitt 1997; Bresnahan et al. 2000). The inability of the non-production section to make a good use of Information Equipment sheds the spotlight on the problems of the manpower and organization of the non-production section. It is extremely important whether it has the people who can see the information from the unique viewpoints which no one else has, whether it has someone who can properly assess such viewpoints, and whether it has the organization flexible enough to change its policies in accordance with such viewpoints.

## 6    APPENDIX A

The industries included in each sector in this paper, are as follows:

Table A.1 Industries Included in Each Sector

| Industrial Sectors | Industries |
|---|---|
| Manufacturing Related to Consumption | Food, beverages, tobacco, feed |
| | Textile mill products |
| | Apparel and other finished, products made from fabrics and similar materials |
| Manufacturing Related to Materials | Pulp, paper, and paper products |
| | Chemical and allied products |
| | Ceramic, stone and clay products |
| | Iron and steel |
| | Non-ferrous metal and products |
| | Fabricated metal products |
| Manufacturing Related to Machinery | General machinery |
| | Electrical machinery, equipment and supplies |
| | Transportation equipment |
| | Precision instruments and Machinery |
| Non-Manufacturing | Construction |
| | Wholesale and retail trade, eating and drinking places |
| | Transport and communications |
| | Electricity, gas, heat supply and water |

## 7 APPENDIX B

The method described in Figure 4 was applied to calculate $k_i^h(t)$, due to the reason accounted below.

Generally, the perpetual inventory method is used to measure Capital Stock, but it requires the following conditions to be satisfied:

1) Its depreciation rate is given and constant.

2) Highly reliable capital expenditure data sequence for a long period is available. However, though the database used for this paper, "Survey in Information Processing Activities by Industry", does have capital expenditure data sequence for Information Related Assets such as Hardware Depreciation, their depreciation rates are unknown and the analysis period of 1985-1998 is not long enough to apply the perpetual inventory method. Therefore, several assumptions were adopted in order to compensate the lack of conditions required to apply the perpetual inventory method. The technique employed here is equivalent to setting the following term,

*if $n < 6$ then $d = 0$ else $d = 1$*

in estimating Capital Stock with the perpetual inventory method, which is,

$$K(t) = \sum_{j=0}^{n} (1-d)^{t-j} I(t-j)$$

where

$K(t)$ : Gross capital stock in the year t

$I(t-j)$ : Investment in the year (t-j)

$n$ : The longest lifetime of assets

$(1-d)^{t-j}$ : Survival function

$d$ : Depreciation rate

This is the technique in which the principles of perpetual inventory method are applied in their simplest forms. In other words, survival function used is the "sudden death" method. This technique was adopted because of the method of creating the data used in this paper as Capital Expenditure data sequence. The amounts of depreciation in "Survey on Information Processing Activities by Industry" gathered by the questionnaire survey to the firms, are supposed to be the accounting values, because many Japanese firms adopt the 6-year fixed-installment depreciation on the information equipment investment for the accounting purpose. This means that the average investment amount for the past 6 years can be calculated by multiplying the depreciation amount of relevant year by six, and that the Capital Stock data consistent with this data creation method can be prepared by using the simplest perpetual inventory method in which "sudden death" method is used for the survival function. For this reason, we employed the estimation method of Hardware Capital Stock described in this paper. The same assumption as for depreciation is adopted for Rental, Lease, and Other Hardware Expenditures.

## 8　APPENDIX C

The results of Malmquist Productivity Index measurements are shown in the Figure C.1.

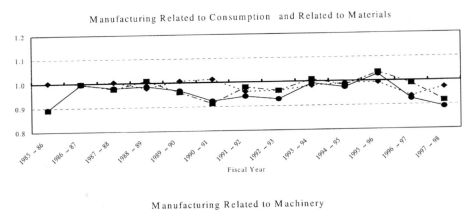

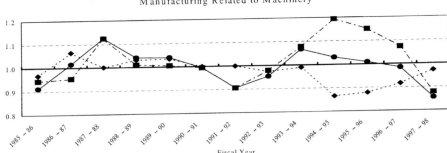

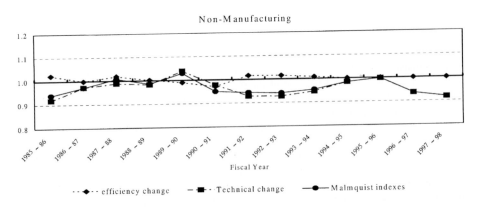

Figure C.1. The Change of Malmquist Index Productivity by Each Sector

In its calculation, it is necessary to bring together the industries with similar business conditions and type of operation, since Malmquist Productivity Index assumes that the industries included in one sector have the same business conditions. Therefore, three sectors are set up under this assumption, which are Manufacturing Related to Machinery including four industries with similar conditions ("General machinery", "Electric machinery, equipment and supplies", "Transport equipment", and "Precision instruments and machinery"), Manufacturing Related to Consumption and to Materials including other manufacturing industries than Machinery, and Non-manufacturing. The same data described in Section 4.2 are employed here.

The chart for Manufacturing Related to Consumption and to Materials shows the consistent, though moderate, decline of productivity for the most part of the period analyzed. For the more detailed examination, Malmquist Index is divided into Efficiency Change and Technical Change. The latter fell below 1 (one) except in the years 1986-87, 1993-94, and 1995-96, but the former was not able to cover the decline of the latter, resulting in the sluggishness of productivity.

The productivity of Manufacturing Related to Machinery showed the significant improvement in the latter half of 1980s, but declined again from the beginning of 1990s due to the business downturn and the fall in product prices too rapid to be covered by the personnel cut and/or the reduction of capital investment. However, the productivity improved together with the business performance in the prosperous period started from 1994 and the firms increased their personnel and the capital investment again. This resulted in the considerable re-decline of productivity in the recession since 1997 when the demands reduced greatly.

The productivity of Non-manufacturing has been deteriorating consistently since 1990 after the slight improvement in the latter half of 1980. The cause is the sluggishness of Technical Change. It is perceived that the unsatisfactory expansion of demands, together with the high cost nature inherent to this sector in Japan and the burden of over investment during the Bubble period, hinders the rise of productivity.

Generally speaking, the productivity in every sector has been hovering low since the latter half of '80s, except a few, very brief periods. It is mainly because no major improvement has been made in Technical Change. However, Information Equipment Ratio has shown a considerable growth in all sectors. This means, as described in Section 3.3, it is very likely that Information Equipment has not been effectively utilized.


## 9   REFERENCES

Bresnahan, T. F., Brynjolfsson, E., Lorin M. H. (2000), "Information Technology, Workplace Organization, and the Demand for Skilled Labor: Firm-level Evidences", *Quarterly Journal of Economics*.

Brynjolfsson, E., Hitt, L. (1997), "Computing Productivity: Are Computers Pulling Their Weight?", http://ccs.mit.edu/erik/cpg/.

Brynjolfsson, E. (1994), "Information Assets, Technology and Organization", *Management Science*, Vol.40, No.12.

Farrell, M. J. (1957), "The Measurement of Productive Efficiency", *Journal of Royal Statistical Society*, 120, pp253-281.

Hiromatsu, T., Kurita, M., Kobayashi, M., Ohira, G., Tsubone, N. (1998), "Information Technology and Value-added Productivity", *The Japan Society of Information and Communication Society Annual Report 1997*, pp. 145-156.

Hiromatsu, T., Kobayashi, M., Tsubone, N., Kurita, M., Ohira, G. (2001), "Effects of IT (Information Technology) on Industries / Firms and its Measurement", *The Japan Association for Social Informatics*, Vol.13, No.2, pp. 47-62.

Hiromatsu, T., Ohira, G., Kobayashi, M., Tsubone, N., Kurita, M. (2002), "Efficiency Analysis on Introduction of IT to Japanese Industries", paper presented at the ITS 14th Biennial Conference IR7, August 18-21 2002, Seoul, pp. 39-60.

CHAPTER 7

# The Impact of Korean Telecommunications Sector on Regional Output and Input Trade: Country-Level Study in the Asia-Pacific Region

Heon-Goo Kim
*Korea National Assembly, Seoul*

Jeonghun Oh
*Graduate School of International Studies, Korea University, Seoul*

**Abstract.** Using the Multi-Regional Variable Input-Output Model, this chapter discusses the industrial linkage among 30 industries in 10 countries in the Asia-Pacific region. Technological improvements in the Korean telecommunications industry are analyzed, and are shown to affect the economic structure of each of the other 9 countries. In the case of Korea, it is found that industries that are disadvantaged due to the improvement in the domestic telecommunications industry become competent industries in the international arena. The change in the Korean economy is accompanied by changes in the production activity of other countries. The analysis of the structural change in the region suggests that the change of telecommunications may affect international division of production. In addition, it is found that the change in output in the region is more closely related to input trade between countries than to telecommunications service use.

## 1   INTRODUCTION

The emergence of new information technology (IT) and its rapid diffusion are based on the belief that spending on IT inputs has enormous potential for reducing costs and enhancing the competitiveness of firms as well as individuals. The rapid price declines and remarkable performance improvements of IT goods and services accelerate this information revolution and lead to the substitution of IT for non-IT inputs in the production. By substituting IT for other types of capital and labor, firms intend to capitalize on the superior returns from IT relative to the other type of inputs.[1]

---

[1] Hitt and Brynjolfsson (1996), Lichtenberg (1993), and Kraemer and Dedrick (1994 & 2001) analyze firm level data to show that IT investments generate returns that are often in excess of the returns on the other types of investments and productivity paradox disappears.

Measuring impacts on IT investment, however, is complicated by the fact that such investments are influential not only in final economic growth, but in some economic factors such as employment, price level of economic resources, intermediate purchases, income, industrial outputs, and trade flow in industrial and regional detail. As a result, there have been inherent problems in showing the detailed outcomes in the models that relate productivity growth to IT investment.

Most of the previous studies of IT impacts on the economy have focused on the simple relationship, which is to discover whether IT capital investment brings about economic growth.[2] These studies have been interested in determining whether IT capital investment made positive contributions to the diffusion of new technology, productivity improvement, reduced unemployment rate, enhanced consumer utility, and the positive management outcome. On the other hand, the studies on the impacts of IT capital investment, whose goal is to identify more detailed outcomes such as interactive relationship between industries, are relatively insufficient. Furthermore, the studies of IT capital investment have focused on the productivity on a single country level but have missed the relation of the productivity with trade between countries.

To compensate for the points we indicated above, we are going to use Multi-Regional Variable Input-Output Model (hereafter, MRVIO) in studying the country level analysis. MRVIO shows its ability to represent the changed technological coefficients of all industries due to a cost reduction in a certain industry in the region. In this chapter, this will be used to identify the impact of the technological development of the Korean telecommunications sector on the production and trade activities in various industries among 10 Countries in the Asia-Pacific region. Our analysis will investigate the validity of the above postulate and it also complements previous research on IT, production change, industrial structure, and trade.

The key research issues to be examined in this chapter are: Does the growth of the Korean telecommunications sector affect production of Korean industries and enhance their competitiveness in the international market? Does the growth of the Korean telecommunications sector cause the demise of the primary sector in developing countries or of manufacturing jobs in developed countries? Does the Korean telecommunications sector foster international division of production? What is the main factor that leads to the change in production of the countries in the Asia-Pacific region?

The rest of the chapter is organized as follows. In section II, the comparison of the characteristics of MRIO and MRVIO is explained. The methodology to be used for analyzing the impact of the Korean telecommunications sector on the production activity in industries of the ten countries in the Asia-Pacific region is explained before introducing the MRVIO model. In section III, we show and explain the empirical results of changes in Korean domestic industries and the subsequent changes in input trade account between Korea and those countries and in industrial structure. Concluding remarks and the future study plans are given in section IV.

---

[2] Those researches from various perspectives on the impacts of IT investment on economic growth are as follows: the improvement of productivity (Kraemer and Dedrick, 2001; Dewan and Kraemer 2000; Oliner and Sichel, 1994; Morrison and Berndt, 1991), and the competitiveness of firms (Brynjolfsson, 1996; Hitt and Brynjolfsson, 1996). For more detailed information on this issue, see Pohjola (2001) and Brynjolfsson and Kahin (2000).

## 2   MRVIO MODEL AND ITS METHODOLOGY

In the Input-Output table analysis, the conventional Leontief model has been widely used as a practical tool for industrial impact analysis. Assuming the technological coefficients to be fixed, a major drawback of the Leontief input-output model is its inability to trace the effect of production associated with a cost or price change failing to permit any input substitution effect (Liew&Liew; 1988). It, however, is a reality that an economy's output is affected by the cost and price change of some input because firm owners look for ways of substituting relatively cheaper inputs. The conventional Leontief model, unfortunately, cannot explain this phenomenon by excluding the input substitution behavior of firms facing the price changes of its present inputs and other outside options.

The Multi-regional Input-Output Model (MRIO), meanwhile, can measure the impact of the IT industry development by describing the change of not only the inter-industry purchase but also the inter-regional trade. The MRIO models that have been developed by Isard (1951), Moses (1955), and Polenske (1970) can be used to describe regional production activities, inter-industry purchase, and inter-regional trade. However, we can find those models are unable to permit input substitution and predict the change of production activities caused by cost variation of input in a specific industry. These models are developed on the basis of the traditional Leontief assumption of fixed coefficient of intermediate goods in the production process.

Liew (1979) introduced the Variable Input-Output (VIO) model in which the input coefficients are affected by the factor cost. Liew (1985) extended the VIO model to a multi-regional case and introduced the Multi-Regional Variable Input-Output (MRVIO) model in which the regional technical and trade coefficients are endogenous to the factor cost, that is, the service price of primary inputs. In other words, all the intermediate goods in the production process can be varied if there is a change in the price of primary factors such as labor or capital.

As the technological innovation in telecommunications industry lowers the price of telecommunications service, it also leads to the substitution of IT for non-IT inputs in production. This substitution effect between IT input and intermediate inputs together with other non-IT inputs such as labor and conventional capital has become active, while a lower production cost has rendered a positive production activity raising the demands for non-IT inputs. The size of input substitution effect will vary across industries.

MRVIO, the model used in this analysis, allows the technological coefficients to change, which represents the input substitution. As a result, this model will give us the impact assessment on the economy due to the input cost reduction through the development of telecommunications technology prompted by R&D. In addition, using this model, it is possible to analyze the prevalent impact not only in the domestic industries but also in industries in foreign countries. The MRVIO model is to be used in analyzing how the technological development in the Korean telecommunications industry affects the industries of Korea and the industries of foreign countries trading with Korea.[3]

---

[3] Korean government announced in 1996 that telecommunication industry would be chosen as one of the strategic industries to make economic structure stronger and healthy. Korea has to find the competitive industries and to make this progress further in the procedure of market globalization where only competitive economy can survive.

## 2.1 Data

For our analysis multi-regional input-output data is used. Industries world-wide are interrelated domestically and internationally. This is also true in the telecommunications industry. In this situation of intermingled economic structure, the main purpose of this chapter is to ascertain whether or not telecommunications can affect industries in the international arena. This inter-industrial relation in the domestic and international market is represented in the Multi-Regional Input-Output table 1990 issued by the Institute of Developing Economies in Japan. The regions in this table cover 10 countries in Asia-Pacific region such as Indonesia, Malaysia, Philippines, Singapore, Thailand, China, Taiwan, Korea, Japan and the US. In this chapter, the original data of 78 industries is revised into 30 industries (see Appendix 1) for each country.

Using this data, each country's industrial dependence on the telecommunications technology may be found. After finding the present status of the Korean telecommunications industry, the steps for finding changes in the industrial share and in the input trade accounts of Korea for those countries will be made. This procedure can be a useful measure to find a trade strategy to enhance Korea's competitiveness in the Asia-Pacific regional market.

## 2.2 Model

The Multi-Regional Input-Output table displays the relations of each industry in both the domestic and international market. The output (production) equation for $x_i^s$ is formed as

$$x_i^s = \sum_{r=1}^{m}\sum_{j=1}^{n} x_{ij}^{sr} + \sum_{r=1}^{m} f_i^{sr} \quad \text{(industry: i= 1,...n, country: s=1,...m).}^4 \tag{1}$$

Each commodity produced by each industry in the country s($x_i^s$) is purchased by industries($x_{ij}^{sr}$) and final users($f_i^{sr}$) of all countries.

$x_i^s$ : the amount of commodity i produced by each industry in the country s
$x_{ij}^{sr}$ : the amount of commodity i produced in country s that is purchased as an intermediate input by industry j located in country r
$f_i^{sr}$ : the final demand of commodity i by households, government, and foreign trade and not by the producers to use as an intermediate input to an industrial production process.

It is assumed that all firms maximize their profit by enlarging the difference between revenue and cost subject to technical constraints reflecting the log-linearized Cobb-Douglas production function frontier. This behavior is represented by the following equation.

Max $\Pi = \Sigma r \Sigma j$ ( $p_j^r x_j^r$ - $\Sigma i$ $\Sigma s$ $p_{ij}^{sr} x_{ij}^{sr}$ - $\Sigma k$ $w_{kj}^r L_{kj}^r$ )

subject to $\Sigma r$( ln $x_j^r$ - $\alpha_{oj}^r$ - $\Sigma s \Sigma i$ $\alpha_{ij}^{sr}$ ln $x_{ij}^{sr}$ - $\Sigma k \beta_{kj}^r$ ln $L_{kj}^r$ ),

where $\Sigma i \Sigma s \alpha_{ij}^{sr} + \Sigma k \beta_{kj}^r = 1$ (production function homogeneous of degree one).

---

[4] From now on, $\displaystyle\sum_{r=1}^{m}\sum_{j=1}^{n}$ will be denoted as $\Sigma_r \Sigma_j$ for simplicity's sake. The other summation signs will be treated in

the same way.

Regions and regional flows are described by superscripts: commodities and commodity flows by subscripts.

$p_j^r$ : unit price of $x_j^r$

$x_j^r$ : the amount of commodity produced by industry j located in country r

$p_{ij}^{sr}$ : unit price of $x_{ij}^{sr}$

$w_{kj}^r$ : unit price of primary input k used by industry j in country r

$L_{kj}^r$ : the amount of primary input k used by industry j in country r

After the derivation of the first order condition by differentiating the Lagrangian function Π with respect to the control variables, the optimal employment level of control variables can be obtained. The optimal profit maximizing employment level of control variables such as intermediate input and primary input can be expressed as;

$$x_{ij}^{sr} = \alpha_{ij}^{sr} \ p_j^r \ x_j^r / p_{ij}^{sr} = \alpha_{ij}^{sr} \ p_j^r \ x_j^r / t_i^{sr} p_i^s ,$$

where $t_i^{sr}$ : trade cost[5] (e.g., exchange rate, tariff, transport cost), $p_i^s$ : price of i th commodity in region s.

$\alpha_{ij}^{sr} = x_{ij}^{sr} / x_j^r$ : technological coefficient

$L_{kj}^r = \beta_{kj}^r \ p_j^r \ x_j^r / w_{kj}^r$

These two optimal level of inputs will lead to the price equation for industries like the following.

$$\ln p = (I-A')^{-1} \Sigma k \beta_k \ln w_k , \qquad (2)$$

where   A : the matrix of technological coefficient of industries

$\beta_k$ : $L_{kj}^r / x_j^r$

The optimal level of intermediate input includes prices of all commodities, which affect the output equation (1). The price prediction of eq.(2) related to the change in input cost derived from the input side is used for the output prediction of industry. The prices that have changed will lead to the changes in intermediate inputs purchase by other industries of all countries in this region. As a result, the technological coefficient(A) will be changed to $(p^* {}^{-1}Ap^*)$[6] by being influenced by the relative prices of commodities.

$$x = ( I-p^* {}^{-1}Ap^*)^{-1}f = ( I-h)^{-1}f,$$

where p*: diagonal matrix of prices, f: final demand.

---

[5] $p_{ij}^{sr} = t_i^{sr} p_i^s = (1+\theta) p_i^s$; the price ( $p_{ij}^{sr}$ ) of $x_{ij}^{sr}$ can be expressed as the change in trade cost(1+θ) multiplied by the priced of jth commodity in region s. θ can be expressed for the rate of change in exchange rate, tariff, transport expense, and etc. In this chapter, we assume there is no change in trade cost (θ=0).

[6] The individual cell of this matrix is expressed as $\alpha_{ij}^{sr} (p_j^r / p_{ij}^{sr})$ in MRVIO. Thus the original technological coefficient $\alpha_{ij}^{sr}$ is changed by the relative price of $p_j^r$ and $p_{ij}^{sr}$ .

If there is a change in the input cost due to the telecommunications technology change, there will be a change in the price (dh). And the change in the price will cause a change in output (dx). This relation can be expressed as follows:

$$dx = ( I - h ) -1 \, dh \, x + ( I - h ) -1 \, df \tag{3}$$

The output change (dx) is influenced by the technological change affected by the relative price and the change in the final demand. This dx for Korea and the other nine countries will be compared before and after technological development in the Korean telecommunications sector occurs. The equation (3) is composed of two parts, of which the former is about the input substitution effect through the change in commodity prices while the latter is about the income effect through the change in GDP. In this analysis, we are going to deal only with the input substitution effect to find the net impact of the changes in the telecommunications sector on the given economic structure.[7]

The purpose of this chapter is to examined the changes when there is a 1% capital cost reduction due to the technological development in the Korean telecommunications industry using the equations (2) and (3). The industrial change in domestic economy and subsequent changes in input trade account between Korea and those countries are to be investigated. We also examine the impact of the Korean telecommunications sector on the production activity in industries of the nine countries in the Asia-Pacific region.

## 3    EMPIRICAL RESULTS

### 3.1   Korea's change in domestic economy and in input trade

As we can see in Appendix 2, six industries and the telecommunications industry show an increase in their production activity, while the remaining 23 industries show a decrease in their production activity. The six industries are the livestock, textile, leather and leather products, electronic and electric products, wholesale and retail trade, finance and insurance, and other services. The size of the 23 industries, on the other hand, shrinks after the techno-logical development in the domestic telecommunications industry. Nevertheless, a develop-ment in one industry in a country makes other industries in this country competitive in the international market.

As the cause of the changes in the region, the Korean telecommunications industry leads to changes in input trade account of each industry of Korea with other countries. From Appendix 3, we found in this industry level analysis that all 30 Korean industries do not lose any competitiveness in the international input trade due to the improvement in the Korean

---

[7] The reason why we ignore the income effect in our analysis is to find out the change of the direction of production activity. The income effect dealing with changes in consumption, investment, and government expenditure will give us the overall positive (or negative) value of the same direction influenced by the change in GDP. Although the change in consumption can be obtained through Liew's HIVIO model, this also gives the information of change in the same direction. Since input substitution effect is for the measure of direction of changes in the industrial production activity, the income effect moving almost in the same direction does not give us further information on the industries' production activity.

telecommunications industry. Seven industries[8] do not have any positive or negative change in the input trade account and remain the same after the improvement of telecommunications industry. The domestically strong industry such as "No.27 finance and insurance industry" and "No.26 telephone and telecommunications industry" do not have any positive effect in the international market. This result should be interpreted that these industries are not much actively involved in input trade with the industries of other countries in the region. At any rate, the technological improvement in the Korean telecommunications industry does no harm to the remaining 29 domestic industries in the international market in the region.

Rather 18 of 23 Korean industries proven to be less competitive in the Korean domestic market become stronger in competitiveness in relation to the same industries of foreign countries. The remaining five industries[9] are found to be incapable of being competitive both in the domestic and in the international market. In addition to these five industries, two domestically competitive industries are not internationally competitive. This makes a total of seven industries which are not internationally competitive. Among the internationally competitive industries, "No.24 Wholesale and retail trade" industry has the biggest volume of input trade surplus increase of $212,573 and the second largest rate of trade increase by about 0.02%. This industry is not only domestically but also internationally competitive. "No.16 Metal products" industry" is domestically less competitive but internationally competitive having the input trade surplus increase of $128,536. "No.18 Electronic and electronic products" industry that is domestically competitive displays itself internationally competitive by reducing input trade deficit by $162,966. If we take a look at the % value aside from money volume, the most competitive and efficient industry in the international input market is "No.19 Other electronic machinery and appliance" industry. Even if it becomes domestically less competitive due to the development of "No.26 Telephone and telecommunications" industry in Korea, it shows the largest improvement in reducing the input trade deficit by 0.23% and by $14,465 in dollar value.

From this industry level study, we can find the manufacturing industries (No.8-No.21) are the group that receives the benefit from Korean telecommunication industry. Overall, this group exhibits international competitiveness judging from the input trade improvement from the range of 5 million dollars of industry No.10 and 163 million dollars of industry No.18. All manufacturing industries exhibit improvements in trade account, while we can see little or no improvement in the primary sector (No.1-No.7) and in the service sector (No.22-No.30). This means the Korean economy has an international competitiveness in the manufacturing sector. Thus, there should be a strategic plan to develop this sector along with telecommunications even if the global trend is toward a knowledge based society.

---

[8] The seven industries are "No.6 Crude petroleum and natural gas", "No.22 Electricity, gas, and water supply", "No.23 Construction", "No.26 Telephone and telecommunication", "No.27 Finance and insurance", "No.28 Education and research", "No.30 Public administration."

[9] These 5 industries are "No.6 Crude petroleum and natural gas", "No.22 Electricity, gas, and water supply", "No.23 Construction", "No.28 Education and research", "No.30 Public administration".

Table 1. Korea's Trade Improvement from 9 Countries

| Trade improvement in trade deficit by country | | | | | | |
|---|---|---|---|---|---|---|
|  | Indonesia | Malaysia | Taiwan | Japan | USA | Total |
| Trade deficit (TD) | -992253 | -1234133 | -135929 | -6533472 | -5706182 | -14601969 |
| Deficit share(%) | 6.80 | 8.45 | 0.93 | 44.74 | 39.08 | 100.00 |
| Trade improvement (TI) | 22.6541 | 14.831511 | 46.9216 | 324.221 | 308.5842 | 717.212411 |
| TI/TD(%) | *0.00228 | *0.00120 | *0.03452 | *0.00496 | *0.00541 | *0.00491 |

The "-" sign implies trade deficit., and the "*" sign implies improvements from trade deficit

| Trade improvement in trade surplus by country | | | | |
|---|---|---|---|---|
|  | Philippines | Singapore | Thailand | China | Total |
| Trade surplus (TS) | 214325 | 139001 | 383671 | 551649 | 1288646 |
| Surplus share (%) | 16.63 | 10.79 | 29.77 | 42.81 | 100.00 |
| Trade improvement (TI) | 21.0198 | 34.9617 | 37.40621 | 22.5604853 | 115.9481953 |
| TI/TD(%) | 0.00981 | 0.02515 | 0.00975 | 0.00409 | 0.00900 |

1,000 US $

Considering the input trade by country level, Table 1 demonstrates that the improvement in technological change in the Korean telecommunications industry enhances the input trade with all 9 countries. Korea has the largest input trade improvement with Japan by $324,221 and then with the U.S.A. $308,584. Japan and the USA are followed by Taiwan ($46,922), Thailand ($37,406), Singapore ($34,962), Indonesia ($22,654), China ($22,560), Philippines ($21,020) and Malaysia ($14,832).

The rate of trade improvement (TI/TD) and (TI/TS) shows the different range for the countries of deficit and surplus. The overall rate is 0.00491% for the countries of trade deficit and 0.00899% for those of surplus. Taiwan, Japan and USA are above the overall rate for the countries of deficit and Philippines, Singapore and Thailand are above the overall rate for those of surplus. Indonesia, Malaysia, and China are considered to be low income countries and are below the rates. From this result, we can say the development of the Korean telecommunication industry makes the Korean economy stronger to derive the reduction of deficit and the increase of surplus from high income and middle income countries. This country level study implies that a high tech industry shows potential to improve the input trade account of a country trading with technologically more advanced countries.

## 3.2  The impact on the industrial structure

Improvements in the Korean telecommunications service also contribute to the structural change of the other countries' economies through spillover effect. To explain this result, the 30 industries are grouped into 4 groups to explain the changes in the industrial structure for the sake of simplicity. The industries from number 1 through 7 are grouped into primary industry (1st), the industries from number 8 through 21 are grouped into manufacturing industry (2nd), the industries from number 22 through 30 except number 26 are grouped into service industry (3rd), and the industry number 26 named as "Telephone and Telecommunications Industry" is independently treated as a single group as a part of IT industry.

Table 2. Country's Structural Change by Industries

| | Industry | | | |
|---|---|---|---|---|
| | 1st | 2nd | 3rd | telecom |
| Indonesia &Malaysia | - | + | + | + |
| Singapore,USA & Philippines | - | - | + | + |
| Taiwan & Japan | + | - | + | + |
| Thailand | - | + | + | - |
| China | - | + | - | - |
| Korea | - | - | - | + |

Following the Korean telecommunications industry's change in production technology, the 10 countries vary in their economic structural changes. Table 2 shows the variety of change in economic structure for each country. Indonesia and Malaysia display a similar trend of change in structure. The size of primary industry is atrophied, while the size of manufacturing, service, and telecommunications industries are expanded. USA, Singapore and Philippines also share common traits, in that they have the same structural changes of shrinkage in primary and manufacturing industries while expanding the service and telecommunications industries. Taiwan and Japan shrink the manufacturing industry and expand the primary, service, and telecommunications industries in the same fashion.

The remaining countries display different structural changes as a spillover effect. Thailand shows an expansion in the manufacturing and service industries and a shrinkage in the primary and telecommunications industries. China expands only in manufacturing industry and shrinks in the primary, service, and telecommunications industries. Finally, Korea expands only in the telecommunications industry and shrinks in primary, manufacturing and service industries. This implies that the development in the telecommunications industry absorbs production inputs of other industries for fattening itself without giving the other industries positive influences through the input substitution effect. A lower price of telecommunications service in Korea with comparative advantages will enforce the Korean economy to be more oriented towards the telecommunications service industry.

The direction of the structural change related to division of production in the region does not follow a certain standard such as developed countries, upper income developing countries, lower income developing countries, natural resource endowed countries, or telecommunications sector share of the economic structure. If one considers the case of three groups of countries following the same trend of structural change, it can be demonstrated that those countries do not follow a certain norm. Indonesia and Malaysia have something in common because they are richly endowed in natural resources. However, among ten countries, Indonesia is second lowest, next to China, in telecommunications share (0.57%) of the total output, while Malaysia has the second largest telecommunications share (1.17%) next to the USA (2.28%). The USA is rich in natural resources and Singapore is a small city-state devoid of natural resources even though they are both high income countries in common. However, Philippines, in the category of the lowest income country, shows the same trend of structural change of shrinkage in primary and manufacturing industries and expansion in service and telecommunications industries as does the USA and Singapore. Even if Taiwan is not as advanced as Japan in economic status, both of these countries exhibit similar characteristics of shrinkage in manufacturing industry and expansion in primary, service and telecommunications industries.

We found that there would be no specific trend or standard to predict the direction of structural changes in industry like previously asserted ideas of change from primary to manufacturing industrial society or from manufacturing to knowledge based society. This analysis does not show significant differences between developed and developing countries with respect to the structural change of economy caused by the prosperity of telecommunications service in Korea. However, what we can say for sure is that such service-oriented growth is observed in Singapore, Japan and USA, categorized as developed countries, along with the growth of their telecommunications service. Also, all of the countries in the developing groups, except Taiwan, show shrinkage in the primary industry. These phenomena approximately meet the idea "the demise of the primary sector in developing countries and of manufacturing sectors in the developed countries."

The development of the Korean telecommunications industry leads the development in all other countries except Thailand and China. The telecommunications industry's shares in these countries are relatively lower than most of the countries in the region. The telecommunications share of Thailand is 0.68% and that of China is 0.32%. These relatively lower rates seem to make telecommunications industries of these countries shrink. This implies the countries in the region will specialize the production in their competitive industry. Appendix 4 shows the change in industrial structures that all the countries in the region respond to the impact from the technological improvement in the Korean telecommunication industry. We find that 27 industries of each country increase or decrease their share in the composition of economy of each country where they belong. These structural changes can be interpreted as the international division of production in the region. "No.6 Crude petroleum and natural gas", "No.7 Other mining" and "No.13 Petroleum and petro products" industries are showing the trend of having smaller shares in the economic composition throughout all the countries. Except these 3 industries, the other 27 industries become smaller or bigger by the country, which is determined through their competitiveness.

As this analysis does not assume the barrier of trading intermediate inputs between countries, all the industries in this region would form structural changes on the basis of their competitiveness in the domestic and international market. The competitive industries will be larger and the less competitive ones smaller, which can be interpreted as the international specialization of production. Amidst the demise of the primary industry in the developing countries and of the manufacturing sector in the developed countries, most of the industries in this region specialize their production by the country.

### 3.3   The factor of change in this regional production activity

We have shown the change in the production and trade in this region from the viewpoint of Korea. Each country in this region experiences its own change in domestic production and trade with nine other countries. For this reason, we seek the factor that is the cause of the change. The output equation for the commodity i in region s is expressed as the following:

$$x_i^s = \sum_{r=1}^{m} \sum_{j=1}^{n} x_{ij}^{sr} + \sum_{r=1}^{m} f_i^{sr}$$

The output of commodity i in this equation is composed of intermediate inputs($x_{ij}^{sr}$) and final demand($f_i^{sr}$). As the change in final demand was not dealt in this analysis, the change in intermediate inputs($x_{ij}^{sr}$) will only affect the change in output($x_i^s$). This intermediate input matrix provides us with the information of input use of all industries of 10 countries in the region.

The initial change in this analysis is cost reduction in the telephone and telecommunications industry of Korea. Thus in this matrix we can select the telephone and telecommunications industry as an explanatory variable for the output in each country. Another variable explaining the production activity in this matrix can be the input trade account of each country. Because multiregional input-output table gives us the information about the flow of all inputs between regions[10], this input trade flow is one of the main factors for forming the production activity. We can set up a functional relation that output (x) is affected by the cost (T) spent on the telephone and telecommunications[11] and the input trade account (XM; Export-Import):

x = f(TEL, XM).

These two explanatory variables are divided into four categories made according to the per capita GDP.[12] The four categories are groups of developed countries (ujs: USA, Japan, Singapore), upper income developing countries (ttm: Taiwan, Thailand, Malaysia), lower income developing countries (ipc: Indonesia, Philippines, China) and Korea (ko). When output as production activity is regressed on the cost spent on IT and input trade account by the four categories, the form of equation can be expressed as follows:

$$x = \alpha\ 1 + \beta\ Tujs\ Tujs + \beta\ Tttm\ Tttm + \beta\ Tipc\ Tipc + \beta\ Tko\ Tko$$
$$+\ \beta\ XMujs\ XMujs + \beta\ XMttm\ XMttm + \beta\ XMipc\ XMipc + \beta\ XMko\ XMko + \varepsilon 1 \qquad eq.(a)$$

When there is a change in explanatory variables and dependent variable after our scenario (1% decrease in the capital cost in the telephone and telecommunications industry of Korea) is applied, the regression equation of the changed value is as follows:

$$x^* = \alpha\ 2 + \beta\ Tujs\ Tujs^* + \beta\ Tttm\ Tttm^* + \beta\ Tipc\ Tipc^* + \beta\ Tko\ Tko^*$$
$$+\ \beta\ XMujs\ XMujs^* + \beta\ XMttm\ XMttm^* + \beta\ XMipc\ XMipc^* + \beta\ XMko\ XMko^* + \varepsilon 2 \qquad eq.(b)$$

---

[10] This international input trade flow for the production can be supported by Findlay and Jones (2001). They introduce the idea that when the productive activity takes place within a country instead of within a firm or industry, international fragmentation is then reflected on outsourcing to other countries for supplies of raw materials and intermediate goods(2001, AER, pp.32).

[11] For the IT analysis, IT capital investment is used for the explanation of productivity. Here in this intermediate inputs matrix, the cost spent on telecommunications service is a part of IT capital investment. The data for this variable is obtained from adding the row vectors of telecommunications industry of each country in the intermediate inputs matrix.

[12] Using per capita GDP as of 1990, the category of developed countries over $10,000 involves USA ($23,221), Japan ($24,053), and Singapore ($12,142). The category of upper income developing countries range between $1,000 and $10,000 involves Taiwan ($7,871), Korea ($5,890), Malaysia ($2,479), and Thailand ($1,528). However, Korea is separated from this category treated independently to avoid influencing the characteristics of Taiwan, Malaysia, and Thailand because Korea is the unique country of having the strong impact from initial change in this analysis. Another category of developing countries to distinguish from the aforementioned 4 counties with a little upper per capita GDP is lower income developing countries. The lower income developing countries below $1,000 involve Philippines ($721), Indonesia ($638), and China ($332).

Table 3 shows the estimates for the IT and XM by the developed, developing, and underdeveloped countries.

Table 3. Output Estimates for IT Use and Trade Account

|            | eq.(a)          | eq.(b)           |
|------------|-----------------|------------------|
| β Tujs     | 44.92(16.71)**  | -42.13(0.08)     |
| β Tttm     | -61.22(0.44)    | 1324.72(0.16)    |
| β Tipc     | -70.04(0.37)    | 5018.16(0.15)    |
| β Tko      | -2.11(0.03)     | 0.19(1.39)       |
| β XMujs    | -11.38(2.19)*   | -22.53(5.63)**   |
| β XMttm    | -0.48(0.02)     | 137.05(2.82)*    |
| β XMipc    | -2.52(0.17)     | 60.04(0.88)      |
| β XMko     | 8.55(0.26)      | -2.83(1.03)      |
| F value    | 38.53**         | 5.15**           |
| R2         | 0.51            | 0.12             |
| DF         | 291             | 291              |

Note. T-statistics are in parentheses,
** and * indicate significance at 1% and 5%, respectively.

Ten countries' production activity before the scenario of lower cost of telecommunications service usage is applied depends only on the developed countries' expenditure on telephone and telecommunications service at 1% level of significance.[13] In addition, the input trade account of the developed countries can also affect the production activity at 5% level of significance. After this scenario is applied, the variables explaining the change of the production activity have turned out to be input trade accounts of the developed and the developing countries.

As many researchers have analyzed the positive effect of IT use on production, the data of the Multi-Regional Input-Output table also shows the positive effect of telecommunications service use on the production in the developed countries. However, this multiregional analysis shows the input trade account to be the main cause of change in production activity of the ten countries instead of telecommunications service after the scenario is applied. The production activity is affected by the developed countries' input trade account changed by the improvement of telecommunications service of Korea. The telephone and telecommunications service,

---

[13] Dewan and Kraemer (2000) analyzed IT capital accounts for higher GDP growth than non-IT capital in the developed countries while non-IT capital accounts for higher GDP growth than IT capital in the developing countries. They obtained this result with the data of computer use rather than the data of telecommunications we use in this analysis. However, the result we obtain also indicates the telecommunication industry in developed countries affects the production activity of 10 countries in the Asia-Pacific countries.

a part of Information Technology, is not the direct cause that affects the production activity of the countries in the Asia-Pacific region.

After the impact of Korean telecommunications, the production activity is more related to input trade account rather than telecommunications use in this multi-Regional Input-Output analysis. The input trade account of the developed countries affects the production activity of countries in the Asia-Pacific region in a negative way, while that of the developing countries affects it in a positive way. The prosperous business of Korean telecommunications leads to trade deficits of all other countries with Korea. The trade deficit of the developed countries will make the production activity of the countries in the region increase and that of the developing countries will make it decrease. In other words, the shrinkage of the export on the side of the developed countries makes the production in this region prosperous and that of the upper income developing countries makes it worse. One dollar decrease in input trade account of developed countries will lead to an increase of 22.53 dollars in production and one dollar decrease in trade account of upper income developing countries will lead to a decrease of 133.05 dollars in production. The Korean telecommunications industry affects regional production activity through the creation of trade deficit in the upper income developing countries more than through that in the developed countries. However, if it affects the trade deficit of the developed countries and the trade surplus of the upper income developing countries, the regional production activity would be prosperous.

## 4 CONCLUSION

Through the MRVIO analysis, we can examine the relations of industrial linkage among the10 countries in the Asia-Pacific region. The technological improvement in the Korean telecom- munications industry, holding all other things constant, affects the production activities of all the other countries. Six industries along with telecommunications prove to obtain beneficial effects domestically. However, 23 industries including all manufacturing sector become competitive in the input trade with other countries. Aside from the telecommunications sector, the manufacturing sector turns out to be internationally competent in the region. There needs to be a strategic plan to develop this sector for international competitiveness along with telecommunications even though the global trend is toward the knowledge based society.

Concerning the country level, the technological improvement in the Korean telecommuni- cations industry also makes Korean economy improve the trade account with all nine countries. The development of a high tech industry shows its possibility to improve the input trade account of a country trading with technologically more advanced countries.

In the structural change of the ten countries in the region, we found a demise of the manu- facturing industry in the developed countries. Japan experiences an expansion in the primary sector instead of a shrinkage. In the developing countries, the demise of primary industry is found with the exception of Taiwan. However, the countries experiencing the shrinkage of the primary industry vary in their movement of their manufacturing industry. Among developing countries, Philippines, Taiwan and Korea have shrinkages in their manufacturing sector, while Indonesia, Malaysia, Thailand and China show expansions in it. These phenomena do not exactly follow a norm, such as changes from agricultural to industrial society or from industrial to knowledge-based society with manufacturing industries' disappearing.

The responses from each country's production activity and the direction of changes in these country's industrial structure provide us information from which we can set up more efficient and strategic industrial and trade policy. For example, even if the Korean manufacturing sector is proved to be internationally competitive, it shrinks in the Korean economic structure. This analysis provides us with the idea that the strategic support of non-IT industries along with telecommunications can possibly affect the overall improvement in the input trade account in a more efficient way.

Another conclusion we can draw from the structural change in the region is that the change of IT may also affect international division of production. The comparative advantage over other countries trading with Korea will also affect non-telecommunications service industries of those countries such as primary or manufacturing industries. As we have observed the results from the MRVIO analysis, an impact from a single industry can lead to various outcomes according to each country's present industrial structure.

Finally, we found that changes in input trade account to be the decisive factor influencing the production activities and structural change rather than the factor of changes in the IT use as many researchers assert to be a main factor of productivity improvement. The change in input trade account due to the Korean telecommunications industry affect regional production activity. The change in production activity is positively affected by the input trade deficit in the upper income developing countries and negatively by that in the developed countries.

This study is derived from the 1990 data. In the future, the study of 1995 data is required for the comparison with this study. Using the same scenario for both years will give us the better information for the comparison of the direction of change in industrial productivity and economic structure.

## 5   APPENDIX 1

INDUSTRIES

1. Paddy
2. Other Agricultural Products
3. Livestock
4. Forestry
5. Fishery
6. Crude petroleum and natural gas
7. Other mining
8. Food, beverage and tobacco
9. Textile, leather, and the products thereof
10. Timber and wooden products
11. Pulp, paper, and printing
12. Chemical products
13. Petroleum and petro products
14. Robber products
15. Non-metallic mineral products
16. Metal products
17. Machinery
18. Electronic and electronic products
19. Other electric machinery and appliance
20. Transport equipment
21. Other manufacturing products
22. Electricity, gas, and water supply
23. Construction
24. Wholesale and retail trade
25. Transport
26. Telephone and telecommunications
27. Finance and insurance
28. Education and research
29. Other services
30. Public Administration

## 6   APPENDIX 2 - OUTPUT CHANGES IN KOREA BY INDUSTRY

| INDUSTRY | X | XA | dX |
|---|---|---|---|
| 1 | 9676577 | 9676222 | -354.9625 |
| 2 | 9908906 | 9908784 | -122.5463 |
| 3 | 5706432 | 5706495 | 63.38373 |
| 4 | 927488 | 927466.8 | -21.24174 |
| 5 | 3993224 | 3993217 | -6.868754 |
| 6 | 0 | 0 | 0 |
| 7 | 3138566 | 3138505 | -60.69587 |
| 8 | 41329509 | 41329191 | -318.2302 |
| 9 | 34821297 | 34821380 | 82.523571 |
| 10 | 4961317 | 4961300 | -17.36979 |
| 11 | 11037588 | 11037436 | -152.4504 |
| 12 | 26516306 | 26516185 | -120.968 |
| 13 | 12402662 | 12402206 | -455.9505 |
| 14 | 7654464 | 7654463 | -0.784862 |
| 15 | 10779654 | 10779588 | -66.04064 |
| 16 | 43172378 | 43172017 | -361.4252 |
| 17 | 22241508 | 22241487 | -20.97161 |
| 18 | 27825878 | 27825960 | 82.343133 |
| 19 | 4862969 | 4862965 | -4.110549 |
| 20 | 30066846 | 30066783 | -63.05051 |
| 21 | 16639384 | 16639360 | -24.29048 |
| 22 | 10294330 | 10293875 | -455.2997 |
| 23 | 61757155 | 61756909 | -246.1403 |
| 24 | 39118534 | 39121453 | 2918.5128 |
| 25 | 22323618 | 22323472 | -146.3062 |
| 26 | 6075187 | 6093746 | 18559.277 |
| 27 | 18596949 | 18597480 | 530.53329 |
| 28 | 13573839 | 13573816 | -23.14987 |
| 29 | 57593772 | 57593790 | 18.146293 |
| 30 | 19226531 | 19226531 | -3.73E-09 |

The shaded rows indicate the industries that are beneficial from the development in telecommunications.
Column X is original output and XA is the output that has changed afterward.
Column dX is the value of subtracting XA from X

## 7    APPENDIX 3 - 30 KOREAN INDUSTRIES' INPUT TRADE IMPROVEMENT BY COUNTRY

| Industry | Indonesia | Malaysia | Philippines | Singapore | Thailand | China | Taiwan | Japan | USA | Total(A) | XM(B) | %(A/B) |
|---|---|---|---|---|---|---|---|---|---|---|---|---|
| 1 | 0 | 0 | 0 | 0 | 0 | 0 | 0 | 0.068 | 0 | 0.068 | -10212 | -0.00067 |
| 2 | 0 | 0.00838 | 0.0472 | 0.0676 | 0.00507 | 0.00496 | 0.0078 | 0.508 | 0.024 | 0.67301 | 40117 | 0.00168 |
| 3 | 0 | 0 | 0 | 0 | 0.03466 | 0.001958 | 0 | 0.038 | 0.005 | 0.079618 | -8733 | -0.00091 |
| 4 | 0.0003 | 0.000831 | 0.0178 | 0 | 0.00153 | 3.73E-05 | 0 | 0.559 | 0.0402 | 0.6196983 | 65789 | 0.00094 |
| 5 | 0 | 0.0004 | 0 | 0 | 0.00825 | 0 | 0.019 | 9.54 | 1.472 | 11.03965 | 204222 | 0.00541 |
| 6 | 0 | 0 | 0 | 0 | 0 | 0 | 0 | 0 | 0 | 0 | 0 | 0 |
| 7 | 0.056 | 0.0278 | 0.0293 | 0 | 0.0563 | 0.0694 | 0.2264 | 2.279 | 0.013 | 2.7572 | 93005 | 0.00296 |
| 8 | 0.31 | 0.06 | 0 | 0.106 | 2.5 | 0.1308 | 0.211 | 15.24 | 1 | 19.5578 | -1284878 | -0.00152 |
| 9 | 6.01 | 1.755 | 2.736 | 0.992 | 7.83 | 4.189 | 5.6 | 26.6 | 32.9 | 88.612 | -740306 | -0.01197 |
| 10 | 0 | 0 | 0.012 | 0.006 | 0.01 | 0.1559 | 0.716 | 3.918 | 0.4 | 5.2179 | -1046594 | -0.00050 |
| 11 | 0.4 | 0.25 | 0.2515 | 0.2411 | 0.3768 | 1.415 | 0.11 | 1.4 | 4.6 | 9.0444 | -775092 | -0.00117 |
| 12 | 3.622 | 0.99 | 2.654 | 1.12 | 5.4 | 7.15 | 6.134 | 15 | 7 | 49.07 | -1788099 | -0.00274 |
| 13 | 0.1 | 0 | 0.0678 | 0.3264 | 0.033 | 0.01185 | 1.119 | 5.51 | 0.1 | 7.26805 | -633084 | -0.00115 |
| 14 | 0.14 | 0 | 0.2102 | 0.022 | 0.27 | 0.01127 | 0.16 | 9.021 | 7.971 | 17.80547 | -256063 | -0.00700 |
| 15 | 0.1829 | 0.101 | 0.762 | 0.1796 | 0.1859 | 0.572 | 0.5426 | 11.43 | 1.9 | 15.856 | 95399 | 0.01662 |
| 16 | 4.035 | 4.167 | 2.79 | 5.44 | 6.83 | 3.73 | 7.534 | 57.51 | 36.5 | 128.536 | 899059 | 0.01430 |
| 17 | 0.4216 | 0.5441 | 0.932 | 0.911 | 0.4444 | 0.3275 | 2.7482 | 10 | 8.1 | 24.4288 | -1312423 | -0.00186 |
| 18 | 1.063 | 2.18 | 0.6 | 16.49 | 2.883 | 4.21 | 7.36 | 36 | 92.18 | 162.966 | -2317501 | -0.00703 |
| 19 | 0.3193 | 0.17 | 0.687 | 0.101 | 0.3451 | 0.02747 | 0.055 | 3.5 | 9.26 | 14.46487 | -6318 | -0.22895 |
| 20 | 0.059 | 0.846 | 0.809 | 0.16 | 0.1549 | 0.01134 | 1.24 | 2 | 10.3 | 15.58024 | -1680660 | -0.00093 |
| 21 | 0.714 | 0.57 | 2.892 | 0.639 | 1.32 | 0.542 | 1.21 | 9.7 | 18.609 | 36.196 | -495502 | -0.00730 |
| 22 | 0 | 0 | 0 | 0 | 0 | 0 | 0 | 0 | 0 | 0 | -868474 | 0 |
| 23 | 0 | 0 | 0 | 0 | 0 | 0 | 0 | 0 | 0 | 0 | -795242 | 0 |
| 24 | 4.688 | 3.049 | 5.332 | 7.87 | 8.327 | 0 | 11.397 | 98.5 | 73.41 | 212.573 | 882333 | 0.02409 |
| 25 | 0.46 | 0.112 | 0.19 | 0.29 | 0.3056 | 0 | 0.4196 | 3.64 | 2.7 | 8.1172 | -340077 | -0.00239 |
| 26 | 0 | 0 | 0 | 0 | 0 | 0 | 0 | 0 | 0 | 0 | -22097 | 0 |
| 27 | 0 | 0 | 0 | 0 | 0 | 0 | 0 | 0 | 0 | 0 | -22809 | 0 |
| 28 | 0 | 0 | 0 | 0 | 0 | 0 | 0 | 0 | 0 | 0 | -59392 | 0 |
| 29 | 0.073 | 0 | 0 | 0 | 0.0847 | 0 | 0.112 | 2.26 | 0.1 | 2.6297 | -238491 | -0.00110 |
| 30 | 0 | 0 | 0 | 0 | 0 | 0 | 0 | 0 | 0 | 0 | -891200 | 0 |
| Total | 22.6541 | 14.831511 | 21.0198 | 34.9617 | 37.40621 | 22.5604853 | 46.9216 | 324.221 | 308.5842 | 833.1606063 | | |
| % | 2.71906 | 1.78015 | 2.52290 | 4.19627 | 4.48968 | 2.70782 | 5.63176 | 38.91459 | 37.03778 | 100 | | |

Numbers except in row and columns of % are values of USD1000

XM(B) is the input trade account from original data of respective 30 Korean industry

The last row named % presents the share of trade improvement by country.

# 8   APPENDIX 4 - INDUSTRIAL STRUCTURAL CHANGES BY COUNTRY

| Ind | Indonesia | Malaysia | Philip-pines | Singapore | Thailand | China | Taiwan | Korea | Japan | USA |
|-----|-----------|----------|--------------|-----------|----------|-------|--------|-------|-------|-----|
| 1 | + | + | + | 0 | - | + | + | - | + | 0 |
| 2 | + | + | + | + | - | - | + | - | + | - |
| 3 | + | + | + | + | - | - | + | - | + | - |
| 4 | - | - | - | 0 | - | + | - | - | + | - |
| 5 | + | + | + | + | - | + | + | - | + | - |
| 6 | - | - | - | 0 | - | - | - | 0 | - | - |
| 7 | - | - | - | - | - | - | - | - | - | - |
| 8 | + | + | + | + | - | + | + | - | + | + |
| 9 | + | + | + | + | + | + | - | - | - | + |
| 10 | - | - | - | + | + | + | + | - | + | + |
| 11 | - | + | + | - | + | + | - | - | - | - |
| 12 | + | + | - | - | - | + | - | - | - | - |
| 13 | - | - | - | - | - | - | - | - | - | - |
| 14 | - | - | + | - | - | - | - | - | - | - |
| 15 | + | + | - | + | - | - | - | - | - | - |
| 16 | + | + | + | - | + | - | - | - | - | - |
| 17 | + | + | + | - | - | + | - | - | - | - |
| 18 | + | + | - | + | + | + | - | - | - | - |
| 19 | + | + | + | + | + | - | + | - | + | + |
| 20 | + | + | + | + | + | + | + | - | + | - |
| 21 | + | + | + | - | + | + | + | - | - | - |
| 22 | + | + | - | - | - | - | - | - | - | + |
| 23 | + | + | + | + | + | + | + | - | + | + |
| 24 | + | + | - | + | - | - | + | + | + | - |
| 25 | + | + | + | + | - | - | + | - | + | - |
| 26 | + | + | + | + | - | - | + | + | + | + |
| 27 | + | + | + | - | - | - | - | - | + | + |
| 28 | + | + | + | + | + | + | + | - | + | + |
| 29 | + | + | + | + | + | - | + | - | + | + |
| 30 | + | + | + | + | + | + | + | - | + | + |

+: industrial share has become bigger
-: industrial share has become smaller

## 9  REFERENCES

Amiti, Mary, (2001), "Regional Specialization and Technological Leapfrogging", *Journal of Regional Science*, Vol. 41, No. 1, pp.149-172.

Beede, D. N., Sabrina L. Montes (1997), *Information Technology's Impact on Firm Structure: A Cross-Industry Analysis*, U.S. Department of Commerce.

Bresnahan, T., E. Brynjolfsson, and L. Hitt (1999), "Information Technology, Workplace Organization and the Demand for Skilled Labor: Firm-Level Evidence," *NBER Working Paper* No. 7136.

Brynjolfsson, E. (1996), "The contribution of Information Technology to Consumer Welfare", *Information Systems Research*.

Brynjolfsson, E. and B. Kahin (2000), *Understanding the Digital Economy: Data, Tools, and Research*, The MIT Press.

Dewan, S. and Kraemer, K. (2000), "Information Technology and Productivity: Evidence from Country-Level Data", *Management Science*, Vol.46, No.4, pp. 548-562.

El-Hodiri Farrokh Nourzad Mohamed A., (1988), "A Note on Leontief Technology and Input Substitution", *Journal of Regional Science*, vol. 28-1, 119(2).

Findlay, R. and Ronald W. Jones (2001), "Input Trade and the Location of Production," *The American economic review*, vol. 91- 2, pp.29 – 33.

Gurmukh Gill, Kan Young, Dennis Pastore, Jess Dumagan, and Isaac Turk (1997), *Economy-Wide and Industry-Level Impact of Information Technology*, Economics & Statistics Administration report, OPD 97-3.

Hitt, L. and Brynjolfsson, E. (1996), "Information Technology and Internal Firm Organization: An Exploratory Analysis," *Journal of Management Information Systems*, vol.14, pp.81-101.

Isard, Walter(1951), "Interregional and Regional Input-Output Analysis: A Model of Space-Economy," *Review of Economics and Statistics*, Vol.33, 167-180.

Jung, K, J. Oh, and I. Shin, (2001), "The Diffusion of Information and Communication Technology and Its Economic Impact in Korea," *Information Technology and Economic Development*, Cambridge: Oxford University Press.

Kim, H. G. & J. H. Oh, (2001), "The Impact of IT Industry: VIO Model Approach," *Korean Telecommunication Policy Review*, Vol.8, No. 2, pp 113-127.

Klein, L. R. (1952 & 1953), "On the Interpretation of Prof. Leontief's System," *Review of Economic Studies*, 131-36.

Kraemer, K., and J. Dedrick (1994), "Payoffs from Investment in Information Technology: Lessons from Asia-Pacific Region," *World Development*, 22 (12): 1921-1931.

Kraemer, K., and J. Dedrick (2001), "Information Technology and Productivity: Results and Implications of Cross-Country Studies," *Information Technology and Economic Development*, Cambridge: Oxford University Press.

Lichtenberg, F. R. (1993), "The Output Contributions of Computer Equipment and Personnel: A Firm-Level Analysis," *NBER Working Paper*, No.4540, November.

Liew, C. K., and C. J. Liew (1988), "Measuring the Effect of Cost Variation on Industrial Outputs", *Journal of Regional Science*, Vol. 28, Nov. 1988, 563-78.

Liew, C. K., C. J. Liew, and Joonmo Cho (1994), "The Effects of Korean Wage Hikes on Korean Trade Structure with the U.S. and Japan," *Southern Economic Journal*, Vol. 61, No.2 , 488-509.

Morrison, J. C. and E. R. Berndt (1991), "Assessing the Productivity of Information, Technology Equipment in U.S. Manufacturing Industries," *NBER Working Paper* No. 3583, January.

Moses, Leon (1955), "The Stability of Inrerregional Trading Patterns and Input-Output Analysis," *American Economic Review*, Vol. 45, 803-832.

Oliner,S and Sichel, D. (1994), "Computers and Output Growth Revisited: How Big Is the Puzzle?", *Brookings Papers on Economic Activity*, Vol. 2, pp.273-334.

Polenski, Karen R. (1970), "A Multiregional Input-Output Model for the United States," *Harvard Economic Research Project*, Economic Development Administration.

Pohjola, M. (2001), "Information Technology and Economic Growth: A Cross-Country Analysis," *Information Technology and Economic Development*, Cambridge: Oxford University Press, pp. 242-256.

Samuelson, P. A. (1951), "Abstract of a Theorem Concerning Substitutability in Open Leontief Models", in *Activity Analysis of Production and Allocation*, edited by T.C. Koopmans, 142-46, Wiley.

Wong, P. (2001), "The Contribution of Information Technology to the Rapid Economic Growth of Singapore," *Information Technology, Productivity, and Economic Growth*, Oxford University Press.

# PART III

# DIGITAL GOODS: THEORETICAL INVESTIGATION

Global Economy and Digital Society
E. Bohlin, S. Levin, N. Sung and C-H. Yoon (Editors)

CHAPTER 8

# Price Dispersion in the Internet Marketplace: Are Service-premium Strategies Relevant?[*]

Luca Grilli

*Dipartimento di Ingegneria Gestionale, Politecnico di Milano and CIRET, Milan*

**Abstract**. As e-commerce has many of the characteristics associated with a perfect or "frictionless" market, the emergence of a very low price dispersion would be expected in a cyber market for a homogeneous good. However, there is broad empirical evidence that e-markets are characterized by significant levels of price dispersion. Past contributions on price dispersion have individuated three main reasons for its occurrence: the immature nature of the market, the play of service-premium strategies by firms, and the presence of uninformed consumers in the market. This chapter presents an empirical investigation that aims at testing the service-premium hypothesis. Results highlight that the superior quality of some services (in particular customer support and reliability in delivery times) allows retailers to raise prices, while other store features (web site quality and ease of ordering) have a negligible or positive impact on price dispersion.

## 1 INTRODUCTION

It is common wisdom that the e-commerce activity represents a different job respect to the traditional "brick and mortar" retailing in several aspects; and there is broad consensus among market operators, analysts and economists that the Internet-environment may revise and in some cases revolutionize stores' business strategies.

Flexibility in meeting customer needs and requirements, 24-hour accessibility, the intangible nature of most of the transactions[1] are only some of the peculiarities of the online retailing. Important differences between virtual and physical stores inevitably occur on many others dimensions concerning selling activity. In particular, the virtual environment on which transactions take place has on average increased the importance respect to the physical scenario of firm's decision variables different from price. In addition, it has probably contributed to enlarge the "traditional" strategy space at disposal of firms to rival each other: variety and security of available methods of payment, return policy choices, ability to deliver

[*] Financial support from the MIUR 2000 Research Project "Il commercio elettronico: nuove tecnologie e nuovi mercati per le piccole e medie imprese" is gratefully acknowledged. I am indebted to Massimo G. Colombo for helpful comments on an earlier draft. All errors remain my sole responsibility.

[1] Potential customers do not usually have the opportunity to control good conditions and quality before buying, they actually "touch" the item only some days after the purchase. Moreover, it exists the non trivial problem for consumers of verifying the counterpart's identity and reliability.

on time goods, shipping conditions and options, the level of personal data requested by stores to customers in order to effectuate the purchase, the ease of ordering and the overall web performance of the site (layout, links, pictures, images & speed) are all important factors (other than price naturally) on which Internet shoppers base their purchase decisions [see Helander and Khalid (2000)]. Therefore, they may represent all possible strategic tools at disposal of vendors to compete each other[2]. Along with this increase in the number and importance of firms' strategic variables, Internet has sensibly lowered search costs for products and has made every store extremely "close" to the relative competitors. In the e-marketplace, potential customers are only a click away from leaving the virtual store and do not have any social pressure to stay, and moreover they can switch very easily to substitute shops. In other words, when Internet shoppers are searching for the "desired" product, they can monitor, bearing negligible costs, all the existing supply present on the Web for that item at that particular time. The use of intelligent search engines ("software agents") and the presence of infomediaries or shopbots ("price and quality comparison portals") make all the Internet shops very easily comparable not only by potential clients but also by competitor retailers. So, each potential consumer can almost instantly individuate the best offer for the product he is willing to purchase; but at the same time, each store selling that particular product on the Web can immediately observe selling conditions offered by other firms. If we consider a market for a homogeneous good and we assume that price is the only strategic variable at disposal of a virtual store in order to differentiate itself from competitors (or similarly the only parameter on which customers base their purchase decision), it is straight-forward to note that Internet might confer to the retailing activity those characteristics of perfect information that should drive prices towards the Bertrand equilibrium level. Even admitting some degree of collusion among firms, the "law of one price" should still hold, if we think for example to Sweezy (1939) and Hall and Hitch (1939), in the formulation of the old "kinked demand curve" theory[3].

But as many recent scientific empirical works [see for example Brynjolfsson and Smith (2000a), Clay et al. (2001), Clay et al. (2002)] have shown (and personal experience of any Web shoppers may confirm), this is not often the case, since most of the time identical products are sold by different virtual stores at significantly different prices. The paper is therefore devoted to the analysis of the motives why we do not often observe a low degree of price dispersion and the occurrence of a "price focal" strategy in many Internet markets for homogenous goods, as instead it would have been legitimate to expect on a priori ground. In

---

[2] Some other "strategic tools" can be deemed important both in a virtual and in a physical scenario (customer care, shop pleasantness and atmosphere, brand reputation, are only some few possible examples).

[3] The Sweezy's conjecture states that a "corner" at the current market price might occur in the perceived demand by the firm operating in a non-perfectly competitive market. The line of reasoning which can be easily applied to the e-market environment, is the following: on one hand, each virtual store is aware that once it decides to reduce its price respect to the one settled by rivals, these latter can immediately react, lowering the price as well (moreover no menu-costs exist in the web). On the other hand, a price increase is likely to be unsuccessful, since consumers do not incur in any search costs and they can easily move to another store. If this is the case, the "imagined demand curve" by the representative firm will therefore present a corner in correspondence to the current price with a (strongly, given the Internet-environment here considered) elastic upward side and a (strongly) inelastic downward side. As a direct result, almost no price dispersion should emerge in a virtual market for a homogenous good. The theory has been widely criticized [see for example Stigler (1978) and Friedman (1983)] and revised by more recent contributions which most of the time adopt an explicit game theoretic approach [Maskin and Tirole (1988), Bhaskar (1988), Rotschild (1992)].

particular, we aim at investigating if and to what extent service-premium strategies pursued by virtual stores have an impact on the level of price dispersion in virtual markets for homogeneous items. At this scope, next section will analyse previous empirical findings on price dispersion in Internet markets for homogeneous goods and will illustrate the main hypotheses formulated in the literature for explaining its occurrence. Then, Section 3 provides an empirical investigation carried out on a sample of cross-sector Internet stores selling homogeneous items which aims at investigating the relevance of the service-premium hypothesis. This latter predicts that customers do not care only about the product they are buying but also about the quality of transaction-related services, which implies that they are willing to pay a premium for a high quality level of such services. Stores have been selected through one of the most known shopbots, Bizrate.com, which permits to immediately compare prices together with terms and conditions of sale of various homogeneous goods offered by a conspicuous number of virtual stores. In particular, Bizrate.com rates vendors on the basis of consumers' evaluations concerning several dimensions of the transaction other than solely price, in particular: ease of ordering, web-site performance, customer support and on-time delivery. Finally, while Section 4 draws some concluding remarks, Appendix A outlines a two-stage game model which aims at illustrating the possible arise of an equilibrium characterized by the play of service- premium strategies by a firm operating in a duopoly e-marketplace.

## 2    THE EMPIRICAL LITERATURE ON PRICE DISPERSION ON THE INTERNET

Numerous previous studies have detected the presence of substantial price dispersion in Internet markets for homogeneous goods. Bailey (1998) found that the range of prices of books, CDs and software in 1996 and 1997 was roughly the same and eventually greater in the electronic rather than in the physical marketplace. Clemons et al. (1998) analysed the online travel industry and found that differences on airline tickets could vary by 20%, even after controlling for product heterogeneity. Brynjolfsson and Smith (2000a) compared posted prices (i.e. actual price except tax, shipping and handling, transportation charges) for books and CDs from February 1998 to May 1999, finding that Internet store prices differed by an average of 33% for books and 25% for CDs, with price differentials across Internet retailers that could reach a maximum of 47%. At the same time, they found that once prices are weighted by retailer popularity as a proxy for market shares, the price dispersion on the two virtual markets decreases significantly and becomes lower than in conventional channels. They interpret this result as possible evidence that retailers' heterogeneity in terms of branding, awareness and trust is relevant in explaining the observed price dispersion on the Internet. Brynjolfsson and Smith (2000b) and Smith and Brynjolsson (2001) found very similar results in their empirical analyses of consumer behavior at shopbots. In particular, data gathered by a shopbot specialised on the sale of books reveal that the lowest priced offer is on average 32% more convenient than the tenth lowest priced offer. Always referring to the book industry, significant price dispersion in the cyber marketplace is also detected by Clay et al. (2001). They examined the prices of 399 books on a daily basis between August 1999 and January 2000, exploring, among the other issues, the relationship between market structure and price dispersion on the Internet. They found that more competition seems first to increase and then to decrease price dispersion in the virtual marketplace. Substantial levels of price dispersion are also found by

Clay et al. (2002) and Baylis and Perloff (2002). The first paper considers a sample of 107 book titles collected in April 1999 and finds that standard deviation as a fraction of average price ranged from 0.10 for hardcover books to 0.18 for paperback bestsellers. The second one analyses the digital camera and scanner retail markets, and in particular 41 firms that sold the Olympus C2000Z camera and 28 firms that sold the HP 6300 scanner, for a collection period that went from September to December 1999. Again, the authors find enormous price differentials for both goods: over the observation period, the price range for the camera and the scanner were $342 (42% of the average price) and $106 (29% of the average price) respectively.

So, overall, the presence of significant price dispersion on the Internet is near universally recognized. But for what concerns the cause of the violation of the "law of one price" in Internet markets for homogeneous goods, there is no general consensus. Basically, three distinct hypotheses have been formulated by previous contributions. The first one, investigated by Baylis and Perloff (2002), points to the immaturity of the market. In fact, price dispersion could be the result of the behavior of firms that are adjusting to the competitive equilibrium, trying to frequently undercut rivals. If this is the case, we should observe vigorous competition and price dispersion will be only a temporary phenomenon that will end when price will converge to marginal cost. The empirical evidence produced by Baylis and Perloff (2002) strongly rejects this hypothesis since price-rank ordering of virtual stores is persistent along time. A similar conclusion is also drawn by Clay et al. (2001) who found a very low intertemporal standard deviation of book prices, implying that virtual stores do not change prices very often.

The second hypothesis deals with the violation of one of the Bertrand assumptions: product homogeneity. In Appendix A, a two-stage game model is outlined in order to highlight how services heterogeneity pursued by firms in a market for a homogeneous good can lead to an equilibrium characterized by significant price dispersion. As already said, the virtual environment has enlarged the strategy space at disposal of vendors to rival each other and has probably increased the relevance of retail strategies different from price. If we let the typical Internet shopper base its purchase decision not only on price and brand reputation, but also on the other several characteristics connected with the implied transaction, and if we reasonably assume that virtual stores can pre-determine to a great extent the "quality" level of the transactions effectuated in their web sites (through customer care, delivery and shipping conditions, return policy choices, etc.), each virtual store is not forced anymore to adopt a pricing policy similar to those of its rivals. Rather it has room to maneuver over the levels of its strategic variables: it can change them in such a way that the damaging effect of a variation in one policy variable on the firm's market share or its rivals' will be offset by the change in an other policy variable. If purchase decisions are influenced by the level of customer care and all the other transaction-related services settled by virtual stores, a firm may have the incentive to raise its efforts respect to rivals in one or more of these strategic variables in order to increase the price of its items. On the other way round, a virtual store which decides or is forced to invest less resources than direct competitors on the well-functioning of its web site or in the infrastructure supporting goods order and delivery, will presumably have the chance to settle a lower price without expecting retaliation from its opponents. If this holds true, as highlighted by Varian (1999) and de Figueiredo (2000), two groups of virtual stores will emerge: those with low services and low prices and those offering high services at relatively high prices. Various tests on the service-premium hypothesis have not yielded clear results yet. Brinjolfsson and Smith (2000a) acknowledge the potential role played by services heterogeneity in explaining price dispersion in the on-line book industry, albeit their empirical analysis do not support this view. They find in fact that observed services do not vary significantly across retailers or are negatively correlated with price. They suggest that heterogeneity in unobserved store characteristics may account for a significant portion of the price dispersion they detect. Brinjolfsson and Smith (2000b) in their first study on consumer behavior at shopbots, find that branded retailers hold significant price advantages versus unbranded stores, while branded retailers offer only slightly better services than those provided by unbranded retailers. Smith and Brinjolfsson (2001) put on evidence that shopbot customers are very sensitive to price, but they also find that those who care about delivery times are less sensitive to price convenience and more sensitive to brand reputation. Clay et al. (2002) regress the price of books on some means of differentiation used by virtual stores such as reviews, recommendations, loyalty programs, gift certificates and many others: their empirical study suggests that these amenities are not significantly correlated with price, but that some stores (i.e. Amazon) succeed in temporarily differentiating their products respect to direct competitors (i.e. Barnesandnoble.com and Borders.com). The analysis of Baylis and Perloff (2002) is the only one that strongly rejects the service-premium hypothesis. In fact, both equations modelling the price of the digital camera and the price of the flatbed scanner on a series of covariates capturing various firm characteristics including shipping and restocking fees, website performance of stores and the Bizrate overall store rating reveal a null or negative impact of the above mentioned variables.

Other than product homogeneity, price dispersion on the Internet is usually explained with the violation of another Bertrand assumption: that of zero search costs and hence perfectly informed consumers. In the presence of positive search costs bore by a portion of consumers, price differentials would reflect different firm strategies, with some stores selling at relatively high prices to only uninformed consumers (i.e. inefficient searchers) and other stores which target also informed consumers (i.e. efficient searchers) and therefore charge lower prices (see Salop 1977, Salop and Stiglitz 1977, Varian 1980). Also in this case, the empirical evidence is rather mixed. On one hand, Clay et al. (2001) suggest that many Internet shoppers may not be engaging in search despite of its low cost. On the other hand, Brinjolfsson and Smith (2000a) consider heterogeneity in customer awareness another possible source of price dispersion, but their data reveal that the presence of asymmetrically informed consumers can not be regarded as a crucial factor[4]. Finally, Baylis and Perloff (2002) consider the presence of consumers characterised by different time preferences as the main cause of price dispersion on the Internet. In particular, the negative impact of many firm characteristics on the price of both products (digital camera and flatbed scanner) are interpreted by the authors as a proof that virtual stores providing relatively high level services, are incentived to charge low prices so to attract informed other than uninformed consumers.

The foregoing analysis of the existing literature in price dispersion on the Internet suggests some important remarks and draws some possible implications for future research directions. First, following Brynjolfsson and Smith (2000a), the mixed results produced by previous studies suggest that price dispersion on the Internet may not strongly rely on a single source

---

[4] A straightforward prediction of models of asymmetrically informed agents and models of positive search cost (Salop and Stiglitz 1977, Varian 1980) is that retailers with the lowest prices should attract more consumers, since they are able to get sales from all the informed consumers in addition to the share of uninformed consumers. The on-line book industry analysed by Brinjolfsson and Smith (2000a) does not support this prediction, since Amazon.com is the industry leader in market shares but not in price convenience.

but instead it is likely that several factors jointly contribute to price differentials. Second, the tests conducted so far on the service-premium hypothesis have been prevalently carried out only on the basis of the number and the level of promised services without taking into account consumers' evaluations of the effective quality of these. Since stores may largely differ in reliability, many of these tests are likely to be only partially informative. Consequently, the inclusion into the analysis of some measures of customer satisfaction or of some other reliable proxy for service quality would be desirable in order to better assess the effective importance of service-premium strategies. Third, if price dispersion in many Internet markets is effectively caused by the large presence among shoppers of uninformed consumers, it remains to be explained why this occurs if stores are only a click away one from the other. In other words, why consumers do not engage in search in markets served by shopbots, which reduce so significantly search costs for products compared to "brick and mortar" markets? If brand loyalty, strong time preferences among consumers, limited awareness of infomediaries or shopbots are all plausible reasons and are often advocated as possible explanations for such behavior, a real assessment of their effective role remains to be fully investigated.

## 3   THE EMPIRICAL ANALYSIS

The main aim of the present paper is to shed some light on the relevance of the service-premium hypothesis in explaining price dispersion in virtual markets for homogeneous goods. At this scope, an empirical investigation is carried out through data collected on a "price and quality comparison" web site, Bizrate.com, which reports consumers' evaluations about price convenience and other characteristics of various retailers[5]. In particular, in the second week of June 2002, I selected the whole sample listed by Bizrate.com of 31 virtual stores which sell exclusively homogeneous physical items (books and magazines, CDs, videos), taking into account only those stores which have received more than 500 reviews of customers in the previous three months and that participated in the Bizrate.com "Customer certified" program[6]. Data on the selected sample have been also collected in the last week of April 2003: in this case, information was available only for 26 virtual stores, since 5 firms were found not to be "customer certified" or were not present in the shopbot list anymore. Bizrate.com provides ratings (on a 0-10 scale) for several services bundled to the sale of products and these ratings are based both on information collected from customers who have directly purchased from stores and on reviews provided by Internet shoppers members of Bizrate.com. In particular merchant's rating is computed as follows for the various conditions of sale:

---

[5] Bizrate.com does not charge stores for evaluation or listing in order to provide consumers of unbiased information. Bizrate.com updates ratings weekly.

[6] Stores participate in the program if they allow Bizrate.com to collect feedback continuously and directly from their customers as they check-out and after the date of fulfillment through follow-up e-mails. Some few stores have been initially excluded from the econometric analysis because of their niche nature.

$$\frac{\left(\begin{array}{cc}\text{Average Survey} & \times & \text{Number of} \\ \text{Scores} & & \text{Surveys}\end{array}\right) + \left(\begin{array}{cc}\text{Average Member} & \times & \text{Number of} \\ \text{Scores} & & \text{Member Reviews}\end{array}\right)}{\left(\begin{array}{ccc}\text{Number of} & + & \text{Number of} \\ \text{Surveys} & & \text{Member Reviews}\end{array}\right)}$$

Figure 1. Method of Computation of Stores' Ratings. Screen image from Bizrate.com

Following the line of reasoning developed in the previous section, data on store ratings based on consumers' evaluations should enable us to better assess services heterogeneity across virtual stores. In this way, we are in fact able to take into account the actual quality of the services associated to the delivery of the homogeneous item. Moreover, as shown in Figure 1, note that Bizrate ratings are based both on reviews filled out by consumers who are presumably frequent users of Bizrate.com (Bizrate members) and on surveys collected from consumers who did not necessarily access stores using this or any other shopbot. Allegedly, data are likely to reflect a significant level of heterogeneity across stores' reviewers in terms of sensitiveness towards price and service quality and therefore provide a reasonably adequate testbed of the hypothesis we are concerned with in this work.

Turning to the core of the empirical analysis, collected information on store ratings was about the following selling-related dimensions: price convenience (PCONV), customer support (CS), ease of ordering (EASE), web site performance (WEB), ability to delivery on time goods (DEL). Table 1 illustrates descriptive statistics of these variables.

Table 1. Descriptive Statistics of Bizrate's Store Ratings

| Variables | Min | Max | Mean | S.D. |
|-----------|-----|-----|------|------|
| PCONV | 4.8 | 9.5 | 8.65 | 0.64 |
| CS | 4.8 | 9.5 | 8.17 | 1.04 |
| EASE | 6.9 | 9.4 | 8.74 | 0.48 |
| WEB | 7.7 | 9.2 | 8.58 | 0.38 |
| DEL | 4.4 | 9.7 | 8.40 | 0.98 |

Legend: N° of observations is 57.

On average, ratings are quite high and significantly concentrated around mean values. As a practical matter, no firm was found to score a rating inferior to six in more than two categories in the same week. For what concerns ratings on price convenience, it does not emerge a picture of fierce competition. Considering only virtual stores observed in both periods, two firms were within the five top-ranked firms as in the first as in the second week. Looking at the bottom of the ranking, three virtual stores were within the five least price convenient stores in both weeks. These results seem not to be consistent with the hypothesis that price dispersion reflects an immature market that is adjusting toward a competitive equilibrium, since this explanation should predict vigorous price competition, with firms that change very often their price-rank position because they continuously try to undercut rivals. On the other hand, data seem more consistent with those of Baylis and Perloff (2002) and Clay et al. (2001), with high-price firms that tend to remain high-price firms over time.

Focusing on the test of the service-premium strategies hypothesis, Table 2 reports estimates of the ceteris paribus impact of consumers' evaluations of transaction-related services on the perceived price convenience of virtual stores. In particular, column (1) illustrates the estimation of a fixed effects model and column (2) shows OLS regression results on pooled data.

Before commenting the results, two technical remarks are in order. First, it appears from the goodness of fit statistics that the fixed effects account for a large part of the variation in the endogenous variable. Moreover, a likelihood ratio test rejects the null hypothesis of no group effects ($\chi2 =125.0$). These results point to the existence of a significant bias of the estimated parameters of the pooled regression model due to omitted variables (group effects). Second, the Hausmann statistics argues in favor of the fixed effects model over the random effects model ($\chi2 = 60.9$).

Table 2. Fixed Effects and Pooled Estimates of Stores' Price Convenience

| Variables | Fixed Effects Model | | Pooled Model | |
|-----------|---------------------|---------|--------------|---------|
| CS | -0.511** | (0.197) | -0.039 | (0.216) |
| EASE | 0.434* | (0.247) | 0.123 | (0.353) |
| WEB | 0.048 | (0.336) | -0.131 | (0.461) |
| DEL | -0.387** | (0.159) | -0.010 | (0.216) |
| Constant | - | - | 2.272*** | (0.640) |
| R2 | 0.889 | | 0.007 | |

Legend: variables have been transformed into logarithms. * Significance level greater than 90%; ** Significance level greater than 95%; *** Significance level greater than 99%. Standard errors in parentheses. N° of observations is 57.

Given these results of the diagnostic tests, I exclusively focus on the estimated parameters of the fixed effects model. Only two transaction-related services have a negative effect on the price convenience of stores: customer support and ability to deliver on time goods. The coefficients associated to these variables are statistically significant at 95%. In particular, everything else being equal, a 10% increase in consumers' evaluations about shopper support and delivery times reduces consumers' ratings on price convenience of circa 5.1% and 3.8% respectively. For what concerns the other two regressors, website performance does not have any influence on the price convenience of a virtual store, while the parameter associated to the variable capturing the ease of ordering is positive and statistically significant at 90%. Therefore, as expectations based on the service-premium hypothesis, price convenience of virtual stores appears to be negatively correlated with the effort produced by retailers in some selling-related activities, and in particular in customer care and in fulfilling promised delivery schedules. In this respect, the competitive structure of the market appears to be consistent with the vision suggested by Varian (1999): the more a virtual store devotes resources to those policies which usually sustain its sales in the e-marketplace, the more it is able to command high prices. Clearly investing in selling-related policies with the scope of better satisfying consumer needs and increasing customer loyalty can be profitable for a virtual store as long as these high quality services make Internet shoppers less dependent on the own and the rivals' pricing policies (see Appendix A).

But not all services appear to be the same. In other words, the service-premium hypothesis appears not to hold true for every type of service. Virtual stores' strategies in fact which aim at improving the overall web performance of the site or easing the items ordering process do not allow virtual stores to lessen price convenience. Therefore, from stores' point of view, spending a large amount of resources in these latter policies clearly appears to be less convenient than investment in customer care and in capabilities to delivery on time items. Summarizing, if the main question that addresses this paper is: are service-premium strategies relevant for explaining price dispersion in the Internet marketplace? The answer is yes, but it is limited to some specific transaction-related activities.

## 4   CONCLUSION

The structural conditions on which e-commerce takes place have led to the prediction that Internet retailers will charge the same price for homogeneous goods. But as many empirical contributes have highlighted, the "law of one price" does not hold in cyber markets. This paper analyses the motives individuated by the existing empirical literature for explaining why a conspicuous level of price dispersion emerges in an e-marketplace, and concentrates its attention on one in particular: the service-premium hypothesis. According to this view, consumers are willing to pay a high price provided that a high quality level of related services is associated to the transaction, and naturally firms avoid to compete directly on price because of low profits and therefore try to differentiate themselves in the quality of such services. If this holds true, in a market for a homogeneous good, we should expect the coexistence of virtual stores which offer low prices but also low levels of service quality and virtual stores which target those consumers who are less sensitive to price but also more willing to pay a premium for high-level services. Existing empirical research on the test of the service-premium hypothesis has so far produced mixed results, but overall, there is little evidence in support of this view. The present work differs from the previous ones especially because it uses data on consumers' evaluations about the characteristics of the virtual stores. This approach permits to better control differences in the quality of the services bundled to the sale of the homogeneous item. The analysis conducted on a sample of Internet retailers selling CDs, books, magazines and videos and listed in one of the most known shopbot, Bizrate.com., suggests that service-premium strategies exist but do not apply to the whole universe of the selling-related activities. In particular, to an increase of store ratings in customer support and in the ability to deliver on time goods is associated a reduction in price convenience perceived by Internet shoppers. The same negative effect on price convenience do not hold for other selling-related dimensions as the overall website performance in terms of layout, links, pictures, speed and the ease of ordering.

# 5   APPENDIX A

The following analysis aims at studying if virtual stores operating in a market for a homogeneous good may optimally choose to differentiate themselves from direct competitors through the provision of selling-related services of high quality, thus enabling them to charge higher prices than rivals. At this scope, consider a virtual market, with two stores that sell quantities $q_1$ and $q_2$ of the same good. Demand is derived from a continuum of identical consumers with quasi-linear utility functions to yield:

$$q_1 = a_1 - b_1 p_1 + c_1 p_2$$
$$q_2 = a_2 - b_2 p_2 + c_2 p_1; \tag{1}$$

where $p_i$ indicates firm's i price and $a_i$, $b_i$ and $c_i$ (i = 1,2) are positive parameters.

In order to effectuate a positive level of sales both stores have to invest $E_i \, \varepsilon \, [\bar{E}; \infty[$ in selling-related activities (customer care, web site performance, etc.). The chosen level of $E_i$ affects price elasticity ($b_i$) and cross price elasticity ($c_i$) of the demand faced by each virtual store, and more specifically $b_i'(E_i) \leq 0$ and $c_i'(Ei) \leq 0$: an increase in the efforts produced by a store in order to make easier and more pleasant the transaction process makes in turn its perceived demand less dependent on the own and the rival's pricing policies. Competition among stores can be modeled as a two-stage game: in stage I, firms simultaneously choose investment levels ($E_1$; $E_2$); in stage II, firms choose prices given the particular perceived demands determined by the choice of ($E_1$; $E_2$) in stage I. Then, it is assumed that $a_1 > a_2$, that is store 1 has a "brand reputation" advantage versus store 2. I focus on sub-game perfect equilibria for this game, so that in choosing $E_i$ in the first stage, each firm takes into account its optimal play in the second stage. In particular, I will analyze if and under which conditions a Bertrand-Nash equilibrium characterized by heterogeneity on stores' selling-related policies emerges. The game is solved recursively. In stage II, store i chooses $p_i$ to maximize its profits. Stores 1 and 2 will maximize respectively:

$$\Pi_1 = p_1(a_1 - b_1(E_1)p_1 + c_1(E_1)p_2) - E_1$$
$$\Pi_2 = p_2(a_2 - b_2(E_2)p_2 + c_2(E_2)p_1) - E_2. \tag{2}$$

This yields the following prices as solutions to the second-stage of the game:

$$p_1 = \frac{2a_1b_2 + a_2c_1}{4b_1b_2 - c_1c_2}$$
$$p_2 = \frac{2a_2b_1 + a_1c_2}{4b_1b_2 - c_1c_2}. \tag{3}$$

Virtual stores' reduced-form payoffs in stage II are found by substituting (3) into (2):

$$\Pi_1 = \frac{b_1(4a_1^2b_2^2 + 4a_1a_2b_2c_1 + a_2^2c_1^2)}{(4b_1b_2 - c_1c_2)^2} - E_1$$
$$\Pi_2 = \frac{b_2(4a_2^2b_1^2 + 4a_1a_2b_1c_2 + a_1^2c_2^2)}{(4b_1b_2 - c_1c_2)^2} - E_2. \tag{4}$$

In stage I, firms will have to choose the optimal level of $E_i$. Consider first, a symmetric possible configuration of equilibrium, given by $E_1 = E_2 = E$. In this case, the homogeneous good is sold with the same level of associated services by the two virtual stores, so that $b_1 = c_1 = b_2 = c_2 = \alpha$.

Substituting $b_1 (E^*) = c_1 (E^*) = b_2 (E^*) = c_2 (E^*) = \alpha$ into (3) and (4), we therefore obtain the level of prices and the consequent profits of the two stores once they match each other strategies in selling-related activities:

$$p_1 = \frac{2a_1 + a_2}{3\alpha}; p_2 = \frac{2a_2 + a_1}{3\alpha}$$

$$\Pi_1 = \frac{(2a_1 + a_2)^2}{9\alpha} - E^*; \Pi_2 = \frac{(2a_2 + a_1)^2}{9\alpha} - E^* . \tag{5}$$

Store 1 will always settle a higher price and will earn a greater profit than store 2. In this case the level of price dispersion and the difference in the payoffs between the two stores will exclusively depend on the relative "brand reputation" advantage possessed by store 1. Then, consider the opposite case represented by an asymmetric possible configuration of equilibrium, and more specifically assume that while firm 2 plays $E^*$, firm 1 overcomes its competitor and chooses to play $E_1 = E^+ \geq E_2 = E^*$. Own price elasticity and cross-price elasticity will now be defined by $b_1 = c_1 = \beta$ and $b_2 = c_2 = \alpha$; with $\beta < \alpha$.

Prices settled by the two virtual stores will now be given by the following expressions:

$$p_1 = \frac{2a_1\alpha + a_2\beta}{3\alpha\beta}$$

$$p_2 = \frac{2a_2\beta + a_1\alpha}{3\alpha\beta} \tag{6}$$

and firms' payoffs by:

$$\Pi_1 = \frac{4a_1^2\alpha^2 + 4a_1a_2\alpha\beta + a_2^2\beta^2}{9\alpha^2\beta} - E^+$$

$$\Pi_2 = \frac{4a_2^2\beta^2 + 4a_1a_2\alpha\beta + a_1^2\alpha^2}{9\alpha\beta^2} - E^* . \tag{7}$$

Focusing on the asymmetric configuration $(E^+, E^*)$, this will be a Nash equilibrium of the decision game only if $\Pi_1 (E^+, E^*) \geq \Pi_1 (E^*, E^*)$ and $\Pi_2 (E^+, E^*) \geq \Pi_2 (E^+, E^+)$ are both fulfilled, more specifically if both the following expressions are verified:

$$\frac{4a_1^2\alpha^2 + 4a_1a_2\alpha\beta + a_2^2\beta^2}{9\alpha^2\beta} - E^+ \geq \frac{(2a_1 + a_2)^2}{9\alpha} - E^*$$

$$\frac{4a_2^2\beta^2 + 4a_1a_2\alpha\beta + a_1^2\alpha^2}{9\alpha\beta^2} - E^* \geq \frac{(2a_2 + a_1)^2}{9\beta} - E^+ . \tag{8}$$

Having defined $\Delta E = E^+ - E^*$; (8) reduces to:

$$\frac{(2a_2 + a_1)^2}{9\beta} - \frac{4a_2^2\beta^2 + 4a_1a_2\alpha\beta + a_1^2\alpha^2}{9\alpha\beta^2} \le \Delta E$$

$$\le \frac{4a_1^2\alpha^2 + 4a_1a_2\alpha\beta + a_2^2\beta^2}{9\alpha^2\beta} - \frac{(2a_1 + a_2)^2}{9\alpha} \tag{9}$$

Necessary condition for (9) to be fulfilled is:

$$4\alpha\beta(\alpha - \beta)(a_2^2 - a_1^2) + (\alpha - \beta)(a_2^2\beta^2 - a_1^2\alpha^2) < 0; \tag{10}$$

which is always verified for $\beta < \alpha$. Therefore, as long as an increase in E reduces the elasticity of the perceived demand by virtual stores respect to their and rivals' prices [and $\Delta E$ is bounded as indicated in (9)], a Nash equilibrium characterized by the play of different strategies in selling-related activities always emerges[7]. The equilibrium price charged by store 1 (high services) is always greater than the equilibrium price settled by store 2 (low services). Note also price dispersion associated to the asymmetric configuration of equilibrium is always greater than the one originated by matching selling-related policies.

## 6   REFERENCES

Bailey, J. P. (1998), "Intermediation and Electronic Markets: Aggregation and Pricing in Internet Commerce", Ph.D. Dissertation, Technology, Management and Policy, Massachusetts Institute of Technology, Cambridge, MA.

Baylis, K. And Perloff, J. (2002), "Price Dispersion on the Internet: Good Firms and Bad Firms", *Review of Industrial Organization*, Vol. 21, pp. 305-324.

Bhaskar, V. (1988), "The Kinked Demand Curve – A Game-Theoretic Approach", *International Journal of Industrial Organization*, Vol. 6, No. 3, pp. 373-384.

Briynjolfsson, E. and Smith, M. D. (2000a), "Frictionless Commerce? A Comparison of Internet and Conventional Retailers", *Management Science*, Vol. 46, No. 4, pp. 563-585.

Briynjolfsson, E. and Smith, M. D. (2000b), "The Great Equalizer? Consumer Choice Behavior at Internet Shopbots", *mimeo*.

Clay K., Krishnan R. and Wolff, E. (2001), "Prices and Price Dispersion on the Web: Evidence from the Online Book Industry", *Journal of Industrial Economics*, Vol. 49, No. 4, pp.521-540.

Clay K., Krishnan R., Wolff E. and Fernandes, D. (2002), "Retail Strategies on the Web: Price and Non-price Competition in the Online Book Industry", *Journal of Industrial Economics*, Vol. 50, No. 3, pp. 351- 367.

Clemons E. K., Il-Horn H. and Hitt, L. M. (1998), "The Nature of Competition in Electronic Markets: an Empirical Investigation of Online Travel Agent Offering", *Working Paper*, Wharton School of the University of Pennsylvania.

---

[7] Note that the opposite case where the less advantaged store increases its effort in selling-related activities respect to the rival and plays $E^+$ (i.e. $a_1 < a_2$), it is relatively more difficult to be observed. Necessary but not sufficient condition for the emergence of such Nash equilibrium is that the disadvantage in terms of consumers' perception ($a_1 - a_2 < 0$) is offset by the returns of the additional investment in $E$ ($\alpha - \beta > 0$).

de Figueiredo, J. (2000), "Finding Sustainable Profitability in Electronic Commerce", *Sloan Management Review*, Summer, pp.41-52.

Friedman, J. W. (1983), *Oligopoly Theory*, Cambridge University Press, Cambridge.

Hall, R. L. and Hitch, C. J. (1939), "Price Theory and Business Behavior", *Oxford Economic Papers*, Vol. 2, pp. 12-45.

Helander, M. J. and Khalid, H. M. (2000), "Modeling the Customer in Electronic Commerce", *Applied Ergonomics*, Vol. 31, No. 6, pp. 609-619.

Maskin, E. and Tirole, J. (1988), "A Theory of Dynamic Oligopoly, II: Price Competition, Kinked Demand Curves and Edgeworth Cycles", *Econometrica*, Vol. 56, No. 3, pp. 571-599.

Rothschild, R. (1992), "A Simple Proof of Sweezy's 'Kinked Demand' Conjecture", *Scottish Journal of Political Economy*, Vol. 39, No. 1, pp. 69-75.

Salop, S. C. (1977), "The Noisy Monopolist: Imperfect Information, Price Dispersion and Price Discrimination", *The Review of Economic Studies*, Vol. 44, No. 3, pp. 393-406.

Salop, S. C. and Stiglitz, J. E. (1977), "Bargains and Ripoffs: a Model of Monopolistically Competitive Price Dispersion", *The Review of Economic Studies*, Vol. 44, No. 3, pp. 493-510.

Smith, M. D. and Brynjolfsson, E. (2001), "Consumer Decision-making at an Internet Shopbot: Brand Still Matters", *Journal of Industrial Economics*, Vol. 49, No. 4, pp. 541- 571.

Stigler, G. (1978), "The Literature of Economics: The Case of the Kinked Oligopoly Demand Curve", *Economic Inquiry*, Vol. 16, No. 2, pp. 185-204.

Sweezy, P. M.(1939), "Demand Under Conditions of Oligopoly", *Journal of Political Economy*, Vol. 47, No. 4, pp. 568-573.

Varian, H. R. (1980), "A Model of Sales", *American Economic Review*, Vol. 70, No. 4, pp. 651-659.

Varian, H. R. (1999), "Market Structure in the Network Age", *Paper for Understanding the Digital Economy Conference*, Department of Commerce, Washington D. C.

Global Economy and Digital Society
E. Bohlin, S. Levin, N. Sung and C-H. Yoon (Editors)

# CHAPTER 9

# Disclosure of Source Code
# to a Technologically Advanced Entrant

Yong Yeop Sohn[*]
*Department of Economics, Chonnam National University, Gwangju*

Hun-Wha Yang[*]
*Korea Information Management Institute for Small and Medium Enterprises (KIMI), Seoul*

**Abstract.** This chapter examines the effect on the market of enforced disclosure of private technological information by an antitrust agency, and the role played by compatibility choices and the technological gap between competing goods in determining market structure. To this end, a two-period two-firm model, in which a firm exists as a monopoly in the first period, and another firm with a technologically advanced good enters in the second period, is applied. On the basis of this modeling and a review of case studies, it is concluded that, in situations where a monopolistic incumbent wields its private technological information as an entry barrier, disclosure of source code to competitors contributes to improving social welfare by addressing inefficient allocation of resources caused by path dependence. An open source software policy can also be justified for getting rid of an entry barrier when technology improves gradually.

## 1    INTRODUCTION

For the last few years, there have been a number of discussions on various issues with regard to the Microsoft Case. The controversial debates seem to be attributed not only to the size of Microsoft but also to the characteristics of its business. Of course, Microsoft is the biggest software company in the world, taking over 90% of the operating software of PCs worldwide. On the other hand, antitrust agency in the United States is not familiar with information goods of high technology. Behaviors of firms producing goods, which have different characteristics from the goods of the conventional industrialized era, are measured by old judiciary standards.

---

[*] The authors gratefully acknowledge the valuable comments and suggestions of anonymous referees, which improved the paper significantly. This study was financially supported by a special grant for promoting joint research in the Humanity and Social Sciences of Chonnam National University.

Compared to traditional industries, information goods require high fixed costs to develop but trivial marginal cost to reproduce the already developed good. That means that information goods have strong economies of scale in supply. Furthermore, operating systems software like Windows has another special feature of network externality, which means that a good's value increases as the number of its consumers increases. In that sense, network externality means economies of scale in demand. The positive feedback between the economies of scale in demand and supply is likely to induce the winner-take-all market structure, as mentioned by Varian (1998), Shapiro and Varian (1999), and Lee and Sohn (2001).

Even though that is the case, the first mover does not always take the whole market, as seen in the VCR industry. To take the first-mover advantage, it is necessary for the first mover to secure a certain size of the installed base of customers. That is, the firm has to take a considerable position in the market in advance of potential competitors. With those conditions fulfilled, the firm can enjoy positive profits for a long time because of double economies of scale. However, a technological standard established by the dominant firm might lock consumers in its particular good and then hinder an entrant of advanced technology from entering the market. Accordingly, the new technology may not survive in the market.[1] Hence it is not easy to forecast the survival of a certain good and the subsequent market structure, based only on the technological superiority of the goods.

Shapiro and Varian (1999) have suggested that firms producing information goods would take one of two strategies of compatibility. The monopolistic incumbent takes either open or control strategy; the new entrant employs either compatible or performance strategy. With the incumbent taking an open strategy that allows an entrant to write its software for the incumbent's, it is the entrant's choice to make its goods compatible or incompatible with the incumbent's. In this game, a combination of the open strategy by the incumbent and the compatible strategy by the entrant brings about the stable market and a smooth transition, since the entrant cooperates with the incumbent in expanding the market itself. But if the entrant takes the performance strategy while the incumbent has an open strategy, the incumbent cannot get any benefit from the entrance of a firm of high technology, because the market would shift to the entrant with some discontinuity. On the other hand, the incumbent can choose to control its technology and charge royalty to anyone who wants to draw its goods on the base of the incumbent. Then, the entrant is forced to make a decision on whether to pay royalty for making its goods compatible or to go forward to fierce warfare to make its good the market standard.

Shapiro and Varian have found that the technology of the entrant's good is a meaningful factor for the entrant in deciding on the compatibility strategy and hence in determining the market structure. The more advanced in technology the entrant is, the more likely it relies on the performance strategy. However, though they understand the relationship between the technological advance of the entrant and the compatibility choice of rival firms correctly, they have failed to investigate the strategic behaviors precisely of those firms involved in the war. Firms are more strategic in the real world than Shapiro and Varian think to be, when they are to decide whether to make their goods compatible or to foreclose their private technological information from access of their competitors.

In the history of antitrust suits in the United States, there have been some cases that are directly related to the strategies of revealing its technological secrets; Eastman Kodak (1979)

---

[1] This phenomenon is called path dependence in the information goods market. Liebowitz and Margolis (2000) provide us with three different types of path dependence.

and Microsoft (2001), among others. Firms in the lawsuits are accused of keeping secrets from all the competitors or opening them discriminatorily only to some of their favorable competitors. Usually those firms do not rely on the patent system. Patent system is supposed to guarantee profitability of a new development at the cost of revealing its private information to the public. But firms capable of controlling its technological secrets are self-confident enough to protect their own secrets by themselves and do not apply for a patent right. These self-protective measures have been the object of legal suits by the antitrust agency or their competitors.

In this paper we examine the relationship between the technological superiority of the entrant and the market structure, and analyze the firms' choice of disclosure of their technological secrets and the effect of their enforced disclosure on the market, provided that both firms in the game know the entrant's technological prowess. In this situation, the incumbent's control policy toward its source code can deter a new competitor from entering. Market equilibrium and social welfare are accordingly affected by the firms' choice of controlling technological secrets. Then, there is a legitimate room for antitrust agency to intervene.

To deal with compatibility choice of firms, and specifically with the effect of disclosure of the technological source code on the market, Section 2 introduces a few legal cases for the source code revelation and a brief trend of open software policies of various governments. Section 3 surveys the literature on technology and compatibility choice of firms. In Section 4 the relationship between the technological superiority of the entrant and market structure is analyzed theoretically, assuming that compatibility is given exogenously. Section 5 investigates firms' strategic choice of compatibility and deals with effectiveness of the source code revelation policy of the antitrust agency. Summary and conclusion are in Section 6.

## 2    CASES RELATED TO DISCLOSURE OF SOURCE CODE

### 2.1    Eastman Kodak Company

Technological information of a good, which is directly related to its function, is one of the vital factors for its success in the market. If the good is operated in a system with various kinds of complementary goods, its technological secrets should be shared among the firms producing at least one of those complementary goods, in order to make them more interoperable in the system.

If a firm discloses its technological secrets to a specific firm while excluding others, which are at the same stage in the vertical stream of industries, then the firm offered with the technological information has a strategic advantage over its competitors. When the original firm has market power in its market, it would be easier for its downstream firm with the technological information to take more share of its own market. This kind of leverage strategy has often been found to exist among goods working complementarily in a system.

In the 1970s, Berkey Photo, Inc. alleged in a private antitrust suit against Eastman Kodak Co. that Kodak had monopolized markets for amateur conventional still cameras, conventional photographic film, photo-finishing services, and color print paper. Kodak's market shares all of those markets except for the photo-finishing services reached over 60% at the time of the suit. In the amateur still cameras market, Kodak had taken 60 to 65% of market share since the 1950s. Its share of the film market had been stable at 80 to 90% since 1952. Kodak also took 67% of color print paper market.

Kodak maintained its strong position in the cameras market, thanks to a series of its collateral innovations of films and film formats. In 1963 Kodak introduced the 126 instant-loading format with Kodakcolor X film, and its sales increased by 22%. More decisively, Kodak introduced the 110 film format with Kodakcolor II film in 1972. The new camera that used the 110 cartridges was so successful that it sold 5.1 million units in 1973 while competitors sold 800,000 units. As a result, Kodak's share of the amateur conventional still cameras market jumped to 90% in the U. S.

Berkey Photo, Inc. contended that Kodak, as a dominant firm, was required to get Berkey to the starting line by advising Berkey technical requirements film would need to have when Kodak began shipping new cameras. Kodak is accused of not disclosing technological secrets strategically to take the stronghold in the film market altogether, and that this kind of tying would violate the Section 2 of Sherman Act.

The court accepted that Kodak monopolized cameras, film, and color print paper markets, and that it had secured its monopoly through patents and technological innovations. That is, the court accepted that the technological innovation of Kodak had contributed to building its monopolistic position, and Kodak strategically kept secret its private technological information on their new cameras and films from outside competitors in closely related markets. However, the court ruled that Kodak was not required to advise Berkey about its new cameras prior to their release. Instead, Kodak was entitled to reap the benefits of its technological innovations. It said: "If a firm that has engaged in the risks and expenses of research and development were required in all circumstances to share with its rivals the benefits of those endeavors, this incentive to innovate would very likely be violated. Withholding from others advance knowledge of one's new products, therefore, ordinarily constitutes valid competitive conduct." (Berkey Photo, Inc. v. Eastman Kodak Co., 603 F. 2d 263, 281 (2d Cir. 1979)) In summary, the court conceded that the technological innovation of a branch of business would help build monopolistic market power in its own market, and that access to information on the monopolist's product is essential for manufacturers of collateral products or services to compete effectively in their markets. But the court had consistently held that there was no obligation for the firm to pre-disclose the information because the requirement would tend to discourage aggressive competition in innovation.

## 2.2  Microsoft

The Microsoft case has been attracting many audiences since the U. S. Department of Justice and the attorney generals of 19 states sued against it. As is well known, Microsoft took the dominant share of the operating systems market for personal computers. It was alleged that, attempting to monopolize the internet browser market, it tied anti-competitively its internet browser, Internet Explorer, to its own operating systems software, Windows. (Though the tying behavior was found not guilty in the appeals court)

Both the district and appeals courts found that Microsoft was guilty of monopolizing the operating systems market for personal computers. It suppressed Netscape not to create a cross-operating systems platform on which various applications could be run. Other anti-competitive acts under Section 2 of Sherman Act taken by Microsoft to keep its monopoly position strong are: (1) restrictions on OEM licenses that made OEMs difficult or prohibited to include a second browser, (2) exclusion of Internet Explorer from the add/remove program utility and mixing of browser and operating systems code together, and (3) exclusive arrangement with internet access providers.

Finding these problems, the district court Judge Jackson ruled that, though some of them were not upheld in the appeals court and in the final settlement, Microsoft should take following remedies: (1) breaking up Microsoft according to the lines of business (operating systems and applications) or breaking up Microsoft in three equal parts, (2) forcing Microsoft to disclose applications programming interfaces (APIs) that allow it to include Internet Explorer in the operating system, and (3) forcing Microsoft to give away the Windows source code or to license it to successful bidders in an auction imposed by the government on Microsoft. We are going to look into the issues of the third remedy further afterward.

In the following district court, Judge Kollar-Kotelly again ordered that Microsoft disclose APIs and related documentation to independent software vendors, independent hardware vendors, internet connection providers, and OEMs for the purpose of interoperating with the Windows Operating System Product. The judge also ruled that the Technological Committee (TC) have the power to access to Microsoft's source code to investigate enforcement and compliance with the final judgment and to handle complaints and other inquiries from non-parts.

Though both Judges ordered Microsoft to disclose the source code of the Windows operating system, their meanings of source code were not exactly the same. According to Judge Jackson, Windows operating system product meant the software code (including source code and binary code) of Windows 95, Windows 98, Windows 2000 Professional and their successors, whereas Kollar-Kotelly meant Windows operating system product to be the software code (as opposed to source code) distributed commercially by Microsoft for use with personal computers as Windows 2000 Professional, Windows XP, and their successors. The difference of their meanings of source code caused disparities of remedies. Judge Jackson enforced Microsoft to disclose the source code of Windows free, but Judge Kollar-Kotelly ordered Microsoft to disclose its source code for commercial terms rather than for free by the force of the government.

Even if those remedies had been changed in their contents during the judiciary process up to the final settlement between Microsoft and the Justice Department and some of states involved in the suit, the notion that disclosing the source code of a good of an influencing firm is very important to make the market structure more competitive has been generally accepted. Forcing Microsoft to give away the Windows source code for free or by commercial trade would help lose its monopolistic market power.[2] And other firms having access to the source code would write different applications for each of the evolving version of Windows, which might make all the applications incompatible running on the different versions of Windows.

However, network externality enjoyed owing to the identical operating systems program of Microsoft over the world would probably disappear because of incompatibility, and then consumer surplus would suffer. Now the real big question to be answered is: would the change be benevolent, at last, to the public?

During the time that Microsoft case was tossed up in the courts, the European Commission was really aware of risks of lock-in and has initiated the open source software policies by establishing the Information Society Technologies to handle the related technological

---

[2] Recently, Microsoft has got complaints from its competitors that "its communications licensing program is overly costly and onerous." The Justice Department raised concerns about the Microsoft program in a court filing on the Microsoft's compliance with the final settlement. In response to the filing, Microsoft had made a series of changes intended to make it easier and less expensive for its competitors and partners to license technical information from the company. (The New York Times, July 4, 2003)

problems and the Interchange of Data Between Administration to facilitate data exchange among its member countries. The United Kingdom, among others, has been very active in implementing the open source software policies. Recently some states in the U.S. such as California and Oregon have also legislated the open source software program. Those activities of various governments are justified in the sense that they are to address the lock-in problem occurring in adopting and using a certain kind of software by mandating themselves to buy an alternative or by requiring the software provider to open the source code.

To deal with the relationship between compatibility of goods and resulting market structure and the effect of forced disclosure of source code on the market equilibrium, first, we are going to focus on analyzing the effect of interoperability on the market structure after surveying the studies on the relationship between technology and compatibility.

## 3   TECHNOLOGY AND COMPATIBILITY

Information goods such as computer operating systems, word processing softwares, internet access services, and electronic libraries are used daily by a wide variety of industrial and societal sectors. The value of the information goods increases as the number of consumers increases, as shown by Katz and Shapiro (1985), and Liebowitz and Margolis (1994, 1995). With this network externality, compatibility between related goods becomes an important factor for consumers in deciding their purchases. Consumers tend to use goods of popular formats to make it easier to exchange files or data with other users.

Accordingly, firms have to be serious about whether to make its goods incompatible with other related goods or to open its source code to competitors at the time when they begin to introduce a new technology. Compatibility choice tends to affect the market structure by foreclosing competitors.

Shy (2001) defines compatibility using three criteria. First, a software can work with different hardware brands. Second, files made by a software can be read by another software. Third, two computers can be networked with the same storage device: i.e., the same printer and other peripherals. Shapiro and Varian (1999) show that compatibility can be a strategic choice for a firm. If the entrant's goods were not superior to the incumbent's, the entrant would let its goods be compatible with the incumbent's and enter the market, sharing the network with the incumbent. However, if the entrant's goods were superior to the incumbent's, the entrant would introduce incompatible goods and manage to dominate the whole market. In contrast, the incumbent would not allow its goods to be compatible with the entrant's without paying for using its source code.

As for technology, Katz and Shapiro (1986) show that a sponsored firm, which is a firm with private rights to a technology, expands its investment to promote the technology, and illustrates their possible outcomes of their model. First, the incumbent with a superior technology has the strategic advantage when no sponsor exists in the market; second, the sponsored technology has the advantage even if that technology is inferior; and third, the potentially superior technology may be adopted when competition with sponsored technologies exists.

Thum (1994), contrary to other literatures, argues that inefficiency in resource allocation caused by network externality can be attenuated if firms use a variety of contracts to compete for larger market share: simple market contracts where price discrimination between old and new users is impossible; upgrade contracts where firms are allowed price discrimination between new and old users; and service contracts where price paid in the first period includes the delivery of all the future versions. Choi and Thum (1998) show that consumers do not wait for technologically superior goods because firms quickly adopt the existing technology. In addition, a consumer with early knowledge of this aspect accepts goods using the incumbent's technology.

However, Econonomides (1995) analyzes whether the main supplier, which has exclusive rights as the technology creator, has any incentive to share this technology with competitors despite the lack of mechanism for reaching agreement in the market. He asserts that expansion of the network supplies the firm with opportunities for larger production, creating an incentive to invite competition. That is, benefit from increased network externality is greater than loss from more severe competition.

Sohn and Yang (2001) investigate the relationship between the technological superiority of a new firm and the market structure by assuming that compatibility is given exogenously. Their analysis is summarized in Section 4 below.

## 4    MARKET STRUCTURE WITH GIVEN COMPATIBILITY

To investigate how compatibility of a good affects market equilibrium, we applied a two-period two-firm model, in which we took the following assumptions. First, a firm produces one type of information goods that are durable. Second, a firm exists as a monopoly in the first period, and another firm enters in the second period. Third, firms are supposed to choose their goods' compatibility at the time of their decision of production. Fourth, an entrant of the second period produces a technologically advanced good, and finally the size of the second period market is grown at the rate of $g$. Hence the number of consumers reaches $1 + g$ in the second period, with the number of potential consumers in the first period normalized to 1. At the beginning, the third assumption was not applied, and we assumed instead that interoperability between goods is given exogenously.

Consumers are characterized by their own willingness to pay for good 1 produced by the incumbent, firm 1. The type of consumers has a uniform distribution over 0 to 1. The technological superiority of the new good is notated by $a$, meaning an increased willingness to pay of each consumer. Prices of good 1 in the first period and second period, are $p_1$ and $p_{11}$, respectively. Price of good 2 produced by the entrant, firm 2, in the second period is $p_{22}$. A consumer can purchase only one unit each period. If a consumer buys the incumbent's good in the first period but wants to buy a new good made by the entrant in the second period, then the consumer has to pay a switching cost of $s$. Change in network externality from the switching is represented by $b(\underline{b} > 0, \bar{b} < 0)$, which is net network externality of switching from good 1 to good 2.[3]

In the incompatible case, the incumbent has already made its mind not to open its source code to anybody. And hence the entrant's decision on compatibility is meaningless in the sense that it does not affect anything in the market. But in the compatible case, the incumbent firm is forced to disclose its source code by the order of the antitrust agency. Only the entrant has a chance to decide on the compatibility of the goods. In both cases, partial (one-way) compatibility is assumed not to be possible.

---

[3] See the more detail in Yang (2003).

If good 1 is not compatible with good 2, consumers gain network externality only from consumers of good 1. Utility of a representative consumer is the sum of his own willingness to pay for good 1 and network effect from good 1's consumers in the first and second period minus the price of good 1. Demand for good 1 in the first period is defined by the number of consumers whose willingness to pay is greater than the consumer who is indifferent between buying a unit of a good in the first period and waiting and buying in the second period. And demand for good 1 in the second period is the number of consumers whose willingness to pay is located from the cut point of the first period demand down to another point of indifference between buying and not buying in the second period.[4]

Firm 1 maximizes its profit in the first period, and firm 2 also maximizes it in the second period, if it decides to enter, by choosing their own price based on demand for each good determined by consumers. Our calculations revealed that the second period market structure will be divided into three parts with respect to the superiority of the new entrant's good, $a$, as shown by the white blocks in Figure 1: (a) monopoly of the incumbent with no new entrance over the range of small superiority of the entrant's technology, $0 < a < p_{22} - p_{11} + \underline{b}$, (b) duopoly of the incumbent and the entrant over the range of moderate superiority of the entrant's technology, $p_{22} - p_{11} + \underline{b} \le a < p_{22} + s + \overline{b}$, and (c) monopoly of the entrant over the range of significant superiority of its technology, $p_{22} + s + b \le a$.

In the compatible case where the incumbent opens its source code to its competitors, consumers have an opportunity to enjoy an expanded network externality since good 1 and good 2 can be connected to each other. Here, we have two different market structures in the second period, as shown by the shaded blocks in Figure 1. There is no monopoly of the incumbent. But instead the co-existence area in this case is much larger than that in the case of incompatibility, $0 \le a \le p_{22} + s$. And the entrant would be the monopoly in the second period if the superiority of its technology were extremely high, as over $p_{22} + s < a$.

Now we are well prepared to examine the firms' strategic choice of compatibility and then the impacts on market equilibrium and the social welfare of the revelation policy of source code forced by antitrust agency. We will find that the government's disclosure policy has a meaning especially when the incompatibility strategy of the incumbent is a tool of entry barrier against a new firm armoured with an advanced technology.

---

[4] Four different types of utility functions are described in Yang (2003).

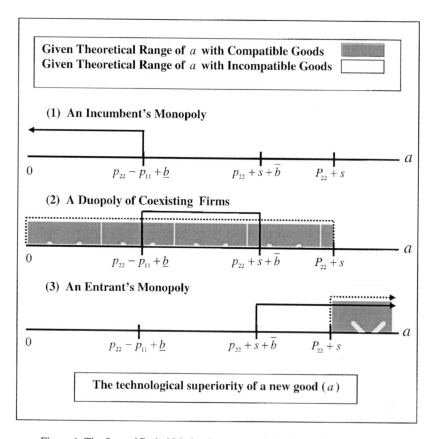

Figure 1. The Second Period Market Structure and the Superiority of a New Good

## 5    COMPATIBILITY CHOICE

To analyze the strategic choice of compatibility, we introduce an antitrust agency that can order firms to disclose their private information on technology to the public. In the real world, the antitrust agency sometimes orders the incumbent to disclose its technological secrets to other competitors just as it did in the Microsoft case when withholding technological information can be used as a tool for establishing monopoly and deterring other firms from entering.

From the analysis in the previous section (and more detailed description in Sohn and Yang (2001), it is not hard to understand that the incompatible case in the previous section is similar to the situation where firms' compatibility choice is endogenous without any government intervention, and that the compatible case in the previous section looks like the situation of government intervention forcing the incumbent to disclose its source code.

In Figure 2, we compare equilibrium profits of firms under government intervention and those of firms without the government intervention. There are a few ranges of technology that show inequalities in profits.[5] Figure 2 tells us that, only when the technological superiority of the entrant is small, the incumbent is interested in the incompatibility strategy. On the other hand, the entrant wants to have its good compatible with the incumbent's in order to use the customer base of the incumbent to its benefit in this case. But the dream of the entrant will not come true because of the incumbent's blocking strategy.

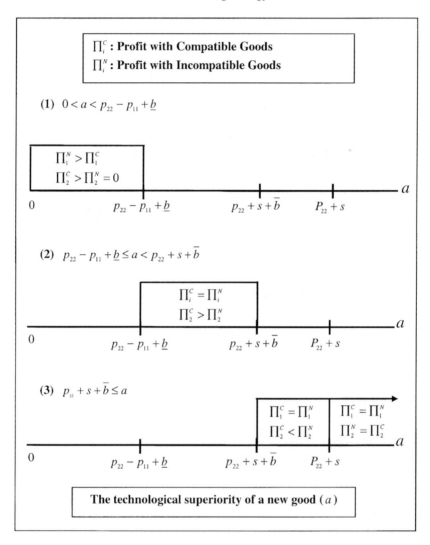

Figure 2. Choice of Compatibility

When the entrant is expected to enter the market with a moderately advanced good, the incumbent does not care about its compatibility strategy since it does know it loses the whole second period market to the entrant. But the entrant is still interested in using the customer base of the incumbent and so makes its good compatible with the incumbent's. If the entrant's good is extremely advanced, even the entrant does not pay attention to get its good to be interoperable since it is capable of taking the whole market without relying on the incumbent's customer base.

It is obvious that, only when the technological superiority of the new good is small, forced disclosure of technological information contributes to the social welfare. Without government intervention, the incumbent would fortify its monopolistic position by using its technological secret as a tool for entry barrier, since the incumbent can get more profit in the incompatible case.

Government intervention on disclosure of the incumbent's source code to competitors contributes to the social welfare only when the technological superiority of the new good is greater than zero but less than the sum of network externality and the gap of prices in the second period, $(a \leq p_{22} - p_{11} + \underline{b})$. In the rest of the cases, $(p_{22} - p_{11} + \underline{b} \leq a)$, government intervention dose not affect market equilibrium.

If the new good is marginally better than the old good in technology, the old one dominates the market without the survival of the new one. Liebowitz and Margolis (1998, 2900) term this phenomenon as path dependence in the network industry. Survival of the QWERTY keyboard in the market through defeating Dvorak is often cited as one of the examples of path dependence. In this very case, government intervention could be justified in addressing inefficient resource allocation.

In the rest of the range, where the technological superiority of the entrant is significant to extreme, the government order to the incumbent to reveal its source code does not affect market equilibrium. The entrant enters the market with technologically advanced good and takes a number of consumers large enough to be profitable in the second period. And if the entrant's technology is extremely advanced, then even the consumers who had bought the incumbent's good in the first period are willing to throw away the old good and buy the new advanced one. In this situation, the entrant cannot find any reason to make its good compatible with the incumbent's. The entrant would take the performance strategy as mentioned by Shapiro and Varian (1999).

In our analysis, when the technological superiority of the entrant is moderate, the entrant finds its interest in making its good compatible while the incumbent does not care much about the compatibility. This situation is similar to the one described by Economides (1995). He shows that the incumbent sometimes takes activities facilitating new entry to enjoy the gains from enlarged network externality with it.

One of the most controversial issues in Microsoft Case was the effect of the revelation of its source code on the market performance. According to our findings in this paper, two interpretations of the Microsoft Case are possible. If Microsoft ships an incompatible operation systems program in a situation where other goods are marginally superior in technology to Microsoft's, the incompatibility strategy of Microsoft could be an entry barrier. However, if Microsoft's good is significantly superior to other goods in technology, and if Microsoft takes the whole market owing to the superiority, it must be the case for the entrant's monopoly established in the past. Now then we can say that the remedy that orders disclosure of the Windows source code is meaningful only when Windows' competitors are marginally superior, if any, to Windows. In that case, Microsoft's strategy to keep its technological information secret without relying on the patent system could be an entry barrier to hold the monopolistic position of Microsoft intact. Open source software policy of the European countries and some states in the U. S. can be justified once again when technology in the targeted software industry improves gradually, in addition to addressing the lock-in problem mentioned previously. If technological development in the area jumps up rapidly, the policy could hardly do anything.

## 6    CONCLUSION

We have seen that the technological difference plays an important role in affecting the market structure and compatibility choice in the expanding information goods market, in which the entrant's good is superior to the incumbent's in technology. The second period market is decisively affected by the technological superiority of the new good. It is found that, with the assumption of incompatible goods, the second period market is, (i) a monopoly of the incumbent with no new entrant when the superiority of the entrant's technology is small; (ii) a duopoly of the co-existing incumbent and the new entrant when it is moderate, and (iii) a monopoly of the entrant when the entrant ships a highly advanced good in technology.

In the compatible case where consumers have an opportunity to enjoy expanded network externality, we have two different market structures in the second period. Without the case of monopoly of the incumbent, the duopoly area is large enough to cover almost the whole range of technological prowess, except for the case of the entrant's monopoly when its technology is extremely high.

It is now clear that, only when the technological superiority of the entrant is small, the incumbent is interested in taking the incompatibility strategy. The entrant's desire to use the customer base of the incumbent by having its good compatible with the incumbent's is infertile because of the incompatibility strategy of the incumbent's. When the entrant tries to enter the market with moderately advanced good, the incumbent does not care about the compatibility strategy whereas the entrant wants to use the customer base of the incumbent and makes its good compatible with the incumbent's. If the entrant's good is extremely advanced, even the entrant does not pay attention to get its good to be compatible. Now, it can take the whole market without relying on the incumbent's customer base.

Consequently, only when the technological superiority of the new good is just small, forced disclosure of technological information contributes to the social welfare. In this case, without government intervention, the incumbent would maintain its monopoly by using its technological information as an entry barrier. The intervention is workable in addressing inefficient resource allocation caused by path dependence.

In this view, the judgment of Judge Jackson to reveal the source code of the Microsoft's Windows has the plausibility of removing an entry barrier of the monopolistic enterprise. However, the final settlement under Judge Kollar-Kotelly advising the release of Windows' source code on a commercial base, which aims to give consistent motivation to developing technology, would help a monopolistic firm set up the entry barrier of charging a high price and hurt technology innovation and the social welfare. This is the problem to face especially when the entrant introduces a good of marginally advanced technology. Open source software policy of the European countries and some states in the U. S. can be justified when technology in the targeted software industry improves gradually.

Here, we do not take into account several important variables for simplicity: costs to develop an improved good, and partial compatibility and/or upgrade of goods. These are factors to be incorporated properly in an extended model in the future.

## 7   APPENDIX

The full features of the theoretical model and mathematical work to derive equilibrium are in Yang (2003). Here we just introduce the beginning part of the model. To the assumptions and notations described in the Section 4, we add one more assumption that the marginal cost of reproduction of an information good is assumed to be zero.

Market demand in the first period is $d_1$, and that in the second period $d_2$. Consumers who use one of the goods in the second period can be divided as follows:

$d_{g_i}$ : consumers who newly come to the market and purchase good $i = 1,2$ in the second period;

$d_{w_i}$ : consumers who enter but do not purchase in the first period, but purchase good $i = 1,2$ in the second period;

$d_{st}$ : consumers who purchase good 1 in the first period and continue to use it through the second period; and

$d_{sw}$ : consumers who purchase good 1 in the first period and switch to good 2 in the second period. (with $d_1 = d_{st}$, $d_{sw} = 0$ ; with $d_1 = d_{sw}$, $d_{st} = 0$ )

### 7.1   A.1 Non-compatible Goods

First, assume that good 1 is not compatible with good 2. Consumers gain network effects only with consumers of the same good. Utility of a representative consumer who buys good 1 in the first period and still use it in the second period, is

$$u_{11}^1 = v - p_1 + kd_1 + \delta kd_2, \tag{1}$$

where $d_i$ is the demand in period $i = 1,2$, $\delta \in [0,1]$ is the discount factor, and $k$ is the network externality factor which affects consumers' purchase, as in Economides(1999).

Denote the utility function of a representative consumer $i$ by $u_{mn}^i$, where the subscripts $m$ and $n$ represent whether a good is bought in the first and second period, respectively; 0 means 'not buy' and 1 is 'buy.' The superscript $i$ stands for the good a consumer uses in the second period.

$$u_{11}^1 = (1-\delta)v - p_1 + (1-\delta)kd_1 + \delta v + \delta k(d_{st} + d_{w_1} + d_{g_1}) \tag{2.1}$$

$$u_{11}^2 = (1-\delta)v - p_1 + (1-\delta)kd_1 + \delta(v + a - p_{22}) + \delta k(d_{sw} + d_{w_2} + d_{g_2}) - \delta s \tag{2.2}$$

$$u_{01}^1 = \delta(v - p_{11}) + \delta k(d_{st} + d_{w_1} + d_{g_1}) \tag{2.3}$$

$$u_{01}^2 = \delta(v + a - p_{22}) + \delta k(d_{sw} + d_{w_2} + d_{g_2}), \tag{2.4}$$

To derive a demand function of each period, we must specify the type of the consumer, $v_{12}^i$, who is indifferent between purchasing a good in the first period or second period, from utility functions (2.1) to (2.4). Similarly, $v_{20}^i$ denotes the type of consumer who is indifferent between purchasing a good in the second period and making no purchase. The superscript from $v_{12}^i$ and $v_{20}^i$ represents good $i = 1,2$, which the critical consumer may buy in the second period.

$$v_{12}^1 = \frac{p_1 - \delta p_{11} - (1-\delta)kd_1}{1-\delta}, \qquad \text{where } u_{11}^1 = u_{01}^1; \tag{3.1}$$

$$v_{12}^2 = \frac{p_1 - (1-\delta)kd_1 + \delta s}{1-\delta}, \qquad \text{where } u_{11}^2 = u_{01}^2; \tag{3.2}$$

$$v_{20}^1 = p_{11} - k(d_{st} + d_{w_1} + d_{g_1}), \qquad \text{where } u_{01}^1 = 0; \text{ and} \tag{3.3}$$

$$v_{20}^2 = p_{22} - a - k(d_{sw} + d_{w_2} + d_{g_2}), \qquad \text{where } u_{01}^2 = 0. \tag{3.4}$$

Consumers whose willingness to pay is higher than $v_{12}^i$ would like to purchase good 1 in the first period and therefore

$$d_1 = 1 - v_{12}^i. \tag{4}$$

Consumers whose type is between $v_{12}^i$ and $v_{20}^i$ wait in the first period and buy goods in the second period and $d_{w_i} = v_{12}^i - v_{20}^i$. The assumption that the market grows at the rate of $g$ implies that all potential consumers are located over [0,1], but the size of the consumer in any interval is increased by $1 + g$ times, as shown in Figure 3. New demand created by the market growth is $d_{g_i} = g(1 - v_{20}^i)$. Therefore, the market demand in the second period is

$$d_2^i = d_{g_i} + d_{w_i} + d_{sw}, \tag{5}$$

where the subscript and superscript, $i = 1,2$ represent the good a consumer buys in the second period.

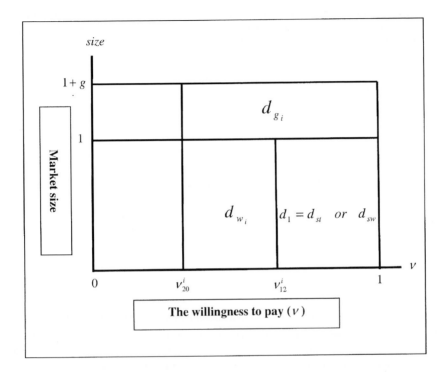

Figure 3. The Market Demand in the Second Period with Non-Compatibility

## 7.2  A.1.2 Compatible Goods

When goods are compatible with each other, consumers enjoy network externality regardless of which good is purchased. Thus, network externality is greater in the compatible market than in the incompatible market. Notations of utility functions for the compatible case are the same as those for incompatible case except for the tilde (~), which indicates the compatible case.

$$\tilde{u}_{11}^{\ 1} = (1-\delta)v - p_1 + (1-\delta)kd_1 + \delta v + \delta k(d_{st} + d_{w_1} + d_{g_1} + d_{sw} + d_{w_2} + d_{g_2}) \tag{6.1}$$

$$\tilde{u}_{11}^2 = (1-\delta)v - p_1 + (1-\delta)kd_1$$
$$+ \delta(v + a - p_{22}) + \delta k(d_{st} + d_{w_1} + d_{g_1} + d_{sw} + d_{w_2} + d_{g_2}) \tag{6.2}$$

$$\tilde{u}_{01}^{\ 1} = \delta(v - p_{11}) + \delta k(d_{st} + d_{w_1} + d_{g_1} + d_{sw} + d_{w_2} + d_{g_2}) \tag{6.3}$$

$$\tilde{u}_{01}^{\ 2} = \delta(v + a - p_{22}) + \delta k(d_{st} + d_{w_1} + d_{g_1} + d_{sw} + d_{w_2} + d_{g_2}) \tag{6.4}$$

The critical consumer, who is indifferent between buying in the first and second periods, or between buying in the second period and not buying at all, is represented in the same way as in the incompatible case, except for the upper tilde

$$\tilde{v}_{12}^1 = \frac{p_1 - \delta p_{11} - (1-\delta)kd_1}{1-\delta}, \qquad \text{where } \tilde{u}_{11}^1 = \tilde{u}_{01}^1; \tag{7.1}$$

$$\tilde{v}_{12}^2 = \frac{p_1 - (1-\delta)kd_1 + \delta s}{1-\delta}, \qquad \text{where } \tilde{u}_{11}^2 = \tilde{u}_{01}^2; \tag{7.2}$$

$$\tilde{v}_{20}^1 = p_{11} - k(d_{st} + d_{w_1} + d_{sw} + d_{w_2} + d_{g_1} + d_{g_2}), \quad \text{where } \tilde{u}_{01}^1 = 0; \text{ and} \tag{7.3}$$

$$\tilde{v}_{20}^2 = p_{22} - a - k(d_{sw} + d_{w_1} + d_{st} + d_{w_2} + d_{g_1} + d_{g_2}), \quad \text{where } \tilde{u}_{01}^2 = 0. \tag{7.4}$$

Demand in the first period is

$$d_1 = 1 - \tilde{v}_2^i, \tag{8}$$

that in the second period is

$$d_2^i = d_{g_i} + d_{w_i} + d_{sw}, \tag{9}$$

where the subscript $i = 1,2$ represents the good a consumer buys in the second period.

With compatibility, when the entrant's good is marginally advanced technologically, as represented by $a < p_{22} - p_{11}$, firm 1 is a monopolistic supplier in both periods but that range is not realized. Firms are now choosing their price to maximize profits with demand for their respective good determined by consumers in the context described above.

## 8   REFERENCES

Cabral, L. M., D. J. Salant, and G. A. Woroch, (1999), "Monopoly Pricing with Network Externalities," *International Journal of Industrial Organization*, Vol. 17, pp.199-214.

Choi, J. P. (1994), "Network Externality, Compatibility Choice, and Planned Obsolescence", *Journal of International Economics*, Vol. 42, pp. 167-182.

Choi, J. P. and M. Thum (1998), "Market Structure and the Timing of Technology Adoption with Network Externalities," *European Economic Review*, Vol. 42, pp. 225-244.

Economides, N. (1995), "Network Externalities, Complementarities, and Invitation to Enter," *European Journal of Political Economy*, Vol. 12, pp. 211-232.

Economides, N. (1999), "Durable Goods Monopoly with Network Externalities with Application to the PC Operating Systems Market," Discussion Paper EC-99-09, Stern School of Business, N.Y.U.

Gilbert, R. J. and M. L. Katz (2001), "An Economist's Guide to U. S. v. Microsoft," *Journal of Economic Perspectives*, Vol. 15, pp. 25-44.

Jackson, T. (2000), "Final Judgment," United States District Court for the District of Columbia, Jun , 2000. about Civil Action NO. 98-1233.

Katz, M. L., and C. Shapiro (1985), "Network Externalities, Competition, and Compatibility," *American Economic Review*, Vol. 75, pp. 424-440.

Katz, M. L., and C. Shapiro (1986), "Technology Adoption in the Presence of Network Externalities," *Journal of Political Economy*, Vol. 94, pp. 822-841.

Katz, M. L., and C. Shapiro (1994), "System Competition and Network Effects," *Journal of Economic Perspectives*, Vol. 8, pp. 93-115.

Kollar-Kotelly, C.(2002), "Final Judgment Prusuant to Rule 54(b)," United States District Court for the District of Columbia, Nov 12, 2002. about Civil Action NO. 98-1233.

Lee, S-H. (1999), "Compatibility Choice of Network Products by a Discriminating Monopolist" (in Korean), *The Korean Journal of Industrial Organization*, Vol. 7, pp. 107-126.

Lee, S-H., and Y. Y. Sohn (2001), *Principles in Cyber Market Competition* (in Korean), Sigmainsight, Seoul.

Liebowitz, S. J., and S. E. Margolis (1994), "Network Externality: An Uncommon Tragedy," *Journal of Economic Perspectives*, Vol. 8, pp. 133-150.

Liebowitz, S. J., and S. E. Margolis (1998), "Path Dependence," in Newman, P. (ed.) (1998), *The New Palgrave Dictionary of Economics and Law*, Palgrave Macmillan, London.

Liebowitz, S. J., and S. E. Margolis (2000), *Winners, Loser & Microsoft*, The Independent Institute, Oakland.

Schmalensee, R. L. (1999), "Schmalensee Testimony," available online at http://www.microsoft.com/presspass/trial/schamal/schaml.asp, [accessed May, 2002]

Shapiro, C. and H. R. Varian (1999), *Information Rules*, Harvard Business School Press, Boston.

Shy, O. (2001), *The Economics of Network Industries*, Cambridge University Press, New York.

Sohn, Y. Y. (2001), "Pricing Strategy of Information Goods" (in Korean), *Journal of the Sungkok Academic & Foundation*, Vol. 32, pp. 47-89.

Sohn, Y.Y and H-W. Yang (2001), "Compatibility Choice of Information Goods with Market Growth" (in Korean). Papers presented at the Winter Conference of the Korean International Economics Association, 1015-1038.

Thum, M. (1994), "Network Externalities, Technological Progress, and the Competition Market Contracts," *International Journal of Industrial Organization*, Vol. 12, pp. 269-289.

Varian, H. R. (1998), "Market for Information Goods," paper presented at Bank of Japan Conference, 18-19, June.

Yang, H-W. (2003), Strategic Pricing and Compatibility Choice of Information Goods with Market Growth, The dissertation for the Degree of Doctor, Chonnam National University, Korea.

Global Economy and Digital Society
E. Bohlin, S. Levin, N. Sung and C-H. Yoon (Editors)

CHAPTER 10

# Weighing the Intangible: Towards a Theory-Based Framework for Information Society Indices

Dan M. Grigorovici, Jorge R. Schement, Richard D. Taylor

*Institute for Information Policy, Pennsylvania State University, University Park*

**Abstract**. This chapter aims to make a contribution to a conceptual model of information indicators. A variety of statistics are currently being used to measure Internet access or level of deployment of ICT at various levels, but the underlying theory is tenuous at best, with data that are often not comparable and indicators chosen subjectively. The chapter includes a critical survey of the literature on Information Society Indicators and of currently used e-readiness measures. It is argued that most existing indicators lack a comprehensive deductive theory to guide them, and that unweighted measures are used too frequently in inter-sector and inter-country comparisons. As an alternative, the steps involved in constructing an "e-readiness" index based on a Structural Equation Modeling approach are presented, and its potential to be applied to issues of social development is discussed.

## 1  INFORMATION SOCIETY INDICES AND DEVELOPMENT: IMPLICATIONS FOR THEORY AND MEASUREMENT

A review of the literature studying the impacts of Information and Communication Technologies (ICT) on development shows a fierce debate and contradictory findings: even if some studies show that the level of ICT provision in a country is highly correlated with income per capita (Grace et al. 2001, p. 13), there is still lack of understanding of the direction and magnitude of their underlying causal links. For example, the household digital divide could be said to be growing as the access gap between those with the highest and lowest levels of ICT access is getting bigger. Conversely, the digital divide could also be said to be shrinking, as rates of growth are faster for lagging groups. Common economic measures of distributional inequalities such as Gini coefficients also show the digital divide to be shrinking.

Although empirical and theoretical studies have continued to grow in the last years, the need for theory-building is still acutely felt within the research community. The lack of an overarching theory of the impacts of ICT on development that can guide research as well as development of measurement instruments is most likely the reason why current advancement is still hard to come by, especially when different researchers use the same concepts to mean different terms, use different ones to mean the same concepts, and the public discourse has seen a proliferation of poorly defined terms such as "Digital Economy", "Information Society", "Information Economy", "Knowledge Economy", etc.

Despite the lack of theory and an operational definition of the concept of information, several indices and measurement instruments exist in the literature, from both academic and corporate sources. Disparities among countries in their capacity to create and use ICT for development have persisted for a long time and are now huge. Yet the nature of those challenges is very different across countries, because countries vary immensely in their technological capacity and needs.

Usually, information indicators (or, using a more current term, e-readiness indices) have been classified in three types, as an OECD-based taxonomy proposes: "Physical indicators" (measuring the need for infrastructure for accessing the Internet, with indicators quantifying host computers, telephone lines, personal computers, etc.), "People Indicators" (studying consumers' level of use of the Internet, and of ICT), and "Policy Indicators" (containing measures of variables thought to have a direct impact on distributive justice issues, such as: ISP market, pricing, or usage). For instance, the SINE (Statistical Indicators for the New Economy) program of the European Union (Statistical Office of the European Communities (2000)) considered that "Indicators for the New Economy"[1] cover the following four distinctive target areas: Technology Domain, Industry Domain, Economy Domain and Social Domain. The Technology domain comprises the major technological changes that constitute the foundations of the New Economy and future economic growth. Briefly, these would cover indicators of enablers and accelerators of the information revolution, such as improvements in processing power, storage and communications through bandwidth enhancements; convergence, and so on. It should be noted that measuring the digital economy implies the measurement of the penetration and use of digital technologies in the public and private sectors, and across regions and countries. It also implies measuring the speed and direction of technological progress. As an illustration, the Technology Domain could contain groups of indicators that concern the new technology and its users such as: Information Technology and Communications (ICT) Infrastructure; Internet Infrastructure; Digitization; Virtualization; Multimedia; Internet users; and Internet penetration.

It is obvious that a vast range of social impacts of ICT needs to be measured and monitored. This list of social impacts includes: the living standards; the life styles; the social usage of Internet; the environment and social inclusion in, or exclusion from, the information society. For instance, UNDP's conceptual linkage between technology readiness of a country and its human development level are graphically represented in the figure below, used from UNDP 2001.

---

[1] "The New Economy is a knowledge and idea-based economy where the keys to job creation and higher standards of living are innovative ideas and technology embedded in services and manufactured products" (Atkinson & Court, 1998, p.8). Several generally agreed upon features of the New, or otherwise called Digital, Economy are thought to be: dynamic, global, networked, digitization-based technology, service-based workforce.

## Links between technology and human development

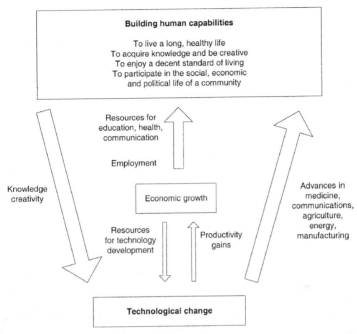

Figure 1. Links between Technology and Human Development. Source: UNDP (2001), p. 41.

Thus, as implied by the above definitions, the required indicators should unequivocally capture the consequences of the New Economy for living conditions and lifestyles, more specifically for wealth creation, income distribution, earnings inequalities, education and training, social protection and social cohesion (including the risks of the emergence of an information underclass), demographic dynamics, individual empowerment, new communities, changing cultural norms, and so on. Taking into account the previous discussion, some groups of indicators which are likely to be in the Social Domain may be the following: Economic and social demography indicators; Lifelong learning/training indicators; Living standards and lifestyles indicators; Cultural indicators; Social inequality indicators; Technology penetration indicators; Internet penetration indicators; Time use.

Before any discussion about what should an Information Society Indicator (ISI)[2] contain, the sheer necessity of having an index and what type of index should it be, needs to be addressed. For instance, economists have long been using GDP statistics (both aggregate and

---

[2] Heretofore, we use Information Society Indices (ISI) or "InforMetrics" as used within the authors' research program, to refer to all the differently named but similar measures reviewed in this paper: "e-readiness", "technology achievement", etc. and to suggest the all-encompassing nature of the theoretical and measurement model proposed by the authors in this chapter. This also contains the advantage of avoiding to use a more value-laden term such as "e-ready" which implies comparisons based on an ideal state of readiness.

per capita magnitude) to measure changes in economic development over time. Thus, a reasonable question to be addressed is: why would an ISI need to contain more than a GDP-based economic development measure, especially non-economic, contextual and quality of life indices, since, it is argued, GDP can be a good proxy for intangibles such as services or innovation systems? First of all, let alone the fact that GDP is not an ideal measurement for economic welfare (proof standing Samuelson's or Nordhaus and Tobin's attempts for a "measure of economic welfare", or Daly and Cobb's "index of sustainable economic welfare" as alternatives), GDP is an economic measurement, while the span of phenomena that ISI encompass extend well beyond economic ones, to social impacts, social and political context moderators that have an important role when attempting to construct a comprehensive model (Horn, 1993; Berger-Schmitt & Noll, 2000; Berger-Schmitt & Jankowitsch, 1999; Cobb, 2000; Cobb & Rixford, 1998; Shifflet & Schement, 1996). While GDP is a direct-objective indicator, the data that we are interested in regarding ICT phenomena require not only direct objective measures, but also indirect-derived ones (Horn, 1993). The permeability of Information Society phenomena into all areas of society and levels of analysis require a measurement instrument beyond economic statistics only, as it is well known (Horn, 1993) that economic indicators "are inadequate for comparing countries that differ in history, culture and value systems" (Horn 1993, p. 68). While all the indices reviewed in this paper make cross-country comparison in terms of their ranking as to how far off they stand from an "e-ready" or "technology achieved" ideal type, even the selection of variables included assume a chosen concept of development. This "may give a picture of economic development defined ad hoc, but omit sociocultural factors because they do not fit the development concept or because such indicators are not easily available" (Horn 1993, ibid.).

The current ISI statistics are based on concepts, definitions, theories having roots in the agricultural and industrial society and economy. From an economic perspective the industrial economy can be better measured and quantified than the knowledge based economy as there are generally tangible inputs, activities, outputs, which are significantly easier to measure, but in a knowledge based economy cause and effect are not directly linked by tangible assets or activities. Consequently, measurement systems are often indirect and complex, e.g. investment in PCs does not directly relate to economic benefits to an organization (Carss, 2002).

Another important question is whether the structure of the final ISI indicator that we might arrive at should be single variable or combined, that is, whether we should have one single all-encompassing index (as most of the measures reviewed here propose) or a multi-factor one. Our proposal is based on the conclusion that ISI require a multi-stage, multi-factor solution and the issue of whether we combine the weighted factors (sub-indices) into a single one or not should be more of a practical concern, depending on the country studied or level of analysis chosen. For instance, some of the chosen sub-indices could not apply to a certain region (or could weigh less in the overarching index than for another region, hence the need for a reliable weighting procedure), and they should not be included into the single index, while others should. A third, important deficiency of the measurement instruments reviewed is that they offer descriptive statistics which can only point to the level where a country stands in terms of e-readiness, IT development, etc. but neither direction nor magnitude of cause and effect relationships can be explained. This is due to the inexistence of a theoretical model that underlies current indicators. We propose a more inferential-based measurement instrument, including both economic and social indicators, able to explain and predict the impacts of ICT on development at various levels. Also, development itself should be included in the theoretical model as an input or contextual variable, in order to avoid hidden, value-laden political assumptions such as the one referred to above. This chapter suggests that in terms of methodology, structural equation and multilevel modeling could prove as invaluable tools in this process, helping build a more reliable ISI, as we explain in the sections below.

## 2    A REVIEW OF EXISTING INFORMATION SOCIETY INDICES

The number of assessment tools in both academic and corporate settings aimed at quantifying the impacts of ICT on development has been proliferating rapidly in recent years. Theoretical models being almost nonexistent though, it is hard to compare one instrument with another, since "the range of tools uses widely varying definitions for e-readiness and different methods for measurement" (Bridges.org, 2001). For example, Harvard University's model (Computer Systems Policy Project, 2001) looks at how information and communications technologies (ICT) are currently used in a society, while APEC's method (APEC 1999, 2000) focuses on government policies for e-commerce. Bridges.org's excellent review on e-readiness indicators (Bridges.org, 2001) classified two major categories that are used, offering different underlying goals: those that seek to measure "e-economy" metrics, and those that look at "e-society" indicators. E-economy assessment tools look at the ability of ICT to impact the economy, while e-society assessment tools look at the potential impact of ICT on the wider society. Although the theoretical assumptions on which these measures are built are usually made explicit and as stated above, the theoretical side has not been as advanced as the actual index construction work in this area, each of the measurement instruments reviewed has implicit theoretical assumptions about what it means for a society or economy to be "e-ready". More often than not, most of these are politically bound which poses a serious threat to the scientific reliability of the instruments. For instance, some of them operationalize a contextual variable such as "higher education funding type" (private vs. public) as distance from market-based institutions, through using a scale item such as "how viable is higher education as a business?" Obviously, there is here the underlying assumption that the ideal-state of an "e-ready" society should have market-oriented higher education. This is an assumption that misrepresents situations of countries other than North American ones, and this has the consequence of underweighting some of the variables in the measurement models proposed right from the start.

A first step in any approach to the problem of measuring Information Society is to consider a country's ability or "readiness" to integrate information technology (IT) and e-commerce, in order to provide a baseline that can be used for regional comparisons and planning. It is important to understand what it means for a country or economy to be "e-ready" and conduct an evaluation based on objective criteria to establish basic benchmarks. It means considering whether the necessary infrastructure is in place, but also looking beyond, to whether IT is accessible to the population at large and whether there is an appropriate legal and regulatory framework to support its use. If we are to narrow the digital divide, all of these issues need to be addressed simultaneously in a coherent, achievable strategy which is tailored to meet the needs of a particular country. An e-readiness assessment process can then be used as an information-gathering mechanism for governments as they plan their national and international strategies for IT integration. It can help governments focus their efforts from within, and identify areas where external support or aid is required.

Currently, a range of assessment tools have been developed to measure a country's or economy's e-readiness, and assessments have already been conducted in dozens of countries.

The tools use widely varying definitions for e-readiness and different methods for measurement and the assessments are very diverse in their goals, strategies and results. However, the right tool depends on the user's goal. The user should choose a tool that measures what they are looking for (construct validity), and does it against a standard that fits their own view of an "e-ready" society.

Given the discussion above, the need for well-justified country-level information economy and e-readiness metrics is strong. The recent proliferation of various "e-readiness" and similar indexes, and a recently announced initiative by the World Bank's Information for Development Program to fund such studies (Infodev, 2001), underscores the strong interest of policy makers and business people alike. Researchers who are studying how the Internet is influencing and changing the economic, political, and social systems of various countries have been limited by the absence of measures that are more accurate, explanatory, and sophisticated than the simple number of Internet hosts in a country (Menou, 1995a-b, 1993a-b; Wilson et al., 1998). Interest in national level metrics is well-founded on what a user has access to and why, and the answers to these questions depend on the specific legal, economic, political, and social conditions that surround a particular user. Furthermore, users are located within a particular national system of innovation, which also strongly influences the diffusion process and the absorptive capacity of a country.

Mosaic, a consortium of universities, has been doing analysis for some years, and has done case studies and self assessments for some 25 countries. The Mosaic Group's "Global Diffusion of the Internet" (GDI) studies, (Wolcott 2001), focus on the nation as the unit of analysis, and characterizes the state of the Internet along six dimensions: pervasiveness, geographic dispersion, sectoral absorption, connectivity infrastructure, organizational infrastructure, and sophistication of use. In addition to these dimensions, the framework includes an open-ended list of determinants -- factors which influence the development of the Internet, i. e., the values of the dimensions in a nation. Each dimension has five ordinal values ranging from zero (non-existent) to four (highly developed). Table 1 shows the definition of the levels of the first dimension, pervasiveness.

Geographic dispersion was selected as the second variable. While widespread access is desirable, the payoff is in who uses the Internet in a nation. This is accounted for in the sectoral absorption dimension, a measure of the degree of Internet utilization in the education, commercial, health care, and public sectors. These sectors are seen as key to development, as also suggested by their use in the United Nations Development Program's Human Development Index (UNDP 2001). Connectivity infrastructure is the fourth variable. It is a measure based on international and intranational backbone bandwidth, exchange points, and last-mile access methods. Organizational infrastructure is a measure based on state of the ISP industry and market conditions.

Table 1. The Five Levels of the Pervasiveness Dimension. Source: Wolcott et al. (2001).

| | |
|---|---|
| Level 0<br>Non-existent | The Internet does not exist in a viable form in this country. No computers with international IP connections are located within the country. There may be some Internet users in the country; however, they obtain a connection via an international telephone call to a foreign ISP. |
| Level 1<br>Experimental | The ratio of users per capita is on the order of magnitude of less than one in a thousand. There is limited availability, and use of the Internet is embryonic. Only one or a few networks are connected to the international IP network. The user community comprises principally networking technicians. |
| Level 2<br>Established | The ratio of Internet users per capita is on the order of magnitude of at least one in a thousand. The user community has been expanded beyond networking technicians. |
| Level 3<br>Common | The ratio of Internet users per capita is on the order of magnitude of at least one in a hundred. The infrastructure of supporting and related goods and services has become well-established, although is not necessarily extensive. |
| Level 4<br>Pervasive | The Internet is pervasive. The ratio of Internet users per capita is on the order of magnitude of at least one in ten. Internet access is available as a commodity service. |

Using Mosaic's measurement instrument, a highly rated nation ("e-ready") would have many ISPs and a high degree of openness and competition in both the ISP and telecommunication industries. It would also have collaborative organizations and arrangements like public exchanges, ISP industry associations, and emergency response teams. The final variable is sophistication of use, a measure characterizing usage from conventional to highly sophisticated and driving innovation. A relatively conventional nation would be using the Internet as a straight forward substitute for other communication media like telephone and fax machines, whereas in a more advanced nation, applications may result in significant changes in existing processes and practices and may even drive the invention of new technology. In addition to these six dimensions, Mosaic's framework considers determinants of Internet diffusion. One view of these determinants is presented in Wolcott et al. (2001), which organizes them into government policies and non-governmental determinants of Internet success, as shown in Table 2.

Table 2. Factors and Policies Influencing Internet Success within a Nation

Source: Wolcott et al. (2001).

Internet Success Determinants

- Telecommunication infrastructure

- Personal computing and software

- Financial resources

- Human capital

- Sectoral demand and awareness

- Competitive environment

Government Policies

- Markets and choice

- Investment policy

- National security

- Cultural concerns

- Social equity

Understanding how the determinants influence the dimensions in a given country can lead to prescriptive statements, and GDI studies typically include thorough analyses of both dimensions and determinants (Wolcott et al., 1996). The results are presented on a diagram with six spokes representing each of the dimensions. Values for one or more countries at one time or across time can be plotted on the same diagram or compared side-by-side on several diagrams. Figure 2, for example, shows the status of Internet diffusion in Turkey and Pakistan in 1999.

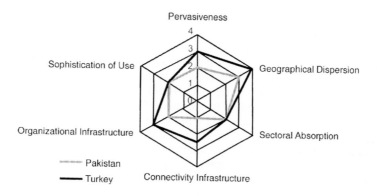

Figure 2. Internet Diffusion Dimensions for Turkey and Pakistan, 1999.
Source: Wolcott et al. (2001).

Figure 3 shows the rapid growth of the Internet in Finland from 1994 to 1997.

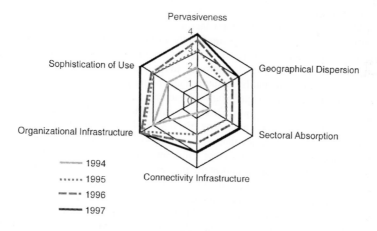

Figure 3. Internet Diffusion Dimensions for Finland, 1994-1997. Source: Wolcott et al. (2001).

The IDC/World Times Information Society Index is the fifth installment of the Information Society Index (ISI) research done at the International Data Corporation (IDC 2000). The index measures information capacity and wealth for 55 nations, accounting for 97 % of the world's GDP and more than 99 % of all IT spending. Based on clustering 23 variables in four classes (computer infrastructure, information infrastructure, internet infrastructure and social infrastructure), the latest figures consulted (with data from 2000) classify countries in "skaters" (ISI score above 3,500, with Sweden, Norway, Finland, and United States occupying the first, second, third, and fourth ranks respectively), "striders" (ISI above 2,000, with New Zealand - 16th, Belgium - 17th, Taiwan - 18th, and Korea - 19th), "sprinters" (ISI score above 1,000, with UAE - 28th, Hungary - 29th, Poland - 30th, and Argentina - 31st), and "strollers" (ISI score below 1,000, with Saudi Arabia - 44th, Brazil - 45th, Colombia - 46th, and Thailand - 47th). ISI variables are: computer infrastructure (PC's installed per capita; Home PC's shipped per household; Government and commercial PC's shipped per non-agricultural workforce; Educational PC's shipped per student and faculty; Percent of non-home networked PC's; Software vs. hardware spending), information infrastructure: (Cable subscribers per capita; Cellular phone ownership per capita; Cost per phone call; Fax ownership per capita; Radio ownership per capita; Telephone line error rates; Telephone lines per household; TV ownership per capita), Internet infrastructure (Business Internet users per non-agricultural workforce; Home Internet users per household; Education Internet users per student and faculty; eCommerce spending per total Internet users), and Social infrastructure (Civil liberties; Newspaper readership per capita; Press freedom; Secondary school enrollment; Tertiary school enrollment). Apparently, there is no analysis in ISI's criteria for bundling these specific variables into the factors. It seems that some of the variables could have been bundled together into only one; others are split into demographic classes when it shouldn't have been necessary to do so. An assessment of what each variable (and percentage variation explained) brings to the cluster, and what should its weight be might very well be needed as much as one of the major issues in constructing ISI metrics is assigning weights to the included variables. Most of the reviewed measures use a rather subjective or convenient weighting system (dividing 100% into equal percentages for factor weights of sub-indices chosen from the start to be part of the overall index). As explained in the last two sections below, our approach calls for a more objective choice of variables to be input into the overall index, a more theory driven approach to weighting and a proper index construction methodology, by using Structural Equation Modeling and Exploratory Factor Analysis methods.

The Economist Intelligence Unit/Pyramid Research e-readiness rankings (The Economist Intelligence Unit 2001) tallies scores across six categories--including the business environment rankings--and 19 additional indicators. Each variable in the model is scored on a scale from one to ten. The six categories that feed into the final rankings (and their weight in the model) are: connectivity (30%), business environment (20%), eCommerce business and business adoption (20%), the legal and regulatory environment (15%), supporting e-services (10 %), and social and cultural infrastructure (5 %). "Connectivity" measures the access that individuals and businesses have to basic fixed and mobile telephony services, including voice and both narrowband and broadband data. Affordability and availability of service (both a function of the level of competition in the telecoms market) also figure as determinants of connectivity. "Business environment" bundles 70 indicators covering criteria such as the strength of the economy, political stability, the regulatory environment, taxation, and openness to trade and investment. The resulting "business environment rankings" measure the expected attractiveness of the general business environment over the next five years. The "E-commerce consumer and business adoption" evaluate the extent of credit-card ownership as well as the existence of secure, reliable and efficient electronic payment mechanisms, the ability of vendors to ensure timely and reliable delivery of goods, and the extent of website development by local firms. "Legal and regulatory environment" considers the extent of legal support for virtual transactions and digital signatures. Ease of licensing and the ability of firms to operate with a minimal but effective degree of regulation are other criteria. "Supporting e-services" include portals and other online intermediaries, web-hosting firms, application service providers (ASPs), as well as website developers and e-business consultants. The rankings assess the extent to which local companies and organizations have access to these services. Finally, "Social and cultural infrastructure" assess the national proclivity to business innovation and receptiveness to web content. No indication of the theoretical reasons for arriving at the index, weighting, and factor solution is provided with the instrument and additional documents.

McConnell International (McConnell International 2000) has comparative data for 42 countries. Its report measures five areas: connectivity (infrastructure, access and pricing), e-leadership (government policies and regulations), information security (intellectual property, privacy, electronic signatures), human capital (ICT education, available skilled workforce), and e-business climate (competition, political and financial stability, foreign investment, financial infrastructure). A quick look at McConnell International's ratings shows how complex is the reality of ICT use. For example, Mexico rated poorly on connectivity, but reasonably well on human capital, information security, government policies and the business climate. The Philippines had good human capital, but rated poorly in all other areas (McConnell International, 2001).

APEC e-readiness has released their fifth version of their annual assessment of Asia-pacific countries in terms of their readiness for the New Economy (APEC 1999, 2000). They define readiness as the degree to which an economy or community is prepared to participate in the digital economy. Readiness is assessed by APEC by determining the relative standing of the economy in the areas that are most critical for e-commerce participation. Six broad indicators of readiness for e-commerce are developed into a series of questions that provide direction as to desirable policies that will promote e-commerce and remove barriers to electronic trade. Six categories are measured for "readiness for e-commerce": "basic infrastructure and technology" (speed, pricing, access, market competition, industry standards, foreign investment), "access to network services" (bandwidth, industry diversity, export controls, credit card regulation), "use of the Internet" (use in business, government, homes), "promotion and facilitation" (industry led standards), "skills and human resources" (ICT education, workforce), and "positioning for the digital economy" (taxes and tariffs, industry self-regulation, government regulations, consumer trust).

The Index of the Massachusetts Innovation Economy measures progress of three key components of the Massachusetts Innovation Economy. It is based on a dynamic conceptual framework that links resources to economic results through an innovation process. The framework measures Massachusetts' progress in leveraging its resources through innovation to create higher levels of economic performance. The Massachusetts Innovation Economy has three interrelated and interactive components: "results" (Outcomes for people and business—job growth, rising average wages, and export sales), "innovation process" (Dynamic interactions that translate resources into results—idea generation, commercialization, entrepreneurship, and business innovation) and "resources" (Critical public and private inputs to the Innovation Economy—human, technology, and investment resources, plus infrastructure) (Massachusetts Technology Collaborative 2000).

The City of Seattle has developed a set of indicators for measuring the community's level of access to the Information Economy. They are arranged into six major categories. Each category has a set of subtopics with a description and one or more measurements. The measurements are intended to cumulatively provide an indicator of the topic presented. The indicator categories are: "access" (ownership and home use, public access and level of use, Information Technology Literacy and Fluency, Business and Economic Development (tracking the workforce and industry needs and impacts to the community), "community building" (measures the extent to which IT is being used in community building activities), "civic participation", "human relationships to technology" (including Quality of Life), and "partnerships and resource mobilization".

Computer Systems Policy Project's (CSPP)[3] "Readiness for the networked world" defined e-readiness as the degree to which a community is prepared to participate in the Networked World (Computer Systems Policy Project 1998). The Index examines 19 different categories of indicators, ranking each by levels of advancement in Stages One through Four. The Guide neither offers specific advice nor suggests that the only route from Stage Two to Stage Four be through Stage Three. Nor does it provide an overall score; it seeks only to offer a starting point in an ICT planning process. The categories are linked, each driving the others, such that a community cannot concentrate solely in one area, but must pay attention to each, noting where it might be able to capitalize on synergies among the categories. The categories fall within five groups: "network access" (Information Infrastructure, Internet Availability, Internet Affordability, Network Speed and Quality, Hardware and Software, Service and Support), "networked learning", "networked society", "networked economy", and "network policy".

Perhaps one of the most objective ISI metrics reviewed by the authors, the Commonwealth of Australia's "E-commerce preparedness Index" (Commonwealth of Australia, 2000) has been assessed using a new indicator: the Allen E–commerce Preparedness (ECP) Index. This is based on key factors illustrating enduring structural differences between the preparedness of the States and Territories to adopt e-commerce. This composite index includes data associated with e-commerce use which are arranged into two clusters: data that indicates capacity to use e-commerce in supply; and indicators of the capacity to use e-commerce in consumption. The analysis in this report is conducted by modeling a "base case" of the economy in which e-commerce is frozen. Another scenario is then modeled with e-commerce factored into the economy thereby enabling the effects of e-commerce to be isolated by comparing the two scenarios. The Monash Multi-Regional Forecasting (MMRF) simulation model results indicate that Australia's economy and the economies of all of its states gain on a medium to long term basis. They are projected to have a higher level of output of between 0.8 per cent to 3.6 per cent by the year 2010, with national GDP rising by 2.9 per cent. The Allen E-commerce Preparedness (ECP) Index has been thus developed to identify and assess the structural regional differences in the impact of greater use of e-commerce. Scores have been normalized to facilitate comparison. The higher the Allen ECP Index the more prepared the specific economy is with respect to the take up of e-commerce. The Allen ECP Index is thus a composite index based on two clusters of factors and data: supply (the preparedness and propensity of producers to use e-commerce and the initiatives of governments in helping to prepare their respective economies for the take up of e-commerce), which was weighted at 0.603; and consumption (the different propensity of consumers to use e-commerce), weighted at 0.40.

Overall, our review found that although current ISI metrics have definite usefulness when considering descriptive types of analyses, they suffer from several deficiencies. First of all,

---

[3] CSPP is a "public policy advocacy group...comprised of the Chairman and Chief Executive Officers" of US information technology companies.

most of them contain blurred boundaries between measuring ICT potential (commonly known as "e-readiness" measures) from actual ICT achievements, or they do not distinguish between ICT inputs and efforts, thus undermining the very sole purpose of index construction in general. On the other hand, as even the act of choosing variables to be included in an index constitutes implicit theory building, the inexistence of an explicit theoretical model to be tested through inferential statistics that can guide index construction has the effect of poor measurement validity. This impacts on variables chosen to be included, their weights, and the factoring solution: specifically, most of the reviewed instruments assign weights rather subjectively and no factor analysis is reported.

In conclusion, a comparative look at several largely diffused measures reveals much too few common findings. One reason why this can be the case is the current lack of theory supporting the measures, and even more, the circularity of the bits of theory that underlie some of them: the assumptions built into the variables chosen to be bundled into different clusters contain assumptions on what the indices are supposed to measure. The logical question that is raised is: what is the cause for contradictions in the different measurement models and how are they related to the conceptual assumptions laying at their foundation? To answer this, we have employed statistical analyses of three indices: UNDP's "Technology Achievement Index", CID's "Networked Readiness Index", Metricnet's "Global New E-Economy Index". The analyses and results for the UNDP index are discussed in the next section[4].

### 2.1 Analysis of UNDP's "Technology Achievement Index"

The uneven diffusion of information and communications technology—the "digital divide"—has caught the public discourse worldwide, already becoming almost a catch phrase. There have long been huge differences among countries but, as stated in the previous sections, the differences are mapped differently by different measures.

One of the measures for instance, the "Technology Achievement Index" was introduced in the 2001 UNDP Report (UNDP, 2001) and presents a snapshot of each country's average achievements in creating and diffusing technology and in building human skills to master new innovations. In addition to the differences across countries, the index reveals considerable disparities within countries. India, for example, home to one of the most dynamic global hubs—Bangalore, which Wired rated 11th among the 46 hubs, ranks 63rd in the technology achievement index, falling among the lower end of dynamic adopters. Why? Because of huge variations in technological achievement among Indian states. The country has the world's seventh largest number of scientists and engineers, some 140,000 in 1994. Yet in 1999, mean years of schooling were only 5.1 and adult illiteracy was 44%.

Descriptive statistics such as this are a good example of the current contradictory findings when comparing different measures. This led to the present inquiry upon what causes or explanations can be found to support the contradictions and different rankings for the same countries across different indices. The statistical analyses reported here use findings from several regressions performed in an attempt to predict technology achievement (based on UNDP's "TAI" index) using both the composite human development index (HDI) for the

---

[4] A more detailed analysis of the UNDP measure, as well as a comparison with analyses done with the CID and Metricnet measures are at different stages of development in the "InforMetrics" research program as part of the authors' institutional affiliation. For more details, contact the corresponding author at dangrig@psu.edu.

same year, as well as specific variables from the index (educational attainment, income, etc.). The HDI measures the overall achievements in a country in three basic dimensions of human development—longevity, knowledge and a decent standard of living. It is measured by life expectancy, educational attainment (adult literacy and combined primary, secondary and tertiary enrolment) and adjusted income per capita in purchasing power parity (PPP) US dollars. The HDI is a summary, not a comprehensive measure of human development. As a result of refinements in the HDI methodology over time and changes in data series, the HDI should not be compared across editions of the Human Development Report (see UNDP 2001 for detailed explanations of the index). As stated in the UNDP 2001 report, (which uses data up to 2000) the TAI aims to capture "how well a country is creating and diffusing technology and building a human skill base—reflecting capacity to participate in the technological innovations of the network age". This composite index measures achievements, not potential, effort or inputs. It is constructed using indicators, not direct measures, of a country's achieve-ments in four dimensions: "technology creation capabilities" (number of patents granted per capita and receipts of royalty and license fees from abroad per capita), "diffusion of recent innovations" (based on Internet diffusion and exports of high- and medium-technology products as a share of all exports), "diffusion of old innovations" (based on electricity consumption in kwh/capita, and telephones per 1000 people) and finally, "human skills" (mean years of schooling, and gross enrolment ratio of tertiary students enrolled in science, mathematics and engineering, as components).

As suggested by its authors, the TAI is not a measure of which country is leading in global technology development, but focuses on how well the country as a whole is participating in creating and using technology. As an example, by the UNDP data, the United States has far more inventions and Internet hosts in total than does Finland, but it does not rank as highly in the index because in Finland the Internet is more widely diffused and more is being done to develop a technological skill base throughout the population. One of the reasons for proceed-ing with the current analyses was to study what are the predictors of such variations in ranking. Using the UNDP 2001 Human Development report containing data until 2000, several statistical analyses were performed. N= 162, after removal, N=157. A simple linear regression was performed to examine HDI level (with "leaders", "potential leaders", "dynamic adopters", "marginalized" and "others" as the categories proposed by UNDP) as predictors of HDI level (with "high development", "medium development" and "low development" as categorized by UNDP). Table 3 reports the statistics associated with this analysis, and shows that HDI level accounted for a significant portion of the variance in the Technology Achieve-ment Index rank.

Table 3. Human Development as Predictor of Technology Achievement

|      | $\beta$ |
| --- | --- |
| HDI  | .80* |

$F(1,160) =293.07$, Adjusted $R2=.64$, $p<.001$
*$p<.001$.

Next, a multiple regression analysis was performed to examine HDI value, GDP per capita, and education index for 1999 as predictors of inclusion in the TAI levels. Table 4 shows that, as common sense would suggest, only GDP per capita accounted for a significant portion of the variance in TAI levels. HDI value only marginally reached significance (p=.10), while education was not significant as predictor of technology achievement.

Table 4. Predictors of Technology Achievement

|  | $\beta$ |
| --- | --- |
| HDI value | .19 |
| GDP per capita | .75* |
| Education index | .02 |

$F(3,158) = 279.19$, Adjusted $R2 = .84$, $p < .001$.
*$p < .001$.

This could be due to the limitations of the data and to the different reliabilities of the different sources of data that the UNDP report computed to arrive at the indices used. Further analysis is suggested to unravel the causes of the two predictor's non-significance, and checking for consistency. There are several theoretical points to be made based on these analyses and the ones not reported here[5]: most importantly, we can see that depending on what variables are included in the analyses as predictors (an issue of variable decision), the significance and explanatory power of the regressions change. This, in our opinion, could explain the disparate findings from the literature on effects of ICT on development. That is, some studies reported an effect of education on IT achievement, while others reported GDP as the most significant predictor. Therefore, the confusion in the field has a twofold explanation: first of all, this is due to the non-existence of a global theoretical model at the foundation of selecting the variables to be included, and second, to the fact that classic regression analyses are somewhat limited in their ability to include a wide range of variables along with possible moderators, include measurement error in the model in the same time. In fact we believe that an appropriate solution for solving this problem is building a consciously objective theoretical model and then use structural equation modeling to test its fit to the data, as explained in the section below, as our proposal for a new model.

The results of the regression analyses above show great disparities among countries at different levels of development. There are four groups of countries categorized by UNDP, with TAI values ranging from 0.744 for Finland to 0.066 for Mozambique. These countries can be considered leaders, potential leaders, and dynamic adopters or marginalized:

- "Leaders" (TAI above 0.5)—topped by Finland, the United States, Sweden and Japan, this group is at the cutting edge of technological innovation. Technological innovation is self-sustaining, and these countries have high achievements in technology creation, diffusion and skills. Coming fifth is the Republic of Korea, and tenth is Singapore—two countries that have advanced rapidly in technology in recent decades. This group is set apart from the rest by its higher invention index, with a marked gap between Israel in this group and Spain in the next.

- "Potential leaders" (0.35–0.49)—most of these countries have invested in high levels of human skills and have diffused old technologies widely but innovate little. Each tends to rank low in one or two dimensions, such as diffusion of recent innovations or of old in-

---

[5] The rest of the analyses are reported elsewhere. For additional analyses as well as access to the original data, the reader should contact Dan Grigorovici at dangrig@psu.edu.

ventions. Most countries in this group have skill levels comparable to those in the top group.

- "Dynamic adopters" (0.20–0.34)—these countries are dynamic in the use of new technology. Most are developing countries with significantly higher human skills than the fourth group. Included are Brazil, China, India, Indonesia, South Africa and Tunisia, among others. Many of these countries have important high-technology industries and technology hubs, but the diffusion of old inventions is slow and incomplete.

- "Marginalized" (below 0.20)—technology diffusion and skill building have a long way to go in these countries. Large parts of the population have not benefited from the diffusion of old technology. These rankings do not shadow income rankings and show considerable dynamism in several countries with rising technological achievement—for example, Korea ranks above the United Kingdom, Canada and other established industrial economies. Ireland ranks above Austria and France. Large developing countries—Brazil, China, India—do less well than one might expect because this is not a ranking of "technological might" of a country. Finally, technology hubs have a limited effect on the index because of disparities within countries. If the TAI were estimated only for the hubs, such countries would undoubtedly rank as leaders or potential leaders.

However, limitations in data series must be taken into account in interpreting TAI values and rankings. Some countries will have undervalued innovations because patent records and royalty payments are the only systematically collected data on technological innovation and leave out valuable but non-commercialized innovations such as those occurring in the informal sector and in indigenous knowledge systems. Moreover, national systems and traditions differ in scope and criteria. High numbers of patents may reflect liberal intellectual property systems. Diffusion of new technologies may be understated in many developing countries. Also, it would be interesting to further this line of research by comparing how different Information Society or E-readiness measures proposed in the literature, can better or worse predict human development as contained in the data of the UNDP report. This line of research would show disparities of prediction between different measures, and this, in turn, could be due either to different reliabilities estimates for each, or to poor construct (concurrent) validity across all of them. Although technological achievements are important for human development, the TAI measures only technological achievements. It does not indicate how well these achievements have been translated into human development. Still, the TAI shows a high correlation with the human development index (HDI), and it correlates better with the HDI than with income.

Many of the assessment models presented above measure all countries against one standard: the optimal state of e-readiness. Two problems can arise from this. First, many developing and emerging countries could be faced with an insurmountable task and not know where to start. These tools place developing countries in the 'early' stages of e-readiness, and indicate that they must undergo massive economic and political changes to become e-ready. Second, it may be faulty to use a single standard of measurement at all. There is no single social, political, and economic model that has been the most successful at harnessing information technology. Comparing a developing country against an "optimal state of e-readiness" may not amount to anything other than biased conclusions and questionable, if not invalid, rankings, based on an absolute standard, which is historically, politically, and culturally dependent. Some authors would argue that the unique cultural and historical environment of a region must be taken into account as part of a national ICT policy to truly gauge the country's e-readiness for the future. A solution to both of these problems could be to base the primary assessment on countries within a particular region or social / economic / political group. Cross-country or region comparisons will be based on multiple-group structural equation modeling methods to test the equivalence of the general model between the countries/regions. The assessment tool could then be adapted for the region using a multilevel modeling-based index, and recommendations could be made based on the experiences of similar countries. Additional data points and recommendations on how to become e-ready could be drawn, with caution, from the best practices and other examples seen in developed countries. This method is far from perfect, though. It is considerably more complicated and costly. It provides detailed description of the state of ICT, but a less detailed action plan for future work. In addition, data points from similar countries may be lacking. For example, what happens when no similar country exists that has been successful at harnessing ICT?

The lesson is that there is a wide range of e-readiness assessment models available, but each has limitations. Every model evaluated would require re-designing to make it a comprehensive assessment tool. The tools that are ready-to-use are either limited in scope or lack detailed description on how to use the tool in practice. Of course, no tool will fit every user's needs. However, one could envision a tool that gave the user control over what was measured, and provided the resources to measure the various aspects of e-readiness. E-assessment measures ask some of the vital questions that are missing in most digital divide policy reports – namely, how is the technology used in everyday life? Where and how often is the technology used in schools, businesses (internal technology and e-commerce), government (internally and e-government), and in health care? Unfortunately, e-assessments do not generally discuss socio-economic divisions in a society. A more comprehensive look at ICT use would combine both e-assessments of the sectors of society (i.e. schools, businesses, health care) and studies of socio-economic divisions (i.e. ethnicity, income, gender). If socio-economic issues are not studied and addressed, then the practical use of ICT will remain the province of a privileged few.

There are thus four main reasons why macro level information indicators, however carefully constructed, cannot approximate the systematic comprehensiveness of traditional economic indicators:

- there are no stable formulae or "recipes" for translating information inputs into knowledge creation or knowledge outputs;
- inputs into knowledge creation are hard to map because there are no information and/or knowledge accounts analogous to the traditional national accounts;
- information lacks a systematic measurement system that would serve as a basis for aggregating pieces of information that are essentially unique;
- new knowledge creation is not necessarily a net addition to the stock of knowledge, and obsolescence of units of the knowledge stock is not documented.

The problem of developing new Information Society indicators that can also take into account knowledge as output at a macro level is itself an indication of the unique character of the "New Economy". Were we faced with trivial modifications to the traditional accounting system, a few add-on measures might suffice. To fully understand the workings of the knowledge-based economy, new economic concepts and measures are required which track phenomena beyond conventional market transactions. In general, improved indicators for the knowledge-based economy are needed for the following tasks: measuring knowledge inputs;

measuring knowledge stocks and flows, knowledge outputs, networks and learning. However, after the discussion above and contradictory findings derived from the different indices, it is safe to ask the question if an Information Society index should be of use at all, and if so, how can it be computed so as to prove itself a valid construct with a reliable measurement instrument. Our review of the current measurement models suggested that due to the lack of theoretical foundation that can guide the pursuit for an index, most of the existing indices suffer from the circularity issue discussed previously: most of the indices are rather ad hoc constructs that contain unexamined theoretical assumptions. This has led, with one notable exception, to the current state of Information Society indices: including in the measurement models variables that are then measured and tested as outcome variables, a "double counting" issue.

## 3   TOWARDS A NEW FRAMEWORK FOR INFORMATION SOCIETY INDICES

We propose in this section the foundations of the "InforMetrics" approach for a new framework that might help the e-learning measurement models have a better starting point. First, it is necessary to clearly differentiate "readiness" from "use". We suggest using two different indices for "readiness" and "use", which will increase the predictive power of the measurement model. More concretely, for instance, if we have measures of "use" and "e-readiness" at the current time, and a well-defined predictive model linking the two, we can project future demand for "use" by subtracting current "use" from the predicted value of "e-use" in future periods. Thus, all the "use" measures should be eliminated from "e-readiness" index, so that we have different / clear indices. Second, for the "e-readiness" index we need to develop specific indicators/ items for each category within each sector. There are only a few, if any, universal indicators that can be applied to all sectors. Because of this, and because the importance of these items is not equal, it would be better giving different weights to different items, as well as different weights to different sectors. For instance, if we had legislation, censorship, and corruption as the contextual factors under the government sector (see the model below), and we considered legislation as the most important factor for our purposes, we would give a weight of maybe 55% to legislation, 25% to corruption (the second important factor), and 20% to censorship. The same goes for sectors as well. If we are primarily interested in industry (as being the largest available market, e.g), we should give it more weight. These weights should be assigned based not on the researcher's subjective judgment, but on analysis of data from various markets and countries on e-learning readiness and use. These sets of weights might differ from time1 to time 2, from country 1 to country 2, based on current state of affairs in specific geographical areas. What we need in this case is both a theoretical framework and a methodological tool able to handle the analyses needed.

A structure for analyzing what statistics and indicators are useful for "underpinning identification, formulation, monitoring and assessing the new economy" has been proposed by Gardin (Gardin, 2002). Figure 4 below illustrates the hierarchy of complexity connected with indicators for the new economy – starting from basic facts to more intricate indicators for capturing the emerging phenomena developing from the new economy. The steps also illustrate the different domains the indicators should bring light to.

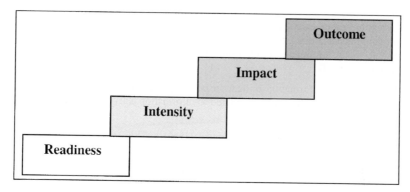

Figure 4. Hierarchy of Complexity and Classification of Information Society Indices.
Source: Gardin (2002).

The "Readiness indicators" indicate the potential for use of ICT and describe variables such as ICT infrastructure, access to and availability of Internet, e-mail, PCs and IT-skills. The "Intensity indicators" indicate the actual use and applications of ICT and describe variables such as ICT investments, the extent of use of Internet, e-mail, PCs, e-commerce, for what purpose they are used by different user groups – people and households, businesses and government. These two families of indicators represent the basic indicators for the Information Society and provide the main basis for eEurope benchmarking and analysis of the digital divide. They relate mainly to the infrastructure and the transfer of possibilities and participation of the people. The following two families of indicators relate to economic and social changes. The "Impact indicators" relate mainly to the micro level, enterprises and governments, but also to the industry level. They describe new ways of organizing work, referring to the relations between individuals as well as between individuals and the enterprise; of organizing production, which refers to inter-enterprise relations such as outsourcing, joint ventures, licensing etc; knowledge supply/human investment/human resources; mobility; innovation/R&D and spin-offs. The "Outcome indicators" relate mainly to the macro or societal level. They describe economic growth, productivity and competitiveness; employment and the labor market; social inclusion and participation. It is on this level the issues about sustainable economic development can be approached (Gardin, 2002).

Among the metrics reviewed earlier there is model that we found closest to our research objectives: the "Information Utilization Potential" (IUP), model proposed in an earlier, almost forgotten paper by M. Menou (Menou, 1985). In our opinion, IUP can provide the theoretical and measurement basis for further work in constructing our proposal for the Information Society Index. Its scope (as cited in Menou 1985, p. 327) can be expressed by the following equation:

IUP= (A+B+C+D)

Where:
A= Information resources and activities,
B=Information needs and uses,
C= Physical, social, administrative environment variables, and
D= Dynamics of (A+B+C)

"In other words, the information utilization potential represents the relative present, future, strengths, weaknesses of the countries related to information activities" (Menou 1985, p. 327).

Table 5. Structure of the IUP model. Source: Menou (1985), p. 330

| Types of aggregation / Levels | Factual data | Structural aggregation (Structural IUP) | Functional aggregation (Functional IUP) |
|---|---|---|---|
| Level 0 | Original data | | |
| Level 1 | Individual statistical data | X data elements | |
| Level 2 | Raw values for national totals +breakdowns | Y data elements | |
| Level 3 | Further aggregation of Level 2 data: relativization to size of country studied | 230 variables | 230 primary factors (+ 885 secondary factors) |
| Level 4 | Aggregation into homogenous groups: structural (components of the information situation); functional (steps in the communication cycle) | 21 structural groups | 18 functional groups |
| Level 5 A | | 3 intermediate composite indices | 7 intermediate composite indices |
| B | | 1 single composite index | 1 single composite index |

The IUP model (tested for the first time in the pilot project developed at the Brazilian Institute for Information in Science and Technology – IBICT) prove to be the most exhaustive attempt to construct an information index to date. Even if for unknown reasons it has not been used as a model for the current indices analyzed in the previous sections, the main advantage of the IUP is its modular structure[6]: not only does it have two composite indices (a structural one and a functional one), but it attempts to use the "information situation" or context as unit of analysis, thus being able to account for more than an information product-based measure. Its process-oriented construction shows itself in the two composite indices found: the "structural IUP" is further broken down into three distinct components (background or enabling conditions, information needs and uses, and information services and activities), while the "functional IUP" is comprised of seven distinct components "to form intermediate composite indices corresponding to the major roles of the various constituencies in the information sector" (Menou, 1985, p. 334). The usefulness of the IUP model lies in the fact that while it uses standardized measures, it is still able and flexible enough to account for the variables bundled into the final indices. In our opinion, this is the most promising suggestion to date of any attempt to construct an information indicator, as the major source of dissatisfaction with the current metrics is that a single index solution cannot account for the specific factors that make a ranking and comparison different than another. After aggregation and factor analysis of the variables included in the IUP model, the indices arrived offer the possibility of "switching" between the two sub-levels of Level 5 (see Table 5 above) and depending on the level of analysis and the objectives of the measurement, using either the lower level composite indices (3 intermediate functional and 7 intermediate structural) or the two overarching ones. As found in the paper in which the model was published, after several linear regressions, "the information factor IUP is highly correlated with the other composite IUP indices – 0.93847" (Menou, 1985, p. 341), thus suggesting its validity. Unfortunately, as this model was not pursued in further research, the only data on which it was tested is limited to 1984-85[7]. It is our intent to use IUP as well as the Gardin 2002 classification of factors as starting point for the theoretical framework of ISI, which will then be tested against current data. The following paragraph describes the general model, the work done and steps involved as part of the "InforMetrics" research program currently advanced by the authors of this chapter.

### 3.1 The "InforMetrics" Theory-Based Approach to ISI: Towards a Multi-level Index

Based on what has been discussed in the preceding sections, our approach starts with an initial theoretical model that will be tested iteratively against data to assess its goodness of fit via structural equation modeling. We decided that the framework that best approximates what we have been looking for is Gardin's (2002) classification which serves of a possible factoring solution and Michel Menou's IUP described above. Based on the results of the goodness of fit

---

[6] Another example of a modular and comprehensive measurement model is the "Index of Technological Progress" (ITP), discussed in Rodriguez & Wilson, 2000. Due to limitations of the present paper, an analysis of ITP and comparison with IUP was not included, but we suspect that by its similar modularity and having two composite indices (ITP-Core and ITP-Broad), this is another example of the same type of indicator suggested as best choice for constructing a valid measure. For more information on ITP, see Rodriguez & Wilson, 2000.

[7] International country ranking tables are available for 1985 in the paper in which the IUP model was first published.

tests, we will repeatedly perform "trimming" of the model until we arrive at a best fit solution. This method has been considered as providing the most practical approach when a global theory of ICT impacts on development does not currently exist. On the other hand, we build our model starting from findings from current research, and do not arrive at a solution simply based on statistical information (letting data show us the model). In order to arrive at a more reliable measurement instrument for quantifying the state of Information Society, several required steps are needed[8]. First of all from a conceptual level, we start with the classification of Gardin (2002) by sectors/contexts, then choose variables of interest based on classification, with differential variables and weights depending on their relevance to each sector/context; following the structural equation modeling terminology, we consider both observed and unobserved/latent variables, and each latent variable (e.g., will contain paths from at least two different observed ones, in order to assess measurement error and ascertain reliability of measurement part of the model). Also, weights will be left free to vary unless clear findings from current research indicate a relationship between two variables is strong enough to be fixed. This way allows for a more objective arrival at a weighting solution, rather than the subjective one used in current measures.

From a methodological point of view, as explained above, structural equation modeling offers a much more rigorous tool than the ones currently used in the reviewed metrics. Compared to classical approaches, our choice was based on the advantages that this tool offers: we can thus assess measurement error by directly including it in the model, improving instrument reliability; SEM allows for the distinction between latent and observed variables, as well as analysis of complex relationships between independent, moderator/mediator, and dependent variables, thus being able to distinguish between direct and indirect effects much better than classical regression approaches (Kline, 1998; Maruyama, 1998). Much of the difficulties existent in the reviewed metrics stems from the fact that too many times direct effects have been occluded by moderators (via indirect effects) that have not been considered, thus causing either an over-estimation of the strength of effects, or mis-appreciation of the true relationships. Structural equation modeling proves much more useful in this respect, due to its ability to include large direct-indirect effects links inside the model.

Last but not least, another reason for using this approach is that it provides us with arriving at a weighting and factor solution based on scientific rigor: Confirmatory Factor Analysis, rather than simply dividing 100% total weight by the number of sectors included in the model (the often used solution).

Currently, our work focuses more closely on the World Economic Forum's Networked Readiness Index (NRI) as an initial model for departure in the index construction process.

---

[8] The Institute for Information Policy is currently working on the development of this model

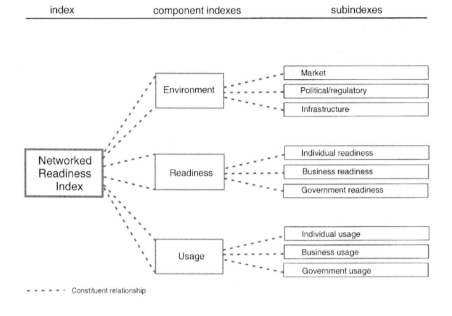

Figure 5. The Networked Readiness Index Framework 2002-2003.
Source: Doutta, Lanvin & Paua, Eds. (2003).

We employ a two group full latent variable modeling approach using data from USA and Italy for 2001-2002 (secondary data). We included a second order Confirmatory Factor Analysis with multiple measures of each observed variable from the NRI sub-indices, in order to assess the measurement error associated with the initial measurement model. The initial structural part of the full latent variable model was based on the conceptual model represented by the NRI (see Figure 5), so that we can test the goodness of fit of the NRI model. We also added Gardin's factors that were inexistent in the original NRI model, so that we can ascertain if a five (Gardin's solution), rather than three (NRI) factor solution improves the fit of the model. Initial findings[9] suggest that not only the overall model is not comparable across the two countries (thus supporting the hypothesis that the NRI index equalizes differences between countries), but the differentially specified models for each country need to be re-estimated due to the initial model's lack of fit.

---

[9] The analyses described here are on going at the time of publication. They are planned to be presented elsewhere. For more information, contact Dan Grigorovici at dangrig@psu.edu.

## 4    CONCLUSIONS AND IMPLICATIONS FOR FUTURE RESEARCH AND POLICY-MAKING

Based on what has been discussed in this paper, we need to address several issues that have been identified to advance Information Society indices: the need for new data (new variables from the different actors within society); the necessity to improve existing methods (classifications and weighting schemes); the need for more analysis (on a micro- and meso-level based on the new variables in combination with existing data); and last but not least, the need for a conceptual framework that define the relevant indicators and to formulate a certain order in the development of these indicators. One such framework has been proposed by Kuipers (2002).

What would a more comprehensive, flexible tool include? Drawing together the perspectives of the existing tools:

1    It should provide (optional) measurements for the range of factors that influence e-readiness. Such as:
    a.   existing technology infrastructure;
    b.   information technology policies (trade, encryption, digital signatures, privacy, etc.);
    c.   distribution, pricing, and usage of the technology in schools, business, government, and throughout society;
    d.   basic "enablers" in society (basic literacy, quality of educational system, political stability, etc.);
    e.   social and cultural factors the influence technology's diffusion and use; and
    f.   market conditions (monopolies, regulation, etc.).

2    It should describe how these measurements could be used for:
    g.   economic growth;
    h.   wide social use of technology; and
    i.   economic growth in the context of social issues such as consumer protection, privacy, etc.

3    It should clearly describe how to use the tool:
    j.   when a policy assessment is needed;
    k.   how the information is to be gathered, and what standards are to be used;
    l.   who is needed to complete the assessment (diverse range of experts knowledgeable about issue, oversight of process to make sure accurate, etc);
    m.  how long it should take;
    n.   what the outcome should look like, including a narrative assessment of the policies, guided by or directly answering the survey questions, with recommendations on what to change;
    o.   how to recognize majority and minority opinions and leave room for dissent; and
    p.   what factors are usually under government control, and which are not.

4    It should indicate how to use the results, including identifying potential difficulties with implementation, such as balancing consumer rights, business and labor issues.

One way of providing a valid, relative and as unbiased as possible measure has to be comprised of two steps[10]: the first logical step is to make use of the tools of structural equation modeling by comprehensively looking at all the important variables that affect the information situation/context, and include them in the model. The advantage of structural equation modeling is that due to its characteristics, it does not lead us into the circularity of assumptions that we discussed previously as the major sources of bias in the existing measures. The data analysis step should be thus able to test several models that provide a best bit solution, and based on this, arrive at an index, if and only if, a single composite index would prove to be adequate. This step should also be able to suggest a way into constructing a theoretical model. The second step should link more closely the information measurement model to Quality of Life models, since ultimately the goal of any endeavor for measuring the "Information Society", "Technology Achievement" or "E-readiness", is to be able to quantify and track their impacts and changes on people's living conditions at various levels of analysis (individual, sectoral, national, international, etc.). Unfortunately, most of the e-metrics research done currently seems to have forgotten the real objective, while driven by the passion for scientific rigidity. Therefore, our current research aims to study the relationships between the information measurement models and those from a mostly independent area of social research: quality of life indices. Examples to be tested in further research are the comprehensive Calvin-Henderson Quality of Life Index (Albery, 1992a-b) and the Genuine Progress Indicator (Anielski & Rowe, 1999; Cobb, 2000; Cobb & Rixford, 1998).

In conclusion, it is hoped that the suggested road would prove a valuable contribution to the work currently done in the field of Information Society macro level metrics which eventually can help both industry and policy communities use a tool in quantifying the Digital Divide gaps in our society. As the first step in trying to alleviate the gaps is being able to correctly "weigh" them, then it is safe to say that valid Information metrics can be important tools for decision-making towards closing the gaps and increasing quality of life by providing access to technology. And as we all know by now, access is not just about physical indicators (teledensity, number of Internet hosts, etc.) and the measure we are looking for needs to take this fact into account.

## 5   REFERENCES

Albery, N. (1992a), "Quality of Life: Its Underlying Philosophy", in N. Albery (ed.) (1995), *The Book of Visions: An Encyclopedia of Social Innovations*, Institute for Social Inventions, London, UK., available online at http://www.newciv.org/GIB/BOV/BV-376.html [accessed January 2003].

Albery, N. (1992b), "The International Index of Social Progress", in N. Albery (ed.) (1995), *The Book of Visions: An Encyclopedia of Social Innovations*, Institute for Social Inventions, London, UK, available online at http://www.newciv.org/GIB/BOV/BV-377.html [accessed January 2003].

Analysys Consulting (2000), "The Network Revolution and the Developing World", available online http://www.infodev.org/library/400.doc [accessed January 2003].

Anielski, M. & Rowe, J. (1999), "The Genuine Progress Indicators-1998 Update", available online at http://www.rprogress.org/pubs/pdf/gpi1998_data.pdf [accessed January 2003].

---

[10] Currently under development under the "InforMetrics" research program under development by the authors of the present chapter.

Asia Pacific Economic Cooperation (2000), "E-Commerce Readiness Guide", available online at http://www.ecommerce.gov/apec/docs/readiness_guide_files/readiness_guide_5.pdf [accessed April 2001].

Asia Pacific Economic Cooperation (1999), "Electronic Commerce Readiness Indicators", report presented at the Meeting of the Steering Group on Electronic Commerce, June 27-28, Auckland, New Zealand. Available online at http://www.apecsec.org.sg/download/virtualib/e-commerce/ sgec.exe [accessed January 2003].

Atkinson, R.D. & Court, R.H. (1998), "The New Economy Index. Understanding America's Economic Transformation", The Progressive Policy Institute: Washington, D.C., available online at http://www.neweconomyindex.org/index_nei.html [accessed January 2003].

Baily, M.N. & Lawrence, R. (2001), "Do We Have a New E-conomy?", National Bureau of Economic Research working paper, No. W8243/2001. National Bureau of Economic Research, Cambridge, MA. Available online at http://papers.nber.org/papers/W8243.pdf [accessed: January 2003].

Barbet, P. & Coutinet, N. (2001), "Measuring the Digital Economy: US and European perspectives", *Communications & Strategies*, No. 42, 2nd quarter.

Berger-Schmitt, R. & Noll, H.-H. (2000), "Conceptual Framework and Structure of a European System of Social Indicators", EuReporting Working Paper No. 9. Mannheim: Centre for Survey Research and Methodology (ZUMA), Social Indicators Department. Available online: http://intraweb.zumamannheim.de/en/social_monitoring/social_indicators/EU_Reporting/pdf_fil es/paper9.pdf [accessed January 2003].

Berger-Schmitt, R. & Jankowitsch, B. (1999), "Systems of Social Indicators and Social Reporting: the state of the art", EuReporting Working paper no. 1. Mannheim, Germany: Center for Survey Research and Methodology (ZUMA). Available online at http://intraweb.zuma-mannheim.de/en/social_monitoring/social_indicators/EU_Reporting/pdf_files/paper1.pdf [accessed January 2003].

Bosworth, B. & Triplett, J.E. (2000), "What's New About the New Economy? IT, Economic Growth and Productivity", The Brookings Institution: Washington, D.C. Available online at http://www.brook.edu/views/papers/bosworth/20001020.htm [accessed January 2003].

Bridges.org (2001), "Spanning the Digital Divide: understanding and tackling the issues", available online at http://www.bridges.org/spanning/report.html [accessed January 2003].

Bruno, L. (2001), "Information Society Index 2001 Trends and Rankings", Bulletin #W23953, abstract available online at http://www.itresearch.com/ [accessed January 2001].

Carss, G. (2002), "The Role of the Statistician in the Knowledge-Based Economy", paper presented at the International Association for Official Statistics conference on "Official Statistics and the New Economy", August 27-29, London, UK. Available online at http://www.statistics.gov.uk/iaoslondon2002/contributed_papers/IP_Carss.asp [accessed May 2003).

Center for International Development (2000), "Readiness for the Networked World", Center for International Development, Cambridge, MA: Harvard University, available online http://www.readinessguide.org/ [accessed April 2001].

Cisco Systems & the University of Texas at Austin (2001), "Measuring the Internet Economy", Austin, TX: The University of Texas at Austin. Available online at http://www.internetindicators.com/execsummry.html [accessed January 2003].

City of Seattle Department of Information Technology & the Citizens Telecommunications and Technology Advisory Board (2000), "Information Technology Indicators for a Healthy Community", Seattle, WA: City of Seattle Department of Information Technology. Available online at http://www.cityofseattle.net/tech/indicators/prelimreport.htm [accessed January 2003].

Cobb, C.W. (2000), "Measurement Tools and the Quality of Life", available online at http://www.rprogress.org/pubs/pdf/measure_qol.pdf [accessed January 2003].

Cobb, C.W. & Rixford, C. (1998), "Lessons Learned from the History of Social Indicators", available online at http://www.rprogress.org/pubs/pdf/SocIndHist.pdf [accessed January 2003].

Commonwealth of Australia, National Office for the Information Economy (2000), "E-Commerce across Australia", available online at http://www.noie.gov.au/publications/NOIE/ecommerce_analysis/eCommerceAcrossAustralia.pdf [accessed January 2003].

Computer Systems Policy Project (1998), "Computer Systems Policy Project Readiness Guide for Living in the Networked World: A Self-assessment Tool for Communities", available online at http://206.183.2.91/projects/readiness/ [accessed April 2001].

Daly, J. (2001), "Measuring Impacts of the Internet in the Developing World", *iMP Magazine*, May, available online at http://www.cisp.org/imp/may_99/daly/05_99daly.htm [accessed April 2001].

Daly, J. (2000), "A Conceptual Framework for the Study of the Impacts of the Internet," available online at http://www.bsos.umd.edu/cidcm/papers/jdaly/concept.htm [accessed April 2001].

David, P.A. (1999), "Digital Technology and the Productivity Paradox: After Ten Years, What Has Been Learned?" paper presented at Understanding the Digital Economy: Data, Tools and Research, U.S. Department of Commerce, Washington, D.C., 25-26 May. Available online at http://mitpress.mit.edu/UDE/david.rtf [accessed January 2003].

Doutta, S., Lanvin, B. & Paua, F., (Eds.), (2003), "The Global Information Technology Report 2002-2003: Readiness for the Networked World", New York, NY: Oxford University Press, World Economic Forum & INSEAD.

European Commission (2000a), "List of eEurope Benchmarking Indicators", European Commission: Bruxelles. Available online at http://europa.eu.int/information_society/eeurope/benchmarking/indicator_list.pdf [accessed January 2003].

European Commission (2000b), "Benchmarking eEurope: Methodology Paper", European Commission: Bruxelles. Available online at ftp://ftp.cordis.lu/pub/ist/docs/2000cpa8-ee-benchmarking.pdf [accessed January 2003].

Gardin, O. (2002), "The New Economy – New Challenges for the Statistical System", paper presented at the International Association for Official Statistics conference on "Official Statistics and the New Economy", August 27-29, London, UK. Available online at http://www.statistics.gov.uk/iaoslondon2002/contributed_papers/CP_Gardin.asp [accessed May 2003].

Gill, G., Young, K., Pastore, D., Dumagan, J.,Turk, I. (1997), "Economy-Wide and Industry-Level Impact of Information Technology", US Department of Commerce: Washington, D.C., Available online at http://netsite.esa.doc.gov/obia/wp-97-3.pdf [accessed January 2003].

Gordon, R.J. (2000), "Does the "New Economy" Measure up to the Great Inventions of the Past?", National Bureau of Economic Research working paper 7833/2000, Cambridge, MA:. National

Bureau of Economic Research, available online at www.nber.org/papers/w7833 [accessed January 2003].

Grace, J., Kenny, C., Qiang, C., Liu, J. (2001), "Information and Communication Technologies and Broad-Based Development: A Partial Review of the Evidence", InfoDev Working paper, World Bank: Washington, DC.

Haltiwanger, J. & Jarmin, R.S. (2000), "Measuring the Digital Economy", in E. Brynjolfsson & B. Kahin (eds.) (2000), *Understanding the Digital Economy*, The MIT Press: Cambridge, MA. . Available online at http://mitpress.mit.edu/books/BRYUH/02.haltiwanger.pdf [accessed January 2003].

Henderson, H., Lickerman, J., & Flynn, P., (eds.) (2000), *Calvert-Henderson Quality of Life Indicators*, Flynn Research: Charlestown, WV. Chs. 1-2 available online at http://www.flynnresearch.com/calvert.htm [accessed January 2003].

Horn, R.V. (1993), *Statistical Indicators for the Economic and Social Sciences*, New York, NY: Cambridge University Press.

IDC (2001), "Sweden Remains the World's Dominant Information Economy While the United States Slips, According to the 2001 IDC/World Times Information Society Index", IDC Press Release, available online at http://www.idc.com/ITOver/press/020801pr.stm accessed April 2001].

IDC (2000), "The 2000 IDC/World Times Information Society Index", available online at http://www.idc.com:8080/Data/Global/ISI/ISIMain.htm [accessed May 2001].

Infodev (2001), "ICT Infrastructure and E-Readiness Assessment Initiative", World Bank: Washington, D.C., available online at http://www.infodev.org/ereadiness/ [accessed April 2001].

Information Technologies Group (2000), "Readiness for the Networked World: A Guide for Developing Countries", Center for International Development, Harvard University: Cambridge, MA, available online at http://www.readinessguide.org/ [accessed April 2001].

Jorgenson, D. W. & Stiroh, K.J. (2000), "Raising the Speed Limit: U.S. Economic Growth in the Information Age", Brookings Papers on Economic Activity, 1, pp. 125-211.

Kenny, C. (2001), "Prioritizing Countries for Assistance to Overcome the Digital Divide", *Communications & Strategies*, No. 41, 1st quarter.

Kirkman, G.S., Osorio, C.A., Sachs, J.D. (2002), "The Networked Readiness Index: Measuring the Preparedness of Nations for the Networked World", in G. Kirkman (ed.), *The Global Information Technology Report 2001-2002: Readiness for the Networked World*, Oxford, Oxford University Press: New York, available online at http://www.cid.harvard.edu/cr/gitrr_030202.html [accessed June 2002].

Kline, R.B. (1998), *Principles and Practice of Structural Equation Modeling*, New York, NY: The Guilford Press.

Krippendorff, K. (2003), "Conceptions of Information that Constrain and that Enable", oral communication presented at the 53rd Annual Conference of the International Communication Association, Information Systems Division, May 23-27, San Diego, CA.

Kuipers, A. (2002), "Building Blocks for the Description of the Digital Economy", paper presented at the International Association for Official Statistics conference on "Official Statistics and the New Economy", August 27-29, London, UK. Available online at http://www.statistics.gov.uk/iaoslondon2002/contributed_papers/IP_Kuipers.asp [accessed May 2003]

Lanvin, B. (2001), "Bridging the Digital Divide: Is it Too Late?", *Communications & Strategies*, No. 41, 1st quarter.

Leadbeater, C. (1999), "New Measures for the New Economy", presented at the International Symposium "Measuring and reporting Intellectual Capital: experience, issues, and prospects", Amsterdam, 9-10 June. Available online at http://www.oecd.org/dsti/sti/industry/indcomp/act/Ams-conf/Technical-meeting/uk.pdf [accessed January 2003].

Loehlin, J.C. (1998), *Latent Variable Models: an Introduction to Factor, Path, and Structural Analysis*, Mahwah, NJ: Lawrence Erlbaum.

Maruyama, G.M. (1998), *Basics of Structural Equation Modeling*, Thousand Oaks, CA: Sage.

Massachusetts Technology Collaborative (2000), "Index of the Massachusetts Innovation Economy", Westborough, MA: MTC, available online at http://www.mtpc.org/theindex/2000index/index2000.htm [accessed June 2002].

McConnell International (2000), "Risk E-Business: Seizing the Opportunity of Global E-Readiness", available online at http://mcconnellinternational.com/readiness/default.cfm [accessed June 2002].

Menou, M., Potvin, J. (2000), "Toward a Conceptual Framework for Learning about ICT's and Knowledge in the Process of Development", The Global Knowledge Learning and Evaluation Action Program background document, available online at: http://www.bellanet.org/ICT_res_pol/docs/LEAP_Concept_2May2000.htm [accessed June 2002].

Menou, M. (1995a), "The Impact of Information – I. Toward a Research Agenda for its Definition and Measurement", *Information Processing & Management*, Vol. 31, No. 4.

Menou, M. (1995b), "The Impact of Information –II. Concepts of Information and its Value", *Information Processing & Management*, Vol. 31, No. 4.

Menou, M. (1993a), "The Impact of Information on Development: Results of a Preliminary Investigation", in M. Feeney & M.Grieves (eds.) (1993), *Changing Information Technologies: Research Challenges in the Economics of Information*, Bowker Saur: London, UK.

Menou, M., (ed.) (1993b), *Measuring the Impact of Information on Development*, IDRC Books: Ottawa.

Menou, M. (1985), "An Information System for Decision Support in National Information Policy-making and Planning", *Information Processing & Management* 2.

Miles, I., Brady, T., Davies, A., Haddon, L., Jagger, N., Matthews, M., Rush, H., Wyatt, S. (1990), "Mapping and Measuring the Information Economy: A Report Produced for the Economic and Social Research Council's Program in Information and Communication Technologies", Library and Information Research Report No. 77, British Library: London.

Mesenbourg, T. L. (1999), "Measuring e-Business: Challenges and Priorities", presented at the Meeting of the Steering Group on Electronic Commerce, Auckland, New Zealand, June 27-28. Available online at http://www.apecsec.org.sg/download/virtualib/e-commerce/sgec.exe [accessed June 2002].

Meta Group (2000), "The META Group Global New E-Economy Index: Facts About the Methodology", available online at http://www.metagroup.com/global/factsheet.htm [accessed June 2002].

Minges, M. (2000), "Counting the Net: Internet Access Indicators", presented at INET 2000, The Internet Global Summit, Yokohama, Japan, 18-21 July, available online a: http://www.isoc.org/inet2000/cdproceedings/8e/8e_1.htm [accessed June 2002].

Minges, M. (1999), "Measuring the Diffusion of the Internet". Presented at INET'99. Dimensions of Internet Diffusion. San Jose, California. June 23, available online at: http://www.itu.int/ti/papers/1999/MM Inet99 Jn99.pdf [accessed June 2002].

Monk, T., & Claffy, K. C. (1996), "A Survey of Internet Statistics/Metrics Activities", available online at http://www.caida.org/outreach/papers/metricsurvey.html [accessed June 2002].

Montagnier, P., Muller, E. & Vickery, G. (2002). "The Digital Divide: Diffusion and Use of ICT's", paper presented at the International Association for Official Statistics conference on "Official Statistics and the New Economy", August 27-29, London, UK. Available online at http://www.statistics.gov.uk/iaoslondon2002/contributed_papers/IP_Vickery.asp [Accessed May 2003].

Moulton, B.R. (2000), "GDP and the Digital Economy: Keeping Up with the Changes", in E. Brynjolfsson & B. Kahin (eds.) (2000), *Understanding the Digital Economy*, The MIT Press: Cambridge, MA. Available online at http://mitpress.mit.edu/books/BRYUH/03.moulton.pdf [accessed January 2003].

Noll, H.-H. (2001), "Social Indicators and Social Reporting: The International Experience", available online at http://www.ccsd.ca/noll1.html [accessed January 2003].

Northwest Research Group (2000), "Information Technology Indicators: City of Seattle Residential Survey", City of Seattle Department of Information Technology: Seattle, WA, available online at http://www.cityofseattle.net/tech/indicators/Data Collection.htm [accessed January 2003].

OECD (2000a), "Measuring the ICT Sector", Organization for Economic Cooperation and Development: Paris, France, available online at http://www.oecd.org//dsti/sti/it/index.htm [accessed January 2003].

OECD (2000b), "Measuring the Digital Divide", Joint WPTISP/WPIE Workshop, Organization for Economic Cooperation and Development: Paris, France, available online at, http://www.oecd.org/dsti/sti/it/infosoc/act/digital_divide/fazio.pdf [accessed January 2003].

OECD (2000c), "A new economy? The Changing Role of Innovation and Information Technology in Growth", Organization for Economic Cooperation and Development: Paris, France, available online at http://www.oecd.org/dsti/sti/stat-ana/prod/growth.htm [accessed January 2003].

Paltridge, S. (1998), "Internet Infrastructure Indicators", OECD Paris, available online at. http://www.oecd.org/dsti/sti/it/cm/prod/tisp98-7e.pdf [accessed January 2003].

Press, L. (1997), "Tracking the Global Diffusion of the Internet", *Communications of the ACM* (40:11).

Press, L., Burkhart, G., Foster, W., Goodman, S., Wolcott, P., & Woodard, J. (1997), "An Internet Diffusion Framework" *Communications of the ACM* (41:10).

Rodriguez, F., Wilson III, E.J. (2000), "Are Poor Countries Losing the Information Revolution?", InfoDev working paper, World Bank: Washington, DC, available online at http://www.infodev.org/library/wilsonrodriguez.doc [accessed January 2003].

Rogers, E. M. (1995), *Diffusion of Innovations* (4th ed.), The Free Press: New York.

Schement, J. R. (1990), "Porat, Bell, and the Information Society Reconsidered: The Growth of Information Work in the Early Twentieth Century", *Information Processing & Management*, Vol. 26, No. 4.

Sciadas, G. (2002), "Monitoring the Digital Divide", Quebec, Canada: Orbicom, available online at www.orbicom.uqam.ca/projects/ddi2002/ddi2002.pdf [accessed May 2003].

Selhofer, H., Mayringer, H. (2001), "Benchmarking the Information Society Development in European Countries", *Communications & Strategies*, No. 43, 3rd quarter.

Shifflet, M., & Schement, J. R. (1996), "Information Indicators: A Review of their Value in Policy Studies of the National Information Infrastructure", paper presented at the International Communication Association, Chicago, IL, May.

Statistical Office of the European Communities (2000), "SINE: Statistical Indicators for the New Economy", available online at http://europa.eu.int/comm/eurostat/Public/datashop/print-product/EN?catalogue=Eurostat&product=SINE-EN&type=pdf [accessed January 2003].

The Economist Intelligence Unit (2001), "The Economist Intelligence Unit / Pyramid Research e-readiness rankings", available online at:
http://www.ebusinessforum.com/index.asp?layout=rich_story&doc_id=367&country_id=VN&ch anne-
lid=6&categoryid=20&title=Introducing+the+EIU%27s+e%2Dbusiness%2Dreadiness+rankings +World [accessed January 2003].

UNDP (2001), "Human Development Report 2001: Making New Technologies Work for Human Development", New York, Oxford: Oxford University Press, available online at http://www.undp.org/hdr2001/ [accessed January 2003].

UNDP (2000), "Driving Information and Communication technologies for Development. A UNDP agenda for action 2000-2001", Oxford University Press: New York, Oxford. Available online at http://sdnhq.undp.org/it4dev/ffICTe.pdf [accessed January 2003].

Wilson, E., Daly, J., & Griffiths, J-M. (1998), "Internet Counts: Measuring the Impacts of the Internet", National Academy Press: Washington, DC. Available online at:
http://www.bsos.umd.edu/cidcm/wilson/xnasrep2.htm [accessed April 2001].

Wolcott, P., Press, L., McHenry, W., Goodman, S. & Foster, W. (2001), "A Framework for Assessing the Global Diffusion of the Internet", *Journal of the Association for Information Systems*, 2, November.

Wolcott, P. (2000), "Global Diffusion of the Internet Project", available online at:
http://mosaic.unomaha.edu/gdi.html [accessed January 2003].

Wolcott, P., Goodman, S., Burkhart, G. (1996), "The Information Technology Capability of Nations: A Framework for Analysis", The MOSAIC Group Working Paper, available online at http://mosaic.unomaha.edu/ITC_1996.pdf [accessed January 2003].

World Bank (2001), "The Knowledge Assessment Methodology and Scorecards", The World Bank Institute: Washington, D.C, available online at:
http://www1.worldbank.org/gdln/Programs/kam/methodology.htm [accessed January 2003].

World Information Technology and Services Alliance (2000), "International Survey of E-Commerce 2000", available online at http://www.witsa.org/papers/EComSurv.pdf [accessed April 2001].

World Times/IDC (2000), "Information Society Index. Measuring the Global Impact of Information Technology and Internet Adoption", available online at:
http://www.idc.com:8080/Data/Global/ISI/ISIMain.htm [accessed May 2001].

# PART IV

# ICT MARKET EVOLUTION AND THE DIGITAL SOCIETY

Global Economy and Digital Society
E. Bohlin, S. Levin, N. Sung and C-H. Yoon (Editors)

CHAPTER 11

# Applying the Principle of Modularity to the Internet QoS Service Model Design

Hak Ju Kim and Martin B. H. Weiss
*Telecommunications Program, Department of Information
Science & Telecommunications, University of Pittsburgh, Pittsburgh*

**Abstract**. As the uncertainty in the markets and technologies of the network industry increases, a flexible architecture is needed by network service providers to maintain a competitive advantage. Since complete replacement of existing networks is not practical, and since it is costly for one operator to manage everything in a network, modularity in network design may be an efficient approach. Although the notion of modularity has recently received some attention in the network industry, its potential value still remains uncertain and its emphasis on flexibility is only loosely related to the goal of creating added value in existing network architectures. The goal of this chapter is to construct a theoretical framework to support the decisions of network service providers in network design: to modularize or not, and if so, by how much. To achieve this goal, a theory is developed to show the extent of modularity in network design by combining two important concepts: modularity from management and complementarity from economics. This will show how the extent of modularity in networks affects the value of networks with complementary components under uncertainty. For empirical testing, a simple QoS service model network is designed and simulated.

## 1    INTRODUCTION

The merger and acquisition boom of the 1990s was driven in part by the synergy effect[1] (Miller, 2002). When AOL merged with Time Warner in 2000, the concept was that the New Economy would lead the Old Economy stalwart into the Internet Age. It was seen as the ultimate triumph of the synergy theory. However, the world economy is now littered with failed or failing corporate giants. Baldwin and Clark (1997) argue that we are living in the age of modularity. Many industries have long had a degree of modularity in their production and design processes as well as their organizational structure. The recent collapse of giants like Enron and WorldCom helps to support their argument.

Mass production (Milgrom and Roberts, 1990) has dominated modern society for several decades. Nowadays, mass customization is emerging as a new way of providing goods and services. What exactly is mass customization? It is increasingly possible both to design

---

[1] The sharing of particularly managerial resources has the potential to reduce costs and to increase revenue through economies of scale (Porter, 1985).

products that have the ability to be configured to meet the preferences of individual customers and to produce those products at costs that do not differ significantly from the cost of mass producing a single product design (Pine, 1993). This trend of mass customization challenges network service providers in the telecommunications industry to increase their flexibility without losing their current economies of scale. Being flexible in this respect can be described as the ability to meet a wide variety of customer requirements in a short period of time. Therefore, new service development has recently been recognized as an important factor for network-based service firms faced with highly competitive environments, as these normally have higher profit margins.

The surviving network service providers, whether ISPs, CLECs, ILECs, or even recent 3G wireless service providers, are facing an environment in which experimentation is needed to find viable business, cost, or service models. With the emerging trend of mass customization (Pine, 1993), customized and rapid service provisioning has recently been identified as an important source of competitive advantage in the network industry. Network service development is no longer about creating the service itself, but also creating a platform. The notion of service architecture is a key concept in service development which is no longer just a technical issue. Creating appropriate modular architectures to support new kinds of service strategies is now central to business strategies. Businesses need to create service and process architectures that are capable of providing the flexibility to customize services for individuals and upgradable them when better components come along.

Traditionally, the analysis of networks has been performed assuming that they are characterized as centralized and monolithic systems. Many academic and field studies in network engineering and economics have focused on whole system replacement and often use a 'green field' assumption for supporting their decision implicitly or explicitly because they consider the existing facilities as a sunk cost. This ignores the reality of networks and the investment behavior of service providers. Although the notion of modularity has received much attention in modern network design as a strategy for managing the complexity of networks efficiently, its potential value still remains poorly understood and its emphasis on flexibility is loosely related to the goal of creating added value in existing networks. So, a better explanatory model is needed to value the modularity in network design.

The main motivation for this paper, then, is the development of a theoretical framework for network service providers to support their strategic design decisions: to modularization or not, and if so, by how much.

The remainder of this paper is organized as follows: Section 2 explains how previous work relates to the issues of modularity considered here and provides the background knowledge of our study, such as modularity and complementarity. Section 3 presents the theoretical framework, such as research model, theory and hypothesis. In section 4 and Section 5, the empirical tests and results analysis are implemented, respectively. Finally, in Section 6, concluding remarks are presented.

## 2  RELATED LITERATURE

### 2.1  The Notion of Modularity

Modularity is not a new concept. It has been applied in many businesses, especially manufacturing, as a lean method of production (Milgrom and Roberts, 1995). The notion of modularity refers to the building of a complex product or process from smaller subsystems that can be designed independently yet function together as a whole (Baldwin and Clark, 2000). That is, each module has a tightly specified interface to the others, allowing modules to be independently changed and upgraded. Because of their independence, modules of a system are driven to evolve through the following design features: splitting, substituting, augmenting, excluding, inverting, and porting.

Modularity is promising as a strategic tool to manage the complexity of networks efficiently (Baldwin and Clark, 1997) by providing high flexibility. This flexibility has real economic benefit, but network designers lack the ability to value flexible networks because of their intangible characteristics. However, the real options approach can be used to analyze the trade-off involved in modular network designs between the upfront costs of developing a modular interface against the value of the options it creates.

Bjorkman (2000) notes that network design is moving from monolithic to modular. He argues that today's switches and routers are typical examples of monolithic design because some parts cannot be easily exchanged for another and must be replaced in whole parts by a single vendor (e.g. Cisco and Nortel). Even though they are separated physically, the software is truly monolithic: for example, since new software releases are related to several functions in the equipment, the operator depends on the vendor. Braun et al. (1995.) suggest a modular de-layered design of communication systems, divided into three categories: (1) application-oriented service interface, (2) communication-oriented components, and (3) network-oriented components. They criticize the use of a simple networking adapter inserted into a system bus and several software modules performing most of tasks to support multimedia applications because this leads to inefficient and highly inflexible implementations. Instead, they suggest efficient implementation with high flexibility by codesigning hardware and software. For example, performance critical components are mapped onto dedicated hardware and less critical components are formed by traditional software modules, especially focusing on protocol support functions.

Zhang et al. (2000) propose a bandwidth broker architecture that decouples the QoS control plane from the packet forwarding plane. They argue that core routers should not maintain any QoS reservation states, whether per-flow or aggregate. Instead, QoS reservation states should be stored at and managed by bandwidth brokers. They point out several advantages of such bandwidth broker architecture. First, it can relieve core routers of QoS control functions such as admission control and QoS state management, and thus enables a network service provider to introduce new (guaranteed) services without necessarily requiring software/hardware upgrades at core routers. Second, it allows us to design efficient admission control algorithms without incurring any overhead at core routers. Wolf (2000) designed the modular network processor through an instruction set (design rule), which pushes the decoding of instructions into the individual modules. Its instructions are tagged with the identifier of the module, and its context mapping unit provides the modules with the appropriate register set. They made example code for processing an IP packet to show how the instruction set could be used. Furthermore they defined several performance metrics and then attempted to compare their modular system and the standard RISC system. They concluded that the performance of the modular system was higher than the standard RISC system design.

Baldwin and Clark (2000) have been the first to observe that the value of modularity in design (of computer systems) can be modeled by the real options approach. Assuming that a product is designed in a modular fashion, they analyze the effect of modular design on product development performance by quantifying the value of modularity in terms of increased design flexibility. They apply the theory of real options to show that the mix-and-match feature of modular design can dramatically speed the rate of performance improvement. But they argue that the costs of testing products made possible by modular design may limit the effectiveness of modular design and modular design requires extensive ex ante product knowledge. They also do not explicitly address the problem of decomposing products into subsystems, like the loss of coordination. Mikkola (2001) developed a mathematical model, termed modularization function, for analyzing the degree of modularity in a given product architecture by taking into account the following variables: number of components, number of interfaces, and substitutability factor of a given product architecture. He assumes that the degree of modularity in a given product architecture is constrained by the composition of its components, interfaces shared among the components, and degree of substitutability. They applied it to two distinct sets of product architectures: Chrysler Jeeps windshield wiper controllers and transmission systems of Schindler elevators. The results showed that the value of modularity was increased by the higher substitutability level and lower new-to-firm component composition. He also discussed some managerial implications for both case studies based on the application of the modularization function.

## 2.2   Complementarity

A new approach to modeling the importance of complementarity (coordination) has been developed in economics by Milgrom and Roberts (1990). They defined complementarity such that if the levels of any subset of activities are increased, then the marginal return of increases in any or all of the remaining activities rises. That is, if the marginal costs associated with some activities fall, it will be optimal to increase the level of all of the activities in the grouping. Their analyses rely heavily on the mathematics of supermodular function. The notion of complementarity was first used by Edgeworth (Schaefer, 1999). Following Edgeworth, two activities or properties are complements if they have positive mixed partial derivatives with respect to a continuously differentiable objective function, like the productivity function or social welfare function. Milgrom and Roberts have considerably extended the initial work of Edgeworth and pioneered its application to economics. Instead of Edgeworth's complements, they use another term, supermodular. It implies that the change in f(x,y) when any component of x is increased is non-decreasing in the other components of y (Schaefer, 1999). If f is supermodular, the arguments of f are complements (Topkis, 1978). The following is a supermodular function:

$$f(x_1, y_1) - f(x_1, y_0) \geq f(x_0, y_1) - f(x_0, y_0).$$

This inequality is equivalent to stating that increasing one or more variables raises the return to other variables. Thus, the supermodularity of a function corresponds with complementarity among its arguments.

## 3   THE MODEL

Figure 1 shows the research model which clarifies the effects of the modularization process and the trade-off between modularization and complementarity in the network design under uncertainty. It is not intended to give absolute numbers or rules for that, but to show general relationships among uncertainty, complementarity, and modularity with regard to network design. Based on this model, we attempt to develop our theory to provide a framework for modularizing the network design with complementary components under uncertainty.

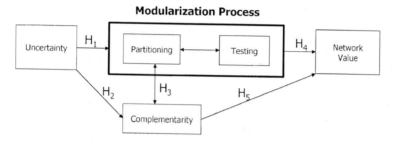

Figure 1. Research Model

Assuming the completely integrated network works very efficiently, its technological variation (uncertainty) is smaller than that of any other system (i.e. less integrated). Now, if we attempt to partition the completely integrated network for a flexible network, the technological variation (uncertainty) will increase because of the loosening of the coordination of the network components by partitioning. The meaning of increasing technological variation (uncertainty) is to increase the potential of technology development (innovation) because of the ease of specialization of that technology, as shown in Figure 2. Rather, if we do several experiments to find the best fitting structure in each module, this will result in increasing the probability of success against that of failure. All of these effects of modularization will be explained in greater detail below.

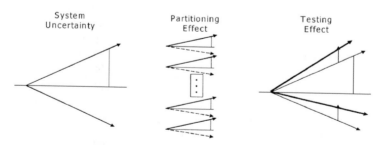

Figure 2. The Effects of Modularity to System

## 3.1   Technological Uncertainty: QoSDEX

Networks are faced with several uncertainties, such as *market uncertainty* (MU) and *technological uncertainty* (TU). The MU is mainly focused on the variation of market conditions, such as customer preferences in market demand and the level of competition in the market for network-based services, while the TU is mainly about the new technologies and unexpected advancements in networks: for example, the unexpected increase of capacity by the development of DWDM technology with fiber. Compared to the MU, there is not much discussion concerning the TU, especially its measurement issues, in academics and industry. Baldwin and Clark (2000) addressed technical potential as a technological uncertainty, but they just suggest a theoretical concept like standard deviation. We attempt to develop a proxy of the technological uncertainty in networks. Then, what are the technological uncertainties in the QoS-enabled networks? The performance volatility of QoS functions are good candidates for technological uncertainties because they are directly related to the performance parameters of a network, such as throughput, delay, loss rate, and jitter.

We propose a QoS Index (QoSDEX), which is defined as the volatility (variation) of network performance by the QoS functions during a certain period, as a proxy for technological uncertainty in the QoS-enabled networks. The QoSDEX is applied to the concept of compound return[2] and the metrics of standard deviation (STD):

(1) The first step for calculating the QoSDEX is to calculate the compounded return of network performance by QoS functions.

$$\mu_t = \ln(QoS_t / QoS_{t-1})$$

where $\mu_t$ is the compound return of network performance by QoS functions between $t$-1 and $t$, $QoS_t$ and $QoS_{t-1}$ are the performance of QoS functions in time t and time t-1.

(2) The next step is to calculate the QoSDEX using the usual formula for the standard deviation in statistics.

$$QoSDEX = \sqrt{\frac{1}{(n-1)}\sum(\mu_t - \overline{\mu})^2}$$

**Assumption 1:** *The technological uncertainty in QoS-enabled network is the variation of network performance of QoS functions (QoSDEX) as a proxy.*

## 3.2   Modular Gains and Losses

Partitioning for modularization is to split an interconnected task structure into modules (Hippel, 1990). It assumes the economies of specialization (or scope) instead of economies of scale. Partitioning is not only simply decomposing tasks but also integrating them by specification and functional interface. The key effects of partitioning are the increasing technical potential (uncertainty gain), the simplicity of management vis-à-vis a complex network (specialization or innovation gain), mix-and-match testing gain, and the loss of coordination.

---

[2] The compounded return equals the logarithm of 1 plus interest rate. For example, if the return rate = 0.1 or 10%, then the compounded return is $ln(1+0.1) = 0.0953$.

To develop a theory concerning uncertainty gain, we use portfolio theory (Markowitz, 1991), which is well known in finance. Like a portfolio of stocks, each network component is interrelated positively or negatively and will affect the whole network's performance, and has its own risk. Using portfolio theory, we assume that the technological uncertainty of a well-constructed and integrated network is smaller than the sum of technological uncertainties of a modularized network. This is generally consistent with the notion that the integrated system is more efficient and reliable than others. Thus, the following formula is induced:

$$\sum_{i=1}^{n} \sigma_i - \sigma_I \geq 0$$

where $\sigma_i$ is the uncertainty of each module and $\sigma_I$ is the uncertainty of the integrated network.

**Hypothesis 1:** *Technological uncertainty is positively related to the modularity. That is, the higher (lower) technological uncertainty is driving the higher (lower) modularization.*

Another effect of partitioning is that the designer can make the network more manageable and productive by decreasing its complexity. This effect is formulized by Baldwin and Clark using the 'root square principle' (Baldwin and Clark, 2000). Assuming that modules are partitioned to the same size and the performance of each module is normally distributed (i.e., N network components are partitioned symmetrically into j modules and are independent of all the other modules.), that E(•) is defined as the expected value, and that M (network) is assumed to have a normal distribution with mean zero and variance $\sigma^2$, then the value of the network is the following:

$$E(M_n) = 0.3989 \sigma n^{\frac{1}{2}}$$

where 0.3989 is the expectation value given that a random variable is greater than zero in normal distribution with a mean zero and a variance and standard deviation of one. If the network is partitioned into j independent modules, the expected value of the modular design by partitioning ($V_{partitioning}$) is:

$$V_{partitioning} = V_{system} + E(M_1) + E(M_2) + ... + E(M_j)$$

where $V_{system}$ is overall system value and $E(M_j)$ is the contribution value of modules.

Under these assumptions, module values will be distributed normally with mean zero and variance equal to $\sigma^2 N / j$. So, each module's expected partitioning value under normal distribution is:

$$E(M_1) = 0.3989 \sigma (N / j)^{\frac{1}{2}}$$

Then, how to calculate the total value of the modules? We substitute this expression for each term in the $V_{partitioning}$ formula, divide by $E(M_n) = 0.3989 \sigma n^{\frac{1}{2}}$, assume $V_{system} = 0$, and then collect terms to get:

$$V_{partitioning} = j^{\frac{1}{2}} V_1.$$

This formula means that the number of modules is proportional to the value of the ease management of network management by partitioning.

**Assumption 2:** *The gain of specialization (innovation) by modularity increases according to the square root of the number of modules. (Square Root Principle)*

The important gain of modularization is the possibility of mix-and-match testing without much cost. Testing can increase the value of a network in a high uncertainty environment because we can get higher expectation of success by picking the best of many tests. To quantify how these tests increase value, we use the extreme order statistics of Lindgren (1968). The value of testing (Q(k)) is calculated by a modified highest order statistic value: in other words, it is the expected value of the highest x among k independent solutions drawn from the distribution F(x). The expectation is truncated in that values of x that are less than zero (the textbook solution's benchmark value) are replaced by zero values. The truncation arises because of the designer's option: if x<0, then the solution drawn from the F(x) distribution is worse than the previously known solution (x = 0). In that eventuality, we assume that a designer can fall back on the previously known solution, and achieve x = 0. This is a basic "designer's option." Q(k) is defined as follows:

$$Q(k) = k \int_{0}^{\infty} z[N(z)]^{k-1} n(z)dz, \text{ where } N(z) = \int_{-\infty}^{z} n(x)dx \text{ and } n(x) = \frac{1}{\sqrt{2\pi}} e^{-z^2}$$

The example values of Q(k) for k = 1 to 10 were computed to three decimal places by using Mathcad (TM) software for numerical integration. Values are shown Table 1.

Table 1. The Value of Mix-and-Match Testing

| k | 1 | 2 | 3 | 4 | 5 | 6 | 7 | 8 | 9 | 10 |
|---|---|---|---|---|---|---|---|---|---|---|
| Q(k) | 0.399 | 0.681 | 0.888 | 1.046 | 1.169 | 1.270 | 1.353 | 1.424 | 1.485 | 1.539 |

**Assumption 3:** *The gain of mix-and-match testing increases the value of the network because the designer chooses the highest order statistic value.*

At a high level of abstraction, a network consists of three sub-systems: operating system, network system, and protocols. Each subsystem has its components: for example, the operating system consists of CPU and memory, the network system has bandwidth, and the protocols have admission control, priority, resource reservation, etc. We assume that there is a complementary relationship between sub-system (across design group) or between its components (within design group). To test complementary in networks, we can use two approaches: the direct method and the indirect method. The direct method focuses on how the components affect performance and the indirect method focuses on the relationship between components.

*Direct Method*

Direct testing for complementarity uses the Supermodular function. It implies that one is interested in imposing one-sided inequality restrictions (e.g. ≥ 0). In a simple two-choice model, there exists a complementary relationship between network components, if

$$\{f(+1, +1) + f(-1, -1)\} - \{f(+1, -1) + f(-1, +1)\} \geq 0$$

where $f(.)$ is performance improvement, $+1$ means the component is on and $-1$ is off. The significance test of the result will be a simple one-tailed t-test.

**Hypothesis 2:** *There exists a complementary relationship between network components.*

*Indirect Method*

Another way to test complementarity is to measure the correlation between network components (within-design group), and between subsystems (across-design group), as seen in Figure 3.

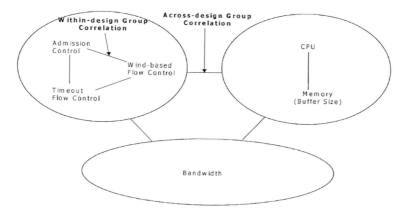

Figure 3: The Relationship Map in Network Components

(1) Between Elements ($\rho$i,j)
We assume that the correlation between elements (within-design group) is greater than or equal to the correlation between elements (across-design group). For example, we assume that there are four network components: $x = \{1, 2, 3, 4\}$. Assuming a completely integrated network design $(\rho1,2) = (\rho1,3) = (\rho1,4) = (\rho2,3) = (\rho2,4) = (\rho3,4) = 1$; now suppose that the NSP creates two design groups: G1 = $\{1,2\}$ and G2 = $\{3,4\}$. The value of $(\rho1,2)$ and $(\rho3,4)$ in the modularized network design is the same value as those in a completely integrated network design. So, the loss of coordination by modularization will be the difference of $(\rho1,3)$, $(\rho1,4)$, $(\rho2,3)$, and $(\rho2,4)$ between the completely integrated network design and the modularized network design.

**Assumption 4:** *Technological uncertainty is more highly correlated within design groups than across design group.*

$$1 \geq \rho_{within} \geq \rho_{across} \geq 0$$

where $\rho_{within}$ denotes the correlation within design group and $\rho_{across}$ denotes the correlation across design group.

**(2) Between Subsystems ($\delta_{a,b}$)**

Assume that correlation between subsystems ($\delta_{a,b}$) in the completely integrated network design is '1'. Then, correlation between subsystems ($\delta_{a,b}$) in the modularized network design is less than or equal to '1' because of decoupling process. So, we can conclude that partitioning and complementarity have a trade-off relationship, which means that more partitioning means more loss of complementarity.

**Hypothesis 3:** *Partitioning and complementarity have a trade-off relationship. That is, the more partitioning, the more loss of complementarity.*

$$(\rho_{i,j})I - (\rho_{i,j})M \geq 0, \ (\delta_{a,b})I - (\delta_{a,b})M \geq 0$$

In summary, Figure 4 shows the above three effects of modularity. That is, the partitioning effect expands the width of standard deviation, testing effect moves it, and coordination effect lowers the height of it, by modularity respectively.

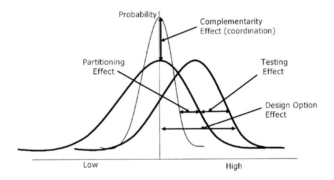

Figure 4: The Effects of Modularity

### 3.3 Real Options Model

A real option is analogous to a financial option contract, which conveys the right but not the obligation, but it is simply differentiated from financial options because they involve real assets rather than financial assets. Flexibility is at the core of real option theory. The main point in the real option approach is to quantify this flexibility in strategic investment projects, which is often not explicitly taken into account by the traditional approaches. It is perhaps not surprising that network engineers or designers tend to overlook the value of flexibility in network design because this is hard to quantify, although it is a real economic benefit. In the real options perspective, the modular network design can be seen as the creation of a portfolio of options (Amram and Kulatilaka, 1998). Since each network module is independently changed and upgraded easily, this will increase the flexibility in network design.

Baldwin and Clark (2000) developed a model to value modularity using the real options approach. Their theory is based on the idea that modularity creates value. At one extreme, a non-modular system (i.e. a fully integrated system) has only one option, which is to replace the whole system, even if only with an incrementally better version, or to leave the old one. In contrast, a modular design creates many options. It isn't necessary to take an all-or-nothing approach. A system of independent modules can be kept as is, or any or all modules can be replaced independently. Thus, a modular design process creates at least as many options as there are modules. The value of a modular system is calculated by adding up the net option value (NOV) of each module:

$$V = NOV_1 + NOV_1 + ... + +NOV_n$$

The NOV is the expected payoff of modularity, accounting for both benefits and exercise costs.

$$NOV_i = \max_{ki}\{\sigma_i n_i^{1/2}Q(k_i) - C_i(n_i)k_i - Z_i\}$$

where $\sigma_i n_i^{1/2}Q(k_i)$ is the expected benefit to be gained by accepting the best positive-valued candidate generated by partitioning modules and $k_i$ independent experiments. For example, a module creates opportunities: (a) technical potential ($\sigma_i$), which is similar to the volatility (uncertainty) in financial option theory, (b) mix-and-match $k_i$ experiments to create the best replacement candidate ($Q(k)$), (c) specialization or innovation by simplifying the complex networks ($n_i^{1/2}$). The second part, $C_i(n_i)k_i$, is the cost to run $k_i$ experiments as a function $C_i$ of the module complexity $n_i$. The last part $Z_i$ is the cost to replace the module given the number of other modules in the system that directly depend on it, the complexity $n_j$ of each, and the cost to redesign each of its parameters. However, they ignore some important factors:

(1) First, technical uncertainty ($\sigma$) is implicitly assumed to be a constant coefficient without considering technological innovation. In reality, technical uncertainty decreases because of the technology innovation.

(2) Second, the effect of the loss of coordination (complementarity) by modularization is not reflected. However, it is a very important factor in network design because most of network components are highly correlated.

As a result of that, we argue that their model may exaggerate the effectiveness of modularization, when the above factors are ignored.

The following is our preliminary model (modified version of Baldwin and Clark's model) to calculate the net option value (NOV) of modularity. This will be developed further through ongoing research.

$$NOV_i = \max_{ki}\{QoSDEX_i X^b n_i^{1/2}Q(k_i) - C_i(n_i)k_i - (\rho_{w,i} - \rho_{a,i})\delta_i\}$$

where   $QoSDEX_i$ : The technical potential (uncertainty),
   $X^b$ : The index of innovation,
   $n_i$ : The number of tasks per module,
   $k_i$ : The number of tests,
   $Q(k_i)$ : The value of testing,
   $C_i(n_i)$ : The cost per module testing,
   $\rho_{w,i}$ : The correlation coefficient within design group,
   $\rho_{a,i}$ : The correlation coefficient across design group,
   $\delta_i$ : The loss of coordination.

**Hypothesis 4**: *The modularity in network design increases the value of network.*

**Hypothesis 5**: *Network components with high complementarity are more likely to become grouped and network components with low complementarity are more likely to become partitioned, to optimize network design.*


## 4    EMPIRICAL TESTS

### 4.1    Network Topology & Traffic Model

In order to evaluate the feasibility of this research, we constructed a simple network model. As shown in Figure 5, the network consists of three nodes and two links.

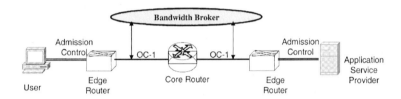

Figure 5. Network Architecture

The edge router handles the QoS control functions of admission control, scheduling, and resource reservation. It interfaces with the application process, which enables inter-process communication. As seen in Figure 6, the edge router is characterized by a queue buffer for adding packets into the queue and a CPU processing rate for packet transmission. The core router is simply a forwarding node, decoupled from QoS control functions. The destination router embodies the same two functions as the edge router. Soon after transmission we collect delay and jitter statistics on the received packets.

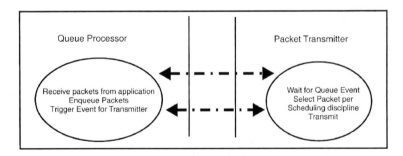

Figure 6. Router Processing

To induce some variation in the measurements, we made the background load 30%. A simple flowchart in Figure 7 depicts the initialization process and the traffic source generation process.

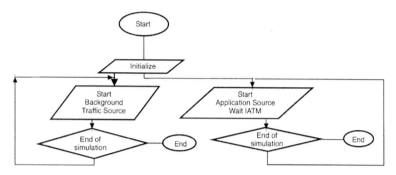

Figure 7. The Flowchart of Initialization and Traffic Source Generation

The video application is modeled with a typical average bit rate of 1 Mbps and a peak bit rate of 10 Mbps. Typically, during a burst, 1,250,000 bytes are transmitted. The call duration is 10000sec (≈2½hours). The video burst is modeled using a Poisson distribution. Each image is transmitted in one second at the rate of 10 Mbps. In one burst period, we transmit 1,250,000bytes*8bits = 10Mbps. To achieve an average bit rate of 1 Mbps, let the average ON and OFF time = t. Each image is transmitted at peak bit rate. Therefore $\tau$ = packet size/peak bit rate. A packet size of 200 bytes was used.

### 4.2 Implementation of QoS Mechanism

In our model, we implemented the following three QoS functions: admission control, packet priority, and resource reservation. QoS functions are implemented in modules and each function can be turned ON or OFF. Admission control is to help meet the required QoS. It helps to prevent network congestion by regulating the amount of traffic accepted into the network. A new traffic application, k, is accepted if and only if:

$$\sum_{i \in A} (a_i) + a_k <= L$$

where A is the set of accepted applications, ai is the average bit rate of an application and L is the link bandwidth.

In our study, we consider only admission control at the edge router. Admission control only admits flows that pass the admission tests for all resource types. The implementation of the admission control mechanism is developed by CSIM simulator.

The interactions of packets from different sources can adversely affect performance experienced by each application. Scheduling endeavors to address this issue. In our investigation, we work with two scheduling disciplines: FIFO and static priority. FIFO is used for the best-effort network. With static priority, the voice application has the highest priority, then the video, followed by the data with the background traffic having the lowest priority. It is implemented in the packet structure, for example, TOS=1(voice), TOS=2(video), TOS=3(data) and TOS=4(background). This is the only QoS function that will transcend the edge router. Bandwidth reservation is based on the application's peak rate instead of the average rate to guarantee service requirements. The bandwidth broker is the central function that checks on the bandwidth availability on all the links that the packets will traverse.

Our simulated network is based on the following configurations:

- The number of total packets at a time: 350,000 packets
- The number of transient (warm-up) packets: 50,000 packets
- Link-speed: OC-1 (52Mbps)
- Propagation delay: 0.00009sec.
- Inter arrival time (IATM): 0.864 sec.
- The speed of CPU: 500Mbps
- The buffer size: 100

To perform the complementarity test between the network resources or components, it is necessary to look at the functions' interconnection. In our model, we use 2k factorial design. The basic approach is to vary each factor for two level values and study all combinations of the various values. According to the 2k factorial design, as seen in Table 2, we make 16 cases for four parameters, such as admission control, packet priority, resource reservation, and bandwidth. Label -1 means "on" or "high level" of that parameter and Label +1 means "off" or "low level" of that parameter. We will simulate the 16 scenarios with 30 times replications and measure mean delay, packet loss rate and jitter.

Table 2. Scenarios for Complementarity Tests

|    | Within design group | | | Across design group |
|----|---------------------|-------|-------------|---------------------|
|    | Admission control   | Priority | Reservation | Bandwidth |
| 1  | -1 | -1 | -1 | -1 |
| 2  | +1 | -1 | -1 | -1 |
| 3  | -1 | +1 | -1 | -1 |
| 4  | +1 | +1 | -1 | -1 |
| 5  | -1 | -1 | +1 | -1 |
| 6  | +1 | -1 | +1 | -1 |
| 7  | -1 | +1 | +1 | -1 |
| 8  | +1 | +1 | +1 | -1 |
| 9  | -1 | -1 | -1 | +1 |
| 10 | +1 | -1 | -1 | +1 |
| 11 | -1 | +1 | -1 | +1 |
| 12 | +1 | +1 | -1 | +1 |
| 13 | -1 | -1 | +1 | +1 |
| 14 | +1 | -1 | +1 | +1 |
| 15 | -1 | +1 | +1 | +1 |
| 16 | +1 | +1 | +1 | +1 |

## 5   RESULT ANALYSIS

*Complementarity Test*

Our test of complementarity is focused around supermodularity. In the case of a supermodular function, f(•) stands for the improvement of network performance. For example, f(1,1) is the performance improvement when admission control and packet priority function is in the "on" state compared to both functions in the "off" state. The data was collected from the above network simulation. To test the significance of this result, we calculate the t-value. The null hypothesis is that admission control and priority are a complementary relationship (complementarity $\geq$ 0). The t-value is significant at $\alpha = 0.05$ (t-value=0.0000000207) and the p-value is 0.0000000383 ($\alpha = 0.001$), which is also significant. So, the null hypothesis is accepted, which means that there exists a complementarity between admission control and priority. Figure 8 shows the complementarity results of the QoS components. Comparing those results, we find that it appears that the evidence of complementarity between network components is supported.

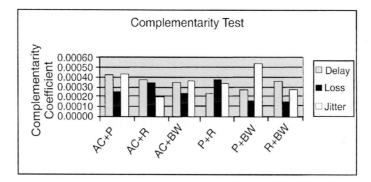

Figure 8. Complementarity Test of Network Components

*QoSDEX Calculation*

Table 3 shows the results of QoSDEXs.

Table 3. QoSDEX of QoS Components

| QoS Types | QoSDEX | QoS Types | QoSDEX |
|---|---|---|---|
| Admission Control | 0.250399 | Admission Control & Priority | 0.122777 |
| Priority | 0.521127 | Admission Control & Reservation | 0.063585 |
| Reservation | 0.121444 | Priority & Reservation | 0.115750 |

Figure 9 shows the change of QoSDEX with a 90% learning rate of QoS technology innovation during a certain period.

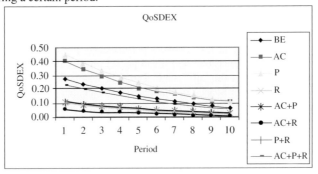

Figure 9. The Change of QoSDEX with Technology Innovation

*The Value of Modularity*

We now apply Baldwin and Clark's NOV model to estimate how much the modular design in the QoS model is worth. For simplicity, we make several assumptions for quantifying the qualitative factors to apply the mathematical model.

- The number of modules is one in case of the whole unmodularized QoS-enabled network design, so the complexity of network (N) is 1. For the modular QoS-enabled network design, the complexity of each module is the proportion of the number of line codes of each QoS function to the total number of line codes of the network.
- If the whole unmodularized QoS design system experiments one time, then its value is 1 ($\sigma N^{1/2}Q(1) = 1$). As a result, the maximum technical potential value ($\sigma$) of a whole system is 2.50689.
- When one experiment on an unmodularized system breaks even ($\sigma N^{1/2}Q(1) - CN = 0$), the design cost per module ($C_i$) is 1.
- The visibility cost of a module is 0 because each module is independent. Each module cannot see its neighbor module.

Figure 10 shows the results of NOV of each module of QoS-enabled network design. The results show that the NOV of packet priority and admission control is increasing continuously with an increasing number of tests, but NOV for most other networks is decreasing. Further, if the loss of coordination is reflected, the NOV will be decreased further. By these results, we tentatively get some inferences as follows. First, each Internet QoS function has different values. This may be used a basis for the Internet QoS pricing. Second, the value of each Internet QoS function is varied according to the research and development activity (e.g. testing). That is, since more research and development activity for the Internet QoS technologies may not always increase their value, the characteristics of the Internet QoS technologies are considered not to lose the benefit of design options.

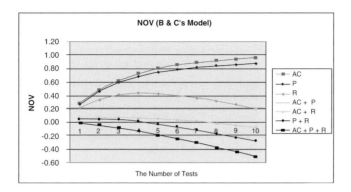

Figure 10. Net Option Value of Modularity (Baldwin and Clark's Model)

## 6   CONCLUDING REMARKS

This study intends to address two main areas related to the potential value of modularity in network design under uncertainty. The first main area deals with the structure of network architecture. We draw the relationship map between network components (within design group), and between network subsystems (across design group). We also test their complementarty. Preliminary results show that there exists complementarity between network elements. The second main area deals with the value of modularity in network design. We have shown that the modularity in network design has a value, but that its effect may be limited by complementarity.

The ultimate contribution of this study is that it will help network service providers in their decisions on whether to upgrade or migrate to the next generation network architecture. More specifically, it will provide a framework to explain how the network-based services interact with the design of networks with complementary components under uncertainty. This will help their strategic design decisions: to modularization or not, and if so, by how much, by establishing the value of modularity in network design.

## 7   REFERENCES

Amram, M. and Kulatinaka, N., *Real Options: Managing Strategic Investments in an Uncertain World*, Harvard Business School Press, 1998.

Baldwin, C. and Clark, K., *Design Rules: The Power of Modularity*, MIT Press, 2000.

Baldwin, C. and Clark, K., "Managing in an Age of Modularity," *Harvard Business Review*, Sep.-Oct., 1997.

Bjorkman, N., *MSF System Architecture Implementation Agreement*, 2000, available online at http://www.msforum.org

Braun, T., Schiller, J., Schmidt, C., and Zitterbart, M. *Design of a Modular and Efficient Communication Subsystem*, ICCC'95, Seoul, Korea, August 1995.

Fields, M., "Capital Budgeting & Learning Curve Phenomenon," in *Capital Budgeting Under Uncertainty, Advances and New Perspectives*, R. Aggrawal, ed., pages 154-168, 1993.

Gaynor, M. and Bradner, S., "The Real Options Approach to Standardization," 2001, Hawaii, IEEE International Conference on Systems Sciences.

Hippel, E., "Task partitioning: An Innovation Process Variable," *Research Policy*, No. 19, pp. 407-418, 1990.

IETF, GSMPv3, 2002, IETF.

IETF, H.248/MEGACO, 2002, IETF.

IEEE, IEEE P1520 Proposed IEEE Standard for Application Programming Interfaces for Networks, 2002, IEEE.

Lindgren, G., *Statistical Theory*, New York: Macmillan, 1968.

Markowitz, H., "A More Efficient Frontier," *The Journal of Portfolio Management*, May 1999.

Markowitz, H., *Portfolio Selection: Efficient Diversification of Investments*, Basil Blackwell, 1991.

Mikkola, J., "Modularity Assessment of Product Architecture: Implications for Substitutability and Interface Management," 2001, Aalborg, Denmark, DRUID's Nelson and Winter Conference.

Milgrom, P. and Roberts, J., "Complementarities and Fit Strategy, Structure, and Organizational Change in Manufacturing," *Journal of Accounting and Economics*, no. 19, pp. 179-208, 1995.

Milgrom, P. and Roberts, J., "The Economics of Modern Manufacturing: Technology, Strategy, and Organization," *American Economic Review*, Vol. 80, pp. 511-528, 1990.

Miller, K., "The Giant Stumble", *Newsweek International*, 2002.

Pine, B., *Mass Customization,* Boston, Massachussett: 1993, Harvard Business School Press.

Saltzer, J., Reed, D., and Clark, D., "End-to-End Arguments in System Design," *ACM Transactions in Computer Systems*, Vol. 2, No. 4, pp. 277-288, Nov. 1984.

Schaefer, S., "Product Design Partitions with Complementary," *Journal of Economic Behavior and Organization*, Vol. 38, pp. 311-330, 1999.

Sharpe, W., "Asset Allocation: Management Style and Performance Measurement," *The Journal of Portfolio Management*, pp. 7-10, 1992.

Softswitch, Softswitch Forum, 2002, Softswitch Consortium.

Topkis, D., "Minimizing a Submodular Function on a Lattice," *Operations Research*, Vol. 26, pp. 305-321, 1978.

Willinger, W. and Doyle, J., "Robustness and the Internet: Design and Evolution," 2002, available online at http://netlab.caltech.edu/internet/

Wolf, T. "Design of an Instruction Set for Modular Network Processor," RC21865 (98398), 10-27-2000, IBM Research Division, IBM Research Report.

Zhang, Z. and et al., "Decoupling QoS Control from Core Routers: A Novel Bandwidth Broker Architecture for Scalable Support of Guaranteed Services", *Sigcomm00*, 2000.

© 2004 Published by Elsevier B.V.
Global Economy and Digital Society
E. Bohlin, S. Levin, N. Sung and C-H. Yoon (Editors)

CHAPTER 12

# Determinants of Customer Retention for Korean High-Speed Internet Services

Min-Kyoung Kim
*Technology Valuation Center, Information Technology Management Research Group,
Electronics and Telecommunications Research Institute (ETRI), Daejeon*

Myeong-Cheol Park
*School of Business, Information and Communications University (ICU), Daejeon*

Gyu-Dong Yeon
*Business Innovation Team, Samsung Networks Inc., Seoul*

**Abstract**. The number of subscribers to high-speed Internet services in Korea, which
has shown a high growth rate every year since it was launched in 1998, reached more
than 10 million by the end of 2002. Until now, service providers have concentrated
on marketing activities to attract new customers, to some extent neglecting the improvement of service quality and customer satisfaction for existing customers. In this
chapter, the relationships between service quality, customer satisfaction, and repurchase intention are analyzed. It is found that quality attributes have a significant effect on customer satisfaction and repurchase intention, and that six key quality elements are major determinants of customer retention. Management implications are,
for instance, that service providers should establish appropriate quality indices to aid
continuous quality management activities, and that service providers may need a
short-term performance improvement plan as well as a long-term network development plan.

## 1   INTRODUCTION

The number of Internet users worldwide has increased by 100 ~ 1000% annually. In Korea,
the high-speed Internet diffusion rate was the highest among OECD members. The number of
subscribers to high-speed Internet services has reached more than 10 million.

When these services were launched in 1998, Hanaro and Thrunet were market leaders.
However, when KT, the dominant fixed network carrier, entered the market in late April
2000, it started to dominate with a market share of around 50%. This was caused by two
factors. One is that almost every household (approximately 90%) is within a 4-km radius of
KT's central office, a feasible region for ADSL (Asymmetric Digital Subscriber Line)
technology. The other is that KT's aggressive marketing activities are based on its own strong
local loop infrastructure and sound financial structure. Other service providers' profitability is
relatively inferior to KT's because they need to lease the networks of Powercom or other

System Operators (SOs). Recently, the monthly growth rate has declined, and the intensity of competition amongst service providers in the market has increased. As shown in Table 1, there are three dominant companies, KT, Hanaro, and Thrunet, sharing most of the current market.

Table 1. Subscriber Profile for each Service Provider

| Items | KT | Hanaro | Thrunet | Dacom | Onse Telecom | DreamLine | Total |
|---|---|---|---|---|---|---|---|
| xDSL | 3,713,743 | 1,064,745 | | | | 96,177 | 4,874,665 (56.9%) |
| Cable modem | | 980,085 | 1,297,800 | 71,101 | 305,334 | 84,704 | 2,739,024 (32.0%) |
| LAN | 529,016 | 318,947 | 9,569 | 80,788 | 8,546 | | 946,866 (11.0%) |
| Satellite | 12,092 | | | | | | 12,092 (0.1%) |
| Total | 4,254,851 (49.6%) | 2,363,777 (27.6%) | 1,307,369 (15.3%) | 151,889 (1.8%) | 313,880 (3.6%) | 180,881 (2.1%) | 8,572,647 (100%) |

Source: Ministry of Information and Communication, August 2002

Despite the very high diffusion rate, service providers have focused on marketing activities for new customers, while putting little effort into improving service quality and customer satisfaction. According to the high-speed Internet user survey by the Korea Consumer Federation (2001), 32.3 % of respondents wanted to cancel their current service.

Because the monthly diffusion rate is gradually decreasing, and the home diffusion rate is about 70%, the Korean high-speed Internet service market appears to have entered the first stage of a mature market. When a market reaches the mature stage, competitive intensity is accelerated due to decreased market demand. Service providers have to protect their competitive strength by recognizing their own market environment and developing a plan to elevate customer loyalty in order to encourage repurchase. Therefore, they need to enhance customer satisfaction rather than focus on attracting new customers. Although it is not the case for other telecommunications services, prior study of high-speed Internet services with respect to service quality and customer satisfaction is rare.

The objective of this chapter is to examine the relationships between service quality, customer satisfaction and repurchase intention for the high-speed Internet service market in Korea. It studies how the attributes of quality influence customer satisfaction and repurchase intention, and identifies the key quality elements that determine customer retention. The chapter also suggests an effective business strategy for elevating customer loyalty and for retaining existing customers.

The remainder of this chapter is organized as follows. In Section 2, we describe research questions and develop hypotheses to be investigated. Further, we define the variables, sample data and collection method. In Section 3, we describe the testing of the hypotheses and report the findings. In Section 4, we conclude with marketing implications and directions for future research.

## 2    RESEARCH QUESTIONS AND DATA COLLECTION

### 2.1    Definition of Terms

*Service Quality*

Service quality can be understood as the customer's judgment of an entity's overall excellence and superiority (Zeithaml, 1987). It can be measured as the difference between the expectations and the perception of the service received (Clow et al., 1997).

In this research, the questions for measuring scale of service quality were written using the SERVQUAL model and the service quality recommendations of ITU-T (International Telecommunications Union - Telecommunication Standardization Sector) (Parasuraman et al., 1985; Bong, 1997). The following three concepts are related to a scope of service quality in this chapter.

- *Overall service quality* is defined as the overall perception of the quality of the high-speed Internet service. Customers' perceptions of each individual quality-element impact on the evaluation of overall service quality. One question for the overall service quality scale was used in the sample survey.
- *Service quality attribute* is defined as a quality that can be classified by generic characteristics. We assume that, in terms of properties of communications services, service quality is classified into six attributes as follows: service performance, service support system, value-added service, service charge, billing, and procedural convenience to use the service. These six attributes are derived and grouped from the service quality elements by factor analysis.
- *Service quality element* is defined as an individual quality element that contributes to overall service quality. A customer perceives overall service quality from the total of individual perceptions of each of the quality elements. Twenty-five questions were asked to measure the scale of quality elements in the survey.

*Customer Satisfaction*

Customer Satisfaction is an affective state that is the emotional reaction to a product or service experience (Spreng et al., 1996). It means a customer's evaluation of the perceived discrepancy between pre-purchase expectation and actual performance felt after consumption of the high-speed Internet service. One question was used to measure the customer satisfaction scale in the survey.

*Repurchase Intention*

Repurchase intention means the behavioral intention of the customer to keep using the same service from the same service provider or not, caused by the result of satisfaction/dissatisfaction. For multi-purpose analysis, the quantitative scale of repurchase intention was measured with two different scales: a seven-point scale and a binomial scale ('yes' or 'no').

## 2.2    Outline of Empirical Analysis

The empirical analysis consists of three parts as shown in Figure 1.

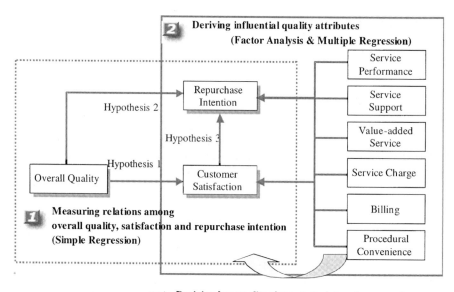

Figure 1. Study Model

*Empirical Analysis 1: Can the general causality of service quality → customer satisfaction → repurchase intention be applied to Korean high-speed Internet services?*

Woodside (1989), and Cronin and Taylor (1992), stated that there was a significant causality between the above variables. Especially, Cronin and Taylor emphasized that overall service quality influenced customer satisfaction and repurchase intention, but the influence of overall service quality was less than that of customer satisfaction for the repurchase intention. The following three hypotheses were established in order to test this relationship in high-speed Internet services.

- Hypothesis 1: Satisfaction with overall service quality is positively related to customer satisfaction.
- Hypothesis 2: Satisfaction with overall service quality is positively related to repurchase intention.
- Hypothesis 3: Customer satisfaction is positively related to repurchase intention.

*Empirical Analysis 2: Which service quality attributes significantly influence customer satisfaction and repurchase intention for high-speed Internet services?*

The quality attributes are derived from 25 individual quality elements of Korean high-speed Internet services by factor analysis. The influence of derived quality attributes on customer satisfaction and repurchase intention was analyzed by multiple regression analysis.

*Empirical Analysis 3: What are the determinants of customer retention among the quality elements of the Korean high-speed Internet service?*

The quality attributes extracted by factor analysis are used as independent variables in the Empirical Analysis 2. Each quality attribute may include more than one individual quality element. Consequently, there is some difficulty in interpreting the real meaning of quality attributes in terms of the implementation perspective of the service provider. In order to put additional marketing effort into increasing customer retention, service providers need to identify individual quality elements that can be controlled directly in the marketplace. Thus, logistic regression analysis with the quality elements as the independent variables was conducted to overcome this difficulty. In particular, the selection of key quality elements, which determine customer retention contribution to future financial performance and profitability in the mature market, is an important step for ensuring competitive advantage through formulation of an efficient business strategy and concentration of resources.

## 2.3   Data Collection

The questionnaire for this research consisted of 41 items for 7 dimensions as follows: demographic information (6), service usage (4), service quality element scale (25), overall service quality scale (1), customer satisfaction scale (1), repurchase intention scale (2), and customer loyalty scale (2).

A quantitative scale was used in the questionnaire. The scale contained seven possible responses: 1 (strongly disagree) to 7 (strongly agree). Two different quantitative scales were used for repurchase intention and intention to recommend to others: the seven-point scale for the dependent variables 1 and 2 in the empirical analysis, and the binomial scale, "Yes" or "No" for dummy dependent variables in the empirical analysis 3.

Data was collected using a web-based survey over eight days. Six hundred and thirty-six replies were collected, but 551 valid replies were used for the analysis after discarding incomplete or insincere responses. The demographic characteristics of the sample are shown in Table 2.

Table 2. Demographic Characteristics of the Sample

| Item | Frequency | Percentage (%) |
|---|---|---|
| Sex | | |
| Male | 487 | 88.4 |
| Female | 64 | 11.6 |
| Total | 551 | 100.0 |
| Age | | |
| Less than 19 | 63 | 11.4 |
| 20 to 29 | 254 | 46.1 |
| 30 to 39 | 201 | 36.5 |
| More than 40 | 33 | 6.0 |
| Total | 551 | 100.0 |

Because the population demographic information is not available, we could not check the sampling bias from the population. However, there does not appear to be a problem related to this sample. Using the ANOVA analysis, we confirmed that there is no significant difference on repurchase intention by sex and age group. The subscriber to a high-speed Internet service is a household, not an individual. Thus, we set the survey replies so as not to overlap within a household.

Table 3 summarizes the composition of samples in terms of service providers and access technology type. The sample distribution for service providers was 259 (47%) for KT, 158 (28.7%) for Hanaro, 77 (14%) for Thrunet, 14 (2.5%) for Dacom, 26 (4.7%) for Onse, and 17 (3.1%) for DreamLine. The sample distribution appeared to reflect actual subscribers in terms of high-speed Internet service providers through a Chi-square test[1] at the 5% significant level.

Table 3. Composition of Samples for Service Providers and Technology Type

| Service Provider | Access Technology Type | | | | Total | |
|---|---|---|---|---|---|---|
| | xDSL | Cable | LAN | Others | | |
| KT | 215 | 0 | 41 | 3 | 259 | (47%) |
| Hanaro | 88 | 55 | 15 | 0 | 158 | (28.7%) |
| Thrunet | 0 | 75 | 1 | 1 | 77 | (14%) |
| Dacom | 2 | 8 | 4 | 0 | 14 | (2.5%) |
| Onse | 0 | 26 | 0 | 0 | 26 | (4.7%) |
| DreamLine | 1 | 9 | 6 | 1 | 17 | (3.1%) |
| Total | 323 | 166 | 54 | 8 | 551 | (100%) |
| | (58.6%) | (30.1%) | (9.8%) | (1.5%) | (100%) | |

---

[1] As the p-value showed 0.17 in terms of the service providers, larger than the 0.05 significance level, we fail to reject the null hypothesis.

## 3 ANALYSIS AND DISCUSSION

### 3.1 Reliability and Factor Analysis

The factor analysis was carried out with 25 questions to investigate the quality attributes of high-speed Internet services. An eigenvalue of more than 1.0 was used as the determinant criterion for each factor. The factor loading and cumulative proportion of variance were calculated using the Varimax rotation method commonly used in factor analysis for better discrimination. One item that did not meet a criterion of 0.4, the general guideline, was removed, and a total 24 items were retained as variables.

Reliability analysis was used to verify the internal consistency of the scales. Cronbach's alpha coefficient ranged from 0.0 to 1.0, reflecting the strength of the relationship between items within the scale. The reliability coefficients for the scale are summarized in Table 4. In this research, if the value of Cronbach's alpha for a factor is greater than 0.6, the factor is considered as "acceptable".

Table 4. Reliability Coefficient of Survey for Service Quality Elements

| Factors | # of Items (24) | Cronbach's α |
|---|---|---|
| Factor 1: Service support | 7 | .905 |
| Factor 2: Value-added service | 4 | .851 |
| Factor 3: Service performance | 4 | .868 |
| Factor 4: Service charge | 3 | .738 |
| Factor 5: Billing | 3 | .643 |
| Factor 6: Procedural convenience | 3 | .757 |

Table 5 shows the result of factor analysis. Service support (factor 1), value-added service (factor 2), service performance (factor 3), service charge (factor 4), billing (factor 5), and procedural convenience (factor 6) were derived as service quality attributes.

- Factor 1 (service support) contains the items related to a business system, such as service maintenance, resolution level for customer complaint handling, etc.

- Factor 2 (value-added service) contains the items related to the offering of various kinds of value-added services.

- Factor 3 (service performance) contains the network performance, such as access or transmission quality, of the communications service as an essential service feature.

- Factor 4 (service charge) contains the customers' assessment of the rationality of the rate level and rate structure.

- Factor 5 (billing) contains the items related to billing procedure.

- Factor 6 (procedural convenience) contains the quality attributes of the procedures related to service use.

Table 5. Factor Analysis Result for Service Quality Attributes

| Dimension/item | Factor 1 | Factor 2 | Factor 3 | Factor 4 | Factor 5 | Factor 6 | Communality |
|---|---|---|---|---|---|---|---|
| *Service support* | | | | | | | |
| Efficiency of dealing with fault | .817 | | | | | | .790 |
| Rapid resolution for the fault | .801 | | | | | | .748 |
| Kindness of fault receptionist | .753 | | | | | | .676 |
| Rapid connection to receptionist | .730 | | | | | | .661 |
| Skillfulness of repairmen | .700 | | | | | | .599 |
| Satisfaction level for solution | .654 | | | | | | .704 |
| Corporate image | .482 | | | | | | .544 |
| *Value-added service (VAS)* | | | | | | | |
| Use convenience of VAS | | .849 | | | | | .793 |
| Various VAS | | .832 | | | | | .764 |
| Various programs for customer | | .735 | | | | | .640 |
| Rationality of VAS charge | | .653 | | | | | .620 |
| *Service performance* | | | | | | | |
| Service stability | | | .827 | | | | .819 |
| Easy access | | | .811 | | | | .740 |
| Stability of access equipment | | | .790 | | | | .738 |
| Guarantee of speed | | | .714 | | | | .634 |
| *Service charge* | | | | | | | |
| Rationality of rate level | | | | .845 | | | .800 |
| Rationality of rate structure | | | | .832 | | | .786 |
| Full explanation of agreement | | | | .488 | | | .492 |
| *Billing* | | | | | | | |
| On-time arrival of bill | | | | | .802 | | .683 |
| Convenience of payment | | | | | .745 | | .618 |
| Accuracy of bill | | | | | .633 | | .501 |
| *Procedural convenience* | | | | | | | |
| Cancellation policy/procedure | | | | | | .717 | .668 |
| Subscription & change | | | | | | .706 | .683 |
| Convenience of fault handling | | | | | | .637 | .733 |
| Eigenvalue | 8.940 | 1.986 | 1.601 | 1.516 | 1.378 | 1.013 | |
| *Total Var. Explained* | | | | | | | |
| Percent of explained variance | 37.2 | 8.3 | 6.7 | 6.3 | 5.7 | 4.2 | |
| Cumulative proportion of variance | 37.2 | 45.5 | 52.2 | 58.5 | 64.3 | 68.5 | |
| Kaiser-Meyer-Olkin Measure of Sampling Adequacy | | | | | .919 | | |
| Approx. Chi-square (Sig.) | | | | | 7,028 (.000) | | |

## 3.2   Empirical Analysis 1

Simple regression analysis was used to test the three hypotheses. The tests can be classified into two categories: firstly, the influence of overall perceived quality on customer satisfaction and repurchase intention; secondly, the influence of customer satisfaction on repurchase intention.

Table 6. Result of Empirical Analysis 1

|  | Hypotheses | | |
|---|---|---|---|
|  | Hypothesis 1 | Hypothesis 2 | Hypothesis 3 |
| *Dependent variable* | Customer satisfaction | Repurchase intention | Repurchase intention |
| *Independent variable* | Overall perceived quality | Overall perceived quality | Customer satisfaction |
| R2 | 0.833 | 0.570 | 0.557 |
| ANOVA |  |  |  |
| F-value | 2,740.9 | 728.5 | 690.8 |
| P-value | 0.000 | 0.000 | 0.000 |
| *Regression coefficient* |  |  |  |
| Constant | 0.086 | 0.445 | 0.716 |
| Beta | 0.967 | 0.898 | 0.838 |
| P-value | 0.000 | 0.000 | 0.000 |

According to the Table 6, the null hypothesis that a linear relationship does not exist was rejected at the 0.01 significance level for all three tests. Therefore, overall perceived quality influences customer satisfaction and repurchase intention, and customer satisfaction is also influential with respect to repurchase intention. The explanatory power for each independent variable to the dependent variable seems to be relatively high, because the coefficient of determination ($R^2$) was more than 55.7%.

Note that the satisfaction with overall perceived quality is a very important determinant of customer satisfaction, as $R^2$ is very high. However, the explanatory power of overall perceived quality with respect to repurchase intention decreased to about 26% in comparison with customer satisfaction. Since repurchase intention is the customer's behavioral intention arising from the result of a consumption experience of a product or service, it can be affected by factors other than quality in comparison with customer satisfaction, a customer attitude. In the end, this result implies that service providers need to manage quality as well as improve repurchase intention.

In conclusion, overall perceived quality is an important variable that has a positive correlation with customer satisfaction and repurchase intention. Customer satisfaction also influences repurchase intention. In this chapter, the causality in previous studies was proved to be applicable to Korean high-speed Internet services.

## 3.3   Empirical Analysis 2

As described in the previous factor analysis, six service quality attributes were extracted. Multiple regression analysis was applied to determine which service quality attributes are influential factors with respect to customer satisfaction and repurchase intention. Results from the two multiple regression equations in Table 7 show that both models are significant. Since R2 was over 50%, the explanatory power of both models seemed to be reasonable.

Table 7. Result of Empirical Analysis 2

|  | Dependent variables | | | |
|---|---|---|---|---|
|  | Customer satisfaction | | Repurchase intention | |
|  | Beta | Sig. (p) | Beta | Sig. (p) |
| *Independent variables* | | | | |
| Service support | 0.623 | 0.000* | 0.719 | 0.000* |
| Value-added service | 0.431 | 0.000* | 0.484 | 0.000* |
| Service performance | 1.043 | 0.000* | 0.925 | 0.000* |
| Service charge | 0.316 | 0.000* | 0.374 | 0.000* |
| Billing | 0.179 | 0.000* | 0.194 | 0.000* |
| Procedural convenience | 0.064 | 0.106 | 0.091 | 0.089 |
| Constant | 3.868 | 0.000* | 3.956 | 0.000 |
| R-square | .677 | | .536 | |
| Adj. R-square | .674 | | .531 | |
| F | 190.5 | | 104.8 | |
| Df | 6 | | 6 | |
| Sig. (p-value) | .000 | | .000 | |

$* P \leq .05$

Table 7 shows that all quality attributes other than "procedural convenience" were statistically significant. Therefore, five of the six quality attributes were proved to be influential predictors of both customer satisfaction and repurchase intention. Procedural convenience was found not significant. This result could be interpreted as a special characteristic of the Korean high-speed Internet service market: "accumulation of experience". Accumulation of experience is generated by long-term service contracts of more than one year for the following two reasons. Firstly, customers want to avoid the additional cost of frequent subscription, cancellation, or switching cost. Secondly, service providers subsidized most of the initial costs, including modem equipment costs, to long-term users only in order to operate their networks efficiently with guarantee of stable traffic volume. Because of this special characteristic of the Korean Internet service market, procedural convenience seems to be a less important factor. Other quality attributes accumulated during the subscription period appear to be more important in influencing customer satisfaction and repurchase intention. This result suggests a managerial implication for service providers: to retain existing customers in this mature market, efforts to improve the quality attributes that customers continuously experience during use of the service are very important.

The order of the degree of importance for each independent variable is as follows: service performance, service support, value-added service, service charge, and billing. As is not the case with other telecommunication services, service charge related items are found to be less important. This is because the flat rate system, independent of traffic volume, is most commonly used in Korean high-speed Internet services. Furthermore, because of the highly competitive climate, rate levels of most service providers are similar.

## 3.4   Empirical Analysis 3

As mentioned above, logistic regression analysis was conducted, based on the values measured by the survey, to find a more detailed meaning of the individual quality attributes investigated in Empirical Analysis 2. We used a binomial scale of customer repurchase intention for the dependent variable, and a few selected important quality elements in each quality attribute for the independent variables.

Table 8. The Result of Empirical Analysis 3

|  | Dependent variable | | |
|---|---|---|---|
|  | Repurchase intention | | |
|  | Beta | Wald | Sig. |
| Constant | -4.490 | 76.943 | 0.000* |
| *Service support* |  |  |  |
| Efficiency of handling fault | -0.036 | 0.101 | 0.751 |
| Rapid resolution for fault | 0.112 | 1.172 | 0.279 |
| Satisfaction for resolution | 0.218 | 3.721 | 0.054** |
| Corporate image | 0.326 | 12.402 | 0.000* |
| *Value-added service (VAS)* |  |  |  |
| Convenience to use VAS | -0.197 | 2.195 | 0.138 |
| Variety of VAS | 0.209 | 3.230 | 0.072** |
| *Service performance* |  |  |  |
| Service stability | 0.486 | 22.648 | 0.000* |
| Easy access | 0.011 | 0.013 | 0.910 |
| Stability of service equipment | 0.058 | 0.323 | 0.570 |
| *Service charge* |  |  |  |
| Rationality of rate level | 0.254 | 4.634 | 0.031* |
| Rationality of rate structure | -0.133 | 1.227 | 0.268 |
| *Procedural convenience* |  |  |  |
| Convenience to report fault | 0.031 | 0.137 | 0.711 |
|  |  |  |  |
| -2 Log likelihood | 512.35 |  |  |
| Chi-square | 217.08 |  |  |
| (Sig. t) | (0.000) |  |  |
| Prediction Rate | 77.3% |  |  |

*$P \le .05$, **$P \le .10$

Twelve quality elements were chosen as the independent variables. Eleven variables were chosen by the communality value, the degree of importance of a special variable in the factor analysis. The criterion value of the communality was greater than 0.7. Although "corporate image" did not pass this criterion, we added it because we thought that, in the high-tech service market, it would be an important factor in selecting a service provider.

The -2 Log Likelihood value and Chi-square value, the fitness of the model including independent variables, appeared significant, as shown in Table 8. The table shows that some of the independent variables are significant and some are not.

Five independent variables were found significant with respect to repurchase intention. "Service stability", "corporate image", and "rationality of rate level", were statistically significant at the 0.05 levels, and "satisfaction for resolution", and "variety of value-added services", were significant at the 0.1 levels.

"Service performance" was the most significant quality attribute in Empirical Analysis 2. In addition, the result of Empirical Analysis 3 tells us that customers perceive "service stability" to be the key quality element among various elements related to the service performance attribute. Customers may recognize "service stability" as one of the most important criteria for making decisions to repurchase after the existing contract period has expired.

Instability of service may be caused by the best-effort service characteristic, an inherent property of the Internet based on TCP/IP, and by technical constraints, such as a relatively high error rate for receiving data, and deterioration of performance in proportion to increased network traffic. Despite these limitations, customers judge that a service should be stable. After all, this implies that the core source of competitive advantage is the ability to overcome technical constraints and to provide a stable service. Therefore, it is necessary for providers to implement various strategies to stabilize service quality, such as positive import of CDN (Contents Delivery Network) or increase of access server capacity.

"Corporate image" appeared to be a very significant factor. It is one of three components of perceived quality suggested by Grönroos (1984). He asserted that "corporate image" is the result of a customer's evaluation of a firm, and is a very important factor because of the intangible property of service. Corporate image is influenced by external variables such as traditional marketing activity. However, as Grönroos mentioned, since corporate image is determined by "technical quality" and "functional quality", this result implies that service providers should energetically undertake marketing activities, such as Public Relations, to improve corporate image. Of course, they should first make efforts to increase the quality of the service in terms of "service stability".

"Satisfaction for resolution" was also an important factor. In this service market, preventive mechanisms are very important. Interestingly, customer satisfaction can be increased, and a positive attitude strengthened, when customer complaints are dealt with quickly and efficiently. The importance of responding to customer complaints adequately has been examined in previous studies. Hirschman (1970) reported that adequate handling of customer complaints could convert a complaining customer into a loyal customer. Therefore, it is very important to build an effective support system for offering maintenance service as well as technical support in order to increase the consumer's repurchase intention.

"Rationality of rate level" was found significant with respect to repurchase intention. This result means that most consumers consider the price level of the service to be an important factor, such as a discount level for a long-term contract. However, rate structure was not a major determinant for repurchase intention because there is no differentiation of price structure, all service providers using the same flat-rate structure.

"Variety of Value Added Service (VAS)" was statistically significantly at the 1% level. Although its importance relative to other influential elements is lower, the result indicates that various value-added services can become an important driving force in increasing a customer's positive behavior. Value-added service has some lock-in effect; thus, it can play a role in influencing the switching cost to customers. Once a customer is accustomed to using a specific valued-added service during the subscription period, that customer would be reluctant to switch to other service providers. Therefore, since customers recognize value-added service as a differential benefit element and tend to become accustomed to the service offering it, the analysis implies that service providers may use value-added service as a differentiator, to retain existing customers in the competitive market.

Findings from this analysis can be summarized as follows. Firstly, when evaluating service quality, the Korean high-speed Internet user recognizes "service performance" as the most important attribute among six quality attributes. Secondly, "service stability" is a major service-quality element in increasing the "service performance" level for customers. Thirdly, the discrepancy between users' expectations and "service stability" performance is the most detrimental factor that determines users' repurchasing behavior after a certain period of consumption experience. Lastly, "satisfaction for resolution", an element of the quality attribute of customer support system, and "corporate image", mostly formed by quality evaluation, are very important elements for quality management.

## 4    CONCLUSION

### 4.1    Summary and Implications

A customer experiences satisfaction or dissatisfaction after purchase, comparing performance with expectation. The experience influences repurchase intention or the formation of a favorable attitude to the service. High-level customer satisfaction may contribute to the increased future financial performance or profitability of service providers.

This empirical analysis was carried out in order to examine the relationships between service quality and its variables, and to derive key quality elements that could improve customer retention for high-speed Internet services. Findings and strategic implications of this chapter can be summarized as follows.

Firstly, the general causality of service quality $\rightarrow$ customer satisfaction $\rightarrow$ repurchase intention is proved to be effective in the Korean high-speed Internet service industry because the influence of overall perceived quality on customer satisfaction is higher than on repurchase intention.

Cronin and Taylor (1992) stated that the influence of customer satisfaction on repurchase intention is higher than the influence of overall service quality. However, the influence on repurchase intention of overall service quality and customer satisfaction was found, in this study, to be similar. Therefore, the causality of service quality $\rightarrow$ customer satisfaction $\rightarrow$ repurchase intention was not fully supported in the Korean Internet service market.

Secondly, the kinds of quality attributes that influence customer satisfaction and repurchase intention were investigated. "Service performance" and "service support" were found to be important factors. However, "procedural convenience" was not a significant factor. Because customers perceive accumulated quality of the service, "accumulation of experience" by long-term contract, which includes changing their experience and evaluating for quality continuously, is much more important than one-time experience such as subscription or cancellation. Therefore, service providers should establish appropriate quality indices that can reasonably be accepted in the high-speed Internet marketplace. Using these quality indices, they should make an effort to conduct continuous quality management activities to evaluate service quality. An example of this approach is the SLA (Service Level Agreement), a policy recently adopted by telecommunication service providers to compensate the customer for deterioration of service quality when the deterioration level falls below a defined quality standard.

Thirdly, another empirical analysis was conducted to identify more detailed quality elements that are determinants of customer retention. "Service stability", "satisfaction for resolution", and "corporate image" were found to be the key quality elements.

This result implies that customers identify service stability as one of the components of service performance that constitutes an important determinant of behavioral intention. Service stability, as the performance of the network itself, is strongly correlated with the technical limitations of the high-speed Internet network, as well as the service provider's own infrastructure. Raising service stability requires a long-term effort. Thus, service providers may need a short-term performance improvement plan as well as a long-term network development plan. For example, increase of access server capacity can be considered.

Corporate image was also an important factor in the Korean high-speed Internet service industry. Grönroos (1982) asserted that corporate image was influenced by external variables such as traditional marketing activity. However, in the Internet service market, corporate image is an important feature of service quality because it is initially determined by an internal variable, quality of the network service. Therefore, service providers need to elevate the quality of their network service internally, as well as marketing activity to improve their image externally.

"Satisfaction for resolution" appeared to be an important quality element. This result can be understood in terms of the technical properties of the communications service. ITU-T recommended that, because problems can occur in the service provision process, service providers should build a service support system to resolve problems rapidly and adequately. The ITU-T recommendation emphasizes the importance of the service support system in the communications service market. Because "satisfaction for resolution" is associated with the SLA mentioned previously, this finding becomes the basis for the urgent introduction of an SLA in the Korean high-speed Internet service industry. One of the significant contributions of this chapter is to present service providers with a reasonable guideline for formulating quality or marketing strategies for retaining customers in the rapidly growing high-speed Internet market. With this guideline, service providers can obtain and maintain a competitive advantage in this competitive marketplace.

## 4.2   Recommendation for Further Study

One of the limitations of this chapter is that the lapse of time has not been considered. This will become the key issue in further study. We mentioned that there is an accumulation of experience in the communications service sector. Because accumulation of experience is a property of communications services as distinguished from other services, further study should be undertaken to measure and analyze the discrepancy between expectation and performance according to the lapse of time.

We analyzed users' responses with respect to service quality for high-speed Internet services, emphasizing perceived quality in terms of subjective perspectives. If some other objective quantitative measurement, such as QoS (Quality of Service) parameters, can be included in the analysis, this could overcome some of the limitations associated with the subjective evaluations of service quality. However, in order to use QoS-related parameters, a considerable amount of performance data would be required.

The ADSL and cable modems are currently two major technologies of broadband communication, but a difference in service quality between the two technologies exists. We have not addressed the issue of difference of perceived quality arising from this technical difference. Therefore, further study may need to address this issue to analyze the differences of perceived quality of different technologies.

## 5    REFERENCES

Bong, S. J. (1997), "Overview on Telecommunication Network and Quality of Service", *Information and Communications Research*, Vol. 11, No. 4, Korea Telecom, Seoul.

Clow, K. E., Kurtz, D. L., Ozment, J., and Ong, B. S. (1997), "The Antecedents of Customer Expectations of Services: An Empirical Study Across Four Industries", *The Journal of Services Marketing*, Vol. 11, No. 4, pp.230-248.

Cronin, J. J. and Taylor, S. A. (1992), "Measuring Service Quality: A Reexamination and Extension", *Journal of Marketing*, Vol. 56, pp.55-68.

Grönroos, C. (1984), "A Service Quality Model and its Marketing Implications", *European Journal of Marketing*, Vol. 18, pp.30-44.

Hirschman, A. O. (1970), *Exit, Voice and loyalty: Responses to Decline in Firms, Organizations and States*, Harvard University Press, Cambridge, Mass.

Korea Consumer Federation (2001), Survey on Consumer Complaints about Telecommunication Services, Ministry of Information and Communication, Seoul.

Parasuraman, A., Zeithaml, V. A. and Berry, L. L. (1985), "A Conceptual Model of Service Quality and its Implications for Future Research", *Journal of Marketing*, Vol. 49, pp.41-50.

Spreng, R. A., Mackenzie, S. B. and Olshavsky, R. W. (1996), "A Reexamination of the Determinants of Consumer Satisfaction", *Journal of Marketing*, Vol. 60, pp.15-32.

Woodside, A., Frey, L. and Daly, R. (1989), "Linking Service Quality, Customer Satisfaction and Behavior Intention", *Journal of Health Care Marketing*, Vol. 9, pp.5-17.

Zeithaml, V. A. (1987), Defining and Retailing Price, Perceived Quality, and Perceived Value. *Marketing Science Institute*, pp.87-101.

CHAPTER 13

# The Analysis of Broadband Demand Using Data on Willingness-to-Pay

Paul Rappoport
*Department of Economics, Temple University, Philadelphia*

Lester D. Taylor
*University of Arizona, Tucson*

Donald J. Kridel
*Department of Economics, University of Missouri-St. Louis, St. Louis*

**Abstract** As has been widely tracked, the 1990's and early 2000's have seen an explosive growth worldwide in the Internet in terms of both users and web sites. As the Internet has grown, access speed has become increasingly important. Although access by dial-up modem is still the standard type of Internet access for the majority of households, an increasing number are demanding higher speed access either in the form of Digital Subscriber Line (DSL) or by cable modem. This chapter focuses on the demand for these two forms of high-speed demand, and makes use of data from an omnibus survey conducted in early 2002 by the Marketing Systems Group of Philadelphia, in which respondents were asked questions concerning their willingness-to-pay (WTP) for cable-modem or DSL access to the telecommunications network. Price elasticities for both cable-modem and DSL access are obtained from the cumulative distributions of willingnesses-to-pay that range from an order of -3 for high willingness-to-pay (and therefore low implied penetration rates) to an order of -1 for low willingness-to-pay (and therefore high implied penetration rates). Other findings include: (1) an (inverse) importance of age as a determinant of willingness-to-pay; (2) the emergence of what would appear to be a material difference between the demand for cable-modem access and DSL access; (3) cable-modem access, but not DSL access, appears to be pretty much independent of income and education.

## 1   INTRODUCTION

As has been widely tracked, the 1990's and early 2000's have seen an explosive growth worldwide in the Internet in terms of both users and web sites. As the Internet has grown, access speed has become increasingly important. Although access by dial-up modem is still the standard type of Internet access for the majority of households, an increasing number are demanding higher speed access either in the form of Digital Subscriber Line (DSL) or by cable modem. The former is offered by local exchange telephone companies over existing copper lines into the home, while the latter is provided by cable television companies via coaxial cable. The present paper focuses on the demand for these two forms of high-speed demand, and makes use of data from an omnibus survey conducted in early 2002 by the Marketing Systems Group of Philadelphia, in which respondents were asked questions concerning their willingness-to-pay (WTP) for cable-modem or DSL access to the telecommunications network. In an initial analysis of this information (Rappoport et al. 2002), the authors focused on the construction of price elasticities for broadband access using a generally overlooked procedure suggested by Cramer (1969). Price elasticities for both cable-modem and DSL access were obtained that range from an order of -3 for high willingness-to-pay (and therefore low implied penetration rates) to an order of -1 for low willingness-to-pay (and therefore high implied penetration rates). The present study extends the analysis of that study to model the survey-elicited WTP's as a function of respondents' income, socio-demographic characteristics, and type of Internet access (if any).[1]

Apart from the elasticities just mentioned (which are generally in accord with existing econometrically derived estimates), the principal findings of the study are:

(1) An (inverse) importance of age as a determinant of willingness-to-pay;

(2) The emergence of what would appear to be a material difference between the demand for cable-modem access and DSL access. While one would think that the two forms of access (assuming that both were available) would be fairly strong substitutes, but a relatively low correlation between the two willingnesses-to-pay suggests otherwise.

(3) Also, probit and regression results show cable-modem access to be pretty much independent of income and education, but not for DSL access.

The format of the paper is as follows. The next section begins with a description of the access/usage framework that guides the analysis, while Section III presents a two-stage probit/regression model for explaining the willingnesses-to-pay for cable-modem and DSL access. In Section IV, price elasticities for both cable-modem and DSL access are calculated from kernel-smoothed cumulative distributions of willingness-to-pay. Conclusions are given in Section V.

## 2    THEORETICAL CONSIDERATIONS

We begin with usual access/usage framework for determining the demand for access to a network, whereby the demand for access is determined by the size of the consumer surplus from usage of the network in relation to the price of access.[2] Accordingly, let q denote usage, and let q(p,y) denote the demand for usage, conditional on a price of usage, p, and other variables (income, education, etc.), y. The consumer surplus (CS) from usage will then be given by

---

[1] In view of the novelty of the Internet phenomenon, it is hardly surprising that the literature on Internet demand is small. Existing studies include several by the present authors [Rappoport, Taylor, Kridel, and Serad (1998), Rappoport, Taylor, and Kridel (1999, 2002a, 2002b 2003c), and Rappoport et al. (2003), as well as papers by Hausman, Sidak, and Singer (2001), Andersson and Myrvold (2002), and Varian (2002).

[2] See Chapter 2 of Taylor (1994).

$$CS \int_p^{\infty} q(z,y)dz. \tag{1}$$

Let $\pi$ denote the price of access. Access will then be demanded if

$$CS \geq \pi, \tag{2}$$

or equivalently (in logarithms) if

$$\ln CS \geq \ln\pi. \tag{3}$$

Perl (1983) was one of the first to apply this framework empirically, doing so by assuming a demand function of the form:[3]

$$q = Ae^{-\alpha p}y^{\beta}e^u, \tag{4}$$

where y denotes income (or other variables) and u is a random error term with distribution g(u). Consumer's surplus, CS, will then be given by

$$CS = \int_p^{\infty} Ae^{-\alpha z}y^{\beta}e^u dz \tag{5}$$

$$= \frac{Ae^{-\alpha p}y^{\beta}e^u}{\alpha}.$$

With net benefits from usage and the price of access expressed in logarithms, the condition for demanding access to the telephone network accordingly becomes:

$$P(\ln CS \geq \ln\pi) = P(a - \alpha p + \beta \ln y + u \geq \ln\pi) \tag{6}$$

$$= P(u \geq \ln\pi - a + \alpha p - \beta \ln y),$$

where $a = \ln(A/\alpha)$. The final step is to specify a probability law for consumer surplus, which, in view of the last line in equation (6), can be reduced to the specification for the distribution of u in the demand function for usage. An assumption that u is distributed normally leads to a standard probit model, while an assumption that u is logistic leads to a logit model. Empirical studies exemplifying both approaches abound in the literature.[4]

The standard procedure for estimating access demand can thus be seen in terms of obtaining information on the consumer surplus from usage by estimating a demand function, and then integrating beneath this demand function. In the present context, however, our procedure

---

[3] Since it introduction by Perl in 1978 in an earlier version of his 1983 paper, this function has been used extensively in the analysis of telecommunications access demand (see, e.g., Kridel (1988) and Taylor and Kridel (1990). The great attraction of this demand function is its nonlinearity in income and an ability to handle both zero and non-zero usage prices.

[4] Empirical studies employing the probit framework include Perl (1983) and Taylor and Kridel (1990), while studies using the logit framework include Bodnar *et al.* (1988) and Train, McFadden, and Ben-Akiva (1987). Most empirical studies of telecommunications access demand that employ a consumer-surplus framework focus on local usage, and accordingly ignore the net benefits arising from toll usage. Hausman, Tardiff, and Bellinfonte (1993) and Erikson, Kaserman, and Mayo (1998) are exceptions.

is essentially the reverse, for what we have by way of information are statements on the part of respondents in a survey as to the *most* that they would be willing-to-pay for cable-modem or DSL service. This "*most*" accordingly represents (at least in principle) the maximum price at which the respondent would purchase that type of access. Thus, for any particular price of access, $\pi^*$, say, access will be demanded for WTP's that are this value or greater, while access will not be demanded for WTP's that are less than this value. Hence, implicit in the *distribution* of WTP's is an aggregate demand function (or more specifically, *penetration function*) for cable-modem (or DSL) access. In particular, this function will be given by

$$D(\pi) = \text{proportion of WTP's that are greater than or equal to } \pi \tag{7}$$

$$= \quad P(WTP \geq \pi)$$

$$= \quad 1 - CDF(\pi),$$

where $CDF(\pi)$ denotes the cumulative distribution function of the WTP's. Once CDF's of WTP's are constructed, price elasticities can be obtained (without intervention of the demand function) via the formula (or an empirical approximation thereof):

$$\text{Elasticity } (\pi) \quad = \quad \frac{d \ln CDF(\pi)}{d \ln \pi} . \tag{8}$$

## 3   MODELING WILLINGNESS-TO-PAY FOR CABLE-MODEM AND DSL ACCESS

As noted, information on willingness-to-pay for broadband access to the telephone network by cable-modem and DSL access was collected in an omnibus national survey of about 2000 households in early 2002 by the Marketing Systems Group (MSG) of Philadelphia. Each of the participants in the survey was asked one (but not both) of the following two questions regarding their willingness-to-pay for DSL and cable-modem access to the Internet:

(a).   What is the most you would be willing to pay on a monthly basis for high-speed Internet service provided by your telephone/cable TV company?

(b).   What is the highest monthly price at which you would consider purchasing high-speed Internet service provided by your telephone/cable TV company?

A total of 2011 households participated in the MSG survey. However, elimination of various non-responses, together with refusals to provide information on income or other variables, reduced the number of usable responses to 1192. Exclusion of responses of "zero" for WTP then yields data sets of 975 observations for cable-modem and 922 observations for DSL that are used in constructing the CDF's for these quantities.[5] The resulting frequency

---

[5] The rationale for eliminating all "zero" responses for WTP is discussed below.

distributions for willingness-to-pay for these two forms of high-speed access are given in Tables 1 and 2.

From the tables, we see that WTP's ranged from highs of $400 and $390 per month for cable-modem and DSL, respectively, to a low of $5, with means, respectively, of $37 and $33 and standard deviations of $22 and $19. Not surprisingly, "pileups" are seen to occur on WTP's divisible by 5 ($50, $45, $40, etc.). Moreover, in a number of cases, it is clear that the values elicited were simply the prices ($45.95, $39.99, $39.95, etc.) that respondents were currently paying for Internet access.

Table 1. Frequency Distribution for WTP's Cable-Modem Service

| WTP | Freq. | % | Cum. Freq | Cum %. | WTP | Freq. | % | Cum. Freq. | Cum. % |
|---|---|---|---|---|---|---|---|---|---|
| 400 | 1 | 0.10 | 1 | 0.10 | 39.95 | 7 | 0.72 | 404 | 41.44 |
| 200 | 2 | 0.21 | 3 | 0.31 | 39 | 6 | 0.62 | 410 | 42.05 |
| 150 | 1 | 0.10 | 4 | 0.41 | 37 | 2 | 0.21 | 412 | 42.26 |
| 125 | 1 | 0.10 | 5 | 0.51 | 36 | 1 | 0.10 | 413 | 42.36 |
| 120 | 1 | 0.10 | 6 | 0.62 | 35 | 65 | 6.67 | 478 | 49.03 |
| 110 | 1 | 0.10 | 7 | 0.72 | 34.95 | 1 | 0.10 | 479 | 49.13 |
| 100 | 7 | 0.72 | 14 | 1.44 | 32.99 | 1 | 0.10 | 480 | 49.23 |
| 90 | 4 | 0.41 | 18 | 1.85 | 32 | 2 | 0.21 | 482 | 49.44 |
| 80 | 7 | 0.72 | 25 | 2.56 | 30 | 137 | 14.05 | 619 | 63.49 |
| 79 | 1 | 0.10 | 26 | 2.67 | 29.99 | 3 | 0.31 | 622 | 63.79 |
| 75 | 13 | 1.33 | 39 | 4.00 | 29.25 | 1 | 0.10 | 623 | 63.90 |
| 70 | 5 | 0.51 | 44 | 4.51 | 29 | 4 | 0.41 | 627 | 64.31 |
| 69 | 1 | 0.10 | 45 | 4.62 | 28 | 1 | 0.10 | 628 | 64.41 |
| 67 | 2 | 0.21 | 47 | 4.82 | 25 | 115 | 1.79 | 743 | 76.21 |
| 65 | 19 | 1.95 | 66 | 6.77 | 24.95 | 1 | 0.10 | 744 | 76.31 |
| 60 | 26 | 2.67 | 92 | 9.44 | 23.45 | 1 | 0.10 | 745 | 76.41 |
| 59.95 | 1 | 0.10 | 93 | 9.54 | 23 | 7 | 0.72 | 752 | 77.13 |
| 59 | 3 | 0.31 | 96 | 9.85 | 22 | 5 | 0.51 | 757 | 77.64 |
| 55 | 31 | 3.18 | 127 | 13.03 | 21.95 | 1 | 0.10 | 758 | 77.74 |
| 52 | 1 | 0.10 | 128 | 13.13 | 21 | 6 | 0.62 | 764 | 78.36 |
| 51 | 1 | 0.10 | 129 | 13.23 | 20.99 | 1 | 0.10 | 765 | 78.46 |
| 50 | 84 | 8.62 | 213 | 21.85 | 20 | 156 | 16.00 | 921 | 94.46 |
| 49.95 | 2 | 0.21 | 215 | 22.05 | 19.99 | 1 | 0.10 | 922 | 94.56 |
| 49 | 6 | 0.62 | 221 | 22.67 | 19.95 | 2 | 0.21 | 924 | 94.77 |
| 48 | 2 | 0.21 | 223 | 22.87 | 19.50 | 1 | 0.10 | 925 | 94.87 |
| 47 | 2 | 0.21 | 225 | 23.08 | 19 | 2 | 0.21 | 927 | 95.08 |
| 45 | 50 | 5.13 | 275 | 28.21 | 17 | 1 | 0.10 | 928 | 95.18 |
| 44.95 | 1 | 0.10 | 276 | 28.31 | 15 | 26 | 2.67 | 954 | 97.85 |
| 44 | 3 | 0.31 | 279 | 28.62 | 14.95 | 1 | 0.10 | 955 | 97.95 |
| 43 | 1 | 0.10 | 280 | 28.72 | 12.95 | 2 | 0.21 | 957 | 98.15 |
| 42 | 3 | 0.31 | 283 | 29.03 | 10 | 16 | 1.64 | 973 | 99.79 |
| 41 | 3 | 0.31 | 286 | 29.33 | 9.95 | 1 | 0.10 | 974 | 99.90 |
| 40 | 110 | 11.28 | 396 | 40.62 | 5 | 1 | 0.10 | 975 | 100.00 |
| 39.99 | 1 | 0.10 | 397 | 40.72 | | | | | |

| Mean WTP: 36.86 | Std. dev.: WTP: 21.82. |
|---|---|

Table 2. Frequency Distribution for WTP's DSL Service

| WTP | Freq. | % | Cum. Freq. | Cum. % | WTP | Freq. | % | Cum. Freq. | Cum. % |
|---|---|---|---|---|---|---|---|---|---|
| 300 | 1 | 0.11 | 1 | 0.11 | 30 | 147 | 15.94 | 507 | 54.99 |
| 200 | 2 | 0.22 | 3 | 0.33 | 29.99 | 2 | 0.22 | 509 | 55.21 |
| 120 | 1 | 0.11 | 4 | 0.43 | 29.95 | 6 | 0.65 | 515 | 55.86 |
| 100 | 5 | 0.54 | 10 | 1.08 | 28 | 1 | 0.11 | 521 | 56.51 |
| 90 | 1 | 0.11 | 11 | 1.19 | 26 | 2 | 0.22 | 523 | 56.72 |
| 80 | 5 | 0.54 | 16 | 1.74 | 25 | 117 | 12.69 | 640 | 69.41 |
| 75 | 3 | 0.33 | 19 | 2.06 | 24.99 | 1 | 0.11 | 641 | 69.52 |
| 70 | 2 | 0.22 | 21 | 2.28 | 23 | 10 | 1.08 | 651 | 70.61 |
| 69 | 2 | 0.22 | 23 | 2.49 | 22 | 6 | 0.65 | 657 | 71.26 |
| 67 | 1 | 0.11 | 24 | 2.60 | 21.99 | 1 | 0.11 | 658 | 71.37 |
| 65 | 9 | 0.98 | 33 | 3.58 | 21.95 | 2 | 0.22 | 660 | 71.58 |
| 60 | 15 | 1.63 | 48 | 5.21 | 21 | 6 | 0.65 | 666 | 72.23 |
| 59 | 1 | 0.11 | 49 | 5.31 | 20 | 173 | 18.76 | 839 | 91.00 |
| 57 | 1 | 0.11 | 50 | 5.42 | 19.99 | 3 | 0.33 | 842 | 91.32 |
| 55 | 21 | 2.28 | 71 | 7.70 | 19.95 | 4 | 0.43 | 846 | 91.76 |
| 50 | 75 | 8.13 | 146 | 15.84 | 19 | 4 | 0.43 | 850 | 92.19 |
| 49 | 3 | 0.33 | 149 | 16.16 | 18 | 1 | 0.11 | 851 | 92.30 |
| 48 | 2 | 0.22 | 151 | 16.38 | 17 | 1 | 0.11 | 852 | 92.41 |
| 47 | 1 | 0.11 | 152 | 16.49 | 16 | 2 | 0.22 | 854 | 92.62 |
| 45.95 | 1 | 0.11 | 153 | 16.59 | 15 | 27 | 2.93 | 881 | 95.55 |
| 45 | 31 | 3.36 | 184 | 19.96 | 14.95 | 2 | 0.22 | 883 | 95.77 |
| 43 | 1 | 0.11 | 185 | 20.07 | 14 | 2 | 0.22 | 885 | 95.99 |
| 41 | 2 | 0.22 | 187 | 20.28 | 12.95 | 2 | 0.22 | 887 | 96.20 |
| 40 | 88 | 9.54 | 275 | 29.83 | 12 | 1 | 0.11 | 888 | 96.31 |
| 39.99 | 1 | 0.11 | 276 | 29.93 | 10 | 29 | 3.15 | 917 | 99.46 |
| 39.95 | 4 | 0.43 | 280 | 30.37 | 9.95 | 1 | 0.11 | 918 | 99.57 |
| 39 | 14 | 1.52 | 294 | 31.89 | 7 | 1 | 0.11 | 919 | 99.67 |
| 38 | 2 | 0.22 | 296 | 32.10 | 6 | 1 | 0.11 | 920 | 99.78 |
| 36 | 2 | 0.22 | 298 | 32.32 | 5 | 2 | 0.22 | 922 | 100.00 |
| 35 | 54 | 5.86 | 352 | 38.18 | | | | | |
| 34 | 4 | 0.43 | 356 | 38.61 | | | | | |
| 32 | 3 | 0.33 | 360 | 39.05 | | | | | |

Mean WTP: 32.93        Std. dev.: 18.89

An interesting question is whether willingness-to-pay, which in principle represents areas beneath demand curves, can in turn be "explained" in terms of the determinants of demand, that is, as functions of price, income, and other relevant factors. To explore this, we return to the expression for consumer surplus in the second line of equation (5), which we now express (in logarithms) as:

$$\ln CS \quad = \quad f(p, y, x, u), \quad (9)$$

where p, y, x, and u denote the price of usage, income, a variety of socio-demographic and other characteristics, and an unobservable error term, respectively. Since information on y and x is available from the MSG survey, expression (9) can be estimated as a regression model with lnWTP as the dependent variable.[6] However, before this can be done, the fact that some of the WTP's are zero - which creates an obvious problem in defining the dependent variable - has to be dealt with.

Two solutions emerge as possibilities. The first is to use WTP as the dependent variable in place of lnWTP (in which case zeros are clearly not a problem), while the second solution is simply to eliminate all of the observations with zero WTP's from the sample. We have opted for the second solution. However, we do this as part of a two-stage procedure, in which, in a first stage, a discrete-choice probit model is estimated that explains zero and non-zero values of WTP. The inverse of a "Mills ratio" is then constructed from this model and used as a "correction" term in a second-stage model, in which the logarithms of non-zero values of WTP are regressed on a set of dummy variables representing income and various socio-demographic factors.[7]

The results for the first-stage probit models are tabulated in Tables 3 and 4.[8] The relationship that most stands out in these tables is the importance of age (or rather the absence thereof) for the negative loadings on age indicate that younger households are more likely to have a non-zero willingness-to-pay for broadband access than older households. The most

---

[6] Since usage is bundled with access for both cable-modem and DSL, usage prices are zero, hence willingness-to-pay and consumer surplus coincide.

[7] Although a value of zero is certainly a valid response to questions concerning willingness-to-pay, to put zero and non-zero values on the same footing in constructing CDF's for cable-modem and DSL access would seem to entail the assumption that penetration rates would be 100% at access prices of zero. Obviously, this need not be the case. By specifying a first-stage model that explains the likelihood of a household having a non-zero WTP, and then incorporating this information as a "correction" in a second-stage model that explains the magnitude of (non-zero) WTP, penetration is thereby determined only with respect to those households that value broadband access positively.

[8] Definitions of the variables are provided in the appendix.

Table 3. Probit Model for Non-Zero, Willingness-to-Pay Cable-Modem Access

| Variable | Coefficient | Standard Error | Chi-Square | Pr > Chi-Sq |
|---|---|---|---|---|
| Intercept | 1.5767 | 0.3133 | 25.33 | <0.0001 |
| dq1 | 0.0162 | 0.1007 | 0.03 | 0.8722 |
| Gender | -0.0633 | 0.1041 | 0.37 | 0.5430 |
| dinc2 | -0.0246 | 0.1824 | 0.02 | 0.8925 |
| dinc3 | -0.0060 | 0.1737 | 0.00 | 0.9725 |
| dinc4 | 0.2795 | 0.1657 | 2.85 | 0.0916 |
| dinc5 | 0.1981 | 0.1780 | 1.24 | 0.2658 |
| dinc6 | 0.0833 | 0.1968 | 0.18 | 0.6721 |
| dinc7 | 0.2666 | 0.2227 | 1.43 | 0.2314 |
| demp1 | 0.1148 | 0.1237 | 0.86 | 0.3532 |
| demp2 | 0.1572 | 0.1875 | 0.70 | 0.4019 |
| hsize | -0.0153 | 0.0397 | 0.15 | 0.6998 |
| dhsize8 | 4.9653 | 6788.513 | 0.00 | 0.9994 |
| Internet_access | 0.5930 | 0.1934 | 9.40 | 0.0022 |
| Age | -0.0329 | 0.0036 | 81.53 | <0.0001 |
| HS | 0.0792 | 0.1934 | 0.17 | 0.6824 |
| S_coll | 0.3024 | 0.2041 | 2.20 | 0.1384 |
| Col_grad | 0.2067 | 0.2117 | 0.95 | 0.3289 |
| Post_col | 0.2151 | 0.2426 | 0.79 | 0.3751 |
| Tech | -0.5198 | 0.3537 | 2.16 | 0.1416 |
| Dial_up | 0.3266 | 0.1914 | 2.91 | 0.0879 |
| Broadband | -0.1174 | 0.3076 | 0.15 | 0.7028 |
| CableModem | 1.2269 | 0.4221 | 8.45 | 0.0037 |

Number of observations: 975
Number of WTP's > 0: 758
Number of WTP's = 0: 217.

Table 4. Probit Model for Non-Zero Willingness-to-Pay DSL Access

| Variable | Coefficient | Standard Error | Chi-Square | Pr > Chi-Sq |
|---|---|---|---|---|
| Intercept | 1.0441 | 0.2804 | 13.87 | 0.0002 |
| dq1 | -0.3477 | 0.0927 | 14.07 | 0.0002 |
| Gender | -0.0514 | 0.0950 | 0.29 | 0.5886 |
| dinc2 | -0.1720 | 0.1724 | 0.99 | 0.3185 |
| dinc3 | 0.0939 | 0.1662 | 0.32 | 0.5723 |
| dinc4 | 0.2429 | 0.1548 | 2.46 | 0.1166 |
| dinc5 | 0.0452 | 0.1611 | 0.08 | 0.7789 |
| dinc6 | 0.1506 | 0.1812 | 0.69 | 0.4061 |
| dinc7 | 0.0417 | 0.1963 | 0.05 | 0.8318 |
| demp1 | 0.1694 | 0.1107 | 2.34 | 0.1261 |
| demp2 | 0.4837 | 0.1802 | 7.20 | 0.0073 |
| hsize | -0.0046 | 0.0364 | 0.02 | 0.9002 |
| dhsize8 | 5.2019 | 6998.477 | 0.00 | 0.9994 |
| Internet_access | 0.3062 | 0.1898 | 2.60 | 0.1067 |
| Age | -0.0267 | 0.0033 | 67.21 | <0.0001 |
| HS | 0.3018 | 0.1770 | 2.91 | 0.0881 |
| S_coll | 0.4524 | 0.1844 | 6.02 | 0.0141 |
| Col_grad | 0.4683 | 0.1927 | 5.90 | 0.0151 |
| Post_col | 0.4929 | 0.2237 | 4.85 | 0.0276 |
| Tech | 0.0160 | 0.3453 | 0.00 | 0.9629 |
| Dial_up | 0.5405 | 0.1911 | 8.00 | 0.0047 |
| Broadband | 0.7874 | 0.3662 | 4.62 | 0.0316 |
| CableModem | -0.2781 | 0.3550 | 0.61 | 0.4334 |

Number of observations: 922
Number of WTP's > 0: 652
Number of WTP's = 0: 270.

important factors after age are the type of Internet access that respondents already have.[9] The effect of income, although positive for both types of access, is seen to have surprisingly little statistical significance.[10] The level of education, on the other hand, is seen to be important only for DSL access. Interestingly, the same is true for the dummy variable (demp2) denoting that the respondent works only part-time. Why there are these differential education and

[9] Because of obvious circularity between WTP and Internet access, readers are cautioned to view these relationships simply as ones of association.

[10] The income dummy variable that has been excluded is the one for incomes less than $15,000 (dinc1), which means that the coefficients for the included income dummy variables are measured in terms of deviations from the coefficient for dinc1. The positive coefficients for dinc4 – dinc7 indicate that the effect of income is positive for household income above $35,000.

employment effects on willingness-to-pay for DSL is not clear. Finally, neither gender nor household size is seen to be of any statistical significance.[11]

The estimated coefficients, standard errors, t-ratios, and p-statistics for the second-stage willingness-to-pay models for cable-modem and DSL access are tabulated in Tables 5 and 6. The dependent variables in these models are the logarithms of the (non-zero) WTP's. The list of independent variables includes all those that appeared in the first-stage models, plus the first-stage "Mills ratios" (M*illscbl* and M*illsdsl*).[12] The results, for the most part, parallel those in the first-stage models, and are probably most notable for what appears not to be important, namely, income and education.[13] As in the first-stage models, the coefficients on age (or rather the logs of age) are both negative, as are the coefficients on the dummy variable denoting dial-up Internet access. The only variables in the cable-modem model with t-ratios greater than 2 (in absolute value) are for dial-up access and broadband access. In the DSL model, on the other hand, the variables with t-ratios greater than 2 include the Mills ratio from the first stage (Millsdsl), both full-time and part-time employment (emp1 and emp2), age, broadband access, and cable-modem access.

As noted, it might seem surprising that income and education are unimportant in the second-stage equations. As it turns out, however, this is actually not the case for DSL access, for the influences of both income and education (because of their significance in the first-stage DSL equation) are represented in the coefficient on the Mills ratio. Thus, the only real surprise would appear to be an absence of income and education effects in the equations for cable-modem access.

---

[11] Linear probability models (i.e., linear regressions with dummy variables denoting zero/non-zero values for WTPas the dependent variable) give results that are similar to those from the probit models, with $R^2$s of 0.28 and 0.25, respectively.

[12] Apart from the Mills ratios, the only difference in the independent variables is that household size and age are now in logarithms. The Mills ratios, it is to be noted, correct for the fact that, because the second-stage model can be interpreted as the conditional expectation of WTP, given that WTP is greater than zero, the error-term in this model is "drawn" from a truncated distribution, and therefore does not have a mean of zero. The Mills ratios are accordingly calculated according to the formula $n(\pi_i)/N(\pi_i)$, where $\pi_i$ denotes the *predicted* value (in the first-stage probit equation) of the probability that respondent i has a non-zero WTP and $n(\pi_i)$ and $N(\pi_i)$ represent the standard normal density and cumulative distribution functions of this event. For a derivation and discussion, see Chapter 6 of Maddala (1983).

[13] Low R-squares in models using cross-sectional survey data of this type are normal.

Table 5. Regression Model For Willingness-to-Pay Cable-Modem Access

| Variable | Coefficient | Standard Error | t-ratio | Pr > \|t\| |
|---|---|---|---|---|
| Intercept | 3.8610 | 0.2052 | 18.81 | <0.0001 |
| Millscbl | 0.1940 | 0.1599 | 1.21 | 0.2252 |
| dq1 | 0.0134 | 0.0290 | 0.46 | 0.6433 |
| Gender | -0.0308 | 0.0302 | -1.02 | 0.3074 |
| dinc2 | -0.0470 | 0.0634 | -0.74 | 0.4588 |
| dinc3 | -0.0202 | 0.0560 | -0.36 | 0.7175 |
| dinc4 | 0.0072 | 0.0530 | 0.14 | 0.8919 |
| dinc5 | -0.0120 | 0.0529 | -0.23 | 0.8208 |
| dinc6 | 0.0225 | 0.0569 | 0.40 | 0.6922 |
| dinc7 | 0.0960 | 0.0609 | 1.57 | 0.1156 |
| demp1 | 0.0319 | 0.0396 | 0.81 | 0.4202 |
| demp2 | 0.0538 | 0.0539 | 1.00 | 0.3181 |
| lnhsize | 0.0342 | 0.0306 | 1.12 | 0.2643 |
| Internet_access | 0.0671 | 0.0751 | 0.89 | 0.3722 |
| lnage | -0.1258 | 0.0745 | -1.69 | 0.0916 |
| HS | 0.0235 | 0.0653 | 0.36 | 0.7194 |
| S_coll | 0.0296 | 0.0680 | 0.44 | 0.6632 |
| Col_grad | -0.0181 | 0.0694 | -0.26 | 0.7942 |
| Post_col | -0.0196 | 0.0777 | -0.25 | 0.8006 |
| Tech | -0.0589 | 0.1464 | -0.40 | 0.6875 |
| Dial_up | -0.1584 | 0.0704 | -2.25 | 0.0246 |
| Broadband | 0.1902 | 0.0937 | 2.03 | 0.0427 |
| CableModem | -0.0738 | 0.0857 | -0.86 | 0.3890 |

$R^2 = 0.0767$     d.f. = 952.

Table 6. Regression Model For Willingness-to-Pay DSL Access

| Variable | Coefficient | Standard Error | t-ratio | Pr > \|t\| |
|---|---|---|---|---|
| Intercept | 3.9188 | 0.2081 | 18.83 | <0.0001 |
| Millsdsl | 0.4272 | 0.2011 | 2.13 | 0.0338 |
| dq1 | -0.0351 | 0.0379 | -0.93 | 0.3538 |
| Gender | -0.0135 | 0.0312 | -0.43 | 0.6652 |
| dinc2 | -0.1095 | 0.0683 | -1.60 | 0.1090 |
| dinc3 | 0.0238 | 0.0577 | 0.41 | 0.6796 |
| dinc4 | 0.0601 | 0.0557 | 1.08 | 0.2809 |
| dinc5 | -0.0469 | 0.0535 | -0.88 | 0.3815 |
| dinc6 | 0.0009 | 0.0593 | 0.02 | 0.9874 |
| dinc7 | 0.0933 | 0.0615 | 1.52 | 0.1296 |
| demp1 | 0.1082 | 0.0426 | 2.54 | 0.0113 |
| demp2 | 0.1275 | 0.0619 | 2.06 | 0.0399 |
| lnhsize | 0.0165 | 0.0316 | 0.52 | 0.6026 |
| Internet_access | 0.0768 | 0.0703 | 1.09 | 0.2752 |
| lnage | -0.2438 | 0.0861 | -2.83 | 0.0047 |
| HS | 0.1180 | 0.0755 | 1.56 | 0.1184 |
| S_coll | 0.1539 | 0.0812 | 1.89 | 0.0585 |
| Col_grad | 0.1080 | 0.0841 | 1.28 | 0.1995 |
| Post_col | 0.1010 | 0.0909 | 1.21 | 0.2264 |
| Tech | -0.0876 | 0.1449 | -0.60 | 0.5457 |
| Dial_up | -0.1079 | 0.0784 | -1.38 | 0.1687 |
| Broadband | 0.2556 | 0.1018 | 2.51 | 0.0122 |
| CableModem | -0.1745 | 0.0799 | -2.19 | 0.0291 |

$R^2$ = 0.0857     d.f. = 899.

## 4    CALCULATION OF PRICE ELASTICITIES

As has been noted, an attractive feature of CDF's of willingnesses-to-pay is that they can be interpreted as penetration functions, from which it is possible to obtain price elasticities in line with expression (8) above. Three procedures come to mind as to how these elasticities might be constructed. The most straightforward procedure would be to define the elasticities as simple arc elasticities between selected adjacent values on the empirical CDF's. Unfortunately, however, because of the 'pileups" just noted, the elasticities that would emerge from this procedure would be highly unstable, and accordingly of little practical use. A second procedure would be to derive the elasticities on the presumption [a la Cramer (1969)] that the WTP's are distributed according to the log-normal distribution. This second procedure was our initial focus, but had to be abandoned when it became apparent that the assumption that the WTP's follow a log-normal distribution is empirically not justified. Finally, a third way, which is the one that we have employed, is to construct the elasticities from a non-parametric approximation to the empirical CDF's.

Specifically, what we have done is to estimate kernel density functions (using the unit normal density function as the kernel weighting factor) as approximations to the empirical frequency distributions of the WTP's, and then calculating elasticities at various points on these functions. Since the use of kernel estimation may be seen as somewhat novel in this context, some background and motivation may be useful. The goal in kernel estimation is to develop a continuous approximation to an empirical frequency distribution that, among other things, can be used to assign density, in a statistical valid manner, in any small neighborhood of an observed frequency point. For example, in Table 1, we see that there are 86 observations at a WTP of $50 (treating $49.95 as $50), but only a single observation at $51 and six at $49. Such "lumpiness", as was noted in the preceding paragraph, makes calculation of an arc elasticity in a neighborhood of $50 a dubious exercise.

Since there is little reason to think that, in a large population, "pileups" of WTP's at amounts divisible by $5 reflects anything other than the convenience of nice round numbers, there is also little reason to think that the "true" density at WTP's of $51 or $49 ought to be much different than the density at $50. The intuitive way of dealing with this contingency (i.e., "pileups" at particular discrete points) is to tabulate frequencies within intervals, and then to calculate "density" as frequency within an interval divided by the length of the interval (i.e., as averages within intervals). However, in doing this, the "density" within any particular interval is calculated using only the observations within that interval, which is to say that if an interval in question (say) is from $40 to $45, then a WTP of $46 (which is as "close" to $45 as is $44) will not be given weight in calculating the density for that interval. What kernel density estimation does is to allow *every* observation to have weight in the calculation of the density for *every* interval, but a weight that varies inversely with the "distance" that the observations lies from the center of the interval in question.

For the analytics involved, let $\hat{g}(x)$ denote the density function that is to be constructed for a random variable x (in our case, WTP) that varies from $x_1$ to $x_n$. For cable-modem WTP, for example, the range $x_1$ to $x_n$ would be $5 to $400. Next, divide this range (called the 'support' in kernel estimation terminology) into k sub-intervals. The function $\hat{g}(x)$ is then constructed as:

$$\hat{g}(x_i) \quad = \quad \sum_{j=1}^{N} \frac{K\left(\dfrac{x_i - x_j}{h}\right)}{Nh} \, , \qquad i = 1, ..., k. \qquad (9)$$

In this expression, K denotes the kernel-weighting function, h represents a smoothing parameter, and N denotes the number of observations. For the two cases at hand (for cable-modem and DSL WTP's), the density function in expression (9) has been constructed for each using the unit normal density function as the kernel weighting function and a 'support' of k = 1000 intervals.[14]

With estimation of the kernel density functions for cable-modem and DSL WTP's, price elasticities can be calculated from the associated CDF's [using a numerical counterpart to expression (8)]. The resulting elasticities, calculated at prices (WTP's) of $70, $60, $50, $40,

---

[14] Silverman's rule-of-thumb,

$$\hat{h} \quad = \quad (0.9)\min[\text{std. dev., interquartile range}/1.34](N^{-1/5}),$$

has been used for the smoothing parameter h. Two standard references for kernel density estimation are Silverman (1986) and Wand and Jones (1995). Ker and Goodwin (2000) provide an interesting practical application to the estimation of crop insurance rates.

$30, and $20, are presented in Table 7.[15] From the table, we see that the elasticities range from less than -3 to a little greater than -1. However, since (from Tables 1 and 2) half of penetration occurs for WTP of $30 or less for both forms of broadband access, the most relevant elasticity can be taken to lie in the range of -2 to -1. This range compares with existing econometric estimates that vary from -0.84 to -1.05.[16]

Table 7. Price Elasticities for Broadband Access Cable-Modem and DSL

|  | Elasticity | |
| WTP | Cable-Modem | DSL |
| --- | --- | --- |
| $70 | 2.97 | 2.21 |
| 60 | -3.29 | -2.57 |
| 50 | -3.17 | -2.99 |
| 40 | -2.35 | -3.10 |
| 30 | -1.53 | -2.10 |
| 20 | -0.95 | -0.97 |

## 5    CONCLUSIONS

This paper has analyzed the demand for broadband access to the Internet using information on willingness-to-pay for cable-modem and DSL access that was collected in early 2002 in an omnibus survey of some 2000 households. A theoretical framework has been utilized that identifies willingness-to-pay with consumer surplus from usage, and allows for willingness-to-pay to be modeled as a function of income, education, and other socio-demographic factors. Perhaps the most interesting findings are (1) the (inverse) importance of age as a determinant of willingness-to-pay and (2) the emergence of what would appear to be a material difference between the demand for cable-modem access and DSL access. One would think that the two

---

[15] The values for the cumulative densities at $70, $60, etc. are taken from the CDF's for the empirical frequency distributions in Tables 1 and 2. The elasticities are then calculated from corresponding points on the kernel CDF's via the formula:

$$Elasticity(x) = \frac{\Delta CDF(x) / CDF(x)}{\Delta WTP(x) / WTP(x)} ,$$

where x denotes the smallest value on the kernel CDF that is greater than x, for x = $70, ...,$20.

[16] See, e.g., Rappoport, Taylor, Kridel, and Serad (1998), Kridel, Rappoport, and Taylor, (1999), Kridel, Rappoport, and Taylor (2002a), Rappoport, Taylor, and Kridel, (2002b), and Rappoport, Kridel, Taylor, Duffy-Deno, and Alleman (2003). In the earlier version of this study, given at the ICFC Conference in San Francisco in June 2002 (also at the European Conference of the International Telecommunications Society in Madrid in September 2002), elasticities were calculated assuming that the WTP's are distributed log-normally [as per Cramer (1969)]. The elasticities obtained by this procedure are, for WTP's of $50 or less, about half those obtained here. However, the empirical frequency distributions provide little support for the assumption that the WTP's are log-normal, hence our decision to use a kernel-based density estimator. Also, the earlier data set included the responses of zero WTP's, which have been excluded in the present data set. Much of the difference is almost certainly due to this exclusion. The decision to exclude zeros was based on the consideration that a response of zero WTP was an expression that the value of cable-modem or DSL access was zero even access were free, rather than that access would be demanded by everyone at prices of zero. Finally, it is to be noted that the non-monotonicity in the elasticities in Table 7 may be due to the "pile-ups" of WTP's at the prices indicated.

forms of access (assuming that both were available) would be fairly strong substitutes, but the correlation between the willingnesses-to-pay suggests otherwise.[17] Also, probit and regression results show cable-modem access to be pretty much independent of income and education, but not for DSL access. Finally, by employing a generally overlooked procedure suggested by Cramer (1969), it has been possible to obtain non-parametric price elasticities for cable-modem and DSL access from the frequency distributions of the willingnesses-to-pay. The elasticities obtained are generally similar for the two forms of access, and range from about -1.00 at a monthly access price of $20 to -3.00 or less for access prices of $40 or more.

Since these elasticities are constructed from information elicited directly from households, and thus entail the use of contingent-valuation (CV) data, the seriousness (in light of the longstanding controversy surrounding the use of such data) with which our elasticities are to be taken might be open to question.[18] However, in our view, the values that we have obtained are indeed plausible and warrant serious consideration. This is especially the case for the values calculated in the part of the WTP CDF's for which half or more of broadband penetration would be projected to occur (that is, at access prices of $30 or less, as per Tables 1 and 2), where the CV-based elasticities are not notably out-of-line with existing econometric estimates. Added credence for our results, it seems to us, is provided by the fact that, with cable-modem and DSL, we are dealing with products (or services) with which respondents are already familiar (and in many instances the respondents already demand), unlike in circumstances (such as in the valuation of a unique natural resource or the absence of a horrific accident) in which there is no generally meaningful market-based valuation can be devised.

In closing, we would like to say that we feel that the findings of this paper are more informative of what is possible to do with willingness-to-pay data of this type, as opposed to the obtaining of substantive results. While it is encouraging that, in view of the fact that the question eliciting willingness-to-pay was posed in two different forms[19], we did not find any apparent "framing" differences, this does not mean that "framing" problems in exercises such as this one are absent. All considered, however, we believe that the results of this paper show that demand analysis involving contingent-valuation data in circumstances in which the products or services are familiar and well-defined is an approach to be encouraged.

---

[17] The $R^2$ between the two willingnesses-to-pay is 0.33. However, a recent paper by Andersson, Fjell, and Foros (2003) suggests that this relatively weak substitution relationship may be a reflection of asymmetric cross-price effects, rather than their absence. Two distinct populations of broadband users may be involved, one whose usage is "TV-viewer" based that requires very high-speed access, and a second whose usage is more "internet-surfer" based that can get by with a lower speed of access. Since cable-modem is in general much faster than DSL, cable-modem access will accordingly be a much stronger substitute for DSL for "internet surfers" than DSL access will be for cable-modem for "TV-viewers."

[18] The critical literature on contingent valuation methods is large. See the NOAA Panel Report (1993), Smith (1993), Portnoy (1994), Hanneman (1994), Diamond and Hausman (1994), and McFadden (1994). On the other hand, particularly successful uses of CV data would seem to include Hammitt (1986) and Kridel (1988). In the present context, one should be skeptical of the largest WTP's, especially for cable-modem access. The respondent providing the highest value ($400) has cable-modem access and an income between $75,000 and $100,000, and thus would not appear to be problematic. However, the next four highest cable-modem WTP's did not report any form of Internet access, and one of them (with a WTP of $200) reported income of less than $15,000. Of course, the latter (who reported an age of 27) may have had high-speed access either at work, and was reporting what cable-modem access would be in the absence of any budget constraint.

[19] Cf., the insignificance of the variable dq1 in Tables 3-6.

## 6   APPENDIX

### 6.1   Definitions of Variables

| | |
|---|---|
| dq1 | dummy variable that equals 1 if respondent was asked question (a) regarding WTP. |
| Gender | dummy variable that equals 1 if respondent is male. |
| dinc1 | income less than \$15 K. |
| dinc2 | dummy variable that equals 1 if respondent's income is between \$15 K and \$25 K. |
| dinc3 | dummy variable that equals 1 if respondent's income is between \$25 K and \$35 K. |
| dinc4 | dummy variable that equals 1 if respondent's income is between \$35 K and \$50 K. |
| dinc5 | dummy variable that equals 1 if respondent's income is between \$50 K and \$75 K. |
| dinc6 | dummy variable that equals 1 if respondent's income is between \$75 K and \$100 K. |
| dinc7 | dummy variable that equals 1 if respondent's income is greater than \$100 K. |
| demp1 | dummy variable that equals 1 if respondent is employed full-time. |
| demp2 | dummy variable that equals 1 if respondent is employed part-time. |
| hsize | size of household (actual number if 7 or less). |
| dhsize8 | dummy variable that equals 1 if household size is 8 or more. |
| lnhsize | log(hsize). |
| Internet_access | dummy variable that equals 1 if respondent has any form of Internet access. |
| Age | age of respondent. |
| lnage | log(Age). |
| HS | dummy variable that equals 1 if respondent graduated from high school. |
| S_coll | dummy variable that equals 1 if respondent has some college. |
| Col_grad | dummy variable that equals 1 if respondent graduated from college. |
| Post_col | dummy variable that equals 1 if respondent has some post-graduate education. |
| Tech | dummy variable that equals 1 if respondent attended technical school. |
| Dial_up | dummy variable that equals 1 if respondent has dial-up Internet access. |
| Broadband | dummy variable that equals 1 if respondent has some form of broadband access. |
| CableModem | dummy variable that equals 1 if respondent has cable-modem access. |
| Millscbl | Mills ratio for cable-modem access, calculated from first-stage probit equation. |
| Millsdsl | Mills ratio for DSL access, calculated from first-stage probit equation. |

## 7  REFERENCES

Andersson, K. and Myrvold, O. (2002), "Residential Demand for 'Multipurpose Broadband Access': Evidence from a Norwegian VDSL Trial," *Telektronic*, Vol. 96, No. 2, pp. 20-25.

Andersson, K, Fjell, K., and Foros, O. (2003), "Are TV-viewers and surfers different breeds? Broadband demand and asymmetric cross-price effects," paper presented at the Norwegian Annual Conference in Economics, Bergen, 2003, Telenor R&D, 1331 Fornebu, Norway.

Bodnar, J., Dilworth, P., and Iacono, S. (1988), "Cross-Section Analysis of Residential Telephone Subscription in Canada," *Information Economics and Policy*, Vol. 3, No. 4, pp. 311-331.

Cramer, J.S. (1969), *Empirical Econometrics*, Elsevier Publishing Co., New York.

Diamond, P.A. and Hausman, J.A. (1994), "Contingent Valuation: Is Some Number Better Than No Number?," *Journal of Economic Perspectives*, Volume 8, No. 4, Fall 1994, pp. 45-64.

Erikson, R.C., and Kaserman, D.L., and Mayo, J.W. (1998), "Targeted and Untargeted Subsidy Schemes: Evidence from Post-Divestiture Efforts to Promote Universal Service," *Journal of Law and Economics*, Vol. 41, October 1998, pp. 477-502.

Hammitt, J.K. (1986), "Estimating Consumer Willingness to Pay to Reduce Food Borne Risk," *Report R-3447-EPA*, The RAND Corporation.

Hannemann, W.M. (1994), "Valuing the Environment though Contingent Valuation," *Journal of Economic Perspectives*, Volume 8, No. 4, Fall 1994, pp. 19-44.

Hausman, J.A., Sidak, J.G., and Singer, H.J. (2001), "Cable Modems and DSL: Broadband Internet Access for Residential Customers," *American Economic Review Papers and Proceedings*, Vol. 91, No. 2, May 2001, pp. 302-307.

Hausman, J.A., Tardiff, T.J., and Bellinfonte, A. (1993), "The Effects of the Breakup of AT&T on Telephone Penetration in the United States," *American Economic Review Papers*, Vol. 83, No. 2, May 1993, pp. 178-184.

Ker, A.P. and Goodwin, B.K. (2000), "Nonparametric Estimation of Crop Insurance and Rates Revisited," *American Journal of Agricultural Economics*, Vol. 83, May 2000, pp. 463-478.

Kridel, D.J. (1988), "A Consumer Surplus Approach to Predicting Extended Area Service (EAS) Development and Stimulation Rates," *Information Economics and Policy*, Vol. 3, No. 4, pp. 379-390.

Kridel, D.J., Rappoport, P.N., and Taylor, L.D. (1999), "An Econometric Model of the Demand for Access to the Internet," in *The Future of the Telecommunications Industry: Forecasting and Demand Analysis*, ed. by D.G. Loomis and L.D. Taylor, Kluwer Academic Publishers.

Kridel, D.J., Rappoport, P.N., and Taylor, L.D. (2001), "An Econometric Model of the Demand for Access to the Internet by Cable Modem," in *Forecasting the Internet: Understanding the Explosive Growth of Data Communications*, ed. by D.G. Loomis and L.D. Taylor, Kluwer Academic Publishers.

National Oceanographic and Atmospheric Administration (NOAA;1993), 58, Federal Register, 4601, January 15, 1993.

Maddala, G.S. (1969), *Limited – Dependent and Qualitative Variables in Econometrics*, Cambridge University Press.

McFadden, D. (1994), "Contingent Valuation and Social Choice," *American Journal of Agricultural Economics*, Vol. 76, November 1994, pp. 695-707.

Perl, L.J. (1978), "Economic and Demographic Determinants for Basic Telephone Service," National Economic Research Associates, White Plains, NY, March 28, 1978.

Perl, L.J. (1983), "Residential Demand for Telephone Service 1983", prepared for the Central Service Organization of the Bell Operating Companies, Inc., National Economic Research Associates, White Plains, NY, December 1983.

Portnoy, P.R. (1994), "The Contingent Valuation Debate: Why Economists Should Care," *Journal of Economic Perspectives*, Volume 8, No. 4, Fall 1994, pp. 3-18.

Rappoport, P.N., Taylor, L.D., and Kridel, D.J. (1999), "An Econometric Study of The Demand for Access to The Internet," in *The Future of The Telecommunications Industry: Forecasting and Demand Analysis*, ed. by D.G. Loomis and L.D. Taylor, Kluwer Academic Publishers, Dordrecht.

Rappoport, P.N., Taylor, L.D., and Kridel, D.J. (2002a), "The Demand for High-Speed Access to The Internet," in *Forecasting The Internet: Understanding the Explosive Growth of Data Communications*, ed. by D.G. Loomis and L.D. Taylor, Kluwer Academic Publishers, Dordrecht.

Rappoport, P.N., Taylor, L.D., and Kridel, D.J. (2002b), "The Demand for Broadband: Access, Content, and The Value of Time," in *Broadband: Should We Regulate High-Speed Internet Access*, ed. by R. W. Crandall and J. H. Alleman, AEI-Brookings Joint Center for Regulatory Studies, Washington, D.C., 2002.

Rappoport, P.N., Taylor, L.D., and Kridel, D.J. (2003c), "Willingness-to-Pay and the Demand for Broadband Access," forthcoming in *Down to the Wire: Studies in the Diffusion and Regulation of Telecommunications Technologies*, ed. by Allan Shampine, Nova Science Publishers.

Rappoport, P.N., Kridel, D.J., Taylor, Duffy-Deno, K., and Alleman, J. (2003), in "Forecasting The Demand for Internet Services," in *The International Handbook of Telecommuni-cations Economics: Volume II*, ed. by G. Madden, Edward Elgar Publishing Co., London.

Rappoport, P.N., Taylor, L.D., Kridel, D.J., and Serad, W. (1998), "The Demand for Internet and On-Line Access," in *Telecommunications Transformation: Technology, Strategy and Policy*, ed. by E. Bohlin and S.L. Levin, IOS Press.

Silverman, B.W. (1986), *Density Estimation for Statistics and Data Analysis, Monographs on Statistics and Applied Probability 26*, Chapman and Hall, London.

Smith, V.K. (1993), "Non-Market Valuation of Natural Resources: An Interpretive Appraisal," *Land Economics*, Vol. 69, No. 1, February 1993, pp. 1-26.

Taylor, L.D. (1994), *Telecommunications Demand in Theory and Practice*, Kluwer Academic Publishers, Dordrecht.

Taylor, L.D. and Kridel, D.J. (1990), "Residential Demand for Access to the Telephone Network," in *Telecommunications Demand Modeling*, ed. by A. de Fontenay, M.H. Shugard, and D.S. Sibley, North Holland Publishing Co., Amsterdam.

Train, K.E., McFadden, D.L, and Ben-Akiva, M. (1987), "The Demand for Local Telephone Service: A Fully Discrete Model of Residential Calling Patterns and Service Choices," *The Rand Journal of Economics*, Vol. 18, No. 1, Spring 1987, pp. 109-123.

Varian, H.R. (2002), "Demand for Bandwidth: Evidence from the INDEX Project," in *Broadband: Should We Regulate High-Speed Internet Access*, ed. by R. W. Crandall and J. H. Alleman, AEI-Brookings Joint Center for Regulatory Studies, Washington, D.C., 2002.

Wand, M.P. and Jones, M.C. (1995), *Kernal Smoothing, Monographs on Statistics and Applied Probability 60*, Chapman and Hall, London.

# CHAPTER 14

# Drivers of Demand Growth for Mobile Telecommunications Services: Evidence from International Panel Data

Aniruddha Banerjee
*NERA Economic Consulting, Cambridge*

Agustin J. Ros.
*NERA Economic Consulting, Cambridge*

**Abstract.** This chapter reports the results from an econometric analysis of global mobile telephony demand growth as a function of various market and regulatory variables and unobservable country and region-specific factors. Using panel data from 1996-2000, the authors investigate the drivers of mobile services demand growth in a selected panel of developed and developing countries. The chapter explores, in particular, the effects on that demand growth of the quality of the existing fixed network, the presence of a separate (and, possibly, independent) regulator, and the offering of innovative pricing arrangements, such as Calling Party Pays and pre-paid services. It is found that although those effects are, for the most part, as expected, there is mixed evidence on the role of the regulator and of the price structure innovations.

## 1    INTRODUCTION

Since becoming commercially available in the early 1980s, and especially in the last decade, mobile telecommunications services have experienced spectacular demand growth worldwide. Between 1990 and 2002, the International Telecommunications Union (ITU) estimates that the number of mobile subscribers worldwide grew from 11 million to 1.15 billion—a compounded annual growth rate of almost 47 percent. In 2002, the number of mobile subscribers worldwide surpassed the number of fixed main lines for the first time.

The importance of mobile services—from both an economic and a sociological perspective—cannot be understated. Consumers have benefited enormously from mobile communications, and the industry has generated considerable wealth for shareholders in a relatively brief period of time. Many consumers now view mobile services as essential to their daily lives, particularly as a growing number of innovative services that go well beyond voice communications become available. Moreover, rapid growth of mobile telephony has non-trivial positive spillover effects on much of the economy. For example, mobile telephony expands communications possibilities between consumers and businesses and lowers transactions costs and other costs of doing business. In addition, technological change embodied in the newer, third-generation (3G) mobile services—which can transmit broadband data and internet services—promises to alter profoundly the way in which we live and work. From a sociological perspective, mobile communications play an indispensable role in helping to connect different populations, especially those located in isolated areas, and in increasing citizens' access to health and emergency services.

In some developing countries, the availability of mobile services has already revolutionized communications. Many such countries have badly lagged more developed countries in the availability and quality of fixed network-based wireline telecommunications. Moreover, it has not been uncommon for prices of fixed network-based services to be based on deeply entrenched subsidies that, in turn, have discouraged private investment in fixed networks, even where such investment has been permitted. As a result, long waiting lists for fixed network services—at times exceeding ten years—have developed in those countries.[1] Now, the availability of mobile services has offered those countries the option to leapfrog existing fixed networks and services with mobile telephony, and millions of consumers now have the opportunity to purchase communications services where they previously did not.

In this paper, we use panel data from 1996-2000 to investigate the drivers of mobile services demand growth in a selected panel of 61 developed and developing countries. The paper reports the results from an econometric analysis of mobile telephony growth as a function of various market and regulatory variables and unobservable country and region-specific factors. The familiar S-shaped diffusion of new technology suggests that the growth rate is low initially, but then accelerates before reaching a natural saturation level. Factors that influence the timing and extent of penetration include income, service price structures and levels, technological change, and consumer tastes and preferences. In addition, supply-side factors, such as the availability and quality of fixed main lines, are expected to have a bearing on the growth of mobile telephony. Apart from these market demand and supply factors, this study also takes account of the regulatory environments in the countries of the panel, in particular whether regulatory agencies separate (or, at least, independent) from government-run telecommunications entities existed during the study period.

## 2    REVIEW OF LITERATURE

Our paper begins with a bifurcated review of the economic literature on international mobile telephony. We first describe the results of empirical studies that use data from various country panels in order to reach conclusions about the determinants of mobile telephony growth. The second part of the review summarizes the results of empirical studies based on the analysis of country-specific data.

### 2.1    Cross-country Analyses

There are several comprehensive empirical studies of the drivers of demand growth for mobile services. Madden and Coble-Neal (2003) used a global telecommunications panel comprising

---

[1] Ros and Banerjee (2000) report evidence from Latin America that fixed network supply constraints (brought on partly by subsidized and unremunerative rates for certain fixed services) were historically responsible for significant unmet demand and long waiting lists. In recent years, a combination of privatization and tariff rebalancing have gone a long way toward relieving supply bottlenecks and meeting pent-up demand.

56 countries and annual data for the period 1995-2000 to estimate a dynamic demand model. Their study examined the substitution effect between fixed and mobile telephony while controlling for the consumption externality associated with telephone networks. The authors modeled optimizing economic agent behavior directly in order to derive mobile demand equations for estimation, and found that, for enhancing network mobile subscription, mobile network size has the greatest long-run impact, followed by the reduction of mobile service prices. Moreover, Madden and Coble-Neal also discovered a substantial substitution effect, specifically that price increases for fixed main lines induce growth of mobile subscriptions. Among the significant factors that affect mobile growth, they concluded that income was the least important.

Using sample data for several African countries, Hamilton (2003) investigated whether mobile services are substitutes or complements for fixed services. Given the conventional wisdom that mobile and fixed telephony are complementary in developed countries, she established that they appear to be substitutes in developing countries where fixed network access is low or non-existent. Studying a possible reverse causality between mobile and fixed telephony in environments with low levels of economic development, Hamilton suggested that mobile telephony acts as a competitive force that encourages providers of fixed services to improve access to their networks. She concluded that mobile and fixed services are sometimes substitutes, and at other times complements, even where access to fixed networks is relatively low.

Another recent study is by Gruber and Verboven (2001a), who estimated a diffusion model for mobile services and analyzed, *inter alia*, the effects of government policies on the global evolution of mobile telephony. This study produced useful evidence on the main drivers of growth in mobile services. Specifically, Gruber and Verboven analyzed how entry and standards regulations affect the diffusion of mobile services, after controlling for various other country-specific factors. Their study was based on data for 140 countries (representing about 94 percent of the world's population) in which mobile services were offered during the period 1981-1997 (except for Japan for which data from 1979 were available).

Gruber and Verboven's main finding from estimating a logistic diffusion model was that diffusion rates of different countries are generally slow to converge. They attributed this slowness partly to the delay in some countries in issuing first licenses and partly to persisting initial cross-country differences. They also found that introducing competition has a strong immediate impact on diffusion but a weak subsequent impact, and that setting a single technological standard accelerates the diffusion of analog technologies considerably. In addition, countries with higher per capita GDP and larger fixed networks tend to have higher adoption rates for mobile services, although those rates tend to diminish over time. Gruber and Verboven noted that the latter finding was evidence of a form of complementarity between fixed and mobile network services (to which we refer as "technological complementarity" in this paper).[2] Interestingly, they also found that, relative to countries with short or non-existent waiting lists for fixed line connections, countries with longer waiting lists had lower mobile adoption rates initially but experienced strong and significantly higher annual

---

[2] *Technological* complementarity (which is the phenomenon Gruber and Verboven observed) refers to the parallel growth of mobile and fixed telephony for technological or other reasons, as opposed to *economic* complementarity—in the sense in which that term is typically used—refers to parallel movements in demand in response to mutual relative price changes.

growth subsequently. From this, Gruber and Verboven concluded that mobile services are well-suited to provide telecommunications access in inefficient fixed line markets.

Two similar studies by Gruber and Verboven (2001b) and Gruber (2001) also focused on the diffusion of mobile services in countries in the European Union and Central and Eastern Europe, respectively. Using logistic models of diffusion similar to those in Gruber and Verboven (2001a), Gruber and Verboven (2001b) found that the transition from analog to digital technology during the early 1990s, and a corresponding increase in spectrum capacity, had a major impact on the diffusion of mobile services. Moreover, the authors found that the advent of competition also had a significant effect on diffusion, but that this effect was smaller than the technology effect. The Gruber (2001) study found that the speed of diffusion increased with the number of firms and—similar to the findings in Gruber and Verboven (2001a)—also increased with the size of the fixed network and the waiting list for fixed line services.

Ahn and Lee (1999) studied the determinants of demand for mobile services using cross-sectional data for 64 countries in 1998. Acknowledging the importance of distinguishing between access and usage, Ahn and Lee estimated the demand for access by exploiting the often-observed fact that the subscribership rate in any country depends on factors specific to that country. Ahn and Lee believed that these country-specific factors include the existing tariff systems, national wealth, the levels of technological development and industrialization, and fixed network facilities. They found that the probability of subscribing to mobile services was positively correlated with per capita GDP and the number of fixed lines per person (akin to the teledensity measure).[3] They also concluded that mobile service prices were not strongly associated with the probability of subscribing to mobile services.

In a related vein, Jha and Majumdar (1999) examined the effects of the diffusion of cellular technology on the competitiveness of telecommunications as a whole in OECD countries. Jha and Majumdar's measure of competitiveness of the telecommunications system in a country was based on productive efficiency, based on their belief that a productive telecommunications sector that uses resources efficiently is also competitive. The authors estimated a stochastic production frontier from cross-sectional data employing a single-step estimation procedure that estimated the frontier and the determinants of efficiency simultaneously. The main finding of this study was that the extent of subscribership to mobile services (along with investment per main line, the number of inhabitants, GDP, higher tariffs, and the extent of market liberalization and private participation) were major determinants of telecommunications sector productive efficiency in OECD countries.

Three other non-econometric studies of mobile services are noteworthy in this context. First, Gruber (1999) analyzed the key variables affecting mobile telephony in the European Union and attributed the rapid growth of such telephony in Europe to a favorable technological and regulatory environment. Specifically, Gruber attributed such growth to technological innovation and a new regulatory framework based on liberalization and technical standardization. In contrast, Gruber also found that national regulatory idiosyncrasies became less important as European Union regulation replaced national regulation.

Second, a study by Rossotto, Kerf, and Rohlfs (2000) examined the importance of competition in mobile telephony. Based on summary statistics of data from countries deploying GSM technology for mobile services, rather than a formal econometric analysis, the study found

---

[3] Following convention, we use the term "teledensity" to mean the number of fixed main lines in operation per 100 inhabitants and "cellular density" to mean the number of mobile subscriptions per 100 inhabitants.

competition to be an important determinant of growth in (and benefits from) mobile telephony. In particular, it found that competition in the market for mobile telephony increased the size of that market and drove incumbent fixed network operators to improve their provision of fixed services.

Finally, Banerjee and Ros (forthcoming) performed a cluster analysis of a panel of 61 developed and developing countries. Forming clusters on the basis of the levels and compound annual growth rates of teledensity and cellular density, they identified four clusters of countries with distinctive telephony and socio-economic characteristics. Based on these findings, the study concluded that while mobile and fixed telephony have generally developed apace in the more affluent countries, relatively less affluent/developed countries have favored the leapfrogging of fixed by mobile telephony—a phenomenon that this study labeled "technological substitution."[4] This inference was supported by one of the main conclusions of the study by Gruber and Verboven (2001a).

## 2.2 Country-specific Studies

Several country-specific studies have examined the determinants of demand growth for mobile services. Sung and Lee (2002) examined the impact of rapid growth in mobile telephones on the demand for traditional fixed network access in South Korea. The analysis used South Korean regional panel data for the period 1991-98. The results showed that a 1 percent increase in the number of mobile telephones results in a reduction of between 0.1 and 0.18 percent in new fixed connections and an increase of between 0.14 and 0.22 percent in fixed disconnections.

These results were generally consistent with those of Sung, Kim, and Lee (2001) who also examined the substitutability between mobile and fixed services in South Korea. The authors estimated separate equations for fixed-line connections and disconnections in South Korea and found that fixed and mobile service operators compete on the basis of price.

Rodini, Ward and Woroch (2002) empirically estimated the substitutability of fixed and mobile services using a large U.S. household survey conducted for the period 2000-2001. This study estimated cross-price elasticities that confirmed that second fixed lines and mobile services are economic substitutes.

Cadima and Barros (2000) estimated the diffusion of Portuguese fixed and mobile networks, and concluded that mobile telephony growth slowed the growth of fixed telephony, but there was little impact of the latter on the former.

Finally, Okada and Keiko (1999) reviewed Japan's regulatory scheme for mobile services and examined the interdependence between mobile and fixed networks. Having first estimated price elasticities and network effects between the two networks, they found the own-price elasticities to be relatively high and the substitution and network effects to be quite substantial.

Findings from the empirical literature on the main drivers of growth in mobile telephony are summarized below in Table 1. National income, liberalization (competition), and the size of the fixed network are consistently identified as important such drivers. Gains in national income expand demand for all goods and services, including mobile services. The finding that

---

[4] Technological substitution—as distinct from economic substitution—occurs not in response to relative price changes but when local conditions favor the development of one form of telephony over another. See footnote 2 for the parallel concept of technological complementarity.

competition is associated with growth in mobile telephony suggests that economies of scale in the industry are not so large as to inhibit competition. While the optimal number of mobile operators in any given country is likely to depend on limits to the size of the overall market for mobile telephone services, competition is clearly a catalyst for the demand for mobile services. The finding that the size of the fixed network has a positive impact on mobile services growth suggests technological complementarity between mobile and fixed services. Nevertheless, there is also evidence that, in some countries, mobile services are a substitute for fixed services, particularly given that the quality of the fixed network appears to be inversely related to demand growth for mobile services. The existing literature does not, however, link demand growth in mobile telephony to other factors, such as privatization, regulation, Calling Party Pays (CPP) or Receiving Party Pays (RPP), and innovative pricing arrangements such as multi-part tariffs and prepaid services. We examine the significance of some of these additional factors in the present study.

Table 1. Main Drivers of Mobile Services Demand Growth in Previous Research

| CROSS-COUNTRY STUDIES | | |
|---|---|---|
| Study | Main Drivers | Mobile/Fixed Line Substitution |
| Madden and Coble-Neal (2003) | Mobile network size, prices, GDP | Yes |
| Hamilton (2003) | N/A | Mixed |
| Gruber and Verboven (2001a) | GDP, size of fixed network, quality of main lines, competition, setting single standard | Mixed |
| Gruber and Verboven (2001b) | Technology (transition from analog to digital), competition | N/A |
| Gruber (2001) | Competition, size of fixed network, quality of main lines | N/A |
| Jha and Majumdar (1999) | Mobile size, investment/line, population, GDP, prices, competition and private participation | N/A |
| Ahn and Lee (1999) | GDP, teledensity | N/A |
| Rossotto, Kerf, and Rohlfs (2000) | Competition | N/A |
| Banerjee and Ros (forthcoming) | Socio-economic development status, regional differences | N/A |

| COUNTRY-SPECIFIC STUDIES | | |
|---|---|---|
| Study | Main Drivers | Mobile/Fixed Line Substitution |
| Rodini, Ward, and Woroch (2002), USA | N/A | Yes for second fixed lines and mobile |
| Sung and Lee (2002), South Korea | N/A | Yes |
| Sung, Kim, and Lee (2001), South Korea | N/A | Yes |
| Cadima and Barros (2000), Portugal | N/A | Yes |
| Okada and Keiko (1999), Japan | N/A | Yes |

## 3 DEVELOPMENT OF GLOBAL MOBILE TELEPHONY

### 3.1 Market Entry Conditions

At the time commercial mobile services were first becoming available (in the late 1970s and early 1980s), state-owned (PTT) monopoly providers of fixed-line telecommunications services operated in most countries. It is not surprising, therefore, that the PTTs were the first to be assigned the right to commercially exploit the new mobile technology. At first, commercial mobile services were regarded as simply additions to the line-up of services offered by PTTs, and revenues from those services were considered ancillary to fixed-line revenues. By long-standing tradition, revenues generated from non-basic services had been used to support public policy goals, and the introduction of mobile services simply expanded the list of services offered by PTTs and, hence, of the policy options available. As a result, in the early years of commercial mobile telephony, monopoly provision of mobile services through the PTT became the dominant form of market structure.[5]

During the 1990s, telephony in many countries underwent an important transformation with pervasive shifts from monopoly to competitive provision of telecommunications services, affecting incumbent operators that were both state-owned and privately owned. Such liberalization first exposed value-added services like customer premise equipment, paging, and mobile services to the workings of the competitive market. There were three possible reasons for this. First, unlike conventional fixed network services, these services were not subject to natural monopoly conditions.[6] Second, several interest groups (consumers, large business users, etc.) exerted pressure on governments to open up these services to competition in order to secure lower prices and better quality and customer service than available from incumbent operators. Finally, many developing countries began opening up their economies to meaningful foreign investment, which had the effect of accelerating the transition to competition.

Mobile competition accelerated through the 1990s as a rapid transition occurred from analog to digital technology. This transition resulted in lower average costs, wider range of services, and greater revenue — all conditions that were conducive to increases in the optimal number of mobile operators in a market. As Gruber and Verboven (2001a) found, of the 118 countries that adopted an analog cellular mobile system, 88 countries retained a monopoly structure and only 30 countries opted for oligopoly. This pattern was reversed, however, for digital technology. Of the 87 countries that adopted digital systems, only 39 retained a monopoly structure while 48 opted for oligopoly.

---

[5] There was a notable exception to this rule in the U.S. At AT&T's divestiture, the emerging mobile business was transferred from AT&T to the Regional Bell Operating Companies (RBOCs). Soon after, mobile duopoly in every RBOC-served market became public policy and the norm.

[6] Natural monopoly conditions exist when one firm can supply the entire volume of market demand for a service more economically than two or more firms that share that volume. In other words, the minimum efficient scale of operations exhausts the market demand. Typically, this happens when average costs decline with volume, i.e., there are economies of scale. Scale economies are most likely to arise when the initial or startup fixed costs are very large relative to variable or incremental costs, a phenomenon often found to have characterized traditional fixed telecommunications networks.

Table 2 provides a glimpse of how the market structure for mobile telephony has changed for 61 countries that we selected for our panel.[7] As is readily evident, monopoly provision of mobile telephony has become increasingly a thing of the past. By 2000, of the 61 countries in our panel (which account for over 90 percent of mobile subscribers worldwide), only 5 percent had retained monopoly provision of mobile telephony, the other 95 percent permitting competition among two or more mobile operators.

Table 2. The Increasing Role of Competition in International Mobile Telephony

| Year | Percent of 61 Countries with Two or More Mobile Operators |
|------|-----------------------------------------------------------|
| 1995 | 61 |
| 1996 | 70 |
| 1997 | 79 |
| 1998 | 89 |
| 1999 | 89 |
| 2000 | 95 |

Source: Adapted from various sources including, among others, ITU, *Trends in Telecommunication Reform 2002: Effective Regulation*, 4th edition, 2002 and regulatory web sites of various countries.

As other researchers have found, this increasing trend toward mobile competition is hard to overlook in any study of mobile telephony growth. Accordingly, our own econometric analysis takes due account of the possible impact of such competition—mainly in the form of innovative pricing arrangements—on mobile subscribership and growth rates. Economic theory posits that, in the absence of market imperfections (e.g., natural monopoly, external-ities, and asymmetric information), competition among suppliers helps to maximize economic benefits. One benefit is that competition leads to higher output and lower prices than a monopoly. As a result, to the extent that mobile telephony markets are not characterized by natural monopoly conditions, we would expect mobile competition to have a positive effect on mobile telephony subscribership and growth rates.[8]

## 3.2   Regulatory Conditions

Ever since the early years of commercial mobile telephony, there has been a tradition of mobile operators worldwide—whether privately or government owned—being allowed to price their services unconstrained by regulation. With such services viewed initially as luxuries and non-essential value-added telecommunications services, and revenues from value-added telecommunications services being used to accomplish broad public policy goals, governments were content to permit mobile operators to extract as much surplus as permitted by market conditions. Even today, there is little formal regulation of the retail prices for mobile services. Although mobile services are no longer viewed as luxuries or non-essential

---

[7] These 61 countries represent a broad range of countries at various stages of socio-economic development. However, for reasons explained below, they exclude countries from Africa.

[8] Over the period of observation, all but six of the countries in our panel had permitted competition among its mobile operators. Because of the almost ubiquitously permitted mobile competition, it is more sensible to represent it through the competitive actions of mobile operators themselves (such as providing CPP, prepaid, or other innovative pricing arrangements) than through a simple binary variable or even just the number of mobile operators on record. Hence, in our study, CPP and prepaid service-related variables serve as a proxy for mobile competition.

items, most countries have come to rely on mobile competition for disciplining their retail prices.

The sole exception to the general forbearance from regulation of mobile service prices has arisen in some countries for the wholesale termination prices that mobile operators charge for terminating calls from other networks, whether fixed or mobile. These prices recover costs associated with the use of mobile switches, base stations, transmission between switches and base stations, etc. in the process of terminating incoming calls. Regulating prices, whether retail or wholesale, makes economic sense only when there is some source of market failure and the direct and indirect costs of regulation are less than the gains from regulation.[9] Most countries appear to have concluded that mobile operators would have some degree of market power over their termination services regardless of the state of competition in the retail market, and have refrained from regulating prices for those services. A few countries have, however, bucked that trend and begun to regulate the termination prices that mobile operators charge interconnecting networks. Even then, any form of control over mobile operators (mostly through spectrum allocation, numbering, and licensing) is much more indirect and sparing on mobile service prices than is the case for fixed network-based services. Regulation is far more common for incumbent fixed networks (e.g., through price cap plans for retail services, interconnection tariffs, universal service requirements, resale and unbundling requirements, etc.).

Another important development during the 1990s was the trend toward the creation of specialized regulatory structures and institutions (e.g., specific to telecommunications or public utilities) that were increasingly separate from and, in some instances, independent of various branches of government. While countries like the United States, Canada, and the United Kingdom have had a long tradition of such regulatory institutions, most countries in our panel have only recently begun to develop separate regulatory structures. Table 3 below shows the trend toward separate regulators in our country panel.

Table 3. The Increasing Trend Toward Separate Regulator for Telecommunications

| Year | Percent of Countries in Panel with Separate Regulator |
|------|-------------------------------------------------------|
| 1990 | 18 |
| 1991 | 21 |
| 1992 | 28 |
| 1993 | 34 |
| 1994 | 36 |
| 1995 | 44 |
| 1996 | 54 |
| 1997 | 69 |
| 1998 | 77 |
| 1999 | 77 |
| 2000 | 84 |

Source: Adapted from ITU, *Trends in Telecommunication Reform 2002: Effective Regulation*, 4th edition, 2002.

This increasing trend toward a separate regulator is likely to have an impact on mobile telephony, and our econometric analysis examines that potential impact. With little direct

---

[9] Regulation involves both direct costs (from the need to erect and administer the regulatory apparatus) and indirect costs (arising from allocative efficiency losses when regulation distorts price-cost relationships).

regulation of mobile service prices or service provision anywhere, it may seem that *any* regulator—whether separate or not—can have little impact on the development of mobile telephony. However, as noted above, separate regulators could plausibly have an impact through their policies for spectrum allocation and licensing and service quality standards. This raises the possibility that unnecessary or excessive control exercised by the regulator through such routes could have a negative impact on mobile subscribership and growth rates.

On the other hand, the establishment of a separate regulator could have some beneficial effects as well, if it is also the case that that regulator is *independent*. Taking a new institutional economics approach, Levy and Spiller's (1996) examination of the problems of utility regulation reveals that issues such as commitment, expropriation, and manipulation of utilities could all have an important impact on sector performance. A separate *and* independent regulator could measure the degree to which decision-making can be transparent, non-arbitrary, free (as much as possible) from day-to-day political interference, and representative of the regulator's ability to maintain a credible commitment. All of this could have a positive impact on the development of the telecommunications sector.[10]

It is not clear *a priori* whether a separate regulator *per se* would have a positive or negative impact on mobile telephony. While a separate *and* independent regulator could improve the environment in which carriers operate, the effectiveness or independence of a regulator that is simply separate is harder to call.

### 3.3   New Pricing Structures

There is now little doubt that prices associated with mobile services (beginning with the price paid for the handset, and including connection charges, monthly subscription charges, per-use charges, roaming and long distance charges, etc.) have fallen considerably in most major markets. At the same time, the pricing structure itself of mobile services has undergone significant change. Thus, in some countries (notably, the United States), per-use pricing plans have disappeared for all but the lowest usage levels. Instead, mobile operators are offering variants of "fixed minutes of use" (FMOU) pricing plans which allow customers to purchase a fixed bucket of peak and off-peak minutes and pay no additional usage-related charges as long as the number of purchased minutes is not exhausted. Customers may select from a number of such plans, which vary by the number of minutes pre-purchased and, hence, by the monthly price paid.

One important variant of the FMOU arrangement is the popular "prepaid service." For a fixed charge, customers buy a fixed number of minutes that must be used up within a specified period of time (usually a month). Prepaid service, however, is available *without* committing the customer to a long-term monthly contract, and is, thus, ideal for customers who are unable to qualify for, or unwilling to accept the obligations of, contract services. FMOU plans also typically minimize or eliminate roaming charges that customers pay for the privilege of using their mobile phones in areas served by mobile networks other than those to which they subscribe. As a result, FMOU plans with regional or national footprints have emerged, most notably in the United States. We believe that the introduction of prepaid

---

[10] Gutierrez and Berg (2000) and Wallsten (2001) stress the importance of a truly *independent* regulator, not simply a separate regulator, as described above. While these authors developed different measures of an independent regulator, the regulator must, at a minimum, be separate and not under the control of any branch of government.

services has had a positive impact on the demand for mobile services, a hypothesis we test in our analysis below.

## 3.4 Pricing Regimes Established by Public Policy

Another important development in the pricing of mobile services concerns the choice made by public policymakers in different countries between CPP and RPP as the operative pricing regime.[11] Under CPP, mobile subscribers pay only to make calls to other subscribers of mobile or fixed networks. In many countries, CPP has superseded the older RPP system, which obliged mobile subscribers to pay for *all* uses of mobile phones, whether to make or receive calls. Conventional wisdom has argued that RPP may have depressed the use of mobile services because customers, unwilling to pay for unsolicited or undesirable calls made to their phones, simply shut off their phones or limited the distribution of their assigned numbers to potential callers. By shifting cost recovery to cost-causing callers (whether from fixed or mobile networks) under all circumstances, CPP is likely to make mobile calling more attractive and, hence, to stimulate the demand for mobile services. This could happen independently of whether the price of mobile calls declines as well, i.e., the demand trigger for mobile services may be not only lower prices for mobile calls but also the pricing regime itself.

Three qualifications to this unmitigated positive appeal of CPP should, however, be noted. First, the implementation of CPP for mobile services may be problematic or impossible in some jurisdictions or countries. For example, despite mature markets for mobile services, the United States and Canada remain predominantly RPP-centric for those services, even though much of Western Europe and South America have implemented CPP over the past decade.[12] Second, CPP does not solve the problem of termination monopoly associated with mobile networks. Calls made from the fixed network to the mobile network are likely to cost more than calls in the reverse direction because of higher termination charges that mobile operators can assess on calls from fixed networks. Hence, CPP may not reduce *all* prices associated with mobile calling and, as a result, fail to stimulate the use of mobile services to the degree expected.[13] Third, the principal perceived defect of RPP—that mobile subscribers would remain obliged to pay even for undesirable incoming calls—has, for all practical purposes,

---

[11] Comprehensive counts of countries that have adopted either CPP or RPP are almost non-existent. Based on research we conducted (including surveys of (1) articles and documents written about CPP and (2) regulatory websites at various countries), we estimate that 30 of the 61 countries in our panel had adopted CPP by 1996, and that count rose to 39 by 2000. Countries that adopted CPP by 2000 were predominantly in the OECD and Latin American regions, significant exceptions being India and South Korea (from the Asia-Pacific region) that also adopted CPP and Canada and the United States (from the OECD region) that stayed with RPP.

[12] In the United States (and possibly some other countries), policymakers have chosen to persist with RPP for practical technological, rather than strictly economic, reasons. In the United States, the numbering system in effect for telecommunications does not allow distinguishing between a telephone number assigned to a fixed main line and one assigned to a mobile phone. Callers cannot tell whether their calls are being terminated on a fixed network or on a mobile network. Therefore, asking callers to pay CPP prices (which may vary with the type of network on which their calls are terminated) would be impractical and unfair. Also, as in the United States, separate layers of federal and state regulation that govern fixed-to-mobile interconnection arrangements may also make it extremely difficult to set uniform prices. After an extensive exploration of the feasibility of CPP in the United States, the Federal Communications Commission declined in April 2001, to adopt specific rules for implementing and governing CPP. It left it up to individual mobile operators to offer CPP on their own.

[13] See, e.g., OECD (2000, pp. 45-46).

been cured by the development of FMOU pricing plans. These plans provide blocks of pre-purchased minutes that are generous enough to enable mobile subscribers to easily absorb the cost of undesirable incoming calls, provided that they terminate such calls soon after receiving them. In sum, these three factors may limit CPP as a desirable alternative to RPP, although CPP remains the proper cost-causative mode of pricing despite the presence of call externalities.[14] On the other hand, CPP may remain likely to encourage greater calling of mobile numbers (and greater use of mobile services, generally) despite the problem of termination monopoly on mobile networks.

## 3.5   State of Mobile and Fixed Telephony

To set the stage for the study reported in this paper, it is useful to summarize the state of mobile and fixed telephony in the 61 countries in our panel. This can be accomplished by focusing on four specific measures of telephony and the relationships among them. The four measures are the levels of teledensity and cellular density and the compound annual growth rates (CAGRs) of teledensity and cellular density. Table 4 shows the relationships among these measures in terms of their rank-order correlations.[15]

Table 4. Rank-Order Correlation Statistics Among Levels and CAGRs of Cellular Density and Teledensity for Panel Countries[16]

| Measures of Mobile and Fixed Telephony | Cellular Density, 2001 | Teledensity, 2001 | Cellular Density CAGR, 1990-2001 | Teledensity CAGR, 1990-2001 |
|---|---|---|---|---|
| Cellular Density, 2001 | | 0.8719 (0.0000) | -0.5326 (0.0000) | -0.7270 (0.0000) |
| Teledensity, 2001 | 0.6874 (0.0000) | | -0.6380 (0.0000) | -0.7815 (0.0000) |
| Cellular Density CAGR, 1990-2001 | -0.3541 (0.0001) | -0.4437 (0.0000) | | 0.6529 (0.0000) |
| Teledensity CAGR, 1990-2001 | -0.5093 (0.0000) | -0.5530 (0.0000) | 0.4557 (0.0000) | |

Spearman correlation statistics and their corresponding probability values are shown above the gray cells on the diagonal. Kendall's tau-b statistics and their corresponding probability values are shown below the gray cells on the diagonal.

Source: Based on data from ITU, *World Telecommunication Indicators Database,* 6th Edition, June 2002.

---

[14] See Kim and Lim (2001) for arguments in defense of RPP and a discussion of how call externalities may internalized by RPP.

[15] Rank-order correlation represents the correlation between the ranks occupied by the 61 countries on any pair of measurements, e.g., cellular density and teledensity, cellular density and cellular density growth rate, teledensity and cellular density growth rate, etc. Unlike the ordinary Pearson correlation, it reflects the correlation between the ranks of the measurements, not between the measurements themselves. Two measures of rank-order correlation are reported in Table 4, the Spearman correlation and the Kendall's tau-b statistic. Both appear to be very highly statistically significant for all pairs of measurements considered. The values of these statistics are different because of how they are constructed but, not surprisingly, they both lead to the same statistical inference. For more on the rank-order correlation statistics reported here, see Sheshkin (2000, pp. 863-894).

[16] Other tests of bivariate association (Pearson's chi-square, Cramer's V-statistic, and the gamma statistic) all yield identical inferences. Results are available upon request.

We first note that the rank-order correlation is highly positive between cellular density and teledensity and also between the respective CAGRs of cellular density and teledensity. That is, countries that rank higher (lower) on teledensity tend also to rank higher (lower) on cellular density. Moreover, countries that have the highest (lowest) CAGRs of cellular density also tend to have the highest (lowest) CAGRs of teledensity. While there are exceptions to the rule, this finding is as expected. However, the positive correlation is stronger for the *levels* of cellular density and teledensity than for their respective *CAGRs*.

The more interesting finding from Table 4 is that of the statistically significantly negative correlation between the ranks of countries on one levels measurement and one CAGR measurement. For instance, ranks for cellular density are negatively correlated with ranks for the CAGR of cellular density, implying that countries that have lower (higher) cellular densities tend also to have higher (lower) CAGRs of cellular density. Because cellular density and teledensity are highly positively correlated, this also implies that countries that have lower (higher) teledensities tend to have higher (lower) CAGRs of cellular density.

## 4    SCOPE OF PRESENT STUDY

The history of mobile telephony in the 61 selected countries since 1990 indicates not merely a dramatic pace of diffusion of a new communication technology, but also distinct regional variations in the manner in which such diffusion has occurred. In some countries (and regions), mobile telephony has developed in a complementary manner with fixed network-based telephony, albeit much more rapidly. In others, mobile telephony has tended to leapfrog fixed network-based telephony as the communication technology of choice. These broad patterns raise obvious questions about both demand and supply conditions that may have been responsible for the observed spread of mobile telephony worldwide.

As noted earlier, other studies have pointed consistently to a small set of factors responsible for the rise of mobile telephony. Among these are the size of the existing fixed network in a country, a measure of affordability such as per capita income (or, per capita GDP), the state of competition in both fixed and mobile services, the quality of fixed main lines (including waiting lists for main lines), and mobile technology standards. These factors practically suggest themselves but, with the exception of per capita GDP, they arise arguably from the supply side. A relatively small set of studies has also examined the effects of prices (of mobile services and fixed service alternatives), pricing structures, or other representations of consumer preference. Viewed together, the results of these inquiries are somewhat inconclusive: While Madden and Coble-Neal (2003) found evidence of price-based substitution between mobile and fixed services, Ahn and Lee (1999) could not detect any effect of mobile service prices on the probability of subscribing to mobile services.[17] Therefore, the need to

---

[17] In some preliminary research leading up to this paper, we were unable to find any statistically discernible role of the usage prices for mobile and fixed services in shaping the demand for those prices. We offer two conjectures regarding this failure. First, despite significant reductions in mobile service usage prices in recent years, they still remain discernibly above usage prices in many (if not all) countries for corresponding fixed services. This is not surprising given the traditional policy in some countries of setting fixed network access prices below economically-efficient levels. That is, the increasing popularity of mobile services may be driven more by various non-price factors (including convenience, mobility, and lifestyle issues) than by relative price differences alone. Second, the emergence of new flat-rated or "bucket" style pricing structures (which provide generous allowances of included

determine rigorously whether mobile and fixed services are economic substitutes or complements, or whether they are substitutes in certain market structures (and countries) but
complements in others, remains largely unaddressed. However, with increasing evidence of
technological substitutability or complementarity between mobile and fixed telephony,
questions worthy of serious research remain about the effects of alternative pricing *structures*,
if not price levels.

Aside from supply-side factors, this study begins an exploration of the effects of the CPP
pricing regime and pricing arrangements such as prepaid services in the growth of mobile
telephony worldwide. For the present study, we started out with time series observations for
the period 1996-2000 on 61 selected countries from the four regional blocs described earlier.[18]
These years corresponded roughly to the global "take-off" period for mobile telephony. They
also witnessed important market and regulatory developments in several countries, including
the introduction of CPP and prepaid services, privatization and liberalization, and the rise of
multiple mobile operators within local or national markets. Details of the 61-country panel,
along with some summary statistics, are presented in Table 5.

Several qualifications to such a study should be noted at this point. First, although the
growth of mobile telephony has clearly become a global phenomenon, there remain strong
regional variations not only in market and regulatory environments but also in the growth
performance itself. This suggests that a thorough study of mobile telephony growth would
require digging deeper than merely conducting a quantitative analysis of an international panel
of data. Specific regional and sub-regional analyses would permit a better understanding of
the questions of substitution or complementarity with fixed network-based telephony and the
leapfrogging of technology where fixed networks remain underdeveloped. In fact, the studies
noted above that reached conclusions about whether mobile and fixed telephony are substitutes or complements have almost all been based on country-specific data. While some
accounting for region-specific differences is attempted here, more granular analysis will need
to be done.

Second, the greatest limitation on a study of this scope is with regard to the availability of
complete and reliable data. Although the ITU's database on telecommunications and
economic indicators appears to be the best and most comprehensive repository of the requisite
data, there are still many legitimate questions about the quality and utility of those data. The
ITU's database is an accumulation of responses from appropriate agencies within individual
countries to its annual request for specific data. This makes that database only as good as the
responses themselves, and there may be reasons to believe that not all countries supply data of
equal quality or validity. Also, missing data and gaps in time series, particularly in the early
years of mobile telephony, are fairly common across a wide range of countries. There are also
critical gaps in economic data such as on GDP and mobile telephony prices; e.g., we have
been unable to procure consistent price data for China, arguably a mobile telephony super-
power. As a result, the econometric analysis of international panel data is deprived of any
input from China's remarkable growth performance in mobile telephony. Similar gaps in data
have made it necessary to exclude a large number of countries—in fact, the entire continent of
Africa—from the present analysis.

---

"anytime and anywhere" minutes of use) have made per-minute usage prices less of a driver of demand for mobile
services.

[18] Although the ITU has published its 2002 update on telecommunications and economic indicators, data for 2001
are not yet available for a number of countries or series.

Table 5. Composition and Selected Telephony Statistics (in 2001) of 61-Country Panel

| Country | Economic Development Status* | Cellular Density | Rank | Tele-density | Rank | Cellular Density CAGR | Rank | Tele-density CAGR | Rank | Mobile Subscribers per 100 Main Lines | Rank |
|---|---|---|---|---|---|---|---|---|---|---|---|
| Asia-Pacific Countries | | | | | | | | | | | |
| Australia | H | 57.6 | 25 | 52.0 | 17 | 43.6 | 49 | 1.2 | 57 | 111.0 | 36 |
| China | L | 11.0 | 50 | 13.8 | 45 | 123.5 | 12 | 33.2 | 1 | 80.9 | 49 |
| Hong Kong | H | 85.9 | 2 | 58.1 | 13 | 38.3 | 54 | 2.3 | 49 | 147.1 | 15 |
| India | L | 0.6 | 61 | 3.4 | 60 | 105.9 | 18 | 17.2 | 3 | 18.8 | 61 |
| Indonesia | LM | 3.1 | 59 | 3.7 | 59 | 68.6 | 36 | 18.2 | 2 | 66.7 | 54 |
| Japan | H | 58.8 | 24 | 59.7 | 11 | 49.6 | 48 | 2.8 | 44 | 98.5 | 43 |
| New Zealand | H | 59.9 | 23 | 47.1 | 22 | 39.1 | 53 | 0.8 | 59 | 124.8 | 30 |
| Philippines | LM | 15.0 | 46 | 4.0 | 58 | 76.9 | 28 | 13.5 | 6 | 377.4 | 2 |
| Singapore | H | 72.4 | 17 | 47.2 | 21 | 40.6 | 50 | 2.8 | 45 | 153.5 | 11 |
| South Korea | UM | 62.1 | 21 | 47.6 | 20 | 70.1 | 34 | 4.0 | 37 | 127.8 | 28 |
| Thailand | LM | 12.3 | 49 | 9.4 | 50 | 53.6 | 45 | 13.1 | 8 | 126.4 | 29 |
| Latin American Countries | | | | | | | | | | | |
| Argentina | UM | 19.3 | 40 | 21.6 | 39 | 80.0 | 26 | 8.0 | 20 | 86.0 | 47 |
| Belize | LM | 16.1 | 44 | 14.4 | 44 | 74.1 | 31 | 4.2 | 36 | 111.4 | 35 |
| Bolivia | LM | 9.0 | 52 | 6.0 | 54 | 103.5 | 20 | 7.4 | 23 | 144.5 | 16 |
| Brazil | UM | 16.7 | 43 | 21.7 | 38 | 159.7 | 5 | 11.6 | 12 | 76.8 | 50 |
| Chile | UM | 34.2 | 31 | 23.9 | 36 | 70.0 | 35 | 12.4 | 10 | 142.4 | 17 |
| Colombia | LM | 7.6 | 54 | 17.1 | 42 | 66.0 | 38 | 8.6 | 17 | 44.7 | 59 |
| Costa Rica | LM | 7.6 | 55 | 23.0 | 37 | 61.7 | 39 | 7.8 | 21 | 32.9 | 60 |
| Dominican Republic | LM | 14.7 | 47 | 10.8 | 48 | 71.0 | 32 | 7.8 | 22 | 135.2 | 23 |
| Ecuador | LM | 6.7 | 56 | 10.4 | 49 | 70.4 | 33 | 7.3 | 24 | 64.3 | 55 |
| El Salvador | LM | 12.5 | 48 | 9.3 | 51 | 112.6 | 13 | 13.1 | 9 | 133.8 | 24 |
| Guatemala | LM | 45.5 | 27 | 35.2 | 30 | 106.8 | 16 | 10.7 | 13 | 150.0 | 14 |
| Honduras | L | 3.6 | 58 | 4.7 | 57 | 160.7 | 4 | 9.6 | 15 | 76.7 | 51 |
| Jamaica | LM | 26.9 | 33 | 19.7 | 40 | 75.0 | 29 | 14.5 | 4 | 136.6 | 22 |
| Mexico | UM | 21.7 | 37 | 13.7 | 46 | 68.4 | 37 | 7.1 | 26 | 158.0 | 10 |
| Nicaragua | L | 3.0 | 60 | 3.3 | 61 | 110.1 | 14 | 9.2 | 16 | 90.2 | 45 |
| Panama | LM | 20.7 | 38 | 14.8 | 43 | 140.0 | 10 | 4.4 | 35 | 139.5 | 20 |
| Paraguay | LM | 20.4 | 39 | 5.1 | 55 | 106.4 | 17 | 6.1 | 28 | 398.2 | 1 |
| Peru | LM | 5.9 | 57 | 7.8 | 52 | 83.1 | 25 | 10.4 | 14 | 76.4 | 52 |
| Uruguay | UM | 15.5 | 45 | 28.3 | 35 | 89.1 | 22 | 7.0 | 27 | 54.7 | 56 |
| Venezuela | LM | 26.4 | 34 | 11.2 | 47 | 85.2 | 24 | 3.6 | 40 | 235.3 | 3 |
| Europe Transition Countries | | | | | | | | | | | |
| Albania | L | 8.8 | 53 | 5.0 | 56 | 171.3 | 2 | 13.6 | 5 | 177.2 | 8 |
| Bulgaria | LM | 19.1 | 41 | 35.9 | 29 | 157.2 | 6 | 3.7 | 38 | 53.2 | 58 |
| Czech Rep | UM | 67.5 | 20 | 37.4 | 27 | 141.5 | 9 | 8.2 | 18 | 180.6 | 6 |
| Estonia | LM | 45.5 | 27 | 35.2 | 30 | 108.0 | 15 | 5.1 | 32 | 129.3 | 27 |
| Hungary | UM | 49.8 | 26 | 37.4 | 28 | 103.6 | 19 | 13.2 | 7 | 133.2 | 25 |
| Lithuania | LM | 25.3 | 36 | 31.3 | 31 | 147.8 | 8 | 3.6 | 39 | 80.9 | 48 |
| Poland | LM | 26.0 | 35 | 29.5 | 32 | 154.9 | 7 | 11.8 | 11 | 88.2 | 46 |
| Romania | LM | 17.2 | 42 | 18.3 | 41 | 189.3 | 1 | 5.5 | 30 | 94.3 | 44 |
| Slovakia | LM | 39.7 | 29 | 28.8 | 33 | 165.8 | 3 | 7.1 | 25 | 138.0 | 21 |
| Slovenia | UM | 76.0 | 12 | 40.1 | 26 | 128.0 | 11 | 6.0 | 29 | 189.5 | 4 |

| OECD Countries | | | | | | | | | | |
|---|---|---|---|---|---|---|---|---|---|---|
| Austria | H | 80.7 | 6 | 46.8 | 24 | 50.0 | 47 | 1.0 | 58 | 172.3 | 9 |
| Belgium | H | 74.6 | 14 | 49.3 | 18 | 59.8 | 42 | 2.1 | 51 | 151.6 | 12 |
| Canada | H | 36.2 | 30 | 65.5 | 8 | 29.3 | 59 | 1.4 | 55 | 53.4 | 57 |
| Denmark | H | 73.8 | 15 | 72.3 | 3 | 34.3 | 55 | 2.2 | 50 | 102.0 | 41 |
| Finland | H | 77.8 | 8 | 54.8 | 15 | 28.0 | 60 | 0.2 | 61 | 142.1 | 18 |
| France | H | 60.5 | 22 | 57.4 | 14 | 54.9 | 44 | 1.3 | 56 | 105.8 | 40 |
| Germany | H | 68.3 | 19 | 63.5 | 9 | 60.7 | 40 | 3.4 | 41 | 107.6 | 37 |
| Greece | UM | 75.1 | 13 | 52.9 | 16 | 89.1 | 23 | 2.9 | 43 | 142.0 | 19 |
| Iceland | H | 82.0 | 5 | 66.4 | 7 | 31.9 | 57 | 2.4 | 48 | 123.5 | 33 |
| Ireland | H | 72.9 | 16 | 48.5 | 19 | 52.4 | 46 | 5.1 | 33 | 150.5 | 13 |
| Italy | H | 83.9 | 3 | 47.1 | 23 | 60.5 | 41 | 1.8 | 54 | 178.4 | 7 |
| Luxembourg | H | 96.7 | 1 | 78.3 | 1 | 74.6 | 30 | 4.5 | 34 | 123.5 | 31 |
| Netherlands | H | 76.7 | 11 | 62.1 | 10 | 57.5 | 43 | 2.7 | 46 | 123.5 | 32 |
| Norway | H | 82.5 | 4 | 72.0 | 4 | 29.9 | 58 | 3.3 | 42 | 114.6 | 34 |
| Portugal | H | 77.4 | 9 | 42.7 | 25 | 91.8 | 21 | 5.3 | 31 | 181.4 | 5 |
| Sweden | H | 79.0 | 7 | 73.9 | 2 | 27.7 | 61 | 0.8 | 60 | 106.9 | 38 |
| Switzerland | H | 72.4 | 18 | 71.8 | 5 | 39.8 | 51 | 2.1 | 52 | 100.8 | 42 |
| Turkey | LM | 30.2 | 32 | 28.5 | 34 | 79.0 | 27 | 8.1 | 19 | 105.8 | 39 |
| U.K. | H | 77.0 | 10 | 58.8 | 12 | 39.8 | 52 | 2.7 | 47 | 131.1 | 26 |
| U.S.A. | H | 45.1 | 28 | 66.5 | 6 | 32.1 | 56 | 1.8 | 53 | 67.6 | 53 |
| Mean of Panel | | 41.6 | | 34.4 | | 83.5 | | 6.8 | | 125.7 | |

* Economic development status follows the World Bank (1996) classification system: lower income (L), lower-middle income (LM), upper-middle income (UM), and high income (H).

Third, perhaps the most critical limitation of the analysis as it currently stands is the insufficient information available about the pricing regime (namely, CPP) and pricing structure innovation (namely, prepaid services) that are hypothesized to have had significant impact on the demand for mobile services. Although we model CPP as a binary variable (1 if in place, 0 if not), we do not presently have complete information on this variable for the period 1996-2000 for all countries in our panel. Even more difficult is trying to represent prepaid services. Unlike CPP, prepaid services cannot adequately be represented by a binary variable. This is primarily because prepaid services come in many different flavors and their primary effect on mobile telephony is through the effective prices that result from them, rather than from their presence or absence *per se*.[19]

Finally, given the large number of countries involved in the panel, there is not enough information to construct purchasing power parity (PPP) price series for each individual country. Only such PPP price series can reflect the true burden of mobile service prices for the local population (relative to local income and cost-of-living standards). As such, the best we have been able to do is to convert all nominal country-specific prices into real such prices (by deflating them using country-specific price indices) and convert them again into US dollar-equivalent prices using the currency exchange rate against the US dollar that prevailed in 1995 for each country in the panel.[20]

---

[19] OECD (2000, pp. 56-62).

[20] It may be comforting to find that, say, the peak hour price of mobile calling (where per-use pricing remains in effect) in country *A* is approximately the same (in US dollar-equivalent terms) as that in country *B*, half way across the globe. However, the burden that such a price represents on consumers in the two countries may be quite different

Despite these limitations, we believe that some useful insights into the growth of mobile telephony globally can be obtained from a study of this sort. Our aim is to continue refining the analysis, as the quality and availability of the requisite data both improve.

## 5 DATA

Annual data from the 61 selected countries were collected for the 1996-2000 period on the following variables:

Cellular density (*CELLDEN*)

Annual percent change in cellular density (*CELLDENGR*)

Real gross domestic product per capita, in 1995 $US (*GDPPC*)

Waiting list as percent of main lines in operation plus waiting list (*WAITPCT*)

Separate regulator: 1 if country has a telecom regulator that is separate from any branch of government (even if not completely independent), 0 otherwise (*SEPREG*)

Calling Party Pays: 1 if country has CPP, 0 otherwise (*CPP*)

Interaction regional binary: 1 if country has CPP *and* is in Asia-Pacific region, 0 otherwise (*CPPAP*)

Interaction regional binary: 1 if country has CPP *and* is in Latin American region, 0 otherwise (*CPPLA*)

Interaction regional binary: 1 if country has CPP *and* is in OECD region, 0 otherwise (*CPPOECD*)[21]

Prepaid service: 1 if country has prepaid service, 0 otherwise (*PREPAID*)

Interaction regional binary: 1 if country has prepaid service *and* is in Asia-Pacific region, 0 otherwise (*PPDAP*)

Interaction regional binary: 1 if country has prepaid service *and* is in Latin American region, 0 otherwise (*PPDLA*)

Interaction regional binary: 1 if country has prepaid service *and* is in OECD region, 0 otherwise (*PPDOECD*)[22]

Because of our interest in the growth rate of cellular density in the countries in our panel, *CELLDENGR* was selected for study as the dependent variable.[23] Corresponding to this

---

if income levels and general costs of living vary substantially between them. This, in turn, could produce very different demand responses.

[21] An interaction regional binary was not necessary for the remaining region, the European transition countries, chosen to be the default region. Only three binaries are needed for the four regions, i.e., the case of the European transition countries corresponds to *CPP*. Also, binaries for three of the four regions were considered but dropped for reasons explained later.

[22] Only three binaries are needed for the four regions, i.e., the case of the European transition countries—the default region—corresponds to *PREPAID*.

dependent variable, *CELLDEN* was selected as a proxy for the existing state of mobile telephony.[24] The rest of the variables were chosen as our other explanatory variables following our prior discussion of the likely determinants of mobile telephony growth. Thus, *WAITPCT* was used as a measure of the quality of the fixed network. *GDPPC* was a measure of average personal income and affordability. *SEPREG* was a binary variable representing the regulatory structure, and *CPP* and *PREPAID* were binary variables selected to represent market (or, more specifically, pricing) structure.[25] Finally, *CPPAP*, *CPPLA*, and *CPPOECD* were interaction binaries for the presence of CPP in the Asia-Pacific, Latin American, and OECD regions, respectively, while *PPDAP*, *PPDLA*, and *PPDOECD* were similar interaction binaries for the presence of prepaid services in the three regions. As noted earlier, *GDPPC* was stated in constant 1995 U.S. dollars.

## 6 ECONOMETRIC MODEL AND RESULTS

### 6.1 Model Specification and Estimation

We estimated a panel data econometric model by a variety of estimation techniques using annual data for the 61 countries during 1996-2000.[26] Specifically, we hypothesized a random effects model which allows for country-specific effects qualifying the overall constant term, where those effects are randomly distributed according to a known distribution (usually the Gaussian) and have a zero mean and constant variance.[27] In general, this model is of the form:

$$y_{it} = \alpha + \mathbf{x}_{it}\beta + \mu_i + \varepsilon_{it} \tag{1}$$

where $y_{it}$ is the dependent variable indexed over i (country) and t (year), $\mathbf{x}_{it}$ is the vector of explanatory variables (including the binary variables), $\beta$ is the vector of coefficients, $\mu_i$ are the random effects with a specified distribution (typically Gaussian) with zero mean and a constant variance, and $\varepsilon_{it}$ is a zero-mean, constant variance disturbance assumed to be uncorrelated with the random effects.[28]

---

[23] In addition, we also explored mobile connections as a percent of *all* (i.e., mobile plus main line) connections as an alternate dependent variable. We do not report results for that variable here because our basic conclusions were not altered.

[24] More precisely, one-year lagged values of this variable were used to avoid the problem of joint endogeneity with *CELLDENGR*. Thus, the lagged values served as instruments for the contemporaneous values of *CELLDEN*.

[25] At this stage of model development, it was not possible to represent adequately the impact of prepaid services. Data on such services (initiation date, type of prepaid service, etc.) are incomplete and unreliable for our country panel at present. Introducing complete measures of prepaid services into our econometric model must await improvements in the quality of data.

[26] All estimation and subsequent specification testing was done using the *STATA*©, Version 7 software.

[27] When a Gaussian distribution is assumed, it is entirely characterized by two parameters, namely, the mean and the variance.

[28] This assumption of uncorrelatedness can be tested by use of the standard Hausman (1978) specification test or the Baltagi and Li (1990) version of the Breusch-Pagan test for random effects.

The model in eq. (1) can be estimated by generalized least squares (GLS), which is a weighted average of the "within" or fixed effects estimator and the "between" estimator.[29] Alternately, under the assumption of a Gaussian distribution for $\varepsilon_{it}$, the model can also be estimated by maximum likelihood (ML) methods. Finally, a more general version of the model in eq. (1) can be specified as the generalized linear model (GLM)

$$g(E(y_{it})) = \mathbf{x}_{it}\beta \tag{2}$$

where $g(\bullet)$ is the link function which determines the actual form of the model and $y$ belongs to a family of possible distributions. If the link function is the identity function and $y$ is Gaussian, then the familiar linear regression model (including one with random effects) is obtained. The GLM also permits a very general within-group correlation structure, and the model can be estimated by a population-averaged method that permits robust estimation of the standard errors of the coefficients.[30] We employed this population-averaged (PA) estimator as our third variant besides the GLS and ML estimators.[31]

## 6.2 Summary of Estimates

The results of estimating eq. (1) with our data are presented in Table 6.[32] Some not-so-obvious features of the results should be noted at this stage. First, although the full panel comprised 305 observations (= 61 countries × 5 years), only 165 were ultimately usable. That is because $STATA^{©}$ handles missing observations in any row of the data matrix by deleting that row. As noted earlier, gaps in the data for various countries and series remained a significant obstacle throughout the analysis. The result of such row deletion is, of course, to create an unbalanced panel; fortunately, the software and the estimation techniques used are equipped to handle unbalanced panels.[33] As the quality and availability of data both improve, the stability of the results obtained here can be assessed by using more observations.

Second, the three estimation techniques for random effects panel data models deliver generally similar and stable coefficient estimates. As expected, however, the ML and PA techniques yield lower standard errors of the coefficient estimates and boost z-statistics (and associated probability values). The results obtained from either of these two techniques may be used to draw conclusions about the state of international mobile telephony.

---

[29] See either Hsiao (1986) or Baltagi (1995) on the specification and estimation of panel data models.

[30] When the exact distribution of the disturbance term is not known, robust estimation of the standard errors (based on a distribution-free specification) often results in the greatest precision (i.e., the smallest standard errors).

[31] This estimator is due to Liang and Zeger (1986).

[32] In addition to the model reported in Table 6, we estimated a model that also included three regional binaries (one each for the Asia-Pacific, Latin American, and OECD regions, with the Europe Transition region treated as the default). The estimates for those binaries were not statistically significant; moreover, the presence of the binaries appeared to induce a problem of collinearity with *GDPPC* and *WAITPCT* by inflating the standard errors of their associated coefficient estimates and rendering them statistically insignificant. This effect likely stemmed from the fact that (except for the Asia-Pacific region) GDP per capita and main line waiting list percentage vary systematically with country membership in the different regions. Because the inclusion of regional binaries failed to advance our overall understanding of the factors driving cellular density growth, the model version reported in Table 6 omits those binaries.

[33] See Hsiao (1986) or Wooldridge (2002) for details on estimation from unbalanced panels.

Table 6. Results of Estimation of Panel Data Model

| Dependent Variable: *CELLDENGR* | Estimation Technique | | |
| Explanatory Variable | PA | ML | GLS |
|---|---|---|---|
| *CELLDEN* (lagged) | -0.0063*** | -0.0063*** | -0.0061*** |
| | (-3.84) | (-3.84) | (-3.54) |
| *GDPPC* | -0.0000** | -0.0000** | -0.0000* |
| | (-2.06) | (-2.06) | (-1.84) |
| *WAITPCT* | 0.7784** | 0.7788** | 0.8198** |
| | (2.46) | (2.46) | (2.40) |
| *SEPREG* | -0.1307*** | -0.1307*** | -0.1290** |
| | (-2.60) | (-2.60) | (-2.38) |
| *CPP* | -0.1794 | -0.1794 | -0.1797 |
| | (-1.56) | (-1.56) | (-1.48) |
| *CPPLA* | 0.1532 | 0.1533 | 0.1589 |
| | (1.26) | (1.26) | (1.23) |
| *CPPAP* | 0.0606 | 0.0607 | 0.0695 |
| | (0.43) | (0.43) | (0.47) |
| *CPPOECD* | 0.3322*** | 0.3321*** | 0.3233** |
| | (2.61) | (2.61) | (2.38) |
| *PREPAID* | 0.3213*** | 0.3211*** | 0.3060** |
| | (2.76) | (2.76) | (2.52) |
| *PPDLA* | -0.4028*** | -0.4027*** | -0.3920*** |
| | (-3.04) | (-3.03) | (-2.83) |
| *PPDAP* | -0.1894 | -0.1895 | -0.1913 |
| | (-1.35) | (-1.35) | (-1.30) |
| *PPDOECD* | -0.2622** | -0.2619** | -0.2426* |
| | (-2.02) | (-2.01) | (-1.79) |
| *CONSTANT* | 0.6947*** | 0.6947*** | 0.6914*** |
| | (8.11) | (8.10) | (7.51) |
| No. of Observations | 165 | 165 | 165 |
| Wald /Likelihood Ratio $\chi^2$ (d.f.) | 100.80*** | 78.58*** | 82.89*** |
| | (12) | (12) | (12) |

Note: z-statistics reported in parentheses. Starred coefficient estimates are statistically significant at the 1% level (***), 5% level (**), and 10% level (*), respectively.

Finally, despite the data limitations, the asymptotic test statistics for judging model fit (namely, the Wald and likelihood ratio statistics) are all highly statistically significant (at the 1 percent level) signifying a generally good fit of the specified model to the data, regardless of the estimation technique used. Also, the estimates prove robust to alternative assumptions about error structure, including AR(1) and general stationarity.

## 6.3    Interpretation of Results

Turning next to interpretation of the results, several findings should be noted. First, Table 7 shows the pattern of statistical significance of the estimated coefficients.

Table 7. Pattern of Statistical Significance of Estimated Model Coefficients

| Significant at 1% level | Significant at 5% level | Not Significant at 10% level |
|---|---|---|
| *CELLDEN* (lagged) | *GDPPC**  | *CPP* |
| *SEPREG* | *WAITPCT* | *CPPLA* |
| *PREPAID* | *PPDOECD** | *CPPAP* |
| *CPPOECD* | | *PPDAP* |
| *PPDLA* | | |
| * Significant at 10% level under GLS estimation.[34] | | |

Second, in order to interpret the signs of these estimated coefficients, it is important to understand what the coefficients of the binaries (*CPP* and *PREPAID*) and the interaction binaries (*CPPAP, CPPLA, CPPOECD, PPDAP, PPDLA,* and *PPDOECD*) imply for the effects of CPP and prepaid service in the four regions of our country panel. Table 8 converts the coefficients for these variables (as reported in Table 6) into the implied coefficients for interaction binaries for all four regions. This conversion is helpful because, at present, the coefficients for the three non-default regions, e.g., *PPDAP, PPDLA,* and *PPDOECD* have to be understood *relative to* the coefficient of *PREPAID*, which represents the effect of prepaid services in the default Europe transition region. The "converted" coefficients represent the *stand-alone* effect of either CPP or prepaid services in each of the four regions in our panel.

Table 8. Original and Converted Coefficients for CPP and Prepaid Service Binaries

| Original Coefficients | | Converted Coefficients | |
|---|---|---|---|
| *CPP* | -0.1794 | *CPPET* | -0.1794 |
| *CPPAP* | 0.0606 | *CPPAP* | -0.1188 |
| *CPPLA* | 0.1532 | *CPPLA* | -0.0261 |
| *CPPOECD* | 0.3322 | *CPPOECD* | 0.1528 |
| *PREPAID* | 0.3213 | *PPDET* | 0.3213 |
| *PPDAP* | -0.1894 | *PPDAP* | 0.1318 |
| *PPDLA* | -0.4028 | *PPDLA* | -0.0815 |
| *PPDOECD* | -0.2622 | *PPDOECD* | 0.0591 |

In Table 8, the "original" coefficients are taken from Table 6, which contains estimates from a model in which *CPP* and *PREPAID* represent CPP and prepaid services, respectively, in the default Europe transition countries. The "converted" coefficients are obtained as the sum of the original coefficient for *CPP* (or *PREPAID*) and the original coefficient of each of the interaction binaries.[35] Note that the converted coefficients for the *CPP* interaction binaries are *negative* in three out of four regions, signifying a possible inability of CPP to stimulate

---

[34] The model was also estimated with the lagged teledensity growth rate (*TELEDENGR*) among the explanatory variables, as a proxy for the evolution of the existing fixed network. The coefficient estimate of this variable remained statistically insignificant under all three estimation variants.

[35] Thus, the converted coefficient of *CPPAP* (representing the stand-alone effect of CPP in the Asia-Pacific region) is the sum of –0.1794 (the original coefficient of *CPP*) and 0.0606 (the original coefficient of *CPPAP*). Similarly, the converted coefficient of *PPDOECD* (representing the stand-alone effect of prepaid services in the OECD region) is the sum of 0.3213 (the original coefficient of *PREPAID*) and –0.2622 (the original coefficient of *PPDOECD*).

cellular density growth in those regions. Only the OECD countries appear to have experienced such stimulation as a result of CPP. Similarly, note that the converted coefficients for the *PREPAID* interaction binaries are *positive* in three out of four regions, signifying a possible boost from prepaid services to cellular density growth in those regions. Only the Latin American region seems not to have benefited as expected from prepaid services. Significantly, only the OECD region appears to have benefited from *both* CPP and prepaid services.

On its face, a negative effect of CPP would run counter to the school of thought that credits CPP with expanding demand for mobile telephony. On the other hand, there are several reasons (some of which were noted earlier) for CPP to produce either an opposite effect or no discernible effect at all.[36] Moreover, it is important to note that the negative effect of CPP observed in three out of the four regions in our panel actually pertains to the *growth rate* of cellular density (the dependent variable in our analysis), rather than to the level of cellular density itself. Not surprisingly, in the OECD region—in which the effect of CPP on cellular density growth was positive during the 1996-2000 period—the *average* cellular density was much higher relative to the other regions, possibly (in part) because of the mutually reinforcing effects of CPP and prepaid services on cellular density growth. This fact is confirmed by Table 9.

Table 9. Average Levels of Cellular Density in 61-Country Panel, By Region, 1996 and 2000

|        | Asia-Pacific Region | | Europe Transition Region | | Latin American Region | | OECD Region | |
| --- | --- | --- | --- | --- | --- | --- | --- | --- |
| Year   | 1996 | 2000  | 1996 | 2000  | 1996 | 2000  | 1996  | 2000  |
| Mean   | 9.31 | 34.71 | 1.63 | 24.59 | 1.09 | 10.52 | 12.56 | 61.21 |
| Median | 6.98 | 44.69 | 0.97 | 19.01 | 0.95 | 9.76  | 10.13 | 66.12 |

Source: Adapted from ITU, *World Telecommunication Indicators Database*, 6th Edition, June 2002

Third, of the four variables other than those related to CPP and prepaid services, coefficients of three have the expected signs, while one has an unexpected sign. For example, the negative sign on the coefficient for lagged *CELLDEN* suggests that a country with lower (higher) cellular density in the past has experienced faster (slower) growth of cellular density. This finding confirms the rank-order correlation relationships observed in Table 4, which shows that the cellular density growth rate for our panel countries is negatively correlated with cellular density and teledensity but positively correlated with the teledensity growth rate. From this, we infer that cellular density growth rates tend to be highest in countries (1) where the use of telephony in any form is generally low to begin with, and (2) in which the predominant

---

[36] There is a school of thought that discounts the efficacy of CPP in boosting mobile subscribership. For example, in 1999, the Infocomm Development Authority of Singapore rejected CPP as the operative pricing regime in that island state, contending that CPP was neither necessary nor sufficient to stimulate demand for mobile services. The Authority attributed mobile telephony growth in countries with CPP to other factors like prepaid services instead. Moreover, the Authority doubted that CPP could ever be implemented efficaciously in countries where callers from fixed networks had to confront the real—and confusing—prospect of paying different prices for calling different mobile networks, and the cost to change structures and systems to avoid this confusion could prove to be prohibitively high. In Europe and South America, unlike in the United States and many Asian countries, mobile phones are assigned numbers that can be separately identified from numbers for fixed main lines. In fact, Gans and King (2000) contend that the lynchpin of success for a CPP scheme is the ability of consumers to identify the networks they are calling, and call for restructured billing that enable mobile operators to charge callers from fixed networks directly for calls terminating on their networks.

tactical direction for the growth of telephony has been to allow mobile networks to leapfrog fixed networks that are more expensive and slower to deploy. In addition, there is a "diminishing returns" or saturation effect in countries (such as those in the OECD) in which both cellular density and teledensity have both achieved relatively high levels. The cellular density growth rate tends to be low in those countries.

Similarly, the sign of the estimate for *GDPPC* is also negative, signifying that, over the observed period, the fastest (slowest) growth in the cellular density has occurred in countries with the lowest (highest) per capita GDP. This indicates that countries that are less affluent or developed (as measured by the GDP per capita) have relied more on mobile than on fixed networks to meet their telephony needs, resulting in relatively high cellular density growth rates in those countries.[37]

Finally, as expected, longer waiting lists tend to boost the cellular density growth rate as customers waiting for main line connections opt for mobile service instead. This is confirmed by the positive sign on the coefficient for *WAITPCT*. This is additional evidence supporting earlier research findings that countries with inferior fixed networks or cost-impeded in their efforts to deploy ubiquitous fixed networks have decided to accelerate the deployment of mobile networks instead.

In contrast to the signs of coefficients for lagged *CELLDEN*, *GDPPC*, and *WAITPCT*, the coefficient of *SEPREG* is statistically significant but has a negative sign. In light of our earlier discussion, this was not entirely unexpected, although we did expect that countries with independent or, at least, separate regulators would likely create market and regulatory environments favoring faster mobile telephony growth. However, because our variable could not distinguish between separate regulators that were independent and those that were not, the finding may simply express information about the effectiveness (or lack thereof) of regulation in these countries. The finding of a negative effect of a separate regulator, therefore, could possibly reflect a *net* negative or dampening effect on mobile subscribership growth caused by factors that are not immediately obvious. As noted earlier, market entry by mobile operators could be slowed by protracted regulatory timetables for spectrum allocation, licensing, and standards setting. Alternatively, the negatively-signed coefficient could be attributed to some inherent weakness in the construction of the binary variable *SEPREG* itself.

## 7    CONCLUSIONS

In this paper, we set out to explore the relationship between the rate of growth of mobile telephony (represented by the cellular density) and a host of demand and supply-side variables. Unique to this exercise was the intuition that the growth of mobile telephony internationally has been shaped by more than just the "usual suspects." Whereas usage prices appear not to have mattered much (and, even today, are above the levels of fixed network service prices, though the gap has narrowed), disillusion and bad experiences with existing fixed network services have prompted customers of communications services to look increasingly in the direction of mobile telephony. That is, technological—rather than

---

[37] Although GDP per capita is not the only, or even the best, indicator of the economic development status of a country, there is little consensus on how that status can be captured by a single measure or index. As in Table 5, we follow the World Bank in its long-standing practice of using the GDP per capita for classifying countries according to their economic development status.

economic—complementarity or substitution has been the more powerful underlying source of movement in mobile telephony markets. Moreover, even with its data limitations, these underlying drivers seem to come through loud and clear from our econometric analysis.

As we noted earlier, this marks the beginning of an exploration into the growth of mobile telephony worldwide. The impressive gains made by mobile services in recent years have already taken the mobile services sector past the fixed services sector within international telecommunications. Indeed, ITU data show that that has already happened for nearly four dozen countries. The advent of 3G services can only fuel this momentum and change fundamentally how human beings communicate throughout the globe. With this in view, new data (as they become available) would enable a further refining of our econometric models and provide greater insight into the factors underlying the evolution of global mobile telephony.[38]

## 8   REFERENCES

Ahn, Hyungtaik and Myeong-Ho Lee, "An Econometric Analysis of the Demand for Access to Mobile Telephone Networks," *Information Economics and Policy*, 11, 297-305, 1999.

Arellano, M. and S. Bond, "Some Tests of Specification for Panel Data: Monte Carlo Evidence and an Application to Employment Equations," *Review of Economic Studies*, 58, 277-297, 1991.

Baltagi, Badi H., *Econometric Analysis of Panel Data*, New York: John Wiley & Sons, 1995.

Baltagi, Badi H. and Qi Li, "A Lagrange Multiplier Test for the Error Components Model with Incomplete Panels," *Econometric Reviews*, 9, 103-107, 1990.

Banerjee, Aniruddha and Agustin J. Ros, "Patterns in Global Fixed and Mobile Telecommunications Development: A Cluster Analysis," *Telecommunications Policy* (forthcoming).

Cadima, N. and P.P. Barros, "The Impact of Mobile Phone Diffusion on the Fixed-link Network," Discussion Paper DP2598, Center for Economic Policy Research, London, 2000.

Gans, Joshua S. and Stephen P. King, "Mobile Network Competition, Customer Ignorance and Fixed-to-Mobile Call Prices," *Information Economics and Policy*, 12, 301-327, 2000.

Gruber, Harald, "An Investment View of Mobile Telecommunications in the European Union," *Telecommunications Policy*, 23, 521-538, 1999.

Gruber, Harald, "Competition and Innovation: The Diffusion of Mobile Telecommunications Services in Central and Eastern Europe," *Information Economics and Policy*, 13, 19-34, 2001.

Gruber, Harald and Frank Verboven, "The Evolution of Markets Under Entry and Standards Regulation—The Case of Global Mobile Telecommunications," Centre for Economic Policy Research Working Paper No. DP2440 (revised), 2001a.

---

[38] Apart from model specification and testing, some of the possible refinements could come in model estimation. For example, if we were to use as an alternate dependent variable the ratio of mobile connections to all connections, then we would expect to use an estimation technique that recognizes the special property of such a dependent variable, namely, that, like other ratio variables, it is continuous on and bounded by the unit interval. In these circumstances, a modified panel data estimator employing quasi-maximum likelihood methods has been proposed by Papke and Wooldridge (1996). Moreover, if dynamics were to be introduced into the model through a lagged dependent variable, then the proper instrumental variable estimator for the panel data model would be the one proposed by Arellano and Bond (1991).

Gruber, Harald and Frank Verboven, "The Diffusion of Mobile Telecommunications Services in the European Union," *European Economic Review*, 45, 577-588, 2001b.

Gutierrez, Luis H. and Sanford Berg, "Telecommunications Liberalization and Regulatory Governance: Lessons from Latin America," *Telecommunications Policy*, 24, 865-884, 2000.

Hamilton, Jacqueline, "Are Main Lines and Mobile Phones Substitutes or Complements? Evidence from Africa," *Telecommunications Policy*, 27, 109-133, 2003.

Hausman, Jerry A., "Specification Tests in Econometrics," *Econometrica*, 46, 1251-1271, 1978.

Hsiao, Cheng, *Analysis of Panel Data*, New York: Cambridge University Press, 1986.

International Telecommunication Union, *World Telecommunication Indicators Database*, 6th Edition, June 2002.

Jha, Raghbendra and Sumit K. Majumdar, "A Matter of Connections: OECD Telecommunications Sector Productivity and the Role of Cellular Technology Diffusion," *Information Economics and Policy*, 11, 243-269, 1999.

Kim, Jeong-Yoo and Yoonsung Lim, "An Economic Analysis of the Receiver Pays Principle," *Information Economics and Policy*, 13, 231-260, 2001.

Levy, Brian and Pablo T. Spiller, *Regulations, Institutions, and Commitment: Comparative Studies of Telecommunications*, New York: Cambridge University Press, 1996.

Liang, K.-Y. and S.L. Zeger, "Longitudinal Data Analysis Using Generalized Linear Models," *Biometrika*, 73, 13-22, 1986.

Madden, Gary and Grant Coble-Neal, "Economic Determinants of Global Mobile Telephony Growth" Curtin University of Technology, presented at the International Telecommunications Society's Asia-Australasian Regional Conference, Perth, Australia, June 22-24, 2003.

OECD, Cellular Mobile Pricing Structures and Trends, DSTI/ICCP/TISP(99)11/ FINAL, May 19, 2000.

Okada, Yosuke and Hatta Keiko, "The Interdependent Telecommunications Demand and Efficient Price Structure", *Journal of the Japanese and International Economies*, 13, 311-335, 1999.

Papke, Leslie E. and Jeffrey M. Wooldridge, "Econometric Methods for Fractional Response Variables with an Application to 401(K) Plan Participation Rates," *Journal of Applied Econometrics*, 11, 619-632, 1996.

Rodini, Mark, Michael R. Ward, and Glenn A. Woroch, "Going Mobile: Substitutability Between Fixed and Mobile Access," Working Paper, prepared for the Conference on "Competition in Wireless: Spectrum, Service and Technology Wars," organized by the Public Utility Research Center at the University of Florida, Gainesville, February 2002.

Ros, Agustin J. and Aniruddha Banerjee, "Telecommunications Privatization and Tariff Rebalancing: Evidence from Latin America," *Telecommunications Policy*, 24, 233-252, 2000.

Rossotto, Carlo Maria, Michel Kerf, and Jeffrey Rohlfs, "Competition in Mobile Telecommunications: Sector Growth, Benefits for the Incumbent Trade Policy," *Info*, 2, 67-73, 2000.

Sheshkin, David J., *Handbook of Parametric and Nonparametric Statistical Procedures*, 2nd edition, New York: Chapman & Hall/CRC, 2000.

Sung, Nakil and Yong Hun Lee, "Substitution between Mobile and Fixed Telephones in Korea," *Review of Industrial Organization*, 20, 367-374, 2002.

Sung, Nakil, C Kim and Y. Lee, "Is POTS Dispensable? Substitution Effects Between Mobile and Fixed Telephones in Korea," paper presented at the 76th Annual Western Economic Association International Conference, July 2001.

Wallsten, Scott J. "An Econometric Analysis of Telecom Competition, Privatization, and Regulation in Africa and Latin America," *Journal of Industrial Economics*, 49, 1-19, 2001.

Wooldridge, Jeffrey M., *Econometric Analysis of Cross Section and Panel Data*, Cambridge, MA: The MIT Press, 2002.

World Bank, Social Indicators of Development. Available from http://www-wds.worldbank.org/servlet/WDSContentServer/WDSP/IB/1996/04/01/000009265_3970128130330/Rendered/PDF/multi_page.pdf, 1996.

# PART V

# POLICY ASPECTS OF THE DIGITAL SOCIETY

Global Economy and Digital Society
E. Bohlin, S. Levin, N. Sung and C-H. Yoon (Editors)

# CHAPTER 15

# Institutional Arrangements of Regional Regulatory Regimes: Telecommunications Regulation In Europe and Limits to Policy Convergence

Maria Michalis
*University of Westminster, London*

**Abstract**: The liberalization of telecommunications markets has been accompanied by a growing tendency towards regionalization, for instance in Europe, and internationalization, notably through the World Trade Organization, of regulatory regimes. This chapter examines the Europeanization of telecommunications regulation, focusing on the European Community (EC), by far the most advanced regionalization movement at present. It provides insights into the problems of strengthening supranational regulatory capacity and its limits. In particular, the chapter concentrates on the regulatory and institutional arrangements following the 1999 Communications Review. Two main arguments are put forward. First, despite the transfer of regulatory competences to the European arena, the chapter suggests that the role of national regulation remains significant. Second, it maintains that the greater flexibility of the new EC communications regulatory framework is likely to result in renewed diversity at the national level. Although the resulting degree of harmonization may be low, the new framework will give national governments more freedom to pursue their own policy objectives.

## 1    INTRODUCTION

The liberalization of telecommunications markets has been accompanied by a growing tendency towards regionalization – for instance in Europe and the Asia Pacific – and internationalization – notably through the World Trade Organization – of regulatory regimes. This chapter examines the regionalization of telecommunications regulation in the European Community[1] (EC), the most advanced regional integration movement at present. The European experience can inform the debate on other regionalization initiatives as well as the broader debate on the process of economic globalization.

The chapter addresses two central issues surrounding the shift of regulation beyond the nation-state and provides insights into the problems of strengthening supranational regulatory capacity and its limits. First, the balance of powers between the national and supranational

---

[1] The subject of this chapter comes under the first EC pillar of the European Union. It is for this reason, and also for simplicity and consistency, that the term EC is adopted.

levels has been a central theme in European integration. Indeed, one of the most contentious issues in the recent review of the EC communications regulatory framework was the division of powers between the two levels. This chapter argues that, despite the transfer of regulatory functions away from the national towards the European arena as part of the liberalization of telecommunications from the mid-1980s onwards, national regulation has remained important, in particular with regard to the actual and effective implementation of European policies.

Second, this chapter suggests that the new EC regulatory framework for electronic communications setting out basic objectives and principles, as opposed to prescriptive rules, is likely to result in renewed diversity at the national level. The greater flexibility of the European regulatory framework will allow national governments to pursue their own policy objectives but with adverse implications for policy convergence.

The structure of the chapter is as follows. Section 2 examines the evolution of the EC telecommunications regulation focusing on the so-called 1999 Communications Review and in particular the ensuing institutional arrangements. Section 3 provides a critical analysis of the effectiveness of EC telecommunications regulation and assesses the implications of the new regulatory framework for the two issues mentioned above, namely the balance of powers between the national and supranational levels, and harmonization. The chapter ends with a summary of the main points.

## 2    EUROPEANIZATION OF TELECOMMUNICATIONS REGULATION

For analytical purposes, the evolution of EC telecommunications regulation has been divided into three broad stages. The main emphasis is on the last one covering the new electronic communications regulatory package adopted in March 2002 and associated institutional developments.

### 2.1    Stage One (1957-1987): A Modest Beginning Emphasizing Information Technology and Industrial Policy

The first stage covers the period from the creation of the European Economic Community (EEC) in 1957 up until 1987. In general, during this period telecommunications was considered a natural monopoly and as such was firmly under the control of national governments. In addition, the founding Treaty of Rome did not grant the European Commission explicit competence in the sector of telecommunications. The absence of political consensus and a clear legitimating base severely handicapped any Commission initiatives for European-level action (Schneider and Werle, 1990). Markets and regulation were divided along national lines.

In the late 1960s, the perceived "technology gap" between Europe and the USA and Japan proved fruitful ground for EC-level action. The apparent continuing decline of the European information technology sector coupled with the manifest failure of divergent national protectionist measures designed to promote national champions rendered the industry, and in turn national governments, more receptive to European-level action. Digitization and the emergence of telematics, coming out of the technological convergence between computing and telecommunications, further facilitated supranational industrial policy initiatives. Digital technologies require high R&D investment and a bigger home market based on common standards. This need was in sharp contrast to the relatively small and fragmented national European telecommunications markets at that time.

Leading European electronics firms working closely with the Commission, had a very influential role in the launch, in 1984, of one of the first and most important European collaborative R&D programs, the European Strategic Program for Research & Development in Information Technologies (ESPRIT). A year later, in 1985, its sister program RACE (R&D for Advanced Communications in Europe) was adopted aiming at the introduction of broadband communications. This program was linked to other EC initiatives aimed at the development of pan-European networks, such as Integrated Services Digital Network (ISDN), one network to support all types of communications (Fuchs, 1992).

In short, up until the mid-1980s, the EC developed an industrial policy around the broader field of information technology. The Commission (notably the DG for industry from which the DG for telecommunications was created in 1986) established alliances with key technology and engineering oriented actors. The big European electronics firms were very influential in the introduction of R&D programs whilst state-owned telecommunications operators and big equipment manufacturers were strong supporters of ISDN as the future common European telecommunications infrastructure. Gradually but steadily the Commission was emerging as an important actor in telecommunications policy.

## 2.2 Stage Two (1987-1998): "Creeping Competence": The 1998 Telecommunications Regulatory Framework[2]

Whereas industrial policy initiatives were the main feature of the first phase, the second phase was a mix of liberalization and harmonization measures. The first European Commission document that placed the introduction of competition in telecommunications markets firmly on the agenda and dealt with associated regulatory issues was the 1987 Green Paper (European Commission, 1987). The decade up to 1998, saw the progressive liberalization of national telecommunications markets and the adoption of common rules aiming at the creation of a single market in telecommunications. This process resulted in the so-called 1998 telecommunications regulatory framework summarized in Table 1.

The Commission, notably the DG for competition, was instrumental in the liberalization of telecommunications markets.[3] All the directives providing for the introduction of competition were issued directly by the Commission on the basis of its strong legal competence in competition policy without formal approval by the European Parliament and the Council of Ministers representing the member states. Nonetheless, tacit political agreement was necessary for the Commission to take such action (Schmidt, 1998).

---

[2] The term "creeping competence" is found in the title of Pollack (1994).

[3] The European Court of Justice with a number of judgments further strengthened the legal base of the Commission.

Table 1. 1998 Telecommunications Regulatory Framework

| Liberalization measures[1] | Main harmonization measures[2] |
|---|---|
| 1988: Equipment Directive (88/301/EEC) | 1986: Mutual Recognition of Equipment Directive (86/361/EEC last amended by 1999/5/EC) |
| 1990: (Value-Added) Services Directive (90/388/EEC) | 1990: ONP Framework Directive (90/387/EEC amended by 97/51/EC) |
| 1994: Satellite Directive (94/46/EC) | 1997: Licensing Directive (97/13/EC) |
| 1995: Cable TV Directive (95/51/EC) | 1997: Interconnection Directive (97/33/EC amended by 98/61/EC) |
| 1996: Mobile Communications Directive (96/2/EC) | 1998: Voice Telephony Directive (97/66/EC) |
| 1996: Full competition Directive (96/19/EC) | |
| 1999: Cable Ownership Directive (1999/64/EC) | |

[1] Liberalization has been introduced through Commission Directives, which do not require approval by the Council, on the basis of article 86 [ex 90]

[2] Harmonization measures have been Council and European Parliament Directives based on article 95 [ex 100]

More specifically, in the 1980s a broader set of developments facilitated the adoption of a pro-competitive EC telecommunications policy (see Braithwaite and Drahos, 2000, Schneider, 2002). First, starting from the USA, the old consensus around the national natural monopoly paradigm was disintegrating. Second, the international liberalization of service industries, in particular finance and travel that depend critically on telecommunications infrastructure and services for their world-wide operations, contributed to calls for liberalization. Third, the breakdown of Keynesian economic consensus and the concomitant shift towards neo-liberalism. Fourth, technological advances, notably digitization, helped draw attention to the significant growth potential of high technology sectors. And last, the relaunch of the European integration process with the "1992" project and the creation of a common market.

Crucially, it was not just market players (such as potential entrants and corporate users) that were supporting the Commission's pro-competitive policy but also European political elites were now more receptive to EC policy action. It is indicative that, from the early 1980s onwards, major European governments had started discussing domestically the reform of their telecommunications sectors. Most notably Britain has led the EC in telecommunications market liberalization and regulatory innovation. Under the recently-elected Thatcher government, Britain was the first EC country to introduce competition in its national telecommunications market in 1982 and to initiate the privatization of its domestic operator British Telecom in 1984 (see Hills, 1986). In other countries, like Germany and the Netherlands, debates and studies on telecommunications were well underway and indeed there were strong similarities between them and the subsequent 1987 Green Paper of the European Commission (Knieps, 1990).

Hence, a conjunction of factors has led to the liberalization of European telecommunications markets. The EC has contributed to this process. It has increased wider international pressures and has provided the overall momentum.[4] With regard to harmonization, as Table 1

---

[4] The EC was also instrumental in the adoption of the 1998 deadline by the World Trade Organization and its landmark 1997 Agreement on Basic Telecommunications.

depicts, the 1998 EC regulatory framework, aimed at the creation of the single market in telecommunications, established the Commission as a central policy actor. Effectively, the framework struck a delicate balance in relation to the separation of powers between the European Commission and the individual member states, as we shall see below.

## 2.3 Stage Three (1998-2002): The New Regulatory Framework for Electronic Communications

In 1999 the Commission launched a far-reaching Communications Review (European Commission, 1999). The Review aimed at updating and streamlining the entire EC communications regulatory package. Whereas the 1998 regulatory framework was designed for a newly liberalized market, the revised framework had to cater for a fully liberalized and technologically convergent market environment.

The new framework was formally adopted in April 2002 and member states had till the end of July 2003 to transpose it into national legislation. It comprises a package of directives covering all electronic communications networks (e.g. fixed, mobile, television broadcast, cable TV) and associated services and facilities (e.g. conditional access systems) with the exception of broadcast content and e-commerce (see table 2).

Table 2. 2002 Electronic Communications Regulatory Framework

| Liberalization measures | Main harmonization measures |
| --- | --- |
| 2000: Regulation on Local Loop Unbundling (Regulation 2887/2000/EC) 2002: Liberalizations Directive (2002/77/EC) | 2002: Access and Interconnection Directive (2002/19/EC) |
| | 2002: Authorization Directive (2002/20/EC) |
| | 2002: Framework Directive (2002/21/EC) |
| | 2002: Universal Service and Users' Rights Directive (2002/22/EC) |
| | 2002: Data Protection and Privacy Directive (2002/58/EC) |
| | 2002: Spectrum Decision (676/2002/EC) |
| | 2002: Guidelines on Market Analysis and Significant Market Power |
| | 2003: Recommendation on Relevant Markets |

The new regulatory framework is available online at
http://europa.eu.int/information_society/topics/telecoms/regulatory/new_rf/index_en.htm [accessed May 2003]

In addition to technological neutrality, the new framework aims to link the degree of regulation to the degree of competition and in turn limit regulatory intervention to a minimum. Based on competition analysis, the Commission has listed eighteen market segments, such as mobile call termination, in which specific regulation, for instance price controls, may be warranted[5] (European Commission, 2003). It has also provided guidelines, again in accordance with competition law principles, for determining the presence or absence of market

---

[5] National regulators may choose to intervene in other market segments but only if, with the Commission's agreement, three criteria are met: the existence of high entry barriers; no possibility to overcome the barriers within a relevant time horizon; and, the inability of competition law alone to correct market failures.

power (European Commission, 2002a). Within each market, national regulators will determine which players possess significant market power and decide whether to impose appropriate obligations.

Besides the balance between competition and sector specific rules, the division of powers between nation-states and the EC was the second central theme in the reform of the 1998 regulatory framework. At the heart of the latter was the idea for a European regulator for telecommunications.

## The Question of a European Regulatory Authority

The question of a European regulatory authority was not new. It was the 1994 Bangemann report of industrial leaders that explicitly advocated the establishment of a European-level authority to address the lack of consistency in implementation (examined below), and to deal with regulatory issues that by their nature are Europe-wide such as licensing, network interconnection and radio spectrum management. At that time, the Commission had the broad backing of leading European telecommunications manufacturers, operators and potential market entrants who, already feeling the pressure of competition in domestic liberalized markets, were eager to expand beyond national borders. At a time when the majority of member states had not set up independent regulatory authorities, the thinking was that a European regulator would facilitate expansion across national borders and could resolve timely and effectively any cross-border regulatory disputes (see Stone Sweet and Sandholtz, 1997). Equally, large corporate users, who would stand to benefit from such transnational operators, were in favor of a European authority. (PNE, 1997)

Not surprisingly, national governments and the limited number of telecommunications regulatory authorities that had been set up strongly opposed the idea for a European regulator. Both regarded the proposed institutional arrangement (i.e., the delegation of regulatory powers to a new supranational institution) as intrusive and restrictive (see NERA, 1997).

By the late 1990s, even the industry interests that had supported the idea for a European regulator in the first place retreated from their original position in response to new market conditions. The new telecommunications environment no longer seemed to warrant the creation of a European authority. First, the euphoria of cross-border alliances which had marked the beginning of market restructuring, had now clearly come to an end (PNE, 1999). Second, all member states had set up national regulatory authorities although, admittedly, their degree of independence, resources, and effectiveness varied. And last, national regulators, partly as a defensive response against the potential creation of a European regulator and partly in recognition of the real need to enhance harmonization, decided in 1997 to set up their own informal forum, the Independent Regulators' Group (IRG).[6]

A report in 1999 confirmed that, although there was support for greater EC involvement in the areas of competition, harmonization, interconnection, and enforcement, these issues could be better addressed by existing, preferably improved, EC structures rather than a new European regulatory institution (Eurostrategies and Cullen, 1999). The Commission accepted the main conclusion of the study and effectively abandoned the idea for a European regulator in favor of other institutional arrangements.

---

[6] The Independent Regulators' Group with 29 members is the wider European coordinating body of telecommunications regulatory authorities. The Group acts as a discussion forum where national regulators share experiences and information, and address issues of common interest and concern.

*New Institutional Arrangements*

As part of the 1999 Communications Review, the Commission came up with new institutional plans setting out two main lines of action (European Commission, 1999, pp. 51-4). The first, concerned provisions to enhance the powers of national regulatory authorities. The Commission stated that "it is essential that [National Regulatory Authorities] are properly resourced, truly independent, and seek actively to open their national markets to competition and innovation" (European Commission, 1999, p. 53).

The second, concerned the adaptation and improvement of existing EC institutional structures (see also European Commission, 2000, arts. 19 & 21). More specifically, the Commission proposed the establishment of two committees. The Communications Committee would be a comitology committee working within the Commission and comprising representatives from the member states.[7] The second, and most controversial, proposal was for a High Level Communications Group composed of the Commission and national regulators. Its ultimate objective would be to promote uniform application of the regulatory framework at the national level. This proposal can be seen as an instance of "policy feedback" (Pierson, 1993): the creation of the Independent Regulators' Group by national regulators provoked a direct response from the Commission who suggested the setting up of its own coordinating body of national regulators.

The response of industry players to the Commission's plans was not surprising in terms of the comments (see Comments on 1999 Review). Telecommunications operators broadly agreed with the Commission's proposals but called for more details and stressed the need that the proposed committees should consult closely with the industry. National governments were generally supportive of the Communications Committee but expressed concerns about the role of the High Level Communications Group, and especially the possibility for national regulators to bypass governments. Similarly, the national regulators' group (IRG) opposed the idea for a rival High Level Communications Group arguing that it would be a "large and diffuse" body, susceptible to political interference and therefore not suitable to deal with detailed practical regulatory matters. The implication was that the IRG was best placed to take on this role of closer co-operation with the Commission. Eventually, in the face of such strong opposition, the proposal for a High Level Communications Group was abandoned (European Commission, 2001).

Another very contentious proposal, at the heart of the balance between EC and national powers, was the so-called "veto-right" (European Commission, 2000, art. 6). The Commission was concerned that the increased flexibility of the new regulatory framework had the potential to result in more fragmentation and restrictive national rules. To address this, and also serving its own institutional interests, the Commission originally proposed a "transparency mechanism" according to which it would have to clear, and could overrule, certain national regulatory measures. The European Parliament (2001) supported the Commission's greater role in national regulatory matters whereas, not surprisingly, national governments, national regulators and their association (IRG) strongly opposed the proposal (see Kurth, 2001). In the

---

[7] According to the comitology procedure, the Commission consults with representatives of national governments on specific issues mainly of a technical nature. Effectively, national governments, through their representatives, have been in a position to keep a check on the Commission's delegated implementation powers.

end, the Council unanimously rejected the so-called "veto right" and limited the Commission's influence over national regulatory decisions (Council, 2001).

The adopted framework provides that, the Commission, in consultation with the Communications Commission, has one month in which to make comments on draft measures dealing with the definition of relevant markets or the designation of undertakings with significant market power whilst the national regulator concerned is under an obligation to take the "utmost account" of these comments (EC, 2002a). If the national regulator in question decides to adopt the measures despite the Commission's recommendation to the opposite, then the national regulator has to publish the reasoning behind its decision. Although its powers have been watered down, it is worth noting that the Commission based on its strong competition powers may still decide to launch an infringement procedure against a national regulatory authority's definition of markets and/or designation of operators with significant market power on grounds of incorrect application of competition law concepts.

The new regulatory package, has provided for the creation of a European Regulators' Group (EC, 2002c). Its formation can be interpreted as a compromise following the rejection of the proposed High Level Communications Group and the conflict between the Commission and national governments and regulators concerning the so-called "veto right". The European Regulators' Group formalizes the co-operation between the national regulatory authorities and the Commission. Its main objective is to encourage co-ordination among national regulators in order to enhance harmonization.

Besides the "veto right", the Council has also narrowed the Commission's interference over radio spectrum matters and in particular the strong role the latter had envisaged for itself in the allocation of radio spectrum. Despite the divergences in the award of 3rd generation mobile licenses (see below) and the problems that the telecommunications mobile sector faces, national regulators and governments strongly opposed any greater involvement by the Commission in this field of radio frequencies assignment. Besides the Radio Spectrum Committee, a comitology committee similar to the Communications Committee dealing with technical issues, a Radio Spectrum Policy Expert Group has been established (EC, 2002b). It is an advisory body, comprising representatives from national regulators and radio spectrum user groups, that deals with radio spectrum issues and liaises with the relevant regional and international bodies.

In sum, within the EC, the allocation of regulatory powers between the European and national levels is a highly political question with important constitutional implications. The result of the 1999 Review confirms the significance of member states to EC telecommunications governance. However, this outcome should not be interpreted simply as an example of national governments acting to protect their autonomy (cf. Schmidt, 1998, Thatcher, 2001). The rejection of the policy proposals for a European regulator did not imply a full reversal to the previous order. This is central to the concept of path dependence (Pierson, 1996). Rather than establishing a European regulator, other institutional arrangements were adopted and a new order was created. The implication of the new committees, summarized in Table 3, is greater reliance on national expert knowledge thereby facilitating the political support of national governments.

Table 3. 2002 Electronic Communications Regulatory Framework: New Institutional Arrangements

---

- **Radio Spectrum Committee** and **Communications Committee** (established by Decision 676/2002/EC, 7 March 2002 and Framework Directive 2002/21/EC, 7 March 2002 respectively):
- EC comitology committees working within the Commission and comprising representatives from the member states. Role: advisory and regulatory.
- **Spectrum Policy Group** (established by Commission Decision 2002/22/EC, 26 July 2002):
- Advisory body comprising representatives from national regulators and radio spectrum user groups. Liases with the relevant regional and international bodies
- **European Regulators Group** (established by Commission Decision 2002/27/EC, 29 July 2002)
- Sectoral formal discussion and coordinating body between NRAs and European Commission. Advisory role. Members: 15 EC national regulators + regulators from accession countries + Commission representative

---

Source: Author's own compilation

## 3     EFFECTIVENESS OF EUROPEAN TELECOMMUNICATIONS REGULATION

### 3.1     Balance of Powers and Limits to Policy Convergence

The formulation of the EC telecommunications policy has been a gradual process. The numerous consultation documents, proposals, public hearings as well as the number of technical committees and expert panels involved in the process attest to the complexities of the process and the problems faced. But how effective has the EC telecommunications regulation been?

Despite the 1998 deadline for full liberalization, competition has yet to establish itself in telecommunications, particularly local access, markets. The formal abolition of monopoly rights has not automatically translated into a real competitive environment and in effect market structures have not changed sufficiently. According to the Commission's latest implementation report, incumbent operators still have 89% of the local calls market in terms of retail revenues (this ranges from complete control in some countries such as Belgium and Germany to 66% in Britain). The situation in the long-distance and international calls markets is slightly different. In these markets, the incumbents' market share has fallen to 73.5% and 67.6% respectively. (European Commission, 2002d, p. 16)

The Commission and national governments have become particularly concerned about the lack of competition in the local loop market and the implications for the information society initiative (Michalis, 2001). At the Lisbon European Council in March 2000, the leaders of EC governments endorsed an ambitious ten-year plan, *e*Europe, aiming at transforming Europe into the world's most competitive and dynamic knowledge-based economy (Lisbon European Council, 2000). They identified local loop unbundling[8] as central to the promotion of

---

[8] This measure requires incumbent operators to make their access networks available to competitors who can install their own, rather than rely on the incumbent's, DSL equipment and provide services to end users.

competition in local access markets and the expansion of the internet and broadband communications on a mass scale. Reflecting the urgency of the issue, in December 2000 and well before the adoption of the revised regulatory package, the EC adopted a regulation requiring operators with significant market power to provide unbundled access to their local loops (EC, 2000). A regulation is the toughest legislative instrument available to the Commission as, unlike directives, it does not have to be transposed into national legislation but is directly applicable and binding in all member states.

Yet, local loop unbundling has not promoted competition in the local loop as initially expected and its prospects in doing so look poor. This failure can be attributed to genuine complexities encountered during the implementation of this measure- in particular technical, operational and pricing problems – but also the reluctance of incumbent operators to facilitate the introduction of competition in one of their last bastions. It is revealing that, as of end of 2002, within the EC, around 80-95 per cent, out of a total of just over eight million Digital Subscriber Line (DSL) connections, were provided by incumbents (ECTA, 2003).

The market situation raises questions about the effectiveness of EC policy to actually promote competition since most markets still do not seem to be liberalized sufficiently in many member states. The challenge to create and maintain a truly competitive market environment remains. As the experience of countries such as the USA and the UK, that initiated liberalization in the early 1980s, shows real competition takes time and its effective introduction requires the active involvement of national regulators.

Indeed, national regulation has been instrumental for the actual implementation of EC policy. As Majone (1996) explains, the cost of regulatory policies, unlike directly redistributive policies, has to be borne by member states rather than the Commission. By implication the national level remains important, especially in the implementation of European policies. Hence, the development of a comprehensive European regulatory framework has not led to a weakening of member states' regulatory powers. Rather, member states' regulatory responsibilities have increased as a result of EC policy.

The centrality of the national level is further confirmed by the fact that most EC harmonization measures take the form of directives. The Commission proposes directives and submits them to both the European Parliament and the Council of Ministers for endorsement. The very need to accommodate diverse interests during policy-making means that the provisions of directives tend to be vague. They leave to member states sufficient leeway as to "the choice of form and methods" to put them into practice. This flexibility is consistent with the principle of subsidiarity[9] and formalizes the duality of regulation at EC and national levels.

Significantly, the implication is that a range of regulatory issues, even those central to the promotion of competition such as cost methodologies and cost accounting, remain the responsibility of relevant national authorities (see Kiessling and Blondeel, 1998). The implementation reports of the EC telecommunications regulatory package that the Commission publishes regularly document the consequent heterogeneity in national regulations and markets in areas such as authorization and interconnection regimes, availability of networks and services, and consumer protection.

A recent example where harmonization has clearly failed is the award of third generation mobile licenses. The EC framework did not specify a selection method for their award and member states have used different methods. Some – such as Britain, Germany and the

---

[9] According to the principle of subsidiarity, incorporated in the Maastricht Treaty of 1992, issues should be dealt with at the most appropriate level.

Netherlands – have used auctions while others – such as Finland, Sweden and Spain – have used comparative selection procedures. In this way, national regulators have affected market entry conditions and in particular the cost of entry with adverse implications for the creation of a level playing field.

Not only are directives vague but also during their incorporation into national legislation, they are filtered through the political, economic, social and institutional characteristics of each member state. This process has contributed to variations among national regulatory responses. There is little guarantee that national regulators – having different powers, priorities and organizational structures, and enjoying different degrees of legitimacy – will implement the EC rules in the same way. The result is a "regulatory patchwork" (Héritier, 1996). The Europeanization of telecommunications regulation has allowed differentiation between the national regulatory frameworks of individual member states (see Eliassen and Sjøvaag 1999; Hulsink, 1999; Thatcher, 1999).

In short, the formal transposition of EC rules into national legislation is different from actual compliance with the spirit and principles of the rules. Through transposition a member state fulfils its formal obligations by complying with the letter of the EC law. But "*de jure* integration" does not necessarily result in "*de facto* integration" (Thompson, 2002). The latter is linked more to the willingness and ability of individual countries to, for instance, assist the creation of and sustain a competitive market environment.

The European Commission, as the guardian of the Treaties, can use various enforcement mechanisms. These are "both informal and formal and constitute a combination of peer pressure, increased monitoring, persuasion and penalties, and policy re-formulation." (Dimitrakopoulos and Richardson, 2001, p. 350). Besides the publication of regular implementation reports[10], the Commission relies on complaints, for example from market players ("whistle blowers"), to find out what is happening on the ground. Cases of infringements may culminate by bringing a case in front of the European Court of Justice (see European Court of Justice, 1999). And since the Maastricht Treaty of 1992, member states may incur financial penalties if they ignore Court judgments.

Overall, although the EC telecommunications policy of liberalization and harmonization is binding on member states, the EC does not possess sufficient authority to actually make this a reality. In effect, the EC provides the momentum. It helps diffuse and it amplifies global pressures. At the heart of its functioning is the relationship between national and supranational levels. Despite the Europeanization of policy, national regulation remains crucial for the actual implementation of EC rules. The European Commission plays an important monitoring role whilst the European Court of Justice, as the regulator of the last resort, has powers to impose compliance. Nevertheless, the creation of a single market is still hampered by the low level of harmonization in European telecommunications markets. The 2002 regulatory package, as we shall now see, has introduced new elements aiming at minimizing litigation and at promoting timely implementation of EC rules and consistency in national regulatory responses.

---

[10] In May 1997, just before the deadline for complete liberalization, the Commission produced its first implementation report. A number of regular updates have since been published.

## 3.2 Implications of the New EC Telecommunications Regulatory Framework

A central feature of the new EC regulatory framework for electronic communications is its greater flexibility compared with the 1998 framework. Although binding, it sets out basic objectives and principles rather than detailed and prescriptive rules. Three main reasons can explain the shift of emphasis away from a hard-law towards a soft-law approach in the area of telecommunications. First, the shift has to be set against the background of changing market and technological conditions. A fully liberalized market place and the convergence in communication technologies underway require a less rigid regulatory framework. Interestingly, the reconfiguration of policy measures at the EC level reflects a parallel reconfiguration at the national level (see, for instance, Oftel, 2001). Second, the emerging consensus is that regulation should take place closest to the market and by implication national regulators are best placed to adapt regulation to meet national demands. Any initiative to promote consistency in the application of EC law in different member states has to involve, rather than replace, national regulators. And last, there is a political need to accommodate diverse interests. Harmonization is about to become a more difficult exercise with the imminent enlargement of the EC towards Central and Eastern Europe and the consequent increase in the diversity of member states.

The soft harmonization approach of the 2002 regulatory framework has potential advantages and disadvantages. On the one hand, the EC's increasing reliance on flexible policy measures provides testimony that there can be no one-size-fits-all regulatory solutions. It allows for significant national autonomy, essential for the pursuit of domestic policy objectives. However, on the other hand, this light-handed approach by increasing the scope for regulatory discretion at the national level is likely to adversely affect the creation of a level playing field and strict policy convergence (Bennett, 1991). Therefore, despite the need for a coherent regulatory framework, the new regulatory package could increase fragmentation. Instead of a single market, it is likely to result in a multi-speed market. In turn, this scenario will undermine the legitimacy of the EC.

In an effort to encourage consistency of national regulatory responses, the new EC framework will be supplemented by non-binding measures such as recommendations, guidelines, benchmarking of best practice and comparative implementation reports. The greater use of soft policy instruments is also accompanied by a growing reliance on soft institutions, such as the European Regulators' Group. The Group, bringing together the national regulators of the member states, will primarily have a coordinating role rather than substantial regulation making powers. Its creation allows national regulators to influence regulation at both national and supranational levels thereby consolidating their participation in the entire policy-making process. Yet, importantly, for the first time, it allows the Commission to have formal involvement with the implementation of EC directives at the national level.

Hence, the new institutional arrangements attempt to induce convergence in national policy frameworks not so much directly by prescribing specific rules but rather indirectly via processes of socialization and policy learning. These are "geared towards changes in attitudes and behaviour" (Wallace, 2001, p. 588). In effect, the European Regulators' Group institutionalizes policy learning and can help spread best practice regulatory models thereby promoting policy improvement and possibly policy convergence.

However, the legal uncertainty surrounding soft policy measures may undermine their potential to enhance harmonization. Indeed, market players expressed their concern that the increased use of soft-law instruments, although necessary, had the potential to result in non-transparent processes from which the European Parliament and interest groups could effectively be excluded (see for instance ETNO, C&W, BEUC comments on the 1999 Review). Soft policy instruments involve to various degrees the sectoral interests whose behavior they aim to regulate. Regulatory matters tend to become de-politicized whilst questions of transparency and effectiveness arise.

Overall, the pattern that is emerging with the new EC telecommunications regulatory framework, characterized by increased flexibility and an emphasis on soft-law instruments – such as policy guidelines, benchmarks, best-practice models, comparative implementation reports and scoreboards – draws on the "open method of co-ordination" adopted at the Lisbon European Council in March 2000. The extent to which this approach can act as a force toward greater harmonization remains to be seen.

## 4 CONCLUSION

The liberalization of telecommunications has been marked by the establishment of governance regimes that have shifted regulation beyond the nation-state. Two central themes surrounding the move towards regionalization and globalization have been the balance of regulatory powers between supranational institutions and nation-states and the degree of harmonization that can be achieved. This chapter examined the Europeanization of telecommunications regulation in the EC.

The EC telecommunications framework relies on national governments and regulators for effective implementation. However, the 1998 regulatory package failed to produce sufficient consistency in national regulatory responses. Delays in the creation of truly competitive markets and the lack of consistency in how different member states applied the EC rules contributed to calls for a European telecommunications regulator. The allocation of regulatory powers between the European and national levels is a highly political question. A European regulator, if created, would have entailed a shift of the locus of regulatory activity from the national to the European arena. For reasons explained above, the idea for a European regulator for telecommunications failed to stabilize and result in concrete action.

The new regulatory framework adopted in March 2002 entails new institutional arrangements. On the one hand, it has greatly increased the discretionary powers of national regulators. On the other, the European Commission, although it did not manage to increase its competencies and control over national regulatory matters by as much as it originally sought for, has acquired more powers to intervene in the implementation of EC directives and has a greater coordinating role in enhancing harmonization. The cooperation between the European Commission and national regulators has been formalized and national regulators are in a stronger position now to influence regulation at the European level.

The new EC regulatory package for electronic communications relies significantly on flexible policy measures. This allows for significant national autonomy, essential for the pursuit of domestic policy objectives. National regulators can tailor regulation to the specific circumstances of their countries while respecting the overall objectives and principles set out at the European level. National regulators need to have sufficient powers and resources to fulfill their tasks in a timely, efficient and transparent manner. In turn, effective national regulation can help increase the credibility and acceptability of the EC. The main implication of the new European regulatory regime drawing attention to the importance of national regulation is that the EC promotes effectively policy co-ordination rather than strict policy convergence.


## 5   REFERENCES

Bangemann High Level Group on the Information Society (1994), Europe and the Global Information Society: Recommendations to the European Council, 26 May [Bangemann Report]

Bennett, C. (1991), "What is Policy Convergence and What Causes it?" *British Journal of Political Science*, Vol. 21, pp. 215-233.

Braithwaite, J. and Drahos, P. (2000), *Global Business Regulation*, Cambridge University Press, Cambridge.

Comments on the European Commission's 1999 Communications Review available online at http://europa.eu.int/ISPO/infosoc/telecompolicy/review99/comments/comments.html   [accessed June 2002]

Council of the European Union (2001), 2340th Council meeting: Transport/ Telecommunications, Luxembourg 4-5 April 2001, Press 131, Nr: 7587/01.

Dimitrakopoulos, D. and Richardson, J. (2001), "Implementing EU Public Policy," in Richardson, J. (ed.) (2001), *European Union: Power and Policy-Making*, Routledge, London and New York.

EC (2000), "Regulation 2887/2000/EC of the European Parliament and of the Council of 18 December 2000 on unbundled access to the local loop", *OJ L*, Vol. 336, No. 4, 12 December, Brussels, available online at: http://europa.eu.int/information_society/topics/telecoms/regulatory/new_rf/index_en.htm#ull, [accessed August 2002]

EC (2002a), "Directive 2002/21/EC of the European Parliament and of the Council of 7 March 2002 on a common regulatory framework for electronic communications networks and services (Framework Directive)," *OJ L* Vol. 108, No. 33, 24 April, Brussels.

ECTA [European Competitive Telecommunications Association] (2003), ECTA DSL Scorecard – End of December 2002, available online at http://www.ectaportal.com/ectauploads/dsl_feb03.xls, [accessed in May 2003].

Eliassen, K. A. and Sjøvaag, M. (eds) (1999), *European Telecommunications Liberalisation*, Routledge, London and New York.

European Commission (1987), Towards a Dynamic European Economy-Green Paper on the Development of the Common Market for Telecommunications Services and Equipment, Communication by the Commission, COM (87) 290, Brussels.

European Commission (1999), Towards a New Framework for Electronic Communications Infrastructure and Associated Services. The 1999 Communications Review, COM(1999) 539, Brussels.

European Commission (2000), "Proposal for a Directive of the European Parliament and of the Council on a Common Regulatory Framework for Electronic Communications Networks and Services, COM(2000)393 final – 2000/0184(COD) Submitted by the Commission on 23 August 2000", *OJ C*, Vol. 365 E, No. 198, 19 December, Brussels.

European Commission (2001), Communication Concerning the Common Position of the Council on the Adoption of a Directive of the European Parliament and of the Council on a Common Regulatory Framework for Electronic Communications Networks and Services, SEC(2001) 1365, Brussels.

European Commission (2002a), "Commission Guidelines on Market Analysis and the Assessment of Significant Market Power under the Community Regulatory Framework for Electronic Communications Networks and Services," *OJ C,* Vol. 165, No. 6, 11 July, Brussels.

European Commission (2002b), "Commission Decision of 2 July 2002 establishing a Radio Spectrum Policy Group," *OJ L,* Vol. 198, No. 49, 27 July, Brussels.

European Commission (2002c), "Commission Decision of 29 July 2002 establishing the European Regulators Group for Electronic Communications Networks and Services," *OJ L,* Vol. 200, No. 38, 30 July, Brussels.

European Commission (2002d), Eighth Report from the Commission on the Implementation of the Telecommunications Regulatory Package, COM(2002) 95, Brussels.

European Commission (2003), Commission Recommendation of 11/02/2003 on Relevant and Services Markets within the Electronics Communications Sector Susceptible to Ex Ante Regulation in Accordance with Directive 2002/21/EC of the European Parliament and of the Council on a Common Regulatory Framework for Electronic Communication Networks and Services, C(2003)497, Brussels.

European Court of Justice (1999), Commission of the European Communities v Grand Duchy of Luxembourg (Case C-59/98), [1999] ECR I-1181.

European Parliament (2001), "Position of the European Parliament of 1 March 2001 on the Proposal for a European Parliament and Council Directive on a Common Regulatory Framework for Electronic Communications Networks and Services, COM(2000)393 final; A5-0053/2001", *OJ C,* Vol. 277, No. 91, 1 October, Brussels.

Eurostrategies and Cullen International (1999), The Possible Value Added of a European Regulatory Authority for Telecommunications, A report for the European Commission.

Fuchs, G. (1992), "Integrated Services Digital Network: The Politics of European Telecommunications Network Development," *Journal of European Integration,* Vol. XVI, No. 1, pp. 63-88.

Héritier, A. (1996) "The Accommodation of Diversity in European Policy-making and its Outcomes: Regulatory Policy as a Patchwork," *Journal of European Public Policy,* Vol. 3, No. 3, pp. 149-67.

Hills, J. (1986), *Deregulating Telecoms: Competition and Control in the United States, Japan and Britain,* Pinter, London.

Hulsink, W. (1999), *Privatisation and Liberalisation in European Telecommunications. Comparing Britain, the Netherlands and France,* Routledge, London and New York.

Kiessling, T. and Blondeel, Y. (1998), "The EU Regulatory Framework in Telecoms. A Critical Analysis," *Telecommunications Policy,* Vol. 22, No 7, pp. 571-592.

Knieps, G. (1990), "Deregulation in Europe: Telecommunications and Transportation," in Majone, G. (ed.) (1990) *Deregulation or Reregulation?: Regulatory Reform in Europe and in the United States,* Pinter, London.

Kurth, M. [President, German Regulatory Authority for Telecommunications and Posts] (2001), "The Independent Regulators Group and its future Role in the new European Regulatory Framework", PowerPoint presentation to ECTA, Brussels (Available online at: http://www.regtp.de/aktuelles/reden/02371 [accessed July 2002].

Lisbon European Council (2000), Presidency Conclusions. Lisbon European Council. 23 and 24 March 2000, available online at http://ue.eu.int/en/Info/eurocouncil/index.htm, [accessed September 2002].

Majone, G. (1996), "The European Commission as Regulator," in Majone, G. (ed.) (1996), *Regulating Europe*, Routledge, London.

Michalis, M. (2001), "Local Competition and the Role of Regulation: The EU Debate and Britain's Experience," *Telecommunications Policy*, Vol. 25, Nos. 10-11, pp. 759-776.

NERA (1997), Issues Associated with the Creation of a European Regulatory Authority for Telecommunications, a report by NERA and Denton Hall for the European Commission (DG XIII).

OFTEL (2001), The Benefits of Self- and Co-regulation to Consumers and Industry. Statement issued by the Director General of Telecommunications, July, London.

Pierson, P. (1993), "When Effect Becomes Cause: Policy Feedback and Political Change," *World Politics*, Vol. 45, pp. 595-628.

Pierson, P. (1996), "The Path to European Integration: A Historical Institutionalist Analysis," *Comparative Political Studies*, Vol. 29, No. 2, pp. 123-63.

PNE [Public Network Europe] (1997), "The Terrible Truth about EC Regulation," *The Economist Group*, London Vol. 7, No 6, pp. 31-33.

PNE (1999), "Not-so-urgent Need for Review," *The Economist Group*, London, Vol. 9, No. 9, pp. 33-6.

Pollack, M. A. (1994), "Creeping Competence: The Expanding Agenda of the European Community," *Journal of Public Policy*, Vol. 14, No 2, pp. 95-145.

Schmidt, S. (1998), "Commission Activism: Subsuming Telecommunications and Electricity under European Competition Law," *Journal of European Public Policy*, Vol. 5, No. 1, pp. 169-184.

Schneider, V. (2002), "The Institutional Transformation of Telecommunications Between Europeanization and Globalization," in Jordana, J. (ed.) (2002), *Governing Telecommunications and the New Information Society in Europe*, Edward Elgar, Cheltenham.

Schneider, V. and Werle, R. (1990), "International Regime or Corporate Actor? The European Community in Telecommunications Policy", in Kenneth D. and Humphreys P. (eds) (1990), *The Political Economy of Communications: International and European Dimensions*, Routledge, London.

Stone Sweet, A. and Sandholtz, W. (1997), "European Integration and Supranational Governance," *Journal of European Public Policy*, Vol. 4, No. 3, pp. 297-317.

Thatcher, M. (1999), *The Politics of Telecommunications. National Institutions, Convergence and Change*, Oxford University Press, Oxford.

Thatcher, M. (2001), "The Commission and National Governments as Partners: EC Regulatory Expansion in Telecommunications 1979-2000," *Journal of European Public Policy*, Vol. 8, No. 4, pp. 585-603.

Thompson, G. (ed.) (2002), *Governing the European Economy*, Sage, London.

Wallace, H. (2001), "The Changing Politics of the European Union: An Overview," *Journal of Common Market Studies*, Vol. 39, No 4, pp. 581-594.

CHAPTER 16

# Effects of Prices for Local Network Interconnection on Market Structure in the US

Mark A. Jamison*

*University of Florida, Gainesville*

**Abstract**. This chapter examines how incumbents and entrants respond to prices for network interconnection in telecommunications, including prices for unbundled network elements. Most studies of the effects of these prices find that lower prices encourage entry and encourage entrants to use more unbundled network elements. Missing from this literature are studies of how incumbents respond to the interconnection prices they charge. US telecommunications laws place an obligation on incumbents to provide interconnection at any technically feasible point, implying that interconnection prices should not affect incumbents' provision of interconnection services. Using data from 1998, evidence is found that low unbundled network element prices, relative to retail prices, result in lower entry, perhaps indicating that US incumbents limit entry. No evidence is found that incumbents hinder entrants from gaining market share for customers who receive more calls than they make (such as Internet Service Providers) or from gaining market share using resold services.

## 1 INTRODUCTION

The situation often arises in which one firm sells an input to another firm and then competes against the other firm in the market for the final product. Examples include local exchange telephone companies selling access to long distance companies and then competing in the long distance business themselves (Willig, 1979), vertically integrated electricity companies or natural gas pipeline companies selling transport to their generating or gas supplier competitors (Economides and White, 1995), railroads providing trackage to other railroads (Baumol, 1983), Internet backbone providers competing with Internet Service Providers (Crémer et al., 2000; Kende, 2000) and incumbent local exchange telephone companies interconnecting their networks with and selling services to new entrants (Katz, 1997). The

* I would like to thank David Sappington, Steve Slutsky, Chunrong Ai, James Prieger, William Taylor, Dean Foreman, and an anonymous referee for their comments, as well as discussants at the Southern Economic Association, Transportation and Public Utilities Group, and International Telecommunications Society meetings and at the US Department of Justice workshop on local competition. I would also like to thank Melis Uygur, Eric Chiang, Eileen Pun, and Janice Hauge for their assistance in gathering data, Verizon, SBC, Sprint, and US West for providing data, and AT&T for funding data collection. All errors and omissions are my own. This chapter was previously titled Incumbent and Entrant Incentives with Network Interconnection: The Case of US Telecommunications.

issue of how to price this input is often couched in the context of a regulated firm interconnecting its network with a new entrant, but the issue could also apply to an unregulated monopolist providing an essential facility to downstream competitors (Economides and White, 1995). For purposes of this chapter, I consider the inputs to be interconnection services, which include incumbent local exchange companies (incumbents) providing unbundled network elements (UNEs) and services for resale to new entrants (entrants), and incumbents and entrants terminating local telephone calls for each other. I explain UNEs, resale, and terminating calls in more detail below.

An extensive theoretical literature has developed on pricing these inputs. Most empirical studies in telecommunications examine entrants' responses to prices for interconnecting networks. Indicative of these studies, Ros and McDermott (2000) and Rosston and Wimmer (2000) find that low prices encourage entry and encourage entrants to expand their market shares.[1] Missing from this literature is an empirical test of whether and how incumbents respond to interconnection prices. This test is important because price signals that encourage more entrants to enter or to compete intensely to expand their market share may also encourage incumbents to hinder entrants in order to protect profits, contrary to regulatory policies that place an obligation on incumbents to provide interconnection services regardless of the price. In this chapter, I take an initial step to fill this void by testing how retail and interconnection prices in US telecommunications affected the early development of competition in local telephone networks.[2] Using data from 1998, my main findings indicate that greater positive differences between retail prices and prices for leasing incumbents' facilities result in fewer entrants, perhaps because incumbents hinder entry to protect profits. Higher prices for exchanging traffic increase entrants' market share, presumably because they successfully target customers who receive more calls than they make. Entrants appear to resell incumbent services as part of a strategy to gain customers while building networks. Before proceeding, I summarize entry under the US Telecommunications Act of 1996 (1996 Act).

The 1996 Act made allowing competition in almost all telecommunications markets a national policy and provides three methods of entry for local telephone service. Some entrants use more than one method. Entrants can build their own facility-based network, lease portions of an incumbent's network, or buy an incumbent's services and resell them.[3] The 1996 Act places an obligation on an incumbent to provide entrants with these interconnection services. Exchanging calls between competing networks is necessary for customers of one company to

---

[1] Jamison (2002) provides a partial survey. These studies did not examine the relationship between retail and interconnection prices.

[2] Telecommunications has traditionally been divided between long distance service and local exchange service. Local exchange service in the US consists of a telephone line and calling within a local calling area, which is typically a city or town. Long distance is calling between local exchange areas. This distinction between local and long distance was based on late 1800's technological limits and the original city-by-city franchising arrangements under which the US telephone system developed. These reasons lost their relevance long ago, but the distinction has remained for regulatory purposes. The AT&T divestiture agreement of 1982 restricted the Bell Operating Companies from providing long distance service, except in limited areas (called Local Access Transport Areas, or LATAs).

[3] Traditional voice telecommunications networks consist of lines and switches. Lines either connect customers to the network or connect switches in the network. Switches route calls between customers. Switches are of two types: local switches (also called central offices) that customers connect to and that switch local calls, and long distance switches (also called tandem or toll offices) that route long distance calls from one local switch to another.

be able to call customers of another company. Payment for exchanging calls is called reciprocal compensation in the US.[4]

Leasing portions of an incumbent's network is called purchasing UNEs. For example, an entrant could lease a local telephone line from the incumbent. The line would connect to the incumbent's building. It could then connect to the incumbent's switch or the entrant's switch, depending on how the entrant wishes to use the incumbent's facilities. Entrants that have their own switches must interconnect their switches with those of an incumbent and pay reciprocal compensation for terminating telephone calls on the incumbent's network. Likewise, an incumbent must pay reciprocal compensation for terminating calls to an entrant.[5] The 1996 Act states that prices for UNEs and for reciprocal compensation are to be cost-based, which regulators have generally concluded means that they should be based on incremental cost.[6] Reselling is little more than rebranding the incumbent's service. The 1996 Act says that wholesale prices must be based upon retail prices minus the portion attributable to marketing, billing, collection, and other costs avoided by the incumbent when it does not provide the retail service. The percent discount given off of the retail price is called the wholesale discount.

The rest of this chapter is organized as follows. In section 2, I describe the hypotheses that I am testing. Section 3 describes my data and methods. Section 4 presents my findings and Section 5 is the conclusion.


## 2    THEORY AND HYPOTHESES

Assuming that entrants seek to maximize profits, I expect more entrants to seek to enter and for entrants to seek to expand their market shares in markets where regulatory policies are more favorable to entrant profits. This can be thought of in terms of an entrant demand curve for entry or interconnection services. Lower prices for UNEs and higher wholesale discounts encourage more entrants to enter and to buy more of these services. Higher prices for UNEs and lower wholesale discounts have the opposite effect. In the case of reciprocal compensation for exchanging calls, entrants are both buyers and sellers of interconnection. Some entrants are more successful at targeting customers (such as Internet Service Providers) who are net receivers of calls, making these entrants net sellers for reciprocal compensation. More of these entrants seek to enter and to expand in markets where reciprocal compensation prices are higher. Other entrants are successful in the market for customers that make calls and so either pay as much or more reciprocal compensation than they receive.

---

[4] "Reciprocal" means that both companies involved in an interconnection are obligated to make payments. "Symmetric" reciprocal compensation means the companies charge the same prices to each other. Reciprocal compensation prices are generally symmetric in the US, so I assume symmetry in my models.

[5] An exception to the payment of reciprocal compensation occurs in the case of bill and keep, the situation in which the service providers do not charge each other for exchanging traffic.

[6] This is based on a review of state commission interconnection decisions located on the National Regulatory Research Institute's web site (NRRI, 1998) for 1998, the time period for my study, the FCC and all state regulators but Arkansas determined that incumbents' prices for UNEs should be based upon incremental cost. Arkansas chose an accounting cost allocation approach called fully distributed cost as its method. Twenty-nine percent of the states also chose to base reciprocal compensation prices on incremental cost and the rest chose bill and keep. The FCC's policies allow for bill and keep, but do not mandate it. Some states that adopted bill and keep applied the policy only as long as the traffic exchange is relatively balanced.

Furthermore, the relationships between the retail prices and the prices entrants pay to incumbents affect entrant demand for interconnection services. Greater positive differences between retail prices and the prices for interconnection services that entrants purchase encourage more entrants to enter and to gain market share. The opposite holds if retail prices are lower. This conclusion should hold for UNEs and resold services for all entrants that use these services and for reciprocal compensation for entrants that are net payers. Higher retail prices and higher reciprocal compensation prices encourage more entrants that are net receivers of reciprocal compensation to enter and to increase their market share, so the effect of the relationship between retail prices and reciprocal compensation prices is ambiguous.

Interconnection prices also provide incentives to incumbents. If incumbents do not respond to these incentives, then an examination of the entrants' demand for interconnection services is adequate for predicting the effects of interconnection prices on the number of entrants and on entrant market share. If incumbents do respond, they might do so by changing the demand for their services relative to the demand for entrants' services. For example, if retail prices are higher relative to interconnection services that incumbents sell, such as UNEs and services for resale, then incumbents might respond by increasing their marketing activities or by improving the quality of their retail services relative to their interconnection services. Either response, if successful, would have the effect of decreasing the retail demand for entrants' services, which would in turn lower entrants' demand for interconnection services. Incumbents could also respond by restricting their supply of interconnection services, implying that incumbents have a supply curve for interconnection services that they provide and do not simply comply with their obligation to provide these services.[7] Incumbents might restrict supply for interconnection services by delaying negotiations with entrants, making ordering of interconnection services difficult, or by other means.

My first hypothesis (which I call H1) is that incumbents comply with their obligations to provide interconnection services. I test this hypothesis by examining the effects of incumbent marketing, incumbent service quality, and the relationship between retail prices and prices for UNEs, reciprocal compensation, and services to be resold on the number of entrants in a market, the volume of calls exchanged between incumbents and entrants, and the volume of resold services. For UNEs and reciprocal compensation, I express this relationship as the ratio of the interconnection price to the retail price. I place the UNE and reciprocal compensation prices in the numerator because in the case of Bill and Keep, the reciprocal compensation price is zero. For resale, I use the wholesale discount. I reject H1 if, controlling for incumbent marketing efforts and service quality, a lower ratio of UNE prices to retail prices or higher wholesale discounts lead to fewer entrants or smaller entrant market share.

My second hypothesis (H2) is that the volume of calls exchanged between the incumbent and entrants is primarily determined by entrants that are successful in attracting customers that are net receivers of calls. I reject H2 if higher reciprocal compensation prices result in lower volumes of exchanged calls. My third hypothesis (H3) is that most entrants are not of the type that attracts customers that are net receivers of calls. I reject H3 if higher reciprocal compensation prices result in a greater number of entrants.

Some observers express concern that entrants take advantage of large wholesale discounts to simply resell services and not build networks. (Harris and Kraft, 1997) If entrants avoid building facilities when wholesale discounts are large, then large discounts should be

---

[7] I would like to thank William Taylor for this insight.

associated with (i) a low market share for entrants using their own facilities or UNEs and (ii) higher levels of service resale. This leads to my last hypothesis (H4), which is that entrants resell services to gain customers with the intent of eventually serving those customers using UNEs or entrant facilities. I reject H4 if higher wholesale discounts increase the number of resold services and lower UNE prices have either no effect on or increase the volume of resold services.

## 3  METHODS AND DATA

I consider three types of models. The first describes the number of entrants, without distinguishing entry methods. The second describes how entrants expand their market share by constructing their own networks and using UNEs. The third describes how entrants expand their market share by reselling incumbents' services. Because my sample size is small, I use reduced form rather than structural form models. I first describe the models for number of entrants.

### 3.1  Models for Number of Entrants

I analyze entry by extending Bresnahan and Reiss's (1991) and Berry's (1992) ordered probit models for entry, which apply a zero-profit equilibrium for entrants. These models assume that markets that are more profitable for entrants attract a larger number of entrants than other markets, all other things being equal. Ordered probit models are used when dependent variables are discrete and represent ordered outcomes. Because of data restrictions, I consider each incumbent's traditional local exchange areas in a state to be a market.[8] The number of entrants ranges from 0 to 164 in these 59 markets. A large range of values in the dependent variable in an ordered probit model causes the analysis to computationally intensive. To remedy this problem, I take advantage of there being only 36 observed levels of entry – many markets have the same number of entrants (for example, five markets have four entrants each) and many levels of entry are unobserved (for example, no markets have entry levels in the 61- to 74-entrant range) – and create an ordinal variable with values from 0 to 35 that is a monotonic transformation of the observed number of entrants per market.

I control for other factors that may affect the number of entrants in a market. The 1996 Act mandates collocation, the process by which entrants locate their equipment in incumbents' buildings. Collocation can increase entry when it decreases entrants' costs of interconnection and using UNEs, relative to entrants placing their equipment some distance away from the incumbents' facilities. I control for the effects of the availability of collocation by including in

---

[8] This causes distortions because for a given incumbent, an entrant may choose to enter some of the incumbent's local exchanges and not enter others, and may choose to supply only some areas of a local exchange. Because regulators generally require incumbents to average retail prices across exchanges and to charge lower retail prices in rural areas than in urban areas, and because per customer costs are generally lower in high density, urban areas than in rural areas, I expect entrants to serve urban areas first. Therefore, regions with higher than average proportions of urban areas should have more entry than areas that are below average. To control for this effect, I include in my models a measure of customer density. Higher customer density indicates markets with higher than average proportions of urban areas.

my models the percent of the incumbent's telephone lines that can be accessed through collocation arrangements.

The 1996 Act also requires competitively neutral means for subsidizing local telephone service. Some regulators have chosen to implement this policy in part by rebalancing prices, the process by which incumbents increase some prices and decrease other prices in order to remove implicit subsidies and align prices with incremental cost. Another common method for implementing this policy is for regulators to develop a "tax" on telephone services, the monies from which are distributed to companies based on their serving customers who the regulators determine should have subsidized prices. I control for the effects of rebalancing by including in my model the ratio of the incumbent's revenues from local telephone services to its cost of providing a telephone line. Higher ratios indicate higher profits for local telephone services. Higher ratios would be associated with (i) more entry and higher market share for entrants if they are willing and able to respond to this incentive or (ii) less entry and lower market share for entrants if incumbents protect these profits. Following Ros and McDermott (2000), I test for the effects of early reforms to the subsidy system by including in my models a dummy variable that indicates whether the state regulator for the market has begun reforming these subsidies.

More entrants are expected in larger and more densely populated markets. I control for market size by including as an explanatory variable the total revenues of the incumbent company in the market. I control for customer density by including the incumbent's number of telephone lines per central office. Because competition in local networks was new at the time of this study, it is unlikely that the data represent a long-run equilibrium. I adjust for this disequilibrium by including as an explanatory variable the amount of time that has elapsed since entrants were allowed to enter each market. Lastly, I include dummy variables for incumbent telephone companies. Table 1 summarizes the explanatory variables that I include in my models for number of entrants.

Table 1. Descriptions of Explanatory Variables for Models of Number of Entrants

| Explanatory Variable | Description |
| --- | --- |
| UNE Price | The price per month for leasing a 2-wire local line in urban areas.[9] I choose local line prices to represent UNE prices because the sunk nature of line investment and the need for right-of-way and conduit space make lines the most difficult facilities for entrants to build. Two-wire lines are the most common technology used for local telephone service. I choose urban prices because I expect most entrants to serve urban areas. |
| Reciprocal Compensation Price | The price per minute for symmetric reciprocal compensation. This variable is zero in the case of bill and keep. |
| Residential Wholesale Discount | The wholesale discount regulators give entrants for buying wholesale services for residential customers. In states where discounts vary by service, I use the smallest percentage discount. |
| Lines per Central Office | The total number of billable telephone lines that the incumbent has in the market divided by the incumbents' number of central offices. This represents density. |
| Local Service Revenue to Cost Ratio | The ratio of the incumbent's local service per-line revenue to the incumbent's cost of providing a telephone line. This represents the incumbent's local service profit margin. |
| Percent of Voice Lines Assessable through Collocation | The percent of incumbent's voice telephone lines that could be accessed by entrants through collocation arrangements. This represents the ease of collocation. |
| Number of Quarters | For each market, the number of quarters prior to 1996 that the first entrant was given telephone numbers. This represents the amount of time that entrants have had to enter the market and gain market share. |
| Service Complaints in 1997 | The total number of customer complaints to state and federal regulators about the incumbent's service in 1997. This indicates the incumbent's service quality. |
| Total Revenue | The incumbent's total operating revenue for 1998. This indicates market size. |
| Ratio of UNE Price to Retail Revenue per Line | The ratio of the incumbent's UNE price to the incumbent's average retail price. |
| Ratio of Reciprocal Compensation Price to Retail Revenue per Minute | The ratio of the incumbent's price for reciprocal compensation to the incumbent's average retail revenue per minute. |
| Universal Service Reform | A dummy variable indicating whether a state has taken steps to develop competitively neutral methods for subsidizing local telephone service. A value of 1 indicates that the state has done so. |
| Marketing Expenses per Line 1997 | The ratio of Total Marketing Expenses in 1997 for regulated services to the number of billable telephone lines. I use 1997 data to ensure that the market expenses were not a response to the number of entrants in 1998. |
| Incumbent Indicators | Dummy variables that associate markets with incumbents. Incumbent dummy variables may reveal differences in how incumbents respond to entry. |

---

[9] A two-wire local line has two wires twisted together that are used to connect the customer to the telephone company central office.

## 3.2    Models for Entrant Market Share

Now consider the second and third types of models, those that describe how entrants expand their market share. I use ordinary least squares regression and examine two measures of entrant output. The first measure is the number of entrant interconnections to the incumbent. These interconnections, called trunks, are necessary for exchanging calls between entrant and incumbent customers. Higher numbers of trunks indicate higher amounts of entrant output for customers that are net receivers of calls and that are served by entrant facilities or UNEs. Trunks understate traffic exchange if the entrants are large because, as an entrant grows, the number of minutes that stay on the entrant's network generally increase. This happens because the probability of a call originating on an entrant's network also terminating on that entrant's network generally increases as the entrant attracts more customers. Trunks overstate traffic exchange if there are many small entrants, or many entrants whose customers are dispersed geographically. This happens because these entrants' low traffic volumes keep them from making efficient use of their local interconnection trunks. I do not include incumbent marketing expenses per line as an explanatory variable in the entrant interconnection models because the variable is too broad of a measure of incumbent marketing to reasonably measure incumbent marketing efforts to Internet Service Providers. My second measure of entrant supply is the proportion of business local telephone lines that are resold by entrants.

For models of entrant market share, I divide the dependent variables and certain explanatory variables by the number of incumbent telephone lines in the market. This indexes these variables according to market size. Table 2 describes the explanatory variables in my market share models that are not also in my entry models.

Table 2. Descriptions of Explanatory Variables for Market Share Models

| Explanatory Variable | Description |
| --- | --- |
| Business Wholesale Discount | The discount regulators give entrants for buying wholesale business services. In states where discounts vary by service, I use the smallest percentage discount. This variable is used in the model of resold business lines. |
| Local Revenue Per Line | The incumbent's per-line revenue from local service. |
| Service Complaints in 1998 Per Line | The total number of customer complaints to state and federal regulators about the incumbent's service in 1998 divided by the number incumbent telephone lines. |
| Total Revenue Per Line | The incumbent's total operating revenue for 1998 divided by the number of incumbent telephone lines. |
| Total Plant in Service Per Line | The net book value of the incumbent's assets in the market divided by the number of incumbent telephone lines. |
| Minutes of Use Per Line | The number of telephone minutes of use for the incumbent in 1998 divided by the number of incumbent telephone lines. |
| Central Office Total Plant in Service Per Line | The net book value of the incumbent's central office assets divided by the number of incumbent telephone lines. |

### 3.3    Data

Table 3 describes the data I use for my dependent variables, which are from the United States Telephone Association's (USTA) report to Congressman Thomas Bliley on December 9, 1998 (USTA, 1998).[10] Data are for 1998. There were no reported entrants in West Virginia in Bell Atlantic's territories in 1998, so I omit this market from the market share models. Table 4 describes the data for the explanatory variables for my entry models. Table 5 describes data for the market share model explanatory variables that are not also used in the entry models.

Table 3. Descriptions of Dependent Variables

| Variable | Name in Model | Mean | Mini-mum | Maximum | Standard Deviation | Obser-vations |
|---|---|---|---|---|---|---|
| Number of Entrants | COMPT | 13.898 | 0 | 35 | 10.22 | 59 |
| Number of Interconnec-tion Trunks | NA | 30,536.4 | 0 | 289,299 | 50,946.3 | 58 |
| Interconnection Trunks Per Line | TRNKPLN | 0.0096 | 0 | 0.0243 | 0.0066 | 58 |
| Number of Business Resold Lines | NA | 27,474.7 | 0 | 183,594 | 42,918.38 | 58 |
| Fraction Business Lines Resold | RSLBSPR | 0.0336 | 0 | 0.3303 | 0.0524 | 58 |

Data for UNE and reciprocal compensation prices and wholesale discounts are from state commissions (NRRI, 1998; Alabama, 1998), X-Change (1998-1999), and interviews with incumbents.[11] Some states have separate prices for terminating minutes at a central office or a tandem office and for different times of the day. To express these prices as a single price, I follow the convention of assuming 6.25% of the minutes terminate at local central offices and the remaining minutes terminate in a tandem. In states where residential service discounts are different from business service discounts, I use the residential discount for the models explaining number of entrants and market share using UNEs and entrant-owned facilities. Business and residential discounts are highly correlated ($R^2$ = 0.88). In tests of various models, business and residential discounts have similar results. To avoid multicollinearity, I use only the residential discount for these models.

---

[10] Observations include Ameritech (all states), Bell Atlantic (all states), BellSouth (all states), GTE (California, Florida, Hawaii, Illinois, Indiana, Kentucky, Michigan, North Carolina, Ohio, Oregon, Texas, Virginia, Washington, and Wisconsin), SBC (Arkansas, California, Oklahoma, and Texas), and US West (all states) for 1998.

[11] In cases where there are discrepancies, I employ the data provided in state commissions' decisions (NRRI, 1998) when available, and other public data when the commission data are not available.

Table 4. Descriptions of Explanatory Variables for Models of Number of Entrants

| Variable | Name in Model | Mean | Minimum | Maximum | Standard Deviation | Observations |
|---|---|---|---|---|---|---|
| UNE Price | UNEPRC | $16.82 | $3.72 | $32.00 | $6.16 | 59 |
| Reciprocal Compensation Price | RCP | $0.0057 | $0 | $0.0283 | $0.0067 | 59 |
| Residential Wholesale Discount | RESRSL | 0.1788 | 0.0700 | 0.2500 | 0.0405 | 59 |
| Incumbent Total Billable Lines | NA | 2,286,606 | 235,862 | 16,071,707 | 2,785,059 | 59 |
| Number of Incumbent Central Offices | NA | 230.1 | 29 | 752 | 174.2 | 59 |
| Lines Per Central Office | LNSPRCO | 10,424.9 | 881.1 | 29,786.8 | 6,851.7 | 59 |
| Incumbent Local Service Revenues (000) | NA | $749,773 | $71,863 | $4,731,829 | $902,587 | 59 |
| Incumbent Line Cost Level | NA | $265.72 | $65.68 | $408.81 | $57.71 | 59 |
| Local Service Revenue to Cost Ratio | LCLPUSF | 1.3290 | 0.7967 | 5.0431 | 0.5551 | 59 |
| Percent of Voice Lines Assessable through Collocation | COLCV98 | 23.66% | 0% | 72.62% | 17.54 | 59 |
| Number of Quarters | NUMQRT | 10.75 | 0 | 18 | 15.44 | 59 |
| Service Quality Complaints in 1997 | SCMPAM-97 | 274.29 | 6 | 2,637 | 466.18 | 59 |
| Total Revenue (000) | REVT | $1,511,887 | $170,463 | $8,460,236 | $1,721,406 | 59 |
| Ratio of UNE Price to Retail Revenue per Line | PRCST-UNE | 0.1969 | 0.0546 | 0.4460 | 0.0739 | 59 |
| Local Calling Minutes for Incumbent (000) | NA | 7,056,890 | 820,771 | 36,441,427 | 7,740,706 | 59 |
| Ratio of Reciprocal Compensation Price to Retail Revenue per Minute | PRCST-RCP | 0.1601 | 0 | 0.8236 | 0.1919 | 59 |
| Universal Service Reform | USFFUND | 0.2881 | 0 | 1 | 0.4568 | 59 |
| Marketing Expenses per Line in 1997 | MKTGSTS-97pl | $25.76 | $13.75 | $37.90 | $5.72 | 59 |

Table 5. Descriptions of Explanatory Variables in Market Share Models and not in Models of Number of Entrants

| Variable | Name in Model | Mean | Minmum | Maximum | Standard Devia-tion | Obser-vations |
|---|---|---|---|---|---|---|
| Business Wholesale Discount | BUSRSL | 0.1792 | 0.0800 | 0.2601 | 0.0377 | 58 |
| Local Revenue Per Line | LCLPRLN | $329.98 | $228.47 | $458.84 | $49.69 | 58 |
| Service Complaints in 1998 Per Line | SCMP98-PL | 0.00016 | 9.03 x 10-6 | 0.00097 | 0.00019 | 58 |
| Total Revenue Per Line[12] | REVTPL | $678.02 | $502.90 | $955.18 | $98.80 | 58 |
| Incumbent Total Assets (000) | NA | $4,532,754 | $493,351 | $27,585,598 | $5,118,892 | 58 |
| Total Plant in Service Per Line | TPISPL | $206.07 | $140.24 | $305.62 | $37.87 | 58 |
| Minutes of Use Per Line | MOUPL | 3,288.7 | 2,188.4 | 4,592.0 | 599.3 | 58 |
| Central Office Total Plant in Service Per Line | COTPILPL | $364.44 | $225.44 | $639.74 | $89.82 | 58 |

Data for incumbent total billable lines, number of central offices, local service revenues, service quality complaints, total revenues, local calling minutes, marketing expenses, and total plant in service are from FCC ARMIS reports.[13] I use the ratio of total revenues for basic local telephone services and total billable lines to indicate incumbents' price levels for local exchange services. Firms charge many prices, so using a single price is inappropriate. I use incumbents' Universal Service Fund costs per line reported to the FCC in 1998 to represent incumbents' costs for telephone lines.[14] I use total numbers of customer complaints to state and federal regulators for 1997 and 1998 in metropolitan statistical areas as my measure of incumbent service quality. Data for 1997 are used to examine number of entrants because these data represent ex ante entry information. Per line data for 1998 are used in models for entrant market share because these data represent the quality that customers and entrants experienced at the time supply and purchasing decisions were put into effect. I use the incumbent's total operating revenues for 1998 for the market, to indicate market size.

I use the percent of incumbent voice telephone lines accessible by entrants through colloca-tion in 1998 to represent the ease of collocation. Data are from Tables 3.6 and 3.7 of the FCC's 1998 Local Competition report. (FCC, 1998) There is a risk of endogeneity because higher entrant interest in a market should increase entrant demand for collocation. Higher demand for collocation should increase the incidence of collocation, which could cause a

---

[12] Total revenue per line, total plant in service per line, and central office total plant in service per lines are expressed as $1000 per line in the model. Minutes of use per line is expressed as 1000s of minutes per line in the model.

[13] All ARMIS data are from http://fcc.gov and were downloaded between March 1999 and December 2002.

[14] USF costs are based on incumbents' regulatory accounting records and provide an average cost for all of an incumbent's operations in a state. Regulatory costs are an imperfect measure of economic costs. The accounting processes (Gabel, 1967) and distortive efficiency incentives caused by methods of regulation (Sappington and Weisman, 1996) cause these regulatory costs to deviate from economic costs.

higher percentage of incumbent lines to be in central offices with collocation. However, differences between markets should also reflect the ease of obtaining collocation.

I use the number of quarters in a state from the time the first entrant was given telephone numbers until the 1996 Act took affect to represent the amount of time that entrants have been operating in a state. Data are from Table 4.8 of the FCC's December 1998 Local Competition report (FCC, 1998).

For the models for number of entrants, I include two price ratios, PRCSTUNE and PRCSTRCP, as explanatory variables. PRCSTUNE is the ratio of the incumbent's UNE price to the incumbent's 1998 total operating revenues. PRCSTRCP is the ratio of the incumbent's reciprocal compensation price to the incumbent's average retail revenue per minute.

I use dummy variables to indicate state efforts to reform universal service subsidies and to identify incumbents. According to a National Regulatory Research Institute survey (Rosenberg and Wilhelm, 1998), fourteen states had revised or were revising their subsidy policies in 1998. I have a dummy variable for each incumbent, but omit the Ameritech dummy from models to avoid multicollinearity.

Multicollinearity problems occur between the reciprocal compensation variables RCP and PRCSTRCP ($R^2$ = 0.97), between the service complaint variables SCMPAM97 and SCMPAM98 ($R^2$ = 0.92), among variables that indicate market size (for example, REVT and TPIS), and between PRCSTUNE and the variables that are included in it. To avoid multicollinearity in the models for number of entrants, I include no more than one variable from each of the collinear groups, with the exception of collinear groups involving PRCSTUNE and PRCSTRCP. I need these variables in some entry analyses to perform likelihood ratio tests of entrant and incumbent incentives. Regarding multicollinearity in the entrant market share models, dividing market size indicators such as REVT by LINES resolves much of the multicollinearity. Otherwise, I include in each model no more than one variable from each collinear group.

## 4    MODEL RESULTS

In this section I examine the results of my models. I examine the number-of-entrants models first. I then investigate the models for market share with respect to calls exchanged. Lastly, I examine models for resale. Tests of log linear models did not improve the overall fit, so I report only the linear results.

### 4.1    Results for Models of Number of Entrants

Table 6 provides the coefficients and t-statistics for these models. One asterisk (*) indicates significance at the 0.10 level. Two asterisks (**) indicate significance at the 0.05 level. Three asterisks (***) indicate significance at the 0.01 level. I estimate two models. Model 1 examines how UNE prices, reciprocal compensation prices, wholesale discounts, customer density, local service price-cost margins, service quality, market size, and UNE price-cost margins affect the number of entrants. The signs of coefficients can be misleading in ordered probit models, so I calculate the marginal effects of explanatory variables on each level of entry in Table 7. A negative marginal effect for a particular explanatory variable and entry level indicates that a higher value for the explanatory variable decreases the probability of a market having that level of entry. A positive marginal effect indicates that a higher value for the explanatory variable increases the probability of a market having that level of entry. For example, the marginal effects for UNE price imply that a higher UNE price would increase the probability that a market would have less entry and decrease the probability that the market would have more entry. Before reviewing the marginal effects further, I examine whether other explanatory variables should be included in entry models.

Table 6. Regression Results for Entry (COMPT)

| Explanatory Variable | Model 1 | Model 2 |
|---|---|---|
| UNE Price | *-0.1370 | *-0.1347 |
| | (-1.89) | (-1.81) |
| Reciprocal Compensation Price | **-57.4441 | -55.4438 |
| | (-1.96) | (-0.56) |
| Residential Wholesale Discount | ***12.1078 | ***12.2769 |
| | (2.85) | (2.85) |
| Lines Per Central Office | *0.0001 | 0.0001 |
| | (1.90) | (1.16) |
| Local Service Revenue to Cost Ratio | **-1.4155 | *-1.1159 |
| | (-2.49) | (-1.82) |
| Percent of Voice Line Assessable through Collocation | | 0.0147 |
| | | (1.18) |
| Number of Quarters | | -0.0164 |
| | | (-0.31) |
| Service Quality Complaints in 1997 | **-0.0010 | **-0.0011 |
| | (-2.01) | (-2.04) |
| Total Revenue | ***1.25e-06 | ***1.35e-06 |
| | (4.88) | (4.99) |
| Ratio of UNE Price to Retail Revenue per Lines | *10.9565 | 8.8917 |
| | (1.86) | (1.45) |
| Ratio of Reciprocal Compensation Price to Retail Revenue per Minute | | 0.4409 |
| | | (0.12) |
| Universal Service Reform | 0.4581 | 0.4967 |
| | (1.15) | (1.23) |
| Marketing Expenses per Line in 1997 | 0.0087 | -0.0083 |
| | (0.27) | (-0.23) |
| GTE dummy variable | | 0.3410 |
| | | (0.41) |
| Bell Atlantic dummy variable | *0.9818 | **1.2968 |
| | (1.84) | (1.98) |
| BellSouth dummy variable | ***2.2178 | ***2.6699 |
| | (3.77) | (3.35) |
| SBC dummy variable | ***3.6751 | ***4.1259 |
| | (4.22) | (3.93) |
| US West dummy variable | | 0.9301 |
| | | (1.13) |
| $\chi^2$ | 107.77 | 109.52 |
| | d.f. = 15 | d.f. = 18 |
| Log Likelihood | -147.7770 | -146.9014 |

Model 2 in Table 6 provides the results of adding other variables to Model 1. Using a likelihood-ratio test, I fail to reject at the 0.10 level the joint hypothesis that the coefficients for these variables are all zero ($\chi^2(3) = 1.75$). I conclude that Model 1 is the most appropriate model for examining how regulatory policies affect entry decisions.

The marginal effects in Table 7 show that there is less entry if the ratio of UNE prices to retail revenue per line is lower, so I reject H1. This result implies that incumbents do not simply comply with their obligations to provide interconnection services to entrants, at least to the extent that these services affect the number of entrants. The marginal effects also show that entry is lower if UNE prices are higher, wholesale discounts are lower, and incumbent ratios of local service revenue to cost are higher, which supports my conclusion that incumbents have a supply curve for interconnection services. The marginal effects also show that there is less entry if reciprocal compensation is higher, so I fail to reject H3 and conclude that most entrants are net payers of reciprocal compensation. Universal service reform and incumbent marketing have no significant effects on entry.

## 4.2    Entrant Market Share Model Results

Tables 8 and 9 provide the results for the entrant market share models. Model 3 in Table 8 shows the results of including most of the explanatory variables in a model for number of interconnection trunks. This model forms the basis for testing hypotheses. Using an F-test, I fail to reject the hypothesis at the 0.10 level that coefficients for the ratio of UNE prices to incumbent retail revenue per line, incumbent local revenue per line, universal service reform, and the GTE, BellSouth, and US West dummy variables are equal to zero ($F(7, 38) = 0.41$). Model 4 shows the Model 3 with these variables. This F-test does not form a basis for rejecting H1, but H1 is already rejected based on the results of Model 1. This difference in model results implies that incumbents may not hinder entrants from gaining market share for customers that are net receivers of calls. The coefficient for reciprocal compensation prices is positive and significant, so I fail to reject H2, that the volume of calls exchanged between incumbents and entrants is largely determined by the calls received by entrants who are successful in attracting customers who are net receivers of calls. Taken together, the analysis of H1 and H2 may explain why incumbents asked regulators to prohibit entrants from receiving reciprocal compensation for terminating calls to Internet Service Providers; i.e., it may be that incumbents were unsuccessful in targeting Internet Service Providers as customers and so sought to prevent entrants from benefiting from their successful marketing to Internet Service Providers.

**Table 7. Marginal Effects for Model 1**

| Entry Level | UNE Price | Reciprocal Compensation Price | Residential Wholesale Discount | Local Service Revenue to Cost Ratio | Service Quality Complaints in 1997 | Ratio of UNE Price to Retail Revenue per Lines | Universal Service Reform | Marketing Expenses per Line in 1997 |
|---|---|---|---|---|---|---|---|---|
| | | | | *Selected Explanatory Variables* | | | | |
| 0 | 0.0002079 | 0.08714273 | -0.0183675 | 0.00214736 | 1.55371E-06 | -0.0166211 | -0.000695 | -1.324E-05 |
| 1 | -0.0002026 | -0.0849369 | 0.01790258 | -0.002093 | -1.51438E-06 | 0.01620034 | 0.00067742 | 1.2901E-05 |
| 2 | 0.00019417 | 0.08138683 | -0.0171543 | 0.00200552 | 1.45109E-06 | -0.0155232 | -0.0006491 | -1.236E-05 |
| 3 | 0.00047191 | 0.19780883 | -0.0416932 | 0.00487438 | 3.52683E-06 | -0.0377288 | -0.0015776 | -3.005E-05 |
| 4 | 0.00111252 | 0.46632562 | -0.0982898 | 0.01149114 | 8.31435E-06 | -0.0889441 | -0.0037192 | -7.083E-05 |
| 5 | 0.00525195 | 2.20141952 | -0.4640044 | 0.05424711 | 3.92502E-05 | -0.4198853 | -0.0175575 | -0.0003344 |
| 6 | 0.00372893 | 1.56302578 | -0.3294469 | 0.03851589 | 2.7868E-05 | -0.298122 | -0.0124659 | -0.0002374 |
| 7 | 0.00704959 | 2.95491979 | -0.6228235 | 0.07281477 | 5.26847E-05 | -0.5636033 | -0.023567 | -0.0004488 |
| 8 | 0.0027985 | 1.17302616 | -0.2472447 | 0.02890557 | 2.09145E-05 | -0.2237358 | -0.0093555 | -0.0001782 |
| 9 | 0.00332454 | 1.39351967 | -0.2937192 | 0.03433894 | 2.48458E-05 | -0.2657914 | -0.011114 | -0.0002117 |
| 10 | 0.00388077 | 1.62667387 | -0.3428623 | 0.0400843 | 2.90028E-05 | -0.3102618 | -0.0129736 | -0.0002471 |
| 11 | 0.00409192 | 1.71517802 | -0.3615168 | 0.04226521 | 3.05808E-05 | -0.3271426 | -0.0136794 | -0.0002605 |
| 12 | 0.00387262 | 1.62325594 | -0.3421419 | 0.04000007 | 2.89418E-05 | -0.3096099 | -0.0129463 | -0.0002466 |
| 13 | 0.00359386 | 1.50640886 | -0.3175135 | 0.03712074 | 2.68585E-05 | -0.2873232 | -0.0120144 | -0.0002288 |
| 14 | 0.00943033 | 3.95283904 | -0.83316 | 0.09740538 | 7.04771E-05 | -0.7539403 | -0.0315259 | -0.0006004 |
| 15 | 0.00231213 | 0.96915698 | -0.2042742 | 0.02388185 | 1.72796E-05 | -0.1848511 | -0.0077295 | -0.0001472 |
| 16 | 0.00351692 | 1.47415973 | -0.3107162 | 0.03632606 | 2.62835E-05 | -0.2811722 | -0.0117572 | -0.0002239 |
| 17 | -0.0032167 | -1.3483284 | 0.28419405 | -0.0332253 | -2.404E-05 | 0.25717191 | 0.01075361 | 0.0002048 |
| 18 | -0.0060902 | -2.5527707 | 0.5380605 | -0.0629051 | -4.55146E-05 | 0.48689987 | 0.02035966 | 0.00038775 |
| 19 | -0.0035091 | -1.4708912 | 0.31002723 | -0.0362455 | -2.62253E-05 | 0.28054878 | 0.01173111 | 0.00022342 |
| 20 | -0.0084286 | -3.5329685 | 0.74466178 | -0.087059 | -6.29911E-05 | 0.67385679 | 0.02817724 | 0.00053663 |
| 21 | -0.0088631 | -3.7150951 | 0.78304952 | -0.0915469 | -6.62383E-05 | 0.7085945 | 0.02962979 | 0.00056429 |
| 22 | -0.0044362 | -1.8594891 | 0.39193401 | -0.0458213 | -3.31538E-05 | 0.35466758 | 0.01483038 | 0.00028244 |
| 23 | -0.0042759 | -1.792314 | 0.37777516 | -0.044166 | -3.19561E-05 | 0.341855 | 0.01429463 | 0.00027224 |
| 24 | -0.0037688 | -1.579742 | 0.33297028 | -0.0389278 | -2.8166E-05 | 0.30131033 | 0.01259926 | 0.00023995 |
| 25 | -0.0033006 | -1.3834727 | 0.29160159 | -0.0340914 | -2.46666E-05 | 0.26387512 | 0.01103391 | 0.00021014 |
| 26 | -0.0030118 | -1.2624322 | 0.26608927 | -0.0311087 | -2.25085E-05 | 0.24078859 | 0.01006855 | 0.00019175 |
| 27 | -0.0027359 | -1.1467857 | 0.24171387 | -0.028259 | -2.04466E-05 | 0.21873089 | 0.00914621 | 0.00017419 |
| 28 | -0.0015836 | -0.6637898 | 0.13991036 | -0.016357 | -1.1835E-05 | 0.1266072 | 0.00529406 | 0.00010082 |
| 29 | -0.000658 | -0.275795 | 0.05813071 | -0.0067961 | -4.91729E-06 | 0.05260344 | 0.00219961 | 4.1891E-05 |
| 30 | -0.0003601 | -0.1509229 | 0.0318108 | -0.003719 | -2.69088E-06 | 0.02878612 | 0.00120369 | 2.2924E-05 |
| 31 | -0.0002909 | -0.1219366 | 0.02570121 | -0.0030047 | -2.17407E-06 | 0.02325745 | 0.00097251 | 1.8521E-05 |
| 32 | -0.0001047 | -0.0438816 | 0.00924914 | -0.0010813 | -7.82386E-07 | 0.0083697 | 0.00034998 | 6.6653E-06 |
| 33 | -1.657E-06 | -0.0006947 | 0.00014643 | -1.712E-05 | -1.23862E-08 | 0.0001325 | 5.5406E-06 | 1.0552E-07 |
| 34 | -8.812E-10 | -3.694E-07 | 7.7853E-08 | -9.102E-09 | -6.58561E-12 | 7.0451E-08 | 2.9459E-09 | 5.6104E-11 |
| 35 | -7.962E-20 | -3.338E-17 | 7.0346E-18 | -8.224E-19 | -5.9506E-22 | 6.3657E-18 | 2.6618E-19 | 5.0694E-21 |

Table 8. Regression Results for Entrants Using UNEs and Facilities (TRNKPLN)

| Explanatory Variable | Model 3 | Model 4 |
|---|---|---|
| UNE Price | -0.0002 | -0.0002 |
|  | (-1.25) | (-1.47) |
| Reciprocal Compensation Price | *0.1966 | *0.2158 |
|  | (1.92) | (1.77) |
| Residential Wholesale Discount |  | 0.0134 |
|  |  | (0.79) |
| Local Revenue Per Line |  | 0.00002 |
|  |  | (0.81) |
| Percent of Voice Lines Assessable | ***0.0002 | ***0.0002 |
| through Collocation | (3.79) | (3.22) |
| Number of Quarters | ***0.0006 | ***0.0006 |
|  | (3.36) | (2.69) |
| Service Complaints in 1998 Per Line | **7.4731 | 7.2727 |
|  | (2.02) | (1.65) |
| Total Revenue Per Line | **0.0350 | 0.0303 |
|  | (2.55) | (1.56) |
| Total Plant in Service Per Line | **-0.0079 | *-0.0083 |
|  | (-2.19) | (-1.76) |
| Minutes of Use Per Line | ***0.0043 | **0.0037 |
|  | (2.95) | (2.10) |
| Central Office Total Plant in Service | ***0.0416 | *0.0338 |
| Per Line | (3.05) | (1.85) |
| Universal Service Reform |  | 0.0007 |
|  |  | (0.37) |
| Ratio of UNE Price to Retail Revenue |  | 0.0036 |
| per Lines |  | (0.36) |
| Central Offices per Line[15] | ***-14.6356 | **-11.6152 |
|  | (-3.48) | (-2.18) |
| GTE dummy variable |  | 0.0033 |
|  |  | (0.68) |
| Bell Atlantic dummy variable | ***-0.0071 | -0.0049 |
|  | (-3.68) | (-1.36) |
| BellSouth dummy variable |  | 0.0024 |
|  |  | (0.62) |
| SBC dummy variable | **0.0055 | *0.0063 |
|  | (2.21) | (1.92) |
| US West dummy variable |  | 0.0027 |
|  |  | (0.61) |
| Constant | ***-0.0337 | ***-0.0358 |
|  | (-4.26) | (-4.01) |
| F | 7.57 | 4.49 |
|  | d.f. = 12, 45 | d.f. = 19, 38 |
| $R^2$ | 0.6688 | 0.6919 |

---

[15] This is the inverse of the explanatory variable Lines per Central Office. I use the inverse for convenience.

Table 9 shows the results for entrant market share using resold business services. Model 5 forms the basis for testing hypotheses. The coefficient for the business wholesale discount is insignificant and the coefficient for UNE prices is negative and significant, so I fail to reject H4, that entrants resell incumbent services to gain customers with the intent of eventually serving these customers using UNEs or entrant facilities. This conclusion is further supported by the coefficient for the percent of lines that are assessable through collocation. This coefficient is negative and significant, indicating that entrants use fewer resold lines if they can use collocation to interconnect their facilities with incumbent facilities. The results from Model 5 support the rejection of H1 – the coefficient for business wholesale discount is insignificant, which is counter to the incentive the discount provides to entrants. Incumbent marketing does not appear to affect entrant market share from resold business lines and, as one would expect, lower incumbent service quality causes entrants to resell fewer business lines.

Model 6 shows the effects of including additional incumbent dummy variables. Using an F-statistic, I fail to reject at the 0.10 level the null hypothesis that the coefficients for these variables are zero ($F(4, 38) = 0.52$).

## 5  CONCLUSION

This chapter shows that incumbents are able to hinder entry in newly opened markets when incumbents' profit margins for inputs sold to entrants are lower than incumbents' retail profit margins. This confirms the theories of Shepherd (1997), Noll (1995), Gulati et al. (2000), and Ordover et al. (1985). I do not find evidence that incumbents in local telephone markets have limited entrants' abilities to gain market share for serving customers that are net receivers of calls, such as Internet Service Providers. I find that most entrants are not of the type entrant that serves primarily customers who are net receivers of calls. Lastly, I find that entrants resell business lines to gain market share with the intent of eventually serving its customers using UNEs or entrant facilities.

Table 9. Regression Results for Resold Business Lines (RSLDBPLN)

| Explanatory Variable | Model 5 | Model 6 |
|---|---|---|
| UNE Price | ***-0.0012 | **-0.0010 |
|  | (-2.70) | (-2.02) |
| Reciprocal Compensation Price | 0.3115 | 0.2506 |
|  | (0.88) | (0.64) |
| Business Wholesale Discount | 0.0278 | 0.0234 |
|  | (0.55) | (0.43) |
| Local Revenue Per Line | 0.0001 | 0.00004 |
|  | (1.67) | (0.56) |
| Percent of Voice Lines Assessable | **-0.0003 | **-0.0004 |
| through Collocation | (-2.04) | (-2.27) |
| Number of Quarters | 0.0007 | 0.0011 |
|  | (1.19) | (1.65) |
| Service Complaints in 1998 Per | *-24.4591 | *-24.2993 |
| Line | (-1.85) | (-1.78) |
| Total Revenue Per Line | **-0.1208 | *-0.0997 |
|  | (-2.45) | (-1.71) |
| Total Plant in Service Per Line | 0.0141 | 0.0096 |
|  | (1.16) | (0.70) |
| Minutes of Use Per Line | -0.0029 | -0.0020 |
|  | (-0.74) | (-0.04) |
| Central Office Total Plant in | -0.0299 | 0.0271 |
| Service Per Line | (-0.71) | (0.46) |
| Universal Service Reform | **-0.0120 | **-0.0123 |
|  | (-2.47) | (-2.29) |
| Marketing Expenses per Line in | 0.0007 | 0.0006 |
| 1997 | (1.47) | (1.10) |
| Central Offices per Line | 15.8692 | 11.2574 |
|  | (1.07) | (0.67) |
| GTE dummy variable |  | -0.0179 |
|  |  | (-1.24) |
| Bell Atlantic dummy variable |  | -0.0092 |
|  |  | (-0.86) |
| BellSouth dummy variable |  | -0.0046 |
|  |  | (-0.41) |
| SBC dummy variable |  | -0.0003 |
|  |  | (-0.02) |
| US West dummy variable | ***0.0256 | 0.0171 |
|  | (3.40) | (1.38) |
| Constant | *0.0474 | 0.0367 |
|  | (1.94) | (1.37) |
| F | 3.31 | 2.61 |
|  | d.f. = 15, 42 | d.f. = 19, 38 |
| $R^2$ | 0.5421 | 0.5660 |

## 6   REFERENCES

Alabama Public Service Commission (1998), *Order In the Matter of Generic Proceedings: Consideration of TELRIC Studies*, Docket No. 26029, August 25.

Baumol, W. J. (1983), "Some Subtle Pricing Issues in Railroad Regulation," *International Journal of Transportation Economics*, Vol. 10, pp. 341-355.

Berry, S. T. (1992), "Estimation of a Model of Entry in the Airline Industry," *Econometrica*, Vol. 60, pp. 889-917.

Bresnahan, T. F., and Reiss, P. C. (1991), "Entry and Competition in Concentrated Markets," *Journal of Political Economy*, Vol. 99, pp. 977-1009.

Economides, N., and White, L. J. (1995), "Access and Interconnection Pricing: How Efficient is the 'Efficient Component Pricing Rule?'" *Antitrust Bulletin*, Vol. 40, pp. 557-579.

Federal Communications Commission (1998), "Local Competition," Report by the Industry Analysis Division, Common Carrier Bureau.

Gabel, R. (1967), Development of Separations Principles in the Telephone Industry, East Lansing, Michigan: Institute of Public Utilities, Michigan State University.

Gulati, R., Nohria, N., and Zaheer, A. (2000), "Strategic Networks," *Strategic Management Journal*, Vol. 21, pp. 203-217.

Harris, R. G., and Kraft, C. J. (1997), "Meddling Through: Regulating Local Telephone Competition in the United States," *The Journal of Economic Perspectives*, Vol. 11, pp. 93-112.

Jamison, M. A. (2002), "Competition in Networking: Research Results and Implications for Further Reform," *The Law Review of Michigan State University Detroit College of Law*, Vol. 2002, pp. 621-640.

Kahn, A. E., and Taylor, W. E. (1994), "The Pricing of Inputs Sold to Competitors: A Comment," *Yale Journal on Regulation*, Vol. 11, pp. 225-240.

Katz, M. L. (1997), "Economic Efficiency, Public Policy, and the Pricing of Network Interconnection Under the Telecommunications Act of 1996," In G. L. Rosston and D. Waterman, eds., *Interconnection and the Internet: Selected Papers from the 1996 Telecommunications Policy Research Conference*, Mahway, New Jersey: Erlbaum Associates Publishing.

Kende, M. (2000), "The Digital Handshake: Connecting Internet Backbones," *Mimeo*, Office of Plans and Policy, Federal Communications Commission.

National Regulatory Research Institute, Interconnection Arbitration Decisions, <http://www.nrri.ohio-state.edu/interconnect.html>, downloaded September - December 1998.

Noll, R. G. (1995), "The Role of Antitrust in Telecommunications," *Antitrust Bulletin*, Vol. 40, pp. 501-528.

Ordover, J. A., Sykes, A. O., and Willig, R. D. (1985), "Nonprice Anticompetitive Behavior by Dominant Firms toward the Producers of Complementary Products," in F. M. Fisher, ed., *Antitrust and Regulation: Essays in Memory of John J. McGowan*, Cambridge, Massachusetts: MIT Press.

Ros, A. J., and McDermott , K. (2000), "Are Residential Local Exchange Prices Too Low? Drivers of Competition in the Local Exchange Market and the Impact of Inefficiently-Set Prices," in M. Crew, ed., *Expanding Competition in Regulated Industries*, Boston: Kluwer Academic Press.

Rosston, G. L., and Wimmer, B. S. (2000), "From C to Shining C: Competition and Cross-Subsidy in Communications," *Mimeo*, Stanford Institute for Economic Policy Research, Stanford University.

Sappington, D. E. M., and Weisman, D. L. (1996), *Designing Incentive Regulation for the Telecommunications Industry*, Cambridge, Massachusetts: MIT Press.

Shepherd, W. G. (1997), "Dim Prospects: Effective Competition in Telecommunications, Railroads, and Electricity," *Antitrust Bulletin*, Vol. 42, pp. 151-175.

United States Telephone Association (1998), Report to House Commerce Committee Chairman Thomas Bliley.

Willig, R. D. (1979), "The Theory of Network Access Pricing," in H. M. Trebing, ed., *Issues in Public Utility Regulation*, Proceedings of the Institute of Public Utilities Tenth Annual Conference, East Lansing, MI: Division of Research, Graduate School of Business Administration, Michigan State University.

X-Change (1998-1999), "Status of State Local Competition Proceedings," *X-Change.*

Global Economy and Digital Society
E. Bohlin, S. Levin, N. Sung and C-H. Yoon (Editors)

CHAPTER 17

# Rationalizing Interconnection Arrangements in Competitive Communications Markets

Mark Kolesar
*Regulatory and Public Policy,*
*TELUS Communications, Calgary*

Stanford L. Levin*
*Department of Economics and Finance,*
*Southern Illinois University Edwardsville, Edwardsville*

**Abstract**. This chapter examines interconnection and unbundling policies that will be required for packet networks. The paper explores these policies both for the case where packet networks interconnect and for the case where packet networks interconnect with circuit-switched networks. Required regulations are identified both for end-state packet networks and for the transition period, and the negative consequences of alternative regulatory approaches that depart from the preferred regulations are brought to light.

## 1 INTRODUCTION

Communications networks are evolving from circuit-switched networks to packet networks. Current regulation, however, generally addresses only the circuit-switched model, even though it is widely recognized that changes will be required in a world of packet networks. The purpose of this paper is to explore what an end-state next generation packet network will probably look like and, consequently, the regulatory policies that will be required for interconnection and unbundling. While this paper is written in the context of North American networks and regulation, there are obvious similarities and implications for the rest of the world as well.

The paper begins by examining a principled approach to interconnection and unbundling for circuit-switched networks. This provides a starting point for the issues of interconnection and unbundling for packet networks. This is followed by a brief overview of packet networks, with some discussion of one type of packet network, the Internet. Next, interconnection and unbundling requirements and the regulation of packet networks are discussed, followed by some comments on the transition from an environment of predominantly circuit-switched

---

* This paper was developed with the assistance of Andre Jerome, General Counsel –Regulatory, Cesky Mobil a.s. OSKAR, Prague, Czech Republic.

networks to one that is predominantly made up of packet networks. Finally, some conclusions are offered.

## 2  BACKGROUND

While many traditional telephone companies have a next generation packet network in development, other carriers have already begun to provide communications services, including voice, over packet networks. These packet networks present an entirely new challenge to the current interconnection and unbundling arrangements, all of which are based on circuit-switched concepts. Consequently, interconnection and unbundling rules developed for circuit-switched networks may need to be re-examined for packet networks.

Because of the fundamental differences between circuit-switched and packet networks, imposing circuit-switched rules for interconnection and unbundling on packet networks may not be workable or sustainable. Attempting to do so may only serve to hinder the development of packet networks and efficient, market-based solutions to consumers' communications needs. More importantly, imposing the wrong rules on packet networks may have a chilling effect on the development of facilities-based competition, particularly for local exchange telephone service. This is because facilities-based competition for local exchange service is likely to arise from companies, including cable television companies and companies with data networks, that will use packet networks to provide voice service. Adverse regulatory rules for packet networks will hinder such investments, harming the emergence of additional facilities-based competition in the local exchange market.

Regulators and policy makers, therefore, need to carefully examine the following three issues.

- What are the fundamental economic principles on which interconnection and unbundling policies are to be based? What are the conditions that will ensure competitive parity and symmetrical regulation for all communications service providers, so that the outcome of competition among them will be exclusively determined by their comparative efficiencies?

- What are the terms, conditions, and pricing of the minimum mandated interconnection arrangements among all suppliers of communications services in order to ensure sustainability, efficiency, and full connectivity to all subscribers? Are these minimum requirements different in a circuit-switched environment than in a packet environment?

- What are the conditions under which network element unbundling should be mandated? Are these minimum conditions different in a circuit-switched environment than in a packet environment?

The outcome of such an exercise, and the rules adopted thereafter, will survive the technological evolutions in the network, as these determinations will be based on sound, basic principles that will provide the telecommunications industry with clear guidelines and expectations upon which market participants can develop their business plans. However, the resolution of these issues should be done in a manner that will not dictate how the industry will evolve nor which services will be provided by whom or using which technologies. Rather, in the words of Alfred E. Kahn (1996, p. 6), "the purpose instead is to establish a framework consistent with principles of efficient competition under which the *market* can be relied upon to determine those outcomes over time."

David Teece (1995, para. 57-8) provides a related warning:

> …good regulatory policy can promote the right kind of competition, that which responds to real market demands and reflects real economic efficiencies. Regulators should avoid policies that stimulate artificial competition wherein participants exploit regulatory distortions and arbitrage uneconomic pricing schemes.
>
> …Therefore, regulatory policies should be competitively neutral. Policies that treat competitors differently can bias customers' choices and distort entry and investment decisions. Policies should provide competitors with an opportunity to compete but should not attempt to guarantee their success. Policies should promote and protect competition, not protect competitors from competition.

## 3   INTERCONNECTION FOR CIRCUIT-SWITCHED NETWORKS

As a basis for developing interconnection rules for packet networks, it is helpful to understand the issues surrounding interconnection for circuit-switched networks. The advent of competition raises the issue of interconnection among networks in order to permit any customer from any network to call all customers on all other networks. Without such mandatory interconnection, some networks might refuse to accept calls from another network, and some customers would not be able to call all other customers connected to the public switched telephone network (PSTN). It would be particularly likely that larger networks would refuse to interconnect with smaller networks, abusing their market power and inhibiting competition. There seems to be no serious debate around the need for networks to interconnect; only the terms and conditions of such interconnection arrangements remain contentious.

The regulatory rules governing interconnection must be based on sound economic principles. As stated by Laffont and Tirole (1999, p. 8), "Regardless of the exact mode of entry, the various networks will need to interconnect to have access to their mutual bottlenecks, namely, the final access to the consumer." Interconnection should, therefore, only be mandated when and where there is a network bottleneck. In practice, on a circuit-switched network, bottlenecks will only be present at the local switch providing customers with connectivity to the network via a local loop. Consequently, mandated interconnection should only take place at this bottleneck, because it represents the last technically feasible interconnection point on the network required to complete a call to the terminating customer.[1]

On a circuit-switched network, the termination point of the customer's local loop at the local switch is the only genuine bottleneck. This is because once a customer selects a service provider and receives a telephone number, the only way this customer can be reached is by using that telephone number to send calls over that local loop. Control over access to the local loop gives the customer's service provider market power by virtue of controlling access to the customer. This necessitates mandated interconnection, which is, in this case, nothing more than call termination, at a price that will most likely need to be regulated.[2]

---

[1] Many countries, including the U. S., provide for mandatory interconnection at points other than the last technically feasible point on the network. They do so at some risk to facilities-based competition, as is explained later in the paper, not to mention the issue of equity to the LEC that is required to modify its network to provide such interconnection.

[2] Of course, service providers may voluntarily reach other arrangements. The interconnection arrangements outlined here are those that the regulator insures as a minimum standard of interconnection.

The service provider originating a telephone call has the obligation (and a variety of means) to transport the call and to deliver it to the local access switch of the called party's local access provider, or to make arrangements for such delivery. Interconnection regulation need only insure that the service provider of the customer receiving the call will terminate it. Although carriers should be free to negotiate alternative terms and conditions for interconnection with the called party's local access provider, regulatorily mandated terms and conditions must be provided, absent such a commercially negotiated interconnection agreement, in order to prevent the abuse of market power and to ensure full connectivity to all subscribers.[3]

Setting the mandated point of interconnection at the last feasible point in the network (the call termination bottleneck), rather than at any technically feasible point, minimizes the functionality that must be unbundled, maximizes the functionality that is competitively provided, and gives freedom to carriers to negotiate economically efficient and mutually beneficial alternative interconnection arrangements.[4]    Mandated network interconnection arrangements should also be technically reciprocal and efficiently provided, given time and space constraints and available technologies, subject to ensuring customer service quality on the PSTN. It is a common fallacy to assume that smaller players do not have market power with regards to call termination and therefore should not be required to reciprocate on the terms and conditions of interconnection. Indeed, any terminating carrier has market power, as they exercise control over the bottleneck providing access to their customers for the call termination function.

It is an important and fundamental characteristic of circuit-switched architectures that the originating customer's carrier is responsible for setting up an end-to-end circuit for delivering the originating customer's call to the terminating customer. In so doing, the originating customer's carrier provides for the means (and bears the cost of providing for the means) by which the terminating customer will send messages back to the originating customer.[5] As will be explained later, this is a different state of affairs than in a pure packet environment, where the originating and terminating service providers' obligations differ from those of service providers using circuit-switched architectures.

---

[3] It may be that in a fully competitive market there will be sufficient incentive for carriers not to exercise market power over call termination and to negotiate interconnection arrangements, thereby making regulated interconnection arrangements unnecessary.

[4] A discussion of the anti-competitive effects of unbundling non-essential facilities, such as would result from a policy mandating interconnection at any technically feasible point on the network, can be found in the next section of the paper. Many countries, including the U. S., have adopted the "interconnect at any technically feasible point" approach, and they are not immune from the negative consequences of such a policy.

[5] Interconnection, traffic sharing, and transiting agreements among carriers in the PSTN recognize, at least implicitly, this characteristic of a circuit-switched architecture.

## 4    UNBUNDLING FOR CIRCUIT-SWITCHED NETWORKS

The essential facilities doctrine dictates that the mandatory unbundling of network elements should only be undertaken when those elements exhibit the characteristics of an essential facility. A network component is an essential facility if it is (1) controlled by a monopoly provider, (2) necessary for the provision of service, and (3) not technically or economically feasible to duplicate. Only network elements that are essential facilities should be subject to mandated unbundling.

The consequences of mandating the unbundling of non-essential facilities on the incumbent's incentive to invest in maintaining and upgrading such facilities are significant. This negative effect has been well documented (see, for example, Kahn, 1998, Sidak and Spulber, 1997, and Harris and Kraft, 1997). For example, Jenny Brannan points out that "open access requirements discourage firms from risky and costly investments because they fear that they will not reap the economic benefits normally associated with risk-taking."[6] This reasoning was also adopted by U. S. Supreme Court Justice Breyer in the Iowa Utilities Board case when he stated that "a sharing requirement may diminish the original owner's incentive to keep up or to improve the property by depriving the owner of the fruits of value-creating investment, research or labor."[7]

Any rule requiring incumbent companies to share their investments in new or existing facilities, outside of what is necessary to ensure reasonable and nondiscriminatory access to facilities that are truly essential, will necessarily curtail the incentives to make these investments in the first place. There is no middle ground in competition or antitrust law; either the facility is essential, in which case it should be unbundled, or it is not, in which case there is no rationale for mandating its sharing.

A broad mandated unbundling policy, and more particularly a policy that would mandate the unbundling of non-essential facilities, also has some detrimental effects on new entrants' incentives to invest. Soma, Forkner, and Jumps (1998) noted that open access requirements encourage firms to refrain from significant investment because they anticipate the ability to utilize the investment of their competitors. Also as pointed out by Jorde, Sidak and Teece (2000, p. 14), "mandatory unbundling . . . is the equivalent to the government's grant to the CLEC of a *free option* to consume, at incremental cost, the fruits of the ILEC's investment." Of course, this option will be exercised each time the short-term cost of providing the service over the CLEC's own facilities exceeds the cost of leasing the facility from the incumbent. Indeed, even if the CLEC's investment in its own facilities has a higher net present value, many CLECs may still prefer to use the incumbents' networks as a means to avoid the risks associated with making a sunk capital investment, given the rapid technological advances witnessed in the industry.

A policy of mandating interconnection at any technically feasible point on the network is nothing other than a policy to unbundle all network elements, whether or not they are essential facilities. For example, if a carrier avails itself of permitted mandatory interconnection at a tandem switch instead of the local switch providing access to the bottleneck, that is equivalent to the mandatory unbundling of the transportation service between the tandem switch and the local switch. When such transport is not an essential facility, as it is not likely to be, such a

---

[6] Jenny Brannan, "Open Broadband Access: An Essential Facility Doctrine Analysis," at http://www.ku.edu/~cybermom/CLJ/brannan/Broadband.htm.

[7] AT&T Corp. v. Iowa Utilities Board, 119 S.Ct. 721,753 L.Ed.2d (1999).

policy leaves the door open to all of the inefficiencies resulting from the mandatory unbundling of non-essential facilities.

Such a policy of limiting mandatory unbundling to essential facilities does not mean that entrants must duplicate the entire network of the incumbent, however. A particular entrant has the option of choosing where it provides service, and it can avoid areas where costs are unusually high. Because the remaining, non-unbundled parts of the incumbent's network are not essential facilities, not only can they be economically and technically duplicated by the entrant, they may also be available from other companies that have invested in such facilities. Finally, just because the incumbent is not mandated to unbundle portions of its network does not mean that it will not do so voluntarily, when a good business case can be made. Avoiding the mandatory unbundling of non-essential facilities, however, will avoid the inefficiencies and perverse incentives described, while at the same time providing reasonable entry options to efficient competitors.

## 5    PRICING OF INTERCONNECTION AND UNBUNDLING FOR CIRCUIT-SWITCHED NETWORKS

Voluntary interconnection and unbundling arrangements should be priced at unregulated, commercially negotiated rates. However, the rates charged for any mandated interconnection and unbundled network elements will need to be regulated. Such prices should be based on marginal or incremental cost rather than average or historical cost (Kahn, 1998) and should include an approved mark-up to recover a portion of shared and common costs (Laffont and Tirole, 1999). Indeed, as noted by Kahn (1998, p. 110), incorporating "a mark-up in access charges...(or charges to CLECs for unbundled elements) equivalent to the mark-up incorporated in the corresponding retail rates of the ILECs is not just *compatible* with efficient competition in the affected retail markets but *necessary* to ensure it is efficient."

For mandated interconnection, fees should exclude the cost of the local loop and include only the portion of costs directly causal to receiving the call from the originating carrier, determining where it must terminate, and switching it to the appropriate location. Indeed, the cost of the loop itself should be borne by the receiving customer and included in the customer's local access charge, in order for the customer to fully internalize the cost of the type of loop chosen by him, be it a traditional copper loop, broadband fiber, or a wireless loop.

Such interconnection costs are most likely very small and largely composed of fixed costs. It is possible that these costs are now (or will be in the near future) so small as to render attempts to measure, monitor and track traffic for billing purposes financially non-viable. Indeed, it is very likely that the cost of call termination is so small, or will become so small as technology evolves, that the cost of measuring the traffic for billing purposes would be greater than the actual interconnection cost incurred. In this case, it may be that call termination should be free or that carriers should have the option of not charging for it.

## 6    NEXT GENERATION PACKET NETWORKS

Circuit-switched networks were primarily designed to carry voice traffic. However, the emergence of high-speed data communications is now the primary driver of traffic growth on today's networks. The volume of data traffic is now greater than voice traffic, and industry projections are that within the next few years voice will account for a very small portion of total traffic. According to a draft report for the Asia-Pacific Economic Cooperation (APEC) Ministerial Meeting on Telecommunications and Information Industry (APEC Telecommunications Working Group, para. 2.1.6), "data traffic, primarily Internet Protocol traffic, is already more than half of global telecommunication traffic and would comprise 95% of global traffic within four years." Circuit-switched networks are not well suited to an environment in which most of the traffic is data.

Meanwhile, new packet technology has enabled the consolidation of traditionally disparate data and voice networks and improved bandwidth utilization, thus considerably reducing network costs. Carriers are reconfiguring their networks in order to optimize them for data rather than voice traffic and unifying multiple networks into a single multi-service network. New competitive carriers are taking advantage of the potential cost savings and greater flexibility in service development by adopting and implementing these new technologies right from the outset. They are building vast global networks, based around packets, on which voice service is being provided alongside data (McTaggart and Kelly, 2000).

While many packet networks use Internet Protocol (IP), other protocols for packet networks are or will become available. Recent developments have considerably improved the capability of IP to deliver delay-sensitive traffic, leading to dramatic quality improvements for applications such as voice. This has in turn led to a migration away from circuit-switched networks in order to benefit from the lower costs and service creation flexibility offered by packet technologies. In addition, the development of gateways that allow the exchange of traffic between networks using different protocols is facilitating the adoption of packet-based networks. Eventually, existing circuit-switched networks will be subsumed into packet networks, as there are no fundamental technological barriers remaining to prevent this evolution.

The end result will be a new public network that is data-centric in nature and capable of efficiently carrying and routing any form of digital communication. While the emergence of packet networks is often associated with the rise of the Internet itself, it is important to appreciate that next generation packet networks do not necessarily involve the public Internet at all. Indeed, mostly for reasons of service quality, voice communication is much more likely to rely on closed, managed packet networks, at least for the next few years, than it is to make extensive use of the public Internet.

This ability of packet-based networks to carry simultaneously any type of traffic, be it voice, data or video, will bring about some significant challenges to the interconnection and unbundling rules developed for traditional circuit-switched networks. For example, any framework relying on the ability to distinguish and measure different types of traffic in order to determine which rules should apply is unworkable on a packet network, where such distinctions are irrelevant and cannot be made. Similarly, the use of minutes for a variety of purposes is common on circuit-switched networks, but the concept of a minute is incompatible with packet networks, where only packets exist.


## 7    INTERNET INTERCONNECTION

To understand the interconnection arrangements that might be necessary for a next generation packet network, it is helpful to understand the interconnection arrangements for the Internet, a public packet network. The Internet is a network of networks, spanning a highly diverse set of more than 50,000 component networks, and it is still growing (Huston). Unlike the telecommunications network, the Internet grew in the absence of any specific regulatory framework. Rather, it developed in response to market conditions and is, therefore, instructive for analyzing next generation packet networks.

A key difference between circuit-switched and packet networks involves the way in which information is passed from the originating party to the destination party and, when required, returned. In a circuit-switched network, a dedicated circuit is opened for the duration of each call. This dedicated circuit is opened by the service provider serving the originating party, and this circuit is used both for sending information to the recipient and for receiving information back from the recipient.

Packet networks, which do not operate on the principle of a circuit, are quite different. Communications are decomposed into data packets that are sent over the network and reassembled at the destination, and each packet may or may not take the same route along the way. A packet network customer, using the Internet or some other public packet network, only expects his service provider to deliver, or to make arrangements to deliver, his packets anywhere in the world. He expects to be able to receive packets from anywhere in the world, by virtue of the fact that other customers have made similar arrangements with their service providers to deliver packets to him. In a packet network environment, the service provider of the customer originating the communication does not open a circuit and accept the responsibility of arranging for returning packets. The service provider of a customer receiving a communication on a packet network is responsible for arranging for the delivery of packets that this customer might wish to return to the originating customer.

It is also worth noting that on a packet network the service provider of the customer receiving packets does not generally know the origin of those packets. This is another significant difference from the situation in a circuit-switched network where the service provider offering terminating service knows the origin of a call, and it removes the ability of the service provider to discriminate among terminating packets.

For these reasons, the obligations of service providers in a packet network environment, and the costs imposed on them, differ in important ways from those of a service provider on the PSTN. These differences provide both an explanation for why interconnection arrangements across packet architectures have evolved differently than on the PSTN (and in the absence of regulation) and an explanation for why mandated interconnection is unlikely to ever be required for packet networks.

On the Internet, interconnection is provided through peering arrangements. Internet interconnection issues became controversial in the early 1990s, and even more so between 1996 and 1998, when large Internet service providers (ISPs) radically changed interconnection terms between themselves and smaller ISPs. While the largest ISPs, and, indeed, similarly-sized ISPs, kept peering arrangements, unequal-sized ISPs switched from peering to a customer-supplier relationship. These larger Tier 1 ISPs argued that the cost of infrastructure investment to sustain growth required that they recoup these costs through settlement fees from smaller ISPs.

Peering is a business and technical framework that enables ISPs to exchange traffic between their networks, usually on a bill-and-keep or sender-keeps-all basis (Baake and Wichmann, 1998). Peering is generally judged worthwhile when the traffic exchanged between networks is roughly equal or when there is a commercial or technical benefit, such as improved quality of service. Without peering, ISPs must pay fees (called transit fees) to purchase connectivity to a national backbone network. In the current Internet model, local

ISPs enter into peering relationships with other local ISPs but then purchase transiting services from regional ISPs. These regional ISPs in turn enter into peering relationships with other regional ISPs but purchase connectivity from national backbones, thus creating a mesh of interconnections at various levels (see, for example, Laffont and Tirole, 1999, p. 269, note 3, Frieden, 1999, and Kende and Oxman, 1999).

In order for ISPs to interconnect their networks, they need to agree on a financial settlement model to govern their relationships. Traditionally, the Internet has dealt with this issue by adopting just two models of interconnection, a customer/provider relationship with payments to providers and the peering relationship without any form of financial settlement.

However, the industry is moving towards more bilaterally negotiated financial settlement agreements,[8] not unlike the telecom industry. Until now, ISPs had little incentive to devise traffic metering and tracking systems (Mackie-Mason and Varian, 1998). However, it is very likely that the financial settlements between larger and smaller ISPs could become traffic-based, although not minute-based, in the near future, not unlike traditional telephony settlement models (Frieden, 1999, note 21). Some economists are even arguing that to be efficient and equitable, that is, to impose market-based discipline on ISPs and consumers alike, the pricing system should be based on a per-connection model or even on a next-hop model, taking into account the number of routers involved in transporting the packets from the content requester to the content provider (Clark, 1997, and Kende and Oxman, note 21). As noted by Maria Farnon and Scott Huddle, "introducing a fee-based settlement system promotes more interconnection among network providers as ISPs are now properly compensated for network expansion. Settlements allow small providers to grow their networks and reduce their costs, and allow incumbent large providers to be fairly compensated for their larger infrastructure cost of handling more customers."[9]

In this context, a potential alternative to bill-and-keep is the adoption of a financial settlement structure based on both parties effectively selling traffic termination services to each other. This implies the need to measure the volume of traffic being passed in each direction and to use a single accounting rate for all traffic. The negotiated rate should, however, have a strong relationship to the average marginal cost of transit traffic in both ISP networks for the settlement to be attractive to both parties and to avoid business instability.

## 8    INTERCONNECTION AND UNBUNDLING FOR PACKET NETWORKS

On the Internet, service providers originating packets can deliver these packets onto the network and be assured that they will be delivered to their destination. This is because the receiver of those packets has accepted an obligation to hand them off to successive routers on his network or on another network to route the packets to their intended destination. Returning packets requested by the originator can also be delivered onto the network with the assurance that they will be delivered, for the same reason. This result is achieved because the originating and terminating service providers either incur the expense of being a peer on the Internet or they purchase transit services from someone who has incurred the expense to be a peer, either

---

[8] Kende and Oxman (1999, p. 5, note 21). Laffont and Tirole (1999, p. 270, note 3) believe the bill-and-keep model is "probably a leftover of the transition process."

[9] Farnon, Maria, and Huddle, Scott, "Settlement Systems for the Internet," at http://www.ksg.harvard.edu/iip/cai/farnon.html.

directly or indirectly by purchasing transit services. However, as noted above, one important characteristic of packet networks is that the service provider of the party to whom packets are delivered incurs the obligation to terminate the packets as well as the obligation to provide for the delivery of returning packets. This is unlike the obligations of carriers over the PSTN, where the originating carrier has the obligation to set up and pay for both the originating and returning elements of a call.

Next generation packet networks will not necessarily involve the public Internet at all but are more likely to rely on closed, managed packet networks. Even over such alternative packet networks, however, the distinctions between the PSTN and packet networks will persist. In particular, there will still be no circuit, and the obligations for originating and returning packets will be significantly different in comparison to a circuit-switched network. This raises the question as to whether regulators will be required to mandate interconnection or unbundling arrangements for service providers employing end-to-end next generation packet networks.

To the extent that mandated interconnection arrangements may be necessary, as the market for services over packet networks further evolves, interconnection should only be mandated where a genuine bottleneck exists and where that bottleneck provides sufficient market power to allow a service provider to extract monopoly rents. In a packet network architecture, the only bottleneck is the final link to the customer's computer or other device where the customer's packet network address terminates. This is analogous to the call termination bottleneck in a circuit-switched environment. This final connection from the last router (which is controlled by the terminating customer's service provider) to the terminating customer's device is the only bottleneck and the only point of interconnection that theoretically could require regulatory intervention. Any necessary regulatory intervention should be limited to ensuring that a service provider maintains an obligation to accept and deliver packets and that the price for delivering packets is no more than is required to recover the prudently incurred costs of doing so.

The need for any such regulatory intervention, however, is unlikely. Given the manner in which packet networks operate and the incentives of packet network providers to collaborate and interconnect their networks, coupled with their inability to discriminate among packets,[10] it is not likely that there will be a need to mandate interconnection. Certainly, the recent history of the Internet supports the thesis that there are sufficient commercial incentives to negotiate interconnection arrangements and little opportunity for a monopoly or oligopoly of service providers to gain sufficient market power to adversely affect consumers. This thesis is also supported by the robustness of the routing protocols, which provide a prodigious level of connectivity, allowing network providers to have access to resources located on other networks without the prior requirement to directly interconnect with these networks through transiting arrangements. In this context, there are no incentives for larger backbone providers to discriminate or deny interconnection to smaller providers who are willing to abide by commercially negotiated terms and conditions (Milgrom, *et al.*, 1999). Furthermore, consumers have high expectations with regards to universal connectivity and a choice of many local network access providers. Consumer demands will drive backbones to interconnect with each other and local access providers to allow access to their customers for packet termination.

---

[10] This inability can technically be overcome with subsequent Internet protocols. There is, however, little economic incentive to incur the cost of tracking the origin of incoming packets merely because the potential exists to bill service providers delivering packets for termination.

It is not clear that any essential facilities exist on a packet network except perhaps for the last router connecting to a customer. Indeed, the development of the Internet and other emerging packet networks is consistent with the absence of essential facilities. As with any network, and consistent with the unbundling of network elements on circuit-switched networks, the mandatory unbundling of network elements on packet networks should be limited to essential facilities. Consequently, if interconnection is mandated at some point in the network other than the last router (which provides the final connection to the customer), it would be equivalent to the mandatory unbundling of non-essential facilities, with all of the related inefficiencies and anti-competitive consequences.

An issue that will arise with the further evolution to packet networks is the matter of which service provider, the originating service provider or the terminating service provider, should be responsible for any necessary protocol conversions to allow for the exchange of traffic between networks. Consistent with the basic interconnection rule, that the only obligation of the terminating service provider is to accept traffic and deliver it, it should be incumbent upon the originating service provider to deliver traffic to the terminating service provider in a format in which it can be delivered (or to bear the cost of the conversion). There are two qualifications to this obligation, however. First, industry participants are expected to agree on one or more standard industry protocols, and the obligation of any protocol conversion will fall on the originating service provider only as long as the terminating service provider uses an industry-standard protocol. Second, in a special case of the first qualification, where the terminating service provider uses proprietary protocols that are not available to the originator, the terminating service provider must accept traffic in any industry-standard protocol and accomplish the protocol conversion at his own expense.

## 9  INTERCONNECTION AND UNBUNDLING IN THE TRANSITION TO PACKET NETWORKS

Thus far, this paper has considered interconnection and unbundling arrangements where carriers with circuit-switched architectures interconnect with each other and where service providers with packet networks interconnect with each other. However, consideration must also be given to the potential for regulatory intervention in situations where circuit-switched and packet networks are to be interconnected. This latter circumstance is now occurring, as new entrants in the competitive local exchange market are employing packet-based network architectures in advance of incumbent local exchange carriers.

The basic interconnection model proposed in this paper, interconnection at the last switch or router respectively on circuit-switched and packet networks (which in both cases is the last technically feasible point of interconnection and the only bottleneck) for the purpose of call termination, is equally applicable when circuit-switched and packet networks are to be interconnected. In this scenario, the originating service provider should be required to deliver traffic to the terminating service provider in a format in which it can be understood (or to bear the cost of conversion). Generally speaking, if traffic is delivered pursuant to an industry standard protocol, the receiving carrier that is required to deliver the call should bear any cost of conversion if the receiving carrier is not using an industry standard protocol. Likewise, if the receiving carrier is using an industry standard protocol, but the sending carrier is not, the sending carrier should be required to pay for any conversion costs.

In current practice, this latter part of the model is not yet being adopted. New entrants with packet networks are voluntarily agreeing to adopt circuit-switched PSTN interconnection arrangements and to bear the cost of any necessary data or protocol conversions, whether they are the originator or terminator of traffic. This is a purely pragmatic decision on the part of new entrants that are in the minority and that prefer speedy market entry to protracted negotiations or regulatory interventions.

As the balance in the market shifts from a predominately circuit-switched architecture to a predominately packet-based architecture, however, service providers with circuit-switched architectures will be less able to dictate the terms of interconnection. They will become akin to any other service provider with a proprietary protocol in a predominately packet-based environment. Like any other service provider with a proprietary protocol, those with a circuit-switched architecture will have the same incentives that packet network operators have today. Circuit-switched network operators, when they are in the minority, may voluntarily incur the costs of all protocol conversion both when sending and receiving traffic to packet networks. It is not likely that regulation will be necessary.

This transition period is not likely to be smooth, however. Operators of circuit-switched networks cannot be expected to relinquish their dominant position without a fight, and the transition period to either dual standard protocols (circuit-switched and packet) or to a packet network standard protocol may be fairly long. Operators of both circuit-switched and packet networks may approach regulators to gain an advantage in the transition and in the final state. Depending on the response of the regulators, their intervention may permit a speedy transition or it may prolong the transition and hinder the emergence of a market-based solution of the type that is proposed here. Given the machinations that are already underway in North America and in Europe, one cannot be particularly optimistic regarding a speedy transition or regulatory assistance in reaching a desirable outcome.

## 10  CONCLUSIONS

This paper has examined whether regulatory policies regarding interconnection and unbundling will be required in a market dominated by next generation packet networks. It has concluded that the final connection from the last router (which is controlled by the terminating customer's service provider) to the terminating customer's device is the only bottleneck and the only point of interconnection that theoretically could require regulatory intervention. Any necessary regulatory intervention should be limited to ensuring that a service provider maintains an obligation to accept and deliver packets and that the price for delivering packets is no more than required to recover the prudently incurred costs of doing so. However, no such regulatory intervention is likely to be necessary because of the manner in which packet networks operate and the incentives for packet network providers to collaborate and interconnect their networks, coupled with their inability to discriminate among packets.

The paper has also examined the issue of which service provider should be responsible for any data or protocol conversions necessary to allow for the exchange of traffic between networks, the originating service provider or the terminating service provider. It has concluded that it is the responsibility of the originating service provider to deliver traffic to the terminating service provider in a format in which it can be terminated (or to bear the cost of conversion), as long as the terminating service provider uses an industry standard protocol. If the terminating carrier does not use an industry standard protocol, then the terminating carrier will be responsible for protocol conversion.

Finally, the paper has considered the potential for regulatory intervention in situations where circuit-switched and packet networks are to be interconnected. It has again concluded that the interconnection model proposed for a packet-to-packet interconnection will prevail for interconnections between packet and circuit-switched networks, because providers of circuit-switched networks will adopt the same obligations and incentives as any other service provider with a proprietary protocol.

## 11 REFERENCES

APEC Telecommunications Working Group (2000), Task Force for the Study of International Charging Arrangements for Internet Services (ICAIS), Report to the 4th Ministerial Meeting on Telecommunications and Information Technology, Cancun, Mexico, 24-26 May 2000, draft, April 19, 2000.

Baake, Pio, and Wichmann, Thorsten (1998) "On the Economics of Internet Peering," *Netnomics*, Vol. 1, pp. 89-90.

Brannan, Jenny (1999) "Open Broadband As: An Essential Facility Doctrine Analysis" at http://www.ku.edu/~cybermom/CLJ/brannan/Broadband.htm.

Clark, David D. (1997), "Combining Sender and Receiver Payments in the Internet," in Gregory L. Rosston and David Waterman, eds, *Interconnection and the Internet*, Lawrence Erlbaum Assoc., pp. 95-112.

Farnon, Maria, and Huddle, Scott, "Settlement Systems for the Internet," available online at http://www.ksg.harvard.edu/iip/cai/farnon.html

Frieden, Rob (1999), "When Internet Peers Become Customers: The Consequence of Settlement-based Interconnection," paper presented at TPRC.

Harris, Robert G., and Kraft, C. Jeffrey (1997), "Meddling Through: Regulating Local Telephone Competition in the United States," *Journal of Economic Perspectives*, Vol. 11, No. 4, pp. 93-112.

Huston, Geoff "Interconnection, Peering, and Settlements," available online at http://www.isoc.org/inet99/proceedings/1e/1e_1.htm

Jorde, Thomas M., Sidak, J. Gregory, and. Teece, David J. (2000), "Innovation, Investment, and Unbundling," *Yale Journal on Regulation*, Vol. 19, No. 1, pp. 1-37.

Kahn, Alfred E. (1998), *Letting Go: Deregulating the Process of Deregulation, or Temptation of the Kleptocrats and the Political Economy of Regulatory Disingenuousness*, Institute of Public Utilities and Network Industries, Michigan State University.

Kahn, Alfred E. (1995), "Preconditions of Efficiently Competitive Local Exchange Markets," prepared for AGT Limited and submitted as Appendix A-2 to Stentor Resource Centre, Inc.'s submission in CRTC Public Notice 95-36, Local Network Interconnection and Network Component Unbundling.

Kende, Michael, and Oxman, Jason (1999), "The Information Interchange: Interconnection on the Internet," paper presented at TPRC.

Laffont, Jean-Jacques, and Tirole, Jean (1999), *Competition in Telecommunications*, The MIT Press.

Mackie-Mason, Jeffrey K., and Varian, Hal R. (1998), "Economic FAQs About the Internet," in Lee W. McKnight and Joseph P. Bailey, eds., *Internet Economics*, The MIT Press.

McTaggart, Craig, and Kelly, Tim (2000), International Telecommunications Union, IP Telephony Workshop – Background Paper.

Milgrom, Paul, Mitchel,l Bridger, and Srinagesh, Padmanabhan (1999), "Competitive Effects of Internet Peering Policies," paper presented at TPRC.

Sidak, J. Gregory, and Spulber, Daniel F. (1997), *Deregulatory Takings and the Regulatory Contract: The Competitive Transformation of Network Industries in the United States*, Cambridge University Press.

Soma, John T., Forkner, David A, and Jumps, Brian P. (1998), "The Essential Facilities Doctrine in the Deregulated Telecommunications Industry," *Berkeley Technology Law Journal*, Vol. 13, p. 565.

Sullivan, Maev (1999), "The Basics of Interconnection," ITU Workshop on Telecommunications Reform.

Teece, David (1995), "Telecommunications in Transition: Unbundling, Reintegration, and Competition," *Michigan Telecommunications and Technology Law Review*, Vol. 1, pp. 47-78.

Global Economy and Digital Society
E. Bohlin, S. Levin, N. Sung and C-H. Yoon (Editors)

# CHAPTER 18

# Interconnection Policy Regimes and Global Strategic Alliance Activity in the Telecom Industry

Jai Joon Lee

*Joseph M. Katz Graduate School of Business, University of Pittsburgh, Pittsburgh*
*Korea Information Society Development Institute (KISDI), Kwachun*


Ravindranath ("Ravi") Madhavan

*Joseph M. Katz Graduate School of Business, University of Pittsburgh, Pittsburgh*

**Abstract.** This chapter investigates how interconnection policy regimes influence strategic alliance activity in the telecom industry. The relationship between telecom traffic networks and strategic alliance networks is analyzed using data on cross-border strategic alliances and international traffic flows (as a proxy for interconnection) between 1995 and 1999. Maps of alliance networks and traffic flow networks are visualized at the country level. While the alliance networks point to several dynamic features of the alliance landscape, including increasing complexity, decreasing centralization, and increasing regionalization, the traffic flow network appears to be relatively stable, although there is some evidence of increasing regionalization in traffic volume as well. An attempt is made to compare lagged cross-year correlations between alliance activity and traffic flow, but fails to throw light on whether traffic drove alliances or vice versa. Further causal analysis of these interrelated phenomena is a promising area for future research. From the managerial and public policy standpoints, both regulators and managers will be interested in how interconnection policy and firm strategy interact with each other through the mechanisms of interconnection networks and strategic alliance networks.

## 1  INTRODUCTION

The telecom industry has gone through dramatic structural changes during the last decade or so. Two of the most significant forces driving these changes have been the efforts in various national markets to promote effective competition and the global expansion of telecom services aided by the widespread diffusion of new telecommunication technologies. These structural changes have transformed the industry landscape from that of a largely state-owned, monopolistic environment to a privatized, more competitive one by eliminating market entry barriers and opening national telecom service markets to world-wide competitors. The 1996 Telecom Act has been updated and refined in order to reflect these industry changes in the US, and similar regulatory changes are under way in many other countries.

Against this backdrop, two critical elements of the global telecommunications industry – interconnection networks and strategic alliance networks – are investigated here with a focus on how the two networks influence each other. In particular, this chapter is concerned with how strategic alliance decision making is influenced by physical interconnection networks among global telecom operators, or vice versa. This chapter specifically focuses on country-level international telephony traffic volume and the country level alliance activities (aggregated from firm level data).

The following sections will outline the motives of this research on the telecom industry, and then go over some of industry specific characteristics, in particular for the international telephony market. Next, the research questions are presented, followed by a detailed analysis of country-level international traffic flow networks and alliance network activity during the years 1995-1999. After noting the limitations of the study, we conclude with implications for further research.

## 2    INTERCONNECTION POLICY & STRATEGIC ALLIANCE ACTIVITY

A recent article in *The Economist* (2003) describes an intriguing current scenario from the telecom market in India: "To counter *Reliance Infocomm* [the telecom arm of the huge Reliance group offering new 'limited mobile' services], the mobile firms slashed mobile-to-mobile long-distance rates. And they refused to carry calls from fixed-line to mobile networks without payment of access charges. This was immediately opposed by the regulator, which ordered the mobile operators to carry the calls. But the state-owned fixed-line firm then started blocking calls to mobile operators, which led to tens of thousands of mobile users being cut off from fixed lines in Delhi last weekend. A truce has been brokered by the communications minister, who referred the question of access charges to the regulator. But the uncertainty remains, the battle between the fixed and mobile firms is far from over..." This scenario is relevant for two reasons. One, it illustrates, strikingly, the importance of interconnection between different components of the telecom system. Two, it highlights the manner in which interconnection policy and firm strategy intersect—in this example, the fixed-line firm attempting to use interconnection as a competitive strategy tool. It is precisely this interesting intersection between interconnection policy and firm strategy that will be further explored in this chapter.

The telecom industry provides a natural research setting in order to understand an increasingly complex web of networks among different operators with multiple services. Beginning in the last decade, telecom liberalization and privatization efforts in many countries forced state-owned monopoly operators to compete with new entrants, and these competitive market forces have dramatically transformed the telecom industry. (To name just a few of these forces: active cross-border flows of foreign capital investment, substantial growth in various telecom services, and threats by new entrants with more efficient network infrastructure and services.) The recent surge of Internet and broadband services and the resultant "leapfrogging" of markets serve to hasten the convergence and globalization of telecom services. In the US, AT&T's dominant position, at least in terms of traffic volume, has been long gone with the telecom and information technology industries evolving from fixed-line telephony to a variety of alternative telecommunication methods such as mobile and Internet technology.

For mobile and Internet data services, interconnection policy regime becomes even more crucial in expanding their customer bases. Differences in the number of mobile subscribers in

China and in India, compared in a recent article on Asian Mobile Telecoms in *The Economist* (2003), indicate how different regulatory arrangements will determine the competitive landscapes in the telecom industry. Among those regulatory arrangements, it is apparent that interconnection policy regimes, including access charges between mobile and fixed-line networks, have great impact on the growth of telecom market development in different regions. Thus, even in an era of privatization and liberalization, telecom operators' strategic decisions are closely related to the changes in the regulatory framework.

## 2.1   Interconnection Policy

Interconnection is crucial for communicating across networks in a competitive telecom market structure. While the telecom industry is highly interconnected, the operator who controls the essential facilities (e.g. the local loop) is in a very different strategic position relative to competitors without such a "last mile" infrastructure to their customers. In terms of different structural forms, interconnection networks can be divided into three types - vertical interconnection, horizontal interconnection and parallel or cooperative interconnection networks (Noam, 2001).

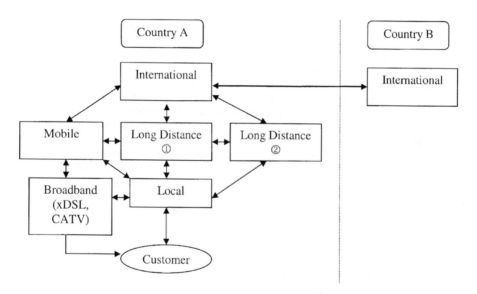

Figure 1. Simplified Interconnection Networks in Telecom Industry

Figure 1 graphically shows how different interconnection networks operate with each other. International interconnection networks among global telecom operators can be considered as a good example for parallel or cooperative interconnection networks.

In order for vigorous competition to become actual (rather than potential), the terms and conditions of interconnection networks need to be determined in such a way as to promote an efficient configuration of suppliers and provide incentives for innovative investment (Berg and Jamison, 1998). Very often, however, incumbents do not voluntarily provide their own networks to their competitors. Even if incumbents are willing to provide their own essential networks to other operators, careful regulatory oversight and the arbitration of interconnection policy, including technical and costing aspects of interconnection, may need to be incorporated in order to avoid incumbents' misuse of information asymmetry and dominant market power in the market.

Thus, interconnection policy (or interconnection networks) is one of the most critical elements in promoting effective telecom competition. Based on interconnection agreements set up among operators, new entrants have three different choices to select in order to start their telecom services: leasing the network from incumbents, being interconnected with incumbents, or building their own network infrastructure. The first two choices are commonly used by the new entrants since the third choice is associated with high initial capital expenditure. Given this, interconnection pricing – e.g. whether it is set extremely high or extremely low - will affect efficient market entry and network investment. Ultimately it has the potential to dramatically affect the whole structure of telecom industry. Recently, the wide use of new telecom services such as high-speed Internet and mobile services also changed the way telecom networks need to be interconnected among operators around the world.

For international telecommunication services, the terms and conditions of interconnection agreements are usually referred to as international settlement and accounting rate systems. At ITU, international settlement and accounting rate systems were developed as a means of dividing the revenues from international services among origin, destination and transit countries. The underlying assumption was that traffic flows between two countries are balanced and the service costs are reduced at a similar rate.

As already indicated, telecom reforms in many countries have led to a transition from monopoly to a competitive environment with multiple operators entering the market. However, the liberalization process did not proceed evenly throughout the globe. Further, alternative calling procedures such as callback and Internet telephony took significant portions of traffic flows, setting up arbitrage opportunities as a result of the different market conditions at the global level. These alternative calling procedures led to a broader imbalance of settlement rate among countries. Furthermore, significant variations in the way global operators are interconnected with each other are also the result of the continuing search for the most efficient, cost-saving traffic routes to serve international telecommunication services. For example, international refilling and transit arrangement over certain countries are often used to bypass countries with higher international settlement rates. Also, Mobile roaming has become more popular as mobile standards of GSM and CDMA technology are implemented in many different countries, and this will further make the networks of international telecommunication service more complex. All these changes had an impact on the way operators interconnected with other operators in different regions, and ultimately, operators' global strategic alliance activities also had to reflect such institutional changes.

## 2.2   Strategic Alliance Activities

In response to such institutional changes at the industry level, operators adjust their firm-level strategic actions or even attempt to influence policy formulation and implementation. In other words, the above changes in interconnection policy generated tremendous market changes, and telecom industry itself has witnessed active market expansion and new service introductions as well as the convergence of telephony, data and multimedia across the world. One of the most significant phenomena accompanying this shift has been global strategic alliance activity among telecom operators. Note that, in this chapter, strategic alliances refer to the wide spectrum of inter-firm linkages, including joint ventures, the cross-acquisition of the existing operator's equity stakes, and various kinds of contracts and cooperative agreements.

Since telecom services require physical interconnection between two operators, inter-firm relationships among telecom operators are not a new trend. However, market liberalization and industry globalization have led to an increase in operator-to-operator inter-firm relationships. Global strategic alliances among telecom operators are very effective and popular ways of expanding product and service coverage beyond national boundaries.

In previous studies in the strategy field, strategic alliances have been studied from many different viewpoints. For example, Nohria and Garcia-Pont (1991) suggested that the pattern of strategic alliances could have important implications for the structure-conduct-performance relationship and concluded that the emergence of strategic blocks indicates homogeneity of strategic capabilities across firms in an industry. Vanhaverbeke and Noorderhaven (2001) argued that competition between alliances blocks was superimposed on competition between individual firms. Daussage, Garrette and Mitchell (2000) investigated the outcome and duration of two different types of strategic alliances - link alliances and scale alliances, concluding that inter-firm learning and skill transfer appear to occur more often in link alliances than in scale alliances.

Madhavan, Koka and Prescott (1998) found that inter-firm relationship networks could be viewed as strategic resources which are subject to change as the industry itself changes. Thus, different alliance patterns and different levels of alliance intensity are good indicators of how operators are shaping their network positions in the fast-changing marketplace in a search for market share and profitability. For example, WorldCom, once a regional network operator in the US, made an effort to build its strong global network through aggressive mergers and acquisitions as well as strategic alliances. (Ironically, though, its aggressive expansion strategies may have been at least partly supported by wrongful accounting practices as reported in the business press over the last few months.) Building on this existing literature, our broader research initiative is based on the idea that some industry events, such as fundamental regulatory reform, potentially change the basis of competition in an industry, and lead to an observable impact on the network of relations within the industry (Madhavan, Koka and Prescott, 1998). Specifically, it focuses on interconnection policy as a key driving force in the telecom industry, and develops a research framework to understand how strategic alliances are formed, expanded and modified in different regulatory settings and regions.

## 3   OVERVIEW MODEL OF INTERCONNECTION AND ALLIANCE NETWORKS

Figure 2 depicts an overview model of how interconnection policy directly affects how and why firms form interconnection networks, and in turn, strategic alliance networks.

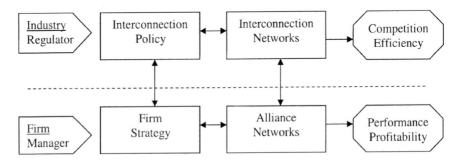

Figure 2. Interconnection Networks vs. Alliance Networks

The keys to successful interconnection policy from a regulatory standpoint are transparent interconnection pricing schemes and technical network interoperability, stemming from the policy objective of industry efficiency through competition. Firm managers, on the other hand, have a chance to make their inputs in the formulation and implementation of interconnection policy in order to maximize their market performance. They also have to weigh different strategic options, such as whether to deploy their own telecom networks or to be interconnected with those of incumbents. Based on the firm's assessment of policy change, managers decide whether to seek competitive advantage on their own or to form different types of inter-firm relationships. Their objectives may be to expand their regional coverage and telecom services or to obtain specific resources and capabilities through alliance networks. Therefore, firm strategy interacts with interconnection policy, and both will play roles in linking the relationship between interconnection networks and alliance networks.

Taken from firm managers' perspective, motives for alliance formation can vary. Adaptation to new product and geographic markets through strategic alliances represent an effective way of rapidly establishing the firm in that specific market. Market expansion into foreign markets and service expansion into new services such as Internet telephony are good examples. However, for cross-border strategic alliances, foreign operators will have to go through a series of regulatory hurdles, including foreign ownership restrictions. These may limit operators to consider different patterns of strategic alliance networks from non-binding equity sharing investment to full scale mergers and acquisitions. Just as patterns of strategic alliances differ, telecom operators will differ in their strategic positioning, with each operator engaging in a number of different types of alliance activities. Depending upon the regulatory conditions in target countries, both the pattern and intensity of strategic alliances may show regionally different trends. Also note that international settlement and accounting rates, one of the key determining indicators for global interconnection networks, will depend upon country-level interconnection policy.

Another characteristic of global strategic alliances in telecom industry is that alliance formation takes time to get an approval from the regulatory bodies (e.g. FCC in the US, EU in Europe) of different countries. Therefore, time lags may be expected in the relationship between interconnection networks and alliance networks. Furthermore, there may be a two-phase sequence of strategic alliances from horizontal market expansion to vertical service modulation through the convergence of telecom and multimedia services. The first phase of global strategic alliances mainly focuses on expanding the service market from the narrow local base to the broader regional market base (Smith et al., 1996). After liberalization and privatization processes in telecom sector stabilize in many industrialized countries, major US and European telecom operators formed cross-Atlantic strategic alliances with their counter-parts. For example, three major partnerships were formed; 1) World Partners of AT&T and several European operators; 2) Concert of British Telecom and MCI and 3) Global One of Deutsch Telecom, France Telecom and Sprint. And then, the second phase of global strategic alliances takes place, being directed toward vertically modulated services in order to provide seamless telecom services at a lower cost to a large number of different customers. In sum, the interconnection networks can be structured in many different forms and services, and as interconnection networks evolve over time, corresponding corporate strategies have to be formulated - e.g., various forms of strategic alliances.

## 3.1   Research Questions

The main research question, thus, is how interconnection policy influences telecom strategic alliance activities in the different regions of the world. As discussed in the previous sections, different attributes of strategic alliances are related to interconnection policy in various ways. As countries vary in market structure and interconnection policies, the geographical patterns of alliance networks will also be different from with each other.

This chapter is focused on addressing the interaction of two different network structures, specifically focusing on the link between interconnection networks and global alliance networks. Changes in the international traffic volume represent an important attribute of the international interconnection network. The more the traffic volume on a given international route, the more the telecom network needs to be interconnected physically (e.g., bandwidth, backup capacity), and the more will be the strategic interactions among participating opera-tors. Depending on the level of traffic volume, the magnitude of international settlement and accounting rates also become more crucial in determining the issues around the interconnec-tion policy at country level. Also, as the importance of traffic volume increases, it will take more time and effort to consider different aspects of interconnection policy regimes, including access charges, technical point of interconnection and different contractual provisions covered in the bilateral interconnection agreement. In other words, the levels of the traffic volume may be related to the complexity of interconnection policy regimes. Thus, while traffic patterns are determined by factors other than the physical interconnection networks, it may be argued that traffic volume between two countries is a useful measure for explaining the attributes of interconnection networks.

## 4   DATA COLLECTION & ANALYSIS

### 4.1   Data Collection

The primary goal of this chapter was to explore the relationship between interconnection networks and strategic alliance networks. For global telecom strategic alliance data, a one-mode data set[1] from 1995 to 1999 was compiled from various sources, including major news services (such as Dow Jones News Publications Library) and "Telecom Chronicle Mergers and Acquisitions: 1995 – 2001" compiled by IDATE, a French telecom consultancy group (www.idate.fr). Out of more than 400 records of telecom strategic alliances reported during this period, 168 records were global (or cross-border) strategic alliances. The key criterion for global alliances, used in this chapter, is the country origin of the operators involved. Therefore, some of the biggest strategic alliances in the US telecom market were not included due to the fact that they were domestic. Multiple news sources, online search engines as well as annual reports of major international telecom operators were used to provide additional contextual data on telecom alliance activity.

Once the alliances were identified, they were aggregated to the country level—e.g., an alliance between a U.S. firm and an Australian firm was coded as an alliance between U.S. and Australia. A unique feature of the data was that several alliances were reported in which one of the partners was itself an alliance—e.g., Concert, a BT-MCI joint venture, may in turn, enter into an alliance with, say, a South American provider. These alliance forms are accommodated by treating such alliances as another network actor in addition to the countries - represented by the category "Global."

In the analysis reported in this chapter,  primary attention is focused on the top 50 most heavily connected international traffic routes at the country level during 1995-1999, in order to capture the relationship between alliance activity and traffic flows along international telephone routes. The underlying assumption was that some properties of alliance networks would be related to properties of traffic flow networks volume among international routes or vice versa. The level of traffic volume, in turn, would proxy the terms and conditions of interconnection networks among operators. For example, the more the traffic volume being carried on specific international routes, the more will be the priority given to quality mainte-nance, and favorable settlement charges will be assessed accordingly. If there is a significant imbalance of traffic flows between outgoing and incoming calls, alternative calling procedures such as callbacks and Internet telephony will be sought by customers, and this will gradually influence the interconnection policy as well.

For traffic data, 1995-1999 traffic routes data were obtained from *TeleGeography*, a Wash-ington, D.C.-based international traffic research group. All data are in millions of minutes of telecommunications traffic. To be consistent with strategic alliance networks (which are symmetric), total minutes of outgoing and incoming traffic between two countries are used for the top 50 traffic routes. ITU's World Telecommunication Indicators Database (www.itu.int) was also used to obtain the total traffic size of each represented country. Data from 1995 to 1999 are chosen see if there are any differences in the pattern of strategic alliance formation

---

[1] In network analysis, the label "one-mode" implies that both rows and columns refer to exactly the same objects (referred to as actors). Actors can be people, groups, organizations, corporations, nation-states, etc. (Everton, 2002). In this chapter, participating countries (note that inter-firm alliances were aggregated to the country level) are considered a single set of actors.

between pre-1996 Telecom Act and post-1996 Telecom Act in the US. US telecom operators played a significant role in shaping both alliance and traffic networks during the five-year period even though market liberalization and privatization in other countries occurred at the different time intervals.

## 4.2   Data Analysis

One-mode network data on alliances and traffic volumes were entered into separate network data matrices, and the corresponding network graphics were drawn using the network analysis and graphic software tool *Pajek*. The following figures visualize the country level patterns of the alliance networks among global telecom operators and the traffic flow networks of the top 50 global traffic routes from 1995 to 1999. Note that the bubbles in the following figures stand for participating actors in both alliance and traffic networks. The size of bubble in the even-numbered figures (traffic networks) indicates the total traffic volume of each country. The arrows in the following figures are two-way, since both networks are symmetric.

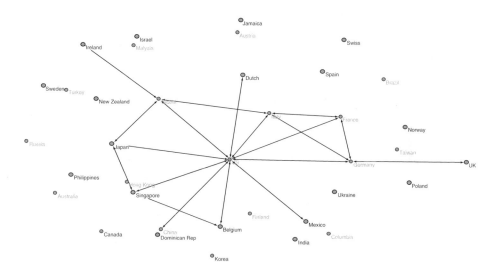

Figure 3. 95 Alliance Network

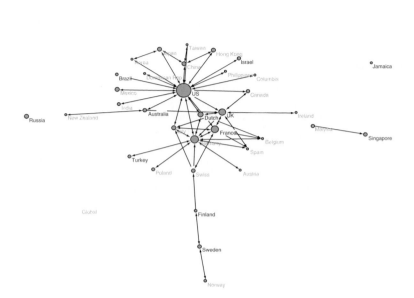

Figure 4. 95 Traffic Network

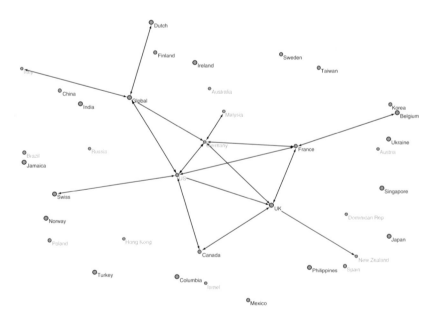

Figure 5. 96 Alliance Network

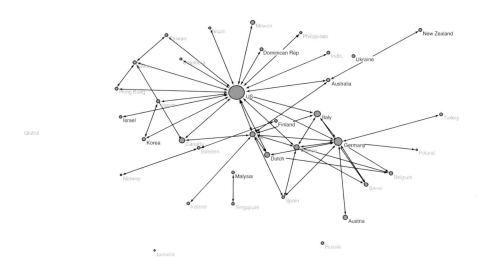

Figure 6. 96 Traffic Network

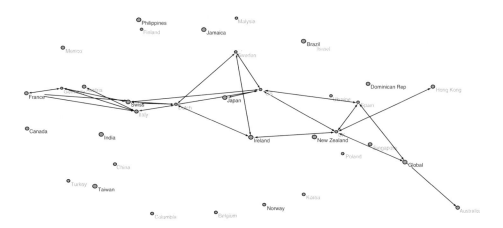

Figure 7. 97 Alliance Network

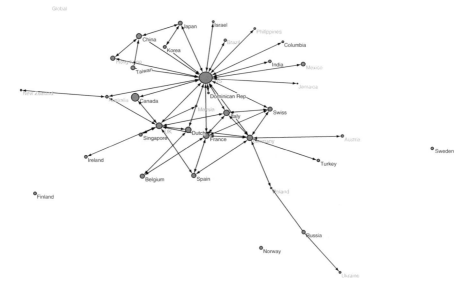

Figure 8. 97 Traffic Network

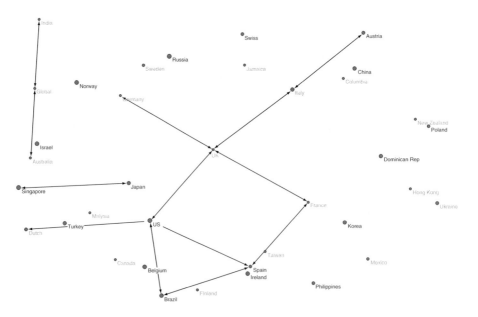

Figure 9. 98 Alliance Network

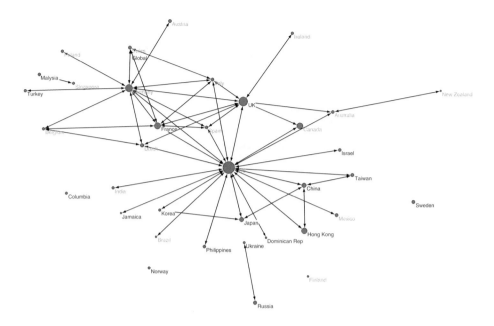

Figure 10. 98 Traffic Network

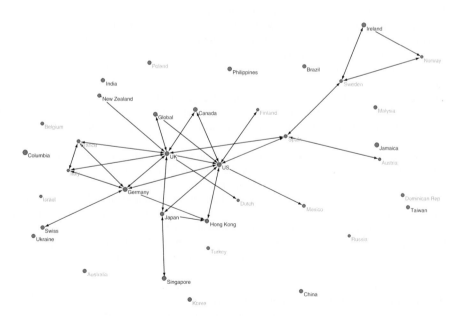

Figure 11. 99 Alliance Network

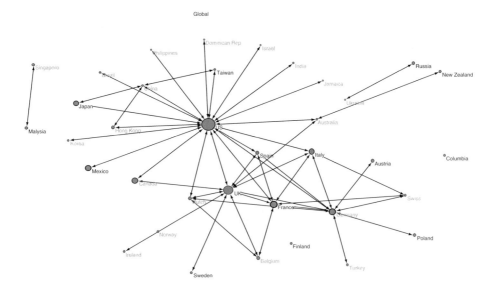

Figure 12. 99 Traffic Network

## Alliance Networks

The network maps demonstrate that US operators clearly took first mover advantage by expanding their strategic alliances with European and Asian operators. As mentioned in the previous section, the role of governments and public policy constraints are key issues in cross-border strategic alliance activity. Varying stages of the telecom deregulation in different countries often limit the selection of the possible alliance partners and the way alliances are structured. All three US global operators (AT&T, MCI and Sprint) as well as several regional bell operators (e.g. Bell South) participated in the global strategic alliances, including Global One, Concert and World Partners. In the case of Europe, four national operators, BT (UK), FT (France), DT (Germany) and Telecom Italia (Italy) took leading roles in forming the global strategic alliances.

The dominating role of the US telecom operators in building the alliance networks from 1995 to 1999 may have originated from the 1984 AT&T's divesture that had significantly contributed to the later US telecom reform processes such as 1996 Telecom Act. Smith and Zeithaml (1996) described how two regional bell operators in a regulated, monopoly environment transformed themselves (e.g. through international expansion strategies) to prepare for the hypercompetitive conditions. With the removal of regulatory barriers and legal roadblocks to competition in local telecom telephony segment in the US, regional bell operators have gained enough strategic flexibility and ability (Smith and Zeithaml, 1996) to be involved in the dynamics of global strategic alliance networks.

Several additional observations emerge from the alliance network figures. First, it appears that the alliance networks are becoming more complex over time, from the 1995 alliance network in Figure 3 to the 1999 alliance network in Figure 11 , with more participating actors, more links between those actors, and more links between disparate regions of the network. The numbers of alliance networks being formed increase from 1995 alliance network to 1999 alliance network. As we move toward 1999, more operators are involved in the global strategic alliance activities not only to expand their geographical markets but also to increase their market position in different services, a series of moves to provide cost-effective, technology-upgraded and converged telecom services across the national markets. The underlying motives for global strategic alliances can include improving network efficiency, increasing the customer base, acquiring technology and know-how, establishing footholds in emerging markets, and enabling carriers to better serve their multinational corporate customers (Rieck, 2002). As telecom operators are faced with more competitive domestic market conditions, they look for additional revenue streams and growth from the global telecom market—and this is reflected in the network pictures.

The second observation is that the alliance network appears to be becoming less centralized over time. In the early stages, the alliance network demonstrates the classic hub-and-spoke pattern, with the US positioned at the center, and a large periphery of isolates. However, over time, other countries increase their network centrality, reflecting greater activity in global alliances. Thus, the gap between the highly central actors, such as the U.S., and the other actors, appears to be on the decline. Even with less central position of US in the later years, however, many alliance partners are indirectly connected through the US many times over. The large global traffic volume (both incoming and outgoing) from the US has played a major role in the formation of strategic alliances among operators at country level.

Third, a regionalization trend is apparent in the network. In conjunction with the reduced centrality of the U.S., regional clusters are forming in Europe and Asia, and appear to be strengthening over time, as can be seen from the 1995 alliance network in Figure 3 to the 1997 alliance network in Figure 7. This may be due to the fact that more inter-regional trade is executed, in keeping with the emergence of regional trading blocs. Also, one may speculate that standards for the telecom equipments and physical networks are more compatible by the regions. In 1995, most European and Asian countries were still in the process of liberalizing their domestic telecom markets, and the target firms in such countries, usually the dominant incumbent operators heavily owned by the government, were still new at the business of forming alliances. In 1999, regional economic blocks like EU and APEC enacted the interconnection directives and a series of competitive market mechanism, and the incentives for the inter-regional trades and strategic alliances increased accordingly. In addition, cultural aspects of inter-region telecom operators are similar with each other. Therefore, strategic alliance activities are more frequent among countries in the same region.

The above second and third observations can be explained by the notion that there are three different kinds of network usage patterns[2] (Coyne, et al., 1998). Value to customers depends increasingly on network interconnections. Therefore, the priorities for alliance formation will be assigned to the heavy traffic volume routes, for example traffic networks between the US and the UK. It can be considered as lane concentration where customers heavily use individual links in a network (Coyne, et al., 1998). But for less demanding traffic routes, operators may prefer zone concentration to lane concentration since large numbers of customers concentrate their usage in some portion or portions of the network (Coyne, et al., 1998). Also, regional economic blocks (e.g. EU, NAFTA, ASEAN, APEC) may prefer intra-region alliances to inter-region alliances.

---

[2] Three different kinds of network usage patterns are zero concentration, zone concentration and lane concentration.

Fourth, there appear to be two different types of actors in the alliance networks – one being consistently active in alliances (e.g., U.S., U.K.), whereas others are sporadically active, less frequent players in the alliance networks (e.g., Australia, India). One may speculate that the consistently active countries either possess large domestic markets (attracting a variety of inward alliances) or have globally aggressive firms (who initiate a number of outward alliances). Since our present data do not allow us to distinguish between inward and outward alliances, we have not investigated this further. Clearly, future studies could fruitfully explore the motives and performance of these two distinct network positions. Absent either a large market or globally aggressive firms, the sporadically active countries engage in brief periods of alliance activity and then fall back into isolation.

Fifth, the "global" category (entities such as World Partners, Concert and Global One) does not appear to represent a key network actor. In other words, while "global" is an active player, as it appears from 1995 alliance network in Figure 3 to 1999 alliance network Figure 11, it appears that the firms that set up such global partnerships do not rely extensively on them as vehicles for international expansion. Perhaps the individual firms prefer to keep their critical alliances to themselves, and utilize their global partnerships as tools of last resort. If this is indeed the case, it would be interesting to ask why this specific relational form has not been successful in telecom industry. By way of contrast, note that multi-party global partnerships play a very important role in airline alliance networks. Such a comparison would suggest the value of analyzing the strategic consequences of multi-party global partnerships in different network-based industries. Note, further, that all three entities of "Global" category are recently in the process of dissolving (or at least minimizing) their roles as a global alliance networks.

*Traffic Networks*

The significant dominance of global traffic volume by the US is evidenced in the central position of the US in the traffic networks over the five year period. However, some of the later Figures show regional clusters forming—and strengthening—in several geographic regions. From 1995 to 1999, the US is dominant in the total traffic volume as well as the number of international routes ranked in the top 50 routes throughout the periods. In Europe, UK, France, Germany and Italy were the four largest traffic volume countries in 1995. As we move toward 1999, the rank of European operators appears stable, but the traffic volumes of Spain, Swiss, Netherlands and Austria have increased at a higher rate, being recognized significantly in the top 50 routes in 1999.

From the figures of international traffic networks, there are several issues to be addressed in more detail. First, only three countries, Russia, Ukraine and Jamaica, were added to the top 50 traffic routes from 1995 to 1999. The US and European countries dominated the international traffic volume as well as the number of strategic alliances. Combining the top 50 international traffic routes with the total traffic volume at country level, we would hypothesize a plausible relationship between interconnection networks and global strategic alliance networks. Specifically, the way interconnection policy regimes developed in certain countries, combining with unbalanced traffic flows, nudges operators to redirect their strategic alliance activities accordingly.

Second, it is worthwhile to look at the less than significant international traffic between European and Asian countries. By contrast, international traffic routes between US and Asian countries show significant increases in the total traffic volume between 1995 and 1999. It is possible that the proximity of European countries to each other generate enough traffic volume within European countries. Therefore, European operators first look for the possible strategic alliances within European blocks, and only then expand their alliance strategy into other areas subsequently. The years included in the data happen to represent the initial stage of European operators' alliance activities within the region. US operators, on the other hand, have existing ties with Asian operators with quite significant traffic volume across the Pacific (due to increasing trade and business partnerships, and perhaps also due to increasing Asian immigrant and foreign student populations). With all these, European operators would have different patterns of alliance activities in other parts of the world, when compared with US operators. As witnessed in some alliance failures recently, it would be interesting to look at what happened since 1999, as well as to assess the different performance outcomes of global strategic alliances.

Overall, the pattern of traffic networks is relatively more stable than the patterns of alliance networks. There was not much change in the traffic volume rankings except in the case of a couple of operators. However, the total volume of international traffic increased significantly, in particular for the year 2000 (TeleGeography, 2002). Note that this chapter uses country-level traffic volume as a proxy for interconnection policy regimes. Even though not specifically pursued in this chapter, however, rankings by the revenue size and the number of new entrants in each national market might have changed dramatically over the five-year period. Also, it should be noted that top 50 traffic routes are based on the total traffic volume from a traditional fixed-line telephony services under the international settlement mechanism. The recent popularity of mobile and other alternative calling procedures (e.g. Callback services, Internet telephony) has led to their accounting for significant portions of international traffic volume nowadays. It is as yet uncertain how these services will impact the changing patterns of alliance and traffic networks.

### Correlations between Alliance Networks and Traffic Networks

With all these network-related changes in the market, operators have to change their firm level strategic behavior in order to sustain competitive advantage. Strategic alliances are one of the most frequently used tools in the newly created competitive framework of the telecom industry. Thus, it would be interesting to look into how alliance activity is related (correlationally or causally) to traffic flows. As shown in Table 1, the network correlations are computed using the QAP (Quadratic Assignment Procedure) routine of UCINET V in order to examine the correlations between the alliance networks and traffic flow networks.

Table 1. Correlation Table between Alliance Activities and Traffic Volume

|            | Alliance 99 | Alliance 98 | Alliance 97 | Alliance 96 | Alliance 95 |
|------------|-------------|-------------|-------------|-------------|-------------|
| Traffic 99 | 0.551       | 0.187       | 0.219       | 0.455       | 0.272       |
| Traffic 98 | 0.544       | 0.181       | 0.203       | 0.450       | 0.258       |
| Traffic 97 | 0.525       | 0.163       | 0.194       | 0.436       | 0.242       |
| Traffic 96 | 0.529       | 0.145       | 0.192       | 0.428       | 0.249       |
| Traffic 95 | 0.531       | 0.149       | 0.210       | 0.412       | 0.241       |

Reference: QAP Correlation computed using UCINET IV Network Analysis Software (1999)

Table 1 presents the correlations between the strategic alliance activities and international traffic volume from 1995 to 1999. For example, alliance activities in 1999 have the correlation of 0.551 with traffic volume in 1999, whereas alliance activities in 1995 have the correlation of 0.241 with traffic volume in 1995. Also, alliance activities in 1996 have the correlation of 0.455 with traffic volume in 1999.

While static correlation analysis, needless to say, cannot throw light on possible causation, it is explored whether the compiled data helps us to address whether alliance activity is driven by traffic flow, or vice versa. This was done by focusing on correlations across the years—e.g., if traffic drives alliance activity, the year $t$ traffic would have a higher correlation with year $t + 1$ alliance activity, as compared to the correlation between year $t$ alliance activity and year $t + 1$ traffic.

However, the results were inconclusive on that front. Overall, the average correlation between year $t$ alliance activity and year $t + 1$ traffic volume was 0.269 while the average correlation between year $t$ traffic and year $t + 1$ alliance activity was 0.328 (both differences are insignificant). A Wilcoxon signed rank test was conducted to compare the correlations between alliance activity in each year and traffic volume in all subsequent years. The correlations between traffic volume in each year and alliance activity in all subsequent years were also calculated. However, this test also suggested no significant difference. Thus, it is premature to conclude anything about the directionality of the relationship between alliance activity and traffic volume. For instance, if both 1999 alliance network and 1999 traffic network are carefully analyzed, the relationships among UK, Japan and Singapore are only present in the alliance network map and not in the traffic flow map. Thus, these alliance networks may imply the motive of market expansion with little increase in traffic volume among three countries. On the other hand, alliance networks between the US and other countries are highly correlated with traffic volume among participating countries. In order to further analyze these interrelated phenomena, in-depth causal analysis tools such as path analysis and LISREL could be explored to investigate the relevant research questions. In addition, newer tools such as Hierarchical Linear Modeling may be warranted for further analyses, since the model incorporates multi-level effects at country, firm, and alliance levels.

## 5   LIMITATIONS

While our pilot data set reveals several interesting features of the telecom alliance landscape, its limitations have kept us from further analyzing the relationship between interconnection networks and alliance networks.

First, this chapter has limited the analysis only to the traffic volume of international fixed-line telephony services, but as the type of strategic alliances expands to the services other than fixed-line telephony, it becomes necessary to consider additional information on the different directions of traffic volume (outgoing and incoming) separately in order to capture more accurately the direction of alliance activity diffusion. Also, mobile traffic volume is overlooked in the analysis. Mobile telecommunication services represent different types of interconnection networks - mobile to fixed (most Europe and Asia's case; existing settlement mechanism is maintained), fixed to mobile (existing mobile interconnection network structure maintained with higher margins), and mobile to mobile (bill and keep roaming arrangement in the US; extra charges for the global roaming provisions), and these networks might result in different consequences for network structure and pricing schemes. As a result, mobile operators will seek to change industry structure, and execute different strategic moves, including in terms of strategic alliances. Also, our data set does not include the more recent strategic alliances among wireless operators during the 3G service licensing period.

Second, Internet alliances with telecom operators in particular are not included in the analysis. The recent increase in the usage of Internet networks poses a challenge to the network environment as a whole. Viewing Internet telephony as cheaper and lower quality technology, Internet networks were initially considered to be complementary to the conventional fixed-line interconnection networks. However, technology is advancing rapidly, and Internet networks will generate enough traffic volumes soon, so that their shares cannot be overlooked in directing the firm's strategic alliance activities. Compared to the conventional fixed-line interconnection networks, these two networks are rather voluntarily-structured, with a greater degree of strategic choices, and entry barriers are not usually a problem given the nascence of the market. However, mobility barriers in terms of firm capabilities are a factor. Clearly, a more complete analysis will have to take these factors into account.

Third, both alliance and traffic data were collected from secondary sources at the country level, and further data collection and analysis will help to investigate the present issues at different levels, in particular at the level of firm strategy. Combining industry news with company press releases, it will be possible to expand and enrich the alliance database and investigate a broader range of strategic alliance formations at firm level. In addition, it may be necessary to develop a reasonable proxy for the international traffic data at the firm (rather than country) level. Most of the data were from the US and European-based data sources, and there might have been both regional and size selection bias on the lists of traffic and alliance networks.

Lastly, accounting for different levels of dynamic interactions between interconnection and alliance networks will increase the robustness of the empirical testing, as well as the richness of theory. In that sense, this chapter represents only a first step in understanding the evolution of global inter-firm relationships in the telecom industry, and in particular, the relationship between traffic and alliance activities at country level.


## 6   IMPLICATIONS

In addition to the implications already pointed out, it should be noted that global strategic alliances in the telecom industry need to be analyzed combing both competitive and corporate strategy lenses. Diversification through strategic alliances is one of the reasons why operators take part in the global strategic alliances. The telecom industry used to have somewhat clear organizational boundaries between generalists and specialists. In many developed countries, telecom regulations have a tendency to keep operators from being too much of generalists, while developing countries have encouraged state-owned monopoly operators to become generalists. Now, the twists are turning another turn for these organizational boundaries of generalists and specialists. One of the key aspects in 1996 Telecom Act was to abolish the business restrictions among local and long distance services, given that the regional Bell operating companies (RBOCs) were required to open their local loops to other competitors. As telecom services are converging with each other, being a generalist is becoming a more acceptable strategy. Strategic alliance activities are sure to help in further enhancing this process. The evolution of alliance networks and traffic networks should be analyzed longitudinally with different strategic motives and actions at firm-level in the future, keeping in mind that prior studies (Chan-Olmsted and Jamison, 2001; Kashlak and Joshi, 1998) have focused on the identification of the business factors and environmental variables that influence the firm's strategic direction in the global telecom market.

In subsequent studies, it would also be worthwhile to address the performance question, such as whether firm-level strategic alliance activity is really a good strategic move to sustain competitiveness in a complex and fast growing environment. By way of analogy, a recent *Harvard Business Review* article (Rovit and Lemire, 2003) provides some insightful ideas of evaluating the M&A strategy, suggesting that companies making frequent acquisitions perform best when they buy systematically through economic cycles. Similarly, are constant "alliancers" more likely to be successful than occasional "alliancers"? Also, Chang (1996) looked at the diversification and corporate restructuring activities of the US manufacturing firms in the US from 1981 to 1989. His evolutionary perspective on firm's entry, exit and economic performance implied that the firm's knowledge base played an important role in predicting which businesses a firm enters or exits. It would be interesting to see whether the outcomes of these two studies apply to the telecom industry context. Furthermore, as Chang (1996) noted, well-directed entry and exit (with emphasis on the human resource profile similarities) would contribute to the improvement of a firm's profitability. Thus, it will be useful to look at the underlying reasons why telecom firms form strategic alliances, what the different types of strategic alliances are, and how firms formulate the magnitude of strategic alliances locally, regionally as well as globally, as well as what factors distinguish high performance strategic alliances from less successful ones.

The recent series of policy changes and the global market expansion in telecom industry have given us some interesting research questions for strategic management and public policy. In addressing these research questions, this chapter hopes to build on previous studies of alliance networks, in particular, on how alliance networks evolve and adapt in response to policy regimes and their correlates (in our case, interconnection networks). While these two networks have different goals for regulators and managers, they interact in ways that have implications for both sets of outcomes (e.g. market efficiency for regulators and profitability for firm managers). More broadly, all four elements highlighted in Figure 2 - interconnection policy, interconnection networks, firm strategy and alliance networks - are interrelated with each other in subtle and interesting ways. From the managerial and public policy standpoint, both regulators and firm managers will be interested in how interconnection policy and firm strategy interact with each other through the network mechanisms of interconnection networks and strategic alliance networks.

## 7    REFERENCES

Barnett, George A. (2002), "A Longitudinal Analysis of the International Telecommunication Network: 1978-1999", paper presented to the Conference at Beijing Broadcast Institute, National Centre for Radio and Television Studies, 13-14 April, Beijing, China

Berg, Sanford V. and Jamison, Mark A. (1998), "Telecommunication Policy: Alliances, Interconnection, and Universal Service", *Public Utility Research Center Working Paper*, University of Florida, Gainesville, USA

Chan-Olmsted, Sylvia and Jamison, Mark. (2001), "Rivalry Through Alliances: Competitive Strategy in the Global Telecommunications Market", *European Management Journal*, Vol. 19, pp. 317-331.

Chang, Sea Jin (1996), "An Evolutionary Perspective on Diversification and Corporate Restructuring: Entry, Exit, and Economic Performance during 1981 – 89", *Strategic Management Journal*, Vol. 17, pp. 587-611.

Coyne, Kevin P. and Dye, Renee (1998), "The Competitive Dynamics of Network-Based Businesses", *Harvard Business Review*, January-February, pp. 99-109.

Dussauge, Pierre, Garrette, Bernard and Mitchell, William (2000), "Learning from Competing Partners: Outcomes and Durations of Scale and Link Alliances in Europe, North America and Asia", *Strategic Management Journal*, Vol. 21, pp. 99-126.

Everton, Sean F. (2002), "A Guide for the Visually Perplexed: Visually Representing Social Networks," *mimeo*, Stanford University, Economic Sociology Research Group, Version .41, www.stanford.edu/group/serg/siliconvalley/documents/networkmemo.doc, [accessed May 1, 2003].

Kashlak, R. J. and Joshi, M. P. (1998), "How Alliances are Reshaping Telecommunications", *Long Range Planning*, Vol. 31, pp. 542-548.

Madhavan, Ravi, Balaji, R. Koka and Prescott, John E. (1998), "Networks in Transition: How Industry Events (Re)shape Interfirm Relationships", *Strategic Management Journal*, Vol. 19, pp. 439-459.

Noam, Eli M. (2001), *Interconnecting the Network of Networks*, The MIT Press, Cambridge, Massachusetts.

Nohria, Nitin and Garica-Pont, Carlos (1991), "Global Strategic Linkages and Industry Structure", *Strategic Management Journal*, Vol. 12, pp. 105-124.

Rieck, Olaf (2002), "Value Creation in International Telecom Acquisitions", paper presented at the ITS 14th Biennial Conference, 18-21, August, Seoul

Rovit, Sam and Lemire, Catherine (2003), "Your Best M&A Strategy", *Harvard Business Review*, March, pp. 16-17.

Smith, Anne D. and Zeithaml, Carl (1996), "Garbage Cans and Advancing Hypercompetition: The Creation and Exploitation of New Capabilities and Strategic Flexibility in Two Regional Bell Operating Companies", *Organization Science*, Vol. 7, pp. 388-399.

TeleGeography, Inc. (1996), TeleGeography 1996/97: Global Telecommunications Traffic Statistics and Commentary, TeleGeography, Washington, D.C.

TeleGeography, Inc. (1997), TeleGeography 1997/98: Global Telecommunications Traffic Statistics and Commentary, TeleGeography, Washington, D.C.

TeleGeography, Inc. (1998), TeleGeography 1999: Global Telecommunications Traffic Statistics and Commentary, TeleGeography, Washington, D.C.

TeleGeography, Inc. (1999), TeleGeography 2000: Global Telecommunications Traffic Statistics and Commentary, TeleGeography, Washington, D.C.

TeleGeography, Inc. (2000), TeleGeography 2001: Global Telecommunications Traffic Statistics and Commentary, TeleGeography, Washington, D.C.

The Economist (2003), "The Tortoise and the Dragon," 25 January, pp. 65, London.

Vanhaverbeke, Wim and Noorderhaven, Niels G. (2001), "Competition between Alliance Blocks: The Case of the RISC Microprocessor Technology", *Organization Studies*, Vol. 22, pp. 11-30.

Global Economy and Digital Society
E. Bohlin, S. Levin, N. Sung and C-H. Yoon (Editors)

# CHAPTER 19

# Convergence Phenomenon and New Service Development in the Telecommunications Industry

Sang-Pil Han
*Graduate School of Management, KAIST, Seoul*

Jae-Hyeon Ahn
*Graduate School of Management, KAIST, Seoul*

Ann Skudlark
*AT&T Labs, Florham Park*

**Abstract**. In the telecommunications industry, there is an emerging phenomenon of convergence. Under this convergence phenomenon, the conventional one-service via one-network concept is changing to multiple services via multiple networks. However, our understanding for this convergence phenomenon is vague, thereby resulting in confusion and uncertainty about the market environment. Also, there is limited literature regarding new service development processes under the emerging convergence phenomenon from business perspectives. To address the issues related to the convergence phenomenon, a *Service-Network matrix* is introduced. Using this matrix, the convergence phenomenon is explained from both service and network viewpoints. Such a framework helps managers to identify new service opportunities, especially during the idea generation stage of the new service development process. Furthermore, a scenario planning approach is suggested for initially screening the new service concepts. Finally, the Service-Network matrix and scenario planning approach are applied to a new service development process for *wireless ADSL service at home*.

## 1. INTRODUCTION

As part of the worldwide growth of the telecommunications industry, there is an emerging phenomenon, *convergence*. Under the convergence phenomenon, the conventional one-service via one-network concept is changing into multiple services via multiple networks concept (Blackman, 1998, Tadayoni and Kristensen, 1999). For example, due to the digitalization and ADSL (Asymmetric Digital Subscriber Line) technologies, PSTN (Public Switched Telephone Network) can provide broadcasting, data/Internet access, and Internet phone services. Voice services such as conventional wire-line voice and Internet phone services are now provided via various networks, such as PSTN and cable networks. Also, with a future vision

vision of one integrated network, there is a transition period where current and new infrastructures compete at the end user market and adjust to emerging types of services (Henten and Tadayoni, 2001)

The convergence phenomenon introduces both opportunities and challenges from business and regulatory perspectives (European Commission, 1997). From the business perspective, it generates opportunities for new services. The capacity utilization rates of most networks are extremely low (Solomon and Walker, 1995). Thereby, incumbent network operators can leverage their potentially underutilized resources to provide a variety of new telecommunications services. Also, new entrants can take advantage of the service opportunities by accessing incumbent's networks. For example, as cable companies are able to provide Internet access services using their cable networks, new comers can also enter the Internet access service market by utilizing other operators' cable networks, which they do not own.

Moreover, with the deregulation of the industry, there are fewer restrictions on providing services thereby opening the door for new opportunities. For example, as both traditional telephone companies and cable companies are able to provide Internet access services, they become competitors. The convergence phenomenon produces fierce competition and uncertainties regarding competitors' strategic actions in the industry. Therefore, telecommunications companies face significant difficulties concerning how to develop or identify new competitive telecommunications services and how to evaluate the viability of those service concepts under the convergence environment.

From the regulatory perspective, many cross-industry activities do not neatly fall under a traditional regulatory framework, such as one-service via one-network paradigm. For example, the issues of network regulation and content regulation cannot be entirely separated (Garnham, 1996). Hence, there exists confusion and uncertainties regarding how regulatory bodies regulate the telecommunications industry under the convergence phenomenon (Blackman, 1998, Clements, 1998). For example, should interactive TV and web casting service be considered a broadcasting service or a data service? Its dual nature introduces challenges to the traditional sector-specific regulation – such as universal service obligation (Blackman, 1995), content regulation, regulatory asymmetry, etc. (McGougan, 1999). Also, should Internet phone service be regulated as a conventional telephone service or a new data service? The Internet phone service raises similar regulatory challenges.

Despite the challenges and opportunities from the business and regulatory perspectives, most of the convergence-related research has been based on different definitions of the convergence (Yoffie, 1996, European Commission, 1997, Burols et al., 1998, Nourouzi and Baker, 1999, Tadayoni and Skouby, 1999, Sheldon 2001); therefore, our understanding for this convergence phenomenon is still vague. Also, studies regarding new service development process under the emerging convergence phenomenon are limited.

The conceptual ambiguity of the convergence phenomenon especially complicates new service development from the business perspective. For example, the introduction of new convergence service - Internet via wireless local area networks (WLAN) provides wireless Internet access service within a limited range of areas such as hotels, airports, campuses, etc. In order to fully develop this new convergence service, it is needed to specify which networks will be utilized and which markets will be targeted. However, there is no conceptual framework to consider both network and market characteristics in the new service development process.

To address the issues related to the convergence phenomenon, a Service-Network matrix and scenario planning approach are introduced. Using the matrix helps managers to identify and exploit the new service opportunities, especially during the idea generation stage of the new service development process. Also, the scenario planning approach would be helpful for initially screening the new service concepts.

This paper is organized as follows. Section 2 reviews the current literature on different perspectives of the convergence phenomenon and the new service development process. Section 3 suggests the Service-Network matrix with its drivers, examples, and implications. Section 4 specifies the preliminary stages of a new service development process under the convergence environment, and examines the *wireless ADSL service at home* case using the convergence framework and scenario planning approach. Section 5 contains conclusions and limitations.

## 2.     LITERATURE REVIEW

Even though the word *convergence* is used frequently in the telecommunications industry, its concept is still ambiguous. Previous research has illustrated the convergence phenomenon from either a service perspective or a network perspective. For example, the European Commission (1997) explained in the Green Paper that convergence enables the provisioning of essentially similar kinds of services through different kinds of networks. But Edwards (1999) and Sheldon (2001) regarded that convergence enabled a single network to carry different kinds of services – voice, data, and broadcasting.

The scope of the research on convergence has been also limited to a specific area. For example, Burols et al. (1998) and Harrison and Hearnden (1999) focused on fixed-mobile voice convergence. On the other hand, Yoon et al. (1999) and McGougan (1999) mainly focused on the broadcasting-telecommunications convergence. However, they used the term convergence in an interchangeable manner. Therefore, it is reasonable to say that there exists no general framework for the study of the convergence phenomenon in the telecommunications industry.

Several different perspectives have been developed to clarify the concept of the convergence phenomenon (Yoffie, 1996, European Commision, 1997, Burols et al., 1998, Harrison and Hearnden, 1999, Nourouzi and Baker, 1999). They are service convergence, network convergence, and industry/commercial convergence[1].

### 2.1.  Service Convergence

Service convergence has been discussed from two aspects; seamless services and multi-characteristic services. Burols et al. (1998) and Nourouzi and Baker (1999) and Harrison and Hearnden (1999) have defined the service convergence as a seamless delivery of fixed/mobile telephony and support services irrespective of the underlying delivering networks. Typical examples are one-phone service and one-mailbox service.

Many new telecommunications services such as VOD (Video On Demand) and Interactive TV are the result of both the technological progress within sectors and cross-fertilization between sectors (European Commission, 1997). They could be arbitrarily classified into one of the telecommunications services such as broadcasting service or data service, under the

---

[1] Business convergence is also interchangeably used with industry/commercial convergence.

traditional network-specific regulatory boundaries. The multi-characteristic properties can be considered a unique characteristic of service convergence.

## 2.2. Network Convergence

Network convergence has been also argued from two aspects - network integration and network utilization. Burols et al. (1998) and Harrison and Hearnden (1999) defined network convergence as a common use of the physical network infrastructures, such as backbones and local exchange capacity. For example, network operators with both wired and wireless networks can share the overlapping parts of the backbone network, so that they can avoid redundant investment. This is called a physical integration or network integration. The overlapping area in figure 1(a) shows the shared network when network 1 and network 2 are integrated.

On the other hand, existing access networks can be best utilized to provide additional services without incurring large incremental network installation costs. For example, digital technologies enable a telephone line to be used as a medium not only for voice but data and video services. This is called network utilization. Network utilization involves a virtual integration of two or more networks. Figure 1(b) shows that network 1 integrates with network 2 and 3 when a network convergence takes place in network 1. In this case, functions of both network 2 and 3 can be provided through network 1.

(a) Network integration                              (b) Network utilization

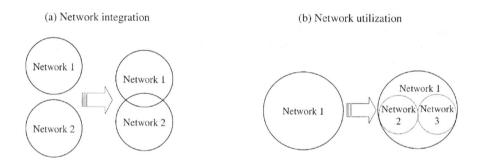

Figure 1(a), 1(b). Two Perspectives of Network Convergence

## 2.3. Industry/Commercial Convergence

Industry convergence (European Commission, 1997) means alliances, mergers and joint ventures by sharing technical and commercial know-how of the partner. These are sometimes referred as horizontal integration (Yoffie, 1996). However, industry convergence is not a telecommunications industry-specific phenomenon, but a common activity also observed in other industries. Therefore, industry convergence is not further discussed in this paper.

Under the convergence phenomenon, voice, data, and broadcasting services are delivered through several kinds of networks. Previous studies on convergence have mainly focused on either network convergence or service convergence. Table 1 shows several convergence services classified from the current service and network perspectives.

Table 1. Current View of Convergence Services

| Perspective / Service | Service convergence | | Network convergence | |
|---|---|---|---|---|
| | Seamless service | Multi-characteristic | Network integration | Network utilization |
| Cordless phone | | X | | |
| One-phone service | X | | X | |
| Internet phone | | X | | |
| Internet service with PSTN | | | | X |
| Wireless LAN | | X | | |
| Cable Modem | | | | X |
| Interactive TV | | X | | |
| Web-casting | | X | | |

**Note:** X denotes relevance.

Most convergence services with the exception of one-phone service are explained by either network perspective or service perspective. Neither network perspective nor service perspective can explain a specific convergence phenomenon in a unifying way. That is, current definitions of convergence are conceptually ambiguous. The vague definition of convergence makes it hard to explain convergence phenomenon in a logically consistent way. Furthermore, poor understanding of convergence phenomenon increases uncertainty on regulatory policy and makes it hard to predict where convergence services will evolve.

Henten (1999) also argued that the establishment of rules and borderlines would enhance the innovative potentials in the technological convergence between the formerly separate sectors[2]. Therefore, the uncertainty regarding the convergence phenomenon may influence managers in the telecommunications industry to become more risk-averse and ultimately delay the growth in the telecommunications industry.

Harrison and Hearnden (1999) emphasized customers' perspectives and argued that consumers want consistent delivery of telecommunications services irrespective of user environments, terminals, locations, etc. Also, as services are delivered through various networks, those networks have to be able to provide both traditional and new services. For example, in order for data service to be provided by cable network, the cable network needs to be upgraded. Therefore, it is reasonable to say that the convergence phenomenon should be considered from both network (or suppliers) and service (or customers) perspectives in a unifying way.

---

[2] For example, the unbundling of hardware and software by IBM in 1969 in the U.S. constituted a boost to the development of a software sector.

## 2.4. The Stage-Gate Process

The convergence phenomenon generates numerous opportunities for new telecommunications services. Therefore, telecommunications companies need a new service development process that adequately addresses the convergence phenomenon. One of the most widely used new product development process is a Stage-Gate process originated by Cooper, which outlines a tried-and-proven process for bringing new products from idea to market launch quickly and successfully (Cooper, 2001).

The Stage-Gate breaks the innovation process into a predetermined set of stages, each stage consisting of a set of prescribed, cross-functional, and parallel activities: The entrance to each stage is a gate. These gates control the process and serve as the quality control and go/no-go checkpoints (Cooper, 2001). Figure 2 shows a general flow of the typical Stage-Gate process from idea generation to service launch.

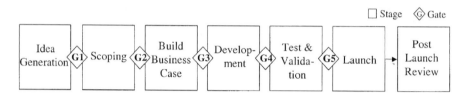

Figure 2. A Stage-gate Process

There is mounting evidence that new product success and failure is often decided before the new product project enters the development phase. That is, upfront or predevelopment activities, which happen in the idea generation, scoping, and build business case stages as shown in figure 2, stand out as activities that separate winners form losers (Cooper, 1988). That is, activities such as initial screening, preliminary market and technical assessment, and undertaking a detailed market study were strongly correlated with product outcomes (Cooper and Kleinschmidt, 1986).

At the idea generation stage in the Stage-Gate process, new product or service opportunities are discovered, and they need to pass the first gate or decision point to scoping stage for further investigation. The screening is based on criteria such as strategic alignment, technical feasibility, market attractiveness, synergy with the business's resources, etc. Financial criteria are not typically used as first screen criteria. At the scoping stage, a preliminary investigation is made into market, technology, business, and alliance/vendor using mostly secondary research, and then the project is reevaluated as a business case based on the new information obtained in the previous stages. Also, a rough financial return is assessed using simple financial calculations, such as Net Present Value (NPV) analysis. In fact, our paper focuses on the predevelopment activities in the idea generation and scoping stages (Cooper, 2001, Cooper and Edgett, 1999).

## 3. THE CONVERGENCE FRAMEWORK

### 3.1. Service-Network Matrix

To address the issues related to convergence phenomenon and explain them in a unifying way, a Service-Network matrix is introduced. Both service and network perspectives are considered at the same time in the Service-Network matrix. In the matrix, service is generally viewed from the customer's perspective and network is generally viewed from the provider's (i.e., network operator or service provider) perspective[3].

Figure 3 shows a Service-Network matrix represented in a two-dimensional space. The vertical axis represents generic services that are delivered through specific networks, and the horizontal axis represents different kinds of networks that deliver generic services. Services and corresponding conventional networks can be selected based on the purpose and level of the analysis.

Let denote $S_{ij}$ as a specific service $i$ that is provided by a network $j$ where $i, j=1,..., n$. Then, $S_{ii}$ is a service $i$ provided by the corresponding network $i$. Using the notation, service $i$ provided by any network can be represented by a $i$-th row in the matrix or $S_{i\bullet}$. Therefore, $S_{ij}$ is an essentially same service as service $S_{ii}$. In the same way, $S_{\bullet j}$ are set of services that are provided by network $j$. Traditionally, a single network provided only one service, which is represented as the diagonal element $S_{ii}$ in the figure 3. For example, PSTN used to provide a voice service only, and a cable network used to provide a cable TV service only. However, the convergence has made it possible for a single network to provide different kinds of services, which are represented as the off-diagonal elements in the matrix.

Network 1 Network 2 Network $i$ Network $j$ ⋯ Network $n$

| | | | | | |
|---|---|---|---|---|---|
| Service 1 | $S_{11}$ | | | | |
| Service 2 | | $S_{22}$ | | | |
| Service $i$ | | | $S_{ii}$ | $S_{ij}$ | |
| ⋮ | | | | ⋮ | |
| Service $n$ | | | | | $S_{nn}$ |

Figure 3. A Service-network Matrix

The convergence phenomenon in the telecommunications industry is viewed from the service and network perspectives. For our purpose, *network convergence* is defined as the

---

[3] European Commission (1998) stressed the need to define convergence from the user perspective rather than provider perspective.

phenomenon that multiple services are provided through a single network. In the same way, *service convergence* is defined as the provision of a service through different kinds of networks.

Naturally, convergence in the telecommunications industry can be defined as the phenomenon that multiple telecommunications services are provided through a single network and a service is provided through distinct networks. In fact, as shown in Table 1, some services were previously viewed only from the service convergence perspective, while others only from network perspective. However, under the Service-Network matrix framework, convergence service can be better explained from both perspectives.

Figure 4 shows typical examples of the telecommunications services in the Service-Network matrix. In the following section, convergence services are viewed both from the service convergence perspective and network convergence perspective respectively, and drivers for the convergence phenomenon are examined.

|  | Cable network | PSTN | PSDN |
|---|---|---|---|
| Broadcasting service | Cable TV Service | Web Casting Service | Web Casting Service |
| Voice service | Internet Phone Service | Wired Telephone Service | Internet Phone Service |
| Data service | Cable Modem Service | ADSL and Dial-up Modem Service | Dedicated Data Service |

Figure 4. Examples of Telecommunications Services

## 3.2. Service Convergence

Consumers generally lack knowledge of the underlying technology enabling the service provisioning. For example, differences between fixed and mobile networks are irrelevant to users (Nourouzi and Baker, 1999) as long as services are successfully delivered. Their main concern is service ubiquity. Also, some policymakers regard convergence service such as web casting to be a "like service" because it delivers content to users in a way that sometimes closely resembles other traditional broadcasting services (OECD, 1997).

Customers may not be concerned with multi-characteristics of convergence services. Instead, they simply interpret those services as being one of the basic services. For example, consumers may consider Internet phone service as voice service rather than data service. Assuming that their voice telecommunications needs are adequately satisfied, customers perceive them the same whether they were serviced through PSTN or PSDN.

*Examples*

Service convergence can be explained for different services such as broadcasting, voice, and data services, which are shown in figure 4. Essentially similar kinds of services would be grouped or considered as one of the basic telecommunications services. If we select a service in the *i*-th row in the Service-Network matrix, those elements in the same row would represent convergence services made possible by service convergence.

For example, broadcasting services are provided via broadcasting, voice, and data networks. Cable TV service used to be provided through cable networks, however, other networks such as PSTN and PSDN became alternative media to provide customers with similar services such as interactive TV and web casting. Also, voice services are provided via voice, data, and broadcasting networks. Until recently, voice service had been provided mostly through wired telephone networks. However, other networks such as cable network and PSDN now can provide voice service in the form of Internet phone service. Finally, data service had been primarily provided by data service dedicated PSDN. However, PSTN and cable networks are now able to provide the same data service in different forms.

*Drivers*

The driving forces of service convergence can be identified from several points of view - network operators, customers, and technology.

Network operators can provide value-added services by utilizing the current network infrastructures to provide seamless services. For example, one-phone services are based on both fixed and mobile networks to provide a seamless voice service thereby delivering extra customer value as well as competitive advantages against competitors. The service convergence enables the network operators to expand their scope of services, so that they can offer 'one-stop service' which is an effective way to retain their current subscribers.

Consumers want easy and ubiquitous access to services, and they want options to a variety of services. Service convergence may satisfy those customers' demand. For example, Internet access service was offered only by wired networks with limited bandwidth. However, a new convergence service (e.g., wireless LAN service) provides both Internet access and increased mobility, thereby, supporting users' preference for access and convenience needs.

Finally, Internet Protocol (IP) technology enabled platform-independent telecommunications services. Seamless services are provided across multiple networks with standardized technologies and protocols.

### 3.3. Network Convergence

Network convergence enables network operators to leverage their existing networks, so that they can save additional network installation costs and thereby reduce consumer prices when providing new telecommunications services. Due to the keen competition in the telecommunications market, network operators have incentives to pass the cost savings to customers in the form of lower prices. As a result, one of the major drivers for network convergence is the incentive to reduce costs when providing new telecommunications services.

*Examples*

Network convergence can be explained for three different kinds of networks shown in the figure 4. If we select a network in the *j*-th column in a Service-Network matrix or $S_{\bullet j}$, then the column would represent convergence services made possible by network convergence.

For example, as the cable network is digitalized, it can provide broadcasting, data, and voice services. With advanced modulation technologies, cable operators can provide their subscribers cable modem service and Internet phone service with the cable TV service. Public Switched Telephone Network (PSTN) provides not only traditional voice service, but also web casting service and data service using ADSL & dial-up modem technologies. In the same way, Public Switched Data Network (PSDN) can provide not only dedicated data service, but also web casting and Internet phone services, which are all available from other networks such as cable and PSTN.

*Drivers*

The driving forces to the network convergence can be identified from several points of view - network operators, customers, government, and technology.

With low capacity utilization rates, the greatest benefits of network convergence to network operators are to leverage the existing networks (Solomon and Walker, 1995). They can expand or initiate new business by selecting the market where a firm's unique resources can earn the highest revenue (Teece et al., 1997). It is economical to extend services by re-using an existing highly reliable infrastructure, which requires only small incremental installation costs. For example, incumbent PSTN operators can provide both voice and Internet access services via a single PSTN; thereby utilizing its unique resource - local loop network - in the most effective way.

The most important customer benefit from network convergence may be convenience. Single billing (Burols et al., 1998) and consolidated customer interface are among the key benefits of network convergence. For example, customers may prefer a single provider who can supply conventional telephone service as well as Internet access service with discounts in a single bill. Furthermore, as consumer habits are not easily changed, and the market needs time to be educated (Bores et al., 2001), the existing network interfaces or installations may act as switching costs.

From the regulatory viewpoint, deregulation in the telecommunications industry has intensified market competition. Companies providing a single service were forced to compete against other companies who provide diverse or bundled services. That has led telecommunications companies to look for a better way of utilizing networks by the network convergence.

Finally, digital technology is a key driving force to convergence. It has demonstrated its efficiency, flexibility and effectiveness in relevant sectors – computer and telecommunications industries (European Commission, 1997). Digitalization has spawned services across conventional industries or sector boundaries (Tadayoni and Skouby, 1999), thereby facilitating the convergence at the technical level (Henten, 1999).

### 3.4. Implications

The Service-Network matrix helps to make a clear and comprehensive description of the convergence phenomenon from both service and network perspectives. Once cells in the matrix are filled with currently available services, managers can identify potentials for new services. They can decide whether to deliver currently available services through alternative networks[4] or to provide new services through currently available networks[5].

From the regulatory point of view, the Service-Network matrix provides an opportunity to see the convergence phenomenon from provider and customer's view. The network perspective helps regulators to understand the extent of network providers' capability to deliver different kinds of services. In the convergence era, conventional regulations based on one-service via one-network concept are not adequate any more. Therefore, Service-Network matrix will help to change the conventional regulatory practices. Also, the service perspective helps to understand that which services consumers consider equivalent. The understanding of customer perception may dictate the direction of regulation. For example, regulation on the Internet telephony will be decided depending on how the customers perceive the service: Are they perceiving it as a voice service or as a specific application of data service?

## 4. NEW CONVERGENCE SERVICE DEVELOPMENT PROCESS

This section illustrates how we can use the Service-Network matrix in the Stage-Gate process shown in figure 2.

### 4.1. Predevelopment Process

The Service-Network matrix can be used to identify new business opportunities in the idea generation stage. Additionally, tools for screening out potential candidates would be needed to deal with uncertainties inherent in the new convergence service development process. A scenario planning approach is suggested as an effective way to deal with the issue. A scenario is a description of potential future states presented in the logical and internally consistent manner (Linneman et al, 1985, Schoemaker, 1991). It helps not to overlook potential negative impacts of the consequences (Schwatz, 1991). Therefore, the scenario planning is well suited to thoroughly understand the uncertainties involved in the new convergence service development process, especially in the feasibility assessment stage. Incidentally, Ahn and Skudlark (2002) used the scenario planning approach to develop a new telecommunications service concept or *Phoneweb service* that allows Internet access through the telephone rather than a computer interface. Figure 5 compares a general predevelopment process to a proposed convergence predevelopment process.

---

[4] It is defined as service convergence.

[5] It is defined as network convergence.

General predevelopment process     Convergence predevelopment process

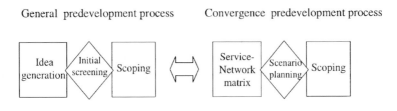

Figure 5. Predevelopment Process: General vs. Convergence

The convergence predevelopment process shown in figure 5 is applied to a new convergence service. A new convergence service or wireless ADSL service at home is identified by building Service-Network matrix under the convergence environment, and then evaluated by the scenario planning approach from the technological change and customer demand dimensions.

## 4.2. An Example: Wireless ADSL Service at Home

Currently, different types of Internet access services are available. Mobile Internet access service, narrowband Internet access service using dial-up modem, and broadband Internet access service using ADSL and cable modems are examples. Recently, public wireless LAN (WLAN) service was introduced to provide wireless Internet service in public places, such as airports, hotels, cafes, etc. In the following, a new convergence service is identified by building a Service-Network matrix for those services and the new service is evaluated by the scenario planning approach.

*Idea Generation Using the Service-Network Matrix*

Each diagonal element in figure 6 shows a specific service provided by the conventional network. However, a specific service in the off-diagonal matrix can be a potential convergence service. For example, public wireless LAN service is provided where fixed Internet can be accessed in public. But a new convergence service can provide Internet access service at home in the form of home ADSL service through wireless LAN. It is shown as a shaded rectangular. We can call it *wireless ADSL service at home.*

It is a service that wireless LAN service is provided at the public places and wireless ADSL service is provided at home. If private wireless LAN can connect multiple PCs at home economically, that would give multiple home PC users access to Internet by sharing a single ADSL line. This feature could help to address the customer retention problems that most of the Internet service providers face.

However, this convergence service would be different from an Internet access solution that connects PCs at home with a personal router. Specifically, personal router solution can't address security issue. However, wireless users of ADSL service at home can be authenticated by the service provider, which would enable serious transactions.

|  | Mobile network | PSTN | Wireless LAN |
|---|---|---|---|
| Mobile Internet service | 2.5G or 3G Service |  |  |
| Wired Internet Service at Home |  | ADSL Service | Wireless ADSL Service at Home |
| WLAN Service in Public |  |  | Public WLAN Service |

Figure 6. New Convergence Service: Broadband Internet Access with Mobile Capability

### Initial Screening Using a Scenario Planning Approach

Despite the benefits of convergence services, they do not always produce a market success. For example, uncertainties regarding customer demands and technological advances may determine the level of market success. To deal with those uncertainties, scenario planning can be used to evaluate the concept of new convergence service or wireless ADSL service at home.

Three major uncertainties in the broadband Internet access market were identified: level of mobile multimedia demand (U1), extent of progress in network technology (U2), and level of terminal convenience (U3). Those uncertainties might affect one another; therefore some combinations of assumptions may not be internally consistent (Porter, 1985). Figure 7 shows three consistent scenarios developed in the broadband Internet access service market.

In scenario I (Wireless World), the performances of the wireless technologies have become significantly enhanced in terms of bandwidth and QoS (Quality of Service). The inherent wireless constraints – interference and noises - are resolved; therefore every telecommunications service can be delivered wirelessly. Terminals are user-friendly and easy-to-carry; smart phones are ubiquitous. Whether at home or on the move, consumers are accustomed to access to the Internet and to mobile applications – commerce, games, music, etc. Hence the wireless ADSL service at home could satisfy many of customers' wireless needs.

In scenario II (Seamless Internet), mobile and fixed network technologies have similar level of performances in terms of bandwidth and speed. However, wireless technologies are still constrained by interference and noise. While mobile multimedia demands are high, terminal technologies are not convenient enough; for example, people have to carry notebooks to access the wireless Internet rather than smart phones. The use of mobile Internet is limited inside building areas – such as, airports, hotels, etc. Hence the wireless ADSL service complements conventional wired ADSL service at home.

In scenario III (Separate Market), the wireless data transmission rate is not enough to compete with wired Internet. Advanced fixed network technology is prevailing and even fiber network technology is to be commercialized. However, mobile terminals still remain to be developed in terms of size, weight, display, processing power, memory, etc. Consumers have become accustomed to using Internet services, especially multimedia services, through fixed-networks using their PCs and notebooks inside buildings or at home. Therefore, wireless ADSL service at home satisfies Internet access demand using desktops or notebooks while leveraging the current ADSL line.

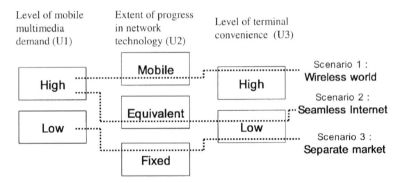

Figure 7. Consistent Scenarios in the Broadband Internet Access Market

Based on the three developed scenarios, newly proposed wireless ADSL service at home was judged to be viable under any of the circumstances. In other words, the service has competitive advantage irrespective of future market conditions. Through this example, it was shown that a new convergence service can be identified by the Service–Network matrix and the meaningful feasibility analysis can be made through scenario planning.

## 5.    CONCLUSION

The convergence phenomenon is prevalent in the telecommunications industry. However, our understanding of the convergence phenomenon is vague resulting in confusion and uncertainty about the future business environment. This paper proposed the Service-Network matrix to better explain the convergence phenomenon, and also illustrated a new service predevelopment process suitable in the convergence environment by utilizing the Service-Network matrix and the scenario planning approach.

Using the Service-Network matrix helps to make a clear and comprehensive description of the convergence phenomenon from both network and service perspectives. Thereby, managers in the telecommunications industry can identify the potential for a new service or the opportunities to deliver services economically through alternative networks. Also, the scenario planning approach is quick and easy to implement, therefore, satisfies the urgent need for the telecommunications companies facing convergence phenomenon.

Activities such as initial screening, preliminary market and technical assessment, and undertaking a detailed market study were strongly correlated with product outcomes (Cooper and Kleinschmidt, 1986, Cooper, 1988). Therefore, activities properly exercised in the predevelopment process would enhance the market performance of the new telecommunications services. Telecommunications companies could apply this approach easily and quickly in order to gain competitive advantage in the fast-changing convergence environment.

There are three areas that warrant further research. First, if we identify opportunities for new convergence services, then we may want to anticipate and prepare for competitor's actions. A scenario analysis that incorporates competitive responses coupled with the insight from the Service-Network matrix may be helpful in the effort. Second, regulatory issues such as universal services, taxation, and content regulation need to be investigated, especially when similar convergence services were regulated as a single basic service. Third, the application of the Service-Network matrix is not limited to the convergence phenomenon in the telecommunications industry. Telecommunications companies may enter into alliances with other parties such as entertainment companies, financial institutions, or fast-food franchises in order to provide augmented services. Therefore, service provisioning (e.g. mobile banking services, reservation services, etc.) through different networks or channels are possible and they can be analyzed as convergence services.

## 6. REFERENCES

Ahn, J.H. and Skudlark, A. (2002), "Managing Risk in a Telecommunications New Service Development Process through a Scenario Planning Approach", *Journal of Information Technology*, Vol. 17, No. 3, pp. 103-118.

Blackman, C.R. (1995), "Universal Service: Obligation or Opportunity?", *Telecommunications Policy*, Vol. 19, No. 3, pp. 171-176.

Blackman, C.R. (1998), "Convergence Between Telecommunications and Other Media: How Should Regulation Adapt?", *Telecommunications Policy*, Vol. 22, No. 3, pp. 163-170.

Bores et al (2001), "Technological Convergence: A Strategic Perspective", Working Paper, Department of Economics, University of Girona, Spain.

Burols, O., Garner, M. and Nourouzi, A. (1998), "Fixed and Mobile Convergence: Dream, Reality or Red Herring?", Short Report 7 Mobile@Ovum, April.

Clements, B. (1998), "The Impact of Convergence on Regulatory Policy in Europe", *Telecommunications Policy*, Vol. 22, No. 3, pp. 197-205.

Cooper, R.G. and Kleinschmidt, E. (1986), "An Investigation into the New Product Process", *Journal of Product Innovation Management*, Vol. 3, pp. 71-85.

Cooper, R.G. (1988), "Predevelopment Activities Determines New Product Success", *Industrial Marketing Management*, Vol. 17, pp. 237-247.

Cooper, R.G. and Edgett, S.J. (1999), *Product Development for the Service Sector: Lessons from Market Leaders*, Perseus publishing, Cambridge, Massachusetts, USA.

Cooper, R.G. (2001), *Winning at New Products: Accelerating the Process from Idea to Launch*, 3rd edition, Perseus publishing, Cambridge, Massachusetts, USA.

Edwards, J. (1999), "Convergence Reshapes the Networking Industry", *Computer*, Vol. 32, Issue 5, pp. 14-16.

European Commission (1997), Green Paper on the Convergence of the Telecommunications, Media and Information Technology Sectors, and the Implications for Regulation Towards an Information Society Approach, COM(97) 623, Brussels.

European Commission (1998), Summary of the Results of the Public Cnsultation on the Greenpaper on the Convergence of the Telecommunications, Media, and Information Technology Sectors: Areas for Further Reflection, SEC(98) 1284, Brussels.

Garnham, N. (1996), "Regulatory Issues", paper presented at a meeting organized by the European Commission, Legal Advisory Board, on "Convergence between Telecommunications and Audiovisual: Consequences for the Rules Governing the Information Market", April, Brussels.

Harrison F.G. and Hearnden S.R. (1999), "The Challenge to Realize Convergence of Fixed and Mobile Communications", *Electronics & Communication Engineering Journal*, pp. 164-168.

Henten, A. (1999), "Convergence: Synergies and Media Power", paper for Policy and Regulatory Summit Telecom 99, 10 Oct, Geneva.

Henten, A. and Tadayoni, R. (2001), "Implications of Internet on Broadcasting", paper presented at the 15th Nordic Conference on Media and Communications Research, 11 August, Reykjavik.

Linneman, R.E. and Harold, E.K. (1985), "Using Scenarios in Strategic Decision Making", *Business Horizons*, Vol. 28, No. 1, pp. 64-74.

McGougan, J. (1999), "Policy and Regulatory Issues in Convergence", IEEE Seminar on Home-Net.TV Plus, June.

Nourouzi, A. and Baker, D. (1999), "Fixed-mobile Convergence Services: Integration and Substitution", Competitive Communications@Ovum, August.

Organization for Economic Co-operation and Development (1997), "Webcasting and Convergence: Policy Implications", OCDE/GD(97) 221, Paris, France.

Porter, M.E. (1985), *Competitive Advantage: Creating and Sustaining Superior Performance*, The Free Press, New York, NY.

Schoemaker, P. (1991), "When and How to Use Scenario Planning: A Heuristic Approach with Illustration", *Journal of Forecasting*. Vol. 10, pp. 549-564.

Schwartz, P. (1991), *The Art of the Long View*, Currency Doubleday.

Sheldon, T. (2001), *Encyclopedia Networking & Telecommunications*, McGraw-Hill, Berkeley, California, USA.

Solomon, J. and Walker, D. (1995), "Separating Infrastructure and Service Provision: The Broadband Imperative", *Telecommunications Policy*, Vol. 19, No. 2, pp. 83-89.

Tadayoni, R. and Kristensen, T. (1999), "Universal Access in Broadcasting: Solving the Information Problems of the Digital Age?", paper presented at the 9th annual INET conference, San Jose, USA.

Tadayoni, R., Skouby, K.E. (1999), "Terrestrial Digital Broadcasting: Convergence and its Regulatory Implications", *Telecommunications Policy*, Vol. 23, pp. 175-199.

Teece, D.J., Pisano, G. and Shuen, A. (1997), "Dynamic Capabilities and Strategic Management", *Strategic Management Journal*, Vol. 18, No. 7, pp. 509-533.

Yoon, C.B. et al. (1999), "The Policy Development under the Convergence Phenomenon in Broadcasting and Telecommunications Industries", Korea Information Society Development Society (KISDI), Seoul, Korea.

Yoffie, D.B. (1996), "Competing in the Age of Digital Convergence", *California Management Journal*, Vol. 38, No. 4, pp. 31-53.

# PART II

Global Economy and Digital Society
E. Bohlin, S. Levin, N. Sung and C-H. Yoon (Editors)

# CHAPTER 20

# What the World Trade Center Attack has Shown us About our Communications Networks

Eli M. Noam

*Columbia Institute for Tele-Information, Columbia University, New York*

**Abstract**. This chapter addresses how communications networks coped with the aftermath of the attacks on the World Trade Center and the Pentagon, and the lessons for the future about the nature of emergency communications. The chapter documents how domestic and international fixed-line and mobile networks, business communication systems, and the internet responded to the huge increase in traffic volume that followed the attacks. While the limitations of cellular networks and major internet content servers in serving millions of users simultaneously were demonstrated, decentralized forms of communication such as email, instant messaging, and bulletin boards performed well. The author concludes that we should revise the basic philosophy of emergency communication from that of the traditional military-style, top-down approach of public safety agencies to a more decentralized system building on lessons from the spontaneous efforts of using internet technology following September 11.

When tragedy strikes, people communicate enormously driven by objective need and subjective compulsion. Have communications networks been up to the task of coping with the aftermath of the attack on the World Trade Center and the Pentagon? What are the lessons? The implications are important to others, since natural and man-made disasters will recur more often than one would wish.

Within minutes of the attack on September 11, 2001, traditional telecommunications were stretched and overloaded. In New York, the collapse of the buildings took out a big phone switch with 200,000 voicelines and a large number of private line circuits, right in the middle of the downtown financial district, and about 20 cellphone antenna sites, and 9 TV broadcast stations using the World Trade Center, but that was only part of the problem. Phone networks are not so much destroyed as congested into uselessness. Networks are designed to handle about 10-15 percent of their subscribers at any one time, to maintain a desired quality of service in terms of blocking probability. But in New York, local traffic volume shot up 2-3 times the usual peak (exact figures are hard to get, since so many calls never made it through to be counted). Long distance voice service on the East Coast became non-functional for a while though it seems to have worked well enough for data traffic. Long distance companies pleaded for people to make only essential calls. They gave priority to calls going out of emergency areas in preference to calls coming in. Some people learned how to beat the system by calling collect, which often worked, but at a price.

A key issue is hence the delicate question of how to allocate scarce capacity in emergency situations when demand is high and supply may be disrupted. Using higher prices as a market-clearing device, as economists might propose, is not likely to be an acceptable solution. Demand is likely to be highly price-inelastic, and the notion of charging grandma $50 per minute to find out if the kids are safe is not likely to be something a phone company's PR department would recommend. Indeed, Verizon, the local phone company, made payphones free for several days. Hence, emergencies require, as a very short-term arrangement, a rationing of scarce capacity that works better than the present random allocation by busy signal. Such a system already exists for official and semi-official use. It is known as GETS (Government Emergency Telecommunications Service) and provides priority to users with special calling cards. Participants include emergency and responsibilities, such as utilities, transportation, and banks. 95 % of GETS calls in New York got through, but that still leaves open how to allocate the remaining capacity among non-official users.

International communications experienced the greatest problems. Trans-Atlantic traffic from Britain was reportedly ten times its normal volume. Less than half of calls from Finland to America got through. 90% of calls from Sweden and Taiwan were blocked. Normally, networks are engineered for congestion of less than 2 percent. Such congestion indicates a huge increase in traffic volume, especially given the vast increase in transatlantic capacity that has come on line in the last few years. What clogged the network was the switching capacity. Transmission has become plentiful, but other bottlenecks remain. To overcome them will be even more important in a society that needs to protect itself against terrorist attacks. Inevitably, various forms of electronic sensors will proliferate, as will the scanning – airport like – of vehicles and cargos. Such scanning is enormously data-intensive, and will require transmissions of high capacity and resiliency.

Cellphones were put to heroic uses, from under the rubble and from hijacked planes. Rescuers got free cellphones from service providers. It seems hard to imagine how after this experience people would ever want to step out without their electronic security blanket. But the cellphones also showed their limitations. For some mobile service providers traffic quadrupled. Everywhere, it seemed, people walked down the street, cell phones glued to their ear, tears in their eyes, but frustration in their face, as they encountered chronic circuit busy signals and eventually ran out of battery power. The cellphone-less huddled around payphones, which seemed to be mostly working, this demonstrating the usefulness of such a "legacy" backup system. The chronic problem of calls not getting through demonstrates the need for the wireless companies to institute a better priority system. A national priority system for mobile phones has been in planning since 1995, but had not been concluded due to insufficient planning funds. For example, one could institute an automatic emergency cutoff of a mobile call after a certain number of minutes. Another solution is to shift cellphone users from voice to short messaging of text. With an 'always-on' technology, as demonstrated in Japan by NTT Docomo's popular i-mode technology, large numbers of users could always be connected at the same time, because they would occupy a frequency only when they send or receive some bits of information, which for text is not much. More spectrum is needed. But even more important is flexibility in using the available spectrum. This includes enabling handheld transceivers of cellular communications to reach other providers and other wireless services such as unlicensed wireless LAN hotspots. Another possibility is to enable the handset to function in peer-to-peer mode. All this would mean reducing the control of cellular service providers over the subscribers' equipment and its uses.

Business communications, such as companies' private networks and data networks, performed quite well. Financial firms might be expected to be reluctant to discuss internal communications breakdowns, but there were few outside reports about encountering such problems. A record number of SOS "disaster declarations" went out to firms that specialize in running computer backup facilities, but they mostly originated from small firms. Big companies are sophisticated users of information. Their data is backed up, and their networks are configured to adjust instantaneously to emergency conditions. Thank you, hackers of the world, for having kept everybody on their toes.

When it comes to the internet, the experience was mixed. The internet backbones functioned well. But some of the major servers of content and transactions slowed down annoyingly. In particular, the internet did not perform particularly well as a mass medium. News sites like CNN.com, MSNBC.com congested almost immediately as the number of users shot up to record levels. The sites did not scale well. Alter encountering congestion, they were stripped down to basic text information. Before the attacks, CNN.com got typically14 million page views per day. On September 11, there were 9 million page views per hour. The lesson is that if one wants to rapidly provide information of interest to millions of people, more or less at the same time, a superior technology is readily available. It is called broadcasting. Aficionados of news websites may protest vociferously, but in peak situations internet news sites are less efficient and effective, and "synchronous" information shared by millions beats in those situations the "asynchronous" provision of information. The websites are then best deployed to serve the specialized or distant users for whom TV news sources tend to be inadequate. Examples are Argentineans who want to get more information than they can get over their national TV; Americans who wish to see how Arab media cover the event; as Norwegians who, are in the shipping business and want to know the impact of the attack on the price of oil tanker charters.

But where the internet shone brightly was in email, and instant messaging, and bulletin boards. Email messages had no problems in getting through. Maybe they were a bit slower in arriving, but the difference rarely mattered. Instant messaging was even faster, enabling distant correspondents to be in touch in real time. It all worked beautifully. After all, that was exactly what the Internet's predecessor was originally designed for by the American military: as a network that could not be easily destroyed, because it was decentralized. Furthermore, it diverted billions of voice calls from the long distance telephone networks, thereby also benefiting the email-less. A 5-minute voice phone call consumes as much transmission capacity as about 4,000 typical emails. By sending a batch of email messages instead of making phone calls, people free up congested networks. It's a bit like donating blood. Another great contribution of the internet was the bulletin board systems. Here, people could post that they were well, that someone else was fine, and how could they be reached. The information was available to the visitors of the sites from all over the world, thus reducing the anxiety that accompanies the frustrations of searching by phone for news about loved ones. Other boards listed unofficially the names of persons reported missing. Still others included requests for help locating missing friends and relatives, and it was hard to read them with dry eyes. Some of these bulletin boards are set up by some official organization, or by large portals such as Prodigy. But most seem spontaneous attempts by volunteers. The bulletin sites tend to be linked to each other. In time, sites with search engines emerged, such as elbnet.com/wtc, that would search many of them automatically so that one would not have to visit each.

The internet chat rooms were sometimes touching, occasionally inspiring, and frequently maddening considering people's argumentativeness even in the face of tragedy. But that may have a positive function in letting people blow off steam.

The emergence of these internet tools and practices provides us lessons for the future about the nature of emergency communications. Disasters are a physical problem first, but soon an information problem. Government authorities are just as much in the dark in a catastrophe as individuals are. During the Los Angeles quake, President Clinton's early information sources were his brother and the TV news. When an earthquake hit the city of Kobe, in Japan, the Japanese government labored for hours in the belief that the number of dead was only 5 percent of the actual figure.

It is time to learn from these experiences and revise the basic philosophy of emergency communication from that of the traditional military-style, top-down, public safety agencies, in which information travels up the hierarchical chains-of-command. Traditional emergency communication is exemplified by the '911' system, in which citizens report to the authorities when something goes wrong, and the authorities provide the public with information whose timing and completeness is in the hands of officials working under great pressure.

A more affective approach would be to learn from the spontaneous efforts of using internet technology and supplement 911 by what might be called the '811' system: by dialing 811(or typing an equivalent URL) over internet-enabled phones, cellphones, or computers, individuals would gain access to a regional 'emergency portal' which links to a variety of official, non-profit, and spontaneous websites, as well as to other portals, and "meet me" points.

Much of the information would also be available to distant parties and reduce the workload on "hotlines" that are chronically busy. It would give news organizations detailed information and sources, could link world-wide donors with actual needs, provide "how-to" information, and reach specialized data bases, for example protection against about toxic substances. Certain communications could have to remain confidential or private and require special levels of access authorization, but that could be easily accomplished.

The aftermath of the World Trade Center disaster shows that such a system is emerging spontaneously. It also demonstrates that the public agencies are still far behind in making use of it, encouraging it, or contributing much to it beyond official announcements. One of the main conclusions is that it is essential to have communications systems that are decentralized and duplicative instead of centralized and monopolized by a single firm or technology. All this demonstrates the importance of decentralization: of information sources and of information channels. If one put all one's eggs in one basket they will break. In New York, the public services emergency control center was right in the WTC complex and was destroyed within minutes. A centralized system will in fact attract attacks because to destroy a vital communications mode will have major repercussions.

There is strength in decentralization. Diversity protects. The data packets of the internet found their own way around disasters just as their creators in the 1960s envisioned. Technology is not the solution to the problem of terrorism, but the latter's challenge might spur innovations. What we have seen in New York is that the communications system is much more resistant to attack, than physical assets like skyscrapers or subway lines were. As the physical realm of society becomes more vulnerable, the virtual realm is becoming increasingly robust. This may be a comforting thought, though one wishes for the opposite to have been true on September 11, 2001.

Global Economy and Digital Society
E. Bohlin, S. Levin, N. Sung and C-H. Yoon (Editors)

# CHAPTER 21

# Network Resilience and its Regulatory Inhibitors

James Alleman

*College of Engineering and Applied Science, University of Colorado, Boulder*

Jonathan Liebenau

*Department of Information Systems, London School of Economics, London*

**Abstract**. This chapter explores the rules, regulation, and company actions that impede network resilience. The chapter starts with a definition of network resilience and a discussion of factors that affect it, falling into the three interacting categories of standards, regulation, and government practices and policies. This analysis allows the authors to identify barriers to network resilience related to local exchange carriers (LECs) and electromagnetic spectrum issues, with a focus on rules and regulation that resulted from the Telecommunications Act of 1996. The chapter proposes four main action areas, involving pro-active roles for industry and government actors, for enhancing network resilience: Ensuring inter-modal competition; Stimulating demand for resilience by raising standards; Subsidies to build out critical infrastructure; Devising new governmental roles and priorities. Addressing these concerns, while expensive in parts, will stimulate new business development in the telecommunications industry and is therefore economically justifiable.

## 1  INTRODUCTION

With the events of 9/11, the concern for network resilience has been foremost on the agenda of the country. The desperate, but often unsuccessful, attempts of people to communicate immediately after the attack on the World Trade Center are the most poignant reminder of the need for communications. While the telecommunications companies responded heroically, and service was restored quickly (Elby 2002, Aduskevicz 2001), many experienced trouble and firms in the Wall Street area and beyond found that the redundancy they thought they had did not exist (United States General Accounting Office 2003a). These firms did not understand that some of the complex rules developed by the Federal Communications Commission (FCC) and mandated by Congress rendered the networks less resilient than they could have been. Many changes are expected in response to the revelations about weaknesses, and also in the normal course of adapting to new conditions of security consciousness and newly available technologies.

However, the current economic weakness of the telecommunications industry is the dominant factor inhibiting investment in network resilience. This weakness has roots in the disillusion of financiers following the "dot.com bubble", the mismanagement of some leading companies, and the detrimental effects of severe competition during a period of high spending for acquisitions, licenses and market share. Many blame the Telecommunications Act of 1996 for some of this weakening; others focus on poor strategic choices and mismanagement in the face of high costs and price-cutting among competitors (Noam 2003). Here we will consider the environment around the telecommunications industry to show what forces are at play and to what extent the network suffers from delay or distortion to the goal of increased resilience.

New opportunities will arise with new thinking about the use of spectrum and the efficient application of new technologies, especially those associated with novel wireless communication devices and architectures. New theories on how to charge for spectrum and how new technologies will allow for spectrum sharing could generate a revised economics of wireless communication that will provide the incentives for investment in resilience.

Effective interoperability and interconnection, a central requirement for resilience, is at least as much a fraught business problem, with policy implications, as it is a technical problem. The current systems of interconnection are also difficult to monitor, to the point where lines are now commonly shared, or conduits are used in common, even where higher levels of independence are expected. How would the disclosure of routing paths affect judgments about reliability and resilience, and what are appropriate rules for interconnection and co-location?

The purpose of this paper is to explore the rules, regulation, and company actions which impede network resilience. We will only be concerned with technical issues insofar as they have impact on the economic and regulatory themes. Initially we address the definition of network resilience and consider the economics and policy areas which affect network resilience. We then explore the ways in which regulation and commercial service and equipment providers create impediments to network resilience. We conclude with an outline of recommendations to enhance the economic/business aspect of network resilience.

## 2    DEFINITION OF NETWORK RESILIENCE

Before proceeding with the discussion, we need to define what we mean by network resilience. The engineering concept is straightforward: it combines the concept of the "robustness" of a system with the ability to reconstitute itself or to be easily repaired. But what would determine the economic/policy definition of resilience? Resilience must be affordable such that investment and maintenance of a resilient network ensures business viability or at least affordability where subsidies are offered. However, in the long term resilient communications will have to be economical within the normal course of charges for services and any governmental involvement will have to be justified as a reasonable cost to ensure national priorities of infrastructure security.

We combine these ideas by adapting the working notion that network resilience lowers the probability that an event will occur that destroys or disables part of a network such that it cannot be reconstituted – a self-healing network. An example of a resilient network would be a long distance network that, when a major transmission link was cut, was capable of rerouting calls such that the calls were unaffected. Similarly, in a metropolitan network, a SONET ring can provide resilience such that when a cut occurs service can be restored by rerouting around the ring within the accepted 50 millisecond period that allows for transparent voice communication handover. Improvements in network resilience could include incentives to invest in order to make a more robust innovative system or to have more redundancy built into the existing system. It might include the technical ability to make use of alternatives by switching from one form of the network to another (as in transferring calls from the PSTN to the internet through voice over IP). Or, it might be the capability built into systems such that functions can be switched between standard and non-standard usages.

## 3    FACTORS AFFECTING NETWORK RESILIENCE

Economic and policy factors, in addition to technical ones, have long influenced the engineering character of networks and will increasingly affect their resilience. These fall into three main interacting categories: standards, regulation, and government practices and policies.

### 3.1    Standards

Standards lie at the heart of network resilience in three ways. Firstly, there is the accepted definition of what constitutes resilience and the tolerance allowable for networks. Currently for voice networks a restoration time of 50 milliseconds is regarded as necessary to ensure transparent handover, and that standard can be met by SONET rings but not by many other standard architectures. The tolerance for handover of data streams can be lower, and a slight lowering of the standard could even now open up a variety of new technologies for consideration as resilient network components. This might especially affect voice over the internet (VoIP) and some of the wireless technologies, including potential networks composed of wireless local area network, IEEE 802.11 standards (especially the widely used WiFi 802.11b technologies).

The other key element of standard concerns the compatibility of hardware and software, and of the use of spectrum, which we address below. Standardization of systems can allow alternative providers of equipment to interface with others when breaks occur and most especially in times of emergency (a necessary but not sufficient condition). The prime example of the lack of compatibility in the United States is the current cellular system. Europe, and much of the rest of the world, adopted the global system mobile communications (GSM) standard, which allows for inter-country roaming and economies of scale in the production of handsets; in principle, the standard also allows for subscribers to utilize the service of alternative providers in time of emergency. New handsets with multiple standards and separate antennae are currently available, but the business model for their use in the United States as well as the regulatory context in which they might operate trail behind the available technology.[6]

For example, the trade-offs between standardization and non-standardization could be examined in the context of using 4-G (and even 3-G) technologies in imaginative ways that provide greater resilience to networks (Techapalokul, Alleman & Chen 2001). There remain many imponderables for future wireless telephony architectures, most especially since the pace of commercial development has slowed following the financial crisis of the telecommunications industry. The extent of consolidation of the industry, and the extent to which

---

[6] There are those who argue that the development of CDMA technology will be seen in the long run as a positive outcome of the lack of imposed mobile telephone standards in the United States.

competing service providers will be allowed to share networks, will have a major impact on how we might bring forward greater resilience.

One of the concrete proposals to accommodate the financial pressures of the industry insofar as it is overextended in wireless investment is to share certain standard resources. In Europe various types of sharing have been initiated, in some cases, as in Germany, limited to sharing towers (a proposal also popular in other places where property rights and planning permissions make the proliferation of towers problematic, as in Britain) and in others stretching to the sharing of significant elements of the network. Where sharing has occurred it has brought about increased levels of interoperability, sometimes to a limited degree, while in other cases it has been more extensive. Interoperability is usually regarded as a contribution to resilience, but the collocation of facilities, and the multiple usage of apparently redundant elements of infrastructure also have the characteristic of being more vulnerable to attack—one destroyed tower or shared switching facility then doubles the network damage, or worse. In sum, this raises the question, would shared networks, in principle, raise or lower resilience?

### 3.2   Regulatory Opportunities and Impediments

Legislative and political forces upon the communications industry can enhance network resilience or create roadblocks that inhibit innovations toward more resilient networks. For example, choices about the character of allowable competition have affected the market structure, which, in turn, have an effect on network resilience, as we demonstrate below. Similarly, constraints upon the use of spectrum have an impact on network resilience. A further means would be in adjusting the form of regulation and standards set by bodies such as the Securities and Exchange Commission to guide the way in which financial institutions must ensure that data and communications are adequately protected (United States General Accounting Office 2003b).

Regulators in this industry have usually been mindful of the need to ensure that major investments in commercial technology and in built infrastructure need to be encouraged and to some degree protected. This has meant, in effect, that disruptive technologies have been constrained when they threaten to undermine huge sunk costs early in the investment cycle. Proponents of voice over internet protocol (VoIP) hold this opinion, and many of those enthusiastic about the potential of recent "bottom-up" spreading of wireless local area networks, especially the 802.11b standard (WiFi), believe that the tentative attitude of regulators is delaying what might turn out to be a disruptive technology that could contribute to network resilience. Evidently in Europe the very slow development of WiFi can be attributed to the willingness of regulators to inhibit its use, often on the grounds that it will interfere with spectrum reserved for police and the security services (in Britain and France). It also is seen as a disruptive technology in the context of massive investment in 3G mobile telephony networks (most especially in Britain and Germany).

Regulators do have numerous opportunities to enhance resilience. Currently, for example, the outage reporting system, unchanged for ten years and almost unreformed since its establishment, demands that service providers file memoranda of cuts to service and compile copious data, but fails to use that data in any strategic manner. Outage reports are rarely referred to when issues such as license renewals are discussed, and they are not used to sanction poor performers.[7] Another example of the potential for regulatory involvement could come with requirements to register details of built infrastructure. The absence of accurate maps of switching and conduit systems is a major missed opportunity which regulators, perhaps at the state level, could remedy, especially given the potential for the application of advanced digitalized geographical information systems.

### 3.3   Government

Although many national security applications such as military communications and the Government Emergency Telecommunication System (GETS) are not directly constrained by commercial financial factors, local governments and civilian applications (including emergency services) are. Government bodies are major consumers of communications services and devices and have the potential to exert more customer pressure on network providers to raise the priority of resilience.

Government users affect prices and demand, and also the opportunities to build out commercial infrastructure to enhance resilience. They also distort the market through their control of large amounts of spectrum. In the years preceding September 2001 much discussion occurred about how new blocks of spectrum could be made available to telecommunications users. It was often noted that the large blocks reserved for broadcasters, especially television broadcasting, were not being used efficiently in the sense that new compression and other technologies are more sparing of spectrum, offering opportunities to relieve some amounts of spectrum. The other large block of spectrum is reserved for military use. Prior to the recent concerns for national security and the needs of the armed forces, there was much discussion of the possibility of releasing some of that spectrum. This proposal is no longer on the table. However, the distorting effects of this kind of governmental control over spectrum has severely limited the availability of non-licensed spectrum, in some cases pressing developers of new technologies to use less efficient spectral bands (such as bands where transmissions are diminished by rain, fog or other atmospheric conditions).

Resilient network improvements must take into account the access prioritization policies of governmental bodies. Currently there are, appropriately, a number of alternative prioritization approaches, ranging from dedicated secure lines to switching priorities in times of network congestion. One of the evident needs of new designs for resilient networks is to ensure that critical services of many kinds, from emergency service workers to national security officers to political leaders, are able to maintain communication when breaks occur in networks. The government is a consumer, a provider, a source of control and an inhibitor of network reliability all at the same time.

In the recent report by the General Accounting Office (2003b), the effects of the physical damage caused by the destruction of the World Trade Center are reviewed and the actions needed to restore services are described. What is perhaps most revealing is the fact that whereas the Security and Exchange Commission has long paid attention to risk reduction efforts, these have not been uniformly applied. In particular, they had not reviewed the broker-dealers' efforts, and it was these members of the financial services community who were most severely hurt and whose continuity of business was seen to be the critical link at the time.

---

[7] The fact that data are publicly available can be regarded as a service to consumers, and some further analysis is provided by the Alliance for Telecommunications Industry Solutions (ATIS).

Similarly, several federal organization are involved in regulating banks and other depository institutions, including the Treasury, the Federal Reserve and the Office of the Comptroller of the Currency, and all of them have at various times been involved in setting standards or commenting on best practices concerning business continuity and communications.[8]

## 4   ANALYSIS

In this section we explore the barriers to network resilience, which are the result of government rules, regulation or policy.[9] While these are not deliberate barriers, and indeed, the issues raised by the attacks of September 11th were not considered when the policies were put in place, they nevertheless have significant implications for network resilience.[10] We focus on the 1996 Telecommunications Act (1996 Act), and rules and regulation which resulted from its passage. The 1996 Act was passed single-mindedly to promote competition. However, the impact of the 1996 Act and the resulting FCC rules on network resilience were profound. In this context, we focus on two areas, local (exchange) carriers (LECs) and electromagnetic spectrum issues.

### 4.1   Local Exchange Carriers

One of the unintended side effects of deregulation following the 1996 Act was that newly introduced players complicated the ability to devise new programs related to resilience. This was largely because such agreements relied on the need to solicit voluntary participation. They also introduced complex coordination of large numbers of key personnel. This affected the way previously existing programs were to work when no longer part of a monopoly. Competition rules are difficult to interpret in practice and most newcomers in the industry are extremely cautious about the appearance of collusion. New players are all competitors, making the sharing of information problematic.

Competition and the consequent larger number of independent players also complicated the ability to react to disaster situations because of coordination problems. Various responses to this have arisen in and around government, including the FCC-linked, industry-organized Network Reliability and Interoperability Council (NRIC) and the Alliance for Telecommunication Industry Solutions (ATIS). We now see a variety of interested bodies, some of which are government influenced (or intended to influence government, both of which can describe NRIC). Others are encouraged or supported by government, and yet others are internal mechanisms. The variety of such bodies has been proliferating and some of them are likely to be better coordinated as the new Department of Homeland Security brings together functions that had been split among bodies such as the FCC, the Department of Commerce and the Department of Defense.

Deregulation falsely raised expectations of users of the ability to have resilience in services by using different carriers when in fact many carriers share the same core network, conduits or

---

[8] This list could be further expanded to include the Federal Deposit Insurance Corporation, the Office of Thrift Supervision and the National Credit Union Administration.

[9] We will collectively refer to these as policy. The context should indicate whether they are rules, legislation, etc.

[10] We do not pretend that this is an exhaustive list, but merely note what features of policy contribute to reduced resilience.

co-location facilities. This concern was especially raised by customers in the aftermath of the destruction of the World Trade Center when many corporate customers were dismayed to find that whereas they thought they had two independent service providers, what they in fact had were two independent bills for service that passed through some of (or almost all) the same physical infrastructure.

In the United States, the local PSTN is highly concentrated as the result of the historic monopoly of the incumbent local exchange carriers, only four of which are left from the AT&T divestiture in 1984 (Verizon, SBC, BellSouth, and Qwest). In order to promote the development of competition, the Telecommunications Act of 1996 and the FCC's rules implementing the Act required these companies to interconnect with competitors and to unbundle the network and make the unbundled elements available for use by competitors. There are contentious debates about whether such unbundling and interconnection encourages or discourages competition, which we will not deal with here.[11] However, implementation of this "competition" discouraged the deployment of independent, redundant facilities for local communications.

In its attempt to promote competition in the telecommunications exchange market place, the FCC did not distinguish between facilities based or shared facilities competition. It developed three methods through which a (competitor) service provider (so called CLECs) could enter the exchange market – by providing its own facilities, by leasing, at wholesale prices, or by sharing the facilities of incumbent carriers (ILEC). The fastest, easiest, least-risky, and least capital-intensive method of entering the market was by sharing or leasing the facilities of an ILEC. This had several consequences in the development of viable competition in this market. The service was commoditized; that is, there was little to distinguish the various service providers. CLECs were all providing the same service, with no distinguishing features. Thus, they all competed on the basis of marketing.[12]

Financing during the period after the passage of the 1996 Act was easy and abundant. Since competitors did not make investments in facilities, because of the lease/sharing possibilities, they put money into the acquisition of customers. As a result, when terrorists struck, an end-user who thought she had multiple service providers, with multiple paths into the public switched network (PSTN), was distressed to find that all she had was multiple bills, but only one transmission facility – which was no longer operative! Thus, the means by which competition policy was developed had a significant consequence for network resilience. Of course, a monopoly policy might have had much the same effect if this concern were not taken into account, but under monopoly, resilience was a mainstream routine issue, inseparable from other matters of architecture, design and maintenance.

## 4.2 Electromagnetic Spectrum

Another example in which network resilience is impeded is with electromagnetic spectrum policy. The first issue is the assignment and allocation of spectrum. Both the FCC and other government agencies have responsibility for allocation. Agencies jealously guard the spectrum

---

[11] This is the topic of work in progress by Alain de Fontenay and Jonathan Liebenau, but one discussion of it can be seen in de Fontenay, Savin & Kiss 2003.

[12] Other issues arose in the drive to develop competition in this market. Bad management contributed to the demise of many of these CLECs; for example, competitors over-estimated the size of their potential markets. (If you added all the projections, many cities show a market more than five times actual size.) But these do not have a direct impact on the subject of this paper.

which they have been allocated, even if they do not use it; the military is the key culprit, but not exclusively. The availability of additional spectrum could enhance network resilience.

The FCC has assumed that proceeds of the spectrum auctions accrue to the government. This has led to inefficient behavior in setting up the auctions. The rationale for auctions is to allocate the resource to its best use. However, because government views the auctions as a revenue source, it attempts to maximize the return from the auctions. This has several effects. The ones we are concerned with are its impact on investment, competitors and resilience.

With respect to investment impacts, the profit maximizing behavior of the FCC reduces the number of potential competitors in this market due to the large, up-front capital requirement which is part of the bid on the spectrum. With fewer competitors, there is less redundancy through duplicate networks. This, coupled with the service suppliers' lock-in behavior (see below), affects resilience. Indeed, in Germany, it is the high cost of 3G spectrum that has driven the winning competitors to petition the regulator for permission to share in the building-out of their networks, with a consequent reduction in redundancy. One can only conjecture about the additional impacts of the high cost of spectrum on the availability of cellular service, the lost R&D etc., which may have indirect impact on resilience.

We must also consider the providers' side, and so we will focus on the wireless industry and its equipment manufacturers. The current cellular markets are robustly competitive, but the competing networks are less interoperable and less interconnected than the PSTN networks. Numerous reasons exist for this lack of interoperability, including purposeful exclusion by the wireless providers in order to "lock in" their customers for business reasons via different protocols, handsets designed exclusively for their systems, and lack of number portability (Shapiro & Varian 1999). As mentioned above, spectrum limitations also inhibited the development of more competitors. However, the prospect of the next generation of wireless offers the possibility of correcting some deficiencies. The statutory and regulatory policies could be changed to improve wireless interoperability and interconnection in order to increase network resilience.

To sketch out the example, in a hypothetical future mobile market we can discern some of the deficiencies of the current system when we consider cellular mobile service. If the regulations/standards for the future cellular mobile system are developed with both competition and resilience in mind, with the various service vendors having to cooperate in questions concerning shared standards for networks and handsets, there would be marked improvements in comparison to today's environment. Thus, if for example the Verizon network were incapacitated, Verizon customers could use Sprint's or others networks that survived. The handset would be designed to work on multiple frequencies and protocols—so called software-defined radio. It could serve as a device that can address WiFi (802.11b) networks, if available. At the next level, if all of the cellular antennas were destroyed, the handset would act as part of an ad hoc network, in effect, each serving as an antenna-relay in order to provide service in the affected area(s). With the handset capable of addressing multiple frequencies, lower bandwidth may be used in self-configuring ad hoc networks because of their promulgation characteristics or other desirable attributes of this spectrum. If the congestion on the network caused the quality of service in the voice network to deteriorate, the wireless IP capability of the handset could still provide communications for the users, either in the traditional mode or the ad hoc network mode.

For emergency personnel (and, perhaps, others), other sensors could be embedded into the handset. The sensors, in addition to locating features, could include gas/bio-warfare detectors that are directly linked to transmission functions. The handsets could contain local building schematics and other attributes of the local buildings—exits, hazard storage areas, etc.— in their memories, serving as enhanced PDAs for emergencies. Of course, with IP capabilities, they could transmit and receive updated information as required (Liebenau 2003).

## 5   RECOMMENDATIONS

This leads us to a set of recommendations that will be useful in guiding policies both in government and in the private sector over the next few years. Some of these recommendations refer to existing trends, such as the increasing interoperability of handsets, some refer to issues that have long been discussed but which have particular pertinence to resilience concerns, and some are derived from the preceding analysis.

### 5.1   Categorizing the Problem

Improvements in resilience can be seen to emerge from general changes in the industry; that is, either the continuation of current trends or the application of recommendations broadly agreed upon by observers of the industry. However, there is also a broad category of recommendations that emerge from specific resilience concerns, such as the promotion of particular technologies and direct subsidies (from government or through charges to customers). We address the first only briefly because issues such as spectrum reform and competition policy, while of great importance to resilience, have long been separate areas of debate. While we can show the importance of appropriately resolving these issues, we feel that our major contributions will come from our understanding of new problems and opportunities associated with resilience. The five major problem areas associated with resilience that are in focus in this paper are outlined in Table 1.

Table 1. Resilience Problem Areas

| Problem area | Summary description |
|---|---|
| Congestion | The overloading of pathways, especially in emergencies such that traffic must be rerouted. Denial of service attackers generally use congestion maliciously to overload pathways. |
| Collaboration and interconnection | The ability to share resources and alter routes and modes. In emergencies and in times of serious congestion mutual aid agreements must be made to work and to accommodate inter-modal communications. |
| Physical resilience | Protecting facilities from damage; including central stations, conduits, towers, airwaves, etc. Ensure communications and business continuity through distributed facilities and shared capabilities to minimize the effects of physical damage. |
| Security | Ensuring that routes, messages, procedures, equipment, etc. are safeguarded from intrusion, tampering, distortion, etc. |
| Emergency response | Immediate patching of damage, rerouting of traffic, and new approaches to communications for emergency workers and those caught up in crises that take into consideration both effective transmission capabilities and appropriate content to inform those involved. |

## 5.2  Solutions

The effort to improve resilience should be undertaken on all fronts and by industry as well as government actors. Below, we describe four solution areas, including specific actions that can be initiated immediately, that should be prioritized:

- Ensure inter-modal competition
- Stimulate demand for resilience by raising standards
- Subsidies to build out critical infrastructure
- Devise new governmental roles and priorities, e.g. support spare capacity

Our first proposal is to maintain inter-modal competition in balance with consolidation. No one system is invulnerable but layers of networks create options, as we currently have in many areas where wireless local area networks, cable modems, personal communication devices, emergency communications systems, mobile telephones, and even powerline communications systems exist alongside plain old wireline telephone systems. This will allow a spread in facilities and avoid the problems associated with, for example, excessive and sometimes uncharted confluence of conduits. We should also encourage moves towards enabling functionality at the network edge (and "dumb pipes") to open networks more and to do this through alliances rather than vertical integration strategies. This is likely to foster solutions such as VoIP and stimulate business and investment, possibly at the cost of traditional wireline service providers. This implies that regulators allow for the imaginative use of spectrum and other delivery mechanisms (we welcome, for example, the recent FCC statements encouraging powerline communications developments) and that competition policies be reassessed to allow for and encourage companies to plan for coordination. We would also wish to see stimulation through experiments sponsored by large users, property developers, local communities, etc. This helps to address elements of all five problem areas associated with resilience.

Second, demand should be stimulated by raising standards for business continuity and communications security. Some mechanisms are straightforward and will attract relatively little objection, such as encouraging best practices for data protection and back-up in critical industries. This could be done with industry cooperation through bodies such as the Securities Industry Association and regulators including the Securities & Exchange Commission, the Treasury and the Federal Banking system. Precedents exist in recommendations for business continuity, and we can learn from the Y2K software improvement campaign. A targeted awareness campaign, bringing together Federal, state and in some places local authorities could educate major commercial customers in all sectors about the value of raising resilience standards. Governmental bodies would also stimulate demand as they improve the resilience of their use of networks, and local authorities should speed up the deployment of E-911 facilities. In the medium term these improvements may not add expenses, especially where high quality solutions reduce risks and maintenance costs. This especially addresses the problem areas of physical resilience and security and encourages spending.

Third, technical solutions need to be investigated and subsidized despite the current inability of companies to invest heavily in traditional research and development. This will require considerable direct funding from government, mainly federal, but also state. Given the current weaknesses at Lucent's Bell Laboratories as well as Telcordia and other commercial sources of telecommunications R&D, competition should be open and available to universities and small independent laboratories, commercial and otherwise. We would prefer to see increases in spending spread widely rather than focused on a small number of special institutions. The National Institute for Standards and Technology might play a bigger role, and large companies should be encouraged to collaborate through neutral bodies, but we would not wish to see the establishment of a national research laboratory. Investments should be made to ensure continued improvements to wireless technologies, especially those like the 802.11xx series of standards. Other areas for special investment might include new approaches to congestion relief, ultra wide band and spectrum switching technologies as well as voice over IP. Considerable further improvements are needed before appropriate customized content can be developed and deployed for emergency uses. This addresses many elements of the five problems areas and will stimulate business development.

Fourth, new roles of governments and some civil society solutions need to be explored, for example as follows.

## Federal Jurisdiction

The federal government could make a number of interventions with the potential to improve network resilience. The Department of Homeland Security and other agencies should quickly clarify the role of secure and emergency communications and extend the Government Emergency Communications System (GETS) using wireless, IP and other modes. Federal mandates are needed to ensure spare communications capacity set aside by service providers for emergencies. These would be emanating presumably from the Department of Commerce or the Federal Communications Commission and might be funded by something like the universal services charge. This has long been done with spare capacity requirements for port operators and shippers and for airports and airlines. Federal support is also needed to build up special functions of local law enforcement and emergency services. Here, as in some other areas, there is a need for more transfer of technology from military to civilian uses. Finally, federal grant giving bodies such as the NSF and the Departments of Defense and Commerce should make resilient and emergency communications a top priority.

## State Jurisdiction

Public services commissions need to take on more responsibilities for resilience, such as the proposed New York State Public Service Commission's statutory responsibility for protecting infrastructure, which would include specific requirements to maintain vigilance in collaboration with not for profit research, professional and consumer groups and other non-commercial bodies. In addition, state authorities need to ensure that resilience concerns are applied to interconnection rules and offer opportunities to experiment with different approaches.

## Local Jurisdictions

At a local level, municipal governments can contribute to resilience in several ways. Resilience associated with local economic development and the defense of local infrastructure and businesses needs to be factored in to municipal functions, as with New York City's Department of Information Technology and Telecommunications. Mutual aid and restoration schemes are also most important in local areas, and municipal governments can encourage compliance by using their market power and through public awareness campaigns.

## Civil Society Groups

Voluntary civil action in preparation for emergencies and in times of disaster have been highly effective in solving some problems, such as using advanced communications to notify friends and family, organizing groups to respond where needed, and offering advice to those affected. We could encourage the common use of best practices for solutions such as emergency web portals (E-811), messaging systems, electronic sniffing systems (such as that employed by the Wireless Emergency Response Team—WERT) and other high technology applications. Furthermore, the provision of emergency information content might best be left to civil society groups. For example, voluntary fire departments could coordinate the provision of data suitable for mobile devices to transmit emergency instructions or access special databases relating to property, procedures, risks, etc. Some legal provision might be necessary to ensure compliance and perhaps governmental funding should be provided to meet the cost of data management.

In summary then, we propose to enhance network resilience through the following measures:

1. Encourage inter-modal competition by fostering development and experimentation with new resilient technologies and architectures.
2. Stimulate demand by raising standards for business continuity and communications security.
3. Subsidize new network architecture technologies that promote high capacity and flexibility, especially with regard to wireless and IP technologies.
4. Reassess governmental roles to reflect national security priorities in building out and using communications networks in the manner commonly applied to assure spare capacity in transportation infrastructure.

## 6    CONCLUSION

We believe that addressing these resilience concerns, while expensive in parts, will all in all contribute to revenues for the communications industry and is therefore economically justifiable. Resilience is functionality worth paying for. Furthermore, funds for homeland security are better spent in the long run in improving communications resilience than, for example, in deploying more armed guards at unlikely targets or inhibiting international trade and travel. The recommendations given will stimulate new business development and provide the means by which service providers can compete based on levels of resilience. They also ensure that innovation and variety are encouraged during this period of economic stringency for the industry.

Each of the capabilities listed above requires engineering, business and regulatory design. For example, software defined radio as described above could currently not be designed and multiple frequencies of electromagnetic spectrum could not be used because of regulatory constraints and rules, even if it is technically possible. Current business practices of the cellular providers contribute to the non-compatibility among handsets. These same business practices do not allow the development of cellular handsets that could take advantage of the unlicensed spectrum used for wireless networks – the 802.11b system (Markoff 2002). Indeed, because of the business conflict among the carriers' own data services planned for the 3G (and beyond), it is highly unlikely that these types of features would be built into the handsets.

The fundamental economic policy question is, who bears the costs of improving network resilience? That question arises not only in relation to our hopes for better architectures or widespread ad-hoc and IP environments, but also with regard to emergency services. We believe that new approaches to enhanced emergency telephony (E-911) should be investigated from a policy and commercial point of view. We have excellent proposals to design emergency content for mobile communication devices, but they raise a flurry of legal, economic and managerial questions that need to be investigated. And there are more imaginative suggestions that are emerging from the interaction of social scientists with communications engineers about the use of the internet during emergencies, as well as other IP-related solutions. These should form the focus of high priority research in the coming years.

# 7  REFERENCES

Aduskevicz, PJ, "AT&T Response, Terrorist Attack, September 11, 2001" presentation to the Network Reliability and Interoperability Council V, October 30, 2001.

de Fontenay, Savin, Kiss, Submission to the New Zealand Commerce Commission on "Unbundling the Local Loop Network and the Fixed Public Data Network", May 26, 2003.

Elby, S., "Network Design and Resilience", Presentation to Columbia University course ELEN 6901, October 30, 2002.

Liebenau, J., "Wireless Emergency Content" in Valerie Feldmann (ed.), *Wireless Content*, Berlin: 2003.

Markoff, John, "The Corner Internet Network vs. the Cellular Giants," *The New York Times*, March 4, 2002.

Noam, Eli, "How to Cope with the New Volatility", *America's Network*, October 1 2003.

Shapiro, C & Varian, H., "The Art of Standards Wars", *California Management Review*, Winter 1999.

Techapalokul, S., Alleman, J., Chen, Y., "Economics of Standard: A Survey and Framework", Proceedings of the 2nd IEEE Conference on Standardization and Innovation in Information Technology, October 2001.

United States General Accounting Office (a), Report to the Subcommittee on Domestic Monetary Policy, Technology, and Economic Growth, Committee on Financial Services, House of Representatives, Critical Infrastructure Protection, "Efforts of the Financial Services Sector to Address Cyber Threats", Washington D.C., GAO-03-173, January 2003.

United States General Accounting Office (b), "Potential Terrorist Attacks, Additional Actions Needed to Better Prepare Critical Financial Market Participants", Report to the Committee on Financial Services, House of Representatives, GAO-03-414, February 2003.

# AUTHOR INFORMATION

## BIBLIOGRAPHICAL INFORMATION

**Jae-Hyeon Ahn** is Professor of Telecommunications Management at Korea Advanced Institute of Science and Technology (KAIST) in Korea. His current research interests are customer loyalty and value model, telecommunications service realization process, data mining applications, e-Business strategy development, and telecommunications strategy analysis. He has been a Senior Research Staff member at AT&T Bell Laboratories in New Jersey, USA. He received his B.Sc. (1984) and M.Sc. (1986) degrees in Industrial Engineering from Seoul National University, Seoul, Korea, and his Ph.D. degree in Decision Analysis from Stanford University (1993).

**James Alleman** has returned to the University of Colorado, Boulder, after two years as Visiting Associate Professor at the Columbia Business School, Columbia University, and Director of Research at Columbia Institute of Tele-Information (CITI). He continues his involvement at CITI as a Senior Fellow. Prior to joining the University of Colorado in 1991, Dr. Alleman was the Director of the International Center for Telecommunications Management, University of Nebraska at Omaha, Director of Policy Research for GTE, and an Economist for the International Telecommunication Union. His research includes: network pricing, demand, costing, regulation, and international telephony settlements. More recently, he has focused on corporate governance, real options and financing the ITC sector. Dr. Alleman holds patents (numbers 5,883,964 & 6,035,027 ) on the call-back process widely used by the industry. He obtained a Ph.D. in Economics from the University of Colorado in 1976.

**Aniruddha Banerjee** is a Vice President at NERA Economic Consulting and a consultant on telecommunications matters. His research and consulting has spanned local and long distance competition, interconnection and inter-carrier compensation, universal service, regulatory reform, telephone service quality, demand for mobile services, antitrust and damage analysis, and econometric analysis of various telecommunications-related issues. Dr. Banerjee has presented professional papers widely (including at several international forums), published in journals like *Telecommunications Policy* and *Information Economics and Policy*, and serves as an expert witness on telecommunications matters before regulatory agencies. He has a B.A. from the University of Delhi, an M.A. in Economics from the Delhi School of Economics, and a Ph.D. in Agricultural Economics from the Pennsylvania State University.

**Erik Bohlin** is currently Associate Professor ("Docent") at the Department of Innovation Engineering and Management, School of Technology Management and Economics at Chalmers University of Technology, Gothenburg. Bohlin has published in a number of areas relating to the information society - policy, strategy, and management. He is Vice Chair of the International Telecommunications Society; member of the Scientific Advisory Boards of *Communications and Strategies*, *Info* and *Telecommunications Policy*; Research Fellow of the Institute of Management, Innovation and Technology (IMIT); and Jury Member of the Telenor Nordic Research Award in Telecommunications. He has been visiting researcher at Osaka University (1994), East-West Center in Honolulu (19997), Keio University in Tokyo (1997, 2001) and Institute for Prospective Technological Studies (1998-1999), a European Commission Research Agency in Seville, Spain. He obtained his graduate degree in Business

Administration and Economics at the Stockholm School of Economics (1987) and his Ph.D. at Chalmers University of Technology (1995).

**Grant Coble-Neal** is a member of the Communication Economics and Electronic Markets Research Centre (CEEM) at Curtin University and a Ph.D. candidate in communications economics. During his time at CEEM, Grant has co-authored a number of articles analyzing aspects of the telecommunications industry. Prior to joining CEEM, Grant worked for the Australian Commonwealth Department of the Treasury and at Western Australia's state-owned electricity utility, Western Power.

**Martin Fransman** is Professor of Economics and Founder-Director of the Institute for Japanese-European Technology Studies at the University of Edinburgh in Scotland. His current research is on the changing structure and dynamics of the telecommunications industry, and the economics of innovation. His recent books include: *Telecoms in the Internet Age* (Oxford University Press, 2002), *Visions of Innovation* (Oxford University Press, 1999) and *Japan's Computer and Communications Industry* (Oxford University Press, 1995).

**Dan Grigorovici** is a Fellow of the Institute for Information Policy, Pennsylvania State University and a Ph.D. candidate in Mass Communication at Penn State's College of Communications. He has recently been awarded an IBM Ph.D. Fellowship for his work on Information Indicators. As part of the macro approach to Information Technology, he is involved in a research program aiming to provide a valid, flexible and multi-level composite measure of the Information Society and study its relationship to Quality of Life indicators. Before joining the Pennsylvania State University, he held several creative and research positions in the Advertising and Public Relations industries. From 2000, he has taught and given guest lectures in several undergraduate classes in Penn State's College of Communications. He received his M.A. in Policy Studies from the University of Bucharest in 2000.

**Luca Grilli** is a Research Fellow at Politecnico di Milano and takes part in the research activities of CIRET (Centro Interdipartimentale di Ricerca nell'Economia delle Telecomunicazioni). He received a B.Sc. cum laude from the University of Siena (Italy, 1997), a M.Sc. from the University of York (United Kingdom, 2000), and he is completing a Ph.D. in economics at the University of Siena. His research interests include economics of innovation, network and Internet economics, economic and policy issues in new technology industries. He has previously worked as an industrial economist at the "Social and Economic Research Studies Office" of the Italcementi Group.

**Sang-Pil Han** is a Ph.D. Candidate at the Graduate School of Management at Korea Advanced Institute of Science and Technology (KAIST) in Korea. His current research interests are agent based modeling, social complex networks, convergence phenomenon, and data mining. He received his B.Sc. (2000) and M.Sc. (2002) degrees in management engineering from KAIST Graduate School of Management.

**Takeshi Hiromatsu** is Professor of Statistics and economics at the Graduate School of Arts and Sciences, College of Arts and Sciences, the University of Tokyo and also advisor to the government and commentator in the field of economics. His work focuses on quantitative analysis on economic phenomena, specializing in IT industry and efficiency of IT at the

industry level. He is a member of the Statistical Council of the Ministry of Public Management, Home Affairs, and Telecommunications, the Social Security Council of the Ministry of
Health, Welfare and Labor, and the Quality-of-life Policy Council of the Cabinet Office. He
received his MA in economics from the University of Tokyo, Japan.

**Mark Jamison** is the Director of Telecommunications Studies for the Public Utility Research
Center at the University of Florida. His responsibilities include developing training programs
and conducting research on telecommunications issues. He is also Associate Director for
Business and Economic Studies for the Center for International Business Education and
Research, and a Research Associate with the Center for Public Policy Research. He previously
served as the Special Academic Advisor to the Chair of the Florida Governor's Internet task
force. From February 1993 through June 1996, he was a manager of regulatory policy for
Sprint, where he developed policies on pricing, costing, and market structure issues. Prior to
joining Sprint, he worked nine years for state regulatory commission staffs in the US. His
current research covers the convergence of information industries and the international
development of telecommunications competition.

**Hak Ju Kim** is a Ph.D. candidate at the Department of Information Science and Telecommunications at the University of Pittsburgh. Before studying at the University of Pittsburgh, he
worked at SK Telecom for 6 years as a research engineer. His academic background consists
of an MBA from Korea University, an MS (major: telecommunications) from the University
of Colorado at Boulder, and a Master of International Management (MIM) from Thunderbird
University in Arizona. His main research areas are technology (innovation) management in
networks (i.e. wireless technologies and Internet QoS technologies), risk management with
technology investment (real options), E-business in network (e-Content Pricing), utility
networking with the grid theory, network economics (pricing/costing/investment), bandwidth
management and trading, Internet accounting and charging.

**Heon-Goo Kim** is currently working for the Korea National Assembly as a research officer
specializing in Industry and Trade. He has published in various areas relating to industrial
policy and strategy analysis of education, biotechnology, environment, and information
technology. He obtained his M.A.(1988) and his Ph. D.(1993) in Economics at the University
of Oklahoma.

**Min-Kyoung Kim** is a Research Staff member in the Information Technology Management
Research Group of Electronics and Telecommunications Research Institute (ETRI) in
Daejeon, Korea. Her current research interests are competitive strategy in the IT industry. She
received a B.A. from Handong University in Pohang, Korea, in Management and Economics
(2001) and M.A (2003) in Management from the Information and Communications University
(ICU), Daejeon, Korea.

**Minoru Kobayashi** is Professor in the Department of Business Administration at Wako
University in Tokyo, where he teaches courses in Management Information Systems and
Advanced Information Networks. He has been studying how Information Communication
Technologies influence the management of Enterprises, and Business Models that apply
Advanced Telecommunication Technologies. He has conducted research works at NHK
(Japan Broadcasting Corporation) Science & Technical Research Laboratories, and Daiwa

Institute of Research Ltd. from 1987 to 1996. He joined the faculty of Wako University in 1996. He received an M.S. degree from Hokkaido University (1987) and a Ph.D. degree from The University of Tokyo (1996).

**Mark Kolesar** is currently Assistant Vice-President Regulatory and Public Policy at TELUS Corporation, the second largest telecommunications company in Canada. He has worked in the areas of regulation, government policy and external relations, marketing, and business development. Mr. Kolesar has also taught for over fifteen years at the University of Alberta and the University of Calgary. He now teaches Strategic Management and Business Planning at the University of Calgary. His areas of research include New Media, E-Commerce, Regulatory Policy, and Regulatory Strategy. Mr. Kolesar is on the Advisory Committee to the Centre for Information and Communications, a joint venture of the University of Calgary and the University of Alberta. He is also a Board Member of the Van Horne Institute for International Transportation and Regulatory Affairs and the Chairman of the Van Horne Institute's Center for Regulatory Affairs. Mr. Kolesar has an Honors Degree in Philosophy from the University of Ottawa and an MBA in Managerial Economics and Finance, also from the University of Ottawa.

**Donald J. Kridel** is Associate Professor of Economics at the University of Missouri-St. Louis, where he has been teaching since 1993. Prior to joining the faculty at UM-St. Louis, Kridel was Director-Strategic Marketing at Southwestern Bell where he had held various positions since 1982. He publishes in the area of applied econometrics and regularly addresses industry and academic groups on telecommunications demand analysis. Kridel earned his Ph.D. in economics from the University of Arizona.

**Manabu Kurita** is senior researcher of the Information Technology Research and Development Division, at Daiwa Institute of Research Ltd., Tokyo. His main research interests are the analysis of the economic impacts of introduction of information technology on firms, and the marketing of information security system.

**Jai Joon Lee** is a Ph.D. student in strategy and telecommunication policy at the Joseph M. Katz Graduate School of Business, University of Pittsburgh. He is also on a leave as a research fellow from Korea Information Society Development Institute (KISDI). His research interests are competitive strategy, telecommunication policy, and global strategic alliances in the telecom industry. He holds an MBA from the University of Rochester, and a BS from Purdue University.

**Stanford L. Levin** joined the Department of Economics in the School of Business at Southern Illinois University Edwardsville in 1972, became Professor of Economics in 1985, and was Chairman of the Department of Economics from 1986 to 1994. He became Professor Emeritus in 2002. In November, 1984, he was appointed Commissioner of the Illinois Commerce Commission, the state utility regulatory agency, where he served until March, 1986. In addition, Dr. Levin is President of the Resource Group, Inc., an economic consulting firm, and he is a member of the Board of Directors and Chairman of the Membership & Nominations Committee of the International Telecommunications Society. He was a consulting economist to the Chicago Regional Office of the Federal Trade Commission from 1979 to 1983, and he spent a sabbatical leave in 1978 at the Energy Service of Data Resources, Inc., in Washington, D.C. Dr. Levin has a B.A. in Economics from Grinnell College and a Ph. D. in Economics from the University of Michigan. He has published numerous articles, papers and reports in professional publications, and he has edited two books.

**Jonathan Liebenau** teaches at the London School of Economics in the Department of Information Systems. He specializes in two areas: fundamental concepts of information, and the problems and prospects of information technology in economic development. He is the author or editor of several books and over 40 other major publications. After two years as Visiting Professor in the Management Division at Columbia Business School, and Adjunct Professor of Electrical Engineering at the School of Engineering and Applied Sciences, Columbia University, and a fellow at the Columbia Institute of Tele-Information (CITI), Dr. Liebenau has returned to the London School of Economics. He continues his involvement at CITI in research projects as a Senior Fellow. He is currently conducting research on small business networks and their use of ICTs and is writing on the economics of the telecommunications industry. He holds a Bachelor of Arts in Science Policy from the University of Rochester, and a Ph.D. in History and Sociology of Science from the University of Pennsylvania.

**Gary Madden** is Director of the Communication Economics and Electronic Markets Research Centre (CEEM) and Professor of Economics in the School of Economics and Finance at Curtin University. His recently published articles appear in among others *Applied Economics, Economics of Innovation and New Technology, International Journal of Forecasting, International Journal of Social Economics*, and *Review of Economics and Statistics*. Gary is Editor of the Edward Elgar series, *The International Handbook of Telecommunications Economics, Volumes I-III*. He is also an Associate Editor for *Information Economics and Policy* and a member of the Editorial Board of the *Journal of Media Economics*. Gary was recently appointed to the Board of Management of the International Telecommunications Society. In 2003 he was Chair of the 1st Asia-Australia International Telecommunications Society Regional Conference held in Perth at the Hyatt Regency. He was the *CBS Researcher of the Year* in 1996 and 2002 and received the *CBS Article of the Year* in 1997.

**Ravindranath ("Ravi") Madhavan** is an Associate Professor of Business Administration at the Joseph M. Katz Graduate School of Business, University of Pittsburgh. He earned his Ph.D. in strategic management at the University of Pittsburgh in 1996, and was on the faculty of Business Administration at the University of Illinois, Urbana-Champaign from 1995 to 2001. Prior to his Ph.D., he spent eight years as a manager in the information technology industry, gaining experience in consulting, executive education, and marketing. His research seeks to understand how networks influence competitive advantage. He teaches courses in strategy at the MBA and Ph.D. levels, including elective courses on M&A integration and strategic alliances. In addition, he regularly conducts executive education workshops on various aspects of strategic management.

**Maria Michalis** is a senior lecturer at the University of Westminster and course leader for the MAs in Communication and Communications Policy. She specializes in European communication policy and has published work on digital television, public service broadcasting and the internet, local access competition and the diffusion of broadband technologies, universal service, and the regulatory convergence between telecommunications and broadcasting. She is currently writing a book on the governance of European communications. She has held a BT short-term fellowship and is currently funded by the European Commission Jean Monnet project. She received an M.A. and a Ph.D. in communication policy from City University, London.

**Eli Noam** is Professor of Finance and Economics at the Columbia University Graduate School of Business and Director of the Columbia Institute for Tele-Information. He has also served as Public Service Commissioner engaged in the telecommunications and energy regulation of New York State. His publications include 22 books and about 300 articles on domestic and international telecommunications, television, Internet, and regulation subjects. He served as a board member for the federal government's FTS-2000 telephone network, of the IRS' computer modernization project, and of the National Computer Lab. He is a member of the Council on Foreign Relations, and of the President's IT Advisory Committtee. Professor Noam received an A.B. (1970, Phi Beta Kappa), a Ph.D. in economics (1975) and a J.D. law degree (1975) from Harvard University.

**Jeonghun Oh** is currently Associate Dean at the Graduate School of International Studies at Korea University, Seoul , Korea. He has a special interest in a number of areas relating to the information society and e-business - policy, strategy, and management. He is executive committee chair of the Korea Association for Telecommunications Policies and managing editor of the Korea Review of International Studies. He obtained his B.A. degree in Economics at Korea University (1985), M.A. degree in Economics at Cornell University (1988), and his Ph.D. in Economics at the University of Iowa (1995).

**Gohsei Ohira** is Professor of Economics at Tokyo International University. His research interests are information economy and economics of information network. He received an M.A. (1978) in economics from Tsukuba University, Japan.

**Myeong-Cheol Park** is Associate Professor at the School of Business in the Information and Communications University (ICU). He is also a director of the IT Business Research Institute. He has published numerous papers in areas relating to telecommunications management strategy and economics, and IT venture business management. He has been a Principal Researcher at the Electronics and Telecommunication Research Institute (ETRI). He received his B.S. (1976) and MBA (1978) degrees from Seoul National University, Seoul, Korea and his Ph.D. degree from the School of Business at the University of Iowa (1990).

**Paul N. Rappoport** is Associate Professor of Economics at Temple University. He is also a principal and senior academic consultant with the economics consulting firm, Econsult. He has over 25 years of experience in data analysis, modeling and statistical assessment, with a specialization in telecommunications demand analysis. He was responsible for the development of Bill HarvestingTM, a national database of actual communications bills, a small business panel – which focused on telecommunications and energy – and a large consumer national telecommunication database. Collaborating with Professors Lester Taylor and Donald Kridel, Dr. Rappoport has constructed and estimated demand models and elasticities for a wide array of consumer and business telecommunication products and services. His current research interests include: the construction of internet metrics; modeling the Digital Divide; specifying and modeling business broadband; forecasting internet demand and measuring the nature of network externalities. He received his Ph.D. from The Ohio State University in 1974.

**Agustin J. Ros** is a Senior Consultant at NERA with expertise in the economics and regulation of the telecommunications industry. His articles have appeared in academic journals such as the *Journal of Regulatory Economics, Review of Network Economics* and *Telecommunications Policy* and in numerous industry and trade journals such as, *Public Utilities Fortnightly* and the *Journal of Project Finance*. His research on local telephone competition was cited in *Business Week* and he has written a book on the productivity of employee-owned firms that was published in 2001. He received a B.A. in Economics from Rutgers University and an M.S. and a Ph.D. in Economics from the University of Illinois at Urbana-Champaign and is bilingual in Spanish and speaks fluent Portuguese.

**Jorge R. Schement** is Professor and Co-Director of the Institute for Information Policy, in the College of Communications, and in the School of Information Science and Technology at Penn State University. He holds a Ph.D. from the Institute for Communication Research at Stanford University, and a M.S. in Marketing from the School of Commerce at the University of Illinois. His research interests focus on the social and policy consequences of the production and consumption of information, especially as they relate to ethnic minorities. Schement has served on the editorial boards of seven academic journals, and has edited the Annual Review of Technology for the Aspen Institute. In 1994, he served, at the invitation of the chairman of the Federal Communications Commission, as director of the Information Policy Project and conducted the original research that led to recognition of the Digital Divide. He introduced the idea of Universal Service as an evolving concept, a view adopted in the Telecommunications Act of 1996.

**Ann Skudlark** is a technical manager in AT&T Bell Laboratories in New Jersey, USA. She received a B.S. in Marketing from the University of Rhode Island and an M.B.A. from the University of South Florida. She supervises a decision and intelligent systems group which supports and enhances business decision-making processes. Her current research interests include formalizing scenario planning in the decision analysis process and understanding risk management implications in electronic commerce. She has published in the *Journal of Direct Marketing* and the *Journal of Information Technology*.

**Yong Yeop Sohn** is a Professor in the Department of Economics at Chonnam National University. His research interests are focused on regulation and antitrust policy, strategic choice of information goods market and network economics. He served as researcher at the Korean Institute for Economics and Trade in Seoul, Korea. He received a B.A.(1981) from Seoul National University, Seoul, Korea, an M A. (1985) in economics from the Texas Tech University, and a Ph.D.(1989) in economics from Purdue University, West Lafayette, Indiana, USA.

**Charles Steinfield** is a Professor in the Department of Telecommunication at Michigan State University and recipient of MSU's Teacher-Scholar and Distinguished Faculty Awards. He conducts research on various aspects of electronic commerce including the effects of e-commerce on buyer-seller relations, the influence of e-commerce on intermediation, and the role of physical presence in e-commerce strategy. He holds a PhD in Communication Theory and Research from the Annenberg School for Communication at the University of Southern California. In addition to his faculty position at MSU, Charles Steinfield has been a visiting professor and researcher at a number of institutions in the U.S. and in Europe, including Bell Communications Research, the Institut National des Télécommunications in France, and Delft University of Technology and the Telematica Instituut in the Netherlands.

**Nakil Sung** is Assistant Professor of Economics at the University of Seoul, Korea. Dr. Sung received his Ph.D. degree in Economics from the State University of New York at Buffalo. His principal fields of study include industrial organization, economics of regulation and antitrust, information and telecommunications economics, and applied econometrics. His career began in the Telecommunications Economics Research Labs of Korea Telecom, providing him with a unique insight into the underlying economics of telecommunication production. He has published regularly in leading edge general and filed economic journals on telecommunications production and demand, aspects of competition and productivity, and the measurement of technical change.

**Lester D. Taylor** is currently Professor of Economics and Professor of Agricultural & Natural Resource Economics at the University of Arizona. He has a Ph.D. in economics from Harvard University, and taught at Harvard and the University of Michigan before taking up residence in Arizona in 1972. During the spring semester of 1996, he taught at Charles University in Prague in the Czech Republic. His research in telecommunications covers more than 25 years, and he has published extensively on telecommunications demand, pricing, and costing. His most recent book, *Capital, Accumulation, and Money*, was published in 2000. His most recent book in telecommunications, *Telecommunications Demand in Theory and Practice*, was published in 1994. He has also recently co-edited, with David G. Loomis, *The Future of the Telecommunications Industry: Forecasting and Demand Analysis* and *Forecasting the Internet: Understanding the Explosive Growth of Data Communications.*

**Richard D. Taylor** is Professor and holder of the Palmer Chair in Telecommunications Studies in the Pennsylvania State University College of Communications. He is also Professor of Information Science and Technology in the School of Information Science and Technology, and co-Director of the Penn State Institute for Information Policy. Dr. Taylor's scholarly and research agenda emphasizes the role of information technology in economic development, and policy issues in electronic commerce. He is a member of the Board of the Telecommunications Policy Research Conference and a Trustee of the Pacific Telecommunications Council, and is active in the International Telecommunications Society. Prior to joining Penn State in 1989, he was Vice President and Corporate Counsel of what is now AOL Time Warner Cable. From 1993 to 1998 he was an independent member of the Board of PrimeStar Partners Ltd. He holds an Ed.D. in Mass Communications from Columbia University Teachers College and a J.D. from New York University School of Law.

**Naoki Tsubone** is chief researcher of Information Technology Research and Development Division, at Daiwa Institute of Research Ltd., Tokyo. His current research focuses on networking technology, data mining, electronic government, and financial engineering.

**Martin B.H. Weiss** is Associate Dean for Academic Affairs and Research at the School of Information Science as well as Chairman of the Department of Information Science and

Telecommunications at the University of Pittsburgh. He holds a PhD. in Engineering and Public Policy from Carnegie Mellon University (1988), an MSE in Computer, Control, and Information Engineering from the University of Michigan (1979) and a BSE in Electrical Engineering from Northeastern University (1978). His overall research themes are the analysis of situations where competing firms must cooperate, cost modeling of new technologies in telecommunications systems and the evolution of the telecommunications industry. His industrial experience includes technical and professional work at several R&D and consulting firms in the United States. Together with Phyllis Bernt, he has published the book *International Telecommunications* (Howard Sams, 1993) and he is currently writing a textbook on US Telecommunications Policy with Phyllis Bernt and Christopher Sterling.

**Hun-Wha Yang** is a Researcher of the Survey & Research Team, Korea Information Management Institute for Small and Medium Enterprises (KIMI). Her research is focused on the market structure and the government roles with relevance to information goods (or Digital goods), Internet Economics, and Information & Communication Technology. Her current research interests include policy on ICT for SMEs. She holds a Ph.D.(2003) in economics from Chonnam National University, where she also received her B.A. (1994) and M.A. (1997).

**Gyu-Dong Yeon** is currently a Manager of the Planning and PR team of Samsung Networks in Seoul, Korea. He obtained a B.A. (1992) in Business Administration from Seogang University, Seoul, Korea. He has worked at Samsung SDS since the end of 2000, and he received an M.A. (2002) in Management from the Information and Communications University (ICU).

**Chang-Ho Yoon** is Professor of Economics at Korea University and has been working as Commissioner (non-standing) of Korea Fair Trade Agency since 2000. He obtained a Ph.D. in Economics at Stanford University in 1978, and has published many books and papers (mostly in Korean) on Economics of Information and Industrial Organization. He has recently published a volume on the prospect of North Korean transition (Edward Elgar, 2001 with Larry Lau at Stanford University), and a book on Telecommunication policy and Globalization in Korea (Seoul National University Press, 2000) with his colleagues. His academic involvement includes editorship of the *Korean Economic Review* (1996-1997), Director of the Institute of Economic Research at Korea University (1996-1998), President of Academic Organizations such as Korea Econometric Society (1998), Korean Academy of Industrial Organization (2001) and Korea Association of Telecommunications Policy (2002 – present).

# AUTHOR COORDINATES

Jae-Hyeon Ahn
Graduate School of Management
Korea Advanced Institute of Science &
Technology
207-43 Cheongyangri-Dong Dongdaemoon-
Gu, Seoul, Korea.

E-mail: jahn@kgsm.kaist.ac.kr


James Alleman
University of Colorado
College of Engineering, ECOT 343
C.B. Box 422
Boulder, CO 80309-0422, United States

E-mail: james.alleman@colorado.edu


Aniruddha Banerjee
NERA Economic Consulting
One Main Street, 5th Floor
Cambridge, MA 02142, United States

E-mail: andy.banerjee@nera.com


Erik Bohlin
School of Technology Management &
Economics
Chalmers University of Technology
S-412 96 Göteborg, Sweden

E-mail: erbo@mot.chalmers.se


Grant Coble-Neal
Communication Economics and Electronic
Markets Research Centre
School of Economics and Finance
Curtin Business School
GPO Box U1987
Perth, Western Australia 6845

E-mail: CobleG@cbs.curtin.edu.au


Martin Fransman
Institute for Japanese-European Technology
Studies
The University of Edinburgh
Old Surgeons' Hall
High School Yards
Edinburgh EH1 1LZ, United Kingdom

Email: M.Fransman@ed.ac.uk


Dan Grigorovici
Institute for Information Policy
College of Communications
The Pennsylvania State University
115 Carnegie Building
University Park, PA 16802, United States

E-mail: dangrig@psu.edu


Luca Grilli
Dipartimento di Ingegneria Gestionale
Politecnico di Milano and CIRET
P.zza Leonardo da Vinci 32
20133 Milano, Italy

E-mail: luca.grilli@polimi.it


Sang-Pil Han
Graduate School of Management
Korea Advanced Institute of Science &
Technology,
207-43 Cheongyangri-Dong
Dongdaemoon-Gu, Seoul, Korea.

E-mail: hansangpil@kgsm.kaist.ac.kr


Takeshi Hiromatsu
Graduate School and College of Arts and Science
The University of Tokyo
3-8-1 Komaba, Meguro-ku
Tokyo 153-8902, Japan

E-mail: hirom@waka.c.u-tokyo.ac.jp

Mark A. Jamison
Public Utility Research Center
P. O. Box 117142
205 Matherly
University of Florida
Gainesville, FL 32611-7142, United States

E-mail: mark.jamison@cba.ufl.edu


Min-Kyoung Kim
Information Technology Management
Research Group
Electronics and Telecommunications Research
Institute (ETRI)
161, Gajeong-Dong, Yuseong-Gu
Daejeon, 305-350, Korea

E-mail: gonyang@etri.re.kr


Hak Ju Kim
Dept of Information Science and Telecommu-
nications
University of Pittsburgh
135 N.Bellefield Avenue, Pittsburgh PA15260,
United States

E-mail: hjkim@mail.sis.pitt.edu


Heon-Goo Kim
Korea National Assembly
1 Yoido dong, Young deung po-ku
Seoul, 150-703, Korea

E-mail: hgkim@nanet.go.kr


Minoru Kobayashi
Faculty of Economics
Wako University
2160 Kanai-cho, Machida-City
Tokyo 195-8585, Japan

E-mail: minokob@wako.ac.jp

Mark Kolesar
TELUS Corporation
26, 411 - 1 Street S.E.
Calgary, Alberta, Canada T2G 4Y5

E-mail: Mark.Kolesar@telusplanet.net

Donald J. Kridel
Department of Economics
University of Missouri-St. Louis
8001 Natural Bridge Road
St. Louis, MO 63121, United States

Email: kridel@umsl.edu


Manabu Kurita
Information Technology Research &
Development Division
Daiwa Institute of Research Ltd., Tokyo
15-6 Fuyuki, Koto-ku
Tokyo 135-8460, Japan

E-mail: kuri@dir.co.jp


Jai Joon Lee
Joseph M. Katz Graduate School of Business
247 Mervis Hall
University of Pittsburgh
Pittsburgh, PA 15260, United States

E-mail: jaylee@katz.pitt.edu


Stanford L. Levin
Department of Economics and Finance
School of Business
Southern Illinois University Edwardsville
Mail to:
PMB 110
9648 Olive Blvd.
St. Louis, MO 63132-3002

E-mail: slevin@siue.edu

Jonathan Liebenau
Department of Information Systems
London School of Economics
Houghton Street
London WC2A 2AE, UK

E-mail: J.L.Liebenau@lse.ac.uk


Gary Madden
Communication Economics and Electronic
Markets Research Centre
School of Economics and Finance
Curtin Business School
GPO Box U1987
Perth, Western Australia 6845

E-mail: maddeng@cbs.curtin.edu.au


Ravindranath Madhavan
Joseph M. Katz Graduate School of Business
236 Mervis Hall
University of Pittsburgh
Pittsburgh, PA 15260, United States

Email: rmadhavan@katz.pitt.edu


Maria Michalis
Communications and Media Research Institute
(CAMRI)
School of Media, Arts and Design
University of Westminster
Harrow Campus
Watford Road, Northwick Park
Harrow HA1 3TP, UK

E-mail: M.Michalis@westminster.ac.uk


Eli Noam
Columbia Institute for Tele-Information
Columbia University
801 Uris Hall
New York, NY 10027, United States

E-mail: noam@columbia.edu


Jeonghun Oh
Graduate School of International Studies
Korea University
5-1, Anam-dong, Sungbuk-ku
Seoul, 136-701, Korea

E-mail: ojh@korea.ac.kr


Gohsei Ohira
Faculty of Economics
Tokyo International University
1-13-1 Matoba-kita, Kawagoe, Saitama 350-
1197, Japan

E-mail: goseio@tiu.ac.jp


Myeong-Cheol Park
School of Business
Information & Communications University
(ICU)
58-4, Hwaam-Dong, Yuseong-Gu Daejeon,
305-732, Korea

E-mail: mcpark@icu.ac.kr


Paul N. Rappoport
Department of Economics
Temple University
883 Ritter Hall Annex
1301 Cecil B. Moore Avenue
Philadelphia, PA 19122-6091
United States

E-mail: prapp4@comcast.net


Agustin Ros
NERA Economic Consulting
One Main Street, 5th Floor
Cambridge, MA 02142, United States

E-mail: agustin.ros@nera.com

Jorge R. Schement
Institute for Information Policy
College of Communications
The Pennsylvania State University
115 Carnegie Building
University Park, PA 16802, United States

E-mail: jrs18@psu.edu


Ann Skudlark
AT&T Labs
180 Park Avenue
Florham Park, NJ 07932, United States

E-mail: skudlark@att.com


Yong Yeop Sohn
Department of Economics
Chonnam National University
Yongbong-dong 300, Buk-gu
Gwangju, 500-757, Korea

E-mail: yysohn@chonnam.ac.kr


Charles Steinfield
Department of Telecommunication
Information Studies and Media
Michigan State University
East Lansing, MI 48824-1212
United States

E-mail: steinfie@msu.edu


Nakil Sung
Faculty of Economics
University of Seoul
90 Cheonnong-dong, Dongdaemun-gu
Seoul 130-743, Korea

E-mail: nisung@uos.ac.kr

Lester D. Taylor
University of Arizona
Tucson, AZ 85718, United States

E-mail: ltaylor@bpa.arizona.edu


Richard D. Taylor
Institute for Information Policy
College of Communications
The Pennsylvania State University
115 Carnegie Building
University Park, PA 16802, United States

E-mail: rdt4@psu.edu


Naoki Tsubone
Information Technology Research &
Development Division
Daiwa Institute of Research Ltd.
15-6 Fuyuki, Koto-ku
Tokyo 135-8460, Japan

E-mail: tsubone@dir.co.jp


Martin B.H. Weiss
Dept of Information Science and Telecommu-
nications
University of Pittsburgh
135 N.Bellefield Avenue, Pittsburgh PA15260,
United States

Email: mbw@pitt.edu


Hun-Wha Yang
Survey & Research Team
Korea Information Management Institute
for Small and Medium Enterprises (KIMI)
1F KDB Capital Yeouido-dong 16
Yeongdeungpo-gu
Seoul 150-873
Korea

Email: hhyang@kimi.or.kr

Gyu-Dong Yeon
Business Innovation Team
Samsung Networks Inc.
11F ASEM Tower, World Trade Center
159-1, Samsung-Dong, Gangnam-Gu
Seoul, 135-978, Korea

E-mail: gyudong.yeon@samsung.com


Chang-Ho Yoon
Department of Economics
Korea University
1 Anamdong
Seoul 136-701, Korea

Email: chyoon@korea.ac.kr

# INDEX

# INDEX